Birds of the Texas Panhandle

Number Twenty-nine

W. L. Moody, Jr., Natural History Series

Birds *of the*

Texas Panhandle

THEIR STATUS, DISTRIBUTION, AND HISTORY

Kenneth D. Seyffert

Illustrations by Carolyn Stallwitz

Texas A&M University Press

College Station

Frontispiece: Horned Lark

Library of Congress
Cataloging-in-Publication Data

Seyffert, Kenneth D.
    Birds of the Texas Panhandle : their status,
    distribution, and history / Kenneth D. Seyffert ;
    illustrations by Carolyn Stallwitz.— 1st ed.
        p.   cm.— (W. L. Moody, Jr., natural history
    series ; no. 29)
    Includes bibliographical references (p.).
        ISBN 1-58544-091-4 (cloth — ISBN 1-58544-096-5
    (pbk.)
    1. Birds—Texas—Texas Panhandle. I. Title.
    II. Series.
    QL684.T4 S45 2000
    598'.09764'8—DC21   00-044316

To those who will

write the history of

bird life in the

Texas Panhandle

in the twenty-first

century

CONTENTS

ILLUSTRATIONS

MAP

ACKNOWLEDGMENTS

I little realized when I began assembling material for this book the number of people upon whose work and observations I would come to rely. To all I give heartfelt thanks. When I first began going afield in search of birds, it never occurred to me that my observations could be of value to anyone but myself. I soon learned otherwise when George M. Sutton, editor of the *Bulletin* of the Oklahoma Ornithological Society, took an interest in what I was doing and encouraged me to submit articles to that publication. He and Jack D. Tyler, who followed "Doc" as editor, turned a "birder" into a "student," and without their guidance and encouragement this book would never have come into being. I wish to thank Terry C. Maxwell who, when I first mentioned the intention of writing a work such as this, gave the encouragement and support sorely needed and generously shared materials in his possession. Lastly, and most gratefully, I wish to thank Warren M. Pulich and an anonymous reader for the extraordinary amount of time and attention devoted to reading the manuscript, and for the invaluable advice given toward its improvement.

Perhaps the one person most responsible for planting the idea of undertaking such an endeavor is an obscure artillery lieutenant in the U.S. Army—Charles Adam Hoke McCauley. In 1876 Lt. McCauley, on sick leave from the army, joined the Ruffner expedition as a volunteer to explore the headwaters of the Red River in the Texas Panhandle. His assignment was twofold: to aid in the stadia rod survey and topographic mapping while concurrently acting as the expedition's ornithologist, accepting the responsibility for collecting and recording specimens of the birds, eggs, and nests found in the course of the other work. The expedition left Fort Dodge, Kansas, for the Panhandle on 27 April and returned the following 28 June, during which time McCauley named 103 species of birds found in what are now Hemphill, Wheeler, Gray, Carson, Armstrong, Briscoe, Randall, and Potter counties, a far greater diversity of species than had been named by all previous government expeditions combined—and those few limited almost entirely to gamebirds. Among the earlier expeditions was that of Lt. James William Abert, whose orders were to make a reconnaissance of the Canadian River. On 9 September 1845, Abert made this entry in his journal: "We have the wild turkey in abundance in the neighborhood of our camp, and, as they persisted in retaining possession of their accustomed roosts, our men had a fine opportunity of trying their skill in shooting them." The site was on the Canadian River about four miles east of present-day Tascosa, and some two or three miles west of the Oldham-Potter county line. He went on to name other species, including "quail," "turtle-dove," "prairie-chicken," and "a singular fly-catcher remarkable for their great agility in darting about, which singular movement is greatly facilitated by its long forked tail."

With the publication of McCauley's discoveries there took place the first significant lifting of the veil obscuring knowledge of the composition, distribution, and status of the avifauna of the Texas Panhandle during the nineteenth century, a revelation I found of boundless interest. The thought came to me that, fascinated as I was by this account of a hundred years ago, would not someone a hundred years hence be equally so by what I and others had discovered during the twentieth century? I have joined young McCauley many times on his journey of 1876, discussing around the campfire the many changes in bird life that have come with human settlement, and it is my hope that someone a hundred years from now, with this work in hand, will step into that charmed circle and join us in continuing the discussion.

The twentieth century's first exploration of the Texas Panhandle by an ornithologist occurred when John K. Strecker, Jr., curator of the Baylor University Museum in Waco, accompanied a party from Goodnight in Armstrong County that in May and June of 1910 explored a territory of some 35 miles, including "Goodnight, Mulberry Canyon, Luttrell's ranch (15 miles southwest of Goodnight), Dripping Springs Draw, the Head of Salt Creek, and Rush Creek." In two weeks the party discovered 34 species of birds, including Lesser Prairie-Chicken and House Sparrow. Shortly thereafter T. V. and Luella Reeves (1914) and Anna I. Hibbets, Laura Saunders, and Darthula Walker (1926) began recording their observations. The former couple named 116 and the latter trio 170 species. Observations of both groups were terminated in 1936 and were confined to within forty miles of Canyon. They are of particular value in giving us early looks at the status of several town-dwelling species now common that were then only just arriving on the scene, species such as the American Robin, Blue Jay, House Finch, and European Starling.

Upon graduation from high school in Indiana in 1933, Kenneth D. Carlander, nephew of a prominent Amarillo architect instrumental in the establishment of the Palo Duro Canyon State Park, Guy Carlander, was appointed field ornithologist for the Panhandle-Plains Historical Museum in Canyon—at the handsome salary of $100 a month. Young Carlander was to work in the area three summers (1933–35), during which time he named 167 species of birds. Seventy-three of these received lengthy discussions in a series of articles that ran in the *Amarillo Daily News* from August 2 through December 25, 1934 ("for which I was paid a dollar an article"). He also secured a "collector's license" and prepared a number of scientific skins for the museum, providing others to taxidermist L. E. Simms, who mounted them for display in that institution. These newspaper articles are among the most important accounts published prior to midcentury, for they dealt in detail with the status of many species about which little was then known. After leaving Amarillo Carlander pursued a scientific career, becoming a professor of zoology at Iowa State University.

Soon after Kenneth Carlander completed his work, a team of scientists led by James O. Stevenson of the U.S. Fish and Wildlife Service arrived on the scene to study the development of the new state park. Between 1935 and 1938 they spent 100 field days in the region, resulting in the naming of 152 species of birds. This included work in the summer of 1935 by Paul Russell of the National Park Service, plus "nine short field trips in February, May, August, September, October and December." Included in the final report were data furnished by Philip F. Allan of the U.S. Soil Conservation Service relating to the entire Panhandle. With the publication of Stevenson's *Birds of the Central Panhandle of Texas* in 1942, knowledge of the birds of northwest Texas received a more scientific underpinning.

The work done by Arthur Stewart Hawkins in the period 1943–45 was of equal, if not more, importance in enlarging our knowledge of the Panhandle's avifauna, for it was much more comprehensive in scope, not being limited to the Palo Duro Canyon area as were many of the earlier studies. The results of his work, in which he discusses 229 species of birds, were published in the *Panhandle-Plains Historical Review* in 1945, a work that deserves greater attention than it has received. It was World War II that brought "Art" Hawkins to the Panhandle as a member of the U.S. Army Air Force stationed at Amarillo Army Air Field. He had attended Cornell University, where he majored in zoology under Dr. Arthur A. Allen, and later had taken a research assistantship at the University of Wisconsin, obtaining his master's degree in 1937 under the guidance of the famed early conservationist Aldo Leopold. Hawkins was to say that Leopold was one of the greatest influences on his life. Upon leaving the air force at the end of the war, Hawkins took employment with the U.S. Fish and Wildlife Service, where he became, in the words of F. C. Bellrose (1976), "one of the most knowledgeable waterfowl biologists in North America." He developed groundbreaking methods of surveying North American waterfowl populations, and his methods of counting breeding populations of all manner of ducks are still used today.

William Lay Thompson, while attending the University of Texas, worked in northeastern Hutchinson County between June 8 and July 12, 1950. He studied the summer-resident birds along Bugbee Creek on the Bugbee Ranch, naming 48 species of birds that he found there. Several of the doubtful ones he collected were examined by George M. Sutton before being deposited in the Texas Natural History Collection in Austin. Thompson went on to become a vertebrate zoologist at Wayne State University.

It was with the formation of the Texas Panhandle Audubon Society in Amarillo in January, 1952, that bird observations began being recorded systematically and on a long-term basis. This endeavor was led by Mrs. I. D. ("Peggy") Acord, my long-time companion in the field, whose records were of paramount importance to this work. Many of the "firsts" for the Panhandle are Peggy's, and her wide-ranging observations, along with those of Rena Ross, Esther Waddill, Thelma Fox, Leo Galloway, Mary Moyer, Nancy Elliott, and Vera Deason laid the foundation upon which others have built. Here I must give personal recognition to Leo, my mentor, who opened wide the world of birding and who set the standard for me to follow. In addition to the records kept by Peggy, I have relied extensively on those of Rena Ross, C. D. Littlefield, Leo Galloway, Barry Zimmer, Orilla Bryant, and of late years, Rosemary Scott, Peggy Trosper, and Ed Kutac. Rena's yard at 2807 South Travis Street in Amarillo is the site of some of the most exciting bird finds made in the Panhandle, species such as the White-winged Crossbill, Black-chinned Sparrow, and Golden-crowned Sparrow. Other than for the waterfowl, what is known about bird life in the southwestern Panhandle is due almost entirely to the work done by C. D. Littlefield in the 1960s and 1990s. The Friona area of Parmer County and "Dodd's Woodlot" in Castro County are two of the most closely and systematically birded locations in the region. Particular acknowledgment is due a group of observers outside the Amarillo/Canyon area who over the years have generously shared their observations: Robert and Jerry Askins, Carolyn Stallwitz (Moore County); John Will Bookout (Hartley County); Orilla Bryant (Roberts County); Fern Cain, Maurine Forbus (Hutchinson County); Alice and Don Cocanougher, Tommy Rosson (Deaf Smith County); Richard DeArment (Wheeler County); E. B. Ellis, Jan and Fred Elston, Jack C. Williams (Gray County); Terry Ferguson, Sister Barbara Potthast (Briscoe County), Barbara Lund (Lake Meredith); Joel Reese (Swisher County); Verna Teague (Donley County); Dorothy Hudson, Marian Tomlinson (Hansford County); Roberta Currie, Thomas Johnson (Lake Tanglewood); Rosemary Scott (Oldham County); and Leon and Georgia Swift (Collingsworth County). I relied extensively on waterfowl studies conducted by Max Traweek and James Ray, biologists with the Texas Parks and Wildlife Department, and the U.S. Fish and Wildlife Service's records on file at the Buffalo Lake National Wildlife Refuge. I wish to thank refuge personnel at the latter site for always making me welcome, giving me assistance when needed, and allowing me to roam the refuge freely: Robert Darnell, Gordon Hansen, Richard Gritman, Marie Mayfield, Paul Ferguson, Milton Suthers, Larry Wynn, C. C. Stewart, Johnny Beall, Lynn Nymeyer, Alvin Payne, Kathy Payne. John Hughes (TP&W) and Jim Ray were particularly helpful with the Lesser Prairie-Chicken and Purple Martin accounts. Lastly, I am appreciative of the help given by Cliff Stogner in supplying information on rarities recorded on the South Texas Plains.

It was in the fall of 1964 that I first encountered several "ladybirders" as I sloshed across the mudflats on the Buffalo Lake NWR in search of shorebirds, and thereafter I was drawn into the public world of birding. My observations cover the period 27 October 1963–31 December 1997, during which time I made 1,017 trips to the Buffalo Lake NWR (Randall County), 663 to the Palo Duro Canyon State Park (Randall County), 129 to Lake Meredith (Hutchinson/Moore/Potter counties), 69 to Caprock Canyons SP (Briscoe County), 50 to Taylor Lakes Wildlife Management Area (Donley County), 36 to Ceta Glen (Randall County), 35 to Lake Tanglewood (Randall County), 34 to Lake McClellan (Gray County), 32 to Greenbelt Lake (Donley County), 31 to Lake Marvin/Gene Howe WMA (Hemphill County), and 736 to other points in the Panhandle. I participated in 111 Christmas Bird Counts, conducted 122 Breeding Bird Surveys, and spent over 500 hours atlassing in 23 counties.

Alas, the many hours spent birding were not matched by an equal number in the practice of writing the English language. Along with Proust, I must confess "There is no one who knows less about syntax than me." My heartfelt thanks go to Ruth Galloway for correcting my many errors of composition, although their removal has deprived the reader of the humor he or she would otherwise have derived from this work. Without Ruth's help the author would become known as "The Awk."

When *Window on the Prairie: An Artist's Perspective* was published by the Feather Press of Dumas in 1981, I knew that Carolyn Stallwitz would be the one to illustrate this work. Anyone who has spent countless hours afield observing birds in all kinds of weather and during all seasons will immediately recognize and feel a closeness to the those she so beautifully depicts in their natural settings. Thanks also go to Joseph Cepeda for graciously offering to draw the map and to Pam Allison for secretarial assistance. Lastly, though surely firstly, my thanks go to my sister, Mary Pipes, who believed unwaveringly that I could do it.

The specimen listings given here are by no means complete. I wrote to all the major museums in the country soliciting a list of Texas Panhandle specimens in their collections and received prompt and generous responses from almost all. These institutions are named under "Abbreviations." Several who did not have their collections computerized as yet kindly offerred to open them for my examination. To all of these institutions I am most grateful.

Birds of the Texas Panhandle

Introduction

The two major works on bird life that include the Texas Panhandle within their scope of study are H. C. Oberholser's monumental two-volume *The Bird Life of Texas* and P. A. Johnsgard's *Birds of the Great Plains*. However, other than in showing the county and season of occurrence, the former work, published in 1974, is lacking in data pertaining to the status of each species, while the latter, published in 1979, is directed at nesting birds only. While both were welcomed by observers and students as providing the first comprehensive overviews of the birds of the region, much has been learned since they were published. Oberholser names 355 species occurring in the Panhandle plus five others of questionable status, whereas the present work includes 442 species; Johnsgard discusses 107 nesting species compared to 151 that have now been confirmed.

The purpose of this book is to make known this increase in knowledge and to provide an enlarged as well as a more detailed view of the richness of bird life that exists in the 26 counties of the Texas Panhandle, an area larger than West Virginia. A view often expressed when I began a study of the region's avifauna was: "I have driven across the Panhandle many times and there can't be much of a variety around. If you want to find birds you should go to where there are more trees." Barren and depauperate as the High Plains may appear, of the 606 species of birds confirmed in Texas (1998), 67 percent have been confirmed in the Texas Panhandle.

That such diversity exists should be no surprise. Although the sea of grassland called the Great Plains was long considered a barrier separating, in a rather clear-cut manner, the avifauna of the eastern part of the continent from that of the west, it is in fact much like an ocean that attracts wanderers from both east and west, and its tree-lined waterways provide many avenues of penetration. In any given year it is possible for the Texas Panhandle to be visited by a migrant Golden-winged Warbler bound for the northeastern woodlands and a wintering Golden-crowned Sparrow from the boreal scrub of the Pacific Northwest, or a far-ranging Common Redpoll from the Canadian Arctic and a wandering Tricolored Heron from the Gulf Coast.

The Llano Estacado is a high, isolated plateau that slopes in a southeasterly direction at altitudes ranging from 4,693 feet in Dallam County in the northwest

to 1,782 feet in Childress County in the southeast. The climate is subhumid continental. The average annual temperature is 56°F and winds are frequently south or
southwesterly in direction with an average velocity of 16 miles per hour. The average growing season of 196 days is relatively short compared with other regions
in Texas, and there are usually twelve weeks of freezing temperatures a year. The
average mean minimum in January is 21.1°F, and the average mean maximum in
July is 92.9°F. Rainfall fluctuates greatly and water evaporates quickly due to
windy conditions. The average rainfall ranges from 16 inches in Hartley County
in the semiarid west to almost 23 inches in Lipscomb County in the subhumid
east, and its irregular distribution may cause drought in one area and bountiful
harvests just a short distance away. Rainfall is usually rapid and violent, most of
it falling during May through September, and the region's silty clay loam soil
does not readily absorb moisture. Drought is a natural and common occurrence
(Britten, 1993; *Dallas Morning News*, 1998–99; Haukos and Smith, 1994).

The Texas Panhandle is composed of two ecological areas, the Rolling Plains
and the High Plains (Gould et al., 1960). The Rolling Plains of Permian redbeds
occupy the eastern Panhandle and extend westward via the Canadian River Valley
to the New Mexico state line, and the High Plains consist of Cenozoic alluvium
derived by outwash from the mountains of New Mexico, the conspicuous caprock
escarpment marking their boundary on the east. The Canadian River has cut
through this deposit ("the breaks") to isolate the High Plains of the northern part
from that of the south.

The Rolling Plains are an area primarily of mesquite shrub and mixed grassland (McMahon et al., 1984). Plants commonly associated with it are mesquite,
juniper, yucca, prickly pear, and cholla cactus, and the dominant grasses are
several species of beardgrass and grama, little bluestem, and buffalograss. The
eastern and northeastern sectors contain pockets of sandsage and oak shinnery
("mottes"), along with skunkbush sumac and Chickasaw plum, where a small
population of the Lesser Prairie-Chicken still resides; in much of the far southeastern sector the dominant association is sandsage/mesquite brush. These eastern plains are laced by a number of east-west waterways, among them Wolf Creek,
Sweetwater Creek, McClellan Creek, and the North Fork and Salt Fork of Red
River, providing habitat for a number of woodland species. The Canadian River
Valley and its drainage are dominated by an association of cottonwood, hackberry, and salt cedar woods, while on higher ground mesquite and juniper brush
prevail. The river provides an avenue of westward penetration for such typical
eastern nesting species as the Red-headed Woodpecker, Carolina Chickadee,
House Wren, and Eastern Bluebird, while woodlands in its eastern drainage are
home to species that reach their westernmost limits in the area: Red-bellied

Woodpecker, Great Crested Flycatcher, Warbling Vireo, Indigo Bunting, Baltimore Oriole.

The High Plains (Llano Estacado) make up a vast area of gently rolling terrain with deep and fine-textured soils dominated by blue grama and buffalograss, hence the name "short grass plains." To the inexperienced and unadjusted eye the land appears monotonous and endless in extent. On 14 June 1849, Captain Randolph B. Marcy reached the base of the Llano Estacado and wrote in his journal (Marcy, 1854): "When we were upon the high table-land, a view presented itself as boundless as the ocean. Not a tree, shrub, or any other object, either animate or inanimate, relieved the dreary monotony of the prospects; it was a vast illimitable expanse of desert prairie ... a land where no man, either savage or civilized, permanently abides; it spreads into a treeless, desolate waste of uninhabited solitude, which always has been, and must continue, uninhabited forever."

Although it gives the appearance of uniformity, scattered over the Llano Estacado are topographic irregularities and peculiar soil types that provide habitats for minor communities. A major feature is the abundance of shallow circular basins called playas, localized sites that "are the most significant topographical expression, surface hydrological feature, and only remaining native habitat on the Southern High Plains" (Haukos and Smith, 1994). These depressions average 6.3 hectares in surface area, and 19,340 are found south of the Canadian River and 3,590 north (Guthery and Bryant, 1982). "In terms of diversity, biomass, and sheer numbers, avifauna are the most dominant and recognizable taxa associated with playas" and are found when the playas are "dry, flooded, or in any other moisture condition" (Haukos and Smith, 1994). Although 85 percent of the larger playas have been modified by human activity (Bolen et al., 1989), playas on the southern High Plains provide winter habitat for an estimated 500,000–2,800,000 ducks and 100,000–750,000 geese (U.S. Fish and Wildlife Service, 1988), along with several million migrant shorebirds. During summer they play host to a variety of nesting birds, principally ducks of various species, Ring-necked Pheasants, and Mourning Doves (Bolen et al., 1989), and the food base provided by a variety of wildlife attracts raptors during all seasons. One hundred and fourteen nonwaterfowl species have been found in playas: 63 fall or spring migrants, 25 winter migrants, 15 summer residents, 11 year-round residents (Simpson and Bolen, 1981). Traweek (1978) reported 2,017 duck broods in 12 counties during a single year.

A dominant feature of the southern Panhandle is Palo Duro Canyon, a gorge 600–800 feet in depth carved by the Prairie Dog Town Fork of Red River, which has exposed to view much of the last 230 million years of geologic history. Like a finger poked into the underbelly of the region, the "Big Canyon" reaches as far north as central Randall County and provides an avenue of entrance to such typical southern and southwestern species as the Golden-fronted Woodpecker, Western Scrub-Jay, "Black-crested" Titmouse, Bushtit, Canyon Wren, Canyon Towhee, Painted Bunting, and Black-throated Sparrow. Although the rugged and colorful canyon walls are largely bare of vegetation, the numerous terraces of loamy soils are highly fertile and hold much moisture—with a consequent richness in plant life—while riverine habitats contain an even greater diversity (Wright, 1978). At various levels are found tree species such as one-seeded and redberry juniper, mesquite, hackberry, cottonwood, and soapberry, and brush species such as little-leaf and skunkbush sumac, forestiera, wafer ash, and lotebush. At the lower elevations the dominant grasses are those of medium height—little bluestem, sideoats grama, sand dropseed, alkali sacaton, and Indian grass—while on higher ground short grasses such as blue grama, hairy grama, and buffalograss prevail.

While natural environments determine the makeup of a region's bird life, changes in land use brought about by human settlement can have significant effects in modifying its composition and distribution. This certainly applies to the Texas Panhandle following the arrival of the Anglos (Britten, 1993). With removal of the Indians and elimination of the buffalo, "what had once been a free and open country of communal ownership of lands almost within a decade became a land of individual owners who were fast enclosing their lands" (Sheffy, 1930). The windmill and barbed wire as well as the arrival of railroads allowed settlers to possess land that had formerly been open range. The railroads in particular had an immense effect, for they brought in the latest agricultural equipment and encouraged the establishment of town sites. With development and plantings, these sites have become oases on the prairie that are highly attractive to birds, particularly migrants. As examples of how attractive, a single observer in Vega (population 874) has recorded 188 species there, and at least 311 species have been found within the city limits of Amarillo. By the turn of the century "stock farming" by ranchers—the planting of forage crops to safeguard against inclement weather conditions that might threaten their cattle's food supply—took over as the primary land use, thus forging an alliance between ranchers and farmers that continued through the 1950s. Wheat and sorghum were two crops that could withstand the harsh climate and unpredictable weather patterns of the area, and in the early 1940s a new strain of sorghum was developed that lent itself to mechanized harvesting. The oil bonanza of the 1920s brought in thousands of settlers "and completed the region's transformation from a remote frontier to an industrial powerhouse" (Britten, 1993).

With industrialization came wide-scale irrigation, completing the breakup of the remaining "big spreads" of the cattle ranchers. Irrigated farming has had a significant effect on the region's bird life. Thousands of acres that were once were prairie, the home of meadowlarks, Horned Larks and other grassland species, are now under cultivation and attract swarms of Red-winged Blackbirds instead. The extent of the land conversion is enormous: "In 1954 Carson County possessed 18,598 acres of irrigated land. Twenty years later, the number of irrigated acres had climbed nearly 600 per cent to 101,622 acres" (Britten, 1993). The introduction of feedlots only intensified sorghum production. Again in Carson County, an average of 26,597 acres planted to sorghum from 1940 to 1950 increased to an average of 73,596 acres from 1954 to 1974. Today the southern High Plains is one of the most intensively cultivated regions in the Western Hemisphere, with cotton, wheat, corn, grain sorghum, and various vegetables as dominant crops (Haukos and Smith, 1994). Beginning in 1985, however, this practice of converting prairie to croplands has been mitigated by the return of more than three million acres of marginal land in the South Texas Plains to grassland through the Conservation Reserve Program (CRP), a program proving beneficial to nesting nongame birds (Berthelsen and Smith, 1995).

Concurrent with these changes in land use, other modifications of the environment have occurred that have also had dynamic impacts on the status and distribution of the region's birds: the damming of rivers and streams and the establishment of federal, state, and municipal wildlife refuges, parklands, and sanctuaries. A significant number of sightings noted in this work were made at these sites:

Buffalo Lake National Wildlife Refuge (Randall County/7,664 acres 13.5 miles west of Canyon/344 species). A federal refuge on Tierra Blanca Creek, it once was a major waterfowl refuge on the Central Flyway, holding half a million or more ducks and geese in winter; because of changes in rainfall patterns and a decline in underground water supplies, it is usually dry. Its wooded coves and semiarid grasslands and savannahs, however, still attract a wide variety of birds. During its heyday, out-of-range larids such as Parasitic Jaeger, Glaucous Gull, Black-legged Kittiwake, and Sabine's Gull were among the transients here.

Palo Duro Club/Lake Tanglewood (Randall County/beginning 2 miles northeast of Canyon near the confluence of Palo Duro Creek and Tierra Blanca Creek/250 species). These rural communities in the upper reaches of Palo Duro Canyon comprise an area noted for migrant warblers.

Lake Meredith National Recreation Area (Moore, Hutchinson, and Potter counties/ 44,973 acres 10 miles northwest of Borger/248 species). On the Canadian River and encompassing lake and riverine habitats, wooded canyons, and mesquite/ brush savannahs, it is an important wintering area for Bald Eagles and its marshes are noted for rails.

Palo Duro Canyon State Park (Randall and Armstrong counties/16,402 acres 12 miles east of Canyon/234 species). In the rugged canyonlands traversed by the

Prairie Dog Town Fork of the Red River, several southwestern species reach their northernmost limits of residence here, and the deep canyon provides a winter haven for a number of northern species. Riparian woodlands, mesquite/brush grasslands, and wooded scarps are among its varied habitats.

Caprock Canyons State Park (Briscoe County/15,161 acres 4 miles north of Quitaque/217 species). The uppermost drainage area of the Little Red River, these rugged badlands at the base of the Caprock lack a flowing stream but have the tiny man-made Lake Theo, where Red-throated Loon, Red-necked Grebe, and Surf Scoter have been seen.

Lake Marvin National Grassland/Gene Howe Wildlife Management Area (Hemphill County/576 acres and 6,700 acres 14 miles east of Canadian/215 species). Almost adjoining, the two units lie on the north bank of the Canadian River in an area of rolling sandhills with large natural meadows and extensive stretches of woodland. Nesting Least Terns can be seen in summer and American Tree Sparrows and Harris' Sparrows in winter, and it is almost the only area in the Panhandle where the Barred Owl is found regularly.

Lake Rita Blanca State Park (Hartley County/1,525 acres near the southern outskirts of Dalhart/186 species). Mostly semiarid grassland with but few wooded areas, the park is an important wintering site for waterfowl and Bald Eagles.

Lake McClellan National Recreation Area (Gray County/1,449 acres 13 miles northeast of Groom/183 species). Located on McClellan Creek, the area contains extensive woodlands with a wide variety of woodpeckers.

Taylor Lakes Wildlife Management Area (Donley County/530 acres 7 miles east of Clarendon/186 species). Embracing four shallow lakes along with cottonwoods, willows, hackberries, juniper, mesquite/sandsage, and grasslands, this is a regular stopping point for migrating Tundra Swans.

Greenbelt Lake (Donley County/1,990 acres 5 miles north of Clarendon/174 species). A lakeside community as well as a recreational area, during migration and winter it is noted for its loons, grebes, and mergansers.

Ceta Glen (Randall County/14 miles east of Happy/154 species). Two church camps are located in the upper reaches of South Ceta Canyon; the lower level with springfed stream is densely wooded. Nesting Eastern Phoebes and such out-of-range species as Lewis' Woodpecker, Scott's Oriole, and Pyrrhuloxia have been recorded here.

Palo Duro Lake (Hansford County/8,984 acres 12 miles north of Spearman/145 species). Established only recently on Palo Duro Creek and Horse Creek, the lake holds the only colony of nesting cormorants in the region.

Cactus Lake (Moore County/2 miles east of Etter/115 species). This permanent playa lake winters 250,000 or more ducks and geese and attracts countless Wilson's Phalaropes and swallows during migration.

Wolf Creek Park–Lake Fryer (Ochiltree County/13 miles south and 5 miles east of Perryton/103 species). The association of riverine, lake/woodland, and savannah/grassland habitats on Wolf Creek is underbirded and is one of the few sites in the state where the Common Redpoll has been found.

Many species accounts provide data derived from Breeding Bird Surveys (BBS) and Christmas Bird Counts (CBC). The following is a listing of the survey routes and count circles and the counties in which they lie:

Breeding Bird Surveys: *Childress* (Childress); *Booker* (Lipscomb); *Miami* (Roberts); *Waka* (Ochiltree, Hansford); *Skellytown* (Hutchinson, Carson); *Panhandle* (Gray, Carson); *Pantex* (Armstrong, Carson); *Channing* (Hartley, Oldham); *Dalhart* (Hartley); *Texline* (Dallam).

Christmas Bird Counts: *Amarillo* (Randall, Armstrong); *Buffalo Lake NWR* (Randall, Deaf Smith); *Lake Meredith* (*west*) (Potter); *Lake Meredith* (*east*) (Hutchinson, Moore, Potter, Carson); *Quitaque* (Briscoe).

Plan of Work

When I began thinking of what plan of work I should follow in writing a book of this nature, the question was quickly resolved when I took in hand Warren M. Pulich's *The Birds of North Central Texas.* Numerous other models lay about, but I chose that one primarily for its clarity of presentation. The data are comprehensive and based on a rigorous examination of reported sightings, while its style is open and nontechnical. Unlike that author, however, I make no attempt to give the early and late dates of observations for each county, principally because a good data base is lacking for many of them.

Another work I have always held in high esteem is George M. Sutton's *Oklahoma Birds,* in particular for placing bird sightings in context. Too often the Texas Panhandle is looked upon as a region apart. As did Sutton, I chose to enlarge this view and to place seemingly isolated events in their relation to those occurring in nearby areas. This is most important as regards sightings made in the western, southwestern, and Panhandle regions of Oklahoma, many of which occurred only a few miles from the Texas Panhandle. Under the editorships of "Doc" Sutton and Jack D. Tyler, the *Bulletin of the Oklahoma Ornithological Society* has been invaluable in this regard, and for its role in broadening our knowledge of the avifauna of the region all students must be grateful. Doc also was not content with offering the reader bare facts or statistics; he enlarged his accounts with considerable narrative power.

In writing a work such as this, it is difficult to set a cutoff date for observations and then stick to it. The date I originally set was 1996; however, as it became obvious that the work would not be completed by the end of that year, the date was changed to 1997. The alert reader will note that this date too has been breached and that important later sightings are included. I have tried to be as careful and fair as possible in giving recognition to out-of-range and out-of-season sightings, suggesting caution in those cases where there was some doubt as to authenticity. Often one finds oneself uncertain in assessing the validity of observations submitted by those of whose competence one has no personal knowledge or for which there is little or no supporting documentation. State Bird Records Committees with their strict criteria came into being only recently. Also, one tends to accept rare sightings made by present-day observers, including one's own, but question those made by observers of earlier days. Too often we mistakenly think that better optical equipment and field guides make us more competent and reliable field observers than those who preceded us. A Golden-crowned Kinglet reported in the Texas Panhandle in June of 1876 is scoffed at, but one seen in June of 1996 is accepted without much questioning.

The status and distribution of birds in any given region is never static. Changes in climate and land use and other environmental disruptions have determining effects. In this work I give each species' current status and, when possible, track changes that may have occurred since the species was first reported, the Mississippi Kite being an example. The terms of abundance to use, as well as their definitions, became a puzzle as I reviewed the different practices followed in checklists, field guides, and other publications. In a bid for uniformity, I settled on the terminology adopted by the Academy of Natural Sciences of Philadelphia in its series *The Birds of North America*.

The occurrence and distribution data for species shown in this work are biased to a certain extent by where observers live and work: "It is, I find, in zoology as it is in botany: all nature is so full, that that district produces the greatest variety which is the most examined" (Gilbert White, *The Natural History of Selborne*, 1768). As an example, 410 species of birds have been recorded in Randall County and only 99 in Sherman County, primarily because the latter has received far less attention. This work issues a challenge to future observers to fill in these and other gaps in our knowledge. Finally, the nomenclature used in this book follows that of the seventh edition of the American Ornithologists' Union *Check-list of North American Birds* (1998).

Accounts of Species

This book gives accounts of a total of 442 species, 406 of which are considered valid for the study area. The remaining 36 species are considered in the section "Species of Uncertain Occurrence." The nomenclature used follows that of the seventh edition of the American Ornithologists' Union *Check-list of North American Birds* (1998). In each species account a summary status is given for the 26 counties that constitute the study area. Dates of occurrence and distribution and nesting data are included, along with data derived from Christmas Bird Counts, Breeding Bird Surveys, and the Texas Breeding Bird Atlas Project. Where the information is available, perceived changes in the status and distribution of each species are discussed, with emphasis placed on what observers in the late nineteenth and early twentieth centuries said concerning each. A map shows the principal waterways, bodies of water, parks, wildlife refuges, and towns referenced in the text. Other features mentioned in the text can be located by checking official county maps issued by the Texas State Highway Department and obtainable from that agency's offices in the respective county seats or in Austin. As well as Panhandle counties, adjacent counties in Oklahoma, New Mexico, and the South Plains are shown. Specimens and their locations in various museums complete the species accounts. Abbreviations for museums and frequently used terms, along with definitions for status terminology, are as follows:

ABBREVIATIONS

ACNHM	Amarillo College Natural History Museum, Amarillo, Tex.
BBS	Breeding Bird Survey
BLNWR	Buffalo Lake National Wildlife Refuge, Randall County, Tex.
CMNH	Carnegie Museum of Natural History, Pittsburgh, Pa.
CAS	Chicago Academy of Sciences, Chicago, Ill.
CBC	Christmas Bird Count
CM-NH	Cincinnati Museum of Natural History, Cincinnati, Ohio
FMNH	Field Museum of Natural History, Chicago, Ill.

LMAWM	Lake Meredith Aquatic and Wildlife Museum, Fritch, Tex.
LEAS	Llano Estacado Audubon Society
MCHM	Moore County Historical Museum, Dumas, Tex.
MNH	Museum of Natural History, University of Kansas, Lawrence
MTTU	Museum of Texas Tech University, Lubbock
MVZ	Museum of Vertebrate Zoology, University of California, Berkeley
NPS	National Park Service
NWR	National Wildlife Refuge
NMOS	New Mexico Ornithological Society
OMNH	Oklahoma Museum of Natural History, Norman
OSU	Oklahoma State University, Stillwater
PDCSP	Palo Duro Canyon State Park, Randall County, Tex.
P-PHM	Panhandle-Plains Historical Museum, Canyon, Tex.
PPC	Patrick Pitt Collection, Memphis, Tenn.
SP	State Park
SM	Strecker Museum, Baylor University, Waco, Tex.
SRSU	Sul Ross State University, Alpine, Tex.
TBRC	Texas Bird Records Committee
TBSL	Texas Bird Sounds Library, Huntsville
TBBAP	Texas Breeding Bird Atlas Project: CO (confirmed nesting); PR (probable nesting); PO (possible nesting)
TCWC	Texas Cooperative Wildlife Collection, College Station
TNHC	Texas Natural History Collection, University of Texas, Austin
TOS	Texas Ornithological Society
TPAS	Texas Panhandle Audubon Society
TPWD	Texas Parks and Wildlife Department
TP-RF	Texas Photo-Record File, TCWC
USFWS	U.S. Fish and Wildlife Service
USFS	U.S. Forest Service
USNM	U.S. National Museum, Washington, D.C.
WFVZ	Western Foundation of Vertebrate Zoology, Warren M. Pulich Collection, Camarillo, Calif.
WTAMU	West Texas A&M University, Canyon
WMA	Wildlife Management Area

TERMINOLOGY

Resident: Year-round presence in an area, including breeding, although different populations may occur from season to season.

Breeder: Leaves the area during the nonbreeding season; some birds on a summering ground may actually be birds of passage, not yet on their breeding grounds.

Summer visitor: Visits area during spring and summer but breeds elsewhere.

Fall visitor: Visits in late summer, fall, or early winter; generally postbreeding wanderer.

Winter visitor: Resides in the area during the nonbreeding season.

Migrant: A bird of passage, staying briefly while en route between its summer and winter homes.

Abundant: A species that can be found in quantity without any special search in the appropriate habitat during the appropriate season.

Common: Species noted at least daily with some search in appropriate habitat; the numbers of these birds may be as large as for those in the preceding category.

Fairly common: A species that may require some search to be detected regularly in a locality favorable to it.

Uncommon: Occurring infrequently and yet seen too often to be considered rare.

Rare: Seldom encountered except by chance in a day's search or by a special search of the locality where it has previously occurred or nested.

Casual: A species that is out of its normal range but can be expected to occur again.

Vagrant: Recorded once or twice (rarely more) within a designated area and, on the grounds of reasonable probability, unlikely to occur there again (the term "Accidental" is sometimes employed by other authors).

Spring: March, April, May

Summer: June, July, August

Fall: September, October, November

Winter: December, January, February

CO: confirmed nesting

PR: probable nesting

PO: possible nesting

Blue List: The National Audubon Society list of species that have recently or are currently giving indications of noncyclical population declines or range contractions, either locally or widespread.

ORDER GAVIIFORMES

Family Gaviidae (Loons)

Red-throated Loon *Gavia stellata* (Pontoppidan)
STATUS: Vagrant.
OCCURRENCE: The Red-throated Loon has been reported once. On 24 November 1977, a single bird in winter plumage was observed on Lake Theo, Caprock Canyons SP, Briscoe County (K. Seyffert, J. Garbutt; TBRC). It was watched at length as it swam and dived in the middle of the lake at the deepest point.

This small loon winters in North America primarily along the Pacific and Atlantic coasts, ranging regularly to the Gulf Coast of Florida, and is casual in inland areas of North America south through the Rocky Mountains to Colorado and New Mexico, and in the eastern states to Texas and the Gulf Coast (AOU, 1983). At the time of the Briscoe County sighting only five other Red-throated Loons had been documented and accepted for Texas by the TBRC, all but two of the birds found inland from coastal areas (Lasley and Sexton, 1995a). In recent years more are being reported as observers become alert to possible presence of the species and more skilled in loon identification.

A Red-throated Loon was observed south of Durham, Roger Mills County, Oklahoma, 1 December 1970 (Williams, 1971), and the species is listed on the 1957 "Clayton Area Check-list of Birds" for Union County, New Mexico (Ligon, 1961); its presence there was not recognized by Hubbard (1978).

Pacific Loon *Gavia pacifica* (Lawrence)
STATUS: Casual fall and winter visitor.
OCCURRENCE: The Pacific Loon has been reported in two counties of the Texas Panhandle: *Randall*—BLNWR, 19–20 May 1979 (1); 17 September 1979 (1); extremely early for any loon species, this one must be questioned. *Donley*—Greenbelt Lake, 20 December 1981 (1); 21–23 November (2; TBRC) and 18 December 1997 (1); 5–7 December 1998 (3) and 19 January 1999 (3).

The Pacific Loon winters in North America along the Pacific Coast south to southern Baja California and southern Sonora and "casually in the interior of western North America south to Arizona, New Mexico and Texas" (AOU, 1983). In the past 15 years accepted Pacific Loon observations in Texas have gone from five to over 60 (Lasley and Sexton, 1995a). The species is now expected in low numbers virtually statewide during winter and has been removed from the TBRC's Review List. This is another instance in which increasing alertness and proficiency in identification have resulted in greater numbers of a rare species being reported.

The nearest point to the Texas Panhandle where a specimen has been taken is Clayton, Union County, New Mexico (November 1899), as cited by Hubbard (1978), and one was photographed on Lake Carl Etling, Cimarron County, Oklahoma, on 23 October 1988 (Oliphant, 1990). Others have been observed at Ransom Canyon Lake near Lubbock, 23 November–20 December 1986 (TBRC), and Roger Mills County, Oklahoma, 15 November 1977 (Baumgartner and Baumgartner, 1992).

Common Loon *Gavia immer* (Brünnich)

STATUS: Rare migrant and winter visitor. Vagrant summer visitor.

OCCURRENCE: The Common Loon has been reported in eight counties—Briscoe, Childress, Donley, Hemphill, Hutchinson, Moore, Potter, and Randall—and has been seen in every month.

Rarely have more than 2–3 birds been seen at a time: 10 at BLNWR, 9 November 1963, and 2–10 on Lake Tanglewood 17–24 November 1963—most likely the same birds as these sites are only 20 miles apart. With few exceptions, loons have not been reported on playas but only on impoundments.

This loon's rarity in winter is attested to by there having been only 16 reported since 1960, principally on Lake Meredith in Hutchinson and Moore counties. This body of water is so large and difficult of access that more probably would be found were the area covered thoroughly by boat and at times other than CBCs.

Summer rarities were two winter-plumaged birds on Lake Tanglewood, 28 May–13 July 1989 (TP-RF), and another in South Canyon, Lake Meredith, Hutchinson County, 28 June 1996. Of note are recent summer sightings at Clayton Lake in nearby Union County, New Mexico, where I observed a single loon on 12 June 1982 and two on 22 July 1987 (Hubbard, 1987). One spent all of July near Lubbock in 1966 (Williams, 1966) and another 2–8 June 1978 (Williams, 1978). Scattered summer records of nonbreeding Common Loons are not uncommon on the southern plains, as readers of *Audubon Field Notes* and *American Birds* are aware.

Most migrant loons are recorded during fall, principally in November (10 September–26 November). Unusually early were two at BLNWR on 22 August 1979. Spring dates range from 6 March to 31 May. A Common Loon in breeding plumage remained on the quite small MediPark Lake in Amarillo, 14–22 May 1991. As can be seen, these out-of-season sightings have all occurred in recent years.

ORDER PODICIPEDIFORMES

Family Podicipedidae (Grebes)

Pied-billed Grebe *Podilymbus podiceps* (Linnaeus)

STATUS: Fairly common to common migrant. Uncommon breeder and winter visitor.

OCCURRENCE: The Pied-billed Grebe has been recorded during every month and in all counties of the study area except Dallam, Lipscomb, Roberts, and Wheeler. Oberholser (1974) shows it in six.

Apart from those few that oversummer, most Pied-billed Grebes are encountered from early April to mid-May and from late August to late November, usually singly or in small numbers. Noteworthy were an estimated 50 on Lake Marvin, Hemphill County, 28 April 1956, and 60 at the BLNWR on 21 August 1978.

The earliest mention of the Pied-billed Grebe is that by McCauley (1877), who spoke of it as "occasional upon the Canadian." One is much more likely today to find a grebe on a playa or impoundment than on the Canadian River, for the river's ecosystem has changed drastically during this century: "Hardly more than twenty feet wide, it had no sand bars, but was deep with clear, living water. . . . Its banks along nearly the entire route through the Panhandle were fringed with fruit bushes and trees. . . . Until trappers killed the animals, beaver and beaver dams were numerous. As the dams deteriorated, the water ran unchecked, altering the nature of the river, and cattle, when they came, destroyed the bushes" (Carlson, 1980). Except during flood time, few stretches of the river today have water deep enough to attract grebes.

Temperature largely determines the presence of this grebe in winter, as reflected by the CBCs. For example, on *Lake Meredith* (*east*) counts (1970–87) the Pied-billed has been recorded on all but one (high 17); the lake remains ice-free in winter. On *Quitaque* counts (1975–95), located below the caprock escarpment where some water is always open, it has been recorded on all counts (high 23). Since Lake Tanglewood and the Amarillo sewage pond were brought within the *Amarillo* count circle, the species has been found yearly (high 10); formerly it was recorded irregularly, as the shallow playas were often frozen.

NESTING: Playas with emergent vegetation and marshes with open areas of water are the preferred habitats for nesting Pied-billed Grebes. Many playas are ephemeral, however, and finding nesting grebes every summer is no sure thing. Since this grebe is an opportunist, if sufficient rainfall occurs in mid- or late summer, filling formerly dry lake beds, nesting is initiated. As examples of late nesting: *Carson*—two nestlings, 20 August 1981; adults with four downy young, 3 September 1981. *Castro*—adult with four downy young, 31 July 1988. *Donley*—two juveniles at Greenbelt Lake, 7 November 1996, had heads with prominent black and white markings. *Randall*—adult on nest, 22 July 1989; at BLNWR—pair building nest, July 1939 (Stevenson, 1942); adult on nest, 16–24 August 1975; ten or more young (including several in downy stage), 27 August 1978; one young, 3 September 1984; three adults with six downy young, 25 July 1987; five newly hatched chicks, 29 July 1995; adults on three recently built nests, 29 August 1996; adult on nest, 30 July 1997. The 29 August 1996 observation at BLNWR is illustrative of how late in the season nesting may be initiated. The lake had been dry until rains fell in mid-July; within a few days of its filling, courting grebes were present. It would be of interest to know where these late nesters had spent the summer, for the entire region was undergoing a severe drought and habitat for nesting was limited or absent. Under such circumstances, were they south-bound birds that had interrupted their flight to take advantage of favorable nesting conditions? If so, had they previously experienced nesting failures and were they now attempting to renest?

The TBBAP (1987–92) found CO nesting in ten survey blocks, PR in five, and PO in four. All but two quadrangles were located in the southern half.

Horned Grebe *Podiceps auritus* (Linnaeus)

STATUS: Rare to uncommon migrant. Rare winter visitor.

OCCURRENCE: The Horned Grebe has been recorded in ten counties: Armstrong, Briscoe, Childress, Donley, Hansford, Hemphill, Hutchinson, Moore, Potter, and Randall. Oberholser (1974) shows it in two. It has been seen from September to May.

Prior to the impoundment of Lake Meredith in 1965, almost all Horned Grebes in the study area were recorded during migration. Although the BLNWR had been surveyed regularly and extensively, this grebe was rarely seen during winter. It was only with the establishment of the *Lake Meredith* (*east*) CBC in 1970 that the species was discovered to be a fairly regular winter visitor. Although found on only five of 16 counts, it probably would be recorded with greater frequency if the lake were surveyed by boat, as was done on 3 January 1976, when 14 grebes were tallied in the numerous bays and coves accessible only by water. Such a high number is unusual, for rarely are more than 2–3 seen in a day. The largest single group ever recorded in winter consisted of 40 at BLNWR on 4–8 December 1998, birds that did not overwinter.

The Horned Grebe can be expected from the third week of October to the third week of April. The only May sighting is of one in Randall County, 3 May 1971. A single September sighting is acceptable—two birds still in partial breeding plumage on a park lake in Amarillo, Potter County, 28 September 1952; others reported earlier than October I have dismissed. Pulich (1988) discounts all August and September sightings reported in north-central Texas as probable misidentified Eared Grebes. The two species in winter plumage can easily be confused, and variant plumages in subadult Eared Grebes, a species that nests in the study area, add to the difficulty. This variance is well illustrated by Peterson (1990). Migrant Eared Grebes tend to arrive earlier than Horned Grebes, the former peaking in late September and the latter in early November. Kaufman's (1992) discussion of identification problems is well worth attention. He wisely warns that "even in those eastern regions where the Eared Grebe is considered rare, any purported 'Horned Grebe' seen before mid-October should be scrutinized with great care." The earliest Oklahoma Panhandle date is 29 September (Baumgartner and Baumgartner, 1992), the earliest Kansas date 3 October (Thompson and Ely, 1989), and those found on the High Plains of eastern Colorado before mid-September are considered "casual" or "accidental" (Andrews and Righter, 1992).

Red-necked Grebe *Podiceps grisegena* (Boddaert)
STATUS: Vagrant spring and fall migrant.
OCCURRENCE: There have been five reported sightings of the Red-necked Grebe in the Texas Panhandle, one each for Briscoe, Gray, and Potter counties, and two for Randall: *Briscoe*—one in winter plumage on Lake Theo, Caprock Canyons SP, 3 April 1977. *Gray*—one on Lake McClellan, 26 September 1954. *Potter*—one in winter plumage on Lawrence Lake, Amarillo, 12 March 1971. Oberholser (1974) reported the date in error as 2 March. *Randall*—one in November 1937; on 31 October and 7 and 14 November 1954, 1–2 were seen on a small lake on the southwestern outskirts of Amarillo.

The Red-necked Grebe is a Review List species requiring verification by the TBRC. None of the Panhandle sightings was reviewed. Written documentation of a Red-necked Grebe found in nearby Lubbock County on 5 and 7 January 1989 was accepted, as was a sighting of three on White River Lake, Crosby County, 21–22 January 1978.

Eared Grebe *Podiceps nigricollis* Brehm
STATUS: Fairly common to common migrant. Rare to uncommon breeder and casual winter visitor.
OCCURRENCE: Oberholser (1974) shows the Eared Grebe for Hemphill, Parmer, Potter, and Randall counties; this study adds Armstrong, Briscoe, Carson, Castro, Childress, Dallam, Donley, Gray, Hansford, Hartley, Hutchinson, Moore, Ochiltree, Oldham, Sherman, and Swisher. It has been recorded in every month.

The Eared is the most common of the grebes found in the Panhandle during migration: any large assemblage is almost certain to be of this species. The largest numbers reported have been on the BLNWR (250–300, 10–17 October 1959; 300, 30 April 1966; 400, 29 April 1967; 240, 4 May 1968). At one time the sewage pond southeast of Amarillo, Randall County, would hold 100+ in migration: an estimated 150 were present on 10 May 1981. Most migrants pass through during the periods April–May and September–October. There are a few spring records as early as 11 March and fall ones as late as 26 November. The Eared Grebe is rarely found in winter, and then more often early or late in the season. My records show sightings during only eight winters.

NESTING: Summer sightings of the Eared Grebe are fairly frequent, but few birds have been discovered nesting. Johnsgard (1979) shows the southern limits of its breeding on the Great Plains well north of the Texas Panhandle in northeastern Colorado and northwestern Nebraska (and a possible record in southeastern Colorado), while Strecker (1912) speaks of it as a "summer resident in the western half of the State," without citing nesting. The first report of breeding was that of Hawkins (1945), who classified the Eared Grebe as a "rare summer resident. On August 6, 1945, two adults and four quarter-grown young were observed at close range on a spike-rush-choked lake near Washburn" (Armstrong County). In addition, he found four nests with eggs; but it was not certain if they belonged to Eared or Pied-billed grebes, as the latter species was also observed on the lake. Nestings since mid-century were summarized by Seyffert (1988a) and others have been added (nests with eggs and/or chicks): *Armstrong*—7 August 1988; 26 July 1992; 24 June 1997. *Carson*—2 July 1989; 7 July 1997. *Castro*—2 August 1987. *Gray*—5 September 1982; 29 August 1997. *Moore*—24 August 1996. *Parmer*—10 July 1990; June 1991. Fischer et al. (1982) cited nestings in Castro and Swisher counties without giving dates.

Many of these dates indicate late laying of eggs (late June and after), in that the incubation period of the Eared Grebe is 21 days. Only once have I witnessed nesting activity earlier in the season. During the TBBAP in 1987 (16 May), I observed at least four pairs on a playa in the Dodd NE survey block south of Dimmitt, Castro County. One pair was engaged in courtship activities, calling *poo-eep, poo-eep* almost continuously and performing their "penguin dance" and "habit preening," as described by Palmer (1962). Later in the summer I saw one juvenile. I have never seen this playa without water; it receives runoff from a nearby cattle feedlot as well as adjoining irrigated fields, and it contains a great deal of emergent aquatic vegetation. Perhaps therein lies an explanation for so many late nestings, for most playas depend on local rainfall as a source of water and often it is late May or early June before they are filled, allowing the development of suitable nesting habitat.

SPECIMENS: Two specimens have been taken in Hutchinson County (31 March 1977, WTAMU), one bird found dead in a fish net and both in winter plumage.

Western Grebe *Aechmophorus occidentalis* (Lawrence)

STATUS: Rare migrant and casual winter visitor. Vagrant summer visitor.

OCCURRENCE: Oberholser (1974) shows the Western Grebe in four counties: Hutchinson, Potter, Randall, and Roberts. This study adds seven others: Briscoe, Castro, Childress, Donley, Gray, Hemphill, and Moore. It has been recorded in every month except March.

There have been nine spring, three summer, 18 fall, and eight winter reports of the Western Grebe in the study area. Spring dates range from one on Lake Tanglewood, Randall County, 3 March 1997, to one on Lake Meredith, Moore County, 31 May 1972. Three summer sightings are of single birds: Amarillo sewage pond, Randall County, 24 August 1985; Lake Theo, Caprock Canyons SP, Briscoe County, 23 June–2 July 1988; and Cactus Lake, Moore County, 28 June 1997. Fall dates range from two at BLNWR on 17 September 1978 to two on Lake Childress, Childress County, 26 November 1994. Winter dates range from one at BLNWR on 2 December 1971 to one on Lake Meredith, Hutchinson County, 4 January 1981.

Seldom is more than one grebe reported at a time (five were at BLNWR on 23–30 October 1965 and four on 3 December 1978). The closest to the study area that the species has been reported in summer is northeast Union County, New Mexico, 11 June 1978 (K. Seyffert); one at Lake Carl Etling, Black Mesa SP, Cimarron County, Oklahoma, 21 June 1981 (Williams, 1981); and two nonbreeders on Tucumcari Lake, Quay County, New Mexico, in the summer of 1987 (Hubbard, 1987).

In 1985 the light "color morph" of the Western Grebe was elevated to species status as *Aechmophorus clarkii*, the Clark's Grebe (AOU, 1985). Without evidence to the contrary, it is assumed that all sightings of *Aechmophorus* grebes in the Texas Panhandle have been of nominate *occidentalis*. Area observers should be on the alert as a Clark's Grebe was photographed on Lake Carl Etling, Black Mesa SP, Cimarron County, Oklahoma, on 9 May 1993 (Grzybowski, 1993), another was seen there on 27 November 1993 (S. Patti et al.), and yet another at the Elkhart, Morton County, Kansas, sewage ponds on 5 May 1996 (Cable et al., 1996).

ORDER PELECANIFORMES

Family Pelecanidae (Pelicans)

American White Pelican *Pelecanus erythrorhynchos* Gmelin

STATUS: Uncommon to fairly common migrant. Casual summer and winter visitor.

OCCURRENCE: The American White Pelican has been recorded in 19 of the 26 counties: Briscoe, Carson, Castro, Childress, Dallam, Deaf Smith, Donley, Gray, Hansford, Hartley, Hemphill, Hutchinson, Moore, Oldham, Parmer, Potter, Randall, Roberts, and Wheeler. Oberholser (1974) named it in four counties: Deaf Smith, Potter, Randall, and Wheeler. It has been observed in every month of the year.

Large gatherings of these pelicans, such as occur a short distance to the east at the Great Salt Plains NWR in Alfalfa County, Oklahoma, have never been reported in the study area. The greatest numbers were 160 at BLNWR on 23 October 1959 and 150 on Lake Meredith, Potter County, 11 April 1982. The species can be expected in spring from late March to mid-May (early date 17 March) and in fall from late August to mid-November (late date 20 November). Evidence points to a peak in spring during the last week of April; migration in fall is more strung out.

The southern limits of the American White Pelican's breeding range are extreme northern California, western Nevada, northern Utah, northern Colorado, northeastern South Dakota, and southwestern Minnesota, with sporadic breeding on the central coast of Texas (AOU, 1983). Though it is a nonbreeder in the study area, there are a number of summer records: BLNWR, 1–4 from June to September 1945 (Hawkins, 1945), 8–10 on 6–8 June 1963, one on 8–30 June 1973, 1–24 on 17 June–4 July 1979; Lake Meredith, 7–8 in summer of 1975; Hansford County, four on 14 June 1978; Childress County, one on 12 June 1987; Carson County, 77 on 12–13 June 1997.

There are seven winter records of pelicans: four at BLNWR in 1954–55, one on 1–4 January 1973, one on 27 December 1973; one at Greenbelt Lake, Donley County, 20 December 1981; one at Lake Meredith, Hutchinson County, 27 December 1981; one at Lake MacKenzie, Briscoe County, 26 December 1986; and one at Rita Blanca Lake, Hartley County, 2 December 1995.

SPECIMENS: There is an undated specimen taken in Moore County (MCHM).

Brown Pelican *Pelecanus occidentalis* Linnaeus

STATUS: Casual summer and fall visitor.

OCCURRENCE: There have been six reported sightings of the Brown Pelican in the Texas Panhandle, three of them cited by Oberholser (1974): an unspecified number in Hemphill County, June 1955; one at BLNWR ca. 1 October 1955; and one near Canyon, Randall County, 26 April 1956. The date for the Hemphill County sighting is in error as the observer's notes specify that the year was 1935. There have been three subsequent sightings: an adult on the sewage plant playa near Amarillo, Randall County, 21 June 1986; one on Lake Meredith, Moore County, 10 August 1991; an immature in Bugbee Canyon, Lake Meredith, Hutchinson County, 28 June 1996. The 30-year hiatus in sightings is understandable as the Brown Pelican was almost extirpated from Texas coastal waters beginning around 1958. A word of caution is in order for sightings not supported with details: juvenile or dirty American White Pelicans may appear brown.

Family Phalacrocoracidae (Cormorants)

Double-crested Cormorant *Phalacrocorax auritus* (Lesson)

STATUS: Fairly common migrant. Casual breeder and summer visitor locally. Rare winter visitor.

OCCURRENCE: The Double-crested Cormorant has been seen in 19 counties: Armstrong, Briscoe, Carson, Castro, Childress, Collingsworth, Donley, Gray, Hansford, Hartley, Hemphill, Hutchinson, Lipscomb, Moore, Ochiltree, Oldham, Potter, Randall, and Roberts. Oberholser (1974) cited it in three: Gray, Roberts, and Randall. It has been recorded in every month.

Until recent years, cormorants were expected in the study area from mid-April to mid-May and from early September to late October (24 March–31 May; 2 September–27 November). The species has been recorded on only ten CBCs, six of them on the *Amarillo* CBC at Lake Tanglewood, and there are only four other January–February records.

Until the late 1970s, the Double-crested Cormorant was reported only singly or in very small groups, and then not every year. Eleven at BLNWR on 19 October 1969 and 15 on 15 April 1979 were thought noteworthy at the time. Today its presence is expected throughout most of the year, sometimes in fairly large numbers: 40 in Randall County, 29 April 1995; 40 at Palo Duro Lake, Hansford County, 3 October 1995; and a combined total of 70 at Lake Childress–Baylor Lake, Childress County, 26 November 1994.

NESTING: On 4 June 1994, Double-crested Cormorants were discovered nesting on the recently impounded Palo Duro Lake, Hansford County. Five nests were occupied, three with at least six young visible. The site was visited again on 30 April 1995, when ten occupied nests were present (TP-RF). On the following 2 June 12 nests containing at least 12 young, along with 24 adults and two first-year birds, were observed. On 4 June 1996 the colony held 15 occupied nests; on 7 June 1997, 13 occupied nests; and on 5 June 1998, 18 occupied nests. The colony also contained nesting Great Blue Herons. Prior to this discovery there had been only six reported summer sightings of cormorants in the study area, and then no more than one or two at a time.

The Double-crested Cormorant is a rare breeder in Texas. Oberholser (1974) cited nestings in Matagorda County on the upper Texas coast in 1926 and in Baylor and Wilbarger counties in north-central Texas in the period 1937–39. It was not until 1974 and 1977 that nestings were again discovered, this time at Toledo Bend Reservoir in Newton and Sabine counties in extreme southeastern Texas (Holm et al., 1978). By the early 1990s many summering cormorants were being seen around the state, particularly in the central and northern sectors. In June of 1991, 18 pairs nested on Lake Fork, Wood County, northeast Texas (Lasley and Sexton, 1991), where two birds were seen again in 1992 (Lasley and Sexton, 1992). Totally unexpected was a colony of nesting birds found on Toyah Lake, Reeves County, in the Trans-Pecos in June–July 1992 (Lasley and Sexton, 1992), followed by five pairs that "built nests on pumpjacks on an otherwise barren playa in Midland County" in June 1993 ("still on eggs in July"), a first nesting for the southern plains (Lasley and Sexton, 1993). At the time of the discovery at the new Hansford County reservoir, nesting was also discovered at the recently impounded McNary Reservoir in Hudspeth County in extreme western Texas (Lasley and Sexton, 1994b). The Double-crested Cormorant breeds very locally in inland North America (AOU, 1983).

SPECIMENS: There is a specimen on display (ACNHM) taken at an unspecified location in the study area on an unknown date.

Family Anhingidae (Darters)

Anhinga *Anhinga anhinga* (Linnaeus)
STATUS: Vagrant summer and fall visitor.
OCCURRENCE: The Anhinga has been reported three times, once in Deaf Smith County and twice in Hutchinson County.

Oberholser (1974) places a far western sighting of the Anhinga in Deaf Smith County during May 1939 (H. Saunders) without giving details. On 24 October 1971, a bird was flushed in Bugbee Canyon, Lake Meredith, Hutchinson County, by observers in a boat and then watched as it briefly flew before again alighting (M. Forbus et al.). Thereafter it swam with only its head and neck exposed

("Had a very long neck and a bill which seemed a continuation of the neck"). Three weeks later another Anhinga, possibly the same bird, was seen by Park Ranger E. Day and others off Fritch Fortress. None of the observers, however, had ever seen an Anhinga before, and the possibility that it was a misidentified cormorant must be considered. The Deaf Smith bird may also be suspect as May is the height of the Anhinga's breeding season. An extraordinary seven were seen on Weatherly Lake near Borger, Hutchinson County, 11 October 1976, one remaining until 13 October (F. Cain).

The Anhinga is an uncommon summer resident along the coastal plain and locally in East and Central Texas, with rare postbreeding dispersal to areas west and north of the breeding range (TOS, 1995). In Texas it has been reported no nearer the study area than Wise County (Pulich, 1988) and in Oklahoma at Lake Altus, Greer County (Baumgartner, 1951).

ORDER CICONIIFORMES

Family Ardeidae (Herons, Bitterns, and Allies)

American Bittern *Botaurus lentiginosus* (Rackett)
STATUS: Rare migrant. Casual summer and winter visitor.
OCCURRENCE: Oberholser (1974) places the American Bittern in two counties of the study area, Dallam and Potter. Ten others can be added: Briscoe, Carson, Castro, Gray, Hemphill, Hutchinson, Moore, Oldham, Parmer, and Randall. It has been seen in every month.

The terms "rare" and "casual" are used advisedly in classifying this species' status, for bitterns are secretive and most often go undetected. I have recorded the species but once or twice every third year or so. This conforms to its status on the South Plains, where it is classified as casual (seen at intervals usually every two to five years; LEAS, 1994). This bittern can be expected from early March to late May and from mid-September to late November. There are several winter sightings of single birds: Lake Meredith, Hutchinson County—3 December 1970, 12 February 1971, 11 January 1972, 6 December 1981; BLNWR—16 December 1978 and 6, 14, and 24 December 1986; Amarillo, Potter County—8 January 1995. The American Bittern is a rare to uncommon winter resident along the Texas coast with occasional sightings at inland locations (TOS, 1995).

In summer it is as rare and irregular as in winter: two at BLNWR on 30 July 1954 and one on 27 August 1976, 22 August 1979, and 21 August 1980. On such late dates, they were possibly postnesting wanderers. Two heard "pumping" at a playa near Sunray, Moore County, 31 May 1975, indicated possible nesting, as did one each at BLNWR, 5 June 1978; Lake Meredith, 5 July 1982, Hutchinson County, 18–19 June 1989; and Carson County, 6 June 1997. Two seen and heard at Lake Tanglewood, Randall County, from early May to early June 1987 were thought to be nesting; however, a torrential rain brought a wall of water down the canyon, inundating the marsh, and the bitterns were not seen again. Oberholser (1974) shows a summer sight record for Potter County without giving details, and Johnsgard (1979) includes the northeastern Panhandle in the breeding range of the species but fails to cite the basis for the inclusion.

There has been no certain discovery of the American Bittern nesting at any locality near the Texas Panhandle. In Oklahoma, Sutton (1967) says it "probably" has nested in Beaver County, while Baumgartner and Baumgartner (1992) cite an observer's assertion that it nests every year (Harper County). Hawkins (1945) says that during the spring of 1945 this heron was found to be common in the Blackwater Draw area of Lamb County: "It may nest there." In New Mexico recent summer records at several locations, including Tucumcari Lake in Quay County, indicate it "may breed" (Hubbard, 1978). The AOU (1983) places the southern limits of the American Bittern's breeding range no nearer than central Kansas, generalizing its status in Texas by saying it breeds "locally."

Least Bittern *Ixobrychus exilis* (Gmelin)

STATUS: Rare migrant and casual breeder.

OCCURRENCE: The Least Bittern has been found in seven Texas Panhandle counties—Briscoe, Gray, Hemphill, Hutchinson, Parmer, Potter, and Randall—and has been seen in May, June, July, and September.

When speaking of the distribution and status of the Least Bittern in Texas, most references are rather sweeping in nature and lacking in details. Strecker (1912) said it was a "summer resident of the entire state, breeding from the northern boundary south to Brownsville." Wolfe (1956) cited it as a "summer resident in all areas," and the TOS (1995) gives it as an uncommon to locally common summer resident throughout much of the state. Both Palmer (1962) and Johnsgard (1979) included the extreme southeastern corner of the study area in the Least Bittern's breeding range, and such inclusion is brought forward in a recent publication (Gibbs et al., 1992); this despite Pulich's (1988) assertion that nesting has not occurred in that area (Wilbarger County) since 1929. Oberholser (1974) is somewhat more specific, showing a spring sight record for Parmer County and a summer sight record for Potter/Randall counties and classifying the Least Bittern's status as "casual in the Panhandle." The following account clarifies the Parmer County reference, but I have been unable to discover the basis of any for Potter and Randall.

A reference to the Least Bittern is found in a letter of Philip F. Allen's (1 August 1952), in which he lists it among those species found at Lake Marvin, Hemp-hill County. The first published record pertains to a bird found near Friona, Parmer County, 20 May 1963 (Baumgartner, 1963). Few have been reported since: 1–3 in the Sanford Dam marsh, Lake Meredith, Hutchinson County, 15 June–13 July 1975; one at Weatherly Lake near Borger, Hutchinson County, 24 September 1977; one at Lake Theo, Caprock Canyons SP, Briscoe County, 3 June 1978; one at a playa in Gray County, 6 May 1998. Predating these observations, I find a reference by Harold Saunders to a Least Bittern seen in Hemphill County "prior to '33."

NESTING: On 14 June 1977, I observed an adult Least Bittern at Lake Marvin, Hemp-hill County, standing on what appeared to be a nest placed near the outer perimeter of a growth of cattails. The nest was so positioned that I was unable to examine its contents. It was my belief that the structure was indeed a nest rather than a foraging platform, such as the Least Bittern is known to build at rich feeding sites, for if the bird had been feeding it would have flown the moment it was disturbed. Instead, it slowly crept away and disappeared into the cattails. The summer sightings of Least Bitterns in the Sanford Dam marsh point to a probability of breeding there; should more attention be directed to that site, nesting would likely be confirmed. Only a small portion of the marsh has ever been explored in summer.

The nearest to the Texas Panhandle that the Least Bittern has been documented nesting is at Tucumcari Lake, Quay County, New Mexico (Hubbard, 1987), and in Woodward County, Oklahoma (Sutton, 1967).

Great Blue Heron *Ardea herodias* Linnaeus

STATUS: Fairly common to common migrant. Uncommon to fairly common breeder. Uncommon winter visitor.

OCCURRENCE: The Great Blue Heron has been recorded in all counties of the Texas Panhandle and in every month of the year. It is the most common of the typical herons in the study area.

The major movement in spring takes place in April and in September during fall. The species is fairly evenly distributed during the spring passage, with few groups of any size occurring, but that of fall can be quite different. Illustrative of the latter season are numbers of herons recorded at the BLNWR during the autumn of 1970: 29 August, 44; 5 September, 60; 7 September, 90; 22 September, 40; 23 September, 7. The largest numbers reported at one site were "several hundred" on the refuge on 12 October 1952. Occasionally the Great Blue can be locally common in winter. Records of the USFWS at BLNWR show 10–40 wintering yearly during the period 1958–66, the largest number being 100+ that remained throughout the season in 1952–53. Such high numbers are unusual, however, as reflected in the cbcs. The *Lake Meredith* (*east*) count has averaged 14 birds, and the *Lake Meredith* (*west*) count four. In recent years the inclusion of permanent water within the *Amarillo* count circle has produced an average of 15 herons per count; on 17 December 1988, 34 were tallied at Lake Tanglewood. Almost all wintering herons are found at the larger impoundments, only a few transients appearing in the Palo Duro Canyon.

NESTING: Martin (1989) summarized the then known nesting sites of the Great Blue Heron in the study area and other sites have been added. The species has now been confirmed nesting in 14 counties—Collingsworth, Dallam, Donley, Gray, Hansford, Hartley, Hemphill, Hutchinson, Lipscomb, Ochiltree, Potter, Randall, Roberts, and Wheeler—and has been seen in summer in the others. Many heronries consist of only two or three nests placed in the upper portions of tall cottonwood trees, often far from water, and they can easily be overlooked. On several occasions an active Red-tailed Hawk or Great Horned Owl nest has been found in the midst of a colony. Nesting activities begin early. As an example, on 9 February 1998 eight herons were observed standing on nests at Palo Duro Lake, Hansford County. The earliest reported date of nest occupancy is 11 March 1996 at Jackson Lake, Donley County, and the latest date of a nest with unfledged young is 24 June 1976, Roberts County. As can be seen, the Great Blue Heron is predominantly a breeding bird of the eastern Panhandle and the Canadian River and its tributaries.

SPECIMENS: Great Blue Heron specimens have been taken in Hutchinson (12 July 1950, TNHC), Potter (1 January 1979, OMNH), and Randall (date not shown, WTAMU) counties. Oberholser (1974) refers to a summer specimen from Childress County without giving details. The subspecies found in the study area is *A. h. treganzai* (TOS, 1995).

Great Egret *Ardea alba* Linnaeus

STATUS: Rare summer and fall visitor.

OCCURRENCE: The Great Egret has been seen in 14 Panhandle counties: Armstrong, Briscoe, Carson, Castro, Donley, Gray, Hall, Hansford, Hemphill, Hutchinson, Oldham, Randall, Potter, and Swisher. Oberholser (1974) shows it in two, Hemphill and Randall. It has been recorded from April to October.

Great Egrets are fairly evenly distributed over the period May–September, with somewhat more reported in August. Few are seen earlier, the earliest being a single bird at BLNWR, 9 April 1994. The only October sightings are for 10 October: Lake Meredith, Potter County, 1991 (6); Lake Marvin, Hemphill County, 1995 (1); Lake McClellan, Gray County, 1997 (1).

Since the early 1980s, the Great Egret has been reported in the study area with increasing frequency and in larger numbers. My records show over twice as many during the latter half of the period 1963–93. Prior to 1950, only two observers mentioned the species: Stevenson (1942) called it an "uncommon fall migrant," and Hawkins (1945) cited it once (13 May 1943). Rarely are more than one or two birds seen at a time. On 20 September 1997 a phenomenal 30 or more, along with at least 15 Snowy Egrets, were found on a playa between Panhandle and White Deer, Carson County—a gathering that reminded the observers of scenes downstate.

In Texas the nearest to the study area that the Great Egret has been found nesting is Wilbarger County, but not in recent years (Pulich, 1988).

Snowy Egret *Egretta thula* (Molina)
STATUS: Rare summer and fall visitor.
OCCURRENCE: The Snowy Egret has been recorded in 13 counties: Armstrong, Briscoe, Carson, Castro, Deaf Smith, Donley, Gray, Hansford, Hemphill, Hutchinson, Moore, Potter, and Randall. It has been seen from April to October.

Little or no mention is made of the Snowy Egret in the accounts of early observers. McCauley (1877) speaks of it as "occurring in same localities as *A. herodias*," and Hawkins (1945) cites three dates: 14 May, 29 July, and 3 October. Bailey and Niedrach (1965) point out that it was only with the building of large reservoirs on the eastern plains of Colorado that the species began to be seen with any frequency, and such appears to be the case in the study area.

The Snowy Egret has been recorded from 15 April to 21 October, most often in June and July. No indications of nesting have been observed; however, in adjacent Quay County, New Mexico, Hubbard (1978) gives the status of the Snowy Egret as: "Summers occasionally at Tucumcari L. and may breed there." The nearest to the study area in Texas where it is known to nest is Wichita County (Pulich, 1988).

Unexpected was a gathering of 15 or more Snowy Egrets, along with 30 or so Great Egrets, on a playa between Panhandle and White Deer, Carson County, 20 September 1997.

Little Blue Heron *Egretta caerulea* (Linnaeus)
STATUS: Rare summer and fall visitor.
OCCURRENCE: The Little Blue Heron has been found in ten counties: Armstrong, Carson, Castro, Donley, Gray, Hemphill, Hutchinson, Potter, Randall, and Wheeler. It has been seen from April to November.

The Little Blue Heron is rarely mentioned in the accounts of early observers. McCauley (1877) spoke of it in general terms as seen "occasionally," and Hibbets et al. (1926–36) called it a "rare summer resident." Most sightings have occurred in late summer and early fall (22 July–22 September). The four April sightings are of an adult at Lake McClellan, Gray County, 15 April 1984; an unspecified number near Amarillo, 20 April 1973; one at BLNWR, 27 April 1976; and two in Donley County, 30 April 1973. There have been two November sightings: one near Amarillo on 14 November 1968 and one near Lake Tanglewood on 19 November 1976, both in Randall County. Reports seldom specify whether the bird was an adult or immature. Possibly some thought to be the latter should be discounted, for a young Little Blue Heron can be confused with a Snowy Egret by an inexperienced observer. Only once has the species, been reported in the PDCSP, an adult bird, 12 September 1965.

The nearest to the Panhandle that the Little Blue Heron is known to nest is in central Oklahoma and north-central Texas (AOU, 1983).

Tricolored Heron *Egretta tricolor* (Müller)

STATUS: Vagrant fall visitor.

OCCURRENCE: The Tricolored Heron, formerly known as Louisiana Heron, has been reported twice in the Texas Panhandle, both times in September.

I flushed a subadult Tricolored Heron from a cattail marsh on McClellan Creek a few hundred yards downstream from the dam, Lake McClellan, Gray County, 12 September 1980. The bird flew to a cable supporting a pipeline spanning the creek, where it remained perched in full view for several minutes before continuing upstream toward the lake. The second sighting took place on 19 September 1995, when I encountered a Tricolored Heron at Greenbelt Lake, Donley County. This bird, again a subadult, was viewed at close range for some thirty minutes and was accompanied by an immature Little Blue Heron.

The nearest to the Panhandle that the Tricolored Heron has been confirmed is a bird found in Lubbock County on 23 August 1982 (TP-RF). The species is a common resident along the Texas coast, with postbreeding dispersal to all parts of the state (TOS, 1995).

Cattle Egret *Bubulcus ibis* (Linnaeus)

STATUS: Fairly common summer and fall visitor. Rare breeder.

OCCURRENCE: Since it first appeared in Potter County, the Cattle Egret has been observed in 18 additional Texas Panhandle counties: Armstrong, Briscoe, Carson, Castro, Childress, Donley, Gray, Hansford, Hartley, Hutchinson, Moore, Ochiltree, Oldham, Parmer, Randall, Roberts, Sherman, and Swisher. It has been seen from April to December.

The Cattle Egret was first reported in the Texas Panhandle on 21 September 1966, when a single bird was found on a playa on the eastern outskirts of Amarillo, Potter County (L. and R. Galloway). Thus it took eleven years for this egret to extend its range into northwest Texas from Mustang Island, Nueces County, where the species was first observed in the state, 25–27 November 1955 (Oberholser, 1974). Another egret was seen later in 1966, on 30 October at BLNWR. These were not isolated occurrences on the northern plains, for Cattle Egrets found in Floyd County on 11 October and Dickens County on 16 October 1966 were firsts for those areas as well (Williams, 1967).

Today the Cattle Egret appears yearly and in increasing numbers, the early and late dates being for one at BLNWR, 1 April 1987, and for seven near Hart, Castro County, 2 December 1972. Large gatherings are not normally seen, but their size continues to increase. As examples at scattered locations: 49 in Parmer County, 21–22 September 1992; 60–70 near Sunray, Moore County, 18–24 August 1996; 90 between Amarillo and Canyon, Randall County, 7 September 1997. On 31 August 1996, 90 were tallied at the very site where the first Cattle Egret had been found 30 years earlier. These are all late season reports, but late May–July sightings are increasing. Subadults seen during this period are not presumed to be evidence of local nestings, however, as postbreeding dispersal of juveniles can be rapid and distant (Telfair, 1994). This egret may turn up anywhere, witness four found perched in large cottonwood trees at the first water crossing in PDCSP on 19 September 1992 and one on 18 September 1995.

NESTING: There had long been speculation concerning the probable nesting of the Cattle Egret in the study area, and in the summer of 1994 nesting was confirmed. Feeding adult egrets were observed on 8 July in Parmer County, leading to the discovery of nests with young on 27 August at a site located three miles east and two miles south of Lazbuddie (C. D. Littlefield). The nests were placed in a colony of Black-crowned Night-Herons. Eight to 14 occupied egret nests were estimated, with two nests containing unfledged young still present on 5 September. Other nestings followed: Sunray, Moore County, 19 June 1996 and 2 July 1997; playa southwest of Spearman, Hansford County, 2 July 1997 and 6 June 1999; Wild Horse Lake, Amarillo, Potter County, summer 1997 and 1999; near Clarendon, Donley County, 26 August 1997; and BLNWR, 11 July 1999. The latter colony contained 45 occupied egret nests. The Cattle Egret usually nests with other egret and heron species, particularly when colonizing new areas (Telfair, 1994), and those in the Panhandle, with few exceptions, have done so.

SPECIMENS: There is a specimen on display taken in Moore County (MCHM).

Green Heron *Butorides virescens* (Linnaeus)
STATUS: Uncommon to fairly common migrant and summer visitor. Rare breeder.
OCCURRENCE: Oberholser (1974) shows the Green Heron in three counties of the Texas Panhandle: Hemphill, Potter, and Randall. This study adds 15 others: Briscoe, Castro, Childress, Collingsworth, Dallam, Donley, Gray, Hall, Hans-

ford, Hutchinson, Lipscomb, Ochiltree, Oldham, Roberts, and Wheeler. It has been recorded from April to December.

Earlier references to the status of the Green Heron in the study area are somewhat contradictory. Both Hibbets et al. (1926–36) and Hawkins (1945) classified it as "a rare summer resident." Carlander (1934) thought otherwise. Giving its status as "fairly common," he went on to say: "While walking along a stream, one might come upon a flock of these birds." In sections of the country where the Green Heron is common such flocking is known in spring, but this is the only such instance reported in the study area. Perhaps Carlander's "flocks" were indeed spring migrants.

The earliest date for a returning Green Heron is 9 April 1989 in Wheeler County, and seldom is one encountered past September. In 1979 several remained at BLNWR until late November, the last one leaving during the first week of December.

NESTING: Until recent years the Green Heron was not known as a breeder in the Texas Panhandle (Palmer, 1962; Oberholser, 1974; Johnsgard, 1979), despite summer sightings indicating probable nesting. The nearest locations where nesting was known to occur were in adjacent Ellis and Roger Mills counties, Oklahoma (Sutton, 1967). It was during the TBBAP that nesting was confirmed: at Palo Duro Creek near Canyon, Randall County, 30 July 1987 (adults at nest containing one young); and on Gene Howe WMA, Hemphill County, 12 August 1990 (adults with one young). These late nestings may be explained by Sutton's (1967) belief that the Green Heron is two-brooded and by Pulich's (1988) suggestion that high winds early in the nesting season may destroy this species' fragile nest, causing the birds to renest. Wind would certainly be a factor in nesting success in the study area.

Probable and/or possible nestings at other sites have been discovered in recent years: *Briscoe*—Lake Theo (Caprock Canyons SP); *Childress*—Prairie Dog Town Fork of Red River north of Childress; *Collingsworth*—Salt Fork of Red River north of Wellington and Buck Creek west of town; *Donley*—Greenbelt Lake and Taylor Lakes WMA; *Gray*—Lake McClellan; *Hall*—Indian Creek near Memphis, Prairie Dog Town Fork of Red River, and Turkey Creek west of Turkey; *Hemphill*—Lake Marvin and Canadian River east and west of Canadian; *Hutchinson*—Canadian River east of Sanford Dam at Lake Meredith, White Deer Creek (Duncan Ranch), and Spring Creek (Terry Ranch); *Lipscomb*—Wolf Creek; *Ochiltree*—Lake Fryer (Wolf Creek Park); *Oldham*—Canadian River at Boys Ranch; *Potter*—Canadian River east of Boys Ranch; *Randall*—Palo Duro Creek in Lake Tanglewood area (Currie Ranch) and BLNWR; *Roberts*—Canadian River; *Wheeler*—Britt Ranch, Mobeetie area (Sweetwater Creek), Wheeler Valley

Park, and Young Ranch. These discoveries indicate that the Green Heron is probably more widespread as a breeder in the study area than was previously thought.

Black-crowned Night-Heron *Nycticorax nycticorax* (Linnaeus)
STATUS: Fairly common to common breeder. Casual winter visitor.
OCCURRENCE: The Black-crowned Night-Heron has been recorded in every county except Childress and would be there with better coverage. It has been seen in every month.

In spring, returning Black-crowned Night-Herons may be expected during the first week in April, the earliest date being 13 March 1983 for two in Randall County. Most are gone by late September, the latest 1 November 1996 in Randall County. Nine winter observations are on file: nine birds in the winter of 1960–61 on the outskirts of Amarillo, Randall County; one at BLNWR on 15 December 1962 and three on 26 December 1979; one recovered in Carson County, 27 February 1972; one at Lake Meredith, Potter County, 20 December 1980; one in Amarillo, Potter County, 10 January 1995, and 1–4 on 6 December 1997; three near Amarillo, Randall County, 20 January and 12 February 1996; and one in the upper reaches of the Palo Duro Canyon, Randall County, 3 January 1998. Possibly late February sightings represent returning birds and not overwintering ones. A short distance to the south in the Lubbock area the Black-crowned Night-Heron is commonly found in winter (LEAS, 1994). Prior to Stevenson's (1942) reference (see NESTING), summering herons had been recorded by early observers but none reported the species nesting.
NESTING: The Black-crowned Night-Heron has been on the National Audubon Society's Blue List of species since its inception (Arbib, 1971). What effects the widespread use of toxic chemicals may have had on the species can only be surmised, but an example of deliberate habitat destruction leaves no doubt of one important factor that has contributed to its decline. A thriving colony containing 100 or more nests was found east of Sunray, Moore County, in July of 1973. Two years later I revisited the site and discovered that all the nest trees had been cut down and lay about in heaps. The night-herons had largely abandoned the site, only about a dozen pairs remaining, a few of those carrying nesting materials into the cattail marsh. Still later, on 6 June 1977, I found only four adult birds in the marsh, and on 6 June 1978, not one.

Neither Palmer (1962) nor Johnsgard (1979) shows the Black-crowned Night-Heron nesting in the Texas Panhandle; Oberholser (1974) shows a sight record of breeding in Randall County without giving details. Perhaps his reference is based on Stevenson (1942): "Allan . . . reports a colony along the Canadian River near Canadian, Texas. Mr. L. E. Simms of Canyon informed me that about 100 adults nested in a grove 9 miles west of Canyon in 1934." These sightings would have been in Hemphill and Randall counties respectively. Other heronries have been found in those counties since, as well as in Armstrong, Carson, Castro, Dallam, Deaf Smith, Hansford, Hartley, Moore, Parmer, Potter, Sherman, and Wheeler counties. Probable or possible nestings have been observed in Briscoe, Collingsworth, Donley, Gray, Ochiltree, and Swisher counties. These widespread summer observations make it evident that diligent searching would disclose further nestings throughout much of the study area.

SPECIMENS: Specimens are available from Hall (2 September 1977, WTAMU) and Randall (25 April 1966, WTAMU) counties. The disposition of a specimen collected in Carson County is unknown. Oberholser (1974) shows spring and fall specimens taken in Hutchinson County and a fall specimen in Wheeler County, without naming where these were deposited.

Yellow-crowned Night-Heron *Nyctanassa violacea* (Linnaeus)

STATUS: Rare migrant and summer visitor. Vagrant breeder and winter visitor.

OCCURRENCE: The Yellow-crowned Night-Heron has been recorded in 16 of the 26 Texas Panhandle counties: Briscoe, Carson, Castro, Childress, Donley, Gray, Hall, Hansford, Hartley, Hemphill, Moore, Ochiltree, Parmer, Potter, Randall, and Swisher. Oberholser (1974) shows it in two: Potter and Randall. It has been seen in every month except November–January and March.

With the exception of Hawkins (1945), none of the early observers mentioned the Yellow-crowned Night-Heron. He classified it as a "rare visitor" and gave one citation: "An adult . . . August 4, 1943 . . . about five miles from Amarillo." Its crepuscular and nocturnal habits make the Yellow-crowned less likely to be encountered than the Black-crowned Night-Heron; accounting, perhaps, for the paucity of sightings. The earliest spring record is of a single bird at Lake Marvin, Hemphill County, 21 April 1968, and the latest in fall is of six in Amarillo, Potter County, 6 October 1984. On 13 February 1981, a subadult in a weakened condition was found in Amarillo, Randall County. This night-heron is found occasionally wintering in nearby Lubbock County (TOS, 1995).

NESTING: There have been only two confirmed nestings of the Yellow-crowned Night-Heron in the study area. In neither instance (1970, 1971) was the nest found in an eastern county, where expected; they were in Parmer County in the southwestern sector in a colony of Black-crowned Night-Herons six miles east of Farwell. The Yellow-crowned is known to nest with the Black-crowned as well as with other herons (Bent, 1926). There have been numerous other summer sightings, many indicating possible nesting: *Castro*—Fischer et al. (1982) cited the species in July, without giving details; *Childress*—an adult near Childress,

6 June 1976; *Gray*—two adults along McClellan Creek near Lake McClellan, 14 July 1988, and another on 24 May and 19 July 1990; *Hall*—an adult at Berkley Creek on the outskirts of Memphis, 15 July 1979, and an immature south of Memphis, 30 May 1988; *Hansford*—an adult at a playa in the southwestern sector containing a colony of nesting Black-crowned Night-Herons, Cattle Egrets, and White-faced Ibis, 2 July 1997; *Hartley*—one at Rita Blanca Lake, 24 June 1995; *Hemphill*—one adult at Lake Marvin, 14 June 1977; *Moore*—one juvenile on a playa east of Sunray, 8 July 1973, at a herony of Black-crowneds; *Ochiltree*—an adult at Lake Fryer (Wolf Creek Park), 7 June 1983; *Randall*—one on 29 June and two on 5 and 12 July 1969, one on 5 June 1973, an adult on 25 July 1987, and an adult on 4 July 1988—all at BLNWR; one near Amarillo, 24 June 1973; *Swisher*—an adult on a playa near the outskirts of Tulia, 21 July 1985.

It is in the eastern Panhandle that future nestings will probably be discovered. Sutton (1967) cites nesting in nearby Greer and Roger Mills counties in Oklahoma. On 23 May 1971, I found two nests with adults incubating eggs along Lebos Creek (= Sandy Creek), Jackson County, southwestern Oklahoma, some 35 miles east of the state line. It is in this southeastern region that both Palmer (1962) and Johnsgard (1979) show the Yellow-crowned Night-Heron breeding.

Family Threskiornithidae (Ibises and Spoonbills)

White-faced Ibis *Plegadis chihi* (Vieillot)
STATUS: Uncommon to common migrant and summer visitor. Casual breeder.
OCCURRENCE: The White-faced Ibis has been recorded in every county except Childress, Collingsworth, Dallam, Lipscomb, and Roberts. Oberholser (1974) shows it in two: Hemphill and Randall.

Although recorded from April to November, the White-faced Ibis is most commonly seen between mid-May and early September. The early and late dates range from ten birds near Amarillo, Randall County, 3 April 1976, to one at BLNWR, 23 November 1993. There is but one other November sighting and two exist for October.

The White-faced Ibis was not cited by early observers, and as late as mid-century it was considered rare. Those reported on 1 May 1954, for example, provoked the comment "rarely seen on the Plains" (Baumgartner, 1954). A later observation illustrates an increasing presence: "Migrating White-faced Ibis become more abundant and widespread in the Region each year and tend to linger into October and November" (Williams, 1984). A review of my records shows an average flock size of 8.6 (high 30) for the period 1964–84 and 28.2 (high 275) for the period 1985–94.

NESTING: There have been five confirmed nestings of the White-faced Ibis in the study area. In August 1985 a colony of about 25 pairs was found on a playa near Hart, Castro County (letter, David G. Cook, Department of Range and Wildlife Management, Texas Tech University, Lubbock, 14 August 1986). Nest building and egg laying began in late July and early August; the 23 nests were visited weekly from 20 August to 16 September. The date of nesting is several months later than normal and may be attributable either to delayed nesting or to a re-nesting attempt of birds forced to move from their original nesting site due to drought or habitat destruction. These factors are important to birds that utilize playas as nesting sites, and may account for many of the unusually late nestings reported in this study for other waterbirds.

On 2 July 1997 I observed a number of ibis at a playa southwest of Spearman, Hansford County, two of them on nests built in small willows; on 6 June 1999 I again saw several ibis at this site with two adults on nests. This colony contained nesting Cattle Egrets, Black-crowned Night-Herons, and Great-tailed Grackles as well. Two other sites visited in 1997 in the Spearman area also held ibis that appeared to be nesting in cattails. On 29 July 1997, 6–7 ibis were observed car-rying nesting material at a playa near Claude, Armstrong County. A mixed col-ony of Cattle Egrets and Black-crowned Night-Herons at BLNWR held 15 occupied White-faced Ibis nests on 11 July 1999, two of the latter with chicks being fed. This colony occupied a stand of tamarisk.

Prior to these discoveries, the nearest to the region where the White-faced Ibis was known to nest was Tucumcari Lake, Quay County, New Mexico (Hun-dertmark, 1974; Hubbard, 1983). To the south, nesting ibis were discovered on the Ralls sewage pond, Crosby County, in the summer of 1987 (*fide* C. Stogner). On 16 July 1989, while working on the TBBAP, I found a small colony of nesting ibis at a playa in the Wasson Quadrangle, six miles west and 3.75 miles south of Plainview, Hale County. The same day some 16 miles farther south, I visited another colony that had been discovered earlier and that contained 50 or more nesting ibis. Prior to the 1950s, Hawkins (1945) was the only observer to report a White-faced Ibis in the Texas Panhandle in summer: 1 June 1943. In addition to confirmed nestings in Armstrong, Castro, Hansford, and Randall counties, summer birds have been observed in Carson, Gray, Hartley, Moore, Ochiltree, Oldham, Potter, Randall, and Sherman counties.

Area observers should examine colonies of Black-crowned Night-Herons closely for possible nesting White-faced Ibis, as mixed colonies are known to occur. This relationship was pointed out by Hundertmark (1974) and Zuvanich (in Sutton, 1967), the latter reporting 13 ibis nests in a colony of Black-crowneds found in 1962 at Cheyenne Bottoms, Barton County, Kansas. Bailey and Nie-drach (1962) also found the two species nesting together in the San Luis Valley of Colorado.

Roseate Spoonbill *Ajaia ajaja* (Linnaeus)

STATUS: Vagrant summer and fall visitor.

OCCURRENCE: The Roseate Spoonbill has been reported in the Texas Panhandle four times, once each in Deaf Smith and Donley counties and twice in Randall County.

On the morning of 1 September 1958, an immature Roseate Spoonbill was discovered at BLNWR (D. Acord, P. Acord). The bird was viewed at length as it fed, preened, flew ("like a beautiful pearl in flight"), and rested. That afternoon it was observed again and a three-minute black-and-white motion picture film was taken. At this time the bird "put on a beautiful show, soaring around the lake over and over." The present whereabouts of the film is unknown. In addition to the 1958 sighting, Oberholser (1974) shows two prior ones: a spring occurrence in Randall County and one during fall in Deaf Smith County. The former has reference to a spoonbill seen at McSpadden Lake, Canyon, 28–29 April 1937 (A. I. Hibbets) and the latter to one observed in October 1939 (H. Saunders). The latest sighting was of two birds at Greenbelt Lake, Donley County, on 17 July 1999 (H. Oatmen, K. Moxon).

The Roseate Spoonbill is a locally common resident along the Texas coast and a rare straggler inland (TOS, 1995). On 31 July 1994, two were observed in Dawson County just to the south of the study area (*fide* C. Stogner).

Family Cathartidae (New World Vultures)

Black Vulture *Coragyps atratus* (Bechstein)

STATUS: Casual summer and fall visitor.

OCCURRENCE: The Black Vulture has been reported in five counties—Armstrong, Gray, Oldham, Potter, and Randall—during June, August, September, and October.

With the passing of the buffalo in the late nineteenth century, the status of the Black Vulture on the High Plains changed dramatically. This is brought out clearly by the observations of McCauley (1877), who found both Black and Turkey vultures feeding on the many slain buffalo, the Black Vultures much more numerous. Since McCauley's day, few Black Vultures have been reported. Carlander (1933) makes reference to an unspecified number seen in "several places" between 13 August and 4 September 1932. There was a report of one or more at Lake McClellan, Gray County, 25–26 September 1950, and one was seen "over the rangeland bordering the Canadian breaks" in northwestern Potter County on 5 October 1958. The notes of one observer (P. Acord) say further: "others recorded from the eastern edge of the panhandle in past years." Oberholser (1974) shows summer sight records for Armstrong, Gray, and Oldham counties and a fall sight record for Gray County, some possibly based on McCauley's observations. Inexperienced observers may misidentify immature Turkey Vultures lacking red heads, calling them Black Vultures, and care must be exercised when birds of this age class are encountered during late summer and early fall.

The Black Vulture has occurred hardly more often just to the south of the study area, where it is classified as "accidental" in April, May, July, and September (LEAS, 1994). There are but three records from northwest and southwest Oklahoma according to Baumgartner and Baumgartner (1992). These authors speak of the species' decline with the disappearance of the buffalo, and Sutton (1967) refers to the possibility that in earlier days the birds ranged farther westward in the state.

The Black Vulture is a common summer resident in Texas from the Pecos River northeast and east to the Red and Sabine rivers and south to the coast and the Lower Rio Grande Valley (TOS, 1995).

Turkey Vulture *Cathartes aura* (Linnaeus)

STATUS: Fairly common to common migrant and breeder. Vagrant winter visitor.
OCCURRENCE: The Turkey Vulture has been seen in every Texas Panhandle county and has been recorded in every month.

The Turkey Vulture was included on the first Blue List of birds (Arbib, 1971). In an attempt to validate such placement regionally, I surveyed my records (April–August) for the period 1964–92 and discovered the following: the average number per trip afield 1964–73 was 4.9; 1974–83, 4.2; 1984–92, 6.5. These figures indicate that the species is probably holding its own in the Panhandle. Larger numbers were to be found in the study area in the late nineteenth century, as attested to by McCauley (1877) when speaking of the number of carrion feeders attracted to the many buffalo carcasses hunters abandoned on the plains. Today more efficient and sanitary range practices prevail and fewer dead livestock are left lying about as food for scavengers. The largest congregations of Turkey Vultures have been reported at roosts in late summer and fall. One such roost at BLNWR can hold 200 or more.

The first returning birds in spring can be expected in mid- or late March; the earliest were two birds observed near Canyon, Randall County, on 5 March 1992. One seen flying over Dumas, Moore County, on 17 February 1988 was exceptional. Rarely is a vulture recorded past October. One fledgling observed repeatedly at BLNWR in 1972 remained until 12 November. Three others were found there on 12 November 1986. There have been only two other November sightings. Three winter sightings are on file. Two were at BLNWR, 29 December 1962, and one was recorded by reliable observers on the Lake Meredith (east) CBC in Hutchinson County, 3 January 1987. The bird was on the ground at a prairie dog town near Fritch. On 18 December 1998, a single vulture was seen flying south over Amarillo. Occasionally one is found wintering in the Lubbock area (LEAS, 1994).

NESTING: The Turkey Vulture has been confirmed nesting in four counties: Armstrong, Collingsworth, Lipscomb, and Randall. I know of only three instances in which actual nests have been found. Strecker (1910) found vultures breeding in "caves and under shelving rocks" near the top of Dripping Springs Draw in Armstrong County. I found a nest with two downy young in a shallow cave downstream from BLNWR on 4 July 1967. At the same site, on 27 May 1974, I flushed an adult from a nest containing two eggs. The TBBAP disclosed PO nesting in 56 quadrangles, PR in four, and CO in three, the latter based on the observation of juveniles. The number of POS is likely excessive, for wherever a vulture was seen it was assumed to be possibly nesting in that survey block.

SPECIMENS: Oberholser (1974) references a specimen collected in Randall County but fails to name its present whereabouts.

ORDER ANSERIFORMES

Family Anatidae (Ducks, Geese, and Swans)

Black-bellied Whistling-Duck *Dendrocygna autumnalis* (Linnaeus)
STATUS: Vagrant winter visitor.

OCCURRENCE: The Black-bellied Whistling-Duck has been recorded once in the Texas Panhandle. A single bird was shot by a hunter on 7 December 1980 on the John A. and Mike Smith farm 17 miles NNW of Hereford, Deaf Smith County (letter, Patrick M. Pitt, 12 November 1992).

During winter the Black-bellied Whistling-Duck is an uncommon to locally common resident on the coast and in the Lower Rio Grande Valley, with irregular sightings inland (TOS, 1995). The nearest to the study area that the species has been confirmed is Midland County (Midland Naturalists, 1992).

Fulvous Whistling-Duck *Dendrocygna bicolor* (Vieillot)
STATUS: Vagrant summer visitor.

OCCURRENCE: There has been one reported sighting of the Fulvous Whistling-Duck in the Texas Panhandle: three birds observed on the BLNWR, 5 July 1969 (R. Gritman, USFWS). The present whereabouts of a photograph taken of the birds is unknown.

The Fulvous Whistling-Duck in Texas is a common summer resident and rare to uncommon winter resident in the coastal area from Galveston County south to the Rio Grande (TOS, 1995). The nearest to the study area where it has been reported is Elkhart, Morton County, Kansas, some 65 miles to the north, where a nesting pair was found during the summer of 1971 (Williams, 1971). A lone bird was observed on 1–16 July 1983 in Comanche County, Oklahoma (Tyler, 1983), some 90 miles to the east. The origin of the nesting pair in Kansas must be questioned (Cable et al., 1996), for the Fulvous Whistling-Duck is sometimes held in captivity and may escape or be released.

Greater White-fronted Goose *Anser albifrons* (Scopoli)

STATUS: Uncommon migrant and rare winter visitor.

OCCURRENCE: The Greater White-fronted Goose has been observed in 14 counties: Briscoe, Carson, Castro, Dallam, Donley, Gray, Hansford, Hartley, Hemphill, Moore, Ochiltree, Parmer, Potter, and Randall. It has been recorded from August to April and once in July.

Most sightings of White-fronted Geese occur in the fall, often before the arrival of the first Canada Geese. The earliest date is 16 August 1954 for 30 on a playa near Canyon, Randall County. Besides being early (normal arrival is in late September), this group was exceptionally large, probably twice the average to be expected. Other noteworthy high numbers were 95 observed on a playa south of Umbarger, Randall County, 2 October 1984, and 55 on Taylor Lakes WMA, Donley County, 29 January 1998.

Winter sightings are rare and irregular. During the period 1961–69, the White-fronted Goose was seen fairly regularly at BLNWR, and a few were reported with fair regularity on the Taylor Lakes WMA during the late 1990s. Apart from in these two localities, however, there have been few reported since 1969. A single bird on a playa in Randall County on 17 December 1977 represents the only White-fronted Goose ever found on a CBC in the study area. This lack of birds in winter is comparable to its status of "occasional" and "irregular" in other regions of western Texas (LEAS, 1994; Midland Naturalists, 1992). The species sometimes flocks with the Canada Geese and might be reported more often if groups of the latter were examined closely.

Spring passage occurs within a relatively short period: 1 March–12 April. The sole summer sighting is of one found on a playa in Castro County on 9 July 1989, more than likely an injured bird. Although the mid-continent population that winters in Texas nests across the low arctic from the western shore of Hudson Bay to Alaska, it migrates primarily to the east of the Texas Panhandle before dispersing along the coastal plain (Ely and Dzubin, 1994). It is probable that if the eastern counties were visited more often in winter, more White-fronted Geese would be encountered.

The subspecies found in the Panhandle is *A. a. frontalis* (TOS, 1995).

Snow Goose *Chen caerulescens* (Linnaeus)

STATUS: Common to abundant migrant and winter visitor. Vagrant summer visitor.

OCCURRENCE: The Snow Goose has been recorded in all but four of the 26 Texas Panhandle counties: Childress, Collingsworth, Hall, and Roberts. It has been seen in every month.

Normally the Snow Goose is not reported until late fall. Hawkins (1945) cites a juvenile at the BLNWR on 12 October 1944, calling it a "very early date." Equally unexpected were six at the same location on 7 October 1979. Most first sightings occur around 14–24 November—quite late in relation to the passage of the species east of the Panhandle, where Sutton (1967) places the height of migration in Oklahoma as 4 October–15 November and Pulich (1988) in north-central Texas as mid-October.

There has probably been no greater change in the status of a bird species in the study area than in that of the Snow Goose and Ross's Goose. Until recently it was late winter and early spring before Snow Geese were encountered in numbers in the western Panhandle, birds thought to have wintered in Mexico (Bellrose, 1976). Triggered by a population explosion, another group became established in the study area by the 1990s. As examples, on 25 January 1993 an estimated 44,000 were observed on a playa at the Bovina, Parmer County, feedlot (TPWD), and up to 20,000 were wintering in the Cactus Lake area, Moore County (TPWD). In the winter of 1995–96, the number had grown to an estimated 60,000 in an area bounded by Cactus Lake on the east and Lake Rita Blanca, Hartley County, on the west (TPWD). This group is worthy of further study to determine, among other things, when the birds first arrive in fall and when they leave in spring. The sparse data contained in my records show an estimated 10,000 present as early as 7 November and a like number as late as 13 February.

Prior to these recent changes, the CBCs were illustrative of the Snow Goose's presence in early winter. Out of 124 counts (1961–96) it was recorded on only 18. Thought noteworthy at the time were 1,600 tallied at BLNWR on 5 January 1972. In all my years of birding the refuge, the highest numbers tallied were 1,000 on 21 March 1965 and 11 March 1973. The only recovery of a Snow Goose banded at BLNWR was one banded on 6 December 1963 and recovered near the refuge on 25 October 1964 (USFWS). The few isolated Snow Geese seen during summer have been of injured birds.

The "Blue Goose," formerly a full species, is now considered a blue morph of a polymorphic population. It is quite uncommon in the study area and flocks of "white birds" must be examined closely before one may be seen: "Blue morphs are concentrated in the center of the range, breeding mostly in populations north and northeast of Hudson Bay and wintering primarily on the Gulf coast" (AOU, 1983).

SPECIMENS: There is a specimen on display taken in Moore County (MCHM).

Ross's Goose *Chen rossii* (Cassin)

STATUS: Rare to fairly common winter visitor.

OCCURRENCE: The Ross's Goose has been recorded from mid-November to late April in 13 counties: Carson, Castro, Dallam, Deaf Smith, Gray, Hall, Hansford, Hartley, Hemphill, Moore, Parmer, Potter, and Randall. Oberholser (1974) names it only in Randall County.

The first report of a Ross's Goose in the study area occurred in late December 1966 when two were bagged by hunters near the BLNWR. On 28 December five more were found in a flock of Snow Geese on the refuge itself, and 2–5 continued to be seen until the following 18 February.

That the Ross's Goose had not been reported earlier is understandable, for prior to 1955 its total population was estimated at only 6,000 birds and its wintering grounds were restricted to the Central Valley of California: the species was considered rare and endangered throughout much of western North America (Dzubin, 1965). It is probable that this figure was too low as the very fact of the species being considered rare and endangered ensured that many reported sightings would be discounted, despite numerous claims by reliable observers that the Ross's Goose was more common than was generally thought. With better coverage and methods of censusing, by late 1964 it was estimated that the continental population of Ross's Goose was 34,300–44,000 (Dzubin, 1965). This increase, which occurred during a period of climatic amelioration in arctic Canada, paralleled an increase in the number of Lesser Snow Geese (Trauger et al., 1971). Beginning about 1960 with an expansion of Ross's Goose nesting range in Canada, it was found that the number of birds had increased dramatically in the central United States, with 1–6 percent of the then current world population wintering along the Gulf Coast of Texas and Louisiana (Prevett and MacInnes, 1972). A later study disclosed a continuing increase in population (Frederick and Johnson, 1983).

Ross's Geese are found most commonly in flocks of predominantly white-phase Snow Geese. Of migrating Snows in Iowa, the percentage of Ross's was 0.083–0.086 percent in 1968–69 and 0.38 percent in 1981 (Frederick and Johnson, 1983). Emphasizing a continuing population explosion, aerial surveys in December 1992 of Cactus and Stone lakes east of Etter, Moore County, disclosed an estimated 20,000 "white geese" (TPWD), and of those 3.3 percent at the former site and 14.3 percent at the latter were Ross's Geese. On the same day a survey of Lake Rita Blanca in Hartley County disclosed that 17.8 percent of all white geese were Ross's. Higher ratios have been reported recently. As examples, during the first week of December 1995, 83 percent of an estimated 3,000 white geese on Lake Rita Blanca were thought to be Ross's, and of an estimated 60,000 that wintered in the Etter–Rita Blanca Lake area, 10–30 percent were thought be Ross's. It is difficult to determine with accuracy the species composition of such large mixed flocks. Late February or early March counts would possibly be more accurate, for by that time Snow Geese have started to move north, leaving the Ross's Geese to migrate later (Dzubin, 1965). When viewing large flocks of feeding white geese, I found that it was not always clear whether some were Ross's or Lesser Snow geese, and the question of to what extent intermediates were possibly present also arose. It is known that hybridization and introgression of the Lesser Snow Goose and Ross's Goose are occurring at such a rate that the latter may be in serious jeopardy as a species (Trauger et al., 1971).

There have been only scattered reports of the Ross's Goose in other areas of the Panhandle.

SPECIMENS: A Ross's Goose was taken in Castro County in December 1977 (Dowler et al., 1978; MTTU).

Canada Goose *Branta canadensis* (Linnaeus)

STATUS: Abundant migrant and winter visitor. Rare breeder locally.

OCCURRENCE: The Canada Goose has been recorded in every county of the Texas Panhandle and has been seen during every month. Oberholser (1974) shows it in eight counties.

The Texas Panhandle is graced with large numbers of wintering Canada Geese. When the BLNWR was in its heyday in the 1960s, it was not unusual for 30,000–40,000 to winter yearly. The largest number ever recorded was 78,000 during the week of 2–8 January 1971, a substantial increase over the 4,255 recorded in 1948 when censusing began (Grieb, 1970). Today even larger aggregations are found in other areas, primarily that encompassing Rita Blanca, Cactus, and Palo Duro lakes (Hartley, Moore, and Hansford counties), where an estimated 100,000–150,000+ winter (TPWD). CBC averages reflect early winter abundance: *Buffalo Lake* NWR—7,427; *Amarillo*—1,264; *Lake Meredith (east)*—658; *Lake Meredith (west)*—1,271; *Quitaque*—306; *Friona*—42. Small numbers of returning geese in fall may be seen in September, but it is not until late October or early November that the larger flocks arrive. By the first week in March most have departed.

The results of a banding program conducted by the USFWS in conjunction with the Colorado Game, Fish and Parks Division on the BLNWR and in the Arkansas River Valley in Colorado (Grieb, 1970) disclosed that both groups of geese nested in the Northwest Territories (MacKenzie drainage) south into northern Alberta, Canada. The race most common in the Texas Panhandle was *B. c. parvipes* (Lesser Canada), making up 90–95 percent of wintering birds, with the remainder made up of about equal portions of *B. c. hutchinsii* (Richardson's) and *B. c. moffitii* (Giant Canada). It was determined that the geese passing across the eastern Texas Panhandle on their way to wintering near Vernon, Wilbarger County, were a separate population, having little interchange with the western group.

Two returns of Canada Geese banded on the BLNWR are of particular interest. One was recovered along the Bering Straits, 2,700 miles from the Texas refuge, and another on Midway Island in the Pacific Ocean, some 4,000 miles away. The northernmost recoveries were two at Cape Bathurst, Northwest Territories, 12 July 1976, one bird banded on 12 December 1972 and the other on 16 January 1973. The easternmost recovery was one in lower Michigan, 30 August 1973, banded on 17 December 1963, and the southernmost one at Aransas Bay, Aransas County, Texas, 20 December 1964, banded on 30 December 1961. Two geese at least 22 years of age were recovered in Canada: an immature male banded on 7 December 1962 was recovered on 4 November 1984 at McLairan Lake, Saskatchewan; and a mature male banded on 23 December 1963 was recovered on 9 October 1985 at Edgerton, Alberta. Of 1,188 recoveries, 38 were over ten years old.

A more recent study of small Canada Geese wintering in an urban setting in Lubbock disclosed that although the neckbanded geese originated in areas from the Western Arctic to Baffin Island in the east, the majority had been marked in the Central Arctic (East) (Ray and Miller, 1997). Numbers ranged from 5,600 in December 1990, to 97,300 in January 1993. These were birds thought to have been forced out of their normal wintering grounds on the High Plains north and northwest of Lubbock by harsh winter and poor habitat conditions. It is further thought that they are now conditioned to an urban environment and will continue to utilize its habitats regardless of conditions elsewhere. Increasing numbers of Canada Geese are also wintering within the city limits of Amarillo. As an example, 1,000+ were assembled on tiny MediPark Lake in Amarillo, Potter County, during the winters of 1997–98 and 1998–99.

NESTING: In the spring of 1991, numerous pairs of Canada Geese were discovered nesting in the Canadian River Valley, Hemphill County, east of Canadian to the state line. Most likely the birds had migrated into the area from a population established in Oklahoma in the 1980s by the Oklahoma Department of Wildlife Conservation. Geese have continued nesting at these sites in increasing numbers. Canadas have also been found nesting in the Lelia Lake Creek–Taylor Lakes WMA area near Clarendon, Donley County. About 15 young geese hatched in the vicinity of the Tascosa Country Club in Amarillo, Potter County, in the summer of 1995. The origins of the adults were probably various: birds raised locally and then released; overwintering birds that remained near a reliable source of food; and injured birds. Other summering birds, some nesting, are being reported with increasing frequency throughout much of the Panhandle. The first confirmed nestings of the Canada Goose in Texas reported in the literature were among those released on the Hagerman NWR, Grayson County, in the late 1940s (Pulich, 1988).

SPECIMENS: Despite the number of Canada Geese harvested yearly, I know of only four specimens available: Childress (15 August 1976; OMNH), Deaf Smith (18 February 1981, WTAMU), and Randall (4 February 1969, 4 January 1971, WTAMU) counties. Hunters are encouraged to contribute specimens to museum collections for study purposes. On 25 January 1970 a Canada Goose showing incomplete albinism was captured on BLNWR.

Brant *Branta bernicla* (Linnaeus)

STATUS: Casual fall and winter visitor, vagrant summer visitor.

OCCURRENCE: The Brant has been recorded in six counties of the study area: Castro, Deaf Smith, Hartley, Hutchinson, Randall, and Sherman. Reports of birds found in the twentieth century are for December, January, and March.

The first published reference to the Brant in the Texas Panhandle is that of Abert (1846). On 14 September 1845, while traveling along the north side of the Canadian River east of present-day Plemons, Hutchinson County, he spoke of seeing "large flocks of the green-winged 'teal', and the brant, 'anas bernicla,' and Canadian goose, 'anas Canadensis.'" This picture may be contrasted with that of today, when large flocks of Green-winged Teal and Canada Geese are not expected so early in the fall and a Brant hardly ever. It is of interest that not far to the east, S. W. Woodhouse also noted during this same period that the Brant was "abundant in the large streams of the Indian Territory," a claim that later students in Oklahoma thought possibly mistaken (Tomer, 1997).

There have been four twentieth-century sight records of the Brant in the study area, plus seven birds taken by hunters. The sight records were of one near Hereford, Deaf Smith County, 10 March 1969; Oberholser (1974) refers to a winter sight record in Randall County, without giving details—possibly Harold Saunders's of December, 1937; two on the Bookout farm southwest of Hartley, Hartley County, in early spring 1982; and one or more seen by hunters in Sherman County north of Cactus Lake in the winter of 1995–96.

Seven Brant taken by hunters in recent years were of both the "black-bellied" race (*B. b. nigricans*) and the "white-bellied" race (*B. b. hrota*). Five were taken by Patrick Pitt (letter, 12 November 1992). Pitt took a juvenile *nigricans* on 5 December 1980 and an adult *hrota* on 27 December 1982 in Deaf Smith County. The birds were mounted and photographed (TP-RF). The remaining three Brant were all *nigricans:* two adults taken in Deaf Smith County, 14 January 1984, and Castro County, 12 December 1986, and a juvenile taken in Deaf Smith County, 6 January 1989. Pitt says he knows of one other juvenile *nigricans* for certain taken in Deaf Smith County, and possibly yet another. In the winter of 1989, one (race unspecified) was bagged by a goose hunting guide near Dimmitt, Castro County.

From nearby areas, a Brant (*nigricans*) in Oklahoma was observed in Beaver County, 2 April 1922 (Sutton, 1967), and in Texas there are records of one near Vernon, Wilbarger County, 28 December 1956 (TP-RF); one at Lubbock, Lubbock County, 27 January 1994 (TP-RF); and another (*nigricans*) at Lubbock, 25 November 1994 (TP-RF). The latest sighting was one at Lubbock from 4 January to 20 April 1996 (TP-RF).

Formerly the two races of Brant were recognized as separate species. The "black-bellied" group winters along the Pacific Coast as far south as southern Baja California, and the "white-bellied" group along the Atlantic Coast from Maine to North Carolina (AOU, 1983).

SPECIMENS: The two mounted birds mentioned are in the hunter's private collection (PPC).

Trumpeter Swan *Cygnus buccinator* Richardson

STATUS: Casual visitor fall to spring.

OCCURRENCE: There have been two confirmed Trumpeter Swan sightings in the Texas Panhandle, the first a cygnet recovered near Boys Ranch, Oldham County, 8 April 1993 (D. Swepston; TBRC). The bird wore a white-on-green collar and had been banded on 10 September 1992 near Du Noir, Wyoming, while still too young to fly. The young bird, accompanied by several Canada Geese, had been seen in the area repeatedly several weeks prior to the day it struck a power line and broke its neck. At that time it was thought to be a Tundra Swan. A collar-banded swan thought to be an adult Trumpeter was seen briefly on the BLNWR during the CBC of 24 December 1993 (J. Reese, T. Carlisle, T. Johnson). As in the case of the Oldham County bird, it too wore a green collar; however, the white markings could not be read and confirmation that it was a Trumpeter Swan was unobtainable. It was later learned that in 1992, protocols formulated by the USFWS stipulated that only Trumpeter Swans be banded with white-on-green collars (Howe, 1993–94).

Prior to these confirmations, "Waterfowl Biologist Robert Jessen, a competent Trumpeter observer, saw two pairs of Trumpeters in that area [Texas Panhandle] in January 1990 and 1991" (Burgess and Burgess, 1997). The actual locations where these observations were made is unavailable. On 26 December 1993, what was thought to be a first-year Trumpeter Swan was observed on Lake

Marvin, Hemphill County (E. Stokely, J. Fiedler). The bird was observed from a short distance and a detailed drawing was made of its head. Recent studies, however, have shown considerable overlap in features previously thought distinctive in immature Trumpeter and Tundra swans, and it is virtually impossible to separate the two species in the field without extensive experience (Patten and Heindel, 1994). Documentation of the sighting submitted to the TBRC was rejected; however, it was accepted by the Trumpeter Swan Society (letter, Madeleine Linck, Trumpeter Swan Society, Maple Plain, Minnesota, 5 April 1996). In the absence of a specimen or the observation of a collar-banded bird, clear photographs are probably necessary to substantiate a sighting of an immature Trumpeter Swan.

In recent years there have been several regional sightings of Trumpeter Swans, the latest being two collared birds that wintered on a ranch pond near Justiceburg, Garza County. These were subadults from Hennepin Parks, Minnesota, "on a pioneering migration" (Burgess and Burgess, 1997). A sighting of six near Mangum, Greer County, Oklahoma, 8 February–10 March 1986, was considered valid (Baumgartner and Baumgartner, 1992).

At one time "large numbers of Trumpeter Swans historically wintered in Texas or migrated through Texas enroute to Mexico" (Burgess and Burgess, 1997). It is possible, if not probable, that a number of the swans in recent sightings in the Texas Panhandle reported as tundras were in fact trumpeters. Identifying swans correctly is a challenge to area observers.

SPECIMENS: The specimen secured in Oldham County in 1993 was deposited in the collection at MTTU.

Tundra Swan *Cygnus columbianus* (Ord)

STATUS: Rare migrant and winter visitor. Vagrant summer visitor.

OCCURRENCE: The Tundra Swan, formerly called Whistling Swan, has been recorded in 14 counties: Armstrong, Briscoe, Carson, Donley, Gray, Hansford, Hartley, Hemphill, Hutchinson, Moore, Oldham, Potter, Randall, and Wheeler. It has been seen November–April, and once each in July and September.

Almost all Tundra Swans have been recorded during the period November–February. Seven have been reported in spring, the latest an immature bird near Amarillo, Randall County, 4 April 1987. Two summer sightings were probably of injured birds: one in Oldham County (Oberholser, 1974) and an adult on Cactus Lake, Moore County, 13 July 1985. The lone September sighting was a single bird in a flock of American White Pelicans at McGee playa, Potter County, 21 September 1995. This was exceptionally early as the previous early date was 13 November 1959 at BLNWR.

Most swans are reported as singles or in groups of no more than two or three birds. Notable exceptions: a flock of 20 near Canadian, Hemphill County, November 1956; 25 at Lake Marvin, Hemphill County, November 1991, 12 remaining all winter; and 20 on the Lelia Lake ponds, Donley County, 16 February 1992. At this latter site and nearby Taylor Lakes WMA, swans were again found on 7 December 1995 (8), 11 November 1996 (9), 30 October 1997 (4), and 21 November 1997 (7), indicating that these sites may be regular stops for southbound birds. Eight swans (two adults, six immatures) remained on Lake Tanglewood, Randall County, 25 December 1966–7 February 1967.

It is possible that some Tundra Swans reported in the past were in fact Trumpeter Swans. The presumption was that all swans found in the study area would be tundras, and little attention was given to the possibility of some being trumpeters. This belief is no longer valid, however, for with the introduction of the Trumpeter Swan at various locations in mid- and western North America and the establishment of breeding populations, this species can be expected in the study area with increasing frequency. Every swan should always be scrutinized closely. Inexperienced observers at times report seeing swans that are in fact either American White Pelicans or Snow Geese. The reverse occurred when an Amarillo newspaper ran a picture of a proud hunter with his "Snow Goose" prize, when in reality the bird was an unlawfully shot Tundra Swan.

Specimen: There is a specimen taken 5.5 miles east of Canadian, Hemphill County, December 1955 (TCWC).

Wood Duck *Aix sponsa* (Linnaeus)

STATUS: Rare to uncommon migrant and rare winter visitor. Rare to fairly common local breeder in eastern two-thirds.

OCCURRENCE: The Wood Duck has been recorded in all but three counties of the Texas Panhandle: Collingsworth, Sherman, and Swisher. Oberholser (1974) shows it in two: Randall and Wheeler. It has been seen in every month.

The Wood Duck may formerly have been more common than it is now. McCauley (1877) said of it in the late nineteenth century: "Frequently observed in various streams, canyon localities, and elsewhere," naming Sweetwater Creek in particular. It is in many of those same areas of McCauley's observations that the species is found most commonly today. Indicative of its summer status in the southwestern sector of the study area, a four-year waterfowl study (Traweek, 1978) conducted in June and July produced only a single Wood Duck; a more recent and extensive five-year study (1988–92) conducted in the western High Plains disclosed not one (Ray et al., in prep.).

This strikingly handsome bird is seldom reported in winter. Since the beginning of the annual CBCs in 1954, the Wood Duck has been recorded only four times. In recent years wintering birds are being reported by hunters with greater frequency, probably the result of an increase in population throughout most of its range. The species now comprises more than 10 percent of the annual waterfowl harvest in the United States, and in the Atlantic and Mississippi flyways it is second only to the Mallard in the number of birds shot (Hepp and Bellrose, 1995). This is in contrast to the early 1900s when the species was thought to be verging on extinction. Indicative of its increasing presence in the study area, 23 were observed in one group on Lake MacKenzie, Briscoe County, 29 October 1995, and 60+ on Palo Duro Lake, Hansford County, 22 February 1997, and 30–40 in November that year.

NESTING: Hawkins (1945) classified the Wood Duck as a "rare summer resident" and was the first to report nesting: "On July 11, 1943, at Palo Duro Club, a hen was observed with eleven very young ducklings. . . . On four occasions between April 20 and June 3, Wood Ducks were noted at Happy Glen Hollow, near Canyon. They exhibited typical nesting behavior." Both sites are in Randall County. With the impoundment of Lake Tanglewood in the 1950s, Wood Ducks began appearing there in summer, particularly downstream from the dam, and during the summers of 1990 and 1991, adults with young were observed numerous times. Historically, it is in the Lake Marvin area of Hemphill County that nesting Wood Ducks have been reported most often (Bellrose and Holm, 1994). The ducks nest in the large cottonwood trees surrounding the lake as well as in the river valley and adjacent areas. In recent years a nest box program was initiated on the Gene Howe WMA. As an example of its success, in 1994 26 boxes contained 65 young. A similar program has been in place in Amarillo, Potter County, for a number of years, producing as many as 40–60 young yearly. A two-year nesting study of Wood Ducks along five waterways in the eastern Panhandle (Canadian River, Washita River, Sweetwater Creek, North Fork of the Red River, Salt Fork of the Red River/Lelia Lake Creek) was initiated in 1996 (Magill, 1996). Eighty nest boxes proportionately distributed among the five drainages at randomly selected sites had 6 percent occupancy, with 80 percent nesting success in the first year of the study.

The Wood Duck has been confirmed nesting at other locations as well. Two discoveries were made during the TBBAP: a pair hatched eight young from a nest box at Blair's Lake near Borger, Hutchinson County, during the summer of 1988; an adult female and three young were found during the summer of 1989 on the Gething Ranch, Gray County. On 7 July 1997, a hen and nine ducklings were observed on the Taylor Lakes WMA, Donley County. Two localities where there have been strong indications of nesting but where confirmations are lacking are southeastern Hutchinson County and the Lake McClellan area in Gray County. Wood Ducks may be found in spring in PDCSP but only as transients.

Johnsgard (1979) shows the Wood Duck's breeding range in the Texas Panhandle extending along the Prairie Dog Town Fork of the Red River from Childress County to its confluence with Palo Duro and Tierra Blanca creeks near Canyon in Randall County. Other than as noted in the immediate vicinities of Canyon and Lake Tanglewood, I have been unable to confirm present nesting downriver.

SPECIMENS: Specimens have been taken in Moore (29 October 1972, WTAMU), Parmer (1 January 1973, 22 September 1978, WTAMU), and Randall (March 1972, WTAMU) counties.

Gadwall *Anas strepera* Linnaeus

STATUS: Common to abundant migrant. Fairly common winter visitor. Rare summer visitor with casual breeding.

OCCURRENCE: The Gadwall has been recorded in all but four counties—Collingsworth, Dallam, Roberts, and Sherman—and would be found in those with better observer coverage. It has been seen in every month.

Although Gadwall can be abundant during migration, congregations of the magnitude occurring among several of the other dabbling ducks have never been reported. USFWS records at the BLNWR show a high of 4,000 for 25 November–2 December 1979, but this is exceptional. The 8,500 reported on the CBC of 26 December 1979 was a reporting or publishing error: 85 was more than likely the correct number. CBC averages and incidence of occurrence more truly reflect the Gadwall's early winter status: *Amarillo*—31 (26 of 33); *Lake Meredith (east)*—41 (18 of 18); *Lake Meredith (west)*—6 (10 of 24); *Quitaque*—18 (16 of 21); *Buffalo NWR*—18 (11 of 29). A Gadwall banded on the BLNWR on 17 February 1987 was recovered east of Lariat, Parmer County, 30 November 1987. Fall birds do not arrive suddenly and in large flocks, and their departure in spring is equally gradual. They are most abundant from mid-October to mid- or late November, and from mid-April to early May.

NESTING: Both Oberholser (1974) and Johnsgard (1979) make reference to a single nesting of the Gadwall in the study area, citing Hawkins's (1945) record for Potter County: a hen with two ducklings, 27 July 1945, near the then city limits of Amarillo. Other nesting Gadwalls have been found. The first was reported by Stevenson (1942): "Allan [Philip Allan, U.S. Soil Conservation Service] found a brood of young at Buffalo Lake in July, 1939. He considers the Gadwall to be a common breeding bird throughout the Panhandle wherever conditions are suitable." Such an assessment has not been confirmed by later observers. On 6 August 1972, I encountered a hen with seven young on the BLNWR, and on 5 July 1982 a hen with one young downriver from the Sanford Dam at Lake Meredith, Hutchinson County. A four-year TPWD study (1974–77) of waterfowl

(Traweek, 1978) conducted in the southwestern sector of the study area found Gadwalls with broods only in 1975 (26 adults, 5 broods, 31 ducklings). During the years 1988–92 the TPWD conducted waterfowl surveys during May and June and found a few pairs of Gadwall each year but no evidence of nesting (Ray et al., in prep.). The Gadwall nests with regularity no nearer the Texas Panhandle than southern Nebraska (Johnsgard, 1979).

In nearby locations in New Mexico, Ligon (1961) cites nesting in the Clayton area of Union County and Williams (1994) reports a Gadwall brood "at an e. plains wetland near San Jon," Quay County, 17 June 1993. A female Gadwall attending seven chicks was found on the Boise City, Cimarron County, sewage ponds on 1 August 1985, a first nesting for Oklahoma (Grzybowski, 1987).

SPECIMENS: Specimens have been collected in Hall (13 February 1977, March 1977, WTAMU) and Moore (29 October 1971, WTAMU) counties. Oberholser (1974) shows fall specimens for Armstrong, Hemphill (24 October), and Randall counties without specifying their locations.

Eurasian Wigeon *Anas penelope* Linnaeus

STATUS: Vagrant winter visitor.

OCCURRENCE: The Eurasian Wigeon has been recorded in four Texas Panhandle counties—Deaf Smith, Hemphill, Hutchinson, Potter—and has been seen from November to March.

Oberholser (1974) shows a winter sight record of a Eurasian Wigeon for Deaf Smith County, without attribution. The observation is probably that of Harold Saunders, who recorded one (gender not specified) in that county in December 1947. It was 25 years before another was seen, a male at Sanford Dam, Lake Meredith, Hutchinson County, 18–20 January 1972. On 16 January 1984, a male bird was shot 17 miles NNW of Hereford, Deaf Smith County (letter, Patrick M. Pitt, 12 November 1992). The 1990s produced four sightings of Eurasian Wigeon, a male each time: Lake Marvin, Hemphill County, 23–28 November 1992 (TBRC; TP-RF), and 3–14 December 1995 and 15 January 1996 (TBRC; TP-RF); Thompson Park Lake, Amarillo, Potter County, 20 December 1994–15 March 1995 (TBRC; TP-RF), and 13 November 1995–21 March 1996 (TBRC; TP-RF).

Other sightings of the Eurasian Wigeon have been reported in nearby areas: in Oklahoma one near Guymon, Texas County, 29 April 1955, and one in Roger Mills County, 18 October 1970 (Baumgartner and Baumgartner, 1992); Ligon's (1961) citation of one found near Clayton, Union County, New Mexico, on 10 April 1954 was later reclassified as "hypothetical" by Hubbard (1978); and a male was seen at the Elkhart, Morton County, Kansas sewage ponds, 10 March 1995 (Cable et al., 1996).

This Old World wigeon is found regularly in North America in winter on the Pacific Coast from southeastern Alaska south to northern Baja California and on the Atlantic-Gulf Coast from Labrador and Newfoundland south to Florida and west to southern Texas (AOU, 1983).

American Wigeon *Anas americana* Gmelin

STATUS: Common to abundant migrant and winter visitor. Rare summer visitor.

OCCURRENCE: The American Wigeon has been recorded in all but three counties of the study area: Collingsworth, Lipscomb, and Roberts. Oberholser (1974) shows it in seven. It has been seen in every month.

The Texas Panhandle is the nation's third most important wintering ground for the "baldpate" (Bellrose, 1976), and this is one of the area's most abundant species of waterfowl. The highest number recorded at any one time was 207,000 at BLNWR, 2–9 December 1959 (USFWS). During the 1960s, the Fish and Wildlife Service records show annual peak numbers in the 50,000–100,000 range. The highest number recorded on a CBC was 100,000 on 29 December 1967. The averages and highs on the other area CBCs are considerably less: *Lake Meredith* (*east*)—363 (5,000); *Friona*—177 (1,000); *Quitaque*—76 (500); *Amarillo*—39 (304); *Lake Meredith* (*west*)—43 (102). The species can often be found in winter on city lakes and ponds, rivaling the Canada Goose as a panhandler.

Hawkins's (1945) observation that "a few, probably nonbreeders, remain throughout the summer" has been borne out by later observers. My records (1964–97) show that I found the American Wigeon during summer (June–July) in twelve of the years, and then no more than ten birds in a day. A four-year (1974–77) waterfowl study (Traweek, 1978) found a yearly average of 113 adults during June–July but no broods. During a waterfowl survey conducted in 1990 (Ray et al., in prep.), three pairs were observed in the northern sector of the region and one pair in the southwestern sector; again, nesting was not confirmed. The species is not known to nest any nearer the Texas Panhandle than northwestern Nebraska (Johnsgard, 1979).

Returning birds in fall normally arrive in mid-September, but abundance is not reached until early or mid-October. Overwintering birds, joined by migrants, often reach peak numbers in mid-February, and most are gone by mid-May. An adult male banded on the BLNWR on 29 January 1963 was recovered near the refuge on 10 May 1988, making the bird at least 25 years of age (USFWS).

SPECIMENS: There are specimens available for Deaf Smith (26 December 1984, WTAMU), Moore (MCHM; 9 November 1972, WTAMU), and Parmer (25 October 1973, 7 January 1976, WTAMU) counties.

American Black Duck *Anas rubripes* Brewster

STATUS: Casual winter visitor.

OCCURRENCE: The American Black Duck has been recorded in six counties—
Castro, Deaf Smith, Hemphill, Moore, Parmer, and Randall—and has been seen
October–February.

There have been ten reported sightings of the Black Duck in the study area,
the earliest a single bird in Deaf Smith County, in November 1939. Hawkins
(1945) names three: one taken in Hemphill County in 1943 and mounted; one
in a flight of Mallards at BLNWR on 23 January 1944, and another found dead
("evidently the victim of fowl cholera"), 18 February 1945. The remaining
sightings occurred after mid-century: one in October 1952 and two on 15 December 1963 at BLNWR; one wintering near Dumas, Moore County (1972–73),
captured and banded (letter, James E. Dillard, TPWD, Dumas, 16 June 1973); one
captured and photographed in Parmer County, 26 January 1986 (Fedynich and
Rhodes, 1995); and one on 12 December 1994 at Hart, Castro County.

Because the Black Duck can easily be confused in flight with the dark-phase
Mottled Duck, any sight report must be viewed with caution. A specimen, photograph, or bird in hand is almost a necessity for acceptance, particularly since
the Mottled Duck is being encountered with greater frequency north of its
known range on the Texas coast, and hybrid combinations of Mallard–Black
Duck and Mallard–Mottled Duck occur. Sutton (1974a) avers that in Oklahoma
there is "no acceptable record for Panhandle," and Hubbard (1978), while ac-
knowledging reports of Black Ducks in the area of Clayton, Union County, New
Mexico, places the species on that state's "hypothetical" list. Pulich's (1988) re-
quest should be followed: "Any duck hunter who shoots a duck suspected of
being a Black Duck should save it for proper identification."

Mallard *Anas platyrhynchos* Linnaeus

STATUS: Fairly common (summer) to abundant (winter) resident.

OCCURRENCE: The Mallard is one of the most common waterfowl species in the
Texas Panhandle and has been recorded in all 26 counties during every month
of the year.

Midwinter is the season of the Mallard's greatest abundance. Playa lakes
abound with the "greenhead," and still greater numbers gather on impoundments. At one time the BLNWR was justifiably known for its large wintering
population. USFWS records during 14 consecutive winter seasons (1959–72) show
peak numbers ranging from 62,500 to 510,000. With the draining of the lake in
1973, numbers dropped dramatically, as CBCS reflect: 435 in 1973, 10 in 1974, 200
in 1975. A torrential rain filled the lake in the spring of 1978, and on the following
24 December, 175,350 were tallied. Averages and highs on the other CBCS: *Lake*

Meredith (east)—7,690 (75,000); *Lake Meredith (west)*—1,782 (25,000); *Quitaque*—931 (7,500); *Friona*—958 (3,700); *Amarillo*—356 (2,093). For the period 1961–91, 52 percent of all ducks recorded on the CBCs were Mallards. Of an estimated 120,00 ducks that wintered on Lake Meredith in the winter season of 1970–71, 80 percent were Mallards.

Traversing the eastern and central Panhandle in May and June of 1876, McCauley (1877) commented on the status of the Mallard: "Abundantly found on all the lower parts of water-courses and at suitable places above." The Mallard is still today a fairly common summering bird and has been recorded in all the study area counties during that season. The results of a four-year (1974–77) waterfowl study (TPWD) conducted during June and July disclosed the Mallard as the single most common duck species (Traweek, 1978), ranging from 28 percent of all adults observed in 1974 to 43 percent in 1975—the highest number 824, the lowest 279, and the average 568. The study was based on 25 driving/walking transects in 12 counties: Armstrong, Briscoe, Carson, Castro, Deaf Smith, Parmer, Randall, Swisher, Bailey, Floyd, Hale, and Lamb. The expanded data revealed a yearly average of 8,589 adult Mallards.

Returns of Mallards banded at BLNWR show wide dispersal (USFWS): *Canada*—NWT (3), AB (53), SK(41), MN (2), PEI (1); *United States*—AK (1), MT (14), ND (8), WA (2), SD (7), ID (5), MI (1), OR (1), NE (49), WY (2), UT (3), CO (45), KS (34), DE (1), OK (9), MO (1), TX (Panhandle 67), TX (other 68), NM (10), AR (4), MS (4), AZ (1), LA (7). A Mallard banded on 23 February 1987 was recovered on 1 January 1989 near the northwest tip of the Yucatan Peninsula. The oldest bird was one banded on 11 February 1968 and recovered on 22 November 1988 near Steamboat Springs, Colorado. A Mallard exhibiting partial albinism was netted on the refuge on 4 February 1968.

NESTING: The Mallard has been found in summer in all 26 study area counties and confirmed nesting in all but five: Childress, Collingsworth, Dallam, Hall, and Wheeler. The four-year Traweek (1978) study disclosed as many as 1,528 broods and 10,048 ducklings (expanded data) produced in the best season. The percentage frequency of young Mallards ranged from 64 percent of all young ducks observed in 1975 to 81 percent in 1976. A more recent study (1988–92) covering the western two-thirds of the High Plains, stretching from the northern Panhandle to south of Lubbock, found Mallard breeding pairs the most abundant of 15 species of duck, the mean 0.14 pairs/km² (Ray et al., in prep.). During the TBBAP confirmations were made or evidence of nesting was found in 18 counties: CO in 33 survey blocks, PR in 30, and PO in 16. Of the 79 occupied quadrangles, 20 were located between the 100th and 101st meridians, 35 between the 101st and 102nd, and 24 west of the 102nd meridian, indicating a fairly even distribution.

The Mallard is both an early and a late nester. My earliest record is of a hen flushed from a nest containing four Mallard eggs and twelve teal eggs at BLNWR on 18 April 1987. Broods of young ducklings have been observed quite late in the year. A hen and six small chicks were on a playa near Umbarger, Randall County, 25 September 1982, and on 26 September 1991, I found a hen with seven very young ducklings at BLNWR.

Despite the fact that the Mallard is known as a widespread nester in the Texas Panhandle, many published works, including rather recent ones, fail to reflect this knowledge. Johnsgard (1979) shows the Mallard's nesting range extending into only the northeasternmost tip of the study area; Palmer (1976) does not show the area at all, while Oberholser (1974) tags only three counties with sight records of breeding—and one of them he thought questionable.

SPECIMENS: There are specimens from Castro (3 November 1984, CMNH), Moore (1971, WTAMU), and Randall (3 January 1968, 1972, WTAMU) counties. Oberholser (1974) shows specimens taken in Castro, Deaf Smith, Moore, Oldham, Potter, Swisher, and Wheeler counties, without naming the collections in which they were deposited.

Blue-winged Teal *Anas discors* Linnaeus

STATUS: Common to abundant migrant. Uncommon to fairly common breeder. Vagrant winter visitor.

OCCURRENCE: The Blue-winged Teal has been recorded in every county of the Texas Panhandle and has been seen in every month.

In his journey through the area in May and June of 1876, McCauley (1877) found the Blue-winged Teal to be "more abundant than any other of the *Anatidae*." Today the Mallard would take that honor in most years. Returning teal are normally first seen in early or mid-March, a week or two after the first Cinnamon Teals have returned. Numbers reach a peak in mid-April, then rapidly decline. By mid-August numbers begin to increase once again, and an abundance is reached in early or mid-September. Few are reported past October: 1,575 on the BLNWR on 22 October 1993 were unusual, and 50 on the refuge on 13 November were exceptional. Really large congregations are rarely seen. An estimated 3,050 were tallied on the BLNWR, 5 September 1970.

Winter sightings are rare: three on the BLNWR on 3 January 1965, eight on 12 February and five on 19 February 1966—the latter possibly early migrants; a male on Lake Meredith, Hutchinson County, 29 December 1973; a female on Greenbelt Lake, Donley County, 20 December 1981; 2–30 from 6 to 26 February 1994 on the BLNWR—again, possibly early migrants. The Blue-winged Teal is a common winter resident in the southern third of Texas (TOS, 1995).

An oddity was an adult male Blue-winged Teal I saw with a white head, ob-

served on a playa near Amarillo, Randall County, 9 May 1986. Its plumage otherwise appeared the same as that of other males swimming nearby. The head was
not uniformly white, however, but smudged with gray beside the eyes and down
the sides, faintly outlining a white spot near the base of the bill.

NESTING: The results of a four-year study (1974–77) conducted by the TPWD (Traweek, 1978) disclosed the Blue-winged Teal as the second most common breeding duck in the study area, following the Mallard. Based on 25 transects in 12
southwestern counties, the expanded figures came to a yearly average of 3,112
adults, 93 broods, and 398 ducklings. The summer of 1997 proved an exception
to this ranking, for Blue-winged Teals far outnumbered Mallards as nesters. As
examples of teal abundance, on several playas between Groom and Pampa in
Gray County an estimated 100+ adults with 350 or more young were observed
on 16 July, and on 27 July 75+ adults with 200 or more young on a few playas
in Armstrong County. One small playa in Gray County held 80 or more ducklings, and another a short distance down the road held 70 or more. The species
had been reported breeding in fourteen counties prior to the TBBAP—Armstrong, Briscoe, Carson, Castro, Dallam, Hansford, Hartley, Hutchinson, Moore,
Oldham, Parmer, Potter, Randall, Swisher. The project added five others—Deaf
Smith, Gray, Hansford, Ochiltree, and Sherman. Prior to this, all confirmed
nestings had been restricted to west of the 101st meridian, the majority in the
central and southwestern sectors.

Reports of actual nests with eggs are few, no doubt through insufficient
searching. The dates range from 18 April 1987 at BLNWR to 24 July 1997 in Carson County. There is evidence of later nestings. I observed a hen with a brood
of unfeathered ducklings on 23 August 1992 and a hen with eight ducklings on
1 September 1995, both on playas in Randall County, and two groups of eight
unfledged young on the BLNWR on 3 September 1984.

SPECIMENS: There is a specimen collected in Randall County (WTAMU). Oberholser (1974) names specimens for Dallam and Wheeler counties but fails to
specify their whereabouts.

Cinnamon Teal *Anas cyanoptera* Vieillot

STATUS: Fairly common to common migrant and uncommon breeder. Casual
winter visitor.

OCCURRENCE: The Cinnamon Teal has been recorded in every county except
Childress, Collingsworth, Lipscomb, and Roberts and would be in them with
better coverage. Oberholser (1974) shows it in five counties. It has been seen in
every month.

Returning Cinnamon Teals in spring can be expected as early as February,
occasionally during the first week, and a few stragglers may remain in fall until

mid-November. There have been only ten winter sightings, including birds seen in February. The species has been recorded twice on CBCS: a female 16 December 1989 on Lake Tanglewood, Randall County, and a flock of twelve farther up the canyon from that site, 16 December 1995. Its almost total absence in winter from the High Plains is in contrast to its status below the caprock escarpment, where the Cinnamon Teal is listed on the South Plains checklist (LEAS, 1994) as uncommon ("present, but not certain to be seen").

The Cinnamon Teal has been poorly studied in the Panhandle and an assessment of normal numbers during migration is lacking. Many observers neither take the time nor make the effort necessary to separate teal species in a mixed flock; consequently, these groups are simply tallied as "teal" when arriving at aggregate numbers. This is particularly so later in the year when ducks are in transition plumage. This lack of attention is important to remember when wondering why observers never report significant numbers of Cinnamon Teals.

On 16 April 1995 a male Cinnamon X Blue-winged Teal hybrid was observed on the sewage plant playa southeast of Amarillo, Randall County. The bird was swimming in a mixed group of male and female Cinnamon Teals. Its plumage was seemingly identical with that of other males in the group except for a pronounced white crescent between the eye and the base of the bill and a white patch on the lower side near the tail, features characteristic of the male Blue-winged Teal. Another Blue-winged X Cinnamon hybrid was captured near Hart, Castro County, 20 March 1986 (Godfrey and Fedynich, 1987).

NESTING: The TBBAP recorded CO nestings in four survey blocks in Randall County, and PR nestings in 16 in 11 other counties: Briscoe, Castro, Carson, Deaf Smith, Hansford, Hutchinson, Ochiltree, Oldham, Potter, Sherman, and Swisher. Numerous pairs and small groups of vigorously courting birds were also observed. The expanded data of the Traweek (1978) study, based on 25 transects in 12 southwestern counties, produced a yearly average of 2,043 adult Cinnamon Teals, 40 broods, and 152 ducklings. Prior to the TBBAP, nestings were known for Castro, Dallam, Hutchinson, and Potter counties. All nestings have been found west of the 101st meridian.

SPECIMENS: Specimens are available from Castro (December 1975, MTTU), Parmer (20 January 1974, WTAMU), and Randall (1970, WTAMU) counties.

Northern Shoveler *Anas clypeata* Linnaeus

STATUS: Abundant migrant and fairly common winter visitor. Rare to uncommon in summer, with casual breeding.

OCCURRENCE: The Northern Shoveler has been recorded in all the Texas Panhandle counties except Collingsworth, Lipscomb, Roberts, and Sherman. It has been seen in every month.

The "spoonbill" is most abundant during migration. The highest numbers reported in fall and spring at BLNWR—10,000 on 7 November 1969, 6,000 on 7 April 1960 (USFWS)—are indicative of numbers during peak periods (early October–early November, mid-March–mid-April). There are short periods during spring in which the shoveler may be the dominant species of duck. The CBC averages and highs disclose an erratic presence and normally small numbers during early winter: *Buffalo Lake* NWR—21, 100; *Amarillo*—54, 1,000; *Quitaque*—7, 75; *Lake Meredith* (*west*)—0.75, 6; *Lake Meredith* (*east*)—2, 8; *Friona*—2, 10.

NESTING: Few Northern Shovelers have been confirmed nesting despite numerous sightings in summer. Johnsgard (1979) shows the species breeding in the northern tier of counties: "dependent young have been reported from early March to June 30" (details lacking). Other confirmed nestings have been recorded in the following counties: *Parmer*—3 June 1990; *Castro*—summer of 1994; *Oldham*—3 May 1995; *Carson*—6–7 July 1997; *Gray*—16 July 1997; *Armstrong*—23 July 1997; *Randall*—23 July 1997, 1 July 1998. A four-year study of waterfowl (Traweek, 1978) disclosed a yearly average of 254 adult shovelers in June and July but no broods or ducklings. The study was made in the southern and southwestern sectors. During the period 1988–92 the TPWD conducted waterfowl surveys in much of the central and western sectors in May and June and found a few pairs of shovelers each year but no confirmations of nesting.

SPECIMENS: There are specimens collected in Armstrong (3 May 1973, WTAMU), Deaf Smith (6 December 1967, WTAMU), Hall (March 1977, WTAMU), Moore (MCHM), and Parmer (31 March 1976, WTAMU) counties.

Northern Pintail *Anas acuta* Linnaeus

STATUS: Abundant migrant and winter visitor. Rare to uncommon breeder.

OCCURRENCE: The Northern Pintail has been recorded in every Texas Panhandle county except Collingsworth, Hall, and Roberts. It has been seen the year round.

Second to the Mallard, the Northern Pintail is the most common species of duck in the study area during migration and in winter. It is the earliest to return in large numbers in fall, normally in early to mid-September, although an influx can be detected as early as late July. Its abundance in winter is illustrated by numbers recorded at BLNWR during the period 1959–69 (USFWS), when peak numbers ranged from 70,000 (1961) to 280,000 (1963). Will such numbers ever be seen again? Continental breeding waterfowl surveys conducted in May show high populations of pintails in the 1950s and 1970s (5.5–9.9 million) and record low numbers during extensive prairie drought in 1988–91 (1.8–2.3 million) (Austin and Miller, 1995). Waterfowl can rebound given favorable nesting environments, however; numbers of breeding Northern Pintails increased substantially in 1993–95 with improved prairie water and near-record habitat conditions. Indicative of such a rebound, the estimated 35,000 pintails on Cactus Lake, Moore County, 13 February 1996, were the most recorded there in many years.

Averages and highs on area CBCs are indicators of pintail numbers in early winter: *Friona*—1,281 (5,150); *Lake Meredith (east)*—817 (10,000); *Quitaque*—420 (5,000); *Amarillo*—382 (3,500); *Lake Meredith (west)*—215 (2,000). Thirty-five percent of all ducks recorded on the CBCs (1966–91) were Northern Pintails. Numbers begin diminishing rather rapidly in late winter. As an example, there were an estimated 200,000 at BLNWR on 18 February 1979, 75,000 on 4 March, and 500 on 1 April.

A Northern Pintail banded on 27 February 1971 at BLNWR was recovered on 28 May 1980 at the Velikaya River (Chukchi Peninsula) where it enters the Gulf of Anadyr on the Bering Sea in eastern Siberia (USFWS). The refuge's banding program resulted in other recoveries: *Canada*—AB (3), SK (2), MN (1); *United States*—WA (1), SD (1), IA (1), UT (5), NE (2), CA (6), AR (1), TX (Panhandle 1), TX (other 7), MS (2), LA (1); *Mexico*—Chihuahua (1), Colima (1), Jalisco (1), Nayarit (1), Sinaloa (2). Hawkins (1945) said that of 424 pintails banded in 1943, 6 percent were recovered, the recoveries coming from as far away as Bogota in Colombia, and Nicaragua, Mexico, California, and the Dakotas.

NESTING: The Northern Pintail has been confirmed nesting in seven counties: Dallam, Gray, Lipscomb, Moore, Parmer, Randall, and Sherman. In 1945 Hawkins (1945) "visited nearly every water area in the Panhandle. Eight broods . . . were found."

The results of a four-year (1974–77) nesting study in the southwestern counties (Traweek, 1978) disclosed a yearly average of 77 adults, 6.5 broods, and 46 ducklings. The expanded figures for the 12-county area resulted in a yearly average of 1,168 adults, 97 broods, and 698 ducklings. The TBBAP found two confirmed nestings (Randall County). With the exception of Lipscomb County, all nesting activity has been observed in counties lying west of the 101st meridian.

SPECIMENS: Specimens have been taken in Parmer (6 January 1974, WTAMU), Potter (10 December 1985, WTAMU), Randall (15 November 1939, unspecified date in 1969, 9 February 1971, unspecified date in 1972, 10 March 1974, 21 November 1987, WTAMU), and Wheeler (10 February 1939; P-PHM) counties. Oberholser (1974) names specimens for Castro, Donley, Roberts, Swisher, and Wheeler counties but does not indicate where they are housed.

Garganey *Anas querquedula* Linnaeus

STATUS: Vagrant fall visitor.

OCCURRENCE: The Garganey has been reported once in the Texas Panhandle. An adult male was observed in the company of Buffleheads some three miles downstream from the Sanford Dam at Lake Meredith, Hutchinson County, 22 November 1985 (Cain, 1988). It was seen again later in the day on a cattail-choked pond near the dam and still later on the stilling basin. While at the latter site, it was viewed through a 64-power Questar spotting scope. The only question that arises is the possibility that the bird was an escapee. In reviewing Garganey records in North America from 1957 to 1985, Spear et al. (1988) discussed the possibility of escapes. The investigation resulted in a conclusion favorable to most sightings being of wild birds, citing in support Ryan's (1980) summary "that an unlikely 10% or more (of all captives in North America) would have had to escape, survive, and be seen to account for all the wild sightings."

There have been other Garganey sightings near the study area. In adjacent Roger Mills County, Oklahoma, a drake was observed, 2 May 1979 (Ross, 1982), and another in Custer County, Oklahoma, 15 May 1981 (Klett, 1982).

Green-winged Teal *Anas crecca* Linnaeus

STATUS: Abundant migrant and winter visitor. Rare to uncommon summer visitor, with vagrant breeding.

OCCURRENCE: The Green-winged Teal has been recorded in all Texas Panhandle counties except Childress and Lipscomb, and would be in them with better coverage. It has been seen every month.

The first published account of the Green-winged Teal in the study area (Hutchinson County) is that of Abert (1846); this was one of only a few species of birds that he mentioned. The species today is abundant during winter. As an example, USFWS records at BLNWR show a peak of 35,000 on 30 January 1959. The following 4 January 1960 the species peaked at 42,000, and in subsequent years (through 1971) high numbers ranged from 1,000 to 25,000. Bellrose (1976) estimated the wintering population in the Panhandle at nearly 100,000 birds. Today's high numbers and frequency of sightings during winter cause one to wonder at the observation of Hawkins (1945): "Arriving late in August, this smallest of the ducks stays with us until the lakes freeze, before continuing farther south. Early in February it returns again."

The Green-winged Teal can be found fairly regularly in summer, albeit in small numbers. Sightings typically are of single birds or groups of less than ten. Exceptional were the 30–70, almost all males, that spent the summer of 1973 at BLNWR. Such a large preponderance of males in summer is almost always the case. A four-year study (1974–77) of waterfowl in the southwestern counties disclosed an average of 208 adult green-wingeds (expanded data) during June and July (Traweek, 1978)—no broods or ducklings were observed. During 1988–92 the TPWD conducted waterfowl surveys during May and June over much of the western High Plains area and found a few pairs of green-wingeds yearly, without confirming nesting (Ray et al., in prep.).

Because of summering birds, fall arrival and spring departure dates are somewhat obscured. My records show the Green-winged Teal as normally "common" by late August, becoming "abundant" in the first week of October. By the end of April most have departed. Eleven recoveries have been made of birds banded at BLNWR (USFWS): WA (1); CA (4); KS (1); TX (4); LA (1).

NESTING: There have been two reports of the Green-winged Teal nesting in the study area. Oberholser (1974) notes: "Dallam County, Buffalo Springs (a number nesting, July, 1936, Mrs. R. L. Duke), but details lacking and record questionable." Considering the frequency of this teal's summer presence, it is probably a valid record. On 15 June 1975, I observed a hen and drake with four ducklings at Lake Meredith, Hutchinson County. The birds were on the river, at that point narrow but deep, a short distance downstream from Sanford Dam. A regional nesting was reported by Williams (1982): "In Crosby Co., Tex., a Green-winged Teal nest with 8 eggs [was] destroyed by hail and flood June 18, 1982. . . . The nest represented one of the very few breeding records of the species in the state." In only one other instance has the Green-winged Teal been reported nesting nearer the Texas Panhandle than central Nebraska, that one in Barton County, Kansas, in 1968, some 150 miles north of the study area (Thompson and Ely, 1989).

SPECIMENS: Specimens have been collected in Hansford (2 September 1954, OMNH); Hutchinson (8 November 1987, WTAMU), and Randall (15 November 1939, 1968, 11 March 1969, January 1970, 1971, 18 April 1972, WTAMU) counties.

Canvasback *Aythya valisineria* (Wilson)
STATUS: Fairly common migrant and winter visitor. Casual summer visitor.

OCCURRENCE: The Canvasback has been recorded in 19 counties: Armstrong, Briscoe, Carson, Castro, Childress, Dallam, Donley, Gray, Hansford, Hartley, Hemphill, Hutchinson, Moore, Ochiltree, Oldham, Parmer, Potter, Randall, and Swisher. It has been seen in every month.

The first published account of the Canvasback in the study area is that of McCauley (1877): "Whilst riding up Red River Canyon, May 24, I suddenly came upon a large reedy pool of the stream from which arose . . . two of this species, not met with elsewhere." That he saw the species so late in the season is unexpected, for today it is normally gone from the area by the third week in April and is seldom reported in May. The latest spring date is 9 May 1970: 14 on a playa in Randall County. Hawkins (1945) stated that "a few non-breeders remain during the summer." Since his mid-century observations, I know of only six others seen in summer. Returning birds in fall can be expected in mid-October. There have been three sightings earlier: one at BLNWR, 21 September 1969; three on 13 September 1986 and one on 5 September 1988, Randall County. Canvasbacks winter irregularly and in small numbers. This is reflected by the CBCs: *Amarillo*—10 of 40; *Buffalo Lake NWR*—9 of 29; *Lake Meredith (east)*—6 of 18; *Lake Meredith (west)*—2 of 24; *Quitaque*—15 of 21. The highest number on any count is 105.

Seldom are large concentrations of Canvasbacks encountered. The largest number recorded since mid-century was 450 on the BLNWR on 7 November 1959, and nothing approaching those numbers has been recorded since. The number Hawkins (1945) speaks of is an indication of how the species has declined: "According to old timers, one of the largest flights of Canvasback and other diving ducks in their memory occurred during the fall of 1942. About twelve hundred Canvasbacks remained at Buffalo Lake all winter that year." My records testify to the species' scarcity. During the period 1965–96, I recorded Canvasbacks 232 times at an average of 16 birds per sighting. Only nine observations involved one hundred or more birds, the largest 261 on the BLNWR on 9 November 1969. These figures support the small numbers supplied by Bellrose (1976), who shows the central migratory corridor of the Canvasback running through the Texas Panhandle and estimates their number at 8,100–20,000: "Texas winters 9,400, about half scattered along the coast and the rest inland, mostly in the Panhandle."

NESTING: Prior to a four-year (1974–77) waterfowl study conducted by the Texas Parks and Wildlife Department (Traweek, 1978), the Canvasback was not known as a breeder in Texas. In 1975 the surveyors reported four broods of 32 ducklings, but the county or counties where they were discovered are not given. Four counties (Bailey, Floyd, Hale, and Lamb) of the twelve in the survey are not located in the Panhandle but adjoin it to the south. The nearest locations where nestings have been confirmed are the Bosque del Apache NWR in central New Mexico (Hubbard, 1978), and there only occasionally; Barton County (five summers) in central Kansas (Thompson and Ely, 1989); and south-central Colorado, where nestings are rare and very local (Andrews and Righter, 1992).

Redhead *Aythya americana* (Eyton)

STATUS: Common to abundant migrant. Uncommon to fairly common summer visitor, with casual breeding locally. Uncommon to fairly common winter visitor.

OCCURRENCE: The Redhead has been recorded in all but three of the Texas Panhandle counties—Collingsworth, Lipscomb, and Roberts—and would be in them with better coverage. It has been seen in every month.

The number and irregularity of sightings of wintering Redheads are revealed by the CBCS (with highs in parentheses): *Amarillo*—14 of 40 (40); *Buffalo Lake NWR*—10 of 29 (75); *Lake Meredith (east)*—10 of 18 (104); *Lake Meredith (west)*—2 of 24 (7); *Quitaque*—9 of 21 (38). Large gatherings in winter are seldom encountered. Fairly large numbers of spring migrants can be expected in mid- or late February, the birds peaking during the first two weeks of March and remaining fairly plentiful until mid-April. In some years a noticeable buildup may take place again as early as the last week of July, but fall migration reaches its peak from the second week in October through the last week of November. The largest numbers recorded in spring and fall have been posted at BLNWR: 3,000 on 9 March 1963 and 3,500 for 25 November–2 December 1967.

In some years the Redhead may be one of the more common of the summering waterfowl, particularly in the southwestern sector in Parmer, Castro, and Randall counties, with many of the birds appearing paired. Following is a sampling of numbers I have recorded in June–July: *Castro*—4 June 1978 (17), 24 June 1979 (53+), 4 July 1982 (40); *Parmer*—7 June 1977 (40+); *Moore*—8 July 1973 (16+); *Randall*—17 June 1973 (100+), 4 July 1993 (210+). All the Randall County birds were males, as is often the case with large groups in summer. Of the 53+ in Castro County, only four were females. The Redhead has been recorded in summer (June–July) in 18 of the 26 counties: Armstrong, Carson, Castro, Dallam, Gray, Hall, Hansford, Hartley, Hemphill, Hutchinson, Moore, Ochiltree, Oldham, Parmer, Potter, Randall, Sherman, and Swisher.

Twice have I observed female Redheads with white heads. One was with a male on the sewage pond southeast of Amarillo, Randall County, 12 June 1984. The head was not pure white but a slightly off-white. The other bird was also accompanied by a male, 26 July 1992, on a playa in Armstrong County; its head appeared pure white.

NESTING: It was only fairly recently that the Redhead was discovered nesting in the Texas Panhandle. Oberholser (1974), Palmer (1976), and Johnsgard (1979) do not show it breeding here, and the only confirmation of nesting in Texas was the record cited by Oberholser for Medina County in 1928, far downstate. He refers to the possibility of the Redhead having nested in Dallam County (Buffalo Springs) in the summer of 1933 ("said to breed, Mrs. R. L. Duke").

The first published account of nesting is that of Traweek (1978). During a four-year waterfowl study (1974–77), yearly numbers averaged 2,481 adult Redheads with 22 broods and 110 ducklings (expanded data). The counties encompassed by the study lie in the southern and southwestern sectors. On 2 August 1977 a female with several one- to seven-day-old ducklings was found on a playa a few miles east of Hart, Castro County, and on the following 11 August a second female with brood was sighted south of Summerfield in the same county

(Rhodes, 1979). On 3 July 1988, I observed a female Redhead with nine downy chicks on a playa within the city limits of Hart, Castro County. Although late in the season, these dates are not surprising, for the Redhead evinces a propensity for late nesting. While confirmations of breeding have been few, it is not uncommon to encounter both courting and paired birds; there undoubtedly are more nestings occurring than we have found. As an example, of 17 Redheads I observed on a playa in Castro County on 4 June 1978, ten appeared paired. On another playa that day, three more pairs were encountered, with much interaction, such as flight pursuit and threat posturing, when encroachment of territories occurred.

SPECIMENS: Specimens have been taken in Carson (November 1958, MTTU), Parmer (October 1973, 18 December 1974, WTAMU), and Randall (1969, WTAMU) counties. Other specimens are cited by Oberholser (1974) for Childress, Deaf Smith, Donley, Ochiltree, Potter, and Swisher counties, but the collections in which they were placed are not given.

Ring-necked Duck *Aythya collaris* (Donovan)

STATUS: Fairly common to common migrant. Uncommon to fairly common winter visitor. Vagrant summer visitor.

OCCURRENCE: The Ring-necked Duck has been recorded in 17 counties: Armstrong, Briscoe, Carson, Castro, Childress, Donley, Gray, Hansford, Hartley, Hemphill, Hutchinson, Moore, Oldham, Parmer, Potter, Randall, and Swisher and has been seen in every month except August.

The Ring-necked Duck is seldom found in large gatherings. Most are of 25 birds or fewer and any of 100 or more are exceptional. The largest number ever reported was 400+ on Lake McClellan, Gray County, 25 October 1974. A few winter in the Panhandle, mostly in the southern third. The only CBC on which the species has appeared with regularity is Quitaque in Briscoe County, located below the caprock escarpment. There this duck has been found on every count save one at an average of 23 per count (high 116, low 1). It has been recorded only sporadically on the other counts. The ring-necked is usually found on the smaller bodies of water, some little more than large ponds surrounded by wooded and marshy areas—a large impoundment is not usually the place to look for one.

A movement of returning birds in spring is discernible in late February and early March, the passage usually completed by late April. During the period 1964–96, my records show seeing these ducks only three times in May. The latest May date is for two in Parmer County, 27 May 1962. Two summer sightings have been reported. Hawkins (1945) cites a pair at the Palo Duro Club lake near Canyon, Randall County, 11 July 1943 ("no evidence of nesting was found"), and there is a June record for Castro County. Another report is of two Ring-necked Ducks that summered at Lubbock in 1980 (Williams, 1980b). The nearest to the Texas Panhandle that the species is known to breed is southern Colorado and northern Nebraska (AOU, 1983). Returning southbound birds can be expected from early October to late November. There have been only two sightings reported in September: 12 at BLNWR, 23 September 1961, and three on 19 September 1987.

Greater Scaup *Aythya marila* (Linnaeus)

STATUS: Casual winter visitor.

OCCURRENCE: The Greater Scaup has been reported in six counties: Briscoe, Deaf Smith, Gray, Hemphill, Randall, and Roberts. It has been seen in the period October–March.

Confirmation of the Greater Scaup in the study area consists of birds recovered from hunters' bags. Hawkins (1945) reported the species as a "rare migrant. Among a thousand ducks inspected six were the large 'Bluebills' or 'Broadbills.' Five were recovered in 1942." On 11 November 1972, one was recovered from a hunter's bag in Deaf Smith County (USFWS); it was reportedly shot from a group of three.

McCauley (1877) was the first to note the Greater Scaup in the Panhandle (May–June 1876)—"Fulicula marila, (L.) Steph.—*Greater Blackhead*"—and said it was found "frequenting the Canadian and Lower McClellan Creek." He may have misidentified the birds as he did not record the Lesser Scaup, the species to be expected. It is difficult to separate the two in the field. These may be the source of Oberholser's (1974) spring sightings for Gray and/or Roberts County.

There have been six other reported sightings: *Briscoe*—a male with 14 Lesser Scaup on Dry Creek Lake, Caprock Canyons SP, 1 January 1980; one on Lake Theo, Caprock Canyons SP, 16 November 1990; *Hemphill*—one in October 1937; two on Lake Marvin, 21 December 1966; *Randall*—a male on a playa with 25 Lesser Scaup, 22 March 1985; 1–8 at South East Park in Amarillo, 4–21 January 1998.

The Greater Scaup is a rare to uncommon migrant in all parts of Texas (TOS, 1995). It probably would be recorded more often in the study area if all scaup were examined more closely.

Lesser Scaup *Aythya affinis* (Eyton)

STATUS: Common to abundant migrant. Uncommon to common winter visitor. Casual summer visitor, with vagrant breeding.

OCCURRENCE: The Lesser Scaup has been recorded in all the Texas Panhandle counties except Collingsworth, Lipscomb, Roberts, and Sherman, and would be in them with better coverage. It has been seen in every month.

During migration, the Lesser Scaup is one of the most abundant of the diving ducks. Cumulative numbers recorded in a day's time may be quite large, although single gatherings seldom are. The greatest number recorded at one time is 1,000 at BLNWR, 23 March 1963. The 8,500 reported on the refuge during the CBC of 26 December 1979 is suspect, for the highest number recorded otherwise on a CBC is 72. The Lesser Scaup has been recorded most consistently on the Quitaque CBC in Briscoe County: 20 of 21, high 71.

There have been six reported sightings in summer: a single bird on Lake Marvin, Hemphill County, 7 June 1953; a male on 4 June 1984, four males and one female on 12 June and a male on 31 August 1985, all on the sewage pond southeast of Amarillo, Randall County; and four on Cactus Lake, Moore County, 24 June 1995. In no instance were there indications of possible nesting. A single male that summered in South East Park, Amarillo, Randall County, in 1996 appeared to be an injured bird. Most Lesser Scaup are gone by early May, the heaviest movement taking place in late March and early April. The latest spring date is 30 May 1993. Returning birds in fall do not usually appear until mid- or late October; the earliest were four on 21 September 1968 at BLNWR.

NESTING: There has been one report of the Lesser Scaup nesting: fledglings were observed in southern Swisher County in July 1977 (letter, C. Stogner, 24 April 1995). Neither the name of the observer nor other details were given. The nearest previously known nesting took place in Bailey County (Hawkins, 1945): "According to Refuge Manager Keifer of the Muleshoe Wildlife Refuge, a Scaup nested there in 1942." The nearest to the Texas Panhandle that the Lesser Scaup is known to breed is northern and northeastern Colorado (Andrews and Righter, 1992) and Cowley County in south-central Kansas (Thompson and Ely, 1989).

SPECIMENS: There is a specimen taken in Swisher County (1973, WTAMU).

Surf Scoter *Melanitta perspicillata* (Linnaeus)

STATUS: Casual migrant.

OCCURRENCE: The Surf Scoter has been recorded in six counties—Briscoe, Hemphill, Ochiltree, Potter, Randall, and Swisher—five times during fall and winter and once in spring, as follows: *Briscoe*—a female on Lake Theo, Caprock Canyons SP, 17–18 November 1990 (TP-RF), and another female, 22 October 1992; on 12 November 1995, still another female was found on Dry Creek Lake in the park. *Hemphill*—one on Lake Marvin, 10 April 1968. *Ochiltree*—Hawkins (1945) cites a female recovered from a hunter's bag at Lake Fryer, Wolf Creek Park, 19 November 1943. *Potter*—Oberholser (1974) shows a winter sight record; this is possibly based on Harold Saunders's sighting of December 1939. *Randall*—two at BLNWR during the winter of 1956–57; a female at BLNWR, 22 October–19 November 1972; two at BLNWR, 7 November 1973. *Swisher*—a female on a playa near Tulia, 21 November 1995.

There are five reports of the Surf Scoter from nearby counties of Oklahoma, four from New Mexico, and three from the South Plains area. The species winters primarily along the Atlantic and Pacific coasts, on the Great Lakes, and rarely (but regularly) on the Gulf Coast. It is considered casual in other interior locations (AOU, 1998).

White-winged Scoter *Melanitta fusca* (Linnaeus)

STATUS: Vagrant winter visitor.

OCCURRENCE: There have been three reported sightings of the White-winged Scoter in the Texas Panhandle. A female was seen at BLNWR, 26 January 1963 (USFWS), and another of unspecified gender on the refuge, 6 November 1973 (M. Suthers). Concerning the latter sighting, it should be noted that on the following day two Surf Scoters were reported at this location by a different party. The unlikelihood of any scoter being seen in the Panhandle raises the possibility that one of the identifications may have been in error. The presence of the White-winged Scoter was placed on a firmer basis with the observation of a male on Palo Duro Lake, Hansford County, 16 January 1999 (E. Kutac, R. Scott, P. Trosper, et al.).

Sites near the study area where White-winged Scoters have been reported are Clayton in Union County, New Mexico; the Oklahoma Panhandle; and the South Plains. Several have been recorded in the Clayton area: one on 13 February 1954 (Baumgartner, 1954); "4 individuals . . . seen on two lakes" on 2 November 1954 (Baumgartner, 1955); one on 29 November 1969 (Williams, 1970); and one on 4 December 1970 (Williams, 1971). A specimen was taken (date not given) in Texas County, Oklahoma (Wood and Schnell, 1984), another in Lubbock County during the fall of 1967 (Williams, 1968), and one was found dead on the Muleshoe NWR, Bailey County, 2 January 1985 (Williams, 1985). Others have been seen at Lubbock: 29 October–19 November 1977 (Williams, 1978) and January or February 1981 (Williams, 1981).

The White-winged Scoter winters in North America primarily along the Atlantic and Pacific coasts and on the Great Lakes. It is considered casual in other locations and on the Gulf Coast (AOU, 1983).

Black Scoter *Melanitta nigra* (Linnaeus)

STATUS: Vagrant fall and winter visitor.

OCCURRENCE: The Black Scoter has been reported twice in the Texas Panhandle.

Both are sight records recognized by Oberholser (1974), one for fall at the BLNWR, the other for Deaf Smith County, December 1939. Details are lacking for each.

There have been three sightings reported from nearby areas. A single Black Scoter was seen near Clayton, Union County, New Mexico, 29 November 1969 (Williams, 1970): Krehbiel (1955) classified it as an "accidental transient" on his Clayton list. A male and three females were seen on Lake Lawtonka, Comanche County, Oklahoma, 12 November 1977 (Tyler, 1979b), and two adult hens were collected at Lake Ellsworth near Elgin, Comanche County, Oklahoma, 8 December 1985 (Carden and Rushing, 1987).

The Black Scoter winters in North America primarily along the Atlantic and Pacific coasts and on the Great Lakes. It is considered casual in other interior locations and the Gulf Coast (AOU, 1983) and is a rare visitor along the Texas coast (TOS, 1995).

Oldsquaw *Clangula hyemalis* (Linnaeus)
STATUS: Casual winter visitor.
OCCURRENCE: The Oldsquaw has been recorded in four Texas Panhandle counties—Deaf Smith, Hutchinson, Potter, and Randall—with sightings scattered over a period of eight months, October through May.

Details by county are as follows: *Deaf Smith*—Oberholser (1974) shows a fall sighting without giving details. Possibly it is based on Harold Saunders's record of November 1939. *Hutchinson*—one on Lake Meredith on 5 January, five on 17 March, three on 24 March 1971; a first winter male off South Canyon, Lake Meredith, 3 January 1988; a male at Fortress Cove Marina, Lake Meredith, 2–9 May 1989—the bird appeared to have a fishhook in its mouth, possibly accounting for such a late sighting. *Potter*—a female remained on Thompson Park Lake, Amarillo, 12 January–2 February 1958. The present whereabouts of a film taken of the bird is unknown. *Randall*—one at BLNWR, 27 October 1960, 14 December 1963, 7 April 1979, and 17 November 1979; a female on a playa southeast of Amarillo, 19 November–14 December 1986.

The Oldsquaw winters along the Pacific Coast south to central California, along the Atlantic Coast south to South Carolina, and on the Great Lakes. It is considered as casual in other inland locations (AOU, 1983).

Bufflehead *Bucephala albeola* (Linnaeus)
STATUS: Fairly common to common migrant and winter visitor.
OCCURRENCE: The Bufflehead has been reported in 19 counties: Armstrong, Briscoe, Carson, Castro, Childress, Dallam, Donley, Gray, Hansford, Hartley,

Hemphill, Hutchinson, Moore, Oldham, Parmer, Potter, Randall, Swisher, and Wheeler. It has been recorded in every month except July and August.

The Bufflehead is not to be expected in fall until the third week of October and is normally gone by the second week of May. Extreme dates range from 20 birds at BLNWR, 26 September 1964, to a female on a playa near Amarillo, Randall County, 20 May 1958. The species is most common during migration and can readily be found on playas and impoundments. Up to 350 "butterballs" were recorded on the BLNWR on 22 March 1962, an unusually high number. The 300 recorded there on 17 and 24 December 1966 were also unusual for winter, while a combined total of 250 on Lake Childress and Baylor Lake, Childress County, 26 November 1994, was noteworthy.

In winter the Bufflehead is found more often below the caprock escarpment in the southern sector of the study area, where it has been recorded on all the Quitaque CBCs save one, during a winter when all bodies of water in the count circle were frozen. The average for the count is 17 (high 36). On 15 November 1985, I observed 66 Buffleheads on a playa in Randall County, 90 percent of them females or first winter birds. Birds in spring may be seen courting vigorously.

There have been two summer sightings. Two birds were on the BLNWR on 1 June 1968 (USFWS), and during a four-year (1974–77) waterfowl study conducted during June and July in the southwest sector, a single bird was reported in 1977 (Traweek, 1978).

Common Goldeneye *Bucephala clangula* (Linnaeus)

STATUS: Uncommon to fairly common migrant and winter visitor.

OCCURRENCE: The Common Goldeneye has been recorded in all but nine counties: Childress, Collingsworth, Dallam, Hall, Lipscomb, Oldham, Roberts, Sherman, and Wheeler. It has been seen from November to May.

Normally the Common Goldeneye is present no more than four months out of the year (December–March). It is usually found on the larger impoundments and playas, and then not in large numbers. The most reported in one gathering were 150 at BLNWR in December 1968 and 100 or more on Greenbelt Lake, Donley County, 5 February 1978. Hawkins (1945) observed only a dozen over a three-year period, but later observers have found goldeneyes to be more common. The CBCs reflect early winter status: *Amarillo*—1–40 on 9 of 40 counts; *Buffalo Lake* NWR—1–50 on 5 of 29 counts; *Lake Meredith* (*east*)—1–81 on 17 of 18 counts; *Lake Meredith* (*west*)—1–16 on 13 of 24 counts; *Quitaque*—1–6 on 7 of 21 counts.

Wintering Common Goldeneyes cannot be expected much sooner than the second week in December. The earliest were eight on the BLNWR on 4 November 1967. The species is normally gone by mid-March; extremely late were one near

Canyon, Randall County, 20 April 1945 (Hawkins, 1945); two at BLNWR, 27 April 1963; and one near Friona, Parmer County, 5 May 1960. Although goldeneyes are associated with the larger impoundments, I observed a male coursing the creek in the PDCSP on 6 December 1964 and flushed five near the first water crossing on 2 January 1967. Two were on a small pond downcanyon from Lake Tanglewood, Randall County, 21 December 1996.

SPECIMENS: A Common Goldeneye was collected in Castro County (January 1976, MTTU).

Hooded Merganser *Lophodytes cucullatus* (Linnaeus)

STATUS: Uncommon to fairly common migrant and winter visitor. Casual summer visitor.

OCCURRENCE: The Hooded Merganser has been recorded in 13 counties: Armstrong, Briscoe, Carson, Childress, Dallam, Donley, Hartley, Hemphill, Hutchinson, Moore, Potter, Randall, and Roberts. It has been seen in every month except April, August, and September.

Of late years this strikingly handsome merganser has been seen with increasing frequency and in greater numbers. Hawkins (1945) did not see any during the three years he worked in the area near mid-century, and earlier still it was not listed in any of Carlander's reports (1933, 1934, 1935). When I first began observations in the early 1960s, seeing a Hooded Merganser in the Panhandle was considered a singular event.

The Hooded Merganser is most often found during the period November–February, usually on smaller bodies of water. Early and late dates are 25 October 1996 (Thompson Park Lake, Amarillo, Potter County) and 6 May 1968 (BLNWR). Until recent years only single birds or groups of no more than three or four were expected; when 34 appeared on Thompson Park Lake on 17 December 1991, it was an event of note. Comparable numbers have continued to be seen each winter since. On 23 November 1994, 40 were found on Greenbelt Lake, Donley County, and 35 on Lake Childress, Childress County.

In summer the Hooded Merganser has been seen four times. Singular was a juvenile that I encountered on a playa located approximately 12 miles south and five miles east of Washburn, Armstrong County, 7 July 1985. I viewed the bird from a near distance and at great length and made detailed notes on its appearance and behavior. I am confident that it was a bird in juvenal plumage. The playa, bisected by a dirt road, was quite shallow over much of its area, and there were extensive stands of emergent vegetation growing around its perimeter. Extending some 30–40 yards from the road and for a distance of some 200 yards alongside it, the water was much deeper. It was here that the young bird remained during the whole time of my observations. It was wary but not alarmed, and I could approach it closely while in my car before it would occasionally fly, and then only a short distance before alighting. It flew strongly, dived once, and never made any movement to hide in the nearby vegetation.

I can only speculate as to the bird's origin. I am reasonably sure it was not hatched in the study area. The nearest to Washburn that the Hooded Merganser has been confirmed nesting—and that was a one-time occurrence—is the Great Salt Plains NWR, Alfalfa County, Oklahoma, 21 May 1981 (Clover, 1981), some 225 miles to the northeast. This was only the second Oklahoma nesting record. Pulich (1988) cites a north-central Texas record for Dallas County, 30 May–3 June 1987. Farther north, Thompson and Ely (1989) cite several nestings in Kansas, with hatching occurring as early as 13 April. Interestingly, there is a recent report of a possible male Hooded Merganser seen in summer on a playa in south-central Armstrong County, some 15 miles from where the juvenile was found.

Oberholser (1974) shows a summer sighting of the Hooded Merganser for Roberts County without naming its source: it is probably based on Harold Saunders's observation of June 1933. The latest summer sighting is 21–28 June 1986, when an adult male was observed on the sewage plant playa southeast of Amarillo, Randall County.

Common Merganser *Mergus merganser* Linnaeus

STATUS: Fairly common to common migrant and winter visitor. Casual summer visitor.

OCCURRENCE: The Common Merganser has been recorded in all but seven of the Texas Panhandle counties: Armstrong, Deaf Smith, Hall, Lipscomb, Ochiltree, Roberts, and Sherman. It has been seen in every month.

McCauley (1877) was the first to cite the presence of the Common Merganser in the study area: "A few specimens noted frequenting the Canadian; none observed elsewhere." His trek across the area was made in May and June, when few mergansers are to be expected today. Seeing one on the river is also of interest, for the depth and flow of the river have changed so drastically since the latter half of the nineteenth century (Carlson, 1980) that finding a merganser on the river today is unlikely. However, a female was observed and photographed on the Salt Fork of the Red River in Collingsworth County in late December 1989 when the river was in flood. There are a few May records, the latest a male southeast of Amarillo, Randall County, 27 May 1985.

The Common Merganser arrives during fall in mid- or late November and is most abundant from mid-December to mid-March. There are only three October and three September sightings. In winter it is not unusual to see 100 or more at a time on the larger bodies of water. The largest concentrations reported were an estimated 6,000 on Greenbelt Lake, Donley County, 29 January 1978, and

5,000 on BLNWR, 19 December 1964. Records on file at BLNWR show numbers peaking at 500 to 2,500 in the years 1959–70. Hawkins (1945) observed 2,100 on the refuge during the winter of 1943. The largest number recorded at Lake Meredith was 1,515 on the CBC of 30 December 1970.

Hawkins (1945) cites a summer record for the BLNWR: "A single male was observed on June 17, 1945." An injured male Common Merganser spent the summer of 1953 on Thompson Park Lake in Amarillo, Potter County (last seen 25 October), and Oberholser (1974) cites another for that location in the summer of 1961. A female remained on the Randall County sewage pond 10 August–4 September 1985, and another female was observed there the following year (22 July–13 August). On 4 July 1992, two mergansers were found on Lake Tanglewood, Randall County, where they remained throughout the summer. One to two were seen on the lake intermittently during the summers of 1993–95, the two in 1995 having returned during the week 16–22 April. In 1996 a Common Merganser was found in South Canyon, Lake Meredith, Hutchinson County, on 28 June. The species breeds no nearer to the Texas Panhandle than northern New Mexico (AOU, 1983).

SPECIMENS: Specimens are available for Hutchinson (20 October 1973, WTAMU) and Wheeler (20 February 1939, P-PHM; 20 February 1939, WTAMU) counties. Oberholser (1974) cites one taken in Childress County but fails to name its location.

Red-breasted Merganser *Mergus serrator* Linnaeus

STATUS: Casual fall and winter visitor. Vagrant summer visitor.

OCCURRENCE: The Red-breasted Merganser has been reported in eight counties: Childress, Deaf Smith, Donley, Hemphill, Hutchinson, Potter, Randall, and Roberts. It has been seen from November to February and once each in September, April, and June.

With the following exceptions, all Red-breasted Mergansers have been observed at BLNWR: *Childress*—one on Lake Childress, 26 November 1994; *Deaf Smith*—Oberholser (1974) cites a specimen taken on 25 November (year not given); *Donley*—150 on Greenbelt Lake, 29 January 1978; *Hemphill*—a female on Lake Marvin, 19 April 1997; *Hutchinson*—two on Lake Meredith, 31 December 1973; *Randall*—Oberholser (1974): "1 male, June 28, 1963, J. M. Sheppard." Oberholser may have erred in placing the sighting in Randall County as Baumgartner (1963) reported a Red-breasted Merganser found "on a temporary pond forty miles southwest of Amarillo, Tex. on June 28 (J. M. Sheppard)." Such a distance from Amarillo would place the bird in either Castro or Deaf Smith County; *Potter*—one on Thompson Park Lake, Amarillo, 13–18 November 1995, and another, 12 April 1997; *Roberts*—unspecified number, September 1935.

Seeing 150 birds of this species on Greenbelt Lake was extraordinary. With one exception (13 females on BLNWR, 11 November 1979), all other sightings on record involved no more than three birds. The latest winter date is 21 February 1965, again birds found at BLNWR. The Red-breasted Merganser in Texas is a rare to uncommon winter resident inland, common along the coast (TOS, 1995). Pulich (1988) says they are not seen in north-central Texas every winter; when they are present, it is mainly on large reservoirs.

SPECIMENS: The location of the specimen Oberholser (1974) cites as collected in Deaf Smith County is unknown.

Ruddy Duck *Oxyura jamaicensis* (Gmelin)

STATUS: Common to abundant migrant. Rare to uncommon winter visitor. Rare summer visitor, with casual breeding.

OCCURRENCE: The Ruddy Duck has been reported in every county except Collingsworth, Lipscomb, Roberts, and Wheeler and has been seen in every month.

Few Ruddy Ducks winter in the study area, as illustrated by the CBCs: the species was recorded during three of 42 combined Lake Meredith counts (high 3); four of 29 at BLNWR (high 20); 14 of 21 Quitaque (high 5); and on none of the Amarillo counts (1954–86) until the count circle was shifted to include the Randall County sewage pond; thereafter (1987–96) it was found in six of ten counts (high 77). None of these counts are made in the northern sector; in nearby Oklahoma Sutton (1967) says that of 19,994 ducks banded, only one was of this species. A few begin returning in mid-February and they are common by mid-May, at which time they decline rapidly. Examples of high numbers: 1,300 at BLNWR on 29 March 1962 and 1,000+ on 15 April 1979; 2,000 at Randall County sewage pond near Amarillo on 24 October 1992.

The Ruddy Duck's presence in summer is variable. Hawkins (1945) called it an "uncommon summer resident" and found no evidence of nesting. Of 500 he observed assembled at BLNWR in midspring of 1945, 30 were still present on 3 June, and 25–50 remained in the area throughout the summer. The findings of later observers have been similar: scattered sightings but no confirmation of nesting until recent years. Returning fall migrants begin appearing in late August or early September, become common in October, and by late November have largely disappeared.

NESTING: The first report of Ruddy Duck nesting is by Rhodes (1978): "On 14 September 1977 . . . I observed two Ruddy Duck broods . . . on a playa lake 7.83 kilometers east of Hart, Texas on FM Road 1056, in Castro County. One brood had seven ducklings and the other had eight." On 2 July 1978, eight pairs were observed on a playa 12 miles south and three miles west of Dimmitt, Castro County; one hen had two ducklings and another had a recently hatched chick.

The results of a four-year (1974–77) study of waterfowl in the southwestern sector (Traweek, 1978) showed a yearly average of 409 adult Ruddy Ducks, 18 broods, and 95 ducklings (expanded data). During the TBBAP three other nestings were discovered: one group of six ducklings and another of three on a playa at Hart, Castro County, 31 July 1988, and a hen with one duckling on a playa on the southern outskirts of Amarillo, Randall County, 14 August 1989. During the wet summer of 1997 six more nestings were found: three hens with broods on the playa at Hart, Castro County, 8 August; a hen with nine ducklings on a playa northeast of Groom, Gray County, 29 August; five ducklings on a playa eight miles east of Washburn, Armstrong County, 6 September. All reports of nesting have been from west of the 101st meridian. Closer observation of summering birds would probably result in more confirmations.

There are a few records of Ruddy Ducks nesting in nearby areas. Hawkins (1945) speaks of two broods found at "Blackwater Draw," a drainage that runs through Bailey County. An adult Ruddy with three juveniles was discovered on 31 July 1977 in Crosby County, "the first nesting record for w. Texas" (Williams, 1977). Ligon (1961) refers to the species being classified as a nester on the checklist of birds for Clayton, Union County, New Mexico, but this is unacknowledged by Hubbard (1978), and Sutton (1967) speaks of probable, but only occasional, nesting in Harper and Beaver counties, Oklahoma. Nebraska is usually shown as the southern limit of the breeding range of the Ruddy Duck, with only very local nesting in Kansas (Johnsgard, 1979).

SPECIMENS: Specimens have been collected in Parmer (30 October 1973, 31 March 1976, WTAMU) and Randall (9 September 1968, WTAMU) counties.

ORDER FALCONIFORMES

Family Accipitridae (Hawks, Kites, Eagles, and Allies)

Osprey *Pandion haliaetus* (Linnaeus)
STATUS: Uncommon to fairly common migrant. Vagrant winter visitor.
OCCURRENCE: The Osprey has been recorded in 17 counties: Briscoe, Carson, Castro, Childress, Collingsworth, Dallam, Donley, Gray, Hansford, Hartley, Hemphill, Hutchinson, Oldham, Parmer, Potter, Randall, and Wheeler. Oberholser (1974) shows it in two: Parmer and Randall. It has been seen during the periods February–June and August–December.

The Osprey was seldom mentioned by early observers. McCauley (1877) spoke of seeing a few ("chiefly on the Canadian"), and Stevenson (1942) referred to the U.S. Soil Conservation Service agent P. F. Allan classifying it as a rare migrant. Hawkins (1945) cited only six birds seen during three years of work in the area. Such a paucity of sightings during an era when the species was more abundant throughout its range than at present may be accounted for by the lack of suitable bodies of water. Today it is found almost exclusively at reservoirs and other impoundments (not playas), all constructed since the late 1930s. My records show a greater incidence of sightings since 1977, probably a result of the species' recovery following the banning of DDT and other harmful pesticides.

The first returning Ospreys in spring can be expected in early or mid-April. Of six recorded in March, the earliest was one at Lake Tanglewood, Randall County, 1 March 1973. Two late winter sightings at BLNWR, 14 February 1970 and 20 February 1971, were possibly early migrants. Most are gone by early May, the latest one at Greenbelt Lake, Donley County, 26 May 1995. The only summer sighting is Allan and Sime's (1943a), of a single bird at BLNWR on 18 June 1942. I know of only four summer records from nearby areas: one remained on a small impoundment south of Durham, Roger Mills County, Oklahoma, 13–15 June 1964, and one again 14–21 June 1979; Hubbard (1987) cites one at Tucumcari Lake, Quay County, New Mexico, in June 1987; the LEAS (1994) classifies it as "rare" in June on the southern plains. Ospreys are known to nest no nearer to the Texas Panhandle than central New Mexico (AOU, 1983).

The return of the Osprey in fall can be expected during early September, the earliest being two at Lake Tanglewood, Randall County, 17–18 August 1986. The species has been recorded three times beyond October, all on 11 November: Lake Tanglewood, Randall County, 1964 (1); BLNWR, 1961 (2), Lake Meredith, Hutchinson County, 1973 (1). Unexpected was an Osprey observed standing in the stream in the PDCSP on 13 December 1996. What was probably the same bird was seen again in the park on the morning of the CBC, 21 December, and later in the day at the Boy Scout Camp several miles up the canyon.

Swallow-tailed Kite *Elanoides forficatus* (Linnaeus)

STATUS: Vagrant fall visitor.

OCCURRENCE: The Swallow-tailed Kite has been seen once in the Texas Panhandle. In the early afternoon of 18 September 1995, one was observed soaring above Vega, Oldham County (R. Scott; TP-RF). The bird was seen later in the day by others (D. Acord, P. Acord, E. Kutac, K. Seyffert). Only one Mississippi Kite was seen that day, all others having moved out with the passage of the season's first cool front the previous week. Apparently the Swallow-tailed Kite had been in the area for some time, for when a landowner was shown a picture he recognized it immediately as the bird that had been roosting nightly for the previous two weeks or more at his homesite about two miles east of town.

There have been several reported sightings of the Swallow-tailed Kite at locations in Oklahoma near the study area. The earliest was that of McCauley (1877), who observed one "along Wolf Creek, Indian Territory," in the spring of 1876. This would have been near what is now Fort Supply, Woodward County. On 17 August 1988, a Swallow-tailed Kite was found among Mississippi Kites in Guymon, Texas County (Schaefer, 1988). The author's speculation concerning the origin of this bird is of interest. In 1983, swallowtails were transplanted into Mississippi Kite nests near Newton, Harvey County, southeastern Kansas, and at Meade State Park, southwestern Kansas, the latter location only 70 miles from Guymon. Although unlikely, it is possible that the Guymon bird was one crossfostered by the Mississippi Kites. On 1 June 1980, a swallowtail was seen near the Great Salt Plains NWR, Alfalfa County (Kirk, 1981), and on 24 August 1984, one in southern Caddo County (Wilson, 1984). To the south of the study area in Texas, a Swallow-tailed Kite was seen in Lubbock County, 14 September 1973 (Williams, 1974), and at the Muleshoe NWR, Bailey County, 3 September 1979 (*fide* C. Stogner).

The present breeding range of the Swallow-tailed Kite is largely confined to Florida, with disjunct populations in the coastal plains of South Carolina, Georgia, Alabama, Mississippi, Louisiana, and Texas (Meyer, 1995). Virtually all Swallow-tailed Kites leave the United States by mid-September, wintering in the northern half of South America.

Mississippi Kite *Ictinia mississippiensis* (Wilson)

STATUS: Fairly common to common migrant and breeder.

OCCURRENCE: The Mississippi Kite has been recorded in every Texas Panhandle county except Sherman, and would be there with better coverage. It has been found from March to October.

This kite does not appear prominently in the accounts of any observer until the 1940s. The Long Expedition, after traversing much of the Canadian River drainage from New Mexico eastward, first encountered kites on 15 August 1820 northwest of present-day Canadian in Hemphill County (Weese, 1947). That it was not until the far eastern Panhandle had been reached that a kite was encountered is evidence of the species' more restricted range at that time. Another early encounter was recorded by Mollhausen (1858), assuming his identification was correct. On 16 September 1853, at a point along the Canadian River northwest of present-day Amarillo (an encampment named "Beautiful View Creek"), Mollhausen made this observation: "Antelope were springing about on the dry hills, deer lurking behind the blue-green cedars, eagles and kites wheeling their flight through the air." Bolen and Flores (1993) question the presence of the Mississippi Kite at that latitude in mid-September, pointing out that most have left the area by then. Normally that is so; however, on 14 September 1970, I

Mississippi Kite

tallied 35 passing over Amarillo within a short period of time. Mollhausen was a European naturalist and no doubt was familiar with Old World kites, several species of which resemble the Northern Harrier in flight. No kites were seen by McCauley (1877) during his trek through the northeastern and central sectors of the Panhandle in May–June. Such an absence is noteworthy, for it is in those same areas today that the kite is most abundant, and it surely would have been noted if present: the species is neither shy nor secretive. Bolen and Flores (1993) cited the absence as additional evidence of the dramatic change in distribution that took place in the twentieth century.

Strecker (1910) makes reference to only one kite seen on his trip to Armstrong

County: again a surprise, for his route would have lain through an area where the species is now quite common. Neither Reeves and Reeves (1914–36) nor Hibbets et al. (1926–36) have it on their bird lists for the Canyon, Randall County area. Russell (1935) does not name it in his survey of the Palo Duro Canyon and vicinity, while Stevenson (1942) found it "still a regular summer resident in suitable localities," naming two seen in the Palo Duro park. Hawkins (1945) found it common only "along the Canadian River from Miami, Texas, into Oklahoma."

Returning kites in spring can be looked for during the last week of April or first week of May. A specimen was collected in Vega, Oldham County, 25 March 1981, an exceptionally early date. The earliest April record is of two in Canyon, Randall County, 8 April 1995. In contrast to fall migration, when fairly sizable congregations may be seen, no large flights have been reported in spring. Road surveys made during the summers of 1939–41 (Allan and Sime, 1943a) revealed a kite abundance of 24.4/1,000 miles. In a later study, Allan and Sime (1943b) estimated a density of 1–2 pairs per 2 square miles in prime habitat. They found distribution "confined almost entirely to wooded river bottoms." Such confinement differs from circumstances today, further evidence of the extent to which kites began utilizing other habitats in their westward expansion. More recently, Rideout (1979) conducted a road survey during August and found that "on 120 miles of randomly selected routes driven in Collingsworth, Donley, Hall and Hardeman counties . . . 73 Mississippi Kites were seen. This amounts to .61 kites per mile of road driven, and probably could be considered a good population density for an area in the heart of the nesting range." None of these surveys were walking transects, nor were they made in the canyonlands, another important nesting environment. A breeding bird census made in the riparian bottomlands of the PDCSP (Seyffert, 1967–68) produced an average density of nine kites per 100 acres.

The Mississippi Kite begins leaving the area with the arrival of the first cold fronts, however weak, in late August and early September. Kettles of 50 or more over Amarillo, Potter County, on 27 August 1976 and 22 August 1981 were exceptional for such early dates. These may have been gatherings of local birds preparatory to their migrating. I witnessed a similar event on 27 August 1992, when 15 adults and 33 juveniles were found perched in two trees at a site in the PDCSP where there had been a nesting colony. Seventy-nine were observed in one kettle at Amarillo, 31 August 1986, and 50+ over Lake McClellan, Gray County, 7 September 1981. It is not unusual in late summer and early fall to see large numbers of kites around a 31-story bank building in downtown Amarillo, feeding on flying moths and at times extracting them from crevices in the stone. They may also congregate in the older sections of town where there are many large trees and where cicadas abound. I have seen as many as 20–30 kites in my yard feeding on flying insects as well as those littering the sidewalks and street. There are only seven records of birds seen past September, among them a notable 16 over Amarillo, Potter County, 1 October 1983. Exceptionally late was one seen a short distance south of the study area in Hale County, 12 November 1975 (Williams, 1976).

Is the Mississippi Kite a declining species in the Texas Panhandle? Opinions differ, some sharply. Rideout (1979) refers to the beliefs of A. S. Jackson and Richard DeArment, biologists with the TPWD and longtime residents of the eastern Panhandle, who hold that kites have declined alarmingly since the late 1940s, attributing the decline primarily to the loss of nesting trees. It is Jackson's opinion that "large, mature mesquite trees present in the early 1900s were favorite nesting sites. . . . But brush control programs since 1940 have eliminated these mature mesquites over thousands of acres, and the succeeding bush-type mesquites are not used by kites for nesting purposes." Parker and Ogden (1979) concluded otherwise in a study of the Mississippi Kite in its western range. They affirm that nesting habitat is no longer a limiting factor; not only does the kite use riparian sites for nesting, but it has learned to exploit other tree plantings, such as shelterbelts, farm woodlots, and residential and park settings in urban areas. They cite studies that document "a positive correlation between increased insect numbers and agricultural practices, primarily overgrazing and irrigation, in plains regions," and that summarize the frequent grasshopper outbreaks that have occurred since 1900. Not only is the Mississippi Kite no longer habitat limited; it also is not food limited, for it feeds largely on orthopterans such as grasshoppers and crickets. Another important food item is the cicada. Records I have kept of the cicada in residential Amarillo (1979–96) show them emerging during the first or second week of June and remaining through the second week of October, on average 137 days, a period critical to the raising of young.

There is insufficient data showing clearly what kite numbers were formerly like. It stands to reason, however, that with the wholesale eradication of an important component of its nesting habitat, such as large mesquite trees, kite numbers would be reduced significantly. While it is possible that the Mississippi Kite has declined in the more humid eastern third of the study area, it is evident that with its spread into the more arid western sectors, its numbers there have increased greatly. This regional westward shifting parallels that which occurred on a larger scale within the kite's historical range, a phenomenon noted by the editor of Oberholser's *The Bird Life of Texas*: "The Mississippi Kite's feat of shifting, in only half a century, its nesting metropolis from damp forest landscapes of the southeastern United States to the dry southwestern Great Plains is quite without precedent among American birds" (E. Kincaid). In the study area today, the Mississippi Kite can be found in summer as far west as eastern Deaf Smith County, west-central Oldham County, far western Hartley County, and Dalhart in Dallam County.

NESTING: The Mississippi Kite has been confirmed nesting in all the study area counties except Hansford and Sherman in the northwest, and Castro, Parmer, and Swisher in the southwest. Nesting activity begins soon after the kites' arrival, as early as 8 May. Most young leave the nest during the last week of July. A pair was observed nest building in South Ceta Canyon, Randall County, on the extremely late date of 10 August 1955, and on 2 August 1972 a kite "carrying a foot-long stick" was seen along the Canadian River, Hemphill County. A pair of kites and two quite young birds were seen perched near a nest in the PDCSP on 7 September 1988, and on 10 September another very young bird and an adult were encountered some two miles farther down the canyon. A juvenile was seen in the park on 5 October 1986. The TBBAP resulted in 38 CO nestings, 16 PR, and 15 PO—36 of the quadrangles located between the 100th and 101st meridians, 21 between the 101st and 102nd, and 12 west of the 102nd.

SPECIMENS: Two specimens have been taken in Hutchinson (8 June and 4 July 1950, TNHC), and one in Oldham (25 March 1981, WTAMU) counties. Oberholser (1974) cites specimens collected in Deaf Smith, Hutchinson, and Lipscomb counties, and eggs collected in Randall and Swisher counties, but gives no details as to their locations. The Hutchinson County reference may pertain to those collected by Thompson (1952, TNHC).

Bald Eagle *Haliaeetus leucocephalus* (Linnaeus)

STATUS: Uncommon to common winter visitor locally.

OCCURRENCE: The Bald Eagle has been recorded in 19 of the 26 counties: Armstrong, Briscoe, Carson, Castro, Dallam, Deaf Smith, Donley, Gray, Hansford, Hartley, Hemphill, Hutchinson, Moore, Ochiltree, Oldham, Potter, Randall, Roberts, and Swisher. It has been seen in every month except July.

Wintering Bald Eagles are found primarily at reservoirs and other large impoundments and near playa lakes that hold many ducks and geese. The first birds of fall can be expected in early or mid-November. There are three sightings as early as September: an adult at BLNWR, 6 September 1992; an immature at Lake Tanglewood, Randall County, 12 September 1993; and an adult in Carson County, 21 September 1985. Numbers peak in late January and then decline as waterfowl depart; by early or mid-March most eagles are gone. There are five April sightings, the latest an immature at BLNWR, 13 April 1980.

There has been an increase in the number of Bald Eagle sightings in the study area since Allan and Sime (1943a) and Hawkins (1945) reported their findings.

The former recorded only one—in spring 1939—during four years of work, and the latter saw surprisingly few at the BLNWR during a time when water conditions were optimum and the refuge held large numbers of wintering waterfowl: "Usually about four Bald Eagles winter at Buffalo Lake." During the period 1961–77, eagles were recorded only intermittently on the refuge CBCs (high 5) despite an abundance of waterfowl. The lake became dry during the latter years of the period; when it refilled in early 1978, a dramatic increase in eagle numbers followed. That winter as many as 40 resided on the refuge, and the following winter up to 35.

In 1979 an annual Bald Eagle winter survey was initiated on the Lake Meredith National Recreation Area (Carson, Hutchinson, Moore, Potter counties). On 20 January 1979, 54 eagles were tallied and on 12 January 1980, 56. The average number recorded on the Lake Meredith (west) CBC, which encompasses the eagle roost on the LX Ranch, is 14 (high 49). At one time Lake Tanglewood in Randall County hosted a fair number of eagles, as many as 14 in the winter of 1975–76 and 18 in 1985–86.

NESTING: The Bald Eagle formerly nested in the Texas Panhandle. McCauley's (1877) account reads: "Met with several times in the canyon of Red River. On Mulberry Creek, June 17, a nest of this species was found containing two young about a week old." On that date his party was in what is now Armstrong County (Hunnius, 1876). Oberholser (1974) cites eggs collected in Potter County in 1916 (E. W. Gates), the last reported confirmed nesting.

However, the Bald Eagle continued to be considered a "permanent resident" by some area observers (Hibbets et al., 1926–36). An adult was observed on the Duncan Ranch along White Deer Creek, southeastern Hutchinson County, 25 June 1955, and there have been numerous reports of summering eagles since, none verified. They were very likely either Golden Eagles, buteos, or Turkey Vultures. As examples of how far off some identifications have been, Mississippi Kites perched on power lines were once reported as young Bald Eagles, as were a dozen or more vultures going to roost. Intriguing were two adult eagles observed a number of times at an old hawk nest at the BLNWR during the early spring of 1996 and 1997 (USFWS).

SPECIMENS: Oberholser (1974) cites a specimen taken in Potter County (ca. 1896), now in the R. L. Moore collection in Vernon, Texas, and three others collected near Canyon, Randall County, by L. G. Simms ("1 each winter between 1934 and 1937"), possibly those unlabeled mounted birds now housed in the P-PHM collection in Canyon, where Simms is known to have deposited some of his specimens. Wolfe (1956) states: "The U.S. Fish & Wildlife Service files contain records of specimens taken at . . . Amarillo and Canyon." Their present locations also are not known. There is a mounted specimen on display taken in Old-ham County (unspecified date, 1980s, ACMNH). The subspecies found in the Panhandle is *H. l. alascanus* (TOS, 1995).

Northern Harrier *Circus cyaneus* (Linnaeus)

STATUS: Common migrant and winter visitor. Rare to uncommon summer visitor, with casual breeding.

OCCURRENCE: The Northern Harrier has been recorded in every Texas Panhandle county and in every month of the year.

Because of numerous summer sightings, the early and late dates of fall arrival and spring departure of the Northern Harrier are not always clear-cut. Generally speaking, southbound birds arrive in late July or early August, while those northbound are mostly gone by mid-May.

A reportedly nationwide decline in the Northern Harrier population during the 1950s led to its placement on the Blue List of birds (Arbib, 1971). I analyzed my records for the period 1965–96 (September–April) and found a seemingly long-term stability in the study area. Based on 1,551 trips afield, I recorded an average of 2.5 harriers per trip during the first 16 years, and 2.3 during the last 16. These figures possibly reflect at least partial recovery following the 1950s decline (Palmer, 1988a). Indicative of the species' present status in mid-winter in the northern sector, on a 200-mile stretch of road in Moore, Hansford, Sherman, and Dallam counties on 15–16 January 1998, 81 harriers were recorded, over half of them adult males.

The CBC averages reflect the Northern Harrier's early winter status: *Friona*— 17.2; *Buffalo Lake NWR*—14.4; *Quitaque*—11.6; *Amarillo*—7.9; *Lake Meredith (west)*—7.7; *Lake Meredith (east)*—7.4. The Quitaque average is skewed by the 1996 count, in which 56 harriers were tallied, most of them a stream of birds observed in late afternoon, probably headed for a night roost. It is known that the species roosts communally on the ground. Littlefield (1970) observed one such roost on a 30-acre playa near Friona, Parmer County, 20 December 1967. On that date 43 harriers were counted, and there were 66 on the 21st, 30 on the 26th, and 27 on the 31st: "The hawks continued to use the area until mid-March when the lake vegetation was burned." Between 1960 and 1968, an average of 24 harriers wintered yearly on the BLNWR, with a high of 55 recorded on 17 November 1960.

NESTING: Early observers classified the Northern Harrier as "resident." Stevenson (1942) said "it may nest here"; Hawkins (1945) called it a "year-round resident. . . . During the summer months only a few are present, and their nesting status is uncertain"; and Wolfe (1956) mentioned "nests in suitable localities" without citing locations or dates. Allan and Sime (1943a) are the only observers to report an actual nest: "During the wet summer of 1941 it nested in Randall County. A nest was found May 30, 1941." On 4 July 1985, I encountered an adult female harrier with one juvenal-plumaged bird in the Sanford Dam marsh, Lake Meredith, Hutchinson County. The alarm behavior of the older bird and the reluctance of the young one to fly—when it did the duration was short and the bird persisted in returning to the spot from where it had flown—led me to believe that nesting had occurred somewhere in the near vicinity.

June–July sightings are numerous and widespread. I have watched male harriers in courtship flight as early as 30 March (1968) and as late as 10 April (1986). Stevenson (1942) observed a courting pair at BLNWR on 30 May 1941. Sutton (1967) cites nesting in the adjacent Oklahoma counties of Beaver and Cimarron, and Ligon (1961) for the Clayton area, Union County, New Mexico. Beginning in 1986, six nestings have been discovered in southwestern Oklahoma (Comanche and Stevens counties), suggesting that more of the numerous midsummer sightings of harriers in that area were of breeding birds (Regosin et al., 1991). Unknown to the authors was a harrier nest containing six eggs found south of Durham, Roger Mills County, 15 May 1966, only a short distance east of Hemphill County.

SPECIMENS: Specimens have been taken in Carson (ACMNH), Donley (11 March 1979, TCWC), Parmer (17 February 1977, WTAMU), and Randall (8 and 29 September 1939, P-PHM; 7 October 1939, WTAMU) counties. Oberholser (1974) references a fall specimen ("Nov. 17") taken in Gray County, but its location is not given.

Sharp-shinned Hawk *Accipiter striatus* Vieillot

STATUS: Fairly common migrant and winter visitor. Vagrant summer visitor.

OCCURRENCE: The Sharp-shinned Hawk has been recorded in every county except Carson, Collingsworth, Lipscomb, and Sherman, and has been seen in every month of the year.

The first Sharp-shinned Hawks of autumn can be expected in mid-September, the earliest a subadult at BLNWR on 27 August 1989. Fall is the season when most are recorded. My records reveal that 56 percent of all Sharp-shinneds were encountered in fall (September–November), 26 percent in winter (December–February), and 18 percent in spring (March–May). The species has been recorded on 45 percent of all CBCs, and was found during five of the ten years of a Winter-Bird Population Study conducted in the PDCSP (Seyffert, 1968–78). Many reports of wintering birds pertain to those found frequenting suburban yards. By the second week of May most are gone, the latest date being one at BLNWR on 20 May 1979.

The summer status of the Sharp-shinned Hawk in the study area has changed significantly since mid-century, as formerly there were reports of it in the canyonlands, where it was thought to breed. This belief was based on the occasional sighting of adults and immatures, not on the discovery of nests. The first report is that of Carlander (1934), who was cautious: "Possibly breeds. It has been seen during the summer months when it is usually nesting." Russell's (1935) statement that the Sharp-shinned Hawk is "common in Palo Duro and adults and young birds have been seen several times" is the only indication of probable nesting. Stevenson's (1942) later assessment—"A common summer resident in Palo Duro Canyon; adults and immature birds were observed frequently in 1935 and 1936"—was possibly based on Russell. The last reports of summering birds were made in 1955 and 1956 (P. Acord): "Seen uncommonly but regularly in the Palo Duro Canyon—may have nested"; "Permanent resident mostly of the canyons." However, the field check-list of that time (TPAS, 1955) classified the Sharp-shinned Hawk as a "rare migrant," not as a summering bird. Hawkins (1945) wondered at Stevenson's claim as he had seen only one Sharp-shinned in three years of study, and that one during migration. The text in Oberholser (1974) does not give the basis for the summer sighting in Wheeler County, but a search of the editor's files disclosed the observation as Oberholser's own: a pair seen at Mobeetie, 31 July 1901 (*fide* W. Pulich).

I know of no summer sighting of a Sharp-shinned Hawk in the Panhandle since 1956 and am skeptical that the species was ever common at that season or ever a part of the breeding avifauna. Johnsgard (1979) asserted: "No nesting record exists for the Texas Panhandle or adjacent New Mexico." The nearest to the study area that nesting has been confirmed is Cimarron County, Oklahoma (nest and eggs taken in 1909; Sutton, 1967)—the only record for the state—and Wise County, Texas (eggs collected. 30 April 1888; Oberholser, 1974), a record questioned by Pulich (1988). In Colorado, it is a "definite breeder" in the La Junta latilong in the southeastern sector (Chase et al., 1982).

SPECIMENS: There are three specimens taken in Hall (5 December 1976, 8 February 1977, 5 December 1981, WTAMU) and five taken in Randall (7 May, 25 September, 21 October 1939, and 6 February, 14 November 1977, WTAMU) counties.

Cooper's Hawk *Accipiter cooperii* (Bonaparte)

STATUS: Uncommon to fairly common migrant and winter visitor. Casual summer visitor, with vagrant breeding.

OCCURRENCE: The Cooper's Hawk has been recorded in every county except Deaf Smith, Hall, Lipscomb, Ochiltree, and Sherman. Oberholser (1974) names it in six counties. It has been seen in every month of the year.

The Cooper's Hawk has been reported much less often than has the Sharp-shinned Hawk. My records show a ratio of Cooper's to Sharp-shinned of 1:3. The former species has been found on 22 percent of the CBCS versus 45 percent for the latter, and the Cooper's was not found in any year of a Winter-Bird Population Study conducted in the PDCSP—as against half of the years for the Sharp-shinned Hawk (Seyffert, 1968–78). My records also show that 44 percent of all Cooper's Hawks were observed in fall (September–November) and 30 percent in spring (March–May).

Returning Cooper's Hawks can be looked for around the middle of September. Several sightings earlier are of interest: near Canyon, Randall County, 20 August 1969; BLNWR, 20 August 1972; Donley County, 29 August 1976—age classes not recorded. On 17 August 1980, an immature was encountered in the heavily wooded river bottom at Chicken Creek, Potter County. Another immature was observed in the PDCSP on 24 August 1984, and still earlier an immature at the BLNWR on 11 July 1982. Rarely is the Cooper's Hawk seen past early May. A lone individual east of Clarendon, Donley County, 2 June 1989, and one along the Canadian River, Potter County, 15 June 1964, were exceptions. Oberholser (1974) shows summer sightings in Childress, Dallam, and Potter counties, without giving dates or locations.

NESTING: I know of only one reported nesting of the Cooper's Hawk in the study area. A female was seen flying from a nest "in a tree over the Lake Marvin road just north of Canadian," Hemphill County, 25 April 1954 (P. Acord). Almost every publication shows the Texas Panhandle within the breeding range of the Cooper's Hawk. The single exception is Johnsgard (1979), who limits breeding to those locations where actual nestings have been confirmed. Perhaps it formerly nested, but the accounts of earlier observers give no support for that belief. Speaking of the Cooper's Hawk in north-central Texas, Pulich (1988) noted: "It is difficult to assess the former nesting status, and there is no evidence to substantiate nesting in recent years."

The Cooper's Hawk has been confirmed nesting in nearby areas. Sutton (1967) cites three pairs that nested along the Washita River near Cheyenne, Roger Mills County, Oklahoma, in May 1937, and a nest with eggs in Cimarron County, 30 June 1913. Shackford (1984) found it nesting four miles south of Kenton, Cimarron County, in 1980 and 1981 ("the first reported there since 1922"). On 29 May 1989, while atlassing a rather remote and heavily wooded area along the South Pease River near the Matador WMA in Cottle County, I flushed a female Cooper's Hawk from a nest placed high in a cottonwood tree. I was unable to determine the contents of the nest.

These nearby nestings point to the possibility that some of the immature birds observed in mid- or late summer were produced locally. The countless hours spent afield during the last 50 years by many observers would surely have turned up at least a few adult Cooper's Hawks if nesting was occurring, however secretive the species. In addition to this reclusiveness, which makes the species difficult to census, Oberholser (1974) cites other possible reasons for the lack of summer sightings in comparison to former years: changes in farm and ranch practices resulting in the reduction of the number of exposed barnyard fowl; overpopulation; pollution; and habitat loss.

SPECIMENS: Specimens are available for Collingsworth (24 January 1967, WTAMU) and Randall (23 and 30 September 1939, P-PHM; 15 November 1985, WTAMU) counties. A mounted specimen on display for Carson County (ACMNH) was said to have been taken in the 1980s.

Northern Goshawk *Accipiter gentilis* (Linnaeus)

STATUS: Casual migrant and winter visitor.

OCCURRENCE: The Northern Goshawk has been recorded in the following Texas Panhandle counties, a single bird in each instance unless otherwise noted: *Castro*—18 September 1990. *Hemphill*—Lake Marvin, 1 February 1972. *Moore*—east of Stratford, 3 February 1995 (TBRC). *Potter*—Amarillo, 25 April 1959; Lake Meredith, 31 December 1977. *Randall*—10 and 24 February 1957; BLNWR, 6 March and 25 September 1966, 24 October 1972, 12 March 1973, 30 March 1974, 16 November 1976, 9 May 1977, 24 December 1982, 1 November 1995 (TP-RF), 27 December 1997 (TBRC), 6 January 1998; Amarillo, 13 May 1968; Jokerst Ranch, 25–26 October 1972; two in PDCSP, 30 September 1973, and one 30 December 1992 (TBRC); 14 October 1975. *Wheeler*—near Wheeler, 9 March 1983. Few of these sightings were documented.

Common Black-Hawk *Buteogallus anthracinus* (Deppe)

STATUS: Vagrant.

OCCURRENCE: The Common Black-Hawk has been seen in the Texas Panhandle once. On 21 April 1999 an adult was discovered in Thompson Park, Amarillo, Potter County (L. Sare; TP-RF). The bird was seen later in the day as well as on the following day by many others.

The first appearance of a Common Black-Hawk away from the Trans-Pecos and South Texas was in late May 1982, when one adult and one subadult were discovered in Lubbock County (TP-RF). At least one of the birds summered, remaining until 11 October (Williams, 1983). A Common Black-Hawk, presumably one of the birds seen the previous year, was present 11–31 May 1983 (Williams, 1983); later it was joined by another, and both summered (Williams, 1983). Nesting could not be determined as access to the area was forbidden.

Harris's Hawk *Parabuteo unicinctus* (Temminck)

STATUS: Casual fall and vagrant spring visitor.

OCCURRENCE: The Harris's Hawk has been recorded in four Texas Panhandle counties: Castro, Hutchinson, Moore, and Randall. It has been seen in the period August–November, plus an unspecified date in spring (Oberholser, 1974).

The first mention of a Harris's Hawk in the study area is by Carlander (1933), who says the species was recorded in 1932—without citing number, date, or location. A separate list, headed "August 13 to September 4, 1932," says the species was seen in "several places." Although he covered much of the Panhandle, Carlander's work was concentrated primarily in the Amarillo area ("a few miles south and a few miles west"). Oberholser (1974) shows a spring sighting for Randall County and a fall sighting for Moore County, but details for both are lacking. A search of his files disclosed that the Moore County sighting is based on a bird found west of Dumas on 3 September 1939 (F. W. Miller): nothing was found pertaining to the Randall County sighting (*fide* W. Pulich).

Stevenson (1942) gives more details of the bird he saw in the PDCSP: "One was studied at close range for an hour on September 30, 1937, while it perched in cottonwoods along the creek at the north boundary of the park." The files of the USFWS at BLNWR register a sighting on 17 August 1963; no other details are given. More recently, a Harris's Hawk was observed in east-central Hutchinson County, north of the Canadian River, 5 November 1985 (letter, Josef K. Schmutz, University of Saskatchewan, 21 February 1986): "This hawk gave persistent chase to a flicker who eventually escaped among the tall shrubs. This occurred in the lowlands of dense and tall shrubs bordering the Canadian River." On 11 October 1993, one was observed near Dodd in southwest Castro County.

On 9 October 1972, a Harris's Hawk was discovered in the area of the South Fork of the Red River in extreme southwestern Jackson County, Oklahoma, not far from the state line at Childress County (Ault, 1975). Following the initial sighting, up to three birds were found with some regularity in the Eldorado vicinity until 16 October 1975—all of them fall sightings after 25 February 1973. Ault again found a Harris's Hawk near Eldorado on 29–30 January 1987 (Banta and McMahon, 1987). Banta himself observed one at the Fort Sill Military Reservation in Comanche County, Oklahoma, 15 November 1986, and for 100 days thereafter. These sightings and the increasing frequency of sightings just to the south of the study area, including nesting, should alert Panhandle observers to the possibility of the Harris's Hawk eventually becoming a feature of the regional avifauna.

The Harris's Hawk is a common resident in South Texas, north to the Balcones Escarpment and east to Goliad County (TOS, 1995).

Red-shouldered Hawk *Buteo lineatus* (Gmelin)

STATUS: Casual fall to spring visitor.

OCCURRENCE: The Red-shouldered Hawk has been reported in six Texas Panhandle counties: Briscoe, Gray, Potter, Randall, Roberts, and Swisher. It has been seen August–October, December–January, and April–May.

Both Hibbets et al. (1926–36) and Carlander (1933) classified the Red-shouldered Hawk as a "rare permanent resident," the former without naming locations or dates, the latter simply stating that he had seen it in "several places" between 13 August and 4 September 1932. That this raptor of heavily wooded river bottoms was ever a resident in the central Panhandle is unlikely. Its present range in Texas is limited to the central and eastern portions (TOS, 1995), and in Oklahoma one has never been found west of Alfalfa, Caddo, Comanche, and Jackson counties (Tyler et al., 1989).

There have been but few sightings of the Red-shouldered Hawk since mid-century: one at BLNWR, 5 and 19 April 1969; one near Pampa, Gray County, 10 October 1973; one at the Palo Duro Club near Canyon, Randall County, January 1976; two approximately ten miles west of Tulia, Swisher County, 31 December 1986, and another northwest of Littlefield, Lamb County, a short distance south of the study area, 1 January 1987 (Schmutz, 1987); one at BLNWR, 29 August 1993; and one in Caprock Canyons SP, Briscoe County, 20 May 1995. Oberholser (1974) shows summer and winter sightings for Randall County (questioning both), a winter sighting for Potter County, and a summer sighting for Roberts County. Details for all are lacking. A search of the Oberholser files turned up nothing other than the Hibbets citation already given (*fide* W. Pulich).

Nowhere on the southern High Plains is the Red-shouldered Hawk other than rare. One at Lubbock on 30 May 1982 was the first county record, while two at Midland, 9–16 May 1982, "constituted only the third record in 35 years" (Williams, 1982). A second "well-documented" Lubbock sighting occurred on 11–13 August 1989 (Lasley and Sexton, 1990), and another bird was seen in Crosby County, 10 August 1996. One was observed south of Quitaque in Floyd County, 16 December 1997 and 10 January 1998. The Red-shouldered Hawk is found year-round well east of the Texas Panhandle and generally migrates only from the northern half of its range (Crocoll, 1994).

Broad-winged Hawk *Buteo platypterus* (Vieillot)

STATUS: Rare migrant.

OCCURRENCE: The Broad-winged Hawk has been recorded in eight counties—Castro, Dallam, Donley, Gray, Hutchinson, Potter, Randall, and Roberts—in the periods April–May and August–November.

Almost twice as many Broad-winged Hawks have been seen in fall as in spring. Most fall birds show up in September, and spring ones are divided equally between April and May. Both early and late fall dates are of birds seen at BLNWR: 17 August 1968 and a dark morph on 10 November 1956. Few others have been reported in November. The early and late spring dates are at Amarillo, 13 April 1959, and BLNWR, 31 May 1981. All sightings have been of lone birds except for one record of three. In the period 1976–84, the species was reported yearly; otherwise, sightings have been highly irregular. In addition to the dark morph previously noted, two others have been reported: one in the PDCSP, on 3 May 1978, and another near Lake Tanglewood several miles upcanyon from the previous sighting the following 14 May—possibly the same bird.

Swainson's Hawk *Buteo swainsoni* Bonaparte

STATUS: Common to abundant migrant. Fairly common to common breeder.

OCCURRENCE: The Swainson's Hawk has been recorded in every county and has been seen from late February to late November. Without supporting documentation, those reportedly seen in winter must be disallowed.

The Swainson's Hawk is the most common of the summering buteos over much of the study area, the exception being the Red-tailed Hawk in the eastern counties. Early observers spoke of the prevalence of the Swainson's. McCauley (1877) wrote: "This magnificent hawk was frequently seen along streams passed, and both in Red River Canyon and at the very origin of the waters far up in the Staked Plain. At other times they were noted out on the level plain, miles from timber." Strecker (1910) called it "the common large hawk of the plains. On account of a scarcity of trees, they nest on cliffs in the canyons." Allan and Sime (1943a) were the first to quantify observations, and found the species to be a "common resident . . . nesting nearly everywhere that there are a few cottonwood trees." Their study made during the summers of 1939–41 disclosed an average abundance of 20.9 birds per 1,000 miles traveled (1939 = 40.8; 1940 = 8.9; 1941 = 13.0). Later, Hawkins (1945) found the species less common: "an uncommon summer resident. . . . Throughout the spring and until July an average of about one was seen per hundred miles of road traveled." This decline continued in the postwar years. The Swainson's Hawk was placed on the National Audubon Society's Blue List (Arbib, 1972), where it has remained.

An analysis of my records discloses increases. Dividing 28 years of observations into two equal periods (Period A = 1965–78, Period B = 1979–92) and three seasons (Spring, Summer, Fall), the results reveal an increase in the number of hawks seen per trip afield from Period A to Period B during all seasons, particularly summer and fall: *Spring*—Period A = 1.42, Period B = 1.77; *Summer*—Period A = 1.26, Period B = 3.71; *Fall*—Period A = 1.62, Period B = 2.54. These figures do not include mass movements of migrating birds.

The Swainson's Hawk returns in spring around the first of April, the earliest date for one at Lake Tanglewood, Randall County, 15 March 1981. Several late February sightings must be questioned. The largest spring flight on record was observed near Pampa, Gray County, on 13 April 1974—93 hawks in the air and 100+ on the ground. Four days later the site contained 310+ on the ground. The spring movement continues through the early part of May. The beginning of fall migration can often be detected in late August and early September; however, the larger numbers usually occur during the first two weeks of October. "Several hundred" were on the ground east of Pampa, Gray County, 26 August 1995, and still greater numbers in late September and early October: 2,000 between Dumas, Moore County, and Dalhart, Hartley County, 30 September 1985; three kettles of approximately 300 birds each east of Dalhart, Dallam County, 3 October 1980; more than 1,000 passing over the Sanford Dam at Lake Meredith, Hutchinson County, 9–10 October 1974; and in mid-October 1953, a movement of 7,000 to 8,000 hawks, mostly Swainson's Hawks, took place in the Amarillo area over several days. Unusual were 60 at BLNWR on the late date of 25 October 1980. Very few Swainson's have been reported beyond October. An adult was observed north of Lake Marvin, Hemphill County, 20 November 1965, and one near South Ceta Canyon, Randall County, 25 November 1966. Premigratory gatherings have been encountered. As an example, on 24 July 1989, 75–80 Swainson's were tallied along I-40 west of Bushland near the Potter–Oldham county line, and by the 26th the number had increased to 300 or more. I visited the site on the following day and counted 217 hawks on the ground or perched on fence posts along a one-mile stretch of road; many were feeding in the high vegetation, possibly on grasshoppers. Birds in a gathering of up to 47 observed on 3 October 1969 in Parmer County were feeding on armyworms (Littlefield, 1973).

Can the Swainson's Hawk be found in the Texas Panhandle in winter? Allan and Sime (1943a) gave a date of 7 December 1938; a few others have been reported in later years. None having been documented, all must be dismissed. Those reported on CBCs were never seen on subsequent days. It is only in recent years that a few winter sightings in Texas have been documented, none nearer the Panhandle than the San Angelo area. The AOU (1983) restricts the winter range of the Swainson's Hawk to "primarily on the pampas of southern South America," but a few are reported in North America almost every winter in southern Texas and Florida, and regularly in northern coastal California. Most have been sight records, with few reports stating whether the birds were adults or immatures. In an effort to clarify the winter status of the Swainson's Hawk, Browning (1974) contacted fifteen museums in the United States asking for information on specimens collected from November to February. Of seventeen specimens, only six had been collected in December, January, and February, all those from Texas before 1920. He pointed out the difficulties in identification without the bird in hand and concluded that "assuming the adults are correctly identified, probably less than 18 per cent of all [winter] Swainson's Hawk reports . . . are acceptable."

NESTING: Swainson's Hawks begin nest building soon after arrival on their summering grounds, and most young fledge in late July. An indication of possible late nesting (or renesting) was two juveniles standing on a nest on the Rita Blanca National Grasslands, Dallam County, 27 August 1984. The following are the average numbers of Swainson's Hawks recorded on BBSS: *Texline*—5.0; *Pantex*—4.7; *Channing*—3.5; *Dalhart*—3.0; *Waka*—2.9; *Booker*—2.8; *Panhandle*—2.3; *Clarendon*—1.8; *Miami*—1.5; *Childress*—1.5; *Skellytown*—0.3. The TBBAP found CO nesting in 36 quadrangles, PR in 31, and PO in 43. There is evidence that some subadult Swainson's Hawks may remain together in summer. In Carson County on 8 June 1988, I encountered a loose gathering of 14 birds. In the same area on the previous 10 May I had observed 28 birds, most of them subadults, their plumages ranging from almost all white to very dark, no two alike. The following year (28 June), again in Carson County, I found 17 subadults together in one field and 16 more only a short distance down the road in another.

SPECIMENS: Specimens have been taken in Hutchinson (LMAWM), Oldham (3 June 1920, SM), and Randall (22 May 1939, P-PHM; March 1939, 29 August 1939, 1 and 10 September 1939, 15 April 1968, 19 July 1970, 15 October 1974, WTAMU) counties. One bird in the WTAMU collection is a dark morph. Oberholser (1974) names a specimen record of breeding for Randall County, a fall specimen for Oldham County, and a summer specimen for Roberts County, but fails to say in what collections they were placed. The Randall citation possibly is based on the egg and adult collected by McCauley (1877).

Red-tailed Hawk *Buteo jamaicensis* (Gmelin)

STATUS: Fairly common to common resident.

OCCURRENCE: The Red-tailed Hawk has been recorded in every Texas Panhandle county and has been seen year-round.

The status of the Red-tailed Hawk in the study area in relation to the other buteos has changed since mid-century. Allan and Sime (1943a) found the red-tailed "primarily a winter bird . . . relatively uncommon, but by no means rare." For the winters of 1938–39 through 1941–42, based on numbers seen per 1,000 miles traveled, they found the Red-tailed to be the second most common buteo after the Ferruginous and the least common in spring, summer, and fall. In winter the Red-tailed was far behind the Ferruginous (6.2 average versus 31.9).

Hawkins (1945) corroborated these findings to some degree, for he placed the red-tailed fourth in abundance during migration.

An analysis of my records for the period 1965–92 (2,019 trips afield) reveals different rankings. The following are the average numbers seen per trip in each season:

	Spring	Summer	Fall	Winter
Swainson's	1.60	2.66	2.01	
Red-tailed	0.76	0.43	1.41	2.01
Ferruginous	0.21	0.13	0.67	1.76
Rough-legged	0.18		0.20	0.66

In comparing their numbers in the 14-year period (1) 1965–78 with the 14-year period (2) 1979–92, my records do show an increase in Red-tailed Hawks, particularly in winter:

	Spring	Summer	Fall	Winter
(1)	0.52	0.39	1.34	1.12
(2)	0.99	0.47	1.47	2.89

As these figures show, the Red-tailed Hawk is most common in winter. No flocks of migrants have been recorded, but a noticeable increase occurs in early September and a decrease in late winter and early spring. The averages on the CBCs are another indication of its status in winter: *Lake Meredith* (*west*)—13.3; *Lake Meredith* (*east*)—8.9; *Buffalo Lake* NWR—6.7; *Quitaque*—5.2; *Amarillo*—4.0. On the *Friona* CBC, conducted through grasslands and croplands, the species was recorded only once.

Occasionally a "Harlan's" or "Krider's" is reported. Great care is required in identifying both races for there is considerable variation in Red-tailed Hawk plumages due to color morphs and age and racial differences. Long experience in hawk-watching is of help when identifying some of the variations, and even then certainty cannot always be obtained. Almost all "Harlan's" have been reported in the eastern counties, for its primary wintering grounds lie east of the study area, and the "Krider's," though more widespread, is found only in migration and winter.

NESTING: The Red-tailed Hawk is an early nester. Adults have been observed standing on an old nest or refurbishing one as early as 1 February (Hemphill County) and 2 February (Carson County), while occupied nests have been found as early as 14 March (Roberts County) and 15 March (Hartley County). Recently fledged young have been found as late as the first week of July (Oldham County). On 30 May 1977, I observed a juvenile still on its nest, apparently ready to fledge. The nest was placed in an active Great Blue Heron colony. I know of at least two other instances in which Red-tailed Hawks have been found nesting with this heron.

The BBSS do not accurately reflect the Red-tailed Hawk's summer status as none of the counts are made in the wooded areas of the eastern counties. The following are the averages per count: *Channing*—1.0; *Clarendon*—1.0; *Texline*—0.5; *Miami*—0.5; *Booker*—0.5; *Childress*—0.5; *Waka*—0.1; *Pantex*—0.01. The TBBAP classified nesting as CO in 16 survey blocks, PR in 12, and PO in 22. Sixteen of the COS and PRS were located between the 100th and 101st meridians, nine between the 101st and 102nd, and three west of the 102nd meridian. The species has been confirmed nesting in all but eight of the 26 counties (Sherman, Hansford, Moore, Parmer, Castro, Swisher, Hall, and Childress), and would be in most of those with better coverage.

SPECIMENS: Specimens have been taken in Hansford (27 October 1956, MNH), Hutchinson (5 July 1950, TNHC), and Randall (ACMNH; 10 February 1939, January 1969, WTAMU) counties. The subspecies found in the Panhandle are *B. j. fuertesi, calurus, kriderii,* and *harlani. Fuertesi* is resident; the others are migrants or winter visitors (TOS, 1995).

Ferruginous Hawk *Buteo regalis* (Gray)

STATUS: Fairly common to common winter visitor. Rare to uncommon summer resident in the northwestern sector.

OCCURRENCE: The Ferruginous Hawk has been reported in every Texas Panhandle county except Childress and Collingsworth and has been seen in every month.

Returning Ferruginous Hawks in fall can be expected during the second or third week of September, a month or more earlier than the Rough-legged Hawk. No gatherings of migrants have been reported. The species is thought to be declining and studies are now being conducted by the USFWS and other agencies to see whether placing it on the Endangered Species list is warranted. Area observers are of the belief that as far as wintering birds are concerned, more Ferruginous Hawks are being seen today than formerly. My records support this belief. Dividing the years 1965–92 into two equal periods—(1) 1965–78, (2) 1979–92—the 1,267 trips afield reveal the following averages per trip:

	Spring	Summer	Fall	Winter
(1)	0.13	0.17	0.43	0.50
(2)	0.33	0.11	0.88	2.98

Data from the study area prior to this period are largely nonexistent. The Allan and Sime (1943a) roadside counts for the period 1939–41 disclosed averages of 31.4 Ferruginous Hawks per 1,000 miles traveled in winter, 9.6 in spring, 2.9 in summer, and 9.3 in fall. The routes followed are unknown. On 30 January

1988, a roadside count was conducted beginning south of Amarillo, Randall County, and following a circuit through Armstrong, Briscoe, Swisher, and Castro counties, ending west of Amarillo, Potter County—296 miles (K. Seyffert, P. Acord). Twenty-eight Ferruginous Hawks were recorded (94.6/1,000 miles), only one a dark morph. On 15–16 January 1998 (D. Fisher, J. Windsor), a 200-mile stretch of road running through Hansford, Sherman, Moore, and Dallam counties produced 57 birds (285/1,000 miles).

Recent studies of wintering Ferruginous Hawks are revealing (Schmutz, 1987; Schmutz and Fyfe, 1987). Between 18 December 1986 and 6 January 1987, a raptor research team from the University of Saskatchewan conducted a study in seven counties in the Panhandle (Armstrong, Briscoe, Castro, Deaf Smith, Parmer, Randall, and Swisher), plus three adjacent counties (Bailey, Hale, and Lamb). This area was selected as 46 percent of Alberta Ferruginous Hawks winter in Texas, and 47 percent of 15 recoveries in Texas were made in these counties. The researchers estimated that there were 2,464 individuals in their study area (9.8/100 km^2), and that it wintered about 18 percent of all grassland Ferruginous Hawks.

The research team found that patches of grassland harboring prairie dog towns amidst extensive cultivation are the most attractive to Ferruginous Hawks, and they determined that the hawks were mainly feeding on prairie dogs, mice, and rabbits: "On plots with prairie dogs the mean number of ferruginous hawks seen was 4.5 and on plots without prairie dogs 3.6." They found this close correlation unexpected, for the Ferruginous Hawk avoids cultivated areas on its breeding grounds. They concluded that "ferruginous hawks clearly were not adversely affected by cultivation" on their wintering grounds, and that "agricultural practices themselves and the extensive human activity had no negative effect on this hawk which appears shy and retreating on the breeding grounds." I have found the Ferruginous Hawk to be the least shy of the buteos in winter and have often stood at length beneath a power pole on which one was perched.

Ferruginous Hawks are commonly found in the vicinity of prairie dog towns. As examples, a large dog town located in southwest Amarillo, Randall County, held 17 hawks on 19 January 1991 and 18 on the following 28 November. Up to a dozen birds could be seen congregated around dead prairie dogs, fighting over their remains. Such behavior has been well documented in Carson County (Allison et al., 1995).

There is no question that the number of summering Ferruginous Hawks in the Texas Panhandle has declined since the early twentieth century, drastically so during the latter half. Strecker (1912) said of the species that it "breeds abundantly in the Panhandle (Potter and Armstrong counties)," and Hibbets et al. (1926–36) called it a "numerous permanent resident." Toward mid-century Stevenson (1942) reported that "a few nest in the canyons." Allan and Sime (1943a) recorded only 17 of these hawks in 5,003 miles traveled in summer, and Hawkins (1945) classified the species as a "rare summer resident," with no conclusive evidence of nesting. By 1955, it was no longer listed on the Panhandle checklist as a summering bird (TPAS, 1955).

The majority of summering Ferruginous Hawks today are found in the northern counties, few elsewhere: *Armstrong*—one, 29 May 1997. *Briscoe*—one, 11 May 1998. *Dallam*—recorded on 14 of 22 Texline BBSS; others seen beyond the count route. *Deaf Smith*—one, 23 June 1991. *Gray*—one, 3 June 1978. *Hansford*—one, 8 June 1977. *Hartley*—recorded on 14 of 30 Channing BBSS; at other times west of town and south of Dalhart. *Moore*—a subadult, 30 June 1987. *Ochiltree*—two, 8 June 1977; one, 10 June 1982; one, 10 June 1987; one, 25 June 1990; one, 7 June 1995. *Oldham*—one, 17 July 1996. *Potter*—one, 16 June 1973. *Randall*—one, 3 May 1969, and 9 and 14 May 1970; two, 7 July 1975; one, 9 May 1976; two, 11 May 1985; one, 23–26 May 1985; one, 26 April 1996; one, 14 May 1994. *Roberts*—one, 10 June 1979. *Sherman*—one, 22 June 1975; two, 6 June 1977. Some of these birds may have been breeding, for the Ferruginous Hawk is on its nest by late April.

NESTING: Oberholser (1974) cited four nesting records: 6–25 May 1920 (Deaf Smith County); 24 May 1920 (Oldham County); 1939 (Moore County); 14 April 1966 (Dallam County). His editor predicted that the "next southeasternmost nesting of the species is likely to be northwest of the Lone Star State." The summer accounts previously given point to regular nesting today in Dallam, Sherman, Hansford, Hartley, and Moore counties, with probable or possible nestings in others. The following is a listing of those found subsequent to Oberholser's citations: *Armstrong*—a juvenal-plumaged bird collected, 4 July 1967. *Dallam*—on 7 June 1975, I found an adult on a nest built in an isolated stand of three trees located 21.5 miles east of Texline (Rita Blanca National Grasslands). In the following years I found the nest occupied by adults and/or young on 12 June 1976, 11 June 1977, 10 June 1978, 7 June 1980, 11 June 1981, 14 June 1983, 13 June 1987, 16 May 1993, and 13 June 1996. During these years the nest collapsed twice because of its weight and bulk and was rebuilt, either in the same tree or in one nearby. After 1983, the nest was occupied by a Ferruginous Hawk pair irregularly (one year by Golden Eagles, in others by Swainson's Hawks); however, USFS rangers tell me that a pair continued nesting at a site located farther north in the years when this old site was not occupied. In addition, I have recorded other Ferruginous Hawks in the area during each of the survey years, including juveniles. A windmill nest located about three miles south of the Thompson Grove Picnic Area northeast of Texline held one young, with another on the ground not far distant, 22 June 1995 (TP-RF). This same nest held three young in 1994 and four in 1996. *Hartley*—an adult carrying a stick south of Channing, 15 March 1995. *Moore*—a young bird north of Lake Meredith, 30 June 1987, and a fledgling near the Hartley County line, 24 June 1989; *Randall*—a pair with one young near Amarillo, mid-June 1967; a nest built on a cliffside and containing four eggs, 22 April 1968, on the Jokerst Ranch south of Amarillo—by 2 July at least two young had fledged.

SPECIMENS: There are specimens for Armstrong (4 July 1967, WTAMU), Carson (ACMNH), Deaf Smith (December 1969, WTAMU), Moore (MCHM), Ochiltree (16 February 1972, FMNH), and Randall (30 September 1939, P-PHM; 26 February 1939, WTAMU; 7 December 1980, TCWC) counties.

Rough-legged Hawk *Buteo lagopus* (Pontoppidan)

STATUS: Uncommon to fairly common winter visitor.

OCCURRENCE: The Rough-legged Hawk has been recorded in all Texas Panhandle counties except Collingsworth, Hall, and Roberts. It has been seen from September to April.

Returning Rough-legged Hawks in fall can be looked for in mid-October. Possibly all September sightings should be questioned, while those reportedly seen in August must be dismissed. The September sightings are: BLNWR, 10–15 September 1968; Randall County, 15 September 1985; Potter County, 18 September 1996. The earliest confirmed sighting in Kansas is 20 September (Thompson and Ely, 1989). In spring any seen past the first week of April are exceptional. Allan and Sime (1943a) cite a 21 April 1939 date ("unusually late"), and one was observed near Panhandle, Carson County on 28 April 1977. My records (1964–97) show only seven years in which one was seen in April, the latest being 19 April 1970 at BLNWR. Those reportedly seen in May must be disallowed. Fischer et al. (1982) name a 17 May date for the southwestern sector that is hard to credit. Often dark-morph buteos of various species and age classes are misidentified as rough-leggeds, and it is not uncommon for a hovering buteo to be tagged as this species without being examined closely. Although this is a common behavior of the rough-legged, other buteos also engage in it, particularly on very windy days. These early and late dates conform to those for the northwestern and Panhandle areas of Oklahoma (October 1– April 20; Grzybowski et al., 1992). Most Rough-legged Hawks do not vacate their breeding grounds until mid-September to October, and by the end of April they have left southern Canada on their way back north (Palmer, 1988b).

Accounts of the winter status of the Rough-legged Hawk vary widely. Stevenson (1942) called it a "common winter visitor," while Allan and Sime (1943a) said it was "so scarce that mileage records are hardly significant." Hawkins (1945) observed: "During the winter months it is one of the most common hawks on the Plains." Later observers have disagreed with this latter assessment (see Red-tailed Hawk), placing the Rough-legged Hawk last on the list of area buteos. Its abundance, however, can vary significantly from one winter to the next. Two observers tallied 21 on 15–16 January 1998 on a 200-mile stretch of road running through Hansford, Sherman, Moore, and Dallam counties. A look at my records (1965–92) shows the following incidence of abundance per trip afield: (1) 1965–78; (2) 1979–92:

	Spring	Fall	Winter
(1)	0.13	0.22	0.49
(2)	0.08	0.17	0.83

The averages on the CBCs are another indication of early winter status: *Friona*—4.0; *Buffalo Lake* NWR—3.8; *Quitaque*—1.0; *Lake Meredith* (*east*)—0.8; *Amarillo*—0.8; *Lake Meredith* (*west*)—0.7.

SPECIMENS: Specimens have been taken in Deaf Smith (6 December 1967, 20 December 1969, WTAMU), Donley (10 December 1971, WFVZ), Gray (16 February 1972, FMNH), Moore (MCHM), and Randall (19 November 1939, P-PHM) counties.

Golden Eagle *Aquila chrysaetos* (Linnaeus)

STATUS: Uncommon resident.

OCCURRENCE: The Golden Eagle has been recorded in every Texas Panhandle county except Childress, Hall, and Wheeler and has been seen in every month.

Migrant Golden Eagles and winter visitors arrive in the study area in October; it is from then until late winter that the species is most commonly found. The averages on the CBCs indicate its status in early winter: *Amarillo*—2.2; *Buffalo Lake* NWR—1.2; *Lake Meredith* (*west*)—1.1; *Quitaque*—1.0; *Lake Meredith* (*east*)—0.8; *Friona*—0.3. Each count has shown a decline since 1985. Eight to ten eagles wintered on the BLNWR in 1962–63, 7 in 1966–67, and 6–9 in 1967–68. On the Lake Meredith Recreation Area, seven were present, 26 March 1967; eleven were seen feeding on ducks at the edge of the frozen lake, Bates Canyon, Potter County, 13 January 1968; and thirteen were at Plum Creek, Potter County, 24 February 1975 ("just after a blizzard").

NESTING: Most early references to Golden Eagles in the Texas Panhandle placed nesting sites in the Palo Duro Canyon complex and Canadian River breaks. In the early twentieth century, Strecker (1910) reported the species as a "resident, breeding in the larger canyons." Later, Stevenson (1942) also found it "a regular resident of Palo Duro Canyon" and said it was seen almost daily. Allan and Sime (1943a) found it "a year round resident ... seen mainly during the winter months, and then only uncommonly" and cited it nesting in Randall and Hartley counties. Hawkins (1945) spoke of it as a "rare summer resident. . . . At Palo Duro Canyon a pair probably had a nest."

The information contained in these reports is quite sketchy. To determine the status of the Golden Eagle as a breeder, a study was made in 14 Panhandle counties from 1 September 1979 to 31 August 1983 (Rideout et al., 1984). The study team discovered a total of 34 pairs that nested and produced young or that attempted to nest. Numbers of pairs by county were: Armstrong (9); Briscoe (9); Deaf Smith (3); Donley (1); Hemphill (1); Hutchinson (1); Ochiltree (1); Oldham (4); Potter (2); Randall (3). Four other pairs were known to have nested between 1976 and 1979 but not during the study period—in Collingsworth, Gray, Hartley, and Roberts counties—and "there may be 10–20 additional pairs in unsurveyed areas of the Panhandle." During the TBBAP a pair attempted to nest in Dallam County, and a pair nested successfully in Sherman County in 1998. In addition, spring and summer sightings of eagles have been recorded in four counties: Carson, Lipscomb, Moore, and Swisher (Tule Canyon).

Golden Eagles alternate their use of nesting sites; the TPWD study team found more than one in each pair's nesting area. Numbers of sites by county were: Armstrong (21); Briscoe (22); Collingsworth (2); Deaf Smith (6); Donley (2); Gray (1); Hartley (1); Hemphill (2); Hutchinson (5); Ochiltree (1); Oldham (8); Potter (3); Randall (10); Roberts (1). More than 95 percent of the nests were built on the ledges of steep cliffs and less than 5 percent in the upper branches of cottonwood trees. Several of the nesting areas have long histories of use. The one in Hutchinson County has been occupied since 1917 and a nest in Donley County since 1910. A pair of eagles has been seen in Gray County for 30 years; without, however, a nest ever being found. A nest site in Collingsworth County was last occupied in 1978: it had been in use for over 50 years. Speculation was that the adults were possibly killed or were nesting in nearby Oklahoma. In 1973, three pairs nested in the upper Palo Duro Canyon in Randall County. A female of one pair had been released on the Hugh Currie ranch four years previously after being found injured and then nursed back to health. Nest building may begin as early as mid-December and egg laying around the second week of February. The majority of eaglets hatch during the first two weeks of April and fledge by mid-June (Strandtmann, 1962; Rideout et al., 1984).

SPECIMENS: There are specimens for Dallam (26 September 1947, 21 December 1957, TCWC), and Gray (8 May 1947, TCWC) counties. Oberholser (1974) shows eggs collected in Oldham and Potter counties and specimens taken in Dallam, Gray, and Lipscomb counties, without saying where they were deposited. Numerous Golden Eagles donated by the USFWS are on display in various area collections, but their places of taking are not specified.

Family Falconidae (Falcons)

American Kestrel *Falco sparverius* Linnaeus
STATUS: Fairly common to common resident.
OCCURRENCE: The American Kestrel, formerly known as the Sparrow Hawk, has been recorded in every county and has been seen in every month.

Kincaid in Oberholser (1974) bewailed the fate of the American Kestrel and said that during the period 1900–70 it was "almost eliminated as a breeder in the state." Further: "In Texas during the 1960s and early 1970s, the Sparrow Hawk was still practically wiped out as a breeder and much reduced as a wintering species." He proclaimed it "uncommon and local in northern Panhandle." This assessment of the kestrel's status in the study area needs reexamining.

In the late nineteenth century McCauley (1877) found that "this . . . falcon flourishes . . . throughout the section visited, except upon the Great Plain. Every wooded stream had its quota." Carlander (1934) classified the kestrel as "rather common," and Russell (1935) said it was "common in all of the canyon area and . . . occasionally seen on the surrounding plain"—most of his work was done in July and August. Stevenson (1942) called it a "common resident of the canyons and plains," and Allan and Sime (1943a) found its ranking among the birds of prey to be "fourth in abundance" and called it a "year round resident." Near mid-century Hawkins (1945) continued to find it a "fairly common summer resident," and Thompson (1952) said birds were frequently seen. A study done by Allan and Sime (1943a) is of help as it provides average numbers based on random miles traveled for the period 1938–42. A comparison can be made of their winter results with two recent ones. In the winter of 1938–39, they recorded 20.1 kestrels per 1,000 miles traveled; 1939–40, 5.8; 1940–41, 18.2; 1941–42, 32.9. On 30 January 1988, a roadside survey was made beginning south of Amarillo, Randall County, and proceeding in a circle east, south, and west through Armstrong, Briscoe, Swisher, and Castro counties, ending west of Amarillo, Potter County (P. Acord, K. Seyffert). Twenty-eight kestrels were recorded in 296 miles traveled (94.6/1,000 miles). On 15–16 January 1998, two observers (D. Fisher, J. Windsor) found 23 kestrels on a 200-mile stretch of road in Hansford, Sherman, Moore, and Dallam counties (115/1,000 miles).

Winter is the season of the American Kestrel's greatest abundance, as the following averages attest. They are based on 2,478 trips afield that I made from 1965 to 1996: January (5.0); February (2.6); March (2.6); April (2.9); May (1.1); June (1.1); July (1.0); August (1.3); September (2.8); October (2.5); November

(3.3); December (5.8). CBC averages are: *Quitaque*—28.0; *Amarillo*—16.9; *Lake Meredith* (*west*)—12.6; *Lake Meredith* (*east*)—10.3; *Buffalo Lake* NWR—9.8; *Friona*—1.1.

While the overall seasonal abundance is greatest in winter, there is a short period in late March and early April when a pronounced movement occurs. I made two roadside counts over a route running from Clarendon, Donley County, to Amarillo, Randall County, via the JA Ranch (75 miles). On 1 April 1973, 86 kestrels were counted, and on 5 April 1975, 105. There is another discernible movement in late September.

The American Kestrel summers throughout the Panhandle. It can be found in woodland and riparian habitats, shelterbelts, canyonlands, around farm and ranch buildings, and within the smaller towns and on the outskirts of large ones. During the TBBAP the kestrel was recorded in 74 of 102 survey blocks. It was absent only in Hansford and Sherman counties in the north and Castro and Parmer counties in the southwest. The kestrel has been recorded on all but one of the BBSS, that one a count recently initiated: *Channing*—2.2; *Childress*—2.2; *Clarendon*—1.6; *Miami*—1.6; *Booker*—1.3; *Dalhart*—0.8; *Panhandle*—0.7; *Texline*—0.5; *Pantex*—0.4; *Waka*—0.2; *Skellytown*—0.0.

NESTING: The American Kestrel has been confirmed nesting in 17 counties: Briscoe, Childress, Collingsworth, Dallam, Deaf Smith, Donley, Hall, Hansford, Hartley, Hutchinson, Lipscomb, Moore, Oldham, Potter, Randall, Roberts, and Wheeler. The TBBAP classified 22 survey blocks as CO, 21 as PR, and 26 as PO. Thirty-two were located between the 100th and 101st meridians, 19 between the 101st and 102nd, and 18 west of the 102nd. Nest dates range from 18 April 1958 to 20 July 1952 (both Randall County). The species may be two-brooded. A nest box erected in north Amarillo produced two broods in 1992 (T. Massey); however, it was not known for certain whether they were reared by the same pair or if a young individual in either nest survived to care for itself.

SPECIMENS: Specimens have been taken in Briscoe (15 November 1981, WTAMU), Carson (ACMNH), Hall (23 January 1977, OMNH), Hartley (1 November 1939, P-PHM); Hutchinson (4 January 1981, TCWC; 7 July 1950, TNHC), Moore (MCHM), Randall (3 April 1972, TCWC; 14 January, 4 August, and 8 September, 1939, WTAMU), and Swisher (December 1969, MTTU) counties. Oberholser (1974) shows specimens for Dallam, Deaf Smith, Hemphill, Hutchinson, Oldham, and Randall counties, without naming their locations.

Merlin *Falco columbarius* Linnaeus

STATUS: Rare to uncommon migrant and winter visitor.

OCCURRENCE: The Merlin has been reported in 18 counties: Armstrong, Briscoe, Carson, Castro, Dallam, Deaf Smith, Hartley, Hemphill, Hutchinson, Moore,

Ochiltree, Oldham, Parmer, Potter, Randall, Roberts, Sherman, and Swisher. Although it has been recorded in every month, those reportedly seen in summer must be discounted.

The May and June sightings are based principally on birds observed by McCauley (1877). He refers to the species as "*Falco richardsoni,* Ridg.—Richardson's Falcon," the present-day *F. c. richardsoni,* considered at that time a full species. He found it "very abundant, chiefly in the canyon region of Red River . . . also common, though not in the same abundance, in the lower heavily wooded parts of Mulberry and other creeks. None were observed whilst passing through the Indian Territory." Such dates are unexpected, for the Merlin today is rarely seen before late September or early October and never beyond the third week in April. The earliest fall date is one near Amarillo, Randall County, 28 August 1955, and the latest spring date one at the Palo Duro Club near Canyon, Randall County, 20 April 1945 (Hawkins, 1945).

In addition to believing he was seeing Merlins, McCauley reported the finding of a nest containing two eggs on 19 June at White Fish Creek, three miles beyond the headwaters of Tule Creek. The site, in what is now Armstrong County, was near where his party had crossed the Salt Fork of the Red River (Hunnius, 1876). The nest was built some "20 or 25' up" in the crotch of a cottonwood tree, within six feet of a crow's nest. McCauley does not say whether he or the person who found it ever actually saw a Merlin at the nest. He described it in detail and said the eggs were of a "subspherical shape common to birds of prey."

It is difficult to credit the validity of these observations, not only that of a nest with eggs but also the presence of the species itself. McCauley speaks of seeing the birds in the "lower heavily wooded parts" of creeks: typical habitat of nesting kestrels but not of the Merlin, a bird of semi-open areas. The Richardson's race of the Merlin is found nesting today no farther south than northern Montana and North Dakota (AOU, 1957); Johnsgard (1979) cites recent isolated nesting in northwestern Nebraska (1975, 1978); I find no references in the literature to any nesting occurring farther south. Friedman (1950) recognized McCauley's birds, but only as migrants. Erroneously, he placed the locations of the Red River Canyon and White Fish Creek sites in Oklahoma. I can only believe that McCauley's Merlins were misidentified kestrels. He speaks of both species flourishing in the area but collected specimens of neither.

Early observers in the study area spoke of the Merlin as a "rare migrant" (Carlander, 1934; Hawkins, 1945), or "decidedly rare" (Allan and Sime, 1943a). The only exception is Russell (1935), who reported it as "common in all the canyon area and occasionally seen on the surrounding plains." His work was done in July and August: surely his Merlins also were misidentified kestrels. Even though I have classified the Merlin as a rare to uncommon migrant, it is not every year that one is reported. The CBCs demonstrate how scarce it is as an early winter visitor, for it has been recorded on only 6 percent of them. Five were recorded on the Friona, Parmer County, CBC of 5 December 1973, the most ever recorded in one day. More Merlins are seen during fall than spring: my records reflect a ratio of 4:1. This probably can be accounted for by Merlins having largely left the area by mid-spring. Returning birds have been recorded as early as late February in Alberta and are "quite common by April 1" (Bent, 1938).

Peregrine Falcon *Falco peregrinus* Tunstall

STATUS: Rare migrant. Casual winter and summer visitor.

OCCURRENCE: The Peregrine Falcon has been reported in 13 counties: Briscoe, Carson, Castro, Dallam, Hemphill, Hutchinson, Lipscomb, Moore, Oldham, Parmer, Potter, Randall, and Swisher. Oberholser (1974) shows it in three: Parmer, Potter, and Randall. It has been recorded in every month except June.

Early observers failed to mention the Peregrine in their accounts. Stevenson (1942) was the first, going no further than to say "Phillip Allan [U.S. Soil Conservation Service] has seen a few in the Panhandle." Hawkins (1945) classified it as an "uncommon migrant." Records kept since mid-century show an almost equal number seen in spring and autumn. Four Peregrines have been recorded in July, the earliest two at BLNWR, 15 July 1974, and one during the third week of July 1996. Of unusual interest was one observed flying around the upper floors of a 31-story bank building in downtown Amarillo, Potter County, 5 August 1984, a bird that had reportedly been present for some time. On 9 July 1990, a Peregrine was observed about 50 feet south of the Castro County line in Lamb County.

Winter sightings of the Peregrine have been few, one observed by Hawkins (1945) being of particular interest: "Twice in midwinter this falcon was observed pursuing starlings over the roof-tops of downtown Amarillo." Other winter records are: *Hutchinson*—one at Lake Meredith, 19 December 1982; *Parmer*—one near Friona, 22 December 1961–11 February 1962 ("The first to ever winter there"); *Randall*—one at BLNWR, 1 January 1958 and 21 January–25 February 1961, and one near Lake Tanglewood, 19 December 1982; *Swisher*—one near Kress, 5 January 1985.

The earliest spring date is a bird seen along the Canadian River, Potter County, 23 March 1964. Several late spring sightings are on record: one in the Thompson Grove Picnic Area near Texline, Dallam County, 10 May 1996; one at the sewage pond southeast of Amarillo, Randall County, 12 May 1984; one near Dalhart, Dallam County, 13 May 1966; one at BLNWR, 14–22 May and Castro County, 14 May 1994; one at BLNWR, 14 May 1996.

Prairie Falcon *Falco mexicanus* Schlegel

STATUS: Fairly common winter visitor. Rare summer visitor, with vagrant breeding.

OCCURRENCE: The Prairie Falcon has been recorded in all counties except Collingsworth, Hall, Lipscomb, Roberts, and Wheeler. It has been seen in every month.

One concludes from reading the accounts of earlier observers that the status of the Prairie Falcon in the Texas Panhandle as a summering bird has changed dramatically, particularly since the 1930s. McCauley (1877) wrote vividly of his encounters: "Occasionally observed in open country to Red River region, and thence in canyon localities. At Cañoncito Blanco, after obtaining one of the parent birds, an attempt was made to secure the nest, admirably situated in a crevice, about fifteen feet below the top of the vertical canyon wall. Its height was nearly a hundred feet from the stream's bed, and the wall could not be scaled from below, the top jutted out, a great rock overhanging, preventing anyone from getting down from its edge."

The party did eventually secure three young birds and kept them as captives. This observation is the source of Oberholser's (1974) reference to a Randall County find on 3 June 1876. Cañoncito Blanco is the site of present-day Ceta Glen, South Ceta Canyon.

Strecker (1912) referred to the Prairie Falcon as a "resident along the edge of the plains in the Panhandle," and both Hibbets et al. (1926–36) and Carlander (1934) called it a "permanent resident." To Stevenson (1942) it seemed a "fairly common resident of Palo Duro Canyon, nesting on cliff ledges. This falcon is more common in winter than in other seasons." Shortly thereafter, Allan and Sime (1943a) were less positive, noting that the species was "seen principally in the winter, although occasionally at other times. Summer observations lead us to believe that it may nest in some of the canyons." The last summation of the Prairie Falcon's status as a nester prior to mid-century was that of Hawkins (1945), and it was not encouraging: "Summer sight records during the present study were few, and no nests were found."

Since mid-century there have been a number of summer sightings (May–July): *Dallam*—11 June 1977, 14 June 1998. *Hartley*—27 June 1976. *Parmer*—24 June 1962. *Potter*—14 July 1954, 17 May 1984, 11 May 1985, 14 May 1997. *Randall*—6 June and 18 July 1970, July–August 1973, 29 May 1975, 17 July 1977, 9 July 1988, 21 May and 6 and 22 July 1995. Almost all of the Randall County sightings were made in the PDCSP area. An unusual eight falcons were observed along a 22-mile stretch of road south and west of Vega, Oldham County, 2 May 1996. Perhaps some of the birds listed in these summer sightings were nesting.

Returning falcons in fall can be expected by the first of September and few remain beyond April. The CBCs are indicative of early winter distribution. This falcon has been recorded on 60 percent of the *Amarillo* counts, 59 percent of those on the *Buffalo Lake* NWR, and 50 percent at *Friona,* all grassland counts. The percentages on CBCs in areas predominantly canyonland, river bottom, and lakeshore are lower: *Quitaque,* 29 percent; *Lake Meredith* (*west*), 0.2 percent; *Lake Meredith* (*east*), 0.1 percent. Most longtime observers agree that the Prairie Falcon today is more common than near mid-century. The seven on the Amarillo CBC of 19 December 1992 constituted the greatest number recorded since the CBCs began in 1954.

NESTING: Concerning the Prairie Falcon, Johnsgard (1979) had this to say: "Originally also bred on the Texas Panhandle (Randall County), but there is no twentieth-century record for this area."

Although early twentieth-century observers implied that nesting was still taking place in the canyonlands, none reported the actual finding of a nest. There is a recent report of nesting in Gray County. The observers found two adult falcons attending two, possibly three, fledglings four miles southeast of Pampa in June 1990. On one occasion an adult was seen feeding a young bird. A nest thought to belong to the pair was found placed approximately 60 feet up on the top of an elevator platform at an oil well cement plant. Both observers were sure of their identification and described the adult birds in detail. Workers at the plant site said the pair had been nesting there for several years. As far as I know this discovery represents the only evidence of possible recent nesting.

Sutton (1967) cites nestings in the Kenton area of Cimarron County, Oklahoma, and summer sightings from Beaver and Harmon counties. Other pairs have been found nesting in Cimarron County in recent years (Williams, 1981, 1982).

SPECIMENS: There are specimens for Dallam (September 1973, TCWC), Deaf Smith (19 November 1920, CMNH; 18 December 1968, WTAMU), and Randall (20 October 1939, P-PHM) counties.

ORDER GALLIFORMES

Family Phasianidae (Pheasants, Grouse, and Turkeys)

Ring-necked Pheasant *Phasianus colchicus* Linnaeus

STATUS: Common resident.

OCCURRENCE: The Ring-necked Pheasant has been recorded year-round in every Texas Panhandle county.

There is no mention of this handsome bird in the early literature as pheasants were not introduced into the study area until 1933 and subsequent years, during which time the Texas Fish, Game and Oyster Commission released "nearly one thousand" (Hawkins, 1945). Other releases by local ranchers and sportsmen followed. For example, one of the most successful was 125 birds obtained from a game farm in New Mexico and released near Hereford, Deaf Smith County, in February 1943. In August 1945, 100 more were released. Hawkins says further that by near mid-century there were a "few pheasants in other parts of the Panhandle, especially north of the Canadian River, and in the Tierra Blanca Draw at Canyon." He placed the species' southernmost extension at Frio Draw west of Friona, Parmer County. This history of introduction is somewhat contradictory to that given by Wilson (1981), who said: "The Ring-necked Pheasant immigrated into . . . the Texas Panhandle from Oklahoma in the 1940s." Immigration may account for the origin of many found north of the Canadian River, but not all.

Having arrived during the years when irrigated grain crops were becoming widespread in the High Plains, pheasants expanded rapidly. By the 1980s they had become established over some 3.5 million acres. Their distribution is indicated by annual TPWD roadside counts conducted in 13 study area counties (Wilson, 1981). The census lines are 20 miles long and are run twice each, at two-week intervals, beginning in September. The averages by line for the period 1977–80 (less highs and lows) were: *Briscoe-Swisher* 37.5; *Castro* 23.5; *Dallam* 60.0; *Deaf Smith* 120.0; *Hansford* 19.5; *Hartley* 19.5; *Hutchinson* 23.0; *Moore* 48.0; *Moore-Sherman* 30.5; *Ochiltree* 47.0; *Parmer* 30.5; *Sherman* 34.5; *Swisher* 29.0. The estimated harvest of pheasants during the same period was: *1977*—27,800; *1978*—26,143; *1979*—36,581; *1980*—29,500.

The only comparable counts are the BBSS, initiated in 1967 and conducted in June. The routes are 24.5 miles long, the time period at each of the 50 stops is limited to three minutes, and they are run once. The averages are: *Waka* 30.7; *Texline* 14.5; *Dalhart* 12.3; *Booker* 9.8; *Panhandle* 8.7; *Channing* 2.3; *Pantex* 1.3; *Childress* 0.6; *Skellytown* 0.3; *Miami* 0.1; *Clarendon* 0. As an example of the number of pheasants present on a protected area, an estimated 300+ were resident at BLNWR in the mid-1980s (USFWS).

NESTING: The TBBAP disclosed widespread nesting of the Ring-necked Pheasant, less so in the southeastern sector. CO nesting was determined in 22 survey blocks, PR in 36, and PO in 18. All confirmations save one were based on fledglings observed between 7 June and 11 August: a hen on a nest was found in Wheeler County on 21 May 1987. On 4 May 1969, I found a female sitting tight on a nest at BLNWR. Gently lifting her, I counted 17 eggs.

SPECIMENS: There are specimens taken in Carson (ACMNH), Castro (December 1977, SRSU), Dallam (29 November 1969, SM; 18 March 1978, TCWC), Deaf Smith (6 December 1967, 28 February 1968, 7 February 1977, WTAMU), Hutchinson

Lesser Prairie-Chicken

(LMAWM), Moore (MCHM), Lipscomb (23 February 1971, WTAMU), Randall (18 November 1973, WTAMU), and Swisher (14 December 1977, TCWC) counties.

Lesser Prairie-Chicken *Tympanuchus pallidicinctus* (Ridgway)

STATUS: Rare to fairly common local resident in the eastern third of the Panhandle.

OCCURRENCE: During the latter half of the twentieth century the Lesser Prairie-Chicken was recorded in 14 counties of the Texas Panhandle: Armstrong, Carson, Collingsworth, Deaf Smith, Donley, Gray, Hemphill, Lipscomb, Moore, Ochiltree, Parmer, Potter, Roberts, and Wheeler. Historically its range extended over most of the grasslands of the High Plains and Rolling Plains, but the species today is confined primarily to the eastern counties of Lipscomb, Hemphill, Gray, Wheeler, Donley, and Collingsworth (Litton et al., 1994), with almost all on privately owned land.

There are conflicting accounts of the distribution of the Lesser Prairie-Chicken in the Texas Panhandle prior to the implementation of widespread agricultural and range management practices that resulted in the modification and destruction of habitat. Abert (1846) traversed the Panhandle north of the

Canadian River in 1845 and mentioned seeing many flocks of quails and turkeys; however, he failed to name the prairie chicken. McCauley (1877) partially lifts the veil on its status in the late nineteenth century in his account of his journey through the area in May and June of 1876:

> This magnificent game bird was first observed in traveling along the road south from Ft. Dodge, between the Cimarron and north fork of the Canadian. It was abundant in coveys of from twenty to thirty; south of that less frequently seen. Beyond the Sweetwater, they were not found, nor were they seen in any part of the lower sections visited, until, on our return, we reached the rolling land north of McClellan Creek. This, the only one of the Grouse family proper we met with, avoids the Staked Plain, and ventures near it only where all the conditions of its prairie-life may be fulfilled.

Strecker (1910) also reported a restricted range, calling the species a "rare summer resident, more abundant in winter, but very locally distributed"; he later described it as "resident along the foot of the plains in the Panhandle country, south of the Canadian" (Strecker, 1912). He and his party had observed chickens in the Goodnight area of Armstrong County in May and June of 1910 (Strecker, 1910). Bent (1932), relying on information supplied by Walter Colvin in 1914, placed the Lesser Prairie-Chicken's breeding range no "farther south into Texas than two degrees by air line," and gave its winter range as "confined chiefly to central Texas." He stated further: "No information is available relative to the movements of this species between breeding and wintering areas." Colvin said it was "casual in winter at Lipscomb in the Panhandle area." Aldrich (1963) showed its original distribution as not only covering the entire Texas Panhandle but also extending southward through the southern plains as far as south of Midland. He did not make a distinction between breeding and wintering ranges; however, the AOU (1957) said that the southern plains were occupied only by wintering prairie chickens.

A more recent review of the Lesser Prairie-Chicken's status in Texas is that of Sands (1968), who relied chiefly on a study conducted by Jackson and DeArment (1963):

> Originally the Lesser Prairie Chicken ranged throughout the Panhandle of Texas. Jackson and DeArment state that "the exact limits of the original range . . . cannot be clearly defined. . . . It may have been only a winter migrant in the southernmost part of its range in Texas." These authors place the current populations . . . in small, localized areas of northwest Texas, with the bulk of the population occurring in Wheeler, Hemphill and Lipscomb

Counties. "A few are found along the Texas-New Mexico line from Andrews to Lamb County." The current population in the Texas Panhandle is estimated at 3,000 birds.

The future of the Lesser Prairie Chicken in Texas is "not very promising." These authors sound a warning in the following manner. "In the spring months of 1957, the 6,500 acre Site II study area in Wheeler County was subjected to an aerial application of the hormone-type chemical 2,4,5-T. The objective was to control or eliminate brush and weeds. Although only a 25 percent kill was accomplished, acorn production was prevented for 2 years. The loss of a key supply of winter food could not have been other than an adverse influence on prairie chickens. Its effects were apparent in a lower count in the 1959 census." They further stated that the loss of woody cover followed by heavy grazing resulted in plant communities unsuitable for prairie chickens.

Another factor having an adverse effect on prairie chicken populations was the 1930s drought, and periodic drought conditions have been a limiting factor since. Numbers of prairie chickens in Hemphill and Wheeler counties were at a high in 1942 (after the drought broke), "but only in respect to the numbers which had been resident during the critically dry 1930s" (Jackson and DeArment, 1963). Population levels remained steady until the recurrence of drought conditions in 1953, when numbers again dropped dramatically. The 1962 census showed a 62 percent decline in Hemphill County and a 55 percent decline in Wheeler County, this despite slight increases in the intervening years when better moisture conditions prevailed.

Another study (Wilson, 1981) disclosed a higher population level of Lesser Prairie-Chickens than had been given earlier by Sands (1968). In 1979, the spring population was estimated at 7,469 birds, and in 1980 at 9,483 birds. On 100,000 acres in Hemphill County, the density in acres/bird for 1979 was 135.86, and for 1980 it was 110.86; on 5,440 acres in Wheeler County the respective densities were 18.37 and 12.71.

The results of recent studies are not encouraging for some populations (J. Hughes, TPWD). The counties where the Lesser Prairie-Chicken is most common are Hemphill north of the Canadian River (100,000 acres of sandsage/midgrass rangeland), and Wheeler south of the Canadian River (6,720 acres of shinnery oak/midgrass rangeland). Using hectares per lek as a better indicator of breeding density, the Hemphill County population held relatively steady in 1967–85 at an average of 2,747 ha/lek, and the Wheeler County population at 425 ha/lek. In the succeeding period, 1986–99, however, while the Hemphill County average showed a slight increase to 3,318 ha/lek, the Wheeler County average pointed to a precipitous decline in population at 5,689 ha/lek. The causes of this reduction in the number of leks are unknown. Such a picture is sobering when one reads that in Seward County, Kansas, in the fall of 1904, 15,000–20,000 chickens were seen "in and around this one grain field in a single day" (Bent, 1932), and there may have been as many as two million chickens in Texas prior to 1900 (Litton et al., 1994). Despite today's low numbers, the hunting of these birds continues, although the yearly take is small. As an example, in a two-day hunting season in Wheeler and Hemphill counties during the 1969–70 season, 139 birds were killed (Williams, 1970; W. R. Long).

Many observers of the prairie chicken in earlier years spoke of a southern shift of population during winter. Such a movement is no longer discernible, and the remnant population appears to be stationary. There have been occasional reports of chickens seen in fall and winter at locations outside the eastern counties, indicating a possible longitudinal movement. Two chickens were encountered on the Lake Meredith Recreation Area near Fritch, Carson County, in the fall of 1976. On 4 January 1981, during the Lake Meredith (east) CBC, one was seen at close range near Blue West, Moore County, and four were flushed on 27 December 1981 on the LX ranch near Bonita Creek, northeastern Potter County, during the Lake Meredith (west) CBC. Williams (1967) reported a single bird in winter near Friona, Parmer County, "where none had been seen since 1952," and Oberholser (1974) shows spring and summer sightings for that county, without giving details. A single chicken was seen in Deaf Smith County on 14 August 1993, and a male and three hens in a field west of Garcia Lake in that county during the second week of April 1997. On 4 April 1998, two chickens were again observed in western Deaf Smith County. The Parmer and Deaf Smith birds were possibly wanderers from farther south, where another small population resides on the South Plains along the Texas–New Mexico line from Andrews to Bailey counties (Litton et al., 1994).

NESTING: Other than Bent (1932), who gave egg dates in Colorado and Texas ranging from 5 May to 12 June, data is lacking on both nesting and egg dates for the study area. During the TBBAP, CO nesting was found in one quadrangle (Glazier; nest with 11 eggs, 20 May 1987), PR in five (Mobeetie, Pond Creek NW, Wheeler, Kelton, Shamrock West), and PO in one (Shamrock East). Oberholser (1974) names a breeding record for Potter County ("young bird located at Amarillo on June 13, 1938, Dean Amadon"). One would like to know the details of this observation.

SPECIMENS: Specimens have been taken in Hemphill (10 February 1929, MVZ; 8 April 1948, 21 December 1971, 11 June 1981, TCWC), Moore (MCHM), and Wheeler

(13 May 1929, MVZ; 16 August 1936, 25 September 1936, 18 January 1955, TCWC; 23 October 1984, WFVZ; unspecified date, WTAMU) counties. The origins of two mounted birds on display (P-PHM) are not known. Oberholser (1974) shows specimens taken in Gray and Wheeler counties without naming where they were deposited.

Wild Turkey *Meleagris gallopavo* Linnaeus
STATUS: Fairly common to common resident locally.
OCCURRENCE: The Wild Turkey has been recorded in all of the Texas Panhandle counties except Castro, Dallam, Deaf Smith, Parmer, Sherman, and Swisher.

The history of the Wild Turkey in the Texas Panhandle is one of abundance, followed by eradication and reintroduction. It is the one species of bird mentioned by all early explorers. Oberholser (1974) relates that "the first definite [published] record of any species of bird within the confines of the present state of Texas was of the Wild Turkey; the naturalist with the Long Expedition in the Rocky Mountains noted a flock on August 5, 1820, at a point on the Canadian River thirty miles west of present-day Tascosa (Oldham Co.)." In his west-to-east traverse of the northern Panhandle in 1845, Abert (1846) mentions the turkey several times, always in terms of its abundance. Along the Canadian River approximately four miles east of Tascosa, he speaks of its "abundance in the neighborhood of our camp." Near Lefors, Gray County, in the valley of the North Fork of the Red River, he noticed tracks of the birds in the sand, "which game appeared to be very abundant," while in present-day Wheeler County, "the innumerable tracks of the wild turkey showed that they must be very abundant." East of present-day Plemons, Hutchinson County, he again found it plentiful "and our people killed great numbers of them." Shorger (1966) relates that during the winter of 1868–69 in Oklahoma, "Sheridan was camped in the vicinity of the Antelope Hills, Ellis County, where the trees were black with turkeys." This would have been only a few miles east of the present Texas-Oklahoma state line.

A decline in the Wild Turkey was noted by McCauley (1877) as early as 1876: "This species was first met with at Wolf Creek, Indian Territory, where numbers were observed, but not in the abundance in which it was found as lately as two years ago. It may be said to be common throughout the whole section visited save in the alkali region of Red River proper. The decrease or disappearance of this game bird from this section, particularly from the Palo Duro and the Washita regions, has been very marked during the last few years."

By the 1930s Russell (1935) says there were no turkeys left in the Palo Duro, the last one having been killed "over twenty-five years ago," and in their studies neither Carlander (1934) nor Stevenson (1942) mentions the species. Thompson (1952) quotes from the Texas Game, Fish and Oyster Commission (1945): "It is now believed that none of the original wild turkey stock remains there or elsewhere in the northern one-third of the State as far east as Fort Worth. . . . The present occurrence of Turkeys in the northern one-third . . . is the result of restocking during the last twenty years."

Shorger (1966) names two subspecies of Wild Turkey as having had original ranges including West Texas: *M. g. intermedia,* the Rio Grande Turkey, and *M. g. merriami,* Merriam's Turkey. The *intermedia* subspecies occupied the eastern and central Panhandle north to the Canadian River bottoms; the portion occupied by *merriami* was along the Canadian River "probably as far east as Carson County," where it encountered *intermedia.* He says further that in the restocking program, "Rio Grande turkeys have been liberated in northwestern Texas." Hawkins (1945) has this to say of the Merriam's Turkey: "Introduced and established. Once native to this area, the original stock apparently was exterminated and has since been replaced along the Canadian River and at Palo Duro Canyon. Many of the birds for restocking came from the Cottonwood Ranch in Collingsworth County which reportedly received its original stock from California. Thus, the present turkeys are a badly mixed lot and should not be confused with the birds found here by Coronado."

The Wild Turkey today can be found throughout the eastern third of the study area, locally westward down the Canadian River and its tributaries to Oldham County and the Rita Blanca Creek area of Hartley County, and in the Palo Duro Canyon system. In recent years it has moved into the Tierra Blanca draw as far west as BLNWR. It is recorded fairly regularly on three of the area CBCs, for which averages and highs are: *Amarillo*—22 (62); *Lake Meredith* (*west*)—120 (250); *Quitaque*—14 (130).

NESTING: The TBBAP found CO nesting in 17 survey blocks, PR in 18, and PO in seven. Of the 42 quadrangles, 57 percent lie between the 100th and 101st meridians, 26 percent between the 101st and 102nd, and 17 percent west of the 102nd meridian. The Wild Turkey was found in only two quadrangles in the northwest sector (Hartley County) and in only one in the southwest sector (Randall County). All confirmations but one were based on sightings of young birds. The exception was a nest with ten eggs at BLNWR, 10 May 1987. On the late date of 29 July 1995, a hen with a chick was found in the PDCSP.

SPECIMENS: Specimens are available from Collingsworth (MCHM), Hansford (23 October 1955, MNH), Hutchinson (LMAWM), and Potter (ACMNH) counties. Oberholser (1974) shows specimens for Carson, Childress, and Potter counties without naming where they were deposited.

Family Odontophoridae (New World Quail)

Scaled Quail *Callipepla squamata* (Vigors)

STATUS: Fairly common to common resident.

OCCURRENCE: The Scaled Quail has been recorded in every Texas Panhandle county and during every month of the year.

McCauley (1877) said of the Scaled Quail that "none were observed in any part of the section visited." His trek across the area included Hemphill, Wheeler, Carson, Armstrong, Randall, Potter, and Briscoe counties, with a lengthy stay in Randall County, areas where today the species can be found. Strecker (1912) spoke of it as "rare in the Panhandle, on the edge of the plains (Armstrong Co.) resident." Carlander (1934) was somewhat vague in his assessment of its status: "Common in some localities, particularly the Palo Duro Park." Russell (1935) was more precise: "This species is abundant in the canyon and in the bordering mesquite areas. At least seventeen coveys are known to be present in the park." Hawkins (1945) classified it as a "fairly common permanent resident"; however, "the population density over the Plains as a whole is low."

The BBS and CBC results are good indicators of the Scaled Quail's present-day distribution and abundance. (For a discussion of its relation to the Northern Bobwhite, see that species account.) These counts reinforce those of the TPWD (Wilson, 1981) and conform to distribution as set forth by Johnsgard (1973). In addition, they give a more detailed picture of the overlap in Scaled Quail and bobwhite ranges. The averages and highs on the CBCs are as follows: *Lake Meredith* (*east*)—57 (162); *Lake Meredith* (*west*)—45 (320); *Amarillo*—54 (164); *Quitaque*—35 (129); *Buffalo Lake* NWR—7 (44); *Friona*—2 (29). Scaled Quail often congregate in large coveys in winter, more so than do bobwhite. Hawkins (1945) records one congregation eight miles northeast of Channing, Hartley County, that numbered well over a thousand birds. Of these, "several hundred" were banded: "One was killed at Tascosa twenty miles south a year later; another was taken on the Bivins Ranch, seventeen miles southwest." More recently, 250–350 were observed in the Palo Duro Canyon SP, Randall County, 19 January 1968— "the most I have ever seen" (P. Acord).

NESTING: Few egg dates are available. In the Oklahoma Panhandle Schemnitz (1964) found a clutch as early as 8 May 1956. The Scaled Quail has a long nesting period and the pattern of rainfall governs the optimum time for nesting and raising young. Schemnitz's (1964) late date is 6 September 1954, while Stevenson (1942) gives a later date of 9 September 1935 for the PDCSP (nest with 11 eggs). A nest with nine eggs was found 21 June 1966 at the Girl Scout Camp near Amarillo, Randall County; on 24 June it contained 17 eggs. The TBBAP discovered CO nesting in two survey blocks between the 100th and 101st meridians, PR in 13, and PO in five. Between the 101st and 102nd meridians the respective figures were 6, 9 and 8, and west of the 102nd meridian, 6, 9 and 4. Only one CO nesting and one PR nesting were found in the southwest sector, both near Umbarger, Randall County.

SPECIMENS: Specimens have been taken in Carson (24 and 29 November 1977, 12 November 1987, WTAMU), Dallam (9 September 1958, CMNH), Hall (24 January 1974, WTAMU), Hutchinson (LMAWM), Moore (9 November 1985, WTAMU), Potter (ACMNH; 18 March 1970, 11 November 1987, WTAMU), Randall (10 January 1939, WTAMU), and Swisher (November 1969, MTTU) counties. Oberholser (1974) shows specimens taken in Deaf Smith, Gray, Hall, and Lipscomb counties, but does not give their locations. The race *C.s. hargravei* is resident in the northern third of the Panhandle, probably intergrading with *C.s. pallida* in the central and southern portions (TOS, 1995).

Northern Bobwhite *Colinus virginianus* (Linnaeus)

STATUS: Fairly common to common resident.

OCCURRENCE: The Northern Bobwhite has been recorded in every county of the Texas Panhandle and in every month of the year.

A view of the range of the Northern Bobwhite in the Texas Panhandle in the nineteenth century is provided by McCauley (1877):

> The habitat of this . . . game bird . . . reaches through that part of the Indian Territory we traversed and across the Panhandle to the Upper Canyon region. Strictly avoiding the Staked Plains, their range is south through Texas. . . . At the most southern part of Mulberry Creek, about longitude 101°, two specimens were secured; ten miles or more farther to the west, in the bed of Red River, several hundred feet below the level of the plain, I found them with young, well fledged . . . on June 11. . . . Sixty miles farther up the river, our camps were by the stream in the canyon; and up beyond, on rolling land along the Palo Duro and Tierra Blanca, fine fresh water and rich grassy lands; but in these sections we never flushed a Quail, nor did we ever hear the "bob-white."

In the twentieth century most observers prior to 1950 referred to the bobwhite as present only locally. Strecker (1910) called it a "common resident, most abundant east of the foot of the plains." Carlander (1934) classified it as "fairly common. Permanent resident in canyons and along water courses." In his survey of the PDCSP, Russell (1935) said: "Several coveys were found near the lower boundary . . . and others were reported several miles north." Stevenson (1942) found it "common in scrub oak country of the eastern Panhandle, but it is rarely seen in the Palo Duro region." Hawkins (1945) was somewhat more comprehensive, finding the bobwhite locally common, "but over most of the High Plains area its distribution is spotty." He spoke of bobwhites penetrating into Scaled Quail territory in wet years, and the reverse taking place in dry years. He also gave some ratios of the numbers of bobwhites to Scaled Quails based on birds taken in the hunting season: Oldham County (western Panhandle), all 85 bagged were "Blues"; Hutchinson County (central Panhandle), 72 "Bobs" to 17 Blues; Hemphill County (eastern Panhandle), all 80 bagged were Bobs.

In a discussion on the distribution and preferred habitats of the two quail species, Johnsgard (1973) makes reference to three studies: McCabe (1954), Hamilton (1962), and Schemnitz (1964). McCabe (1954) found the ranges of the two quails largely complementary, with a slight amount of range overlap occurring. In the Oklahoma Panhandle Schemnitz (1964) said the bobwhite is limited largely to river bottom habitats, where tree thickets grow adjacent to pasture lands and relatively dense ground-level cover exists, while Scaled Quail "were usually found in the more xeric uplands, tributary canyons, and mesa slopes above these river bottoms." He spoke, however, of "a certain degree of ecological equivalence between the two species." Hamilton (1962) also spoke of the bobwhite typically occurring in scrub oak woodland, riparian woodland, or juniper-oak woodland, and the Scaled Quail typically found in mesquite or juniper savannah habitats.

The BBSS (1967–97) have produced data that provide further insights into the distribution and relative abundance of the Northern Bobwhite (BO) and Scaled Quail (SQ). They reveal in particular the extent and degree of range overlap, along with the shifting of relative abundance as one moves across the area. The following are the seven BBSS routes, listed in order of progression from east to west. Each route is composed of 50 stops. The table names each count route and (1) the number of stops on which quail were recorded; (2) the number of stops on which both BO and SQ were recorded (not always simultaneously); (3) the number of stops on which BO were recorded exclusively; (4) the number of stops on which SQ were recorded exclusively; (5) the average number of BO per count; and (6) the average number of SQ per count (see table 1).

Some of the routes reveal rather extensive overlap, particularly the Childress, Miami, and Channing counts. The Childress count is near the eastern limits of the Scaled Quail's distribution in northwest Texas, and the Channing count near the western limits of the bobwhite's distribution. As to the average number recorded, the BBSS reflect a distribution that is complementary to assessments made by the TPWD (Wilson, 1981).

CBCS are indicative of the relative abundance of the Northern Bobwhite (BO)

TABLE 1

Count	1	2	3	4	5	6
	Quail	BO + SQ	BO only	SQ only	No. of BO	No. of SQ
Childress	49	42	7	0	46.3	23.4
Booker	39	7	29	3	6.2	1.0
Miami	38	27	2	9	12.7	9.4
Waka	7	0	3	4	0.4	0.7
Pantex	39	15	14	10	3.2	3.4
Channing	47	25	0	22	5.5	17.3
Texline	20	4	1	15	0.3	2.3

and Scaled Quail (SQ) in winter. The averages are as follows: *Amarillo*—BO 15, SQ 54; *Buffalo Lake* NWR—BO 62, SQ 7; *Lake Meredith* (*east*)—BO 17, SQ 57; *Lake Meredith* (*west*)—BO 26, SQ 45; *Quitaque*—BO 38, SQ 35; *Friona*—BO 6, SQ 2. The Lake Meredith counts encompass habitats equally favorable to both species; the fact that on each of these counts the SQ average is much higher than that of the BO can be attributed in part to the tendency of Scaled Quail to congregate in larger coveys in winter than do bobwhite. The higher ratio of BO to SQ on the BLNWR count is exaggerated by the 750 BO recorded on the count of 29 December 1967. Large numbers of bobwhites could be found on the refuge during the 1960s; however, the species today is quite scarce. During the period 1959–69, from 250 to 880 (average 456) were recorded in summer (USFWS), while today there may be only a few coveys.

NESTING: The Northern Bobwhite can be found nesting throughout the study area. The TBBAP classified nesting as CO in seven quadrangles between the 100th and 101st meridians, PR in 29, and PO in three. Between the 101st and 102nd meridians the figures were 4, 19 and 7, respectively, and west of the 102nd, 2, 5 and 8. Nesting and egg dates are unavailable; however, nesting probably begins in mid- or late April. Only one brood is produced unless the first attempt at nesting fails (Johnsgard, 1973). Small fledglings have been reported as late as 20 August in the PDCSP.

SPECIMENS: Specimens are available for Hall (TCWC), Hemphill (15 and 31 January 1929, MVZ; 29 July 1971, TCWC), Hutchinson (LMAWM), Lipscomb (2 November and 28 December 1985, WTAMU), Potter (ACMNH; 11 November 1987, WTAMU), and Randall (9 January 1969, WTAMU) counties. Oberholser (1974) shows specimens taken in Armstrong, Hemphill, Lipscomb, and Wheeler counties, but does not name their locations. None of the collections listed here make reference to subspecies. Aldrich (1946) named the subspecies in the Texas Panhandle as *C. v.*

taylori, and this classification is followed by Oberholser (1974), who calls the bird the "Great Plains Bobwhite."

ORDER GRUIFORMES

Family Rallidae (Rails, Gallinules, and Coots)

Yellow Rail *Coturnicops noveboracensis* (Gmelin)
STATUS: Vagrant fall migrant.
OCCURRENCE: There has been one reported sighting of the Yellow Rail in the Texas Panhandle (Seyffert, 1988b). On 15 August 1987 I flushed a Yellow Rail from a weed-grown ditch bordering a playa lake southwest of Amarillo, Randall County. As I walked along the road bisecting the playa, the rail was observed as it flew from the ditch, crossing the road and pitching into the denser and higher vegetation on the other side. The bird was seen again the following day (P. Acord). There were an estimated two dozen or more Soras at the site.

The nearest to the study area that the Yellow Rail had previously been reported was the Muleshoe NWR, Bailey County, 16 September 1974 (Williams, 1975). On that day it was estimated that 50 Soras were in the area. Another Yellow Rail was observed in Lubbock on 8 September 1994 (Lasley and Sexton, 1995b). The Yellow Rail is a rare migrant throughout most of the eastern half of the state, and a rare to locally uncommon winter resident along the upper and central coast (TOS, 1995). Its status is poorly known in most areas of the state.

Black Rail *Laterallus jamaicensis* (Gmelin)
STATUS: Vagrant migrant and summer visitor.
OCCURRENCE: The Black Rail has been reported four times in the Texas Panhandle—May, June, July, and September.

The first was a bird observed in Roberts County in June 1935 (Oberholser, 1974; H. Saunders), a sighting unsupported with documentation. The second record was at Jim's Lake near Borger, southeastern Hutchinson County, where around midnight of 30 June–1 July 1979 a fisherman captured on tape the strange calls of a marsh bird (R. Bryant). The recording was given to Orilla Bryant of Miami, who identified the calls as those of a Black Rail on territory. The tape was sent to Texas A&M University, where confirmation was made and the tape archived (TBSL). At a cattail-choked playa on the Pantex Ordnance Plant, Carson County, 8 May 1997 (T. Green, S. Pomeroy), a well-described Black Rail was seen briefly as it emerged into the open a short distance from the two observers. On 19 September 1998, a Black Rail was recovered from a backyard garden a mile or so west of Amarillo, Potter County (S. Pomeroy; TP-RF). The bird had probably struck an overhead power line and been killed.

There are other sightings of the Black Rail from nearby areas. Four rails were found on the Muleshoe NWR, Bailey County, 16 September 1974 (Williams, 1975), and one that answered a taped call allowed a brief view on 21 September 1980 in Crosby County (Williams, 1981). Sullivan (1976) cites a 1915 record near Gate, Beaver County, Oklahoma. More recently, a Black Rail was closely observed in Morton County, southwestern Kansas, 17 October 1984 (Cable et al., 1996).

The Black Rail is a rare migrant in the eastern third of Texas, and a rare to locally uncommon resident on the upper and central coasts (TOS, 1995). Johnsgard (1979) names it as a breeder in Finney, Meade, Riley, and Barton counties, Kansas. Those recently discovered and photographed in the Arkansas River Valley of southeastern Colorado, 7 May–22 June 1991, were thought territorial and possibly nesting (Andrews and Righter, 1992). Further work in the study area would possibly disclose breeding here also.

King Rail *Rallus elegans* Audubon

STATUS: Rare migrant and local breeder.

OCCURRENCE: The King Rail has been reported in six counties—Gray, Hemphill, Hutchinson, Potter, Randall, and Roberts—from March to September, April excepted.

Oberholser (1974) shows a sight record for Roberts County, probably Harold Saunders's of June 1935, and believed the King Rail likely nested there. The only other mention of a King Rail prior to mid-century is that of Hawkins (1945), who classified it as an "uncommon migrant." Philip F. Allen (letter, 1 August 1952) names the species on his list of birds for Lake Marvin, Hemphill County. On 26 May 1965, an injured rail was recovered from a suburban back yard in Amarillo, Potter County, and later released (TP-RF). While engaged in the TBBAP on 5 May 1987, I encountered at least three King Rails on territory in the Sanford Dam marsh at Lake Meredith, Hutchinson County. I visited the marsh again on 23 May and found an additional four calling farther downriver. I continued finding the birds on 16 and 30 June and 11 July; nests or young were never discovered. I have heard calling rails in the marsh subsequently, on 12 March 1989, 1 March 1992, 8 September 1997, and 7 July 1998. The beginning of March is an extremely early date; however, a King Rail was found in nearby Texas County, Oklahoma, still earlier: 20 February 1995 (Grzybowski, 1995). Two calling rails were heard at Ceta Glen, South Ceta Canyon, Randall County, 23 March 1995, and another in June 1987 along Spring Creek, southeastern Hutchinson County. On 6 June 1998 a single rail was found on a playa in Gray County.

NESTING: The sole confirmation of the King Rail nesting in the study area is that cited by Thompson (1952): a young male "in down plumage" collected on a tule pond in the Canadian River breaks of Hutchinson County, 7 July 1950.

The nearest Texas counties to the study area where King Rails have been known to nest are Wilbarger, Wichita, and Foard (Oberholser, 1974). They are all old records, however, and Pulich (1988) says the species no longer nests there. There are also nesting records from nearby Gate, Beaver County, Oklahoma (Sutton, 1967)—again old ones. A half-grown King Rail chick was recovered in Tillman County, Oklahoma, 6 July 1960 (Tyler, 1979b).

SPECIMENS: Two birds were collected in Hutchinson (5, 7 July 1950, TNHC) County.

Virginia Rail *Rallus limicola* Vieillot

STATUS: Uncommon to fairly common local resident.

OCCURRENCE: The Virginia Rail has been found in eleven counties: Carson, Donley, Gray, Hall, Hemphill, Hutchinson, Moore, Parmer, Potter, Randall, and Swisher. Oberholser (1974) shows it in three. It has been seen in every month.

There are few references to the Virginia Rail prior to mid-century. McCauley's (1877) was the first: "A very few found at swampy places on lower part of McClellan Creek." This would have been in Gray County during May and June. Carlander (1933) reported a specimen taken between either 15 August and 3 September 1932 or 19 June and 15 September 1933—a confusing report. Another early sighting is Harold Saunders's ("prior to '33"). This is possibly the source of the one in Hemphill County questioned by Oberholser (1974). Two collected in Hemphill County in January 1929 are noted under Specimens.

With the construction of Sanford Dam in Hutchinson County in the mid-1960s, and the formation of Lake Meredith and its marshes, a resident population of Virginia Rails became established. It was in winter and not summer, however, that the birds were first discovered. A chance playing of taped calls in the marsh downriver from the dam during the winter of 1970–71 elicited responses from rails, and subsequent Lake Meredith (east) CBCs established a yearly presence. On 15 June 1975, summering rails were also discovered.

Other observations of Virginia Rails have been scattered, some in summer, indicating possible nesting: *Donley*—Greenbelt Lake, 20 December 1981, 6 November 1993, 26 August 1995; Taylor Lakes WMA, 29 March, 9 and 23 April 1996, 1 October 1997. *Gray*—Lake McClellan, 12 September 1980, 7 October 1981, 26 August 1998; near Kingsmill, 23 June 1985. *Hall*—Prairie Dog Town Fork of Red River in north-central sector, 30 May 1988. *Moore*—South Palo Duro Creek east of Sunray, 8 July 1973. *Parmer*—near Friona, 8 September 1966. *Randall*—near Amarillo, 7 August 1962; BLNWR, 26 July 1962, 1 October 1975, 16 September 1977, 10 September 1979, 28 October 1979, 29 August 1993; near Lake Tanglewood,

20 December 1981, 14 October 1987, 21 December 1996; Ceta Glen, South Ceta Canyon, 30 March 1996. *Swisher*—near Tulia, 21 June 1990.

NESTING: The first confirmation of nesting of the Virginia Rail was made on 30 April 1993 when an adult was observed with two downy chicks in the Sanford Dam marsh at Lake Meredith, Hutchinson County. Previously a juvenal-plumaged bird had been seen at the same site, 11 July 1990.

SPECIMENS: Specimens have been taken in Hemphill (23 and 31 January 1929, MVZ) and Randall (8 May 1979, WTAMU) counties. There is an untagged specimen on display in Canyon (P-PHM), which may be the bird collected by Carlander (1933).

Sora *Porzana carolina* (Linnaeus)

STATUS: Rare to fairly common migrant. Casual summer and rare winter visitor.

OCCURRENCE: The Sora has been reported in 15 counties: Briscoe, Carson, Castro, Donley, Gray, Hartley, Hemphill, Hutchinson, Moore, Ochiltree, Oldham, Parmer, Potter, Randall, and Swisher. It has been found in every month.

Most sightings of the Sora have occurred in late summer through early winter. It has been reported much less often in spring: my records of 33 years show fewer than half a dozen spring observations. Little is known about the timing and routes of this presumed night migrant, but surely it must occur with greater frequency than these few sightings indicate. Perhaps fewer are seen in spring because of rapid passage occurring over a short period of time, while birds in fall tend to congregate where food is abundant, and the passage south is more strung out.

There are three summer records of interest: one heard in the Sanford Dam marsh at Lake Meredith, Hutchinson County, 25 May 1987; a specimen collected in Oldham County on 6 June (Oberholser 1974; year not given); and one calling in a cattail marsh on South Palo Duro Creek east of Sunray, Moore County, 8 July 1973. Nesting Soras are known to occur no nearer the Texas Panhandle than southern New Mexico, eastern Colorado, and central Oklahoma (AOU, 1983).

Returning birds in fall can be expected in the last week of July or first week of August. The earliest date on record is for four at a playa near Amarillo, Randall County, 24 July 1988. At this same playa, on 11–15 August 1987, up to two dozen Soras responded to taped calls or were seen. Surprisingly, many records are for winter: *Hutchinson*—29 December 1972, 29 December 1973, 3 January 1976, 4 February 1979, 3 January 1987, 3 January 1988—all in the Sanford Dam marsh at Lake Meredith. *Randall*—BLNWR, 11 December 1965; Lake Tanglewood, 30 December 1967.

SPECIMENS: Specimens have been taken in Potter (19 May 1976, TCWC) and Randall (2 May 1974, WTAMU) counties. The location of Oberholser's (1974) Oldham County bird is not known.

Purple Gallinule *Porphyrula martinica* (Linnaeus)

STATUS: Vagrant summer visitor.

OCCURRENCE: The Purple Gallinule has been reported twice in the Texas Panhandle. A seemingly uninjured bird recovered from a suburban yard in Amarillo, Potter County, was taken to the city animal shelter and was shown on television before being released, 5–8 July 1963 (P. Acord, K. Whipple; TP-RF). There is a record of one seen "prior to '33 in Hemphill County" (H. Saunders), but nothing else is known about it.

From nearby areas in the South Plains there are three records: White River Lake, Crosby County, 25 June 1978 (Williams, 1978); Buffalo Springs Lake, Lubbock, 11 November 1982 (Williams, 1983); Lubbock, 6 May 1994 (Lasley and Sexton, 1994b). The Purple Gallinule is a rare to uncommon migrant and rare to locally common summer resident in the eastern half of Texas (TOS, 1995).

Common Moorhen *Gallinula chloropus* (Linnaeus)

STATUS: Uncommon to common (local) resident.

OCCURRENCE: The Common Moorhen, formerly called the Common Gallinule, has been found in 12 counties: Briscoe, Carson, Castro, Deaf Smith, Donley, Gray, Hansford, Hemphill, Hutchinson, Potter, Randall, and Swisher. It has been seen in every month.

None of the early observers, with a single exception, mentioned the moorhen in the study area, and it was not until the mid-1960s that observers began encountering the species (Seyffert, 1989b). The exception was one in Hemphill County in August 1938 (Oberholser, 1974). The following is a summary of sightings by county since the initial discovery of a single bird at BLNWR, 17 May 1964: *Briscoe*—Caprock Canyons SP, 11 September 1977; Cottonwood Lake near Quitaque, 1 January 1988. *Castro*—playa near Dimmitt, 24 June 1979; unspecified locality, 30 August and 5 September 1980 (Fischer et al., 1982); playa near Dimmitt, 4 August 1985 and 31 July 1988; playa in Hart, 20 June 1987. *Deaf Smith*—a bird recovered at a cattle feedlot west of Hereford, April 1984, was identified as a "jacana" (!); upon examination it proved to be a Common Moorhen (the bird had been taken to an apartment building in Amarillo, where I found it hiding under a bed). *Donley*—Johnson Lakes, 12 October 1986 (TP-RF); Taylor Lakes WMA, recorded February–October and probably a resident. *Gray*—playa near Kingsmill, 11 and 12 August 1979. *Hansford*—playa near Spearman, 2 July 1997. *Hutchinson*—first sighting for Sanford Dam marsh at Lake Meredith, 11 April 1974; the species is now an established resident. *Potter*—Bates Canyon marsh, Lake Meredith, 10 October 1991. *Randall*—BLNWR, 6–11 May 1968; near Lake Tanglewood, 2 October 1977, 19 December 1982, 14 October 1987, summer 1990; near Amarillo, 5 August 1975, 5 August and 12 October 1995; Canyon, summer of 1983. *Swisher*—near Tulia, 28 March–27 July 1990.

NESTING: Some of the sightings listed involved nesting birds. *Castro*—4 August 1985, three juveniles; 31 July 1988, one juvenile. *Donley*—juvenile, 26 August and 17 September 1997 at Taylor Lakes WMA. *Hutchinson*—first confirmed nesting for the Panhandle was in August 1976, when an adult with one chick was seen on the stilling basin at Sanford Dam. Many confirmations have been made since. *Randall*—a brood at Canyon, summer of 1983; seven immatures at South East Park, Amarillo, 5 August 1995. *Swisher*—sightings for summer of 1990 involved courting and/or copulating birds.

American Coot *Fulica americana* Gmelin

STATUS: Fairly common to abundant resident.

OCCURRENCE: The American Coot has been seen in every county except Roberts and has been recorded year-round.

Early observers had little to say about the coot. McCauley (1877) spoke of seeing it "occasionally," and Hibbets et al. (1926–36) called it a "permanent resident." Hawkins (1945) was more expansive, classifying it as a common migrant and fairly common summer resident, but he said it left the area in winter and returned in late February.

The coot is abundant during migration. Spring migration begins in late February or early March, peaking during the last week of March to the third week of April. Fall migration peaks during the last week of September to the third week of October. More are seen in autumn than in spring. Examples of high numbers are 3,000+ at BLNWR, 8–15 April 1979, and 10,000–14,000 daily, 20 October–10 November 1960. On the late date of 3 December 1978, 5,000 were on the refuge. Smaller numbers overwinter: 2,000+ on Greenbelt Lake, Donley County, 7 December 1996, is typical for that body of water. The following are CBC averages and highs: *Amarillo*—28 (124); *Buffalo Lake* NWR—62 (1,535); *Lake Meredith* (*east*)—113 (366); *Lake Meredith* (*west*)—14 (143); *Quitaque*—89 (225).

NESTING: Many of the lakes and playas with emergent vegetation hold their small contingent of coots in summer. There is a resident population in the Sanford Dam marsh at Lake Meredith, Hutchinson County. A four-year (1974–77) study of waterfowl in the southwest sector (Traweek, 1978) found a yearly average of 3,517 coots during June and July, and 111 broods with 513 young (expanded figures). There are nesting records for 12 counties: Armstrong, Briscoe, Castro, Carson, Gray, Hall, Hansford, Hutchinson, Parmer, Potter, Randall, and Swisher. During the TBBAP the coot was classified as CO in 16 study blocks, PR in six, and

PO in 13. Early and late nesting dates are Randall County, 16 May 1986, and Carson County, 3 September 1981.

SPECIMENS: There is a specimen for Hutchinson County (18 April 1967, WTAMU). Oberholser (1974) names one collected in Childress County (May 12) without giving its location.

Family Gruidae (Cranes)

Sandhill Crane *Grus canadensis* (Linnaeus)

STATUS: Abundant migrant and winter visitor. Vagrant summer visitor.

OCCURRENCE: The Sandhill Crane has been recorded in all counties in the Texas Panhandle except Childress, Hall, and Sherman. It has been seen in every month except August.

Southbound cranes begin arriving in autumn during the first or second week of October. My records show first arrivals during the last week of September in six of the years, the earliest being 19 September 1993 (five at BLNWR). A lone bird was observed in Oldham County, 9 September 1995. Carlander (1933) reported seeing the species at "Wolfing's Lake" between 13 August and 4 September 1932. The majority of cranes pass through the study area and winter farther south, particularly Bailey County (Muleshoe NWR) southward. An exceptional winter was 1979–80, when the number at BLNWR peaked at 28,500 in late January. Another notable exception was the unusually mild winter of 1994–95, when an estimated 15,000–20,000 wintered east of Pampa, Gray County. In some winters large numbers may also be found in Carson and Oldham counties. Unexpected were 5,000+ east of Texline, Rita Blanca National Grasslands, Dallam County, 20 December 1982. It is not known whether the group remained throughout the season. The CBCs give an indication of this crane's presence in early winter, with highs: *Amarillo*—7 of 33 (5,563); *Buffalo Lake NWR*—7 of 29 (7,000); *Friona*—2 of 12 (84); *Quitaque*—11 of 22 (1,500). Cranes have never been recorded on either of the Lake Meredith counts (1970–96).

Sandhill Cranes begin leaving the area in late winter, and most are gone by the end of March. Two wearing tags observed on 2 April 1978 at Lake Meredith, Potter County, had been marked the previous 18 and 22 February near Enochs, Bailey County. Unusual for numbers so late in the season were 300 in Potter County, 12 April 1997; 500+ flying over southwest Amarillo, Randall County, 17 April 1987; and 1,500 at the cattle feedlot at Wildorado, Oldham County, 22 April 1997. The latest spring date is for three in Armstrong County, 5 May 1998. It is in late February and early March that the greatest numbers are seen. As examples, 20,000+ were on the Wildorado feedlot on 26 February 1996. An estimated 10,000 on Milkweed Lake northwest of Vega on the same morning increased to what appeared "a million" in the afternoon ("filling the lake and the entire hillside as far as they could see" [T. Green]).

Oberholser (1974) shows summer sight records for Potter and Roberts counties as well as a specimen collected in Swisher County in June (year not given). On 13 July 1985, I encountered a crane on Cactus Lake, Moore County. Probably an injured bird, it made no attempt to fly when approached. A free-flying Sandhill Crane was found in Caddo County, Oklahoma, 9 July 1990 (Exedine, 1991).

SPECIMENS: The specimen Oberholser (1974) names collected in Swisher County in June was nominate *G. c. canadensis.* Its present whereabouts is unknown. The most abundant race found in the study area is *G. c. tabida,* the Lesser Sandhill Crane (TOS, 1995).

Whooping Crane *Grus americana* (Linnaeus)

STATUS: Casual migrant and vagrant winter visitor.

OCCURRENCE: The Whooping Crane has been observed in five Texas Panhandle counties: Carson, Hutchinson, Ochiltree, Potter, and Randall. One reportedly seen in Swisher County is questionable.

The first reported sighting of the Whooping Crane was that of two adults and one immature on a playa on the D. L. Pratt farm three miles west of Panhandle, Carson County, 9 November 1965, birds that remained until 18 November. Knowledge of their presence was brought to the attention of the public by a local television station's weatherman. The following is a chronology of subsequent sightings:

1973—one in a flock of Sandhill Cranes over BLNWR, 6 November; one in a flock of 30–45 Sandhill Cranes at Lake Meredith, 11 and 16 November. *1977*—four off South Turkey Creek, Lake Meredith, Potter County, 30 October, and 13 on 1 November. *1981*—four over Lake Meredith, Hutchinson County, 9 November; three flying in a flock of approximately 100 Sandhill Cranes over the Bates Canyon area of Lake Meredith, Potter County, 11 November. *1984*—one in a flock of Sandhill Cranes north of Kress, Swisher County, 10 February; around the same time, TPWD game wardens who investigated reports of a Whooping Crane near Kress found an albinistic Sandhill Crane, possibly the same bird. *1987*—an immature on a playa southeast of Amarillo, Randall County, 1 November, and regularly thereafter until 25 December (TP-RF). Bands identified it as #3087, hatched at Wood Buffalo Provincial Park in Canada the previous May–June (USFWS). At the time of the discovery the parent birds had yet to arrive at the Aransas NWR, and their whereabouts was unknown. The young bird was later found on 15 January 1988 in Kent County, between Rotan and Jayton, on the Salt Fork of the Brazos River (USFWS). The bird (identified again by its banding) returned to the study area the following 8 April, where it was seen 19 miles east of Panhandle, Carson County. I was told by the USFWS that the juvenile was the offspring of the same adult pair that had abandoned their youngster the previous year. That outcast was found wintering in nearby Caddo County, Oklahoma (Butts, 1988). Also in 1987, four were seen near a playa west of the PDCSP, 24 March. *1988*—one in a flock of Sandhill Cranes at a playa in Ochiltree County, 31 October. *1990*—three west of White Deer, Carson County, 4 November, observed in late afternoon as they prepared to land. *1995*—six near Kingsmill, Carson County, 21 March, in a flock of Sandhill Cranes; a group of six was again seen downriver from the Sanford Dam at Lake Meredith, Hutchinson County, 24 March. *1996*—three flying south over the Pantex Ordnance Plant, Carson County, 23 October; eight were observed south of that plant the following day; four south of Canyon, Randall County, 2 November. Birds in the last two groups were also heard calling.

Some may question the March birds as the departure of the first Whooping Cranes from the Aransas refuge begins from 25 March to 15 April (Lewis, 1995). However, it is noteworthy that a whooper was observed in nearby Texas County, Oklahoma, 20–24 February 1995 (Grzybowski, 1995). Birds reported as Whooping Cranes have proven upon investigation to be American White Pelicans, swans, Snow Geese, Great Egrets, or light-colored Sandhill Cranes. Possibly some of the large groups reported here can be questioned, for Whooping Cranes usually migrate as singles, pairs, family groups of three, or in flocks of 4–5 adults (Lewis, 1995).

ORDER CHARADRIIFORMES

Family Charadriidae (Plovers)

Black-bellied Plover *Pluvialis squatarola* (Linnaeus)
STATUS: Rare to uncommon migrant.
OCCURRENCE: The Black-bellied Plover has been recorded in 14 counties: Carson, Castro, Dallam, Deaf Smith, Donley, Gray, Hansford, Moore, Oldham, Parmer, Potter, Randall, Roberts, and Sherman. Oberholser (1974) shows it in two. It has been seen April–May and August–November.

I find the Black-bellied Plover named only twice in the accounts of early observers. Hibbets et al. (1926–36) spoke of it as being present "spring and fall" without additional comment, and Hawkins (1945) thought it "rare." It is not plentiful today. That so few are reported can perhaps be attributed to this plover's migrating through interior North America over such a wide front. Most observations are of single birds or of groups of no more than two or three. My records (1963–96) show only six occasions when more than ten were seen at a time. The most ever reported was a group of 22 at the sewage plant playa southeast of Amarillo, Randall County, 11 May 1985.

This handsome plover can be expected in spring during the first or second week of May. Earlier dates are 9 April 1972 and 22 April 1973, both in Randall County. These contrast with early dates of mid-March that Pulich (1988) cites for north-central Texas but are in conformity with Oklahoma dates (Grzybowski et al., 1992). The late dates rarely extend beyond the third week in May, the latest being 27 May 1985 in Randall County. The few records we have point to peak migration in the second week of May. In fall the first arrivals can be looked for during the third week of August—the earliest 11 August 1968 at the BLNWR—and few linger beyond October. I have five November dates on file: 6 and 13 November 1966, 11 November 1974, 14 November 1984—all in Randall County—and 18 November 1993 in Deaf Smith County. There is no discernible fall peak, but the majority of plovers have been recorded from the fourth week of September to the third week of October.

American Golden-Plover *Pluvialis dominica* (Müller)

STATUS: Rare migrant. Vagrant in summer and winter.

OCCURRENCE: The American Golden-Plover has been recorded in five Panhandle counties: Armstrong, Castro, Gray, Parmer, and Randall. It has been seen April–May and August–October and once each in July and December.

McCauley's (1877) account of his encounter with the Golden-Plover is worthy of attention for its indication that the species was formerly more widespread:

Whilst abundant in March along the Upper Rio Grande region of Texas . . . none of this species had, when we were traveling south early in May through Kansas, Indian Territory, and Texas to the Red River, as yet found their way thither or been noticed in that region. The days, especially mornings, were often cold, and northers were not infrequent. On our return, in the latter part of June, this fine game bird had, like the buffalo, come north with the increasing heat, and were abundant on the route, apparently keeping up their journey. As we drove by them, if near the road, they would show no shyness whatever.

Among twentieth-century sightings there are none in the study area in June, nor are there records of any for Colorado (Andrews and Righter, 1992). Baumgartner and Baumgartner (1992) name two early June dates for Oklahoma, and the South Plains checklist says this bird is "casual" in June (LEAS, 1994).

Illustrative of how rare the American Golden-Plover has become in the study area, I have recorded it only seven times in 34 years. Spring sightings are far fewer than fall ones, with most occurring in May. There are two April records of single birds: Gray County, 5 April 1988, and Randall County, 22 April 1959. The latest spring date is for one bird at BLNWR, 25 May 1952. Fall dates range from two birds at BLNWR, 29 August 1964, to five in Randall County, 22 October 1966. There is one sighting each for summer and winter. On 7 July 1985, I encountered a plover in breeding plumage on a playa in west-central Armstrong County. The primaries of one wing dragged the ground. I also observed one on 5 December 1987 at BLNWR. The bird was feeding with several Killdeer and was viewed from a short distance. It called on the few occasions that it flew.

Snowy Plover *Charadrius alexandrinus* Linnaeus

STATUS: Rare to uncommon migrant and casual breeder.
OCCURRENCE: The Snowy Plover has been reported in nine counties—Castro, Childress, Deaf Smith, Hemphill, Moore, Parmer, Potter, Randall, and Roberts—and has been seen from March to November.

Sightings of the Snowy Plover were once fairly common; in recent years, however, they have almost ceased. My records reflect an absence of sightings from 1984 to 1995, whereas prior to then I recorded at least one yearly. Such an absence can be attributed in part to the lack of proper habitat. One might think that the margins of playas would provide ideal habitat for encounters, but this is seldom the case. My records show that I have found this plover in the vicinity of playas only six times. With the disappearance of extensive alkaline flats at BLNWR, the primary source of sightings was eliminated. Other locations may still attract them, such as the sandbars of the Canadian River and other waterways and the alkaline flats at the upper end of Lake Meredith, but such sites are difficult of access and few observers venture near them.

Illustrative of the importance that the BLNWR held for the Snowy Plover are the USFWS records of summering birds: 1959, 10–15; 1960, 20–30; 1964, 20; 1965, 20; 1967, 20–25 (with 10 young); 1968, 10–30; 1969, 25 (with 10 young); 1970, 25–30. Sample numbers in late summer and early fall are: 1968—30, 8 September; 1970—100, 1 August; 1971—50+, 23 August–8 September; 1973—100, 27 August. By the mid-1970s the lake had become dry and few plovers were recorded anywhere. A downpour filled the reservoir in the spring of 1978, alkaline flats developed, and plovers returned: 38 on 5 June and 100 on 27 August 1978; 12 on 5 June 1979 (at least one pair summered). Other than on 16 on 20 June 1983, those were the last reported in summer, as the lake once again became dry.

The first Snowy Plovers of the year may be expected during the first or second week of April. The earliest dates are for one near Dodd, Castro County, 21 March 1991, and six in Dallam County, 26 March 1997. Few linger beyond September, the latest date being for one in Deaf Smith County, 3 November 1995. Large numbers are seldom seen. My records show an average of five birds per group and a high of 30.

NESTING: In addition to the young birds noted at BLNWR, there are several egg dates on file—a nest with three eggs and a nest with a broken egg, a pipped egg, and a newly hatched but dead chick, 4 July 1958; a nest (contents not listed), 13 July 1967. A nest with two eggs was found at an oil well site in the Canadian River bed, Roberts County, 23–24 June 1976. The plover nest was placed in a small colony of three Least Tern nests. No Snowy Plovers were found during the TBBAP years. The most recent nestings were found on the river north of Childress in July 1998.

Semipalmated Plover *Charadrius semipalmatus* Bonaparte

STATUS: Uncommon migrant.

OCCURRENCE: The Semipalmated Plover has been recorded in 13 counties: Briscoe, Carson, Castro, Donley, Gray, Hansford, Hartley, Moore, Parmer, Potter, Randall, Swisher, and Wheeler. Oberholser (1974) shows it in two. It has been seen April–May and July–October.

The Semipalmated Plover is almost always encountered singly: rarely have more than three or four been reported in one group. The greatest number on record is 11 at BLNWR, 25 April 1970. The USFWS records show 100 on 27 April 1963, and 40 during the period 17–31 August 1968. Surely the first number is in error as a one-day total. The latter number could possibly be correct for a cumulative figure. In reviewing the USFWS records, it appears that the figures may at times represent weekly numbers entered under one date. If this belief is incorrect, I cannot but be skeptical of some of their numbers.

The early and late spring dates are for two at BLNWR, 18 April 1971, and one at the sewage pond southeast of Amarillo, Randall County, 20 May 1984. The early and late fall dates are for one at the BLNWR, 23 July 1966, and three at that site, 24 October 1969.

Piping Plover *Charadrius melodus* Ord

STATUS: Vagrant migrant.

OCCURRENCE: The Piping Plover has been reported in the Texas Panhandle once. On 11 May 1975, a single bird was found on the alkaline flats at the upper end of Lake Meredith, Potter County (F. Cain).

Considering the fact that the study area lies in the migratory pathway of the Piping Plover, one would expect it to be reported more often. In addition, the species was recently (1987–88) found nesting at Optima Reservoir on the North Canadian (Beaver) River in Texas County, Oklahoma, some ten miles or so north of the Texas-Oklahoma line (Boyd, 1991). On 4 May 1985, one was seen on the Elkhart sewage ponds in Morton County, southwestern Kansas (Cable et al., 1996), and more recently (1989–91) the species has been found nesting in Kiowa County, southeastern Colorado (Andrews and Righter, 1992).

That the Piping Plover has not been reported more often can possibly be attributed to oversight or to misidentification of Snowy Plovers but is more likely a function of its being a nonstop migrant. Rarely is this plover seen at seemingly appropriate stopover sites, such as the Great Salt Plains NWR in Oklahoma and the Cheyenne Bottoms NWR in Kansas, leading to the belief that most migrants probably migrate nonstop to the Gulf of Mexico (Haig, 1992). The species is known as an uncommon migrant in the eastern half of Texas, west to Wichita, Tarrant, and Travis counties (TOS, 1995). This westward extension could possibly include the southeastern counties of the study area, for a Piping Plover was observed in nearby Jackson County, Oklahoma, 20 April 1993 (Grzybowski, 1993).

It is noteworthy that Piping Plovers at the Optima Reservoir represent the first record of the species nesting sympatrically with Snowy Plovers (Boyd, 1991). Boyd points out that the Piping Plover prefers sites with large amounts of sand and gravel, and the Snowy Plover favors alkaline flats: "The nesting site at Optima Reservoir did consist of sand and gravel." Area observers should be on the lookout for such habitat, particularly in the Canadian River area.

Killdeer *Charadrius vociferus* Linnaeus

STATUS: Common resident (rare to fairly common in winter).
OCCURRENCE: The Killdeer has been recorded throughout the Texas Panhandle and during every month of the year.

The familiar "killdee" is among the few species of nongame birds named by early explorers in the region. On 16 September 1845, near present-day Hoover in north-central Gray County, Abert (1846) spoke of seeing it "along the bed of the stream," a species that was "ever and anon sending up his lone melancholy cry of 'kill-deer.'" Later in the century McCauley (1877) found the Killdeer "very abundant in all sections, including alkaline, throughout our entire trip." There has been little change in its status since.

Other than the few that may overwinter, the vanguard of returning Killdeer in spring can be expected in late February and early March, usually as individuals or in small groups. It is not until mid- or late summer that large gatherings are seen. Some sample late-summer figures for the BLNWR: 160, 11 July 1964; 150, 31 July 1965; 150, 30 July 1966; 160, 11 July 1964; 150, 31 July 1965; 150, 30 July 1966; 150, 22 July 1967; 200+, 17 August 1969. At a playa near Amarillo: 100, 8 August 1995. The Killdeer's status in early summer is provided by the BBS averages and highs: *Childress*—8.4 (41); *Booker*—11.8 (30); *Miami*—4.3 (9); *Waka*—29.8 (53);

Pantex—22.0 (36); *Channing*—4.1 (10); *Texline*—12.2 (16); *Clarendon*—2.6 (5); *Dalhart*—8.3 (10); *Panhandle*—20.0 (24); *Skellytown*—11.3 (16). The routes with the highest counts primarily traverse irrigated croplands.

Most Killdeer are gone by late November, as shown by the CBCs (percentage of counts seen and averages): *Amarillo*—39 percent (1.9); *Buffalo Lake NWR*—41 percent (1.2); *Lake Meredith (east)*—67 percent (1.7); *Lake Meredith (west)*—46 percent (1.9); *Quitaque*—36 percent (1.1); *Friona*—25 percent (0.6). The species was found wintering in the PDCSP during seven years of a Winter-Bird Population Study (Seyffert, 1968–78).

NESTING: The Killdeer has been found nesting in diverse habitats, including roadsides, the margins of playas, shortgrass pasturelands, alkaline flats, prairie dog towns, river sandbars, oil well sites, the lawns around farm and ranch dwellings, golf courses, cemeteries, parks and school grounds, and the graveled roofs of city buildings. The earliest and latest nesting dates: two newly-hatched young at BLNWR, 21 April 1945; nest with four eggs, 4 July 1955. The Killdeer has been found nesting in 21 of the 26 study area counties, and would be in the missing ones (Hall, Hansford, Hemphill, Roberts, and Sherman) given more attention. The TBBAP found CO nesting in 44 survey blocks, PR in 51, and PO in 19. The occupied quadrangles were scattered uniformly across the area.

SPECIMENS: Specimens are available for Castro (6 and 7 September 1980, CMNH), Hutchinson (10 June 1950, TNHC), and Randall (7 May 1939, P-PHM; 8 May 1939, 18 August 1975, WTAMU) counties. Oberholser (1974) shows specimens taken in Gray and Potter counties without naming the collections in which they reside.

Although it was not collected, Thompson (1952) observed a "seemingly-black" Killdeer on the Bugbee Ranch in Hutchinson County in the summer of 1950. He found the condition to derive from a coating of carbon black on the bird's feathers, the cause being the large amounts of that substance spewed into the atmosphere by carbon black plants around nearby Borger and Phillips. Anyone living in that area during the years before pollution control measures were installed can testify to the pervasiveness of these clouds of carbon black smoke.

Mountain Plover *Charadrius montanus* Townsend

STATUS: Uncommon to fairly common migrant in western half, rare elsewhere. Rare summer visitor (possibly breeding) in northwest sector.

OCCURRENCE: The Mountain Plover has been recorded in ten Texas Panhandle counties, all located in the western half: Armstrong, Dallam, Deaf Smith, Hansford, Hartley, Moore, Oldham, Potter, Randall, and Swisher. It has been seen March–June and in August, October, and November.

Returning Mountain Plovers in spring can be looked for in mid-March, the earliest being ten or more at a prairie dog town at BLNWR on 14 March 1987—

the group was seen regularly thereafter until 1 April, when eight were last seen. Thirty or more in a pasture south of Amarillo, Randall County, 27–28 March 1964, represent the highest number reported in spring. Other than two May dates (discussed later), the latest spring sighting is of nine near Dumas, Moore County, 14 April 1972.

Returning plovers in fall are not seen until August or later, the earliest being two at BLNWR, 3 and 9 August 1993. Fairly large gatherings are seen only occasionally: 57 near Amarillo, Randall County, 20 October 1966, and 47 near Wayside, Armstrong County, 16 November 1985, the latest on record. Testimony to the species' former abundance, the following entry appeared in the *Tascosa Pioneer* for 6 August 1887: "It is said that there are immense numbers of plover in the country, many of them to be found adjacent to town" (Archambeau, 1966). This would have been at Tascosa, Oldham County, the present site of Boys Ranch on the Canadian River. As recently as the fall of 1956, approximately 3,000 were observed west of Clayton, Union County, New Mexico (Baumgartner, 1957), numbers unheard of today. Current studies show recent declines in distribution and/or population size of the Mountain Plover ranging from 50 to 89 percent (Leachman and Osmundson, 1990), prompting a proposal to place it on the Threatened or Endangered list.

NESTING: Most observers who worked in the study area prior to mid-century classified the Mountain Plover as a summer resident (Strecker, 1912; Hibbets et al., 1926–36; Bent, 1929; Carlander, 1934; Wolfe, 1956). However—with the exception of Bent, who placed breeding at "Washburn, Hereford," they neither named specific locations nor cited dates. The only plovers noted by McCauley (1877) in his travels through the area in April–June of 1876 were found between Camp Supply, Indian Territory, and Fort Dodge, Kansas. Hawkins (1945), who explored the area just prior to mid-century, did not name the species during any season. The one confirmed nesting is that given by Oberholser (1974) for Swisher County: "20 miles south of Canyon (recently hatched young located, May 31, 1899, Vernon Bailey)."

It was with the initiation of the BBSS that Mountain Plovers were again reported in summer. On the Channing (Hartley County) route, I found two on 15 June 1974, one on 1 June 1980, and four on 12 June 1986. The stops were within a mile of one another and the birds were found in grazed blue grama–buffalograss prairie, the vegetative type in which Graul and Webster (1976) say the species is most likely to nest. In Dallam County farther north, I have found the Mountain Plover on the Texline BBS: 7 June 1975 (1); 10 June 1978 (2); 7 June 1980 (2); 15 June 1985 (6). These were found in sections composed primarily of cultivated land intermixed with patches of grassland. Plovers in such atypical habitat were also encountered by Shackford (1991) in the Oklahoma Panhandle. Forty percent of his breeding-season records were of birds found in plowed fields, with one nest in a field of maize. He concluded that "except where prairie dog colonies are present, Mountain Plover may prefer cultivated land to shortgrass prairie for nesting." Flowers (1985) also found nesting plovers in the Oklahoma Panhandle, all located in severely overgrazed grasslands or in, or adjacent to, prairie dog towns. His and Shackford's nesting sites are only some 15–30 miles north of the Texas-Oklahoma line.

On 8 June 1977, I observed a single plover west of Conlen in Dallam County. A single bird was seen west of Amarillo on 16 July 1968 and another in southern Hansford County on the late date of 29 May 1992. Oberholser (1974) shows a summer sight record for Oldham County. A thorough search of appropriate habitats in the north and northwestern sectors of the study area would possibly turn up a few Mountain Plovers nesting still, although such a search conducted in April–June 1996–98 failed to do so. On 26 March 1997, six plover were observed in a field of winter wheat a few miles south of the Oklahoma line, and one again near mid-April, but nesting was not discovered. Near the same location on 8–15 April 1998, 3–5 birds were observed, some courting, but as far as is known they did not remain to nest.

SPECIMENS: Specimens have been taken in Randall County (20 September 1938, and another undated, WTAMU). Oberholser (1974) cites specimens taken in Armstrong and Dallam (August 6) counties, without naming their locations.

Family Recurvirostridae (Stilts and Avocets)

Black-necked Stilt *Himantopus mexicanus* (Müller)
STATUS: Uncommon to fairly common breeder.
OCCURRENCE: The Black-necked Stilt has been found in 17 counties: Armstrong, Briscoe, Carson, Castro, Dallam, Deaf Smith, Donley, Gray, Hansford, Hartley, Moore, Oldham, Parmer, Potter, Randall, Sherman, and Swisher. All but one of the sightings are from west of the 101st meridian. Observers in the southeastern sector should be on the alert, however, as two stilts were found in nearby Jackson County, Oklahoma, 13–14 May 1995 (Grzybowski, 1995). This species has been recorded from March to October.

Prior to Hawkins (1945), who classified it as a "rare summer resident," the Black-necked Stilt was not mentioned by other observers. Even afterward, the species was reported with such irregularity that a year in which more than one was seen was tagged a "stilt year." Oberholser (1974) placed it in the rare to casual category, showing it in only two study area counties, and Johnsgard (1979) called it a "rare summer visitor." It was only in the late 1970s that the stilt began to be reported with regularity and in numbers. My records reflect this: during the period 1964–76, I recorded it in seven of the years; in the period 1977–96, in all but one.

The first stilts in spring can be looked for in mid- or late April, the earliest date being for one at Caprock Canyons SP, Briscoe County, 14 March 1996. Few are seen past mid-September, the latest date being for one in Briscoe County, 18 October 1997. Not only the frequency of stilt sightings but also the number of birds has increased. Ninety on three playas near Hereford, Deaf Smith County, 5 September 1989, were remarkable, and 31 at Cactus Lake, Moore County, 17 July 1998 unusual.

NESTING: The breeding status of the Black-necked Stilt at the end of 1985 was summarized by Seyffert (1989a). The paper cited confirmed nestings in seven counties: Armstrong, Carson, Castro, Deaf Smith, Parmer, Randall, and Swisher. The TBBAP added Briscoe, Gray, Moore, and Oldham as counties with confirmed and/or probable nestings. Stilts have also been found in summer in Dallam, Hansford, Hartley, Potter, and Sherman counties.

American Avocet *Recurvirostra americana* Gmelin

STATUS: Common (breeder) to abundant (migrant).

OCCURRENCE: The American Avocet has been recorded in every county except Collingsworth and Wheeler.

Returning avocets in spring usually arrive during the third week of March: early dates—Gray County, 1 February 1998; Randall County, 2 February 1964. It is noteworthy that McCauley (1877) did not record a single avocet, Carlander (1934) thought it "uncommon," and other early observers had little to say about it. Today it is one of the most common of the breeding shorebirds and has been recorded in 19 of the study area counties during summer.

Gatherings in spring are much smaller than those of late summer and early autumn. The most avocets ever reported for each season, all at BLNWR, are: 300, 13 April 1980; 65–200+, June 1973; 880–1,200+, 5 July–12 September 1970; 500–1,000+, 15 July–3 September 1973; 1000+, 13 September 1983. Most avocets are gone by the end of October, a few as late as mid-November. The latest date is for nine near Dalhart, Dallam County, 2 December 1995. A seemingly melanistic bird observed at BLNWR proved upon closer examination to have head, neck, and underside coated with petroleum oil.

NESTING: Nesting has been confirmed in 17 counties: Armstrong, Briscoe, Carson, Castro, Dallam, Deaf Smith, Donley, Hartley, Hutchinson, Moore, Ochiltree, Oldham, Parmer, Potter, Randall, Sherman, and Swisher. Oberholser (1974) shows two—Castro and Dallam. Extreme dates: bird on nest, 2 May (Briscoe County); recently hatched chicks, 30 July (Randall County). The TBBAP found CO nesting in 25 survey blocks, PR in 22, and PO in five. All but three of the quadrangles were west of the 101st meridian.

SPECIMENS: Specimens have been taken in Carson (23 June 1985, TCWC), Deaf Smith (13 September 1920, CMNH), Moore (fall 1972, WTAMU), Parmer (31 March 1976, WTAMU), and Potter (ACMNH) counties. Oberholser (1974) shows specimens taken in Potter and Deaf Smith counties.

Family Scolopacidae (Sandpipers, Phalaropes, and Allies)

Greater Yellowlegs *Tringa melanoleuca* (Gmelin)

STATUS: Fairly common to common migrant. Rare winter visitor.

OCCURRENCE: The Greater Yellowlegs has been recorded in every Texas Panhandle county except Collingsworth and Roberts, and would be in them with better coverage. It has been seen in every month.

There is little or no mention of the Greater Yellowlegs in the accounts of early observers. Two who did speak of it—Hibbets et al. (1926–36) and Carlander (1934)—both classified it as a "rare migrant." Perhaps the scarcity of observations can be attributed in part to the severe drought that prevailed during much of the time of their field activities. Dry playa beds do not attract migrating shorebirds, and prior to the mid-1930s there were few man-made impoundments. Certainly today the three-note alarm call of the Greater Yellowlegs is a familiar sound from mid-March to late November.

As is the case with many shorebird species, it is hard to say when spring migration ends and fall migration begins. I have recorded the Greater Yellowlegs as late as 29 June and as early as 1 July. It is only an assumption to say that all June birds are northbound and all July birds are southbound. Likewise, those few recorded in late February and early to mid-December are assumed to be early and late migrants, not overwintering birds. Prior to the recent warm winters of 1994–95 through 1997–98, there were but eight midwinter records (Hutchinson, Donley, and Randall counties). The exceptionally warm winter of 1994–95 found unusual numbers in Randall, Potter, and Hemphill counties. It is not unusual now to find one Greater Yellowlegs or more wintering at Thompson Park Lake and MediPark Lake in Amarillo, Potter County. Below the caprock escarpment on the South Plains, the Greater Yellowlegs is classified as "uncommon" in winter (LEAS, 1994).

At times the Greater Yellowlegs can be abundant. A tour of several playas in the vicinity of Amarillo on 15 July 1966 turned up 200+ in a short time. The species is not normally found in large groups. Fifty were observed on the Canadian River in north-central Potter County on 7 October 1965 and 40 or more at Thompson Park Lake in Amarillo, Potter County, the last week of October 1996.

SPECIMENS: Specimens have been taken in Castro (6, 7, 13, and 14 September 1980, CMNH) and Randall (10 October 1988, WTAMU) counties. The one Carlander (1934) collected and deposited in the "Canyon Museum" is probably the untagged mounted bird still on display (P-PHM). Oberholser (1974) names one taken in Lipscomb County ("June 30"), without giving details.

Lesser Yellowlegs *Tringa flavipes* (Gmelin)

STATUS: Common to abundant migrant. Vagrant winter visitor.

OCCURRENCE: The Lesser Yellowlegs has been found in every county except Childress, Collingsworth, Hall, Ochiltree, and Roberts and has been recorded in every month except January.

The Lesser Yellowlegs is more common in the study area than the Greater Yellowlegs, particularly after mid-June. Examples of numbers at BLNWR (1970) are: 125+ 28 June, 275 5 July, 500+ 12 July, 400+ 18 July, 200+ 1 August. As with most other shorebirds, it is difficult to determine correctly when spring migration ends and fall migration begins. It is possible that some of the June and July birds represent nonbreeding summering birds.

The Lesser Yellowlegs is normally first seen in early or mid-April and last seen in late October—on average not as early or as late as the Greater Yellowlegs. The early and late dates are: one near Amarillo, Randall County, 17 March 1990; one near Amarillo, Randall County, 15 November 1984. It has been reported four times in winter, a single bird each time: Lake Meredith, Hutchinson County, 2 December 1970; BLNWR, 3 December 1993; Greenbelt Lake, Donley County, 5 February 1978; near Friona, Parmer County, 11 February 1962.

Between 17 September and 13 October 1975 a die-off occurred in northeastern Parmer County in which 1,300–1,400 ducks and 300–400 shorebirds perished on four playas. Of the shorebirds, 154 were Lesser Yellowlegs, 137 Least, Western, and Semipalmated Sandpipers, 38 American Avocets, 14 Common Snipe, 7 Killdeers, and the remainder Long-billed Dowitchers and Pectoral and Solitary Sandpipers. In addition, an American Bittern, a White-faced Ibis, and a Northern Mockingbird were found dead. The causative agent of the die-off was determined to be Type C botulism. Seventy-five percent of the casualties were found at a playa located adjacent to a cattle feedlot (Traweek, 1975).

SPECIMENS: Specimens have been taken in Castro (5, 6, 7, and 20 September 1980, CMNH) and Potter (25 September 1977, TCWC) counties. Oberholser (1974) names one taken in Lipscomb County ("Aug. 3"), without giving details.

Solitary Sandpiper *Tringa solitaria* Wilson

STATUS: Uncommon to fairly common migrant.

OCCURRENCE: The Solitary Sandpiper has been recorded in 19 counties: Armstrong, Briscoe, Carson, Castro, Collingsworth, Dallam, Deaf Smith, Donley, Gray, Hartley, Hemphill, Hutchinson, Moore, Oldham, Parmer, Potter, Randall, Sherman, and Swisher. It has been seen from April to November.

One of a very few shorebird species recorded by McCauley (1877) during May and June of 1876 was the Solitary Sandpiper: "Occasionally observed along water-courses, as the Canadian, etc." Indeed, the species is well named, for it is seldom that more than one or two are seen at a time. A notable exception was eleven encountered along Tierra Blanca Creek downstream from the dam at BLNWR, 2 September 1984. Though strung out along the streamside, they were within 20–30 yards of one another.

The Solitary Sandpiper is normally present in spring from the third week in April to the second week in May and in autumn from the second week in August to the second week in September. The early and late sightings for the first half of the year are: one in the PDCSP, 8 April 1995, and one at BLNWR, 15 May 1973. The early and late sightings for the last half of the year are: two on a playa in Swisher County, 3 July 1981, and one at BLNWR, 2 November 1996. Only occasionally can it be found in the PDCSP, one of the few shorebird species that have been encountered on the canyon floor.

Willet *Catoptrophorus semipalmatus* (Gmelin)

STATUS: Rare migrant.

OCCURRENCE: The Willet has been recorded in 14 counties: Armstrong, Briscoe, Carson, Castro, Gray, Hansford, Hartley, Hemphill, Hutchinson, Moore, Ochiltree, Parmer, Randall, and Wheeler. Oberholser (1974) named it in two. It has been seen from March to October.

Willets are not reported in the study area every year. In the period 1965–96 I recorded it in 19 years, at an average of two per encounter. The largest group was 11 at a playa in Randall County, 28 April 1984. Even more unusual was a group of 25 in Briscoe County, 27 April 1997. On 22 April 1973, I observed a group of four, two of the birds with oil-soaked feathers from their bellies up to their chins.

The early and late dates for each half of the year range from one bird in Wheeler County, 23 March 1986, to one at BLNWR, 30 June 1973, and from one in Hansford County, 2 July 1997, to one at BLNWR, 12 October 1969. Sightings for each period are equally divided. The Willet is usually silent during its passage, seldom giving its musical *pill-will-willet* call.

Spotted Sandpiper *Actitis macularia* (Linnaeus)

STATUS: Fairly common to common migrant, with casual breeding.

OCCURRENCE: The Spotted Sandpiper has been recorded in every county except Roberts and Sherman, and not in them through lack of coverage. It has been seen from April to October.

Normally the Spotted Sandpiper is present from the last week in April to the last week in May and from the third week in July to mid-September. The early and late dates: one at BLNWR, 6 April 1968; one at the Palo Duro Club near Canyon, Randall County, 19 October 1987. Seldom is a group of any size encountered; normally one sees only a single bird or a loose gathering of no more than three or four.

NESTING: Most early observers classified the Spotted Sandpiper as a summer resident: Hibbets et al. (1926–36) said "summer, few weeks"; Carlander (1934) called it "rather uncommon . . . possible summer resident"; Stevenson (1942) said it was "a summer resident along Palo Duro Creek in Randall and Armstrong counties and at certain lakes and tanks in the vicinity of Amarillo"; Hawkins (1945) reported that "a few remain in this area throughout May, June and July." The only record of breeding was that of Oberholser (1974): "Deaf Smith County, Glenrio (parent with young, July 14 1920, A. J. Kirn)." The Spotted Sandpiper was not reported nesting again until I encountered two adults with one downy chick at BLNWR on 17 July 1966. A pair engaged in alarm behavior was seen again at this site the following year on 24 July 1967—a single bird had been observed on 10 June and a pair on 1 July. There have been summer sightings of birds in favorable habitats in other counties that pointed to possible, if not probable, nesting: *Castro*—one near Dimmitt, 4 June 1978; *Carson*—one calling bird near Panhandle, 5 June 1980. *Donley*—one, 6 July 1996. *Gray*—Lake McClellan: a pair, 23–24 June 1956 ("acting nesty, no nest found"); one, 24 May and three, 17 July 1990. *Hall*—one near the river in the east-central sector, 30 May 1988. *Hansford*—one, 3 July 1977. *Hutchinson*—the following are those I have encountered downriver from the Sanford Dam at Lake Meredith: a single bird displaying alarm behavior, 15 June 1975; a pair was later seen 13 July. Another pair was found at this site on 20 June 1976, again exhibiting alarm behavior; another pair, 15 June 1977; and single adults, 5 July 1978 and 5 July 1982. A nest or young seemed likely to be nearby on each occasion. On 7 July 1998, a juvenile was observed at length and at close range. A Spotted Sandpiper summered at Lake Weatherly near Borger in 1977. *Moore*—three remained throughout summer 1974 at a playa southwest of Dumas, and one was seen at Cactus Lake, 13 July 1985. *Oldham*—I observed one on two occasions at a small sand and gravel impoundment located south of the Canadian River near Boys Ranch, 26 June 1987 and 21 June 1988. Both times a bird flew from the cattails to an open area where it preened at length before returning to the spot from where it had flown. *Randall*—a pair seen regularly during the summer of 1956 at BLNWR, and a single bird, 29 June 1997; one in the PDCSP, 5 June 1967; a pair seen regularly, summer of 1988, at Lake Tanglewood. USFWS records at BLNWR show birds present during the summers of 1961, 1967, and 1968. Fischer et al. (1982) cite unspecified numbers in a 3 June–8 July period (year or years not named) in Parmer, Castro, and Swisher counties.

There are records of nesting Spotted Sandpipers in areas near the Texas Panhandle. In Oklahoma Ports (1979) reported a pair with one young six miles northeast of Hardesty, Texas County, 16 July 1978. The downy young was caught and examined. Shackford (1983) found and caught a downy chick at Lake Etling, Black Mesa SP, Cimarron County, 14 June 1980. At least four adults were in the area. He was of the opinion that the species "may breed fairly regularly in the Oklahoma Panhandle," and cites the two nests, each with three young, found by R. Crompton Tate near Kenton in 1910 and 1911 (Nice, 1931). In New Mexico, Ligon (1961) says of the Spotted Sandpiper: "Nests sparingly along spring-fed portions of Perico Creek, 6 and 7 miles west of Clayton," Union County. In Colorado Chase et al. (1982) show it as a definite breeder in the extreme southeastern (Springfield) latilong.

SPECIMENS: Three specimens are available from Castro County (6 September 1980, CMNH). Oberholser (1974) cites one taken in Oldham County ("Aug 19"), but does not give its location. He names it as nominate *A. m. macularia*.

Upland Sandpiper *Bartramia longicauda* (Bechstein)

STATUS: Common to abundant migrant and vagrant breeder.

OCCURRENCE: The Upland Sandpiper has been recorded in every Texas Panhandle county except Collingsworth and has been seen April–September.

Upland Sandpipers are heard far more often than they are seen, particularly those that pass overhead both night and day on their way south in late summer and early fall. As Frances Williams of Midland has said so well: "Birders who do not know the flight call of this bird miss one of the greatest pleasures of living on the plains, and are also unaware of how abundant this species really is" (pers. comm.). It is often found in weedy or grassy fields as well as along roadsides and may even be seen standing on fence posts, as typically portrayed in books. The largest group I ever encountered was 45 in a field near Umbarger, Randall County, 2 September 1979, while twice that number were recorded on the nearby BLNWR, 27 August 1976.

As is the case for many shorebirds, exactly when spring migration ends and fall migration begins cannot be clearly defined. Those found in June and early July obscure the problem, as some may be summer residents. Upland Sandpipers begin moving south quite early; birds may be heard passing overhead at night in some years as early as the first week in July. The latest fall date, with one exception, is 25 September—one near Lake Marvin, Hemphill County, in 1979, and one at BLNWR in 1983. One on the refuge on 20 October 1991 was extremely late, but in conformity with the latest Oklahoma date of 25 October (Sutton, 1967). The first birds of spring can be expected by the third week of April. The earliest date is a single bird in Wheeler County, 6 April 1989. Few are encountered past the second week of May.

The present-day summer status of the Upland Sandpiper is unclear. The accounts of early observers read as though the species was once rather common. McCauley (1877) spoke of it as "frequently observed on the prairie-land and near the streams, upon returning in latter part of June." Carlander (1934) classified it as a "summer resident," as did Stevenson (1942): "A regular summer resident of range and cultivated farm lands; observed numerous times in fields within the city limits of Amarillo and at nearby lakes." None of these observers named specific instances of nesting, however. By his time Hawkins (1945) categorized the Upland's status as that of "rare summer resident," citing one nesting record.

In recent years there have been a number of summer sightings of Upland Sandpipers, pointing to possible breeding: *Armstrong*—10 (2 at one stop, 8 at another) on the Pantex BBS, 28 June 1986. *Deaf Smith*—one in a grassy field west of Westway, 27 June 1993. *Donley*—one in a pasture in the east-central sector near the Collingsworth County line, 26 June 1983—when flushed, the bird circled overhead several times before returning to the spot from which it had flown. *Gray*—2–4 birds seen regularly during the summers of 1976 and 1977 one mile east of the southwest corner of the Pampa airport. *Hansford*—one bird each at two sites and four at another in the north-central sector, 3 July 1977; six in one group recorded on the Waka BBS, 10 June 1982; one approximately three miles south of Hitchland, north-central sector, 8 June 1991—it flew from grassland and called once as it flew low over an adjacent wheat field. *Moore*—one southwest of Dumas, 23 June 1987. *Ochiltree*—one in a fallow field surrounded by cultivated fields approximately four miles south of Waka, 7 June 1987; two in a grassy field near a playa, 6 June 1996. *Randall*—one between Amarillo and the PDCSP, 19 June 1958.

NESTING: The only confirmed nesting of the Upland Sandpiper in the study area is that cited by Hawkins (1945): "several plovers nested eighteen miles north of Sunray on the Travis Spurlock Ranch" (Sherman County). On 5 July 1983, an adult Upland Sandpiper with two recently hatched chicks was discovered in nearby Crosby County (Stogner, 1983; Williams, 1983). The discovery was a first for the area. In Cimarron County, Oklahoma, Sutton (1967) cites two nests found on 24 June 1910, both containing eggs. Hubbard (1978) names former summer sightings in Quay County, New Mexico, to the west, but nesting was never confirmed. A nest containing four eggs was found in Baca County, southeastern Colorado, 20 May 1923 (Bailey and Niedrach, 1965). These dates should alert area observers to possible nesting should birds be encountered during that period (20 May–5 July).

SPECIMENS: Upland Sandpipers have been collected in Ochiltree (4 August 1966, MNH), Parmer (30 April 1977, WTAMU), and Randall (1 September 1977, TCWC; 27 April 1971, WTAMU) counties. Oberholser (1974) cites specimens taken in Hemphill and Wheeler counties but does not name the collections in which they were deposited.

Whimbrel *Numenius phaeopus* (Linnaeus)

STATUS: Casual migrant.

OCCURRENCE: The Whimbrel has been observed in five counties: Gray, Hansford, Hartley, Moore, and Randall. It has been recorded in April, May, and July.

Whimbrel sightings are as follows: *Gray*—one near Pampa, 1 May 1991, and three, 10 May 1993. *Hansford*—three near Gruver, 13 April 1998. *Hartley*—two near Hartley, 11 May 1983; one in a group of Long-billed Curlews at the same location during the last week of April 1987, and four more, 8–13 May. *Moore*—five near Dumas, 10 May 1981 (TP-RF)—the birds remained for six hours on a tailwater pond along the road. *Randall*—1–4 at BLNWR, 18–23 May 1965, one on 21 May 1966, and 1–2 on 4–12 July 1970; four near Amarillo, 5 May 1984, and one, 9 May 1992; one, 10 May 1986.

As can been seen, none of these sightings occurred in the fall. This prevalence of spring observations has been noted by other regional reporters (Andrews and Righter, 1992; Hubbard, 1978; Oberholser, 1974; Pulich, 1988; Sutton, 1967).

Long-billed Curlew *Numenius americanus* Bechstein

STATUS: Common to abundant migrant. Fairly common to common breeder in northwest sector. Uncommon to fairly common winter visitor in southwest sector.

OCCURRENCE: The Long-billed Curlew has been recorded in every county except Childress, Collingsworth, and Lipscomb and would be in them with better coverage. It has been seen in every month of the year.

The observations of McCauley (1877) are testimony to the Long-billed Curlew's formerly wide range as a breeder in the study area: "Frequent, and perhaps of as general distribution as any other species throughout the section traversed . . . its range and habitat extended over all the places visited, save in the canyons

Long-billed Curlew

themselves and in the immediate vicinity of alkali water. . . . It was found in the same abundance several miles from water, on the Staked Plain, as upon the prairie or rolling-land lying about the lower parts of the creeks." While journeying south in May he found the birds very shy, and "nidification was in progress" on his return northward in June. The route his party followed included Hemphill, Wheeler, Gray, Carson, Armstrong, Randall, Potter, and Briscoe counties.

Shortly after the turn of the century, Strecker (1912) stated that the Long-billed Curlew "formerly bred north of the Canadian, in the Panhandle." Later, this assessment was revised by Stevenson (1942): "Allan [Philip F. Allan, U.S. Soil Conservation Service] states that curlews nest in the northern part of the Panhandle and are regular breeding birds in Dallam County." Prior to that, Hibbets et al. (1926–36) claimed the curlew was a summer resident within 40 miles of Canyon, Randall County, and Carlander (1934) classified it as a "summer resident." Hawkins (1945) found it to be an "uncommon summer resident in the northwestern Panhandle."

Except in the northwestern and southwestern sectors, the Long-billed Curlew today is encountered solely as a migrant. Returning birds in spring can be looked for in mid- or late March. One in Swisher County, 7 March 1982, and three in Armstrong County, 9 March 1986, are among the earliest sightings. Migration is completed by early or mid-May. Curlews encountered from late May through early July in counties other than Dallam, Hartley, Moore, Oldham, and Sherman, where the species is known to nest, should be observed closely for possible nestings. During a study of nesting curlews in Dallam and Hartley counties, King (1978) discovered that "some curlews migrate early while others remain on the breeding grounds with the young." I have witnessed large groups of curlews migrating south in early and mid-July—105 in one group in Randall County, 7 July 1987, and 500 or more west of Hereford, Deaf Smith County, 19 July 1981, the latter in flocks that followed one another at fairly regular intervals as they flew into a prairie dog town from the northwest.

The averages on three BBSS in the northwest sector indicate the Long-billed Curlew's status in that area: *Texline*—33; *Channing*—1.4; *Dalhart*—15. I have found curlews to be common in other areas of Dallam and Hartley counties as well. It is later in the season (September–November) that the largest gatherings of curlews have been observed. On 9 October 1981, I estimated 3,000 in west-central Castro County. Flocks from all directions were converging on a field where others were already massed. Curlews winter in several southwestern counties, as these examples show: *Parmer*—237, 30 December 1973; *Castro*—300, 21 December 1983; *Swisher*—65, 12 December 1996; *Deaf Smith*—one on the BLNWR CBC of 26 December 1979 was a first for the count, and unexpected was one southwest of Hartley, Hartley County, 14 December 1981.

NESTING: Prior to 1972 the single reference to the nesting of the Long-billed Curlew in the twentieth century was that of Oberholser (1974), who cites Mrs. R. L. Duke's assertion that many nested in the Buffalo Springs area of Dallam County in July of 1936. It is in the northwestern sector today that nesting curlews continue to be found: 9 June 1972, adult with one chick southwest of Dumas, Moore County (TP-RF); 10 June 1978, nest with four eggs near the Thompson Grove Picnic Area northeast of Texline; 11 June 1993, a pair with one downy young one mile north of Texline; 8 May 1981, nest with four eggs southwest of Hartley, Hartley County. The Moore County discovery was the first confirmation of nesting since mid-century. King (1978) observed nest building in the Dumas–Hartley area on 18 April and 19 May 1978 and found that five of seven nests hatched young by 25 May. I observed a courting/copulating pair in Dallam County on 16 April 1996. During the TBBAP, nesting was confirmed in four study blocks in Dallam County. Oberholser (1974) shows sight records of breeding in Dallam (as already noted), Sherman, and Ochiltree counties. His sight record of breeding in Carson County is possibly based on McCauley (1877), who spoke of encountering both nest-building curlews and others flushed from nests.

SPECIMENS: There are specimens for Dallam (2 June 1947, TCWC), Deaf Smith (29 October 1977, another without a date, WTAMU), Hansford (8 August 1954, OMNH), Parmer (6 December 1973 and 3 November 1978, WTAMU), and Randall (14 October 1938, P-PHM) counties. Oberholser (1974) names specimens collected in Dallam, Moore, and Deaf Smith counties, the latter a specimen record of breeding, but fails to supply details. He identified the birds as nominate *N. a. americanus.*

Hudsonian Godwit *Limosa haemastica* (Linnaeus)

STATUS: Casual migrant.

OCCURRENCE: The few sightings of the Hudsonian Godwit in the Texas Panhandle have been limited to five counties—Armstrong, Carson, Deaf Smith, Gray, and Randall—and to the months of May, July, August, and September.

Until recent years, almost all observations of the Hudsonian Godwit occurred on the BLNWR: one, 25 May 1958, two, 15–25 May 1973. The single Deaf Smith County sighting was one bird seen near Dawn, not far from the refuge, in August 1979. Eighteen years elapsed before one was seen again (1997), and that was a banner year indeed. The sequence of sightings began with a single bird in breeding plumage found at a playa in Armstrong County, 22–23 July. This was followed by three birds in nonbreeding plumage observed at a playa between Panhandle and White Deer, Carson County, 23 August, and again three at the same location, 20 September (the same birds?). The latest sighting was of three in Gray County, 25 April 1998.

The Hudsonian Godwit migrates to its breeding grounds in the far north via a Great Plains route lying well east of the Texas Panhandle. Its passage southward in fall, however, follows an entirely different route, the birds gathering July–October along South Hudson Bay and James Bay before flying off the eastern shore of the United States directly to wintering grounds in South America (Hayman et al., 1986). Sightings anywhere inland during that time are noteworthy. There are only three confirmed fall sightings in Colorado (Andrews and Righter, 1992), three or four for Oklahoma (Baumgartner and Baumgartner, 1992), and three for north-central Texas (Pulich, 1988). Although the TOS (1995) classifies the Hudsonian Godwit as an uncommon to common spring migrant near the coast, it deems the bird a "very rare" fall migrant. The single sighting reported on the South Plains occurred in Crosby County, 10 May 1975 (*fide* C. Stogner), and there was one in Texas County in the Oklahoma Panhandle, 28–31 May 1993 (Grzybowski, 1993).

Marbled Godwit *Limosa fedoa* (Linnaeus)

STATUS: Rare to uncommon migrant.

OCCURRENCE: The Marbled Godwit has been reported in nine Texas Panhandle counties: Carson, Castro, Gray, Hutchinson, Oldham, Parmer, Potter, Randall, and Swisher. It has been seen from April to October.

Marbled Godwits in spring can be looked for from mid- to late April, and their passage is normally completed by late May. The earliest sighting was a single bird near Pampa, Gray County, 7 April 1988. Only once has a godwit been reported in spring later than May—nine at BLNWR, 17 June 1973. The extreme dates for the last half of the year range from one at BLNWR on 2 July 1972 to one at the same location on 22 October 1967.

The Marbled Godwit has been recorded most often in fall. My records reveal that 68 percent of all godwits were seen in the latter half of the year, mostly in September, while those of another observer show 69 percent. The largest gathering on record was 38 at BLNWR, 4 May 1999.

Ruddy Turnstone *Arenaria interpres* (Linnaeus)

STATUS: Casual migrant.

OCCURRENCE: Randall is the only county in which the Ruddy Turnstone has been recorded. It has been seen in March, May, and August–October. The sightings are as follows, in each instance one bird: 1 August 1964; 11 and 17 October 1964; 16 May 1965; 30 March and 19 May 1968—all at BLNWR. The exception was one seen southeast of Amarillo, 6 September 1971.

The BLNWR sightings were made during the years when there were extensive mud flats and alkaline flats, principally at the upper end of the refuge. Masses of migrant shorebirds of a wide variety congregated at these sites during the mid-1960s to early 1970s, particularly in the latter years when the lake was being slowly drained. Habitat was optimal and the chances of seeing a number of rare species, including the Ruddy Turnstone, were greatly enhanced. Such conditions have never returned.

Ruddy Turnstones have been recorded three times at the Muleshoe NWR in Bailey County: 16 September 1974 (Williams, 1975); 27 April 1981 and 27 May 1986 (*fide* C. Stogner). Another was seen in Lubbock County, 5 September 1976 (Williams, 1977).

The Ruddy Turnstone is a common migrant and winter resident along the coast but rare and local inland (TOS, 1995).

Red Knot *Calidris canutus* (Linnaeus)
STATUS: Rare migrant.

OCCURRENCE: The Red Knot has been observed in four counties: Armstrong, Gray, Oldham, and Randall. It has been recorded in May and July–September.

Only two sightings occurred during the first half of the year. Oberholser (1974) says that most inland records are for the fall. The following is a listing of reported sightings with number of birds in parentheses: *1966*—near Amarillo, Randall County, 5 September (1); *1968*—BLNWR, 1, 3, and 10 September (1); near Amarillo, Randall County, 4 September (1). *1970*—BLNWR, 9 (3) and 18 July (6), and 7 (1) and 22–26 September (2). *1971*—BLNWR, 8 September (15). *1977*—BLNWR, 8 May (2). *1984*—BLNWR, 8 July (1); near Kingsmill, Gray County, 26 August (3), one with a USFWS band on its right leg. *1985*—near Kingsmill, Gray County, 11 August (1). *1996*—Wildorado, Oldham County, 21 August 1996 (7). *1997*—near Washburn, Armstrong County, 1 August (3).

The Red Knot migrates primarily along the Atlantic and Pacific coasts and through the Great Lakes region and only casually elsewhere through the interior of North America (AOU, 1983).

Sanderling *Calidris alba* (Pallas)
STATUS: Rare migrant.

OCCURRENCE: The Sanderling has been reported in eight counties: Briscoe, Carson, Castro, Gray, Hutchinson, Moore, Potter, and Randall. Oberholser (1974) shows it in one. It has been recorded April–May and July–November.

All but one of the spring Sanderling sightings have occurred within the period 5–30 May. The exception was "several" on the Big Blue Creek mud flats in the Chimney Hollow area of Lake Meredith, Moore County, 2 April 1981. The latest sighting was one bird at BLNWR, 30 May 1967. While the fall migration extends over a longer period, most Sanderlings have been recorded in September and October. The extreme dates are for one at Cactus Lake, Moore County, 17 July 1998, and one at BLNWR, 19 November 1978. Normally only one or two are seen at a time; the highest number on record was seven at BLNWR, 26 September 1964. My records show an equal distribution between spring and fall observations.

Semipalmated Sandpiper *Calidris pusilla* (Linnaeus)
STATUS: Fairly common to abundant migrant.

OCCURRENCE: The Semipalmated Sandpiper has been recorded in 13 counties:

Armstrong, Briscoe, Carson, Deaf Smith, Donley, Gray, Hartley, Hemphill, Hutchinson, Moore, Parmer, Potter, and Randall. Oberholser (1974) shows it in two, Parmer and Potter. It has been seen from March to November.

The true status of the Semipalmated Sandpiper in the study area is not as clear as many may think, and probably will not be until there is a selective collecting of specimens. Identification problems raised in recent years involving the Semipalmated and Western sandpipers have cast doubt on the long-held belief of regional observers that the former species greatly outnumbers the latter. Assuming that all identifications were correct, my records (1965–92) disclose that the Semipalmated was encountered more often than the Western. The Semipalmated was found 197 times and classified as uncommon (less than 10) in 31 percent of encounters, common (10 to 99) in 47 percent, and abundant (100+) in 22 percent. This can be compared to 155 encounters with the Western Sandpiper in which the corresponding figures were 49 percent, 43 percent, and 8 percent.

Phillips (1975) pointed out the difficulties in distinguishing between the two species based on sight observations of bill length and plumage alone. He claimed that call notes are better criteria: "Semi-palmated call or location note has a 'chit-chit' quality, lower pitched than the usual almost shrill 'cheep' of a Western." He concluded that "most Semi-palmated Sandpipers are safely distinguishable [from Western Sandpipers] only by voice or by bill measurements combined with careful determination of sex," and he recommended selective collecting and the use of the word "species" more often when not sure of an identification. Other helpful discussions concerning problems of identification can be found in Hayman et al. (1986) and Gratto-Trevor (1992).

Normally the Semipalmated Sandpiper does not appear in spring until late March. The early date is for 12 at BLNWR, 14 March 1971. Any March sighting is open to question, however, as returning birds are not expected in the continental United States before early April (Gratto-Trevor, 1992). The species is seldom recorded past the last week in May, the latest sighting being two at BLNWR, 10 June 1967. A month or so later, returning birds begin arriving, the earliest several near Amarillo, 10 July 1958, and most are gone by late October, the latest being one near Amarillo, Randall County, 6 November 1966.

The Semipalmated Sandpiper has been reported once in winter. On 17 December 1966, ten were observed at Lake Marvin, Hemphill County. This identification may have been in error, for the species is not recognized as present anywhere in Texas in winter (TOS, 1995). The group probably should have been reported simply as "Ereunetes sp."—the genus name at that time—as were four small "peeps" seen on the Lake Meredith (west) CBC of 27 December 1975.

Western Sandpiper *Calidris mauri* (Cabanis)

STATUS: Fairly common to abundant migrant.

OCCURRENCE: The Western Sandpiper has been recorded in 18 counties: Arm-strong, Briscoe, Carson, Castro, Deaf Smith, Donley, Gray, Hall, Hansford, Hart-ley, Moore, Ochiltree, Oldham, Parmer, Potter, Randall, Swisher, and Wheeler. Oberholser (1974) shows it in three: Deaf Smith, Randall, and Wheeler. It has been seen from February to November.

As with the Semipalmated Sandpiper, the status of the Western Sandpiper in the study area is unclear. Purdue (1969) pointed out that most observers believe the Least and Semipalmated sandpipers to be more common in the region than is the Western, but he is of the opinion this may not be the case. He provides a good discussion of the incidence of the Western Sandpiper in Oklahoma, where it has been recorded by competent observers more commonly in its southward than northward passage, and sets forth morphological and behavioral charac-teristics to watch for in distinguishing between it and the Least and Semipal-mated sandpipers. Many observers tend to base their identifications primarily on bill length and curvature, without regard to the sex of the bird, and to disre-gard the fact that there is an overlap in these characteristics with the Semipal-mated Sandpiper.

Senner and Martinez (1982) concluded, based on birds banded on the Chey-enne Bottoms Wildlife Area in southwestern Kansas, that "although western sandpipers are primarily Pacific coast migrants, some migrate to and from breeding grounds in Alaska through interior North America. On the Great Plains, numbers are small and movements irregular during spring migration, whereas in fall western sandpipers are more numerous and widespread." My records support the findings of both authors as to the preponderance of fall sightings over those of spring (30% spring, 70% fall).

The Western Sandpiper is seldom seen before mid-April or later than mid-October. Unexpected was a single bird at the sewage plant playa near Amarillo, Randall County, 1 February 1986, and two in Deaf Smith County, 18–21 No-vember 1993. Pulich (1988) cites two January and three February sightings for north-central Texas, dismissing all but one. On the South Plains the species is considered rare during January in the Lubbock area (LEAS, 1994) and irregular in January and February in Midland County (Midland Naturalists, 1992). Other-wise, the early and late dates range from four near Amarillo, Randall County, 29 March 1981, to two near Hartley, Hartley County, 24 June 1984, and from one in Parmer County, 7 July 1961, to one at BLNWR, 27 October 1968.

SPECIMENS: Specimens (14) have been taken in Castro County(5–20 September 1980, CMNH).

Least Sandpiper *Calidris minutilla* (Vieillot)

STATUS: Common to abundant migrant. Casual winter visitor.

OCCURRENCE: The Least Sandpiper has been recorded in 18 counties: Armstrong, Briscoe, Carson, Castro, Childress, Deaf Smith, Donley, Gray, Hartley, Hemphill, Hutchinson, Moore, Oldham, Parmer, Potter, Randall, Swisher, and Wheeler. It has been seen from February to December.

The Least Sandpiper is possibly the most abundant of the area's small sandpipers. Skittering flocks are a familiar sight around the margins of playas where, more often than other "peeps," they feed in vegetation growing some yards back from the shoreline. The normal arrival time in spring is early April, the earliest dates being for nine in Hutchinson County, 3 February 1995, and a single bird at the sewage pond near Amarillo, Randall County, 21–22 February 1987. In the Lubbock area the Least Sandpiper is classified as "accidental" in February (LEAS, 1994). Normally a few are still moving through as late as mid- or late May. Fischer et al. (1982) give a 29 June date, the only report for June, probably southbound birds. Few are seen past mid-November. The Least Sandpiper has been reported four times in December: nine at a playa east of Canyon, Randall County, 23 December 1969; eight at BLNWR, 17 December 1973, and five on 3 December 1978; nine at Lake Meredith, Potter County, 31 December 1973.

SPECIMENS: Twenty-three specimens are available from Castro County, all taken 5–20 September 1980 (CMNH).

White-rumped Sandpiper *Calidris fuscicollis* (Vieillot)

STATUS: Rare to uncommon migrant.

OCCURRENCE: The White-rumped Sandpiper has been recorded in four Texas Panhandle counties: Armstrong, Donley, Gray, and Randall. It has been seen from May to August.

The White-rumped Sandpiper has received little attention in the study area and its status is not well defined. Several reasons may account for this. The species is a late migrant, most passing through at a time when many observers are not looking for shorebirds; it may simply be overlooked, for large flocks of "peeps" too often are passed over without regard to species composition; importantly, not all observers are familiar with this sandpiper's high-pitched squeaky *jeet,* a call invaluable in noting its presence. Possibly the most important reason is that "most of its migration is made in a few, long, nonstop flights, each of which can last as long as 60 hours" (Parmelee, 1992)—thus reducing the number of times a flock must break its flight to forage. Hawkins (1945) probably gave the best summary of the White-rumped Sandpiper's status: "Uncommon migrant. First recorded . . . on May 6, its numbers increased until May 28 when fifty-five were counted. On June 3, fifteen were seen, and on June 20 two remained. It was next recorded on July 26." At Cheyenne Bottoms, Kansas, where much work has been done on migrating shorebirds, the extreme spring dates are 29 April and 19 June, with peak numbers occurring the last ten days of May (Parmelee, 1992).

I have dismissed the few April, September, and October sightings on record, including my own. The migratory pathway of the White-rumped Sandpiper is elliptical, passing north through the interior of the United States in spring and returning to the east in the fall along part of the Atlantic Coast (Parmelee, 1992), making most, if not all, reported fall sightings in the study area questionable. All post-July sightings must be carefully documented to be credible.

The 55 White-rumped Sandpipers Hawkins found on 28 May can be typical of numbers in late spring. On the same date in 1984, I recorded 65 in a flock at a playa southeast of Kingsmill, Gray County, and 40 were found at a playa in Armstrong County, 29 May 1997. On 30 August 1986, I encountered an injured bird, one of its legs dangling, near Amarillo, Randall County.

Baird's Sandpiper *Calidris bairdii* (Coues)

STATUS: Common to abundant migrant.

OCCURRENCE: The Baird's Sandpiper has been seen in 16 counties: Armstrong, Briscoe, Carson, Castro, Deaf Smith, Donley, Gray, Hansford, Hartley, Hemphill, Moore, Oldham, Parmer, Potter, Randall, and Swisher. Oberholser (1974) shows it in three: Parmer, Potter, and Randall. It has been recorded from March to October.

Opinions have varied concerning the status of the Baird's Sandpiper in the study area. Carlander (1934) said it was "by far the most numerous of the small sandpipers in the Panhandle," and found it more common in fall than in spring. Hawkins (1945), however, classified it as an "uncommon migrant" and suggested that because of the difficulties in identifying the various "peeps," a special study be made to rank them in order of abundance. No such study has ever been undertaken.

The Baird's is the earliest of the small sandpipers to appear in spring and can be expected in mid- or late March, the earliest record being for one in Armstrong County, 9 March 1986. Seldom are any found past mid-May. One on the BLNWR on 30 June 1973 was possibly an early southbound migrant. The first returning birds usually appear in mid-July, and most are gone by late September. The latest date is for five in Randall County, 28 October 1984.

An analysis of the fall migration brings to light an interesting phenomenon as there are two peaks in Baird Sandpiper abundance—15–30 July and 1–22 September. The latter half of the year also usually produces the greatest number.

The most I have ever encountered at one time were 400–500 (Randall County, 15 July 1966), and 500+ (Randall County, 8 August 1995). Most small sandpipers are found around the margins of playas; however, in Randall County on 15 August 1992, I observed 150 or more Baird's feeding in a recently mowed field some distance from water.

SPECIMENS: Ten specimens are available from Castro County, taken 6–20 September 1980 (CMNH).

Pectoral Sandpiper *Calidris melanotos* (Vieillot)

STATUS: Fairly common migrant.

OCCURRENCE: The Pectoral Sandpiper has been found in 13 counties: Armstrong, Briscoe, Carson, Castro, Donley, Gray, Hall, Hartley, Hemphill, Moore, Parmer, Potter, and Randall. It has been seen during the periods March–May and July–November.

Normally the Pectoral Sandpiper arrives in spring around mid-April, the early date being for four near Umbarger, Randall County, 25 March 1967. Unlike for many of the shorebirds, migration is seldom extended beyond mid-May, the latest date being for an unspecified number at BLNWR, 25 May 1970. Its return in fall is likewise condensed in time: many of the other shorebirds can be common in July, but the Pectoral is normally first seen in mid- or late August and is seldom seen beyond the third week of September. The early and late dates are for 6–8 at BLNWR, 4 July 1957, and one on the refuge, 5 November 1973. This sandpiper is not usually found in large gatherings. An exception was a group of 40+ encountered at a playa southeast of Amarillo, Randall County, 31 August 1968, in the aftermath of a severe storm. There were probably many more birds around the playa that went undetected for the observer was limited to viewing those near the road. On the following 4 September "herds in the pastures" were encountered in the same area, and on 8 September a flock of 100+.

Dunlin *Calidris alpina* (Linnaeus)

STATUS: Casual migrant.

OCCURRENCE: The Dunlin has been recorded in six counties: Gray, Moore, Parmer, Potter, Randall, and Roberts. It has been seen March–May and August–October and once in December.

The number of Dunlin sightings in the study area is quite small: *Gray*—one south of Pampa, 5 and 8 April 1988. *Moore*—four at Cactus Lake, 9 August 1997. *Parmer*—an unspecified number, 12–13 May 1961. *Potter*—three off Bates Canyon, Lake Meredith, 29 April 1979. *Randall*—at BLNWR 3–4, 31 March–11 April 1965; one, 22 October 1967; 30+, 3 September 1968; one, 25 April, 25 May, and 19 September 1970; six, 1 August 1973. The only Randall County sighting not reported from the refuge was of one bird on the sewage plant playa southeast of Amarillo, 17 December 1994; judging from its weak flight, it may have been an ill or injured bird. *Roberts*—unspecified number, September 1935.

The Dunlin is a rare to locally common migrant throughout most of Texas and is found commonly in winter along the coast (TOS, 1995). There are two winter sightings from the Lubbock area: 4 January 1974 (Williams, 1974) and 24 January 1982 (Williams, 1982).

Stilt Sandpiper *Calidris himantopus* (Bonaparte)

STATUS: Common to abundant migrant. Vagrant winter visitor.

OCCURRENCE: The Stilt Sandpiper has been found in 17 counties: Armstrong, Briscoe, Carson, Castro, Dallam, Deaf Smith, Donley, Gray, Hansford, Hartley, Moore, Ochiltree, Oldham, Parmer, Potter, Randall, and Swisher. Oberholser (1974) shows it in three: Deaf Smith, Potter, and Randall. It has been recorded in every month except January and February.

Only one observer prior to mid-century mentioned the Stilt Sandpiper. Even Hawkins's (1945) assessment of its status is unexpected, for he considered it an "uncommon migrant." Surprisingly, at the time of his writing there were few records of the species for New Mexico; Ligon (1961) considered it "one of the rarest of this large family of birds occurring in the state." Hawkins thought it remarkable to find "more than a hundred" on 6 May 1945 at BLNWR, only two counties east of the New Mexico state line.

Perhaps an explanation for this absence lies in identification. At a distance the Stilt Sandpiper can appear quite similar to the dowitcher, a common species in the area and one with which the stilt is often found in close association.

Misidentifications may occur unless close attention is paid to differences in posture, bill shape and length, feeding behavior, and call notes—as well as plumage. While in flight, the Stilt Sandpiper may even be confused with the Lesser Yellowlegs, another common migrant. As examples of its present-day abundance, concentrations of 1,000–2,000+ were recorded on the BLNWR, 1–29 August 1970, and 1,000+ on 14 August 1978. Another example is 350+ in one flock at Cactus Lake, Moore County, 10 August 1995.

With few exceptions, all Stilt Sandpipers reported during the first half of the year have occurred in May, the exceptions being single birds seen as early as 28 March 1967 in Randall County and as late as 23 June in Gray County. Southbound birds return in early July, at first a mere trickle, soon followed by a surge during the last week of July or first week of August. The earliest date is for 11 birds near Amarillo, Randall County, 6 July 1986. Most have passed through by mid-October. On 18 November 1985, a late bird was found at a playa in Armstrong County.

There have been two reported sightings of the Stilt Sandpiper in early winter, the same individual in each instance. One was found on a playa between Canyon and the PDCSP, Randall County, 21 December 1969, and again during the following Amarillo CBC of 23 December. Most likely a late migrant, it was not seen afterward. The Stilt Sandpiper winters primarily in South America from Bolivia and south-central Brazil south to northern Chile and northern Argentina, and only casually to uncommonly northward to southeastern California, the Gulf Coast and Florida (AOU, 1983), and the Lower Rio Grande Valley (TOS, 1995).

SPECIMENS: Nine specimens are available from Castro County (CMNH), all taken 6–13 September 1980.

Buff-breasted Sandpiper *Tryngites subruficollis* (Vieillot)
STATUS: Casual migrant.

OCCURRENCE: The Buff-breasted Sandpiper has been recorded in Castro, Parmer, and Randall counties of the Texas Panhandle. There have been seven sightings, all occurring during the period 28 August–13 September, as follows: an unspecified number near Friona, Parmer County, 31 August–1 September 1963; three at the sewage plant playa southeast of Amarillo, Randall County, 31 August 1968, and two there, 6 September 1971; three near Amarillo, Randall County, 6 September 1974; Fischer et al. (1982) cite an unspecified number in Castro County, 5 September 1980; one at a playa north of Dodd, southwest Castro County, 28 August 1993; and one on the BLNWR, 13 September 1993.

There have been two sightings from nearby areas: one in Crosby County, 24 April 1974, and another, 1 August 1981 (*fide* C. Stogner). The Buff-breasted Sandpiper is a rare to uncommon migrant in the eastern half of Texas (TOS, 1995).

Short-billed Dowitcher *Limnodromus griseus* (Gmelin)
STATUS: Casual migrant.

OCCURRENCE: The only county in the Texas Panhandle in which the Short-billed Dowitcher has been reported is Randall, the few sightings there limited to August and September.

The first report of a Short-billed Dowitcher was on 4 September 1972 (K. Seyffert), when one was observed at length at the sewage plant southeast of Amarillo, Randall County. There were other dowitchers in the area, but the Short-billed remained apart. The bird was also heard calling. Based primarily on calls, 12 dowitchers at the same location on 30 August 1985 (K. Seyffert) were tentatively identified as Short-billeds, as were three in Randall County, 17 August 1986 (R. Ross). Such identifications are less than satisfactory as calls alone can be unreliable. A more certain sighting was that of a group of four found at the sewage plant, 26 September 1992 (K. Seyffert). The birds were observed from a short distance for 30 minutes or longer as they fed, often calling while making short flights when disturbed. No other dowitchers were in the area. For Kansas, Thompson and Ely (1989) say: "Sight records seem to indicate that this species arrives after the Long-billed Dowitcher in the spring and before it in the fall," something area observers should keep in mind.

It is probable that more Short-billed Dowitchers occur in the study area than are reported, for it is assumed that all dowitchers encountered are the Long-billed; little or no effort is made to determine if that is truly the case. Two excellent studies on the identification of dowitchers have been published in recent years, and serious observers should avail themselves of this information (Wilds and Newton, 1983; Kaufman, 1990a). Several seasons of concentrated dowitcher-watching would clarify the status of the Short-billed in the study area.

The nearest location to the Texas Panhandle that the Short-billed Dowitcher has been confirmed is in Oklahoma, as cited by Sutton (1967): "May 18, 1937, a female in breeding feather . . . three miles south of Gate, Beaver Co." It is a rare to uncommon migrant in the eastern half of Texas (TOS, 1995).

Long-billed Dowitcher *Limnodromus scolopaceus* (Say)

STATUS: Common to abundant migrant. Casual winter visitor.

OCCURRENCE: The Long-billed Dowitcher has been recorded in all but eight counties: Childress, Collingsworth, Hall, Hemphill, Lipscomb, Roberts, Sherman, and Wheeler. Oberholser (1974) shows it in two: Parmer and Randall. It has been seen in every month except January.

Often the Long-billed Dowitcher is the earliest of the returning shorebirds in spring: it can be expected by mid- or late March. The earliest are one near Umbarger, Randall County, 6 March 1983, and one near Amarillo, Randall County, 6 March 1987. Dowitchers do not linger late in the season and are rarely found past mid-May. An estimated 180 observed at BLNWR during the last week of May 1978 were unusual. The only June records are of a single bird at BLNWR, 16 June 1973, and four at Cactus Lake, Moore County, 27 June 1998. Of note is the observation of Wilds and Newton (1983): "We are not aware of the existence of specimens or photographs supporting claims of the presence of Long-billed Dowitchers south of the breeding-grounds between June 12 and July 1."

Southbound dowitchers can be expected in the third week of July, the earliest a single bird at BLNWR, 12 July 1970, and one is rarely seen beyond the first week of November. Twelve were on the sewage plant playa southeast of Amarillo, Randall County, 14 November 1984, and five at BLNWR, 19 November 1978. Unexpected were three at BLNWR, 5 December 1987; a single bird there, 27 December 1988; and ten near Lake Tanglewood, Randall County, 19 December 1998. Five in northern Hutchinson County on 3 February 1995 are possibly accounted for by one of the mildest winters on record, while 20 in southwest Parmer County on 16 February 1994 were possibly early migrants. The species is found occasionally during winter as near as the Lubbock area (LEAS, 1994).

Flocks of 100 or more dowitchers are not uncommon and some of 500–1,000+ have been recorded at BLNWR: 10 and 17 October 1964; 5 October 1968; 16 October 1972; 22 August 1973; 27 August 1978; 25 October 1988.

SPECIMENS: Specimens have been taken in Castro (22 between 5 and 20 September 1980, CMNH), Hansford (2 August 1954, OMNH) and Parmer (5 November 1976, WTAMU) counties.

Common Snipe *Gallinago gallinago* (Linnaeus)

STATUS: Fairly common migrant. Rare winter visitor.

OCCURRENCE: The Common Snipe has been found in 19 counties: Armstrong, Briscoe, Carson, Castro, Dallam, Deaf Smith, Donley, Gray, Hall, Hartley, Hemphill, Hutchinson, Moore, Parmer, Potter, Randall, Roberts, Swisher, and Wheeler. It has been recorded in every month of the year.

Common Snipe are reported less often in spring than in fall, the first birds appearing in mid-March; the earliest date is 6 March 1983 in Castro County. By late April it is usually gone, the latest date being for one at BLNWR, 1 May 1967. The first fall sightings normally occur in late August or early September, and though the species may at times be common in mid- or late November, few are reported past then. The occurrence of the snipe in winter is irregular. This is reflected in the number of times it has been recorded on CBCs: *Amarillo*—5 of 40; *Buffalo Lake* NWR—3 of 29; *Lake Meredith* (*east*)—8 of 18; *Lake Meredith* (*west*)—6 of 24; *Quitaque*—2 of 21. There are only a dozen or so other winter records, most notably 12 in the Sanford Dam marshes, Lake Meredith, Hutchinson County, 2 December 1970, and 14 at BLNWR, 11 December 1993.

In recent years there has been speculation concerning the possibility of snipe nesting in the study area. There are two records of snipe found in July: two on the BLNWR, 17 July 1966, and one in western Carson County, 25 July 1993. Oberholser (1974) shows it in summer in Roberts County, but details are lacking. In the spring of 1992 a courting snipe was heard on the Gene Howe WMA, Hemphill County, and two courting/displaying birds were seen at the Hay Meadow Pasture on the WMA, 26 April 1998. The site was checked again on 12 May but no birds were found. The nearest confirmed nesting to the Texas Panhandle is the one in western Oklahoma cited by Sutton (1967): "June 3, 1910, nest and three eggs taken on hay-meadow ... near Kenton, Cimarron County." Ligon (1961) makes reference to snipe shown as nesting on the "Clayton Area Check-list of Birds," Union County, New Mexico.

The Common Snipe is normally seen singly or in very small groups. Notable exceptions were 105 recorded on the BLNWR on 2 November 1971, 60 on 27 March 1972, and 40+ on 23 November 1978. The totals represent accumulated numbers of snipe found scattered around the lengthy lakeshore. Twenty-three in one group were found on a playa southeast of Amarillo, Randall County, 15 November 1985.

SPECIMENS: Specimens have been taken in Hall (3 October 1975, WTAMU) and Parmer (13 November 1976, WTAMU) counties.

American Woodcock *Scolopax minor* Gmelin

STATUS: Casual migrant and winter visitor.

OCCURRENCE: The American Woodcock has been found in Hutchinson, Randall, and Wheeler counties and has been reported in February and October–December.

The first American Woodcock reported was watched from a kitchen window as it fed in a suburban flower bed in southwest Amarillo, Randall County, 14 November 1983 (J. Oelze), and was seen later by others (R. Ross, P. Acord, K. Seyffert). On 18 February 1987, another was flushed at streamside in the PDCSP (K. Seyffert). With the publication of Brown's (1981) paper on the American Woodcock in nearby Elk City, Beckham County, Oklahoma, it was learned that the species had been seen previously in the study area: "Since this sighting I have learned that *Philohela minor* has been seen irregularly during fall migration in Wheeler County, Texas . . . (*fide* Dick DeArment, Texas Parks and Wildlife Department)." An inquiry directed to that observer elicited the following statement: "I've seen them irregularly in the fall during the past 30 years. I've seen them in the Britt Ranch bottomland meadows as well as in other similar areas in the county" (letter, Richard DeArment, Wheeler, 9 February 1982). On 31 October–1 November 1995, a woodcock was observed in a residential yard in Borger, Hutchinson County (B. Foster; TP-RF). Yet another appeared in a suburban yard in Amarillo, Randall County, 25–31 December 1995 (C. and N. Turner et al.; TP-RF), only a few blocks from the 1983 discovery.

Sutton (1974a) places the American Woodcock in Oklahoma "westward exceptionally to Harper, Roger Mills, and Greer counties." The nearest locations in Texas where one has been recorded are Wilbarger County, 12 November 1982 (Pulich, 1988), and Lubbock County, 29 March 1995.

Wilson's Phalarope *Phalaropus tricolor* (Vieillot)

STATUS: Common to abundant migrant. Casual breeder. Vagrant winter visitor.

OCCURRENCE: The Wilson's Phalarope has been recorded in all Texas Panhandle counties except Collingsworth, Hall, Hemphill, Lipscomb, Sherman, and

Wheeler. Oberholser (1974) shows it in four counties: Armstrong, Castro, Deaf Smith, and Randall. The species has been seen from March to December.

The Wilson's Phalarope is the most abundant of the shorebirds in the study area, the largest gatherings occurring during the latter half of the year. This preponderance of fall numbers over those of spring is a reversal of the species' status in other areas. In north-central Texas, Neill and Kuban (1986) found phalaropes to be much more common in spring. Their ten-year study disclosed a 99 percent reduction in the number of fall migrants, and they speculated that such a reversal might be due either to the birds using different seasonal flyways or to their being less inclined toward stopovers on their way south. Spring numbers are also much greater in Oklahoma (Sutton, 1967), and in Midland County on the South Plains the ratio is at least 2:1 (*fide* F. Williams). As examples of numbers in the latter area, an estimated 10,000 phalaropes were tallied at Midland on 28 April 1962 and the same number at Lubbock on 26 April 1981 (Williams, 1981).

There is only one March record, a single bird observed on a playa near Amarillo, Randall County, 26 March 1967. An even earlier sighting was one in Lubbock County, 4 March 1990 ("the earliest on record for that area by 3 weeks"; Lasley and Sexton, 1990). By the second week of April phalaropes begin trickling through and by the last week they are abundant, gatherings often numbering in the 1,000–2,000+ range. Such abundance continues through the third week of May, after which numbers diminish abruptly. Of particular interest are the birds of early summer, for one cannot know for certain whether June phalaropes are late stragglers, early southbound migrants, or summering birds.

The volume of returning phalaropes picks up in the first week of July, and the species can be abundant by the third week (1,000+ at the BLNWR, 18 July 1970). August is the premier month. Flocks of 1,000–4,000+ have been recorded numerous times. It is difficult to estimate phalarope numbers when the birds are widely dispersed over a large body of water, and the figures I have given may well be conservative. The largest group I ever encountered was an estimated 10,000 on Cactus Lake, Moore County, 10 August 1995. Abundance continues through the first week of September, at which time numbers begin tapering off to such an extent that there is an virtual cessation during the last week of the month.

The Wilson's Phalarope is rarely reported in October. My records reveal only nine sightings during that month. The greatest number was 30 on a playa in Randall County, 18 October 1986, and the latest sighting was of two in the same county, 28 October 1986. There is one record each for November and December: a small flock was found near Canyon, Randall County, 10 November 1956, and on 14 December 1986 two were observed on the sewage plant playa in Randall County. The latter were feeding at the outlet where the warm discharge from the plant entered the lake. The Wilson's Phalarope is a bird of the plains: four flying low above the stream deep in the PDCSP on 10 May 1995 made for an unexpected and startling encounter.

NESTING: The first nesting of the Wilson's Phalarope in Texas was discovered in Carson County, 15 June 1980 (Seyffert, 1985b). An adult male with a downy chick only a few days old (captured and later released) were found at a playa one mile east of the Pantex Ordnance Plant. Another adult acting "nesty" was observed on this same playa, 24 June 1997. Five other confirmed or probable nestings have been discovered since: (1) Nine adults and seven juveniles were found at the sewage plant playa southeast of Amarillo, Randall County, 21 June 1987. (2) A pair was attending a bird in juvenal plumage at a playa three miles northeast of Dimmitt, Castro County, 24 June 1989. (3) A juvenile was observed at length on 28 June 1989 at a playa approximately five miles south of Kingsmill, Gray County. (4) Four birds in juvenal plumage were noted on 23 June 1991 at a playa six miles east of Hereford, Deaf Smith County. (5) Two adults were exhibiting alarm behavior, one attending four small downy chicks, on a playa a mile or so east of the sewage plant southeast of Amarillo, Randall County, 26 July 1992—a very late encounter. With a mean incubation period of 23 days (Colwell and Jehl, 1994), the eggs were probably laid during the last week of June. These authors give the date of latest clutch initiation in Saskatchewan as 25 June. A sixth record is of an adult with two flightless young at a playa in Carson County, 13 June 1998. The belief that the juveniles named in this account were probably hatched locally is reinforced by the fact that the first Prebasic molt of young Wilson's Phalaropes on their northern breeding grounds occurs in mid-July through August; in addition, juveniles are the last to migrate in fall, following the females and later the males (Colwell and Jehl, 1994).

There have been numerous summer sightings in other counties (Armstrong, Dallam, Hansford, Hartley, Hutchinson, Moore, Oldham) involving both individual phalaropes and what appeared to be paired birds. Those observed prior to the discovery of nesting in 1980 were always thought to be either late or early migrants. With confirmation, however, individual phalaropes or small isolated groups seen in late May through July should be investigated closely.

These summer sightings are evidence of possible widespread nesting when proper wetland habitats are available. Previous to the 1980 discovery, the Wilson's Phalarope was not known to nest any nearer the Texas Panhandle in the twentieth century than Barton and Meade counties, Kansas, and there but rarely (Johnsgard, 1979). The species formerly bred widely across the interior of North America before wetland habitats were destroyed (Colwell and Jehl, 1994).

SPECIMENS: Sixteen specimens have been taken in Castro County (5–20 September 1980, CMNH), and one in Randall County (5 May 1987, TCWC).

Red-necked Phalarope *Phalaropus lobatus* (Linnaeus)

STATUS: Rare migrant.

OCCURRENCE: The Red-necked Phalarope has been found in six Texas Panhandle counties: Castro, Gray, Moore, Oldham, Parmer, and Randall. It has been recorded May–November.

There has been but one sighting of the Red-necked Phalarope in spring: six at BLNWR, 25–30 May 1970. With the exceptions of one sighting in June, two in July, four in October, and two in November, all others were made in August and September. The June sighting was of two females in Castro County, 1 June 1992, and those in November were an unspecified number in Castro County, 21 November 1980 (Fischer et al., 1982), and a single bird near Umbarger, Randall County, 24 November 1985. In Midland County on the South Plains, all Red-necked Phalarope sightings have occurred in the fall (*fide* F. Williams). The first documentation since mid-century was made in Moore County in early September 1974 (TP-RF). On occasions the species may be seen in sizable numbers. Between 24 September and 3 October 1970, 50+ were found regularly at the BLNWR and 50+ again on 8 September 1971.

The Red-necked Phalarope migrates regularly along the North Pacific and North Atlantic coasts and less commonly but regularly through interior western North America from British Columbia and the prairie regions of Alberta, Saskatchewan, and Manitoba south (AOU, 1983).

SPECIMENS: Oberholser (1974) cites a specimen collected five miles northwest of Boise, in southwest Oldham County, 5 September 1920 ("A. J. Kirn; skin not preserved").

Red Phalarope *Phalaropus fulicaria* (Linnaeus)

STATUS: Vagrant fall migrant.

OCCURRENCE: Randall is the only county in the Texas Panhandle where the Red Phalarope has been found. Stevenson (1937) published an account of this discovery:

> There is a mounted specimen of the Red Phalarope (*Phalaropus fulicarius*) in the museum of the Panhandle-Plains Historical Society at Canyon, Texas. The bird, a female in winter plumage, was collected by L. E. Simms at a wetwater lake six miles south of Canyon, Randall County, on October 12, 1933. The specimen is labeled "Wilson Phalarope," an obvious error in identification. Apparently this is the first occurrence of the species in Texas and the record is remarkable in that this bird was obtained on the high plains of the Texas Panhandle. There are few records of this species from the interior of the United States.

Repeated attempts to correct this mislabeling failed, and it was not until 1998 that the error was corrected.

During the years following the 1933 discovery, 21 documented sightings of the Red Phalarope have been accepted by the TBRC (Lasley and Sexton, 1995a). The one nearest the study area was a single bird on the Muleshoe NWR, Bailey County, 18 September 1982 (TP-RF). Five others reported on the South Plains were undocumented: Crosby County, 14–16 October 1979, and 28–30 September 1984; Lubbock County, 19 September 1982, 12–21 September 1983, 17–22 September 1985, and 16 October 1996. Another specimen was collected on 4 October 1968 just east of Boise City, Cimarron County, Oklahoma (Sutton, 1969), and one in Comanche County, Oklahoma, 10 September 1977 (Tyler, 1979b). A single bird was observed near Clayton, Union County, New Mexico, 24 September 1996 (Williams, 1997).

The Red Phalarope migrates along both coasts of North America and only irregularly and casually through the interior (AOU, 1983).

Family Laridae (Jaegers, Gulls, and Terns)

Parasitic Jaeger *Stercorarius parasiticus* (Linnaeus)
STATUS: Vagrant fall visitor.
OCCURRENCE: There have been two sightings of the Parasitic Jaeger in the Texas Panhandle, both in Randall County. The first was an adult dark-phase bird in breeding plumage that I observed on the BLNWR, 14 September 1969. My attention was drawn to a dark gull-like bird by the loud cries of a Franklin's Gull that it was closely pursuing. The gull was trying desperately to evade the larger bird when the chase was broken off as the two neared where I stood on a point projecting into the lake. The jaeger then flew by at little more than eye level and at no great distance. A dark gull-like bird was again seen on the lake the next day; however, it remained beyond good viewing distance and supporting confirmation by others could not be made.

I observed an adult light-phase bird in breeding plumage on the BLNWR, 22 September 1970, watching it at length through binocular and scope as it rested on the lakeshore and circled overhead in short flights. While it was in the air, the pattern of the tail and its length were seen clearly. Later the bird left the lake, flying in a southwesterly direction and gaining altitude as it disappeared from sight.

The Parasitic Jaeger is a summer resident of the far north, and it migrates along the Pacific and Atlantic coasts and casually inland (AOU, 1983). In Texas it is considered to be a rare to uncommon migrant and winter visitor along the coast and in offshore waters (TOS, 1995).

Laughing Gull *Larus atricilla* Linnaeus

STATUS: Vagrant spring visitor.

OCCURRENCE: There are but two records of the Laughing Gull in the Texas Pan-handle. The eight reported near Friona, Parmer County, in late May 1963 (Baumgartner, 1963) were in fact seen on 2 June (*fide* C. D. Littlefield). A first winter bird was observed on a playa on the southern outskirts of Amarillo, Randall County, 13–14 September 1999 (K. Seyffert, P. Acord, L. Jalbert, E. Kutac, B. McKinney). Just outside the study area, half a mile south of the Castro County line, a single Laughing Gull was seen in Lamb County 30 May 1990, and four on 3–4 June (C. Littlefield). All were subadults.

There have been four reports of the Laughing Gull on the South Plains: an unspecified number in Lubbock County, 24–26 May 1975 (Williams, 1975); one at White River Lake, Crosby County, 7 August 1980 (Williams, 1981); one in Lubbock County, 18–23 October 1983 (*fide* C. Stogner); and one in Lubbock, 21 April 1992 (*fide* C. Stogner).

The Laughing Gull has been reported four times in nearby areas of Oklahoma. Tyler (1979b) names two sight records for Comanche County: one at Lake Ellsworth, 3 June 1971, and one in Altus, 23 June 1967. More recently, Maisel (1985) cites three adult Laughing Gulls a few miles southeast of Arnett, Ellis County, 3 June 1982, and Shackford (1986a) cites one adult gull at the sewage lagoons at Boise City, Cimarron County, 23 June 1985.

The Laughing Gull is an abundant resident along the coast, with an increasing number reported inland in recent years, usually in summer and fall (TOS, 1995).

A word of caution is in order when reporting inland Laughing Gulls. Too often it is assumed that there are no real problems in separating the Laughing Gull and Franklin's Gull in the field. As pointed out by Kaufman (1990a) and Lehman (1994), however, one-year-old Franklin's are often misidentified as adult Laughing Gulls. Some first-summer Franklin's have wingtip patterns with no obvious white and many develop a lot of black on the head, forming almost a complete hood, as in the Laughing Gull. Franklin's Gulls of this age group tend to wander inland in summer away from breeding grounds. Area observers should become conversant with these and other identification problems.

Franklin's Gull *Larus pipixcan* Wagler

STATUS: Fairly common to abundant migrant. Casual summer visitor.

OCCURRENCE: The Franklin's Gull has been observed in 15 counties: Briscoe, Carson, Deaf Smith, Donley, Gray, Hall, Hartley, Hemphill, Hutchinson, Moore, Ochiltree, Oldham, Potter, Randall, and Wheeler. It has been seen from March to November.

This gull is found most abundantly during fall. It would probably be reported in greater numbers in spring if more attention were directed to farming activities, for a characteristic behavior of this species is to follow the plow, feeding on organisms uncovered. The earliest spring date is for one bird at Amarillo, Randall County, 4 March 1984. Normally it is early April before the first ones are seen. In spring they are most common from mid-April to mid-May, and the largest number ever reported at one time in that season was 200+ at the BLNWR, 8 May 1969. There have been a few years in which Franklin's Gulls summered on the BLNWR: an unspecified number in 1957; up to 35 in 1969; ten in 1970; eight in 1973. In each of the years there had been a die-off of fish. On 21 June 1996, six were seen in Potter County, and on 28 June 1997, one on Cactus Lake near Etter, Moore County. No indications of nesting have ever been observed: the species has never been known to nest nearer the Texas Panhandle than Iowa (Johnsgard, 1979). Sutton (1967) says that oversummering Franklin's Gulls in Oklahoma are mostly immatures.

The Franklin's Gull normally returns in fall in late August or early September. Illustrative of high fall numbers are the following from the BLNWR: 2,000–3,000, 21 October; 3,000–5,000, 7–24 October 1959; 1,000–2,000, 23–31 October 1965; 1,000+, 29 October 1967; 1,100, 12 October 1971. Hawkins (1945) speaks of a concentration on the refuge in October as showing up "at a distance as a snowy blanket covering several acres." On one occasion (10 October 1955) "flocks of five or six and up to twenty moved almost continuously over Amarillo from 2:00 to 5:00 P.M." (P. Acord). The latest sighting on record is of one bird at Lake Meredith, Hutchinson County, 26 November 1972. Oberholser (1974) shows a winter sight record for Randall County, but details are lacking.

SPECIMENS: There is a specimen collected in Randall County (23 April 1974, WTAMU). Oberholser (1974) shows specimens taken in Briscoe and Hall counties, without naming where they were deposited.

Bonaparte's Gull *Larus philadelphia* (Ord)

STATUS: Rare migrant and winter visitor.

OCCURRENCE: The Bonaparte's Gull has been reported in nine counties: Briscoe, Castro, Carson, Deaf Smith, Donley, Hutchinson, Moore, Potter, and Randall. It has been seen from October to May.

The first reported occurrence of the Bonaparte's Gull was an unspecified number in Deaf Smith County in November 1949. No others were reported until two were encountered on the BLNWR, 24 November 1966. The species has been seen fairly regularly since, primarily during fall and winter.

There have been one March and two April sightings: one at Lake Meredith, Potter County, 21 March 1971; one at Lake Tanglewood, Randall County, 3–4

April 1976; two on Greenbelt Lake, Donley County, 22 April 1998. The latest spring record is of one at the BLNWR, 19 May 1979. Fall birds are not to be expected until late October, the earliest being one at the BLNWR, 22 October 1972. The Bonaparte's Gull is found in greatest numbers during winter. Notable were 135 on Lake Meredith on 2 January 1972, 30 on 18 December 1971, and 47 on 27 December 1975. The species has been recorded on seven of 42 CBCs at Lake Meredith (1970–96). The latest winter sighting is of eight birds off Bates Canyon, Lake Meredith, Potter County, 15 February 1971.

Ring-billed Gull *Larus delawarensis* Ord

STATUS: Common to abundant winter visitor. Rare to uncommon summer visitor.
OCCURRENCE: The Ring-billed Gull has been recorded in 23 counties. Those missing are Hall, Lipscomb, and Sherman. Oberholser (1974) shows it in two. It has been seen in every month.

The Ring-billed is the most common of the gull species found in the study area. The largest gathering ever reported was 3,000 at BLNWR, 27 October 1962. On 3 January 1970, 75 were wintering on the refuge when a die-off of fish occurred. By 14 January, 500 had assembled, increasing to 2,200 by 4 April. Another notable concentration was 1,500–2,000 on Lake Meredith, 30 December 1971–10 January 1972. This body of water is by far the largest that any CBC encompasses, registering gulls more often and in greater number than any other—in all of the (east) counts (average 115) and all but two of the (west) counts (average 69). During the early years of the Amarillo count, only playas were available, and then only when ice-free, and gulls were never recorded. It was only with the incorporation of Lake Tanglewood and the Amarillo sewage pond that gulls began to be seen—on 21 of 33 counts (average 15). The BLNWR has contained water only intermittently since the early 1970s; as a result, the species has been found on only 15 of 29 counts (average 32). Diminutive Lake Theo on the Quitaque count always contains water but rarely attracts gulls, and the ring-billed has been tallied only three times (5, 2, 1). Wintering gulls are also found in the cities. As an example, 115 wintered on Lawrence Lake in Amarillo in the 1980–81 season, fanning out across town during the day to feed at shopping centers and fast food establishments.

In most years the number of gulls begins declining rather rapidly after February, a few nonbreeders remaining into summer. A movement of returning birds may at times be discerned in late August, but usually it is October before this happens.
SPECIMENS: A specimen on display taken in Potter County (ACMNH) is without date.

Herring Gull *Larus argentatus* Pontoppidan

STATUS: Rare to uncommon winter visitor. Casual summer visitor.

OCCURRENCE: The Herring Gull has been seen in ten Texas Panhandle counties—Castro, Childress, Deaf Smith, Donley, Hansford, Hutchinson, Moore, Parmer, Potter, and Randall—and has been recorded in every month.

The only early observers who mentioned the Herring Gull were Stevenson (1942) and Hawkins (1945), both of whom concur with its present status. Sizable numbers are seldom reported, and those few reports are suspect. As an example, 500 were reported at BLNWR, 31 January 1970. When visiting the refuge in January, I recorded 20 on the 4th and 50 on the 25th. By the 31st, 500 may have gathered, but this seems unlikely. USFWS records also show from 175 to 300 on the refuge between 18 November and 2 December 1961, and 135 on the CBC of 23 December 1968. My records show only six on the refuge on 15 December of 1968. It is probable that many of the gulls identified as Herring Gulls were in fact Ring-billed Gulls. Numbers on the other BLNWR CBCs range from 1 to 40. Other area CBCs more accurately reflect the normal numbers of Herring Gulls present: *Amarillo*—1–2; *Lake Meredith* (*east*)—1–4; *Lake Meredith* (*west*)—1–2.

There does not seem to be a definable pattern in the dates of the Herring Gull's arrival and departure. It is rarely reported before early October or later than mid-April. The following are my own out-of-season sightings, all recorded at BLNWR: one, 3 May 1964; one, 9–23 May 1965; one, 10 June and 23 July 1967; one, 19 August 1973; one, 31 July 1986.

SPECIMENS: There is one specimen each from Castro (4 November, WTAMU), Hutchinson (6 January 1969, WTAMU), and Parmer (May 1977, WTAMU) counties. Oberholser (1974) shows a May 1 bird taken in Childress County without giving details.

Thayer's Gull *Larus thayeri* Brooks

STATUS: Vagrant winter visitor.

OCCURRENCE: There has been one reported sighting of the Thayer's Gull in the Texas Panhandle. On 26 February 1967 a gull identified as a Thayer's was found on a playa south of Amarillo, Randall County—"watched for nearly two hours as it rested and fed with Herring Gulls and Ring-billed Gulls" (L. Galloway). At the time *L. thayeri* was considered a race of Herring Gull (*L. argentatus thayeri*), and it was not elevated to species status until 1973 (AOU, 1973).

While serving on the TBRC and reading numerous accounts of gulls thought to be Thayer's, it became clear to me how difficult it is to identify the species in the field or, for that matter, sometimes when in hand. It is necessary that the observer be thoroughly familiar with both Thayer's and similar gull species of all age classes and plumage phases—Glaucous, Iceland, Glaucous-winged, and

Herring. Even some photographs proved inconclusive. As of 12 September 1995, only 20 of 46 sightings of Thayer's Gulls submitted to the TBRC had been accepted (Lasley and Sexton, 1995a). A discussion of the identification problems surrounding the first accepted specimen for Texas can be found in Pulich (1980). Students also are encouraged to consult Lehman (1980) and Kaufman (1990a).

The Thayer's Gull winters "primarily on the Pacific coast from southern British Columbia south to central Baja California, less commonly in south-coastal and southeastern Alaska, the Gulf of St. Lawrence and the eastern Great Lakes (Erie and Ontario), casually in the interior south to southern Arizona, southern New Mexico, and the Gulf coast of Texas and west-central Florida (St. Petersburg), and casually on the Atlantic coast to Maryland. . . ." (AOU, 1983). It is a rare winter resident on the Texas coast and still rarer inland (TOS, 1995).

Glaucous Gull *Larus hyperboreus* Gunnerus
STATUS: Casual fall to spring visitor.
OCCURRENCE: The Glaucous Gull has been found in Carson, Deaf Smith, Potter, and Randall counties of the Texas Panhandle. It has been reported November–March and once in May.

Lacking details, the first reported sightings of the Glaucous Gull in the study area are those shown by Oberholser (1974). His spring Deaf Smith County reference is based on a bird seen in May 1939. The spring reference for Randall County involved a second-winter bird found on the BLNWR, 10 and 15 March 1957. A third sighting occurred during the BLNWR CBC of 26 December 1979. This individual, also a second-winter bird, was found in close association with Ring-billed and Herring gulls, and was last seen on 2 February 1980 (TP-RF). Another second-winter Glaucous Gull was observed on a playa in Carson County, 14 March 1980 , possibly the same bird seen previously some 50 miles to the southwest on the BLNWR. The two latest sightings, both first-winter birds, were one at the sewage plant playa southeast of Amarillo, Randall County, 7–9 December 1985 (TBRC), and one at MediPark Lake in Amarillo, Potter County, 20 January 1996 (TBRC).

There have been 54 accepted sightings of the Glaucous Gull in Texas, only ten of them inland from the coast (Lasley and Sexton, 1995a). The nearest to the Texas Panhandle that a specimen has been collected is Ute Lake, Quay County, New Mexico, March 1976 (Hubbard, 1978). On the Muleshoe NWR, Bailey County, 3–8 were reportedly seen, 22 February–8 March 1951, and a single bird was reported on 21 January 1985 (*fide* C. Stogner).

The Glaucous Gull winters along the Pacific and Atlantic coasts and in the Great Lakes region (AOU, 1983).

Sabine's Gull *Xema sabini* (Sabine)

STATUS: Casual fall visitor.

OCCURRENCE: The Sabine's Gull has been observed four times in the Texas Panhandle, once in August, twice in September, and once in October. Three of the sightings occurred in Randall County and one in Castro County.

The first sighting was of a subadult at BLNWR, 12 October 1969 (K. Seyffert). The bird was observed for an hour or longer as it foraged along the shore; when at rest it could be approached to within a few yards. In a protected bay not far distant was a mixed group of some 100 or more Franklin's and Ring-billed gulls, but the Sabine's remained apart. The preceding days had been a period of extremely high winds: on the day this gull was seen the wind was blowing 30–40 mph from the north with temperatures in the low 30s. There had been only six reported sightings of the species in Texas prior to this discovery (Lasley and Sexton, 1995a). The second Panhandle sighting took place on 23 September 1973 (TPAS), again a subadult at BLNWR. The bird was approached as closely as 30 yards, and it too kept aloof from the Franklin's and Ring-billed gulls in the area. The third sighting was of two subadults on the sewage plant playa southeast of Amarillo, Randall County, 7–11 September 1987 (D. Myers; TBRC). Lastly, a Sabine's Gull was found in southwest Castro County, 26–28 August 1993 (C. D. Littlefield).

There have been four additional sightings from nearby areas: Lubbock, 24 October 1970 (TBRC; TP-RF); Crosby County, 13 September 1981 (Williams, 1982); Texas County, Oklahoma, 15 September 1988 (Grzybowski, 1989); Lubbock County, 25–31 August 1993 (Lasley and Sexton, 1994a).

During migration the Sabine's Gull is found regularly along the Pacific coast from Alaska to northern Baja California and Costa Rica, and along the Atlantic Coast from Labrador to New England (AOU, 1983).

Black-legged Kittiwake *Rissa tridactyla* (Linnaeus)

STATUS: Vagrant fall to spring visitor.

OCCURRENCE: The Black-legged Kittiwake has been seen in one county in the Texas Panhandle—Randall—in November, December, and March.

The first sighting of this kittiwake was of one in first-winter plumage at BLNWR, 28 November 1967 (P. Acord, M. Mayfield, R. Ross), a bird watched for some 30 minutes or longer. It was seen again on 2 December (USFWS). The second sighting was of one observed on Lake Tanglewood during the Amarillo CBC, 21 December 1975 (P. Acord, E. Stevens), its age class not specified. The latest sighting was of a first-winter bird found in 1978 on Lake Tanglewood (the only gull present), on 19 March (K. Seyffert, P. Acord; TBRC) and 21 March (B. & K. Zimmer).

There have been two sightings of Black-legged Kittiwakes in Lubbock County—6 November 1976 (Williams, 1977) and 15 November 1980 (Williams, 1981), and another in Crosby County on White River Lake, 7 November 1982 (*fide* C. Stogner). The Black-legged Kittiwake winters along the Pacific Coast south to northwestern Baja California and along the Atlantic Coast to North Carolina (AOU, 1983).

Caspian Tern *Sterna caspia* Pallas
STATUS: Vagrant spring visitor.
OCCURRENCE: The Caspian Tern has been reported in two counties of the Texas Panhandle, Randall and Roberts.

A Caspian Tern seen in Roberts County on an unspecified date in 1935 is listed in the notes of Harold Saunders. Oberholser (1974) did not recognize the discovery, although he did accept others submitted by this observer, some of which were of species equally out of range. On 31 May 1964, three Caspian Terns were watched at length at the BLNWR (K. Seyffert). Other than a few Black Terns, no other tern species or gulls were present. Another Caspian was reported on the refuge on 1 November 1969 (USFWS).

There are several reports of the Caspian Tern from nearby areas. In Oklahoma Sutton (1974) named a midsummer record for Roger Mills County (date not given)—perhaps in reference to a sighting south of Durham, 26–28 August 1966—and Byard (1979) reported a single bird three miles south of Keyes, Cimarron County, 1 May 1978. More recently, terns were observed on Clayton Lake, Union County, New Mexico, 5 June 1986 and 22 August 1987 (Hubbard, 1987). The South Plains have provided three sightings: six birds at White River Lake, Crosby County, 14 September, and two in Lubbock, 16–17 September 1975 (*fide* C. Stogner); and one in Lubbock, 15 August 1994 (Lasley and Sexton, 1995b).

The Caspian Tern is a common resident along the Texas coast but only a rare migrant and winter visitor in the eastern half of the state (TOS, 1995).

Common Tern *Sterna hirundo* Linnaeus
STATUS: Casual migrant.
OCCURRENCE: The Common Tern has been reported in Randall and Roberts counties of the Texas Panhandle. It has been seen in May, July, August, and September.

Without a specimen or photograph, the listing of the Common Tern for the study area rests on shaky grounds. The questionable validity of sight records is set forth forcefully by Sutton (1967): "Thirty terns of general appearance of *S. hirundo* collected since 1951 in an effort to obtain that species have proved to be *S. forsteri,* so all sight records of *hirundo* are doubtful and most published

summary statements concerning Oklahoma probably apply to *forsteri*." This belief is supported by Thompson and Ely (1989) for Kansas. Anyone who thinks
identifying medium-sized terns in the field is easy should devote time to reading
what Kaufman has to say (1990a).

The following is a listing of reported Common Tern sightings in the study
area: *Roberts*—one in September 1935. *Randall*—at BLNWR, two on 27 July 1958,
two on 2, 5, and 20 September 1964, one on 19 September 1971, and five on
21 May 1973; one near Amarillo, 30 August and 3 September 1968; one near Canyon, 21 May 1983.

The Common Tern is a common fall migrant along the coast and off-
shore, less common in spring (TOS, 1995). It is considered accidental on the
South Plains (LEAS, 1994). Two were photographed in Lubbock, 7 October 1995
(TP-RF).

Forster's Tern *Sterna forsteri* Nuttall

STATUS: Rare to uncommon migrant.

OCCURRENCE: The Forster's Tern has been found in 15 counties: Briscoe, Carson,
Castro, Donley, Gray, Hansford, Hartley, Hemphill, Hutchinson, Moore,
Parmer, Potter, Randall, Roberts, and Swisher. It has been seen from April to Oc-
tober.

The Forster's Tern can be expected from the last week in April to the third
week in May, and from the third week in July to the last week in September. The
early and late spring dates are: two on Lake Rita Blanca, Hartley County, 16 April
1996; one at BLNWR, 20 May 1979 and 20 May 1984. The early and late fall dates
are: one on a playa south of Amarillo, Randall County, 12 July 1986; two at
BLNWR, 7 October 1979. A bird in first-winter plumage was observed on Palo
Duro Lake, Hansford County, 4 June 1996, and Fischer et al. (1982) name a date
of 10 June (year not given) for either Castro or Parmer County (number not
given). A Forster's Tern was reported at Lubbock on the very late date of
21 November 1991 (Lasley and Sexton, 1992).

My records reflect seeing the Forster's Tern only 59 times in 22 of the 33
years. The sightings by month are: April, 5; May, 16; June, 1; July, 7; August, 13;
September, 14; October, 3. The most I ever recorded at one time were 17 on the
BLNWR, 22 April 1967, and 2.9 was the average number. The 1,000 shown on the
BLNWR by the USFWS for 24–31 October 1964 should perhaps be questioned.

Least Tern *Sterna antillarum* (Lesson)

STATUS: Uncommon breeder locally.

OCCURRENCE: The Least Tern has been recorded in 12 counties: Briscoe, Childress,

Donley, Gray, Hall, Hansford, Hemphill, Hutchinson, Oldham, Potter, Randall, and Roberts. It has been seen from April to September.

Most references to the Least Tern involve birds observed on their nesting grounds. Stevenson (1942) classified the species as a "rare migrant." Of a dozen Least Terns observed in three years of study, Hawkins (1945) considered only four as summering and the others as transients. I have seldom encountered one outside areas of known breeding. Other than Potter and Randall counties, Oldham County is the farthest west that the species has been reported (16 May 1998).

NESTING: The following are the counties in which the Least Tern has been confirmed nesting or where its presence indicated possible nesting. *Childress* and *Hall*—in 1984 and 1985 TPWD biologists conducted helicopter, fixed-wing aircraft, and ground surveys of the Red River for possible nesting sites of the Least Tern (Thompson, 1984; McCament, 1985). On 26 June 1984, a nesting colony was found 1 km east of the Hwy 83 bridge north of Childress, Childress County, and on 28 June, a colony 0.5 km west of the same bridge and another about 16 km northwest of Estelline, Hall County. The latter site is approximately halfway between the Hwy 287 bridge north of Estelline and the FM 657 bridge to the west. In 1985 only the Hwy 83 bridge sites north of Childress were surveyed; nesting terns were again found. In June of 1987 all the sites were surveyed by fixed-wing aircraft. Nesting was observed north of Childress and adults were seen north of Estelline (David Rideout, TPWD, pers. comm.). In July 1998 the Childress site was revisited and two colonies of nesting terns were found. *Donley*—one Least Tern on the Clarendon BBS, 10 June 1969, in the Lelia Creek–Salt Fork of Red River area; six terns approximately five miles downstream from the Greenbelt Lake dam on the Salt Fork of Red River the first week of June 1972; one on Greenbelt Lake, 26 May 1995; one on Taylor Lakes WMA, 7 July 1997. *Gray*—one at Lake McClellan, 12 June 1955 and an unspecified number, 23–24 June 1956. *Hansford*—three at Palo Duro Lake, 4 June 1994, and one, 2 June 1995. This is a recently constructed impoundment on Palo Duro Creek; the birds may have been strays from the tern colony at Optima Reservoir, Texas County, Oklahoma, located some 20 miles to the north, where the species has been reported nesting since 1985 (Hill, 1993). *Hemphill*—it is on the Canadian River east of Canadian that most summering Least Terns have been found. Beginning with McCauley (1877—"Occasionally a few were noted on the Canadian"), the species has been found fairly regularly in summer. The following accounts either entail actual nesting or point to possible/probable nesting: 7–8 adults feeding young at Lake Marvin, 3–5 July 1954; 4–5 adults feeding young, 5 June 1955; and four at the lake, 5 July 1971. On 14 June 1977, I discovered a colony of ten nests with eggs on a sandbar a short distance upriver from Lake Marvin. Nesting terns continue being found fairly regularly in that area. The Thompson (1984) and McCament (1985) studies also involved extensive surveys of the Canadian River in search of nesting terns. On 26 June 1984, the river was flown by helicopter from Borger, Hutchinson County, east to the Oklahoma state line. Twenty-five terns were seen between the Hwy 207 bridge north of Borger and Canadian, but no nests were found. Twenty-one terns were seen between Canadian and the state line. On the previous 8 June, a helicopter/ground survey had turned up nesting terns about 11 km ESE of Canadian, and a ground survey found 17 adults and six juveniles in early July about 16 km WNW of Canadian near the Hemphill-Roberts county line. In 1985, the two sites were again occupied by nesting terns. *Hutchinson*—Thompson (1952) collected an adult male in breeding condition in the Bugbee Creek area, 4 July 1950: "In addition . . . several terns were observed as they flew along Bugbee Creek. Probably the birds were breeding at this locality, but no nests were found." *Potter*—one near the "upper canyon" on the Canadian River, 27 May 1956. *Randall*—4–5 on the BLNWR, 9–10 June, and two, 23–24 June 1956. *Roberts*—three nests with eggs discovered on an oil well site in the Canadian River bed approximately ten miles west of Canadian, 23 June 1976. Four adult terns were seen flying near this site, 4 July 1978.

In 1985 the USFWS listed the interior population of the Least Tern (*S. a. athalassos*) as Endangered (50 *Federal Register* 21, 784–21, 792). All encounters with the species in the study area should be reported, particularly when nesting is found or suspected.

SPECIMENS: There is a single specimen taken in Hutchinson County (4 July 1950, TNHC).

Black Tern *Chlidonias niger* (Linnaeus)

STATUS: Uncommon to common migrant.

OCCURRENCE: Oberholser (1974) shows the Black Tern in seven Texas Panhandle counties: Castro, Dallam, Donley, Hartley, Parmer, Potter, and Randall. Eleven others have been added: Armstrong, Briscoe, Carson, Deaf Smith, Gray, Hemphill, Moore, Ochiltree, Oldham, Sherman, and Swisher. It has been seen from May to November.

The Black Tern is the most common of the tern species found in the study area. First arrivals in spring can be expected in early or mid-May and latest departures in fall during late September. The extreme dates are for one on Lake Theo, Caprock Canyons SP, Briscoe County, 1 May 1977, and one on the BLNWR, 17 October 1964. Ten at Lubbock on 9 March 1975 were "six weeks ahead of schedule" (Williams, 1975), and the early date for Kansas is 20 March (Thompson and Ely, 1989).

Black Terns normally pass through in small groups. My records (1964–92) reveal an average flock size of 14 birds. The most I have ever seen at one time were 200+ on the BLNWR, 7 May 1972. Far larger gatherings for the refuge are on record. As an example, a peak of 4,000 was recorded on 13 October 1960 (USFWS). If that figure is anywhere near correct, it points to a drastic decline in Black Tern numbers since. In recent years, 80 at Canyon, Randall County, 20 May 1983, and 50–70 on the BLNWR, 1 September 1996, were thought remarkable.

In most years it is difficult to tell with accuracy when migration ends in spring and recommences in fall. Generally speaking, it terminates in late May and resumes in mid-July. My records for 33 years (1964–96) show seeing terns in summer (June–July) in 29 of these years, and then only in small numbers. The nearest to the Texas Panhandle that the Black Tern has been known to nest is Barton County, southwestern Kansas, where there is one definite record (Johnsgard, 1979).

ORDER COLUMBIFORMES

Family Columbidae (Pigeons and Doves)

Rock Dove *Columba livia* Gmelin

STATUS: Common to abundant resident.

OCCURRENCE: The Rock Dove is found in every Texas Panhandle county during every month of the year.

In reading past accounts of species of birds found in the study area, the inquirer can only conclude that the Rock Dove has no history worthy of note. Even today it is a bird rarely mentioned although often encountered. As far as birders are concerned, it occupies a corner of consciousness discrete from that of other species and is thought of not as a wild creature to be admired and given attention but rather as a familiar domestic animal that roams free. Few, if any, observer records provide data on the Rock Dove, concerning either its introduction and dispersal or the ebb and flow of its population. For most of us it gained legitimate status when awarded recognition as a species to be included on CBCs. Only then did data begin to be accumulated; however, unless the count circle includes a town or grain elevator, it is seldom recorded.

Rock Doves are widely dispersed across the study area, but large concentrations normally are found only around feedlots, grain elevators, and railroad yards. These doves nest throughout most of the year except during molt and some winter periods. Most nests are found on man-made structures, particularly those of a nonmodern design, although of late years the birds have learned to exploit highway overpasses. Small numbers have reverted to the status of being truly "rock" doves, occupying the rocky escarpments of canyonlands. An accessible location where this can be observed is in the South Prong of Caprock Canyons SP in Briscoe County.

SPECIMENS: Seven specimens are available from Randall County (WTAMU).

Band-tailed Pigeon *Columba fasciata* Say

STATUS: Casual summer, fall, and winter visitor.

OCCURRENCE: The Band-tailed Pigeon has been found in four counties: Hemphill, Parmer, Potter, and Randall. It has been seen June–September and November–December.

This montane species has been recorded six times in the study area: a pair near Lake Marvin, Hemphill County, 13 July 1954 and for several weeks thereafter (Oberholser, 1974); one in Amarillo, Potter County, 4 November 1967; one near Friona, Parmer County, 12 December 1970; one at BLNWR, 3 June 1974 (photo); one in McBride Canyon, Lake Meredith Recreation Area, Potter County, 29 June 1975; and one at BLNWR, 28 September 1980.

A Band-tailed Pigeon was observed on the Muleshoe NWR, Bailey County, 1 October 1941, and another was found dead in Lubbock County, 28 April 1984 (*fide* C. Stogner). The nearest locations to the Texas Panhandle where the Band-tailed Pigeon breeds are the montane areas of Colorado, New Mexico, and western Texas (AOU, 1983).

Eurasian Collared-Dove *Streptopelia decaocto* (Frivaldszky)

STATUS: Resident locally.

OCCURRENCE: The Eurasian Collared-Dove has been found in three counties of the Texas Panhandle: Parmer, Potter, and Randall. It has been seen in every month.

It was on 3 September 1996 that confirmation of the area's first Eurasian Collared-Dove was made, a calling bird videotaped in Canyon, Randall County (A. Schoenhals, M. Schoenhals, K. Seyffert; TP-RF). The lone bird was soon joined by another, and a few days later by yet a third. One to three birds continued being seen in the neighborhood thereafter by several observers. Prior to the confirmation, an unidentified dove had been observed visiting a nearby yard as far back as the previous July. Numerous Ringed Turtle-Doves were visitors also and little attention was paid them other than in noting one bird that appeared somewhat larger and had a much different call. On 1 March 1997 a pair of collared-doves was observed courting at this location, and on 7 July the pair was accompanied by a begging juvenile. A pair acting "nesty" was again observed on

18 February 1998. Several collared-doves are now resident in the city. The species has since been found at other locations: Amarillo, Potter County, 27 January 1997; Farwell, Parmer County, 21 February 1997 (TP-RF); Kerrick, Dallam County, 19 August 1999; Gruver, Hansford County, 26 August 1999 (TP-RF); Stratford, Sherman County, 3 September 1999 (TP-RF); near Wildorado, Deaf Smith County, 28 September 1999; Vega, Oldham County, 1 and 15 October 1999; and Happy, Swisher County, 26 February 2000.

The first Eurasian Collared-Doves in the Americas were brought to Nassau in the Bahamas from the Netherlands in the early 1970s. Some escaped from captivity in 1974 and quickly spread throughout most of the islands. From there, the doves are believed to have immigrated to Florida in the late 1970s or early 1980s (Smith, 1987). The ensuing population explosion and expansion westward brought the species to the borders of Texas in the mid-1990s. That the next reported sightings have come from extreme northwest Texas, far from the initial eastern arrival sites in the state, might lead one to think that the Panhandle birds were either raised locally or brought into the area by bird fanciers. The evidence is otherwise, however, for no collared-doves are known to have been imported, and the history of the species' expansion in Europe shows that it often appeared several hundred miles from the nearest known nesting site, with backfilling eventually occurring in suitable areas (Smith, 1987).

White-winged Dove *Zenaida asiatica* (Linnaeus)
STATUS: Year-round visitor and uncommon resident locally.
OCCURRENCE: The White-winged Dove has been recorded in 15 counties: Armstrong, Carson, Castro, Collingsworth, Dallam, Deaf Smith, Donley, Gray, Hansford, Hemphill, Lipscomb, Moore, Oldham, Potter, and Randall. It has been seen in every month.

Concerning the first report of a White-winged Dove in the study area, McCauley (1877) cited "a single specimen noted along one of the southern creeks." The creek to which he referred was probably located in Armstrong, Briscoe, or Randall county. Another White-winged Dove was not reported until the mid-twentieth century.

Reports by decade are as follows: *1950s*—one in Amarillo, 2 June–29 July 1956. *1960s*—one at BLNWR, 9–16 October 1965. *1970s*—one on the Weymouth ranch in southeastern Moore County, 8 October 1970; one at BLNWR, 6 and 9 May 1972, 19 and 21 May 1973 (TP-RF), 3 June and 30 August 1974, and 15 August 1975; one in Amarillo, Potter County, 11 May 1979. *1990s*—the incidence of sightings exploded during this decade and the species became established in Amarillo and Canyon—in one section of Amarillo 14+ could sometimes be seen in a day. Birds also were found at other locations: one at Lake Marvin,

Hemphill County, 17 July 1990; one near Lazbuddie, Castro County, 18 April 1993; one in Clarendon, Donley County, 23 May 1993; one in PDCSP, 6–7 October 1995, 18 February 1996, 27 April 1997, April–May 1997; one on the Salt Fork Ranch, Collingsworth County, 13 January 1996; one at BLNWR, 20 May 1996; one in Thompson Grove Picnic Area near Texline, Dallam, County, 22 May 1996; one in Pampa, Gray County, 5–7 July 1996; 18–20 on the outskirts of Panhandle, Carson County, first week of August 1996; one or more on the Tom Green Ranch in Oldham County in 1996 and 1998; one near Walcott School north of Boot Leg, Deaf Smith County, 12 August 1997; one in Kress, Swisher County, 26 December 1997; one in Gruver, Hansford County, 23 May 1998; one in Darrouzett, Lipscomb County, 10 June–July 1998. Confirmation of nesting has yet to be made.

The White-winged Dove is a common summer resident in Texas north locally to Waco, and east along the coast to Galveston Island, along the Rio Grande to El Paso County and inland to Jeff Davis County, and spreading in recent years north and east (TOS, 1995).

Mourning Dove *Zenaida macroura* (Linnaeus)

STATUS: Fairly common to abundant resident.

OCCURRENCE: The Mourning Dove has been recorded in all 26 Texas Panhandle counties and in every month of the year.

McCauley (1877) speaks of an abundance of Mourning Doves in the Texas Panhandle in the late nineteenth century. One hundred years later the BBS averages give an indication of its present abundance: *Childress*—107; *Booker*—77; *Channing*—57; *Miami*—45; *Pantex*—45; *Texline*—41; *Waka*—37. All the counts are reflecting a long-term decline. Most Mourning Doves withdraw from much of the northern half of the study area in winter, while in the more southerly portions numbers are highly variable, as reflected in the CBCs. The following figures show number of counts, number of years recorded, average number, and high: *Amarillo*—40, 20, 16, 235; *Buffalo Lake* NWR—29, 17, 10, 86; *Friona*—12, 5, 5, 14; *Lake Meredith (east)*—18, 5, 28, 114; *Lake Meredith (west)*—24, 18, 29, 143; *Quitaque*—21, 21, 72, 503. As can be seen, the Quitaque count situated below the caprock escarpment is the most productive. Interestingly, Hawkins (1945), while classifying the Mourning Dove as a "common summer resident," does not speak of it as being present in winter. In fact, he says most leave the High Plains before the hunting season opens on September 1. In late February or early March there is a noticeable increase in the number of returning doves, and by late March and early April nesting has begun. On 12 July 1997 an albino Mourning Dove was observed in Amarillo.

NESTING: The Mourning Dove is a common nesting species throughout the study area. Is it as common today as formerly? Certainly Russell's (1935) assessment of its status in the PDCSP is no longer true: "Western Mourning Doves are probably the most numerous nesting birds in the Palo Duro Canyon. Hundreds of the doves nest throughout the canyon." A review of my May–July records for the 15-year period 1978–92 shows that the Mourning Dove is the sixth most common breeding bird in that state park, exceeded by the Northern Cardinal (almost three times as many), Northern Mockingbird, Golden-fronted Woodpecker, Painted Bunting, and Scaled Quail. There is an insignificant difference in numbers between the Mourning Dove and the Bewick's Wren, Mississippi Kite, and Bullock's Oriole and a small difference from the Lark Sparrow, Bushtit, and Rufous-crowned Sparrow. If the present trend continues, within the next 15 years the European Starling and Brown-headed Cowbird will equal or surpass the Mourning Dove as a breeding species.

Nesting begins in March and terminates in September: a nest with two young being brooded was recorded in Caprock Canyons SP, Briscoe County, 20 March 1977, and a recently fledged bird was seen at BLNWR, 21 September 1986. The Mourning Dove builds its nest in a wide variety of trees and shrubs, and it is not unusual to find nests early in the season placed on the ground where the vegetation has not yet become too high. A nest once used may be occupied repeatedly. I found such a nest containing one egg at BLNWR, 4 April 1971; on 11 April it contained two eggs, and on 18 April it was empty. The same nest held two eggs on 25 April and two young on 9 May. On 29 May it once again contained two eggs—the third set for the same nest. From 14 May to 10 June 1967 (BLNWR), a period of 28 days, I observed with regularity an adult dove on the same nest; on the latter date it contained two eggs. The TBBAP found CO nesting in 53 survey blocks, PR in 63, and PO in 11, spread throughout the study area.

SPECIMENS: Specimens have been taken in Hall (TCWC), Lipscomb (21 April 1986, WTAMU), Potter (February and June 1969, WTAMU), and Randall (22 February and 1 September 1939, WTAMU) counties. Oberholser (1974) cites specimens from Dallam and Randall counties but fails to give details. He classified the specimen from Dallam County as the race *Z. m. marginella*.

Inca Dove *Columbina inca* (Lesson)

STATUS: Rare to uncommon local resident.

OCCURRENCE: The Inca Dove has been seen in 18 counties: Briscoe, Carson, Castro, Dallam, Deaf Smith, Donley, Gray, Hartley, Hemphill, Hutchinson, Lipscomb, Moore, Oldham, Parmer, Potter, Randall, Roberts, and Swisher. It has been recorded in every month.

A permanent resident from Costa Rica north to Mexico, the Inca Dove spread into the southwestern United States in relatively recent times (Mueller,

1992): to Texas in 1866, Arizona in 1872, and New Mexico in 1924. Expansion northward in Texas continued—it was found at Big Spring, Howard County, in 1958 (Baumgartner, 1958) and in Lubbock County in 1974 (Williams, 1974)—to the extent that in recent years it has become a resident as far north as the study area. Its arrival is part of a widespread population expansion, and extralimital sightings continue to be made in growing numbers in other parts of the North American continent as far north as Canada (Graham and Wormington, 1993).

Eighty-eight years after reaching Texas, the first Inca Dove was reported in the study area on 12–13 October 1954 near Vigo Park, Swisher County. Twenty-three years elapsed before another was found. From the third week of November 1977 to the end of winter, one was seen regularly in west Amarillo, Potter County. The incidence of sightings increased steadily thereafter, as the species continued to spread across the Panhandle. In Amarillo Inca Doves have become rather common in several sections of the city. As examples, 20 were observed in one neighborhood during the summer of 1990, and 50–60 visited another yard during the winter of 1991–92 where an extensive feeding program was in place. A dozen or more wintered in Canyon, Randall County, in 1993–94, where the species has since become resident, and up to 18 at a time were seen in Hereford, Deaf Smith County, during the same winter. The first Inca Dove in the PDCSP was observed on 24 May 1979, and the species has been found there intermittently since. Other sightings in Randall County occurred on the Currie Ranch near Lake Tanglewood, 16 October 1983; at Ceta Glen, South Ceta Canyon, 15–16 October 1988; and on the BLNWR, 2 November 1996.

Inca Doves have been found in other study area counties: *Briscoe*—one at Cottonwood Lake southwest of Quitaque, 19 December 1984, and one in Caprock Canyons SP, 19 October 1997; *Carson*—one in Panhandle in December 1986; *Castro*—one on 5 and 11 October 1992 and 30 July 1993 and six in Dimmitt, 3 February 1996; *Dallam/Hartley*—found with regularity in Dalhart beginning in the early 1980s; *Deaf Smith*—1–3 in Hereford, 4 August 1989 (TP-RF) and regularly thereafter; *Donley*—reported in the Clarendon area in the mid-1990s; *Gray*—one in Pampa in the autumn of 1982, 3 February 1991, August 1994, 8 and 28 November 1996. *Hemphill*—first seen in summer of 1994 on the Gene Howe WMA, and at least two or three in the spring and summer of 1995; *Hutchinson*—an unspecified number in Borger in August 1993, followed by others in later years; *Oldham*—first reported in Vega, 19 October 1992, and regularly and in growing numbers thereafter; *Roberts*—up to 11 at one time in Miami in the second week of February 1995; *Swisher*—two or more in Kress, 9 April 1996 and thereafter. Oberholser (1974) shows a winter sight record for Lipscomb County, without giving details.

NESTING: The first confirmed nestings of the Inca Dove occurred in Amarillo, Potter/Randall County, during the summer of 1992: a nest containing two young late May (TP-RF); a fledgling rescued from a city street on 30 June; and an adult with two young on 16 July. Following these discoveries, a pair was found nesting in Borger, Hutchinson County, in 1995, bringing off a brood in May and renesting on 1 June. Another Inca Dove sitting on a nest, its back covered with snow, was observed in Borger, 21 February 1998. An adult on a nest on 14 April 1996 in Kress, Swisher County, was also early, and one in Canyon, Randall County, was observed on the late date of 8 October 1996.

SPECIMENS: Specimens have been collected in Oldham (3 September 1993, TCWC) and Potter (24 October 1988, TCWC) counties.

Common Ground-Dove *Columbina passerina* (Linnaeus)

STATUS: Vagrant summer visitor.

OCCURRENCE: The Common Ground-Dove has been reported in two counties of the Texas Panhandle, Donley and Randall.

A single Ground-Dove was observed feeding with several Mourning Doves on the BLNWR, 15 May 1974. The USFWS files disclose others reportedly seen on the refuge: one, 28 May 1974; two, 14 June 1975; four, 1 June 1976—all without supporting details. Two flying birds were seen from a short distance on the Taylor Lakes WMA, Donley County, 22 November 1995, by a person familiar with the species.

The Common Ground-Dove is an uncommon to locally common resident from South Texas north to Galveston and Bastrop counties and west to Brewster County (TOS, 1995). It is listed as "accidental" in April, May, September, October, and November in the Lubbock area (LEAS, 1994) and has been reported in nearby Jackson and Woodward counties in Oklahoma (Baumgartner and Baumgartner, 1992).

ORDER CUCULIFORMES

Family Cuculidae (Cuckoos and Roadrunners)

Black-billed Cuckoo *Coccyzus erythropthalmus* (Wilson)

STATUS: Casual migrant.

OCCURRENCE: The status of the Black-billed Cuckoo in the Texas Panhandle is uncertain. All reported sightings have occurred during fall, the time of year when the species could be confused with the juvenile Yellow-billed Cuckoo.

Also, none has been reported since 1978. Have observers become more cautious in their identifications?

The reported Black-billed Cuckoo sightings are as follows: one in the PDCSP, 24 August 1952; one at Friona, Parmer County, 23–28 August 1966; one at the BLNWR, 21 September 1974 and 14 September 1975; one in Amarillo, Potter County, 23 August 1978. Two of the sightings were supported with brief notes, and the Friona bird was seen over a period of several days by a competent observer.

The paucity of sightings is unexpected as the Black-billed Cuckoo has been found nesting in nearby Oklahoma. Sutton (1967) notes that a "female shot on May 26, 1936, in locust shelter belt near Arnett, Ellis County, had been incubating eggs"; moreover, he said the species was "almost as common as the Yellow-billed Cuckoo" in that county. He reported two other specimens collected as well as a bird seen in Cimarron County. On 7 May 1963 and 29 July 1972, one was found near Durham, Roger Mills County. Dowler et al. (1978) cite a specimen collected in Lubbock County in September 1974, and a Black-billed Cuckoo was found in Lubbock, 13 October 1989 (TP-RF). There is one other record for the South Plains: a single bird in Crosby County, 15 September 1979 (fide C. Stogner).

The question remains: since the species does occur in the study area, why have none been seen in spring? Perhaps if the eastern counties were birded more intensively that question would be answered.

Yellow-billed Cuckoo *Coccyzus americanus* (Linnaeus)
STATUS: Fairly common to common breeder.
OCCURRENCE: The Yellow-billed Cuckoo has been found in every county except Carson and Sherman, and has been seen from April to October.

Although placed on the Blue List of the National Audubon Society (Arbib, 1971), the Yellow-billed Cuckoo is thought to be holding its own in the study area. McCauley (1877) spoke of it as "found frequently on Mulberry, McClellan, and other creeks, some distance from their heads," and Thompson (1952), referring to its status along the Canadian River in Hutchinson County, said: "Cuckoos gave evidence of their presence at all times during the morning and afternoon in the cottonwoods and sumac thickets. They were one of the chief components of the riparian avifauna." While perhaps not a "chief" component in that area today, the cuckoo is still an important part of it. Habitat destruction that may have occurred has been offset by the introduction of other habitats favorable to the species, such as settlements (towns, ranch and farm lots) and the planting of shelterbelts. Stevenson (1942) considered the Yellow-billed

Cuckoo a "common summer resident of timbered canyons," and Hawkins (1945) thought it a "fairly common summer resident in wooded canyons." A two-year breeding bird census made in riparian habitat in the PDCSP yielded an average density of seven per 100 acres (Seyffert, 1967–68).

The Yellow-billed Cuckoo is one of the last of the summer residents to return in spring, on average near mid-May. The earliest date is that of single birds at both Amarillo and BLNWR, 26 April 1956. By late September most have departed. There are five October records, the latest one in Pampa, Gray County, 11 October 1996. The BBSS do not give a good indication of the Yellow-billed Cuckoo's status because only a few of the routes include proper habitats. The *Childress* count is the most representative of the eastern counties with an average of six per count. The averages on the others are: *Booker*—0.4; *Channing*—0.4; *Miami*—1.7; *Pantex*—0; *Texline*—0.05; *Waka*—0; *Clarendon*—4.3. The only cuckoo I ever registered on the Texline survey was a single bird on the Rita Blanca National Grasslands miles from nesting habitat (11 June).

NESTING: Nesting dates range from June to September. The earliest is that given by Hawkins (1945), who found two nests in the Palo Duro Club near Canyon, Randall County, 10 June 1945. The latest is 24 August 1974 at BLNWR, a nest with adult; on 1 September it contained two young with pin feathers just emerging. Most egg dates on file are for July and August. The TBBAP found CO nesting in 10 survey blocks, PR in 26, and PO in 11. Other than in the Hereford quadrangle, Deaf Smith County, no cuckoos were discovered in the southwestern sector of the study area. Unreported at the time was a pair that raised young in southwestern Castro County in 1992. The only quadrangles in the northwestern sector where the cuckoo was found were Buffalo Springs (Dallam County) and Dalhart West (Lake Rita Blanca, Hartley County), and none were found in Hansford and Sherman counties in the north-central sector. Cuckoos were found in the Stallwitz Lake quadrangle southwest of Dumas in Moore County, in the Boys Ranch West and East quadrangles along the Canadian River in Oldham and Potter counties, in the Vega North quadrangle in Oldham County, and in the Umbarger and Dawn quadrangles west of Canyon, Randall County. So few discoveries outside the Canadian River Valley point to the scarcity of the Yellow-billed Cuckoo west of the 102nd meridian.

SPECIMENS: Specimens have been taken in Armstrong (10 August 1936, TCWC), Hall (4 September 1976, WTAMU), Hutchinson (10 and 13 June 1950, TNHC), Ochiltree (18 June 1985, TCWC), Potter (31 May 1982, TCWC), and Randall (11 August 1956, June 1992, TCWC; 11 August 1939, April 1970, WTAMU) counties. Oberholser (1974) shows specimens collected in Armstrong, Lipscomb, Oldham, and Randall counties, all without details.

Greater Roadrunner *Geococcyx californianus* (Lesson)

STATUS: Uncommon to common resident.

OCCURRENCE: The Greater Roadrunner has been reported in all the Texas Panhandle counties except Castro and Deaf Smith, and has been seen year-round.

The roadrunner is most often associated with the canyonlands, the Canadian River breaks, and the mesquite-brush plains. It may, however, turn up almost anywhere. I encountered one as it crossed a busy street and entered an alley in downtown Amarillo (25 July 1992) and another walking down my driveway near the central city, 29 August 1998! McCauley (1877) spoke of the roadrunner as "first observed in the Canyon of Red River, below the summit of the plain, where the chaparral surrounded us. . . . The species was frequently observed subsequently whenever we descended from the top of the plain to the canyons of the streams." Stevenson's (1942) assessment of it as a "common resident of the canyons and mesquite-covered plains of the region; occasionally noted on open farm lands," conforms to its present distribution. Hawkins (1945), however, thought it an "uncommon permanent resident of the canyons" and did not speak of finding it elsewhere.

The roadrunner is usually found singly and rarely occurs in groups of more than two or three birds. It perhaps is more appropriate to speak of it in terms of the chances of seeing one in a day's outing rather than as an average number likely to be found. The BBSS reflect those chances in early June: *Childress*—81 percent; *Clarendon*—75 percent; *Channing*—30 percent; *Miami*—9 percent. It has never been recorded on the Booker, Pantex, Texline, or Waka counts. These figures are based on 50 roadside stops, each of three minutes duration, made over a 24.5-mile route. The CBCs reflect the roadrunner's status in early winter. Their results, however, can hardly be compared with those of the summer BBSS, for the rules of the game are much different: a CBC is an all-day count with results based on the efforts of more than one individual. The chances of a roadrunner being recorded on a CBC are as follows: *Amarillo*—74 percent; *Buffalo Lake* NWR—31 percent; *Friona*—8 percent; *Lake Meredith (east)*—89 percent; *Lake Meredith (west)*—79 percent; *Quitaque*—76 percent. I participated in the majority of the counts and the most roadrunners I ever recorded on any CBC was 12 (Quitaque).

The PDCSP is a good location in which to find the roadrunner, but even there the chances of seeing one can be highly variable. To determine just how much so, I selected three years of my records at ten-year intervals, resulting in the following: 1970—32 percent chance; 1980—75 percent chance; 1990—64 percent chance.

NESTING: The earliest date of nesting activity was a courting pair at BLNWR, 16 March 1997. A "cooing" male was encountered in Chimney Hollow, Lake

Meredith, Moore County, 13 February 1996. A nest with four eggs was found at BLNWR as early as 24 April 1998, and another with six eggs in the Buck Creek area west of Wellington, Collingsworth County, 27 April 1991. The latest was a nest with four eggs in the Lake Meredith Recreation Area, Hutchinson County, in August 1968. Such dates indicate that the roadrunner is two-brooded. The TBBAP found CO nesting in 11 survey blocks, PR in 10, and PO in 19. The species was found in only one quadrangle in the southwest sector (Umbarger) and in none of the northern tier of counties.

SPECIMENS: Greater Roadrunner specimens exist for Donley (26 July 1970, WTAMU), Hall (8 February 1977, WTAMU), Hemphill (25 January 1929, MFVZ), Moore (MCHM), and Randall (22 August 1939 and October 1966, WTAMU) counties. Oberholser (1974) shows specimens taken in Armstrong (spring) and Lipscomb (summer) counties, without giving details. The Armstrong County citation may be based on the pair of roadrunners collected by McCauley (1877) in the "Red River Canyon" on 20 May 1876. Oberholser also shows eggs collected in Oldham County, again without giving details. An albinistic bird was killed at Lake Tanglewood, Randall County, in the summer of 1988 but was not preserved.

ORDER STRIGIFORMES

Family Tytonidae (Barn Owls)

Barn Owl *Tyto alba* (Scopoli)
STATUS: Uncommon to fairly common resident.
OCCURRENCE: Of the 26 study area counties, the Barn Owl has failed to be recorded in three—Childress, Roberts, and Wheeler. It has been observed in every month of the year.

Although it is classified as a resident, there are few winter records of the Barn Owl. I have recorded it only four times in winter and it has been reported only three times on CBCs. I cannot but believe that the Barn Owl is more common in winter than these few records indicate, and that with more "owling," more would be found. The Barn Owl is almost strictly nocturnal, and observers are apt to overlook it during the day unless one is flushed by chance.

An increase in Barn Owl activity is discernible as early as the third week in March, continuing through April and mid-May and reaching a climax in the last two weeks of May. A movement in fall can be discerned in late August and early September, and most owls are gone by mid-October. It is probable that these movements are not all of a migratory nature but are the result of increased nesting activity in spring and postnesting dispersal in fall. An increase in activity in spring is a certainty: drive down any busy highway during that season and you will encounter an alarming number of dead or injured owls lying alongside the road. It was thought that 18–20 caught in two wooded migrant traps near Texline, Dallam County, 18 September 1992, may have been migrants (NMOS, 1995). As can be seen, much remains to be learned about the distribution and status of the Barn Owl in the study area.

NESTING: The Barn Owl has been confirmed nesting in 14 counties: Carson, Castro, Dallam, Deaf Smith, Gray, Hansford, Hartley, Hemphill, Hutchinson, Lipscomb, Moore, Parmer, Potter, and Randall. The TBBAP found the species in ten survey blocks, a surprisingly low number. Night searches, however, were not made in any of the quadrangles.

SPECIMENS: Specimens have been collected in Carson (ACNHM; 11 March 1979, TCWC), Hutchinson (LMAWM), Oldham (11 June 1978, TCWC), Moore (MCHM), Parmer (September 1975, MTTU; 29 December 1986, TCWC); Potter (6 June 1977, TCWC); Randall (21 May 1991, TCWC; 23 April 1973, WTAMU), Sherman (1981, WTAMU), and Swisher (December 1975, MTTU) counties. The Carson (TCWC) and Parmer (TCWC) county specimens were identified as the subspecies *T. a. pratincola*.

Family Strigidae (Typical Owls)

Western Screech-Owl *Otus kennicottii* (Elliot)

STATUS: Vagrant fall visitor.

OCCURRENCE: What the distribution and status of the Western Screech-Owl in the Texas Panhandle may be is unknown. Little or no collecting of owls has been done; everything remains to be discovered. The single record of one came to light during the preparation of this manuscript when the Museum of Natural History at the University of Kansas, Lawrence, provided me with a computer printout listing their Texas collection. Therein was listed a specimen of *O. aikeni* that was taken in Parmer County, Texas, 11 September 1957. At the time *O. kennicottii* was known under its subspecific name of *O. a. aikeni*; it was not until recently that it was elevated to species status (AOU, 1983).

The nearest to the Texas Panhandle that the Western Screech-Owl has been collected is Cimarron County in the Oklahoma Panhandle (Grzybowski, 1983). Only specimens of *kennicottii* have been taken along the Cimarron River in the northwest and north-central sections, while farther downriver in the Elkhart area of Morton County, Kansas, only specimens of *asio* have been taken, leaving a gap of about 35 miles between the two populations. The only screech-owls recovered along the North Canadian River farther south were *asio* in central

Texas County. In Colorado the Western Screech-owl is classified as an uncommon to fairly common resident on the southeastern plains as far east as western Bent County and southern Baca County (Andrews and Righter, 1992). There is a record of one heard in northeast Union County, New Mexico ("near the species' easternmost limit"), 24 May 1994 (Williams, 1994), and one responded to a taped call at Tucumcari, Quay County, New Mexico, 25 May 1997 (Williams, 1997).

Discovering and mapping the distribution of screech-owls in the Texas Panhandle is a project worthy of an enterprising student. Attempts at finding the Western Screech-Owl in the study area have thus far been desultory at best. Marshall (1967) collected an owl specimen near Tascosa, Oldham County, that proved to be the subspecies *O. a. maxwelliae.* Taped calls of both screech-owls have been played in the Lake Tanglewood and Timbercreek areas in Randall County without eliciting responses other than from easterns, and alleged sightings of westerns in the PDCSP have been unsupported. Distinguishing between the two species by sight alone is difficult without having the birds in hand, and even then it takes experience to tell them apart. An excellent discussion of these problems of identification can be found in Kaufman (1990a). Efforts to discover the Western Screech-Owl in the Panhandle should be directed to areas in the far western counties.

The Western Screech-Owl is an uncommon and local resident in the Trans-Pecos, occurring east to Kerr County (TOS, 1995).

Eastern Screech-Owl *Otus asio* (Linnaeus)

STATUS: Uncommon to fairly common resident.

OCCURRENCE: The Eastern Screech-Owl has been recorded in 13 of the 26 Texas Panhandle counties: Armstrong, Briscoe, Donley, Gray, Hall, Hemphill, Hutchinson, Lipscomb, Oldham, Potter, Randall, Roberts, and Wheeler. Of these, Oldham is the only far western county. The species has been seen in every month.

The Eastern Screech-Owl is a species for which we have little data. What there is has been acquired in relatively recent years. McCauley (1877), Carlander (1934), Russell (1935), and Stevenson (1942) make no mention of it, and Hawkins's (1945) account is terse: "Rare permanent resident." Oberholser (1974) says it is "largely absent from middle and southern Panhandle (breeding unconfirmed), where rare," and Johnsgard (1979) says it "is not known to breed in the Texas panhandle."

Contrary to these few references, the Eastern Screech-Owl today has a fairly widespread presence, and breeding does occur. It is found throughout the eastern counties, in the more heavily wooded habitats in the Canadian River Valley and tributaries (Hemphill to Oldham County), in Palo Duro Canyon and its feeder canyons, and in the parks, cemeteries, and old-growth wooded residential areas of towns. Prior to the winter of 1988–89, the Eastern Screech-Owl had been recorded only twice on the Amarillo CBC. Those birds had been found by chance; however, when taped owl calls began being used, the species began to be registered regularly. It has been recorded only once each on the Quitaque, Lake Meredith (west), and BLNWR counts. Undoubtedly owls would be found regularly on the Lake Meredith count were taped calls utilized, particularly in the Rosita, Bonita, Chicken, and Coetas creeks and in the McBride Canyon section of the national recreation area.

NESTING: Nesting has been confirmed in five counties: *Gray*—four juveniles at Lake McClellan, 17 July 1977; *Hemphill*—nest with young in Wood Duck box on the Gene Howe WMA, summer of 1988; *Hutchinson*—five young in the Bugbee Creek area, 20 June 1950 (Thompson, 1952); *Potter*—a family group of six juveniles in Amarillo, 29 June 1988; *Randall*—four young in Canyon, summer of 1914 (Reeves and Reeves, 1914–36—"one reddish brown, the others gray"); "In 1945 five young were raised in a nesting box erected for Wood Ducks at Palo Duro Club," near Canyon (Hawkins, 1945); an adult with two juveniles in the PDCSP, 30 June 1967. The TBBAP found CO nesting in two survey blocks (Amarillo East and Canadian East), PR in three (Wheeler, The Palisades, Fortress Cliff), and PO in four (Skellytown NW, Alibates Ranch, Rockledge, Parnell).

SPECIMENS: A specimen has been taken in Hutchinson County (20 June 1950, TNHC). This is the one collected by Thompson (1952): "Its juvenal plumage has made definite subspecific identification . . . impossible, but Sutton has suggested the possibility that it may be *O. a. aikeni*." Marshall (1967) makes reference to an *O. a. maxwelliae* ("of an intermediate population known as *swenki*") tape-recorded at a branch of the Canadian River near Tascosa, Oldham County. Oberholser (1974) names the subspecies found in the Texas Panhandle as *O. a. swenki* based on sight records from Lipscomb (late June 1903, A. H. Howell), Potter (2 February 1921, A. J. Kirn), and Randall (A. I. Hibbets, 1937) counties. *Swenki*, synonymous with *maxwelliae*, is a subspecies not shown by Gehlbach (1995) as present in the Texas Panhandle (although his lines of demarcation are only "approximate"): he names only *hasbroucki*. The TOS (1995) acknowledges both—*maxwelliae* in the north and *hasbroucki* in the south. It is evident that extensive collecting should be done to clarify the distribution of subspecies of Eastern Screech-Owls in the study area.

Great Horned Owl *Bubo virginianus* (Gmelin)

STATUS: Fairly common to common resident.

OCCURRENCE: The Great Horned Owl has been recorded in every Texas Panhandle county except Sherman and would be there with better coverage. It has been seen during every month.

This large owl can be found in a wide variety of habitats, including woodlands, farm and ranch lots, shelterbelts, riparian lowlands, canyonlands, towns, and occasionally on the plains with only a few scattered trees. For so large a bird, its presence often goes undetected. I once encountered a pair with regularity during a period of ten or more consecutive years, roosting in a juniper at the head of a side canyon at BLNWR. CBC averages and highs give an indication of the Great Horned Owl's status in early winter: *Amarillo*—1 (5); *Buffalo Lake NWR*—3 (8); *Lake Meredith (east)*—2 (5); *Lake Meredith (west)*—2 (6); *Quitaque*—0.2 (2). Little or no "owling" was done during these counts. The BBSS give no indication at all of its summer status.

NESTING: Nesting has been confirmed in 13 counties: Armstrong, Childress, Dallam, Deaf Smith, Donley, Hartley, Hemphill, Hutchinson, Lipscomb, Moore, Oldham, Potter, and Randall. The earliest occupied nest reported was for a pair at an old Swainson's Hawk nest at BLNWR, 14 February 1971, and an adult was seen on a nest near Clarendon, Donley County, 18 February 1997. I once encountered a fully grown juvenal-plumaged bird perched on a rocky outcropping at BLNWR, 30 May 1970. I was able to approach the young bird without alarming it and sat down close by, carrying on a one-sided conversation for several minutes before an adult owl flew in and lit on the cliffside opposite. The young owl promptly flew to the older bird with apparent ease. The TBBAP found CO nesting in 11 survey blocks, PR in eight, and PO in ten.

SPECIMENS: Specimens have been taken in Briscoe (17 March 1966, WTAMU), Carson (ACMNH), Childress (15 August 1976, OMNH), Hartley (7 March 1939, WTAMU), Hemphill (31 January 1929, MVZ), Hutchinson (LMAWM; 29 June and 3 July 1950, TNHC), Moore (3 November 1960, TCWC), and Randall (30 September 1939, P-PHM; 18 September 1939, WTAMU) counties. The two from Hutchinson County were identified as nominate *virginianus*, and the one from Hemphill County as the subspecies *pallescens*. Russell (1935) speaks of specimens of both *pallescens* and *occidentalis* in the Panhandle-Plains Historical Museum in Canyon that were taken in the Palo Duro Canyon. These races probably intergrade in the study area.

Burrowing Owl *Athene cunicularia* (Molina)

STATUS: Fairly common to common breeder. Rare winter visitor.

OCCURRENCE: The Burrowing Owl has been found in every Texas Panhandle county and has been recorded in every month.

McCauley (1877) tells of the great number of Burrowing Owls he encountered in the Texas Panhandle when the plains were still occupied by an almost continuous prairie dog town: "Both upon the great plain itself and on the rolling prairies from Dodge, Kansas, to the south, up to its edge, scarcely a town of Prairie

Burrowing Owl

Dogs was without its owlish sentinel. In many of them, they seemed to outnumber the other inhabitants, the road south of the Cimarron being still remembered for its large number of birds." The owls of that day were subject to a danger they no longer face: "We were upon the Staked Plain when the owlets were of just the size for a delicious morsel." Such extensive prairie dog towns no longer exist, and this comical little owl has been greatly reduced in numbers as a consequence.

The status of the Burrowing Owl in winter is unclear and warrants further study. Are the few that are found resident birds or migrants from the north?

Early observers classified the species as a "permanent resident" and made no distinction between summer and winter populations. A study by Butts (1976) on the winter status of the Burrowing Owl in the Oklahoma Panhandle is revealing, and his discoveries perhaps apply to the study area as well:

> Apparently only six Burrowing Owls wintered in prairie dog towns of the eastern Oklahoma Panhandle (5114 sq. km) in 1970–71, or approximately 1% of the population there in late July 1970. Owl populations increased very sharply but sporadically during March. No evidence of extensive winter food caches was found. Although no evidence suggested that wintering owls ever entered a state of hibernation or torpor, they may have fasted for at least 3 days during blizzard conditions without suffering mortality. Results of the limited winter banding studies indicated that the small population of wintering owls were permanent residents rather than migrants from the north.

A study of Burrowing Owls made by Ross (1974) in the southwestern Texas Panhandle (primarily Swisher and Parmer counties) was inconclusive as to whether the birds were sedentary or represented different waves of migratory populations—"or a combination of both." The study cites the recovery of two banded owls: an adult from El Paso, Texas, banded in Swisher County, and an adult female near Jalisco, Mexico, banded in the Oklahoma Panhandle. The fact that others banded in Swisher County in 1968 were recovered two years later at the banding site "confirms that some owls overwinter in the same area of their summer nesting sites or where they were hatched."

The scarcity of wintering Burrowing Owls in the study area is indicated by the CBCs: *Amarillo*—4 of 40, high 1; *Buffalo Lake NWR*—9 of 29, high 4; *Friona*—5 of 12, high 6; *Lake Meredith (east)*—0; *Lake Meredith (west)*—0; *Quitaque*—2 of 21, high 1. Some of the dog towns on the outskirts of Amarillo that are checked regularly disclose a few wintering owls almost yearly. For example, 11 were observed west of town on 11 January 1998. In most years there is a noticeable increase in number beginning in early March, and few are seen past late October.

NESTING: The TBBAP discovered CO nesting in 32 survey blocks, PR in 15, and PO in 12. No nestings were found in the southeastern counties of Donley, Collingsworth, Hall, and Childress, although owls have been recorded in them at other times. The large majority were found west of the 101st meridian. No egg dates are available, but sightings of fledglings are common. One of the largest prairie dog towns remaining in the area is one of 1,100 acres in extent on the Pantex Ordnance Plant in Carson County. The density of owls on this acreage is unknown, but along a short section lying adjacent to a public road, 41 owls were observed on 12 July 1995, many of them juveniles.

SPECIMENS: Specimens have been taken in Deaf Smith (28 October 1981, WTAMU),

Gray (10 June 1979, TCWC), Hutchinson (LMAWM); Moore (MCHM); Potter (11 December 1986, TCWC), Randall (10 September 1939, P-PHM; 17 August 1992, OSU; 30 August 1977 and 10 April 1983, TCWC; 6 August and 30 September 1939, 10 March 1968, April 1981, and 3 October 1987, WTAMU), and Sherman (16 October 1987, WTAMU) counties. Oberholser (1974) names specimens taken in Briscoe, Lipscomb, and Oldham counties without giving details. He placed the birds in the race *A. c. hypugaea,* as was the one from Potter County. Many of these specimens are road kills, a fate to which the Burrowing Owl is highly susceptible.

Barred Owl *Strix varia* Barton

STATUS: Rare resident in the eastern one-third.

OCCURRENCE: The Barred Owl has been recorded in Donley, Gray, Hemphill, Potter, and Randall counties, and has been seen in every month except March, May, August, and October.

The only area where the Barred Owl has been reported with regularity is the Canadian River Valley stretching east of Canadian to Lake Marvin, Hemphill County. Oberholser (1974) cites a summer specimen taken in Gray County, a spring and summer sight record for Potter County, and a winter sight record for Randall County, but I have been unable to determine the basis of all of them. The Gray County specimen is likely the bird collected by McCauley (1877): "This specimen was secured in one of the deeply shaded groves along Lower McClellan Creek. . . . None were noticed at any headwaters of the streams . . . owing to the smaller size of the timber." It was an adult female taken on 21 June 1876. The expedition on that date was in the area of present-day Lake McClellan (Hunnius, 1876), where the habitat remains favorable today. I can account for the spring Potter County sight record (A. J. Kirn, 5 April 1920, Amarillo) but not the summer one. The Randall County sighting is possibly based on the birds reported on the BLNWR CBC of 29 December 1967. The count result lists five Barred Owls and one Great Horned Owl—surely an error in reporting! I am dubious that any Barred Owl was on the refuge, despite the fact that the USFWS records show four Barred Owls still present the following day. My records show that I visited the refuge on 15 December and found four Great Horned Owls, the species to be expected. On 17 December 1996, two Barred Owls were heard in the Lelia Lake Creek area of Donley County, and on 3 January 1997, one owl was observed at close range and another was heard nearby.

The western limits of the Barred Owl in Oklahoma are Woodward, Roger Mills, Greer, and Jackson counties (Baumgartner and Baumgartner, 1992). It is listed as "accidental" in the Texas South Plains (LEAS, 1994). To the southeast of the study area, there are nesting records from as near as Wilbarger County (Pulich, 1988).

SPECIMENS: The only specimen available is McCauley's (1877) for Gray County. The subspecies found in the study area is *S. v. georgica* (TOS, 1995).

Long-eared Owl *Asio otus* (Linnaeus)
STATUS: Uncommon winter visitor. Vagrant breeder.

OCCURRENCE: The Long-eared Owl has been reported in 13 counties: Carson, Castro, Dallam, Deaf Smith, Gray, Hall, Hemphill, Hutchinson, Parmer, Potter, Randall, Sherman, and Swisher. It has been recorded in every month except July and August.

The Long-eared Owl is encountered most commonly during spring (early March–early May). Communally roosting birds have often been observed, particularly in the extensive stands of salt cedar at the upper end of the BLNWR and a wooded ravine near the dam: seven, 14 March 1971; eight, 18 March 1973; six, 24 December 1993–9 January 1994. Smaller numbers have been seen fairly regularly at other times.

Returning Long-eared Owls can be looked for in late September: early dates are 26 September 1965 and 27 September 1981 at BLNWR. It has been recorded twice on the Amarillo CBC, four times on the BLNWR, and three times each on the Lake Meredith (east) and (west) counts. Undoubtedly it is more common than our few records indicate, for the species often goes undetected. I once walked by an owl as it perched head-high in a leafless tree not more than ten feet from me, its contour feathers compressed to the point where it looked like a branch, and it never flushed. Two wintered in the small backyard of an isolated farmstead near Kress, Swisher County, in 1988–89, and others have been found around abandoned farm lots on an otherwise treeless plain. An example of the latter were five owls found east of Texline, Dallam County, 21 February 1997.

NESTING: There are two nesting records of the Long-eared Owl in the study area. Oberholser (1974) cites eggs collected near Glenrio, Deaf Smith County, 9 April 1920. A juvenile with an adult was found at BLNWR, 6 and 18 July 1996. There are numerous sightings made in late April and early May on the refuge, as well as in the Amarillo cemeteries. There are a number of nesting records from nearby locations in Oklahoma (Sutton, 1967): nest with eggs, Cimarron County, 4 June 1915; nest with several half-grown young near Kenton, Cimarron County, 23 May 1937; nest with several young, Beaver County, 9 May 1923; the ovary of a specimen collected in Harmon County, 9 March 1955, contained an egg ready to lay; and an adult was found on an old magpie nest near Boise City, Cimarron County, 30 March 1959. There are several records from the Muleshoe NWR in nearby Bailey County: nesting in February and March 1973 and 1974 ("the young were fledged by the end of March and the owls subsequently left the area—they did not oversummer" (*fide* C. Stogner), and in late February 1975 (Williams,

1975). One summered in Lubbock County in 1976, two were seen on 3 June 1980, and one was in Cochran County on 7 June 1951 (*fide* C. Stogner). These dates of nesting activity point to the need for paying close attention to all Long-eared Owls encountered in the study area beginning in early spring.

SPECIMENS: Specimens have been taken in Hall (25 January 1969) and Randall (29 September and 7 October 1939, P-PHM; 17 December 1977, TCWC; 18 October 1939, WTAMU) counties. Oberholser (1974) shows specimens taken in winter in Potter and Gray counties, without giving details, and places the Potter County bird in the range of the subspecies *A. o. tuftsi* and the Gray County bird in that of *A. o. wilsonianus.*

Short-eared Owl *Asio flammeus* (Pontoppidan)

STATUS: Uncommon to fairly common winter visitor. Vagrant summer visitor.

OCCURRENCE: The Short-eared Owl has been recorded in 17 counties: Armstrong, Briscoe, Carson, Castro, Dallam, Deaf Smith, Donley, Gray, Hansford, Hartley, Oldham, Parmer, Potter, Randall, Roberts, Swisher, and Wheeler. It has been seen in every month except July.

This crepuscular hunter is another of the owl species found in the study area for which much work needs to be done to clarify its status. Few birders are active when it is, and more often than not it is encountered by chance rather than as a result of a purposive search. Most are seen from November through March. Carlander (1934) is the only observer to classify the Short-eared Owl as a "permanent resident," on what basis he fails to say. The single out-of-season sighting he cites is one found at "Hall's Ranch" sometime between 13 August and 4 September 1932 (Carlander, 1933). Otherwise, the earliest fall date we have is 24 October 1972 at BLNWR and the latest spring date 21 May 1991 in Randall County. The only other May bird is one seen at Lake Meredith, Potter County, 10 May 1981.

A June record is the specimen taken by McCauley along McClellan Creek in the eastern Panhandle, 21 June 1876 (McCauley, 1877; Oberholser, 1974). On that date his party was in the present-day Lake McClellan area in Gray County (Hunnius, 1876). The bird was an adult female taken "in a grove immediately by the camp" and alive when brought in. It was soon killed by a Prairie Falcon that was being kept as a pet, and examination of the owl's stomach contents yielded a gopher. Another June record is a bird seen in Hartley County, 23 June 1965.

These May and June records as well as another owl collected in summer (discussed later) are puzzlers—unless the Short-eared Owl's breeding range formerly extended much farther south. Johnsgard (1979) places the southern limits of its known breeding range as northeastern Colorado and eastern Kansas, and there only locally. The one Oklahoma nesting record ("of many years ago") comes from near Freedom, Woods County, in the northwestern sector of the state (Sutton, 1967). Present-day dates when the species is expected in Oklahoma range from 11 October to 22 April (Grzybowski et al., 1992). In recent years, however, "3 . . . flushed from a CRP plot in Texas County, OK, July 12–14. . . . [This and] July 17 in Morton Co., KS, were among the very few summer records for OK and KS" (Grzybowski, 1998). A sighting of one near Durham, Roger Mills County, 17 June 1984, is unpublished. The species is unverified in summer in New Mexico (Hubbard, 1978). Its breeding status in Kansas is uncertain. Prior to the 1930s it was a common resident, but today is rare, irregular, or very local in summer, most sightings occurring between 16 October and 15 April (Thompson and Ely, 1989).

SPECIMENS: There are specimens for Carson (ACMNH; March 1975, MTTU; 14 March 1982, TCWC), Castro (January 1978, SRSU), Deaf Smith (11 February 1979, TCWC), Parmer (13 December 1974, 17 February 1977, WTAMU), Randall (16 February 1970, WTAMU), and Swisher (23 November 1978, TCWC) counties. The number of specimens, most of which were road kills, are evidence that the Short-eared Owl is more common than our relatively few sight records indicate. The whereabouts of McCauley's Gray County specimen is unknown.

Northern Saw-whet Owl *Aegolius acadicus* (Gmelin)

STATUS: Vagrant migrant or winter visitor.

OCCURRENCE: The only Northern Saw-whet Owl confirmed in the Texas Panhandle was a badly decomposed carcass found at BLNWR, 6 May 1979 (P. Acord, R. Ross, K. Seyffert, E. Waddill). The wings and skull were salvaged and sent to Texas A&M University in College Station, where the identification was verified. The owl was found lying on a path alongside an extensive and dense growth of salt cedar. Close examination of such habitat, as well as stands of evergreens, would possibly turn up additional saw-whets.

Sutton (1967) reported two specimens of Northern Saw-whet Owls taken in nearby Oklahoma: "November 29, 1933, female . . . taken Eva, Texas County. . . . January 29, 1957, female . . . shot at Guymon, Texas County; when first discovered bird was sitting motionless high in Chinese elm on school grounds in heart of city." Schwindt (1982) reported another Oklahoma saw-whet found in an Austrian pine (*Pinus nigra*) in Guymon, 21 November 1981. On 1 January 1994 still another was found, in a stand of ponderosa pines (*Pinus ponderosa*) near the Lawrence Regnier ranch house south of Kenton, Cimarron County (Shane et al., 1995). Williams (1967) cited one at Clayton, Union County, New Mexico, 1 May 1967: "first recorded in several years."

SPECIMENS: There is one specimen taken in Randall County (6 May 1979, TCWC).

ORDER CAPRIMULGIFORMES

Family Caprimulgidae (Goatsuckers)

Common Nighthawk *Chordeiles minor* (Forster)

STATUS: Fairly common to common breeder. Common to abundant migrant.

OCCURRENCE: The Common Nighthawk has been recorded in every Texas Panhandle county and has been seen from April to October.

This is one of the few species other than gamebirds that claimed the attention of early explorers of the region. It was identified by Abert's (1846) party as they followed the course of the Canadian River: "Here we observed great numbers of the nighthawk ... which were darting around us in all directions, frequently passing within our reach" (16 September 1845). Later in the century McCauley (1877) found nighthawks "whether camped on the summit of the Staked Plain or in a valley by the water." Later observers concurred in their assessment of the species' status.

In 1975 the Common Nighthawk was added to the National Audubon Society's Blue List of birds (Arbib, 1971). An analysis of my records (1965–92) may throw light on whether a decline may be occurring in the study area. The average number of nighthawks per trip afield (May–September) for the period was 2.5 (1965, 2.1; 1992, 0.09). However, taking summer birds only (June–July), the average was 3.4 (1965, 1.5; 1992 3.1). The following are the BBS averages and highs: *Booker*—8.6, 23; *Channing*—7.3, 20; *Childress*—13.9, 23; *Miami*—13.9, 35; *Texline*—5.6, 14; *Clarendon*—7.6, 14. There is a decrease in nighthawks as one moves west of the 101st meridian.

The first Common Nighthawks of the year can be expected in the first or second week of May. There are four April records, the earliest a single bird at the BLNWR, 11 April 1992. The greatest numbers are recorded during fall migration. As examples, 300 were observed over Amarillo, 17 September 1959, and 50+ over Lake Tanglewood, 17 October 1973—which also represent the latest date for the species. There appears to be an abrupt termination in migration around that time, for many of the yearly late dates cluster around mid-October. The records of the USFWS at the BLNWR show peak numbers from the third week of July to the third week in August. This is confirmed by my records, which also show another surge in late September and early October.

NESTING: There is little nesting data available. McCauley (1877) spoke of flushing adults from nests. Prior to the TBBAP, the only reported nest was one containing two newly hatched young at the BLNWR, 16 June 1973. In 1987 five nestings were confirmed: nest with eggs near Greenbelt Lake, Donley County, 24 May; adult on nest near Lake Tanglewood, Randall County, in early June; adult performing a distraction display (nest not found) near Dumas, Moore County, 12 June; an adult with one fledgling near Nazareth, Castro County, 2 August; a fledgling in Pampa, Gray County, 19 August. In addition to these CO nestings, the TBBAP discovered PR nesting in 46 quadrangles and PO in 35 quadrangles. All categories were evenly spread across the study area.

SPECIMENS: Specimens have been collected in Hutchinson (15, 17, 27, 29 June and 6, 7, 9 July 1950, TNHC), Moore (MCHM), Ochiltree (13 September 1981, TCWC), and Randall (21 and 23 May 1939, P-PHM; 27 June 1956, MNH; 14 September 1984, 24 May 1985, TCWC; 26 May, 3 and 9 August 1939, WTAMU) counties.

The nine specimens from Hutchinson County, all taken in June and July, were identified as *C. m. howelli*. Oberholser (1974) names specimens taken in Lipscomb and Wheeler (July 23) counties, and two young in Oldham (24 June 1920, A. J. Kirn) County, also all *howelli*. He does not specify the collections in which they were deposited. McCauley (1877) took specimens at Red River (May 23), Palo Duro (May 26), and Cañoncito Blanco (June 6), and had this to say: "One specimen differs slightly in appearance from the usual style of the species, and has white spots upon *six* of the outer primaries. Having been sent to Dr. Coues for his examination, he returned it, confirming its identification as '*virginianus*,' although, as might be expected from the locality, it tends toward var. *henryi*.' Other specimens seemed to be more decidedly like this variety." The TOS (1995) names two subspecies in the study area: *howelli* and *sennetti*, the former a summer resident and the latter a migrant. McCauley's possible *henryi* is limited to summer residency in the Trans-Pecos and the extreme southwestern sector of the South Plains.

Common Poorwill *Phalaenoptilus nuttallii* (Audubon)

STATUS: Rare to uncommon breeder.

OCCURRENCE: The Common Poorwill has been recorded in 12 of the 26 Texas Panhandle counties: Armstrong, Briscoe, Castro, Dallam, Hartley, Hemphill, Hutchinson, Oldham, Parmer, Potter, Randall, and Wheeler. It has been seen from March to November.

With the exception of McCauley (1877), none of the observers prior to mid-century mentioned the Common Poorwill in their accounts. This absence was not corrected until the 1950s, when a scattered few began being reported. The species is extremely elusive and seldom seen until almost trodden upon and flushed. Most sightings have occurred in April and May, with fewer in September and October. The earliest date is for one in Caprock Canyons SP, Briscoe

County, 30 March 1996—the only March record—and the latest dates are for one at BLNWR, 18 and 25 November 1973, and a freshly killed bird recovered in the PDCSP, 23 November 1998—the only November records. The 1973 bird, erroneously reported as found in "late October" in Potter County (Williams, 1974), was in a heavily wooded and brushy ravine deeply carpeted with leaves and debris and bordered by rocky outcroppings. Night temperatures were quite cool; however, the bird did not appear torpid when I came upon it in mid-morning.

The late November encounters, particularly the discovery of a bird at the same site on two successive weekends, raises the question of possible wintering. It is not known for certain that the poorwill migrates at all in the southern part of its range—in some areas the movement is thought to be altitudinal rather than latitudinal—and its winter range is unknown (Csada and Brigham, 1992). The canyonlands of the Texas Panhandle provide ideal habitat for hibernation, a condition the poorwill is known to enter. One was found in a torpid state lodged in a crypt in the face of a rock during three successive winters in somewhat similar habitat in California (Jaeger, 1949). Brauner (1952) found that torpidity was entered not as a result of low temperature alone but was also provoked by day length, availability of food, and possible psychological influences. He found that the period of winter inactivity ranged from 28 November to 22 January, while Jaeger (1949) found the inactive period to be 26 November–14 February. Had the November study area birds neared the point of entering hibernation?

It is of interest that "goatsuckers, possibly poorwills, were flushed in Crosby County" only a short distance south of the study area, 28 December 1980 and 3 January 1981 (Williams, 1981).

NESTING: Johnsgard (1979) shows the breeding range of the Common Poorwill as covering the entire Texas Panhandle. Actual nesting records are absent. The only positive evidence of breeding can be inferred from a female recovered in west Amarillo, Potter County, 27 April 1989 (P. Acord). On examination the specimen proved to have enlarging ova (letter, Keith A. Arnold, Texas A&M University, 20 December 1990). There have been numerous summer reports of poorwills at scattered localities, primarily in the PDCSP, Caprock Canyons SP (Briscoe County), and Canadian River breaks (Potter County). In addition to the female collected in Amarillo, the TBBAP turned up poorwills in other survey blocks. It was found a PR nester in five and a PO nester in three.

Nestings from nearby areas in Oklahoma point to a time span in which breeding birds can be expected: 21 May 1972, nest with two downy chicks located on "the side of a mesa near Kenton, Cimarron County" (Weske, 1973); 9 July 1954, nest with two eggs, hatched 24 July, Caddo County (Baumgartner and

Baumgartner, 1992). Hunnius (1876) speaks of finding a nest with three eggs near the Washita River in the northeastern Texas Panhandle, 5 May 1876; however the Common Poorwill lays but two eggs; his three-egg clutch was probably that of a Common Nighthawk. One observed in the Thompson Grove Picnic Area near Texline, Dallam County, 26 May 1996, may well have been nesting.

SPECIMENS: There are specimens taken in Potter (27 April 1989, TCWC) and Randall (27 April 1976, TCWC) counties. Oberholser (1974) shows a spring specimen from Armstrong County that is possibly based on the juvenile female collected by McCauley (1877) in the "Red River Canyon" 18 May 1876.

Chuck-will's-widow *Caprimulgus carolinensis* Gmelin

STATUS: Rare migrant; possible breeder.

OCCURRENCE: The Chuck-will's-widow has been recorded in five counties: Donley, Hemphill, Hutchinson, Potter, and Randall. More time spent in the eastern counties would probably disclose the species to be more widespread than is presently known. It has been found in April–June and September.

One locality where the Chuck-will's-widow has been found consistently in summer is White Deer Creek on the Duncan Ranch, southeastern Hutchinson County. It is there that singing birds are often heard in the evening and at night. The ranchers say the birds have always been present, not just in recent years when they first came to the attention of visiting birders. Although neither nests nor young have been found, the species probably breeds in the wooded creek valley. Another location where singing birds have been encountered during the nesting season is the Canadian River valley from Canadian eastward to Lake Marvin, Hemphill County. On the morning of 19 May 1990, I flushed a singing bird on the Gene Howe WMA. It is probable that the species nests for I am told that in recent years summering birds have been heard commonly in that area.

Almost all sightings of the Chuck-will's-widow have occurred in spring. The two exceptions are one bird on the outskirts of Amarillo, Randall County, 4 September 1964, and one in Amarillo, Potter County, 21 September 1974. Other spring sightings (7) of single birds have been made on the BLNWR (27 April–25 May), and one was observed on the Taylor Lakes WMA, Donley County, 9 May 1996.

From nearby areas in Oklahoma Sutton (1974a) cites the Chuck-will's-widow as breeding "westward regularly to . . . Roger Mills County." It is also found regularly at Boiling Springs SP, Woodward County, and irregularly on a BBS route in Beckham County (Baumgartner and Baumgartner, 1992). In the rest of Texas, it is a common migrant and summer resident in the eastern and central portions (TOS, 1995).

Whip-poor-will *Caprimulgus vociferus* Wilson

STATUS: Casual migrant.

OCCURRENCE: The Whip-poor-will has been reported four times in the Texas Panhandle, twice at the same location.

One was heard calling repeatedly on the night of 23–24 September 1978 on
the Duncan Ranch (White Deer Creek), southeastern Hutchinson County, and
one again on the night of 15 May 1987. The Chuck-will's-widow inhabits this
creek valley and one might question whether the singing fall bird was correctly
identified: the Whip-poor-will seldom sings in fall. On 23 September 1990, a
Whip-poor-will was found in the extreme southwest corner of Castro County,
and yet another in the yard of the observer's house located just 50 feet south of
the Castro County line in Lamb County, 11 June 1993. On 3 May 1996, one was
followed about as it was flushed repeatedly at BLNWR.

The Whip-poor-will has been found in Oklahoma westward to the central
portion of the state, and "exceptionally to Woods County" (Sutton, 1974a). In
north-central Texas Pulich (1988) recognized its presence no farther west than
Palo Pinto and Wise counties. There is a resident population to the south of the
study area in the Chisos, Davis, and Guadalupe mountains of the Trans-Pecos
(TOS, 1995). The LEAS (1994) lists the species in the South Plains region as "accidental" in April (Lubbock, 20 April 1984), May (Lubbock County, 1 May 1988),
and September (Lubbock County, 19 September 1975). The latter bird was
brought in by a cat and later released (TP-RF). It is my opinion that closer scrutiny of all caprimulgids would disclose a greater presence of the Whip-poor-will
in the study area than is thought.

ORDER APODIFORMES

Family Apodidae (Swifts)

Chimney Swift *Chaetura pelagica* (Linnaeus)

STATUS: Fairly common to common breeder.

OCCURRENCE: The Chimney Swift has been found in every county except Castro
in the southwest and Sherman in the northwest. Closer observation in some of
the towns of both counties, such as Dimmitt and Stratford, would possibly disclose its presence there also. It has been recorded from March to October.

Oberholser (1974) shows the Chimney Swift in only eight counties. This is
understandable as the species is a relatively recent addition to the area's avifauna,
no observer having named it prior to 1950. When the Chimney Swift first arrived
in Amarillo is unknown, but the first report of it in the literature was in 1954

(Baumgartner, 1954), when an unspecified number were seen on 7 June. The following year another ("west of normal range") was recorded on 29 March (Baumgartner, 1955). As late as 1957, local observers still thought it exceptional, a flock of 150 at Amarillo 5–11 May particularly so. The Chimney Swift is now well established as a summer resident in towns throughout much of the region and is occasionally found in rural areas. I have recorded swifts four times on the Booker BBS at farm lots. As an example of numbers in the smaller towns, 75 summered in Miami, Roberts County, in 1984.

In surveying its arrival in nearby areas, I find that in Clayton, Union County, New Mexico, only ten miles west of Texline in Dallam County, the Chimney Swift was first reported summering in 1969 (Williams, 1969). Until then it was not listed on Krehbiel's (1955) local list of birds. Sutton (1967) found it not at all in nearby Ellis County, Oklahoma, in 1936, and in 1937 no farther west than Alfalfa County in the north-central sector of the state. One in Cimarron County in June of 1965 was thought unusual.

The Chimney Swift is normally first seen in the third week of April. The earliest date is for one in Amarillo, Potter County, 16 April 1992, and the latest date for one in Amarillo, 14 October 1968. The largest assemblage on record is 500 or more around a schoolhouse chimney in Miami, Roberts County, during the fall of 1982.

NESTING: During the TBBAP the Chimney Swift was classified as CO nesting in three survey blocks, PR in 15, and PO in 15. It occupied 18 quadrangles between the 100th and 101st meridians, ten between the 101st and 102nd, and five west of the 102nd.

SPECIMENS: There is a single specimen taken in Randall County (27 May 1969, WTAMU).

White-throated Swift *Aeronautes saxatalis* (Woodhouse)

STATUS: Rare migrant and winter visitor.

OCCURRENCE: The White-throated Swift has been recorded in five Texas Panhandle counties: Briscoe, Castro, Parmer, Potter, and Randall. It has been seen in April–May, September–November, and December–February.

Prior to 1982 there had been but six reports of the White-throated Swift in the study area: 50+ over Amarillo, 21 May 1953; one at Friona, Parmer County, 17 April 1963; an unspecified number at Amarillo, 7 May 1967; a flock of 38 trapped on the 11th floor of the Santa Fe Building in downtown Amarillo, Potter County, during the stormy night of 21–22 October 1970—the birds were examined the next day and released; six in the PDCSP, 23 November 1971.

It was during the CBC of 19 December 1982 that the White-throated Swift was first found wintering in the PDCSP (Seyffert, 1984). As count participants were eating lunch at Hackberry, two swifts were observed flying low overhead, and at least two again later in the day. On the following 11 January a single swift was observed at the head of Sunday Canyon on the western rim of the Palo Duro, some four miles to the southwest of the previous sightings, and on 28 January three swifts in a single group, plus scattered individuals, were encountered between the first water crossing and the turnaround at the end of the park road. The species was found in the state park in three subsequent winters: two flying along the canyon wall where the road descends into the park, 4 December, and three in Timbercreek Canyon during the CBC of 17 December 1988; in winter of 1991–92, three swifts on 15 December and one on 6 February; and a single bird, 19 January 1997.

It was during this period that White-throated Swifts were also found in the Caprock Canyons SP, Briscoe County. At daybreak on 2 May 1987 I observed approximately 75 swifts leaving a night roost on a canyon wall near the entrance to South Prong, swirling overhead and chattering loudly before disappearing up the canyon en masse. On the CBC of 1 January 1989 a single swift was seen flying over the flats in the central sector of the park, and on the CBC of 1 January 1990 at least six were encountered in the South Prong. No swifts had been seen while the party was going up the canyon in the early morning hours; they were encountered on the return at midday. As far as is known, all the winter birds were seen from around noon to mid- or late afternoon. Presumably they remained in a semitorpid state until the canyon walls warmed up, whereupon they emerged and began foraging. On 29 February 1988 several were seen in the Haynes Boy Scout Camp adjacent to the western boundary of the Caprock Canyons SP. A swift observed flying for some 30 minutes or longer around a house in Lamb County near the extreme southwest corner of Castro County, 21 September 1992, prompted the observer to remark: "Interestingly when it departed it headed due east. I thought it might be heading for its wintering area along the caprock" (C. D. Littlefield).

These discoveries of wintering White-throated Swifts are remarkable in that the species was not known to winter any nearer than from the Davis and Chisos mountains west to El Paso County (TOS, 1984) and in New Mexico in the area of Carlsbad, Eddy County (Hubbard, 1978). Whether this occasional wintering will continue remains to be seen. Only a tiny portion of the Palo Duro Canyon system is kept under close observation by knowledgeable observers, and it may be that the White-throated Swift winters more regularly than is realized.

Family Trochilidae (Hummingbirds)

Ruby-throated Hummingbird *Archilochus colubris* (Linnaeus)
STATUS: Rare migrant.
OCCURRENCE: The Ruby-throated Hummingbird has been reported in four Texas
Panhandle counties: Potter, Randall, Roberts, and Wheeler. It has been seen
from April to October.

The status of the Ruby-throated Hummingbird in the study area is ambiguous and much work remains to be done toward clarifying it. Many reports must
be questioned, for it can easily be confused with the Black-chinned Hummingbird, a species fairly common in the area. One experienced observer who maintains a suburban yard in Amarillo designed to attract hummingbirds has told
me he has yet to see a Ruby-throated Hummingbird in the Panhandle. The earliest mention of the species (Reeves and Reeves, 1914–36) is terse and fails to name
a date: "1925. In trumpet vine blooms." A few years later Hibbets et al. (1926–36)
recorded it in "summer and fall, August, 1931." One was not named again in a
published account until after mid-century.

Even later reports of the Ruby-throated Hummingbird have been rare, the
dates ranging from late April to early October. The earliest date is for a male in
Canyon, Randall County, 29 April–1 May (videotaped), and in Amarillo, Randall
County, 29 April—both in 1996—and the latest date is for one in Amarillo, 12
October 1998. Perhaps Hawkins's (1945) statement concerning hummingbirds
in general provides a clue to such a paucity of sightings: "Several Amarillo residents have observed 'hummers' among their flowers, but no one seems to have
identified them as to species." The majority of hummingbirds reported are either females or subadults, and few observers can be sure of their identifications.
Female Black-chinned and Ruby-throated hummingbirds are virtually impossible to distinguish in the field.

Two summer reports of the Ruby-throated Hummingbird found outside the
eastern counties are of uncertain meaning. A male was seen in Amarillo, Randall
County, 2 June 1985, and another at Lake Tanglewood, Randall County, 7 July
1974, both sightings by experienced observers. The June bird was with a male
Black-chinned Hummingbird and an unidentified female. Recent reports of the
species in Wheeler County point to possible nesting. True (1993) names the
Ruby-throated Hummingbird as nesting in the eastern Panhandle, without giving specifics. I stand to be corrected, but it is my belief that actual breeding
remains to be confirmed.

In areas near the Texas Panhandle, Brown (1973) reported male Ruby-throated Hummingbirds seen regularly by the author and others in Elk City,
Beckham County, and Clinton, Custer County, Oklahoma, since 1940. In Altus,

Jackson County, the species is classified as "rare; reported to nest here" (Baum-gartner and Baumgartner, 1992). Concerning the Brown account, the author says all *Archilochus* hummingbirds found in that area had been taken for granted to be ruby-throateds—until closer examination disclosed some to be black-chinneds. Sutton (1967) says further that the ruby-throated is "believed to breed westward to Woods, Canadian, Caddo, Comanche, and Love counties, but no breeding female has been collected in any of these counties and possibility that Black-chinned Hummingbird nests in western Oklahoma must be borne in mind."

Black-chinned Hummingbird *Archilochus alexandri* (Bourcier and Mulsant)

STATUS: Fairly common breeder locally. Vagrant winter visitor.

OCCURRENCE: The Black-chinned Hummingbird has been reported in 12 count-ies: Castro, Donley, Gray, Hartley, Hemphill, Lipscomb, Oldham, Parmer, Pot-ter, Randall, Roberts, and Sherman. It has been seen in every month except February.

The earliest date for a Black-chinned Hummingbird is for one in Amarillo, Potter County, 29 March 1995. Two hummingbirds, thought probably black-chinneds, were observed in Amarillo, Potter County, 24–25 February 1996, at a site where feeders had hung the previous year. Normally the first birds arrive during the first or second week of April, and most are gone by late September or early October. Other than a few winter sightings, the latest date is for one in Amarillo, Potter County, 30 November 1993.

A male Black-chinned Hummingbird in Memorial Park, Amarillo, Potter County, 5 January 1975, was the first reported in winter: "There were snow drifts all around the honeysuckle vine where he was trying to find nourishment" (V. Deason). Others have been seen since, all males: one in Amarillo, Potter County, remained to mid-December 1993; one came regularly to a feeder in Clarendon, Donley County, September 1993–14 January 1994; another was seen at a feeder in Amarillo, Randall County, 20 July–1 December 1994.

The recent increase in reports of all hummingbird species can be attributed largely to the increase in the number of feeders being maintained, especially since the initiation in 1994 of the Texas Hummingbird Roundup program by the Texas Parks and Wildlife Department. Interest has been widespread and more data is being accumulated as a consequence. In some respects, more has been learned about the status of hummingbirds in the study area since 1990 than in all preceding years.

NESTING: None of the current field guides show the Black-chinned Hummingbird as nesting in the Texas Panhandle, and neither Oberholser (1974) nor Johnsgard (1979) recognized it as a nester. Nevertheless, there are several nesting records on file: a female on a nest containing two eggs near Lake Marvin, Hemphill County, 4–5 June 1955; a female observed nest building in Ellwood Park, Amarillo, Potter County, 19 May 1959; a nest with two young in Amarillo, Potter County, 13 July 1973 (nest built in a light fixture in a garage); occupied nest in a grapevine overhanging a patio on the Hugh Currie Ranch near Lake Tanglewood, Randall County, 14 May 1978; a female on a nest with two young in Amarillo, Randall County, 31 May 1983 (TP-RF); a female with fledglings coming to a feeder at Lake Tanglewood, Randall County, summer of 1990; as many as twelve spent the summer of 1994 in a yard in Amarillo, Potter County, where birds are seen yearly, including hens on nests. Many of the plantings in this yard are set out specifically to attract hummingbirds. The Lake Tanglewood area is another excellent place to observe the species in summer, and more nests would be found there with diligent searching.

Although the Black-chinned Hummingbird has yet to be reported in Dallam County, observers there should be on the alert, for the species was seen regularly at four different homesites in the Clayton, Union County, New Mexico, area during the summer of 1992 (NMOS, 1995). Breeding, however, was not confirmed.

SPECIMENS: There is a specimen for Randall County (ACNHM), the date of its taking not shown.

Anna's Hummingbird *Calypte anna* (Lesson)

STATUS: Vagrant winter visitor.

OCCURRENCE: The Anna's Hummingbird has been confirmed once in the Texas Panhandle. A juvenile male was photographed in Amarillo in December 1989 (True, 1993). Details of the event are lacking.

The Anna's Hummingbird is a rare and irregular migrant and winter resident in West and Central Texas and on the upper coast; the single breeding record is for the Davis Mountains (TOS, 1995). Several Anna's have been reported nearby on the South Plains: Lubbock, 28 September–3 November 1983 (TP-RF); Crosby County, 23 August–16 September 1985 (TP-RF); two different males in Lubbock, 3–15 September (TP-RF) and 16–22 September (TP-RF) 1988; one in Lubbock, winter of 1991–92 (Lasley and Sexton, 1992); two in Lubbock, 29–30 August and 6–13 October 1993 (Lasley and Sexton, 1994b). Since the mid- to late 1970s, wintering Anna's have been encountered with increasing frequency in Texas, particularly along the coast.

Calliope Hummingbird *Stellula calliope* (Gould)

STATUS: Rare migrant.

OCCURRENCE: The Calliope Hummingbird has been recorded in seven counties—

Donley, Gray, Hartley, Lipscomb, Potter, Randall, and Swisher—and has been seen from July to October.

The first reported sighting of a Calliope Hummingbird was a male observed at a feeder in Amarillo, Potter County, 1 August 1991. The following is a listing of subsequent sightings: *1992*—a male in Amarillo, Potter County, 9–12 and 25 July and 2, 4, and 7–13 September (videotaped). *1994*—a male in Amarillo, Potter County, 21–23 and 28–30 August and 6 October. *1995*—a male on 29 July, a male and female on 30 July, and a female or immature male on 6 August in Amarillo, Potter County; a male at two separate locations in Pampa, Gray County, 24–25 July; a male in Amarillo, Randall County, 3 August; a male in Amarillo, Potter County, 14–17 August; a male in Clarendon, Donley County, 26 July–2 August; a male, 27 July, and a female, 20–23 August, in Canyon, Randall County. *1996*—two males in Amarillo, Randall County, 24–25 July, and one male, 1 August; a female on 29 July–6 August, 9–11 August, and 19–23 August, a male on 29 July–2 August, an immature male on 1–2 August, and a female on 5 and 9 September, all at the same site in Amarillo; a female in Amarillo, Potter County, from the last week of September to the first week of October; a male in Kress, Swisher County, 30 July; a female in Canyon, Randall County, 3 August; a male in Canyon, 22 August. *1997*—an immature male in Canyon, 22 July, a female on 15 and a male on 16 August, and a female, 6 September; a male in The Palisades, Randall County, 28 July; a male in Lipscomb County, week of 17–23 August; one in Amarillo, Randall County, 13 September. The reports of the females and immatures must be viewed with caution, as with most hummingbird species. True (1993) gives an early date of 8 July for the Calliope, without providing year or other details.

This small western hummingbird has also been recorded in nearby areas. There are records for Clayton, Union County, New Mexico, 28 August 1956 (Baumgartner, 1957), 14 August 1967 (Williams, 1968), 12–29 July 1989 (Hubbard, 1989), and July 1992 (NMOS, 1991–92). The first Oklahoma record was a male in Cimarron County, 22 July 1989 (Rosche and Rosche, 1991). South Plains records are near Slaton, Lubbock County, 14–17 August 1975 (TP-RF); Crosby County 12 August 1985 (TP-RF); Lubbock, 19 July and 20 August–1 September 1986 (Williams, 1986), 30 July 1988 (Lasley and Sexton, 1989), 29–30 July and 10 and 15 August 1994 (Lasley and Sexton, 1995b). This recent arrival of the Calliope Hummingbird on the High Plains and South Plains of Texas has been paralleled in western Kansas (Morton, Finney, and Rush counties), where 11 birds have been reported since 1990 (*fide* Tom Shane). How much of this is due to a possible westward shift in the Calliope's migratory pathway and how much to a recent increase in the number of feeder watchers is a matter of speculation.

Broad-tailed Hummingbird *Selasphorus platycercus* (Swainson)

STATUS: Uncommon to fairly common migrant.

OCCURRENCE: The Broad-tailed Hummingbird has been recorded in six counties: Castro, Oldham, Parmer, Potter, Randall, and Roberts. It has been seen from April to December.

The Broad-tailed Hummingbird appears in the accounts of early observers more often than any other hummingbird species. Reeves and Reeves (1914–36) spoke of one at their home in Canyon, Randall County, in 1934—apparently in summer, for they searched without success for a nest. Hibbets et al. (1926–36) classified it as a migrant only. Carlander (1934) considered the broad-tailed not only a fairly common migrant but also the most common of the hummingbirds in the area, and a possible summer resident. Later observers have given this ranking and summer residency to the Black-chinned Hummingbird.

This handsome hummer arrives early in the year. The early and late spring dates range from 6 April 1993 (Amarillo) to 15 May 1991 (Amarillo). Three June sightings in Amarillo, Randall County, are on record: one (day not recorded) in 1967; one, 1 June 1995; a male, 5 June 1995. More sightings have been made in fall than in spring. This can be accounted for by an elliptical migratory pathway that most hummingbird species use, following a more westward route in spring than in fall. The early and late fall dates range from 26 July 1983 (Amarillo) to 26 October 1992 (Amarillo). The single winter sighting is one that remained in Amarillo, Potter County, until 23 December 1995. Normally the broad-tailed is not seen earlier than the first week of August or later than the third week of October. On the BLNWR, 27 August 1989, I witnessed an Olive-sided Flycatcher closely pursuing a male Broad-tailed Hummingbird, snapping its bill loudly as it chased the fleeing hummer.

The belief of some that the Broad-tailed Hummingbird nests in the study area is unconfirmed. The nearest location where nesting was thought to have occurred is Cimarron County in the Oklahoma Panhandle (Sutton, 1967: "June 20, 1912, nest (two eggs)." However, Sutton (1974) later questioned the correctness of the report. As a summer resident in Texas, the species is confined to the Chisos, Davis, and Guadalupe mountains of the Trans-Pecos (TOS, 1995). It summers statewide in the mountainous areas of New Mexico, occurring only rarely as a migrant eastward (Hubbard, 1978). Johnsgard (1979), however, shows the breeding range extending as far east in that state as northern Union County, and others (NMOS, 1992) say the Broad-tailed Hummingbird can be found during the breeding season in the Sierra Grande area in the northern sector of the county.

Rufous Hummingbird *Selasphorus rufus* (Gmelin)

STATUS: Fairly common migrant.

OCCURRENCE: The Rufous Hummingbird has been found in ten counties: Castro, Donley, Gray, Hartley, Lipscomb, Oldham, Parmer, Potter, Randall, and Swisher. It has been seen from July to November.

Surprisingly, only one observer prior to mid-century named the Rufous Hummingbird, that being Carlander (1934), who called it a "rare migrant." This is in contrast to present-day experience, when observers expect to see the species regularly; in fact, it is the most common of the migrant hummingbirds in fall. Late July is normally the time of its arrival. The earliest date is for one in Canyon, Randall County, one in Kress, Swisher County, and one in Darrouzett, Lipscomb County, 18 July 1996, and the latest date for one in Amarillo, Randall County, 26 November 1998. True (1993) names an early date of 16 July, without giving details.

Daily from 30 July to 3 September 1993, one Rufous Hummingbird or more occupied a suburban yard in southwest Amarillo, Randall County. On some days several were seen at a time as they fought over territorial rights to a trumpet vine. Another visited a yard daily in Pampa, Gray County, 9–27 August 1994, and the species was seen regularly during the same month at three other yards in town, on one occasion as many as five birds at a time.

ORDER CORACIIFORMES

Family Alcedinidae (Kingfishers)

Belted Kingfisher *Ceryle alcyon* (Linnaeus)

STATUS: Fairly common to common resident.

OCCURRENCE: The Belted Kingfisher has been found in all the counties except Sherman. It is present year-round.

McCauley (1877) had this to say about the Belted Kingfisher in May–June: "Red River and its headwaters, with the streams in many places abounding in fish, and the pools . . . were apparently without any of this species. They were, however, found very abundant on McClellan Creek, the Canadian, etc." Today this kingfisher is found on the Red River and its tributaries but is by no means abundant on McClellan Creek and the Canadian River. The nature of these waterways has changed sufficiently to affect the species' status. The Canadian River is no longer a deep flowing stream (Carlson, 1980), and few kingfishers are found along it. Even in the Lake Meredith area the species is no more than fairly common, and the same is true of McClellan Creek and Lake McClellan. Many of the rivers and creeks are dry for most of the year, except for isolated spring-fed pools, and only small numbers of kingfishers can survive on their limited resources. Small impoundments may also dry up during drought years. This kingfisher can be encountered regularly in the PDCSP, but only in small numbers and more often in summer than in winter. A winter population study in the park (Seyffert, 1968–78) found it wintering in eight years.

The Belted Kingfisher is seldom found around playa lakes, and then only as a transient. The larger impoundments host small numbers during most seasons of the year. No regular censusing has been made except for the CBCs, for which averages are: *Amarillo*—2.6; *Lake Meredith* (*east*)—2.1; *Lake Meredith* (*west*)—0.4; *Quitaque*—1.7. Even when it holds water, the BLNWR rarely hosts a king-fisher in winter.

NESTING: Russell (1935) named several families of young kingfishers that were reared in the PDCSP, and Hawkins (1945) observed that "the steep clay bank below Palo Duro Lake serves as one typical nesting site"—this was near Canyon, Randall County. It is in Randall County that all confirmations of nesting have been made. The TBBAP confirmed nesting at Lake Tanglewood in that county in 1988–90. The Belted Kingfisher was classified as a PR nester in nine other survey blocks and as PO in 15. Sixteen occupied quadrangles were between the 100th and 101st meridians, eight between the 101st and 102nd, and one west of the 102nd (Boys Ranch East on the Canadian River).

SPECIMENS: McCauley (1877) collected two specimens along McClellan Creek in Gray County, 20–21 June 1876. These are probably the ones referred to by Ober-holser (1974). The only specimen available is one taken in Hall County (12 October 1974, WTAMU).

Green Kingfisher *Chloroceryle americana* (Gmelin)

STATUS: Vagrant summer and fall visitor.

OCCURRENCE: The Green Kingfisher has been reported in the Texas Panhandle twice since mid-century, both times in Randall County. Prior to then, Hibbets et al. (1926–36) give the following dates for the "Texas Kingfisher": "April 18, 1924, April 4, 1929, August 4, 1929, May 5, 1935." These are among the more intriguing observations registered by these observers. The birds they recorded were found within 40 miles of Canyon.

During a program given by B. W. VanNoy at a meeting of the Texas Pan-handle Audubon Society on the evening of 15 February 1971, he displayed a color slide taken of a Green Kingfisher along the creek at Camp Don Harrington (Boy Scout Camp), Randall County. At the time, he could not furnish the date it was taken. Later (letter, 18 December 1972), he informed me that he was sure it had been taken in September 1966. Sometime after his death, wishing to secure this valuable photograph for the recently established Texas Photo-Record File, I was permitted to go through his extensive collection of slides but was unable to find this one. The most recent sighting of a Green Kingfisher occurred along Tierra Blanca Creek downstream from the dam at BLNWR in November 1979. The sighting was not made known to others at the time. The observer said he saw the bird on a number of occasions over a period of several days and was sure of his identification.

The Green Kingfisher is a rare to uncommon resident from the Lower Rio Grande Valley west to the lower Pecos River, north to the southern half of the Edwards Plateau and east to Bastrop, Fayette, and Jackson counties (TOS, 1995). The nearest to the study area that one has been reported is in Lubbock County, 16 November 1982 (*fide* C. Stogner).

ORDER PICIFORMES

Family Picidae (Woodpeckers and Allies)

Lewis's Woodpecker *Melanerpes lewis* (Gray)
STATUS: Casual summer and fall visitor.
OCCURRENCE: The Lewis's Woodpecker has been found in four counties: Castro, Hartley, Randall, and Swisher. It has been seen in May, August, September, and December.

With few exceptions, all sightings of the Lewis's Woodpecker have been of single birds seen in May, as follows: Jokerst Ranch south of Amarillo, Randall County, 12–14 May 1967; BLNWR, 22 May 1971; Amarillo, 24 December 1972, the only winter occurrence; and Amarillo, Randall County, 10 May 1973. Twelve years elapsed before another was reported: at Ceta Glen, South Ceta Canyon, Randall County, 4–8 May 1985, the bird was watched from a short distance as it fed on discarded food items, particularly pancakes, strewn on the ground near a dining hall. Subsequent sightings are: BLNWR, 17 September 1989 (TBRC); Reynolds Ranch on Rita Blanca Creek, Hartley County, 5 May 1990 (TBRC); southwest Castro County, 19 May 1992; Canyon, Randall County, 26 August 1998 (TBRC). Some uncertainty surrounds a sighting made in Swisher County during the late 1980s. The bird was observed as it perched on a fence post along FM 86 between Silverton and Tulia—"sometime in May."

Sutton (1967) reported the Lewis's Woodpecker breeding irregularly in the Black Mesa country of western Cimarron County, Oklahoma, "where presumably resident." He reported R. C. Tate finding nests in "dead cottonwood trunk" and "mostly dead" pinyon-juniper. Tyler (1979a) reported: "A pair with a nest was found about 4 miles northeast of Kenton, Cimarron Co., Oklahoma on 14 May 1978"—the first nest found since 1922. The first nesting in the Clayton area, Union County, New Mexico, was reported in the summer of 1955 (Baumgartner, 1955) and the latest at Clayton Lake 14 June 1986 (Hubbard, 1986). Zimmerman et al. (NMOS, 1992) reported breeding in the Perico Creek and Upper Piñabetitos Creek areas of Union County. These nearby locations of breeding, along with the dates, should alert observers to the possibility of the Lewis's Woodpecker nesting in the northwestern Texas Panhandle.

Red-headed Woodpecker *Melanerpes erythrocephalus* (Linnaeus)

STATUS: Fairly common to common breeder in eastern half; rare to fairly common breeder locally in western half. Rare winter visitor.

OCCURRENCE: The Red-headed Woodpecker has been recorded in all the Texas Panhandle counties except Sherman and Swisher. It has been seen in every month.

It is instructive to read the accounts of early observers concerning the status and distribution of the Red-headed Woodpecker prior to mid-century. The earliest is McCauley's (1877): "Very abundant on McClellan, Mulberry and other wooded creeks, except at their headwaters, where they were, however, found occasionally." While not abundant, the species remains common today in those same areas. Strecker (1912) observed: "In the Palo Duro section of the Panhandle, it is not uncommon during the summer months, following up the river valleys almost to the New Mexico line." As for the upper reaches of the Palo Duro (PDCSP), today it is rare to uncommon. Neither Russell (1935) nor Stevenson (1942) named it in listing of birds for the park. My records reflect a declining status in the state park. For the 15-year period 1964–78, the average number recorded per trip was 1.5; for the 15-year period 1979–93, it was 0.46.

Strecker's (1912) assertion that the Red-headed Woodpecker followed "the river valleys almost to the New Mexico line" is true of the Canadian River but not of waterways farther south. A few can be found in Hereford, Deaf Smith County, which they probably reached via Tierra Blanca Creek, but the species is rarely found on the BLNWR astride that waterway to the east except as a spring and fall transient. There have been indications of occasional nesting on the refuge but no confirmations. Hawkins (1945) thought the species a "fairly common permanent resident of the eastern Panhandle," with a few extending "westward along the Canadian River at least to Bivins Station, north of Amarillo. . . . Evidently the Canadian is one of the travel lanes by which this woodpecker has invaded New Mexico." Thompson (1952) thought it "a dominant part of the bird population along the stream" (Bugbee Creek area along the Canadian River,

Hutchinson County). It is common today in the Lake Marvin–Gene Howe WMA areas of Hemphill County and remains common to fairly common in the river valley at least as far west as the Boys Ranch area in Oldham County. It can easily be found along Rico Creek and Tascosa Creek north of the river, and Punta de Aqua and Rita Blanca Creek in Hartley County. I have encountered it in the Thompson Grove Picnic Area in Dallam County, an oasis northeast of Texline (11 June 1977; 7 June 1980; 11 June 1981; 15 June 1985). Reeves and Reeves (1914–36) say they saw the Red-headed Woodpecker only once in Canyon (1938), and Hibbets et al. (1926–36) considered it a "rare migrant." Certainly it is not a bird found often today in towns and cities in the central and western portions of the study area, and it is seen only occasionally in Amarillo in summer.

The Red-headed Woodpecker is present from the last week of April to the first week in October. The early date is for one in Clarendon, Donley County, 8 March 1993. Sightings beyond October are rare, and then for the most part of subadults. My latest sighting is of an immature in the PDCSP, 13 November 1966. A young bird visited a feeder almost daily in Miami, Roberts County, 27 November 1979–15 February 1980, and another was seen in Amarillo from the end of January 1986 until the following 1 April.

NESTING: This woodpecker has been recorded nesting in Armstrong, Childress, Collingsworth, Donley, Gray, Hall, Hartley, Hemphill, Hutchinson, Lipscomb, Ochiltree, Oldham, Potter, Randall, Roberts, and Wheeler counties. During the TBBAP nesting was classified CO in 24 survey blocks, PR in 13, and PO in 10. Twenty-nine were between the 100th and 101st meridians, ten between the 101st and 102nd, and eight west of the 102nd. Oberholser (1974) names the late date of nesting in Texas as 15 August ("young in nest"). An uninjured juvenile that had apparently fallen out of its nest was recovered in the Palo Duro Club near Canyon, Randall County, 5 September 1987.

SPECIMENS: Specimens have been taken in Gray (22 June 1969, WTAMU), Hemphill (22 July 1955, TCWC), Hutchinson (13 June and 7 July 1950, TNHC), Randall (11 August 1939, WTAMU), Roberts (3, 11, 13, and 26 August 1965, TCWC), and Wheeler (3 July 1973, TCWC) counties. In addition, Oberholser (1974) refers to specimens collected in Oldham, Roberts, and Wheeler counties, but does not name the collections in which they reside. The Wheeler County bird may have reference to the specimen collected by McCauley (1877) along Sweetwater Creek, 12 May 1876. He collected another in Red River Canyon, in what is now Randall County, 29 May. Oberholser identified the specimens he examined as the western race *M. e. caurinus*. The two collected in Hutchinson County were identified by G. M. Sutton as belonging to nominate *erythrocephalus* (Thompson, 1952).

Acorn Woodpecker *Melanerpes formicivorus* (Swainson)

STATUS: Casual summer and fall visitor.

OCCURRENCE: The Acorn Woodpecker has been recorded four times, a single bird in each instance: Amarillo, Potter County, 9 May 1965; Amarillo, Randall County, 30 September 1985; near Canyon, Randall County, 27 September 1995; and a winter sight record shown for Potter County by Oberholser (1974), for which details are lacking.

The Acorn Woodpecker is a common resident in the Davis, Chisos, and Guadalupe Mountains of the Trans-Pecos and is rarely found outside its breeding range (TOS, 1995). In Oklahoma, a female was collected in Woods County in 1908, and a female was observed repeatedly from 16 January to 24 April 1960 in the Wichita Mountains NWR, Comanche County (Sutton, 1967). In New Mexico, a first sighting for Clayton, Union County, occurred 11 September 1971 (Williams, 1972), another on 15 May 1983 (Hubbard, 1983), and still another 7–8 October 1993 (NMOS 1992–93; Williams, 1994).

Golden-fronted Woodpecker *Melanerpes aurifrons* (Wagler)

STATUS: Fairly common to common resident in the southeastern sector, extending westward in the canyonlands to Randall County. Rare to uncommon visitor elsewhere.

OCCURRENCE: The Golden-fronted Woodpecker has been recorded in 14 counties: Armstrong, Briscoe, Childress, Collingsworth, Donley, Gray, Hall, Hemphill, Oldham, Potter, Randall, Roberts, Swisher, and Wheeler. It has been seen year-round.

The range of the Golden-fronted Woodpecker extends into the study area via the Pease River, Prairie Dog Town Fork and Salt Fork of the Red River, and their tributaries. It has rarely been reported elsewhere. The observations of Stevenson (1942) concerning distribution are of great interest and raise several questions:

> It is strange that McCauley {1877}, who explored Palo Duro Creek and most of the other streams in the eastern Panhandle in 1876, does not mention this species in his paper; nor does Strecker list it as present in Armstrong County in 1910. . . . Philip Allan . . . informs me that this woodpecker also is found near Canadian, Texas, in the northeastern corner of the Panhandle. It is a fairly common resident among cottonwoods along the Canadian River. . . . These isolated colonies may be the result of rather recent invasions from the southeast or the species may have been overlooked until recent years.

Such a recent intrusion may have taken place, for the Golden-fronted Woodpecker could hardly be overlooked today in the areas of Randall and Armstrong counties explored by McCauley and Strecker. That McCauley failed to record it in the northeastern Panhandle comes as no surprise (it should be noted that he did not record the Red-bellied Woodpecker either); but that Allan found it along the Canadian River (Lake Marvin) is very much a surprise. Thompson (1952) also wondered about the Stevenson report: "The yellow-bellied woodpecker which he mentions as being of common occurrence along the Canadian River was not seen by us." Nor has it been seen along the Canadian River since Allan's day, with one exception—a female in McBride Canyon, Lake Meredith Recreation Area, Potter County, late December 1984–14 January 1985. One may question Allan's assertion, for it is the Red-bellied Woodpecker that today occupies the river valley. Sightings in Gray and Roberts counties are one-time events: two at Lake McClellan, Gray County, 23 February 1972; a female in Miami, Roberts County, 21 October 1968 to near the end of the winter season. Prior to the fall of 1997, the single Oldham County sighting was a bird observed on the Tom Green Ranch north of Vega, 24 October 1976. On 26 September 1997, a female was first seen north of Wildorado on the Barfield Ranch ("breaks"), followed by regular sightings until 13 March 1998.

The winter status of the Golden-fronted Woodpecker at separate locations in the Palo Duro Canyon system is indicated by CBCs. The average number on the Amarillo count is 30.0, and 5.9 on the Quitaque count. A Winter-Bird Population Study conducted in the PDCSP (Seyffert, 1968–78) disclosed an average density of 13 per 100 acres. It was the seventh most common species on the study plot. Two instances of imperfect albinism in the Golden- fronted Woodpecker have been reported: PDCSP, 17 December 1972, and Ceta Glen, South Ceta Canyon, Randall County, 4 March 1973.

NESTING: Oberholser (1974) shows nesting in Armstrong and Hall counties. To these Briscoe, Childress, Collingsworth, Donley, and Randall can be added. Nesting activity in the PDCSP begins in early or mid-March, and young in the nest may still be present in late July or early August. A two-year Breeding Bird Study in the state park disclosed an average density of 17 per 100 acres (Seyffert, 1967–68). During the TBBAP the farthest northwest that the species was found nesting was in the Bivins Lake (the only site west of the 102nd meridian) and Palisades quadrangles, both in Randall County, and the farthest north was in the Lelia Lake Creek (Donley County) and Wellington NW (Collingsworth County) quadrangles.

There is an overlap in range of the Golden-fronted and Red-bellied Woodpecker in the southeastern sector of the study area and adjacent southwestern Oklahoma. In addition, Sutton (1967) says there is another overlapping farther north in Oklahoma along the Canadian River south of Arnett, Ellis County. The presence of the Golden-fronted Woodpecker along the river in that county lends credence to Allan's claim of finding the species along the river a little farther to the west in Hemphill County, Texas. This is certainly possible, for little or no exploration has been done along the Canadian River downriver from Lake Marvin to the state line since mid-century. Perhaps the Golden-fronted Woodpecker could still be found along that stretch of river in what appears a more xeric environment, one more favorable to the species than what exists upriver between Lake Marvin and Canadian. It should be noted, however, that none of the Arnett CBCS (1966–94) has registered the species, although the count circle lies largely south of town near the river.

SPECIMENS: Specimens have been taken in Hall (8 February 1977, WTAMU) and Randall (19 December 1935, MVZ; 15 January 1939, P-PHM; 11 August and 15 November 1939, WTAMU) counties. Oberholser (1974) shows fall and winter specimens taken in Randall County, without providing information as to their locations. He identifies them as the northern race *M. a. incanescens*. The specimen collected in Randall (MVZ) is also of that race.

Red-bellied Woodpecker *Melanerpes carolinus* (Linnaeus)

STATUS: Fairly common to common resident in the eastern third, becoming uncommon to rare along the Canadian River west to northern Potter County. Rare visitor elsewhere.

OCCURRENCE: The Red-bellied Woodpecker has been reported in 17 counties: Armstrong, Briscoe, Castro, Childress, Collingsworth, Donley, Gray, Hansford, Hemphill, Hutchinson, Lipscomb, Ochiltree, Oldham, Potter, Randall, Roberts, and Wheeler. Oberholser (1974) shows it in five. It has been seen year-round.

This species was little noted by early observers. McCauley (1877) did not name it although he spent spring and early summer in the northeastern sector where today it is common. Carlander (1934) classified it as a "rather rare permanent resident . . . found only along wooded streams," and in speaking of PDCSP he noted: "In the cottonwoods along the stream you might see the small Texas woodpecker or the larger Red-bellied woodpecker tapping on an old resonant dead limb." Such an observation for the PDCSP has always puzzled later observers, for it is the Golden-fronted Woodpecker that now occupies the park and the Red-bellied has been reported there only three times: a pair feeding young, 30 May 1952 ("I saw the pure red head and nape—no yellow on either head"; P. Acord); a female, 4 November 1987; a female, 17 December 1994. Down the canyon outside the park (Armstrong County), one was observed on 28 March 1964 and 13 February 1965. Hawkins (1945) considered the species to be "possibly a rare summer resident in a few localities" and names only three sightings in the Lake Marvin area east to the state line. Thompson (1952) did not find any during the time he worked in northeastern Hutchinson County. It is possible that the spread of the Red-bellied Woodpecker into the eastern Panhandle is a recent event, for during the winter of 1966–67 it was reported as increasing (Wheeler County) on the western limits of its range (Williams, 1967).

The Red-bellied Woodpecker today is resident primarily in the eastern third of the study area, where it can readily be found, and in the Canadian River Valley as far west as the LX and Kritser ranches in north Potter County (possibly Boys Ranch, Oldham County). It can be found west along Wolf Creek to Wolf Creek Park in Ochiltree County, Palo Duro Lake on North Palo Duro Creek in northeastern Hansford County, the Washita River and Red Deer Creek to the Miami area in Roberts County (possibly farther southwest into Gray County), Sweetwater Creek and the North Fork of the Red River along McClellan Creek to at least Lake McClellan in Gray County, and the Salt Fork of the Red River to the Clarendon (Lelia Creek) and Greenbelt Lake areas in Donley County. Little work has been done in the valley of Prairie Dog Town Fork of the Red River in Childress and Hall counties; the species could possibly be found there also. If so, it would overlap the range of the Golden-fronted Woodpecker, which it presently does farther north in Collingsworth and Donley counties.

Farther upcanyon from the PDCSP there have been a few reported as far west as the Canyon City Club northwest of town, Randall County. The number of out-of-season Red-bellied Woodpecker sightings at BLNWR on Tierra Blanca Creek farther west is surprising in that they far outnumber those of the golden-fronted, a species resident only a short distance to the east. Evidently the red-bellied is a greater wanderer than the golden-fronted. An increasing number of nonsummering red-bellieds have been reported in recent years in the Quitaque (Briscoe County) and Amarillo (Potter/Randall County) areas. The farthest southwestern sighting is a single bird in Castro County, 28 September 1992. Of interest was one found on 9 December 1992 along Perico Creek near Clayton, Union County, New Mexico (Williams, 1993).

NESTING: During the TBBAP the Red-bellied Woodpecker was found a CO nester in five survey blocks (adults on nest, 7 May–19 July), a PR in four, and a PO in two, all in the eastern sector. The Oberholser files reveal that Carlander found a nest with eggs, 25 July 1933 (*fide* W. Pulich).

SPECIMENS: Three specimens are available from Hemphill County (21 November 1984, OMNH). Oberholser (1974) names a specimen collected in Childress County but supplies no details.

Williamson's Sapsucker *Sphyrapicus thyroideus* (Cassin)
STATUS: Casual migrant and winter visitor.
OCCURRENCE: The three counties in the Texas Panhandle in which the Williamson's Sapsucker has been recorded are Dallam, Potter, and Randall. The species has been seen from October through April, January excepted.

The sequence of Williamson's Sapsucker sightings is as follows: a female in PDCSP, 12 February and 6 November 1955; a male found dead in Canyon, Randall County, 8 March 1955; a female in PDCSP, 5 April 1964; a female on the Jokerst Ranch south of Amarillo, Randall County, 12 April 1964; a male at BLNWR, 27 March 1965; a male in Amarillo, Potter County, 9–10 February 1967—the bird was observed as it went to roost about 40 feet up in an elm, flattening itself against the trunk just below a crotch of the tree; a male upcanyon from the PDCSP, 30 December 1967; a female in the Plum Creek area of Lake Meredith, Potter County, 14–16 October 1971; one in the Lake Tanglewood area, Randall County, 19 December 1971; a female in Amarillo, Randall County, 24 December 1972; one in Amarillo, Potter County, 9 October 1975; a female in Amarillo, Potter County, 20 December 1982; a female at BLNWR, 15 October 1986; a female in South Ceta Canyon, Randall County, fall of 1988; a male in PDCSP, 10–18 November 1990 (TBRC); one in the Thompson Grove Picnic Area near Texline, Dallam County, 23–25 April 1996.

Yellow-bellied Sapsucker *Sphyrapicus varius* (Linnaeus)

STATUS: Uncommon to fairly common migrant. Rare to uncommon winter visitor.

OCCURRENCE: The Yellow-bellied Sapsucker has been recorded in 12 counties: Armstrong, Briscoe, Castro, Childress, Deaf Smith, Gray, Hemphill, Oldham, Parmer, Potter, Randall, and Roberts. It has been seen in every month except June, July, and August.

Almost all data pertaining to the Yellow-bellied Sapsucker presented in this account was accumulated before the Red-naped Sapsucker was elevated to species status (AOU, 1985). The relationship of the two concerning arrival and departure dates, distribution, and winter status remains to be discovered, and what we presently think we know about the Yellow-bellied Sapsucker is subject to clarification and amendment.

This sapsucker neither arrives early in fall nor lingers late in spring. There are few records prior to October, the earliest being 11 September 1974 (Amarillo, Potter County). Indications are that the earlier birds may in fact have been Red-naped Sapsuckers. Few sightings have occurred even as late as April, making the three in May exceptional: one in Amarillo, Potter County, 11 May 1953, and one on the Kritser Ranch, Canadian River, Potter County, 7 May 1983 and 11 May 1985. The largest number recorded in any one day was eight or more in the PDCSP, 16 November 1979.

The Yellow-bellied Sapsucker winters primarily in the Palo Duro Canyon. It has been recorded on 26 of the 40 Amarillo CBCs, a circle that includes the state park. Six is the highest number for a count. Another count circle embracing the canyon is Quitaque, where it has been found on five of 20 counts. It has been recorded once on the Lake Meredith (west) CBC and never on those of Lake Meredith (east) or the BLNWR. A few may winter in the mature wooded sections of the larger towns. Its status in the eastern counties is largely unknown. If its incidence of occurrence on the nearby Arnett CBC in Ellis County, Oklahoma, is any indication, the species is a rare winter resident, for it has been recorded on only three of 29 counts (1966–94).

Red-naped Sapsucker *Sphyrapicus nuchalis* Baird
STATUS: Rare to uncommon migrant and winter visitor.
OCCURRENCE: The only counties in which the Red-naped Sapsucker has been reported are Castro, Oldham, Potter, and Randall. Since its elevation to species status in 1985 (AOU, 1985), data on its occurrence in the study area have begun slowly accumulating; many years are needed before the relationship between the Red-naped and Yellow-bellied Sapsuckers will be clearly understood.

The Red-naped Sapsucker sightings have come almost exclusively from two localities, the BLNWR and the PDCSP. There have been so few that I list them all. BLNWR—16 October 1986; 29 September, 4 and 7 October 1987; 13 September 1992; 2 October 1993. PDCSP—4 and 11 November, 9 December 1987; 8 October 1991; 25 February and 10 March 1992; 24 November 1993; 28 September, 23 October, and 23 November 1994; 18 March 1995; 27 March 1996; 19 October 1996; 17 and 28 October, 22 November 1997. Nothing is known about the Castro County sightings other than that the birds were recorded in March, September, and October. One of only a few spring sightings was a bird in Vega, Oldham County, 13 April 1998. Prior to elevation to species status *S. v. nuchalis* was reported six times, five of them in Amarillo, Potter County: 4 October 1954; 23 September 1956; one, 30 September 1956; two, 9 October 1956; one, 4 October 1957. One was recorded on the Lake Meredith (east) CBC, 23 December 1978.

It is to be noted that as of 1988, all Red-naped Sapsuckers reported in Oklahoma had been found in the Black Mesa country of Cimarron County in the western Panhandle and were seen in late September and early October, "before Yellow-bellieds arrive" (Grzybowski, 1989). As can be seen, almost all study area sightings have also occurred during fall.
SPECIMENS: Two specimens have been collected (13 October 1977, 15 January 1979; TCWC), both in Potter County. At the time they were listed as Yellow-bellied Sapsuckers, race *S. v. nuchalis*.

Ladder-backed Woodpecker *Picoides scalaris* (Wagler)

STATUS: Fairly common to common resident.

OCCURRENCE: The Ladder-backed Woodpecker has been recorded in every Texas Panhandle county except Lipscomb and Sherman and would be in them with better coverage. It is in the northeastern and southwestern sectors that the species is least common.

While its numbers are small in any given locality, the Ladder-backed Woodpecker is the most widespread of the woodpeckers in the study area. Few trips afield at any season will fail to disclose this perky and noisy little bird, particularly in places such as PDCSP and BLNWR. It is mentioned by all early observers, and their accounts point to no change in its status. Averages on the CBCS indicate its winter status in various habitats: *Amarillo*—8.2; *Lake Meredith* (*west*)—8.3; *Lake Meredith* (*east*)—7.1; *Quitaque*—5.1; *Buffalo Lake* NWR—3.8. The BBSS are poor indicators of summer status. A two-year Breeding Bird Study conducted in the PDCSP (Seyffert, 1967–68) disclosed an average density of 5 birds per 100 acres.

An oddity was a male Ladder-backed Woodpecker that I observed east of Boys Ranch, Oldham County, 19 May 1988. The scapulars, secondaries, and greater wing coverts were all brown, with little or no white spotting, and the face was strongly buff colored. I did not see its underside.

NESTING: The Ladder-backed Woodpecker is an early nester. A bird "making a nest" was observed at Lake Tanglewood, Randall County, 23 February 1968. I observed a female disputing possession of a nest hole with House Sparrows as early as 30 March 1968 (Randall County); a pair copulating, 11 April 1988 (Potter County); an adult on a nest, 16 April 1972 (Randall County); and small young in a nest, 2 May 1970 (Randall County). I find no late nesting dates on file; however, an adult ladder-backed feeding nestlings was observed at Lubbock as late as 5 October 1985 (Williams, 1986).

The TBBAP (1987–92) discovered CO nesting in five survey blocks, PR in 14, and PO in 13. With the exception of one quadrangle, all those occupied between the 100th and 101st meridians were found south of 35 degrees latitude, those between the 101st and 102nd meridians south of 36 degrees latitude, and those west of the 102nd meridian, with three exceptions, between 35 and 36 degrees latitude.

SPECIMENS: Specimens have been collected in Hutchinson (17 June and 9 July 1950, TNHC) and Randall (24 February, 7 May, and 1 September 1939, P-PHM; 1, 6, and 22 January 1939 and 29 April 1968, WTAMU) counties. Oberholser (1974) shows specimens collected in Armstrong, Deaf Smith, Hutchinson, Potter, and Randall counties, without giving further details. It is probable that his Hutchinson County birds refer to those collected by Thompson (1952; TNHC). Stevenson (1942) also names "several specimens . . . collected in Palo Duro Canyon in December, 1935. One was collected . . . 10 miles north of Amarillo on September 27, 1938." These were very likely the Randall and Potter county birds referred to by Oberholser.

Sutton classified Thompson's specimens as the subspecies *symplectus*. Those taken in western Oklahoma he found to be *cactophilus* (TOS, 1995). Perhaps both races occur in the study area.

Downy Woodpecker *Picoides pubescens* (Linnaeus)

STATUS: Fairly common to common resident in the eastern and central (local) sectors; a visitor elsewhere.

OCCURRENCE: The Downy Woodpecker has been recorded in 22 counties. Those missing are Carson, Castro, Deaf Smith, and Sherman. Oberholser (1974) shows it in eight. It has been found in every month.

A resident throughout the eastern sector, in the central portion the Downy Woodpecker is largely confined to the Canadian River Valley and tributaries, the upper reaches of Palo Duro Canyon, and the larger towns with many trees. In the western counties, it is resident at least as far west along the Canadian River as the Boys Ranch area in Oldham County. The species has been reported fairly commonly in other localities but only as a transient. As examples, it has been found intermittently in the PDCSP from October to March and at the BLNWR from August to May.

An indication of the Downy Woodpecker's winter status is provided by how often it has been recorded on the CBCs: *Amarillo*—13 of 40; *Buffalo Lake NWR*—5 of 29; *Lake Meredith (east)*—7 of 18; *Lake Meredith (west)*—22 of 24; *Quitaque*—7 of 20. No CBC count circle is located in the eastern sector. The Arnett, Ellis County, Oklahoma, CBC is nearby, however, and perhaps is representative of this woodpecker's status in the northeastern sector of the study area. There the species has been seen on all 31 counts (1966–96) at an average of 7.5 per count.

NESTING: Nest building has been observed as early as March in Amarillo, Potter County (1992), and adults with juveniles as late as 24 July at Lake Marvin, Hemphill County (1977). The TBBAP found CO nesting in 13 survey blocks, PR in four, and PO in 11. Eighteen were located between the 100th and 101st meridians, eight between the 101st and 102nd, and two west of the 102nd meridian.

SPECIMENS: One specimen is available for Randall County (7 May 1939, WTAMU). The subspecies found in the Texas Panhandle is *medianus* (TOS, 1995).

Hairy Woodpecker *Picoides villosus* (Linnaeus)

STATUS: Uncommon to fairly common resident locally in the eastern sector and along the Canadian River and its tributaries westward to eastern Oldham County; a visitor elsewhere.

OCCURRENCE: The Hairy Woodpecker has been recorded in 17 counties: Childress, Collingsworth, Donley, Gray, Hall, Hansford, Hartley, Hemphill, Hutchinson, Moore, Lipscomb, Ochiltree, Oldham, Potter, Randall, Roberts, and Wheeler. Oberholser (1974) shows it in four, all located in the northeastern sector. It has been found year-round.

As a summer resident, the Hairy Woodpecker is largely confined to the eastern third of the study area and the Canadian River drainage westward to Oldham County. My records show that the Downy Woodpecker outnumbers the Hairy Woodpecker at a ratio of 2.5:1. In the Lake Marvin and Lake McClellan areas the ratio is 3:1. The only areas where I have found them at parity are Lake Meredith and Boys Ranch along the Canadian River. These figures are based on year-round sightings. As examples of their status beyond summer ranges, in 30 years I have recorded 41 downies on the BLNWR and only four hairies, and in the PDCSP the respective numbers are 23 and two. It is also of interest that I have found the Hairy Woodpecker in Hartley County in the northwest sector (Punta de Aqua and Rita Blanca creeks) but never the Downy Woodpecker.

The frequency with which it has been recorded on the CBCs gives some indications of the Hairy Woodpecker's status in winter: *Amarillo*—6 of 40; *Buffalo Lake* NWR—2 of 29; *Lake Meredith* (*east*)—6 of 18; *Lake Meredith* (*west*)—20 of 24; *Quitaque*—0. No CBC is located in the eastern Panhandle. The Arnett, Ellis County, Oklahoma CBC is conducted nearby, and the Hairy Woodpecker has been recorded there on 25 of 31 counts.

NESTING: Although there have been numerous sightings during the breeding season, few Hairy Woodpeckers have been confirmed nesting. Thompson (1952) collected an adult female in breeding condition on 22 June and a juvenile male in nonbreeding condition on 17 June 1950, both on the Bugbee Ranch in Hutchinson County. Other sightings have followed: 9 June 1969, female with juvenile at feeder on the Jokerst Ranch, Randall County; 16 April 1988, a copulating pair on the Duncan Ranch (White Deer Creek), Hutchinson County; 7 May 1988, a female carrying food to a nest hole at Lake McClellan, Gray County; 12 July 1996, an adult and juvenile on the Taylor Lakes WMA, Donley County; 22 April 1998, a male excavating a nest hole at Greenbelt Lake, Donley County. The TBBAP found CO nesting in one survey block, PR in two, and PR in 13. Thirteen were located between the 100th and 101st meridians, two between the 101st and 102nd, and one west of the 102nd.

TABLE 2

	Percentage	Average No.
January	12%	1.46
February	6%	1.02
March	6%	0.87
April	5%	0.49
May	5%	0.37
June	4%	0.33
July	3%	0.32
August	1%	0.14
September	7%	0.60
October	17%	1.74
November	14%	1.85
December	20%	2.34

SPECIMENS: Two specimens are available from Hutchinson County (17 and 22 June 1950, TNHC)—the ones collected by Thompson (1952). Oberholser (1974) names one taken in Lipscomb County but fails to name the collection where it was deposited.

Northern Flicker *Colaptes auratus* (Linnaeus)

STATUS: Fairly common to common resident.

OCCURRENCE: The Northern Flicker has been recorded in every Texas Panhandle county except Sherman and has been seen in every month.

The Northern Flicker can be classified as common throughout most of the study area from October through February and uncommon to fairly common from March through September. Broken down by month, my records (1964–95) disclose percentage for the year and average number per man-hour afield (2,151 trips of three hours each) (table 2).

These figures reflect the steady decline from a December peak until numbers begin increasing again in late September with the return of migrants and wintering birds.

The CBCs (averages and highs) are indicative of the flicker's status in the central Panhandle during early winter: *Amarillo*—27.2, 72; *Buffalo Lake* NWR—13.3, 28; *Friona*—0.4, 1; *Lake Meredith* (*east*)—24.2, 64; *Lake Meredith* (*west*)—37.4, 111; *Quitaque*—16.3, 50. The BBSS (averages and highs) are less informative on the summer status, as the routes are quite spotty in their inclusion of flicker habitat. Four counts are conducted in the eastern sector: *Clarendon*—2, 8; *Booker*—1.4, 4; *Miami*—1.7, 6; *Childress*—0.2, 1. Four are in the central sector:

Waka—0.2, 2; *Pantex*—0; *Panhandle*—0.3, 1; *Skellytown*—0.3, 1. Three are in the western sector: *Channing*—0.6, 2; *Texline*—0; *Dalhart*—1.0, 1.

The TBBAP produced a more comprehensive picture of summer distribution. Flickers were found uniformly present throughout the eastern one-third and central sector, fairly widespread in the west-central sector, and absent in the extreme northwest, north-central, southwest and south-central sectors. The Canadian River Valley and the Palo Duro Canyon system are the avenues of western penetration, and the wooded sections of the larger towns provide oases of favorable habitat. On both the BBSS and TBBAP, only Yellow-shafted Flickers were recorded.

In comparing the present status of the Northern Flicker in the study area with that of the past, it is necessary to discuss the species in terms of the two races, *A. a. auratus* ("Yellow-shafted") and *A. a. cafer* ("Red-shafted"). Prior to 1973 the two were considered separate species (AOU, 1973), and earlier observers recorded their observations on that basis. It is of interest to note what pre-1960 observers had to say concerning the status and relationship of the two races and then to compare their findings with ours of today.

McCauley (1877) does not speak of the flicker at all, a surprising omission in view of his spending so much time in favorable habitats during May and June. Both Reeves and Reeves (1914) and Hibbets et al. (1926–36) make only brief references to the species. It is with Carlander (1934) that we first get an assessment of the Yellow-shafted/Red-shafted relationship: "The yellow-shafted (or golden-winged) flicker is found here in abundance in the winter, but we have seen the red-shafted flicker here only once." Stevenson's (1942) references to the Yellow-shafted were limited to a few observations in the Palo Duro Canyon area in fall and winter, while he spoke of the Red-shafted as "common in winter in the Palo Duro and adjacent canyons." Hawkins's (1945) account offers more details:

> *Yellow-shafted:* Uncommon summer resident of the eastern Panhandle. Along the Canadian River in the eastern Panhandle this species and the Red-shafted Flicker seem to be about equally common during the summer months, but in the western Panhandle the Yellow-shafted Flicker was listed by the author only once. . . . *Red-shafted:* Common during migration; uncommon summer resident. In the western Panhandle many of these woodpeckers were present from early March throughout most of April, but only once was noted during the summer months. They are present, however, in fair numbers in the eastern Panhandle during the summer months.

Thompson's (1952) work was limited to a single summer season (1950) in the Bugbee Creek area of Hutchinson County, where he collected only Yellow-

TABLE 3

January	RS:YS = 6.5:1
February	RS:YS = 5.5:1
March	RS:YS = 9:1
April	RS:YS = 1.5:1
May	RS:YS = 1:1
June	YS:RS = 6.5:1
July	no RS recorded
August	no YS recorded
September	RS:YS = 6.5:1
October	RS:YS = 6:1
November	RS:YS = 8.5:1
December	RS:YS = 8:1

shafted Flickers. In assessing the then current status of the two species, the editor in Oberholser (1974) concluded that the Yellow-shafted Flicker was "uncommon and irregular in northwestern Panhandle . . . and almost out of the reproductive business in the state"; and that the Red-shafted Flicker was "scarce and local in northern Panhandle (nesting suspected). In winter, common west of 100th meridian."

We can compare these observations with what my records of later years reveal. Because all of the sightings after 1973 do not specify the race, my summations are based on the ten-year period 1964–73, when the two subspecies were considered separate species. These records disclose a relationship that differs markedly in several ways from those of earlier observers. On a year-round basis, the Red-shafted Flicker outnumbers Yellow-shafted Flicker by a ratio of 5:1. During the nonbreeding season (August–April) the ratio is yet greater—7:1. During the breeding season (May–July), however, there is a complete reversal, for then yellow-shafteds outnumber the red-shafteds at the same ratio of 7:1. It is worth noting how this relationship changes from month to month as the year progresses (table 3).

These figures are in complete contradiction to Carlander's. Where he found the Yellow-shafted Flicker in abundance in winter and recorded the Red-shafted but once, I have found the Red-shafted far outnumbering the Yellow-shafted. My observations also are not in accordance with those of Hawkins in summer. Where he found the two races about "equally common" in summer along the Canadian River in the eastern Panhandle, I have not found the Red-shafted Flicker present at all; and while he recorded the Yellow-shafted but once in summer in the western Panhandle, I have found it to be the sole race present. I have never recorded the Red-shafted after 14 May or prior to 8 August. However, I have observed a number of hybrids.

Perhaps this reversal can be attributed in part to the fact that the zone of hybridization of the two races of flickers bisects the western Texas Panhandle, the area of primary introgression beginning just west of Norman in central Oklahoma (Short, 1965). Short based his assignments on six color characteristics in determining the "purity" between the two races: (1) crown, (2) ear coverts, (3) throat, (4) nuchal patch, (5) shaft, (6) malar color in males. Most observers base their identifications solely on (5) and (6), particularly shaft color. It should be understood that although I speak of "Yellow-shafted" and "Red-shafted" flickers in this text, some of the birds were possibly hybrids.

Recent studies have shown that both Yellow-shafted and Red-shafted Flicker populations are declining in the United States and Canada, a total decline of 52 percent over a 25-year period for the Yellow-shafted and 19 percent over a 23-year period for the Red-shafted (Moore, 1995). My records, based on number of flickers recorded per hour afield during winter (October–February), do not reflect this decline: 1965–74, 1.38; 1975–84, 2.14; 1985–95, 1.73.

NESTING: The editor's statement in Oberholser (1974) that the flicker is "almost out of the reproductive business in the state" is not true of the study area. The TBBAP proved the flicker to be one of the most widespread of the nesting woodpeckers, exceeded in the eastern counties only by the Red-headed Woodpecker and in the Palo Duro Canyon system by the Golden-fronted and Ladder-backed woodpeckers. CO nesting was established in 15 survey blocks, PR in 22, and PO in 12. Twenty-six of the occupied quadrangles were between the 100th and 101st meridians, 14 between the 101st and 102nd, and nine west of the 102nd meridian. All of the 33 quadrangles that I surveyed held Yellow-shafted Flickers. We have no egg dates on file. Adults on the nest have been observed as early as 11 April (Canyon, Randall County), and as late as 10 July (McBride Canyon, Lake Meredith, Hutchinson County).

SPECIMENS: *C. a. auratus* specimens have been collected in Hansford (22 December 1955, MNH), Hutchinson (12, 21, 27 June, and 1 July 1950, TNHC), Oldham (1 February 1982, TCWC), Potter (ACMNH), and Randall (6 January 1939, P-PHM) counties, and *C. a. cafer* in Hutchinson (23 November 1968, WTAMU), Potter (ACMNH), and Randall (1, 22, 29 January, 10 February, and 13 March 1939, P-PHM; 30 September 1957, TCWC; 15 December 1965, WTAMU) counties. It would be of value to know to what extent, if any, these specimens are hybrids. Oberholser (1974) names a specimen of *C. a. luteus* collected in Lipscomb County but fails to give details: perhaps he is referring to the bird collected by Short (1965). Stevenson (1942) also cites a specimen of *C. cafer colaris* collected in Randall County, 30 September 1937, but its present whereabouts is unknown.

ORDER PASSERIFORMES

Family Tyrannidae (Tyrant Flycatchers)

Olive-sided Flycatcher *Contopus cooperi* (Nuttall)
STATUS: Fairly common migrant.
OCCURRENCE: The Olive-sided Flycatcher has been found in 15 counties: Armstrong, Briscoe, Castro, Dallam, Deaf Smith, Donley, Gray, Hartley, Hemphill, Hutchinson, Ochiltree, Oldham, Parmer, Potter, and Randall. Oberholser (1974) shows it in four: Armstrong, Parmer, Potter, and Randall. It has been seen in the periods April–June and August–October.

The first Olive-sided Flycatchers of spring can be looked for during the first week of May. There have been only a few April sightings, one quite early—a single bird near Canyon, Randall County, 12 April 1986. The spring passage extends into late May, occasionally into June. The latest June date, a puzzler, is of a bird that remained in Amarillo, Randall County, until the last of June 1967. These late birds do not imply possible nesting, for the olive-sided is known to be a late migrant, nesting no nearer the Texas Panhandle than the Guadalupe and Davis mountains of Texas (TOS, 1995) and the mountains of central New Mexico (Hubbard, 1978). Just as it may linger late, so does the species return early in fall, usually during the last week of August, the earliest date being for one at BLNWR, 3 August 1968. Rarely is one encountered past September, the latest being for a single bird near Canyon, Randall County, 9 October 1956.

The arrival and departure dates of the Olive-sided Flycatcher and Western Wood-Pewee almost coincide. With the arrival of one one can expect arrival of the other; likewise, the departure of one is followed soon afterward by the other. For the period 1965–95, my records reveal the early and late spring dates for the olive-sided as 26 April–9 June and for the wood-pewee 1 May–10 June. The corresponding fall dates are 3 August–1 October, and 1 August–3 October. While I have seen slightly more than twice as many wood-pewees as olive-sideds, the degree of seasonal movement has been almost identical: I have recorded 62 percent more olive-sideds in fall than in spring, and 57 percent more wood-pewees. Migrants of both species are more evenly spread out in spring than in fall, with hardly discernible peaks and valleys. The single week of greatest occurrence is 16–22 May, when 39 percent of all olive-sideds were recorded and 37 percent of all wood-pewees. While fall migration covers a 64-day span as compared to 47 in spring, there is a pronounced movement in early September for both species. For the Olive-sided Flycatcher, 50 percent of all birds were recorded during the week of 3–9 September, and for the Western Wood-Pewee, 54 percent during the week of 1–7 September.

Western Wood-Pewee *Contopus sordidulus* Sclater

STATUS: Fairly common migrant.

OCCURRENCE: The Western Wood-Pewee has been recorded in 18 counties: Armstrong, Briscoe, Castro, Dallam, Deaf Smith, Donley, Gray, Hansford, Hartley, Hemphill, Hutchinson, Lipscomb, Moore, Ochiltree, Oldham, Parmer, Potter, and Randall. Oberholser (1974) shows it in three: Oldham, Parmer, and Potter. It has been seen from April to October.

The first Western Wood-Pewees in spring can be expected in the first week of May. There have been only three seen in April, the earliest one in Amarillo, Potter County, 25 April 1955. Most are gone by late May. The species is noted for being a late spring migrant and there are numerous June records. Returning birds in fall can be looked for in early August, the earliest a single bird at BLNWR, 1 August 1970—several late July records are probably of early migrants. Few remain past September, the latest a single bird in Vega, Oldham County, 23 October 1992.

The nearest localities to the Texas Panhandle where the Western Wood-Pewee has been found breeding are in the western Oklahoma Panhandle and northeastern New Mexico (Johnsgard, 1979). For Oklahoma Sutton (1967) says "(presumably) summer resident in Cimarron County seen from April 27 to September 26." He cites seven specimens (male and female) taken in summer in Cimarron County, none showing gonads greatly enlarged. Baumgartner and Baumgartner (1992) cite a record of nesting (nest and eggs), 3 June 1920, near Kenton, Cimarron County (R. C. Tate). For New Mexico Hubbard (1978) says: "Eastern limits of main breeding population are the Dry Cimarron, Canadian, and Pecos valleys" in the northeastern sector. In southwestern Kansas singing males on territory in suitable habitat have often been seen, but nesting has never been confirmed (Thompson and Ely, 1992). Although there is no evidence of the Western Wood-Pewee nesting in the study area, the frequency of June and July sightings, particulary of birds found in the northern tier of counties, warrants close attention for such a possibility.

Occasionally during fall the Western Wood-Pewee can be found in abundance: at BLNWR there were 75+ on 3 September 1968 and 35+ on 7 September 1970. For a comparison of its status with that of the Olive-sided Flycatcher, see the species account for that flycatcher.

SPECIMENS: Oberholser (1974) cites a summer specimen collected in Oldham County, 4 June (*C. s. veliei*), but its location is not given.

Eastern Wood-Pewee *Contopus virens* (Linnaeus)

STATUS: Rare to uncommon migrant.

OCCURRENCE: The Eastern Wood-Pewee has been recorded in six counties: Armstrong, Gray, Hartley, Hutchinson, Potter, and Randall. It has been seen May–June and August–October.

The status of the Eastern Wood-Pewee in the study area is poorly known, and much remains to be learned. Few have been reported; it is probable that a fair number of nonsinging birds have been assigned to the more common Western Wood-Pewee in default, particularly those found in the eastern sector. The difficulty in distinguishing between the two species is pointed out by Rising and Schueler (1980) in their study of wood-pewees in the Great Plains: "The Eastern and Western wood pewees are difficult to separate both in the field and in the hand. The most conspicuous difference between the two—their distinctive primary songs—is of restricted use: the females do not sing; spring migrants sing rather infrequently and fall migrants probably do not sing at all. . . . Singing birds were morphologically like those of the species whose song they sang; hence we have no evidence of song switching. . . . We have no evidence of hybridization."

Oberholser (1974) is of the opinion that the Eastern Wood-Pewee "probably nests occasionally in northern Panhandle," and Johnsgard (1979) shows its breeding range as "extending locally into the Texas Panhandle" (Red River up to the junction of Palo Duro and Tierra Blanca Creeks near Canyon, Randall County). Neither author provides supporting data for his claim.

Other than Stevenson (1942), who collected "an adult female, probably a migrant . . . in Palo Duro Canyon on the Elkins Ranch on August 11, 1936," none of the observers prior to mid-century named the Eastern Wood-Pewee in their accounts. Surprisingly, Stevenson did not mention the Western Wood-Pewee at all. Sightings of the Eastern Wood-Pewee have been few and scattered, those few heard singing as follows: BLNWR, 10 June 1967, 7 June 1969, 6 June 1970, 19 June 1983, 14 May 1985, 17 May 1995; Duncan Ranch (White Deer Creek), southeastern Hutchinson County, 18 June 1988; Reynolds Ranch (Rita Blanca Creek), Hartley County, 2 June 1990 (along with five or more singing Western Wood-Pewees); Lake McClellan, Gray County, 10 May 1997. None of the singing birds were observed again when the locations were revisited.

Only one of these observations (Gray County) was made in the eastern sector, where one would expect to find the Eastern Wood-Pewee; however, that area has not been birded with regularity in summer. In north-central Texas Pulich (1988) places "suspected" nesting as near as Wichita County. In Oklahoma Baumgartner and Baumgartner (1992) place nesting as far west as Caddo and Comanche counties and say the species has been recorded irregularly on a BBS route in Roger Mills County, adjacent to Hemphill County, Texas.

SPECIMENS: A specimen is available from Randall County (11 August 1936, TCWC). It is the one collected by Stevenson (1942) and referred to by Oberholser (1974).

Empidonax Flycatchers *Empidonax* spp.

STATUS: Fairly common to common migrant.

OCCURRENCE: Empidonax flycatchers have been recorded in all but four counties: Childress, Hall, Sherman, and Wheeler. Oberholser (1974) shows them in only four: Dallam, Oldham, Potter, and Randall. They have been seen March–December.

Eight species of empidonax flycatchers have been identified in the study area: Yellow-bellied, Acadian, Willow, Least, Hammond's, Dusky, Gray, and "Western" (presumably Cordilleran). Six of these are represented in the six species accounts that follow, and for the other two there are accounts later, under Species of Uncertain Occurrence. Those identified represent only a tiny percentage of the total number of empids seen. With few exceptions, only the Willow and Least flycatchers have been heard singing during their passage, and without extensive experience with each species on its nesting grounds or knowledge gained by the study of specimens, in most cases it is prudent simply to list a nonsinging bird as "*Empidonax* sp." Even observers with such experience and knowledge disclaim 100 percent accuracy in their ability to identify every empid correctly by sight alone. For these reasons, it is desirable that a specimen or series of definitive photographs be secured for each species listed in this work in order to place its reported presence on a firm foundation.

The first empids of spring can be expected the first week of May. There have been few April sightings, the earliest a single bird in Amarillo, Randall County, 10 April 1968. There is one March report: Amarillo, Randall County, 25 March 1956. There is an almost complete termination of sightings after 1 June. The seven-day period of greatest abundance is 16–22 May. Fall birds begin arriving the last week of July, and it is seldom that any are found beyond late September or early October, the latest a single bird in Amarillo, Randall County, 9 November 1958. The fall seven-day period of greatest abundance is 2–8 September. It is in fall that most empids have been recorded (72%), the largest number in a single day being 100 or more on 8 September 1969 in the two Amarillo cemeteries.

Winter sightings are three. The first, reportedly a Least, was observed in South Ceta Canyon, Randall County, 6 December 1936 (Hibbets et al., 1926–36). On 10 December 1994, an empid was found at the Sad Monkey Railroad Station

TABLE 4

Species	Number	Percentage	Period
Least	28	36.4	22 July–2 October
Willow	24	31.2	22 July–15 September
Dusky	11	14.3	28 July–6 September
"Western"	9	11.6	15 August–18 September
Hammond's	5	6.5	9 September–28 September

in the PDCSP, and on 17–25 December another was found less than a mile farther downcanyon at the first water crossing, presumably the same bird. During the same period another empid was discovered south of the study area on the Muleshoe NWR, Bailey County, 18 December. This bird was videotaped and identified as a Gray Flycatcher (TP-RF). While the Palo Duro bird was definitely not of that species, its possible identity remained a matter of speculation. On 2 December 1997, another empid was observed in a suburban backyard in Canyon, Randall County.

There have been a number of June sightings of interest (see individual accounts for others): *Dallam*—one in the Thompson Grove Picnic Area near Texline, 7 June 1980; *Donley*—one in the Lelia Creek area, 10 June 1969. *Oldham*—one along Rico Creek north of Boys Ranch, 6 June 1982. *Randall*—1–2 in the PDCSP, 10 June 1956 and 4 July 1964; three at BLNWR, 28 June 1969, five on 6 June and one on 20 June 1970, and one on 4 June 1972; one at Lake Tanglewood, 9 June 1963.

Of 77 empidonax flycatchers identified by an experienced observer during the fall of 1994 in southwest Castro County, the following is a breakdown by species (letter, C. D. Littlefield, 14 December 1994); how many went unidentified is not known (table 4).

Willow Flycatcher *Empidonax traillii* (Audubon)

STATUS: Uncommon to fairly common migrant.

OCCURRENCE: The Willow Flycatcher has been recorded in 12 counties: Armstrong, Castro, Dallam, Deaf Smith, Donley, Gray, Hansford, Hartley, Hemphill, Oldham, Potter, and Randall. It has been seen from April to September.

Along with the Least, the Willow Flycatcher is the most common of the empids in the study area and the one most often heard singing. It is particularly vocal during late May. The earliest spring date is 26 April 1995 at BLNWR. The early and late fall dates are 30 July 1997 in Armstrong County and 15 September 1933 in Randall County. Several June birds have been reported: one at BLNWR, 1 June 1986; one singing on the Reynolds Ranch (Rita Blanca Creek), Hartley

County, 2 June 1990; one in the Thompson Grove Picnic Area northeast of Tex-line, Dallam County, 7 June 1980, 9 June 1984 and 13 June 1987; one in the Lelia Creek area northeast of Clarendon, Donley County, 10 June 1969; one at the Palo Duro Club near Canyon, Randall County, 10 June 1964; two birds together, plus two singles, near Westway, Deaf Smith County, 14–17 June 1991. The number of summer sightings has led to speculation about the possibility of the Willow Flycatcher occasionally nesting; Carlander (1934) was even led to classify it a "summer resident."

In nearby areas of Oklahoma Sutton (1967) speaks of a male Willow Flycatcher reported as a possible nester: a bird taken on 8 June 1965 in a dense stand of cottonwoods along the Cimarron River in northern Beaver County, northeast of Forgan. Furthermore, he says the species "certainly breeds" in Ellis County, although neither nests nor young were ever found. In northeastern New Mexico, the Willow Flycatcher has been found breeding in the upper Piñabetitos Creek area in Union County, 22 miles west and 6.5 miles south of Clayton (NMOS, 1992). South of the study area on the southern plains, one was found in Crosby County, 1 July 1979 (Williams, 1979). For a further discussion of this group of birds, see Empidonax Flycatchers.

SPECIMENS: Carlander (1933) reported a specimen taken at an unnamed point in the Texas Panhandle sometime between 15 August and 3 September 1932 and 19 June and 15 September 1933. He stated that one specimen was in the "Canyon Museum" (Panhandle-Plains Historical Museum); if so, I have not been able to locate it. Oberholser (1974) cites summer specimens taken in Oldham (June 6), Dallam, and Potter counties, and a spring bird taken in Oldham County, but details for all are lacking.

Least Flycatcher *Empidonax minimus* (Baird and Baird)

STATUS: Uncommon to fairly common migrant.

OCCURRENCE: The Least Flycatcher has been recorded in eight Texas Panhandle counties: Armstrong, Castro, Donley, Hansford, Hemphill, Oldham, Potter, and Randall. It has been seen from May to October.

Most of the Least Flycatcher records on file are based on singing (*"che-bec"*) birds. The earliest spring record is of two singing at BLNWR, 6 May 1985, and the latest another singing bird at Lake Tanglewood, Randall County, 9 June 1963. Unlike the Willow Flycatcher, more often heard during its late May passage, the Least is commonly heard also in early and mid-May. The early and late fall dates range from a singing bird in Amarillo, Potter County, 1 August 1997, to one singing in Amarillo, Potter County, 1 October 1983. Hibbets et al. (1926–36) reported a Least Flycatcher in South Ceta Canyon, Randall County, 6 December 1936. Many of the late June and early July sightings of unidentified empids have probably been Least Flycatchers, for that species leaves its breeding grounds quite early. The Least is remarkable in that it spends no more than 64 days on its breeding grounds, of which at least 58 days are needed to raise broods. Adults leave before hatch-year birds, and studies have shown that at Long Point, Ontario, 90 percent pass through during the 34-day period 11 July–13 August; on the latter date some are already on their wintering grounds in Guatemala (Briskie, 1994).

Specimens of the Least Flycatcher have been taken in Beaver, Cimarron, Greer, Harper, and Texas counties of western Oklahoma (Sutton, 1967): "The one breeding record for the state, a nest and four eggs taken May 29, 1913, near Kenton, Cimarron County . . . must be regarded as questionable in view of the fact that no bird was collected." There is no evidence of breeding in Kansas (Thompson and Ely, 1992).

SPECIMENS: One specimen is available taken in Hemphill County (29 July 1971, TCWC).

Hammond's Flycatcher *Empidonax hammondii* (Xantus de Vesey)

STATUS: Rare migrant in southwestern sector.

OCCURRENCE: The only county in the Texas Panhandle where the Hammond's Flycatcher has been reported is Castro. It has been found in May, August, and September.

Daily spring and fall censusing of a wooded area ("Dodd's Woodlot") in the southwestern corner of Castro County produced the following sightings of Hammond's Flycatcher (C. D. Littlefield): *1990*—9 August (1), 7 September (1); *1991*—17 August (1), 31 August (1), 2 September (2), 3 September (1), 5 September (2), 29 September (1); *1992*—15–16 August (1), 5–6 September (1), 11–12 September (1), 23–24 September (1); *1993*—8 May (1), 13 May (1), 19 May (1), 24 August (1), 26 August (1), 30–31 August (1), 1 September (1), 20 September (1). Such regularity emphasizes the need for closer examination of all empids.

Sutton (1967) speaks of Hammond's Flycatchers found at locations in Oklahoma near the Texas Panhandle: "First found in state in 1932 and 1933, when five specimens were taken in 'oak-lined, rocky gullies along steep mesa-sides' near Kenton, Cimarron County. Specimen taken in Harmon County in 1954 (2 October) was among elms and hackberries in sheltered spot along dry streambed near Vinson." Harmon County, adjacent to Childress and Collingsworth counties, is indicative of the possibility that the Hammond's may appear anywhere in the Panhandle, not just the western counties. Weske (1976) also speaks of finding the Hammond's during field work in the Kenton area, 6–13 September 1974 (specimen). More recently, Gryzbowski (1996) cites a Hammond's "carefully studied" in Cimarron County, 2 September 1995.

In Texas the Hammond's Flycatcher is also known as a rare to uncommon migrant in the Trans-Pecos (TOS, 1995), while in New Mexico it is a summer resident locally in mountainous areas and a migrant statewide, possibly as far east as Clayton in Union County (Ligon, 1961; Hubbard, 1978). That some of the birds that nest in Colorado and New Mexico would pass through the study area when migrating to their wintering grounds in Mexico and Central America is to be expected. A paucity of spring sightings is also to be expected, for most Hammond's are known to migrate farther west during their passage northward (Sedgwick, 1994).

Dusky Flycatcher *Empidonax oberholseri* Phillips

STATUS: Rare migrant in southwestern sector.

OCCURRENCE: The Dusky Flycatcher has been recorded in one Texas Panhandle county, Castro. It has been seen in the periods April–May and July–September.

This is another of the empidonax flycatchers that have recently been added to the list of Texas Panhandle birds. Because of problems in identification presented by all the empids, particularly in the case of nonsinging birds, local observers have been reluctant to place name tags on them, and wisely so. In 1990 an observer familiar with the species on its western breeding grounds began recording the Dusky Flycatcher with regularity in southwestern Castro County. The birds were observed at an abandoned homesite ("Dodd's Woodlot") consisting of some 20 acres of trees (elm, oak, juniper, Arizona cypress), weeds, and shrubs, located adjacent to a playa lake. The lot was surveyed daily from 15 March to 15 June and from 1 August to 15 October. The Dusky Flycatcher was recorded as follows: *1990*—15–20 May, 12 September. *1991*—28 July–10 September; *1992*—25 April–8 May, 29 July–6 October; *1993*—29 August–12 September.

The Dusky Flycatcher has been collected north of the study area in the Oklahoma Panhandle: "Nine specimens have been taken, eight in spring (May 1–19), one in fall (September 23)"—all in Cimarron County in 1954 (Sutton, 1967). In addition, Weske (1976) observed others in the Kenton area of Cimarron County during eight days of field work (6–13 September) in 1974. What was thought to be a Dusky Flycatcher remained in a Lubbock yard, 30 August–1 September 1988 (Lasley and Sexton, 1989). This empid is considered the "most regular of the 'western' Empidonaces in Kansas," and is a "low-density transient" in the western portion of the state (Thompson and Ely, 1992).

The Dusky Flycatcher is a common migrant in the Trans-Pecos (TOS, 1995). In New Mexico it summers locally in mountainous areas as near the study area as Sierra Grande Mountain in western Union County (NMOS, 1992) and is a migrant statewide (Hubbard, 1978).

Gray Flycatcher *Empidonax wrightii* Baird

STATUS: Vagrant migrant in southwestern sector.

OCCURRENCE: The Gray Flycatcher has been recorded twice in the Texas Panhandle, once in Castro County and once in Randall County.

On 30 August 1987, a singing Gray Flycatcher was observed at length at
BLNWR (K. Seyffert), and on 2 September 1992 another was found in southwestern Castro County (C. D. Littlefield). This site is located three miles north of
the Castro–Lamb county line. A few feet south of the line, Gray Flycatchers were
found again on 19 August 1992 and 19 September 1993.

The Gray Flycatcher was classified as an uncommon migrant in the Trans-
Pecos until recently, when nesting was discovered in the Davis Mountains (Pe-
terson et al., 1991). It has been recorded as a migrant in New Mexico only as far
east as Las Vegas and the Sacramento Highlands (Hubbard, 1978), and a speci-
men was taken along the Cimarron River, northeast of Elkhart, Morton County,
Kansas, 29 April 1967 (Thompson and Ely, 1992). One was videotaped on the
Muleshoe NWR, Bailey County, on the very late date of 18 December 1994
(TP-RF).

Cordilleran Flycatcher *Empidonax occidentalis* Nelson

STATUS: Casual migrant in the southwestern sector.

OCCURRENCE: The Cordilleran Flycatcher has been recorded in two western counties of the Texas Panhandle: Castro and Parmer. It has been seen from May
to September.

Almost all Cordilleran Flycatchers have been found in Castro County, and
those only in recent years: *1990*—16 May–27 May, 30 July–3 September; *1991*—
11 August–12 September; *1992*—4 June, 22–23 August; *1993*—2–15 September.
They were found on "Dodd's Woodlot" in the southwestern corner of Castro
County. A few other nonsinging birds have been reported elsewhere, all lacking
supporting details other than shape of eye-ring. As is the case for all empids, a
specimen would place this species' presence in the study area on a more solid
foundation.

An immature female Cordilleran Flycatcher was taken 10 km east of Kenton,
Cimarron County, Oklahoma, 6 September 1974 (Weske, 1976). A. J. Krehbiel
classified it as an "occasional transient visitor" in the Clayton area, Union
County, New Mexico (Weske, 1968); however, the species is considered rare east
of the Rocky Mountains, and Hubbard (1978) pointed out that migrants reported on the eastern plains of New Mexcio had not been verified. Two specimens have been collected from the Cimarron River south of Richfield, Morton
County, southwestern Kansas, 3 and 5 September 1952, and a singing bird was
reported in the same area, 26 May 1984 (Thompson and Ely, 1992). In other

sections of Texas, the Cordilleran Flycatcher is an uncommon summer resident in the Chisos, Davis and Guadalupe mountains (Peterson et al, 1991; TOS, 1995).

Black Phoebe *Sayornis nigricans* (Swainson)

STATUS: Casual summer and fall visitor.

OCCURRENCE: The Black Phoebe has been reported in four counties: Carson, Ochiltree, Potter, and Randall. It has been seen March–May, July–September, and November–December.

Sightings of the Black Phoebe are as follows—all of single birds: *1952*—BLNWR, 18 May. *1954*—Randall County, 4 September. *1955*—Palo Duro Club near Canyon, Randall County, 7 April, and Canyon, 23 May. *1956*—Canyon Country Club near Canyon, Randall County, 13 April. *1961*—Jokerst Ranch south of Amarillo, Randall County, on an unnamed date in April. *1964*—BLNWR, 8 May. *1967*—Amarillo, Potter County, 10 March. *1972*—BLNWR, 19 November. *1980*—Ceta Glen, South Ceta Canyon, Randall County, 9 September. *1981*—BLNWR, 26 July. *1983*—Amarillo, Potter County, 12 September. *1989*—Lark, Carson County, 30 March. *1995*—BLNWR, 6 August. *1998*—Wolf Creek Park, Ochiltree County, 7 December (TP-RF)

The Black Phoebe nests no nearer the Texas Panhandle than south-central Colorado (Pueblo, 1972–74), central New Mexico, and western and west-central Texas (AOU, 1983). It is classified as rare to uncommon from September to March in the Texas South Plains (LEAS, 1994).

Eastern Phoebe *Sayornis phoebe* (Latham)

STATUS: Uncommon to fairly common migrant. Rare to uncommon breeder locally. Vagrant winter visitor.

OCCURRENCE: The Eastern Phoebe has been recorded in 17 counties: Armstrong, Briscoe, Castro, Dallam, Deaf Smith, Donley, Gray, Hall, Hartley, Hemphill, Hutchinson, Moore, Oldham, Parmer, Potter, Randall, and Wheeler. Oberholser (1974) shows it in four: Briscoe, Deaf Smith, Potter, and Randall. It has been found in every month.

One of the earliest of the flycatchers to return in spring, the Eastern Phoebe arrives in mid-March or earlier: Lake Tanglewood, Randall County, 3 March 1974. Most migrants are gone by mid-May. There is considerable irregularity in return dates in fall. More consistency is found in the latest dates, most falling in the mid- to late October range. There have been four November sightings, the latest at PDCSP, 21 November 1990. Two of the three winter records were of single birds recorded in Caprock Canyons SP, Briscoe County—1 January 1976 and 14 and 31 December 1997. The other was a bird that remained on the BLNWR from

11 December 1993 to 26 February 1994. It spent the entire time in the Stewart Dike area at the upper end.

NESTING: Nesting is local and largely confined to the mesic draws and canyons of the Palo Duro Canyon system. While Hibbets et al. (1926–36) named the Eastern Phoebe as a "summer bird (June 1933)," and Carlander (1934) called it a "summer resident," neither mentioned finding nests. The first reference to actual breeding occurred in 1954 when several nests were found in June and July—one at Ceta Glen, South Ceta Canyon, Randall County, and two at the Girl Scout Camp in Randall County. Others have been found since: *Armstrong*—1 July 1990 (Dripping Springs). *Briscoe*—3 May 1998 (Caprock Canyons SP). *Hemphill*—24 June 1999 (Lake Marvin). *Randall*—summer of 1972 (Lake Tanglewood); South Ceta Canyon, 1 July 1973; yearly at Ceta Glen. Probable or possible nestings have been reported in other counties: *Gray* (Lake McLellan); *Oldham* (Vega); *Wheeler* (Wheeler).

To the north in the Oklahoma Panhandle, the Eastern Phoebe "breeds regularly in small numbers in Black Mesa country of Cimarron County" and eastward has nested in Greer and Harmon counties (Sutton, 1967). A pair of phoebes with eggs in the nest was found 17 miles southwest of Clayton, Union County, New Mexico, 9 June 1962 (Baumgartner, 1962).

Say's Phoebe *Sayornis saya* (Bonaparte)

STATUS: Fairly common to common migrant. Uncommon to fairly common breeder locally. Casual winter visitor.

OCCURRENCE: Oberholser (1974) shows the Say's Phoebe in nine Texas Panhandle counties: Armstrong, Briscoe, Dallam, Deaf Smith, Gray, Oldham, Parmer, Potter, and Randall. To these Carson, Castro, Childress, Donley, Hall, Hartley, Hutchinson, Lipscomb, Moore, Ochiltree, and Roberts can be added. It has been recorded in every month.

Today the Say's Phoebe is the most common of the phoebes in the study area, its plaintive call one of the early indicators of spring. Most observers prior to mid-century had little to say concerning it. McCauley (1877) spoke of seeing "several along McClellan Creek and a few other points," and Strecker (1910) found it "a common species in the canyons and arroyos." This was on a trip originating downstate that terminated in Armstrong County. Even more recently, the Say's Phoebe was not named by Reeves and Reeves (1914–36), Hibbets et al. (1926–36), Carlander (1934), or Russell (1935), while Stevenson (1942) and Hawkins (1945) both classified it as a rare migrant only. All of these observers worked in areas where the species can be found today.

The Say's Phoebe returns in early spring, usually in mid-March. The few that have been found in late February were probably migrants rather than wintering birds: one in PDCSP, 23 February 1992 and 26 February 1989, and one at Lake Tanglewood, Randall County, 28 February 1975. One to seven have been recorded in winter in 14 of 46 years. Most are gone by mid-May, and it is not until late August or early September that a southbound movement is detected. Except on the rare occasions when a few are seen in early or midwinter, most are gone by late September or early October. As a migrant, the Say's Phoebe is usually found singly or in very loose congregations: 25–30 at BLNWR on 22 September 1970 and 50 on 30 September 1961. Such large gatherings have never been reported in spring.

NESTING: The Say's Phoebe has been confirmed nesting in five counties: Armstrong, Deaf Smith, Hartley, Ochiltree, and Randall. Summer sightings indicating probable nesting have been recorded for Dallam, Briscoe, Carson, Castro, Childress, Gray, Lipscomb, Moore, Parmer, Potter, Oldham, and Roberts counties. During his trip to Armstrong County, Strecker (1910) spoke of finding nestings "under arched rocks and shelving cliffs and in shallow caves," and this is typical along much of the caprock escarpment today. Nesting phoebes are found regularly at Lake Tanglewood and in the PDCSP, where they occupy sites on and around houses, buildings, and picnic and camping shelters as well as natural sites on cliffsides. Two-broodedness has been observed regularly at Lake Tanglewood: four pairs feeding recently hatched young, 3 June 1973; second clutch of eggs, 28 June 1975. Nest building in the PDCSP has been observed as early as 28 April 1992 and as late as 10 July 1954. A singing bird was found at an abandoned farmstead east of Texline, Dallam County, 15 March 1995. Nests around abandoned homesites on the open plains are not uncommon: a nest containing young was found in Deaf Smith County, 4 July 1975, and a pair were seen nest building in Ochiltree County, 18 May 1991.

SPECIMENS: A specimen is available from Potter County (12 April 1981, TCWC). Oberholser (1974) shows specimens collected in Dallam ("Texline, Aug. 7, 1903, A. H. Howell") and Randall (fall) counties but does not give their present whereabouts.

Vermilion Flycatcher *Pyrocephalus rubinus* (Boddaert)

STATUS: Casual summer and fall visitor, with vagrant breeding.

OCCURRENCE: The Vermilion Flycatcher has been recorded in eight counties: Castro, Donley, Hutchinson, Parmer, Potter, Randall, Swisher, and Wheeler. It has been seen March–July and once in October.

Sightings by county are as follows, a single bird in each instance unless otherwise noted: *Castro*—Dodd, 16 April 1993. *Donley*—Clarendon, 23–27 June 1996. *Hutchinson*—Lake Meredith, 6 July 1967; Borger, 27 March 1971; Duncan Ranch, White Deer Creek, 14 May 1987. *Parmer*—1 October 1961 and 24 April 1963. *Pot-*

ter—Amarillo, 14 May 1995 and 11–13 April 1998 (TP-RF). *Randall*—near Canyon, 24 March 1956 and 19 March 1978; a pair in Amarillo, 8–11 April 1956 and 4 April 1976; one near Amarillo, 30 April 1956; at BLNWR, 18 March 1961 (2), 20–26 March and 3 April 1966, 7 June 1969, 21 May 1973, 1 April 1987, 21 June 1993, 16 May 1997; at PDCSP, 15 April 1987. *Swisher*—near Kress, 9 April 1987. *Wheeler*—near Wheeler, ca. 15 March 1986. The Vermilion Flycatcher reported by Baumgartner (1955) near Childress, Childress County, 10 April 1955, was in fact a male found dead on the M. S. Wells Ranch 15 miles southeast of Childress, Cottle County, outside the study area (*fide* R. DeArment).

NESTING: Two pairs nested in Amarillo in 1959. The female of the first pair was found on the nest on 6 May, and the three newly fledged young were observed on 1 June. On 12 June a second pair was located with three partially feathered young (P. Acord). These events took place in the city cemeteries (Potter/Randall counties).

Tomer (1983) reported finding nesting near Kenton, Cimarron County, Oklahoma, 8 May–11 June 1982, and Webster (1990) nesting in the same vicinity, 17 May–21 June 1990. The species nested for the first time near Clayton, Union County, New Mexico during the summer of 1966 (Williams, 1966): "Two pairs were present, but apparently only one pair raised young." Vermilion Flycatchers have also been found nesting just south of the study area on the South Plains (LEAS, 1994).

SPECIMENS: Oberholser (1974) shows a spring specimen taken in Childress County. Possibly this has reference to the bird found dead in Cottle County but reported in error as Childress County. If the specimen was deposited in a museum collection, he fails to name which one.

Ash-throated Flycatcher *Myiarchus cinerascens* (Lawrence)

STATUS: Uncommon to common migrant and breeder.

OCCURRENCE: The Ash-throated Flycatcher has been recorded in every county except Sherman, Swisher, and Wheeler. Oberholser (1974) shows it in nine. It has been found in every month except December and January.

The Ash-throated Flycatcher arrives early in spring, normally during the first week of April. There are four earlier sightings, the earliest a bird at Lake Theo, Caprock Canyons SP, Briscoe County, 22 February 1991. By late September most have left the area. There are two records beyond September: one near Dodd, Castro County, 10 October 1993, and in the PDCSP, 16 November 1979.

The PDCSP is a locality where the Ash-throated Flycatcher can readily be found in summer. A two-year Breeding Bird Study in the park disclosed an average density of seven per 100 acres (Seyffert, 1967–68). Its presence on BBSS reflect the habitats through which they run. The counts with highest averages are Childress, Channing, and Clarendon, the first traversing mesquite-brush habitat (average 4.1), the second mesquite-shrub/grassland (average 1.7), and the third mesquite-shrub/grassland, sandsage–Harvard shin oak brush, and crops (average 1.8). The other counts have produced far fewer, or none at all, as they run primarily through grasslands and/or croplands.

NESTING: Although this flycatcher arrives early in April, the first reported nesting activity is that of an adult carrying nesting material in the PDCSP, 27 April 1968. The latest date of nesting activity is that of an adult feeding young in a nest in Hall County, 15 July 1979. The Ash-throated Flycatcher can be two-brooded. Nest boxes maintained north of Amarillo, Potter County, have produced two broods regularly.

The TBBAP found CO nesting in nine survey blocks, PR in 24, and PO in six. Of the 39 occupied quadrangles, 18 were located between in the 100th and 101st meridians, 12 between the 101st and 102nd, and the remaining nine west of the 102nd. There was a considerable overlap with the Great Crested Flycatcher in quadrangles lying east of the 101st meridian, where 12 of the 18 were occupied jointly.

SPECIMENS: Specimens have been collected in Randall County (27 and 28 June 1956, MNH). Oberholser (1974) shows one collected in Oldham County, but details are lacking.

Great Crested Flycatcher *Myiarchus crinitus* (Linnaeus)

STATUS: Uncommon to fairly common breeder in eastern third, migrant elsewhere.

OCCURRENCE: Oberholser (1974) shows the Great Crested Flycatcher in six Texas Panhandle counties: Hemphill, Hutchinson, Lipscomb, Parmer, Randall, and Roberts. Thirteen others have been added: Armstrong, Castro, Childress, Collingsworth, Donley, Gray, Hall, Hansford, Hartley, Moore, Ochiltree, Potter, and Wheeler. It has been seen from April to October.

This flycatcher returns in spring during the last week of April, about a month later than the Ash-throated Flycatcher. Most early dates cluster around the 20–24 April period, the earliest being for a single bird in Randall County, 20 April 1926 (Hibbets et al.) (1926–36). Few have been recorded past mid-September, the latest being a bird at BLNWR, 10 October 1996.

NESTING: The Great Crested Flycatcher was a CO nester (Hemphill, Collingsworth counties) in two survey blocks during the TBBAP, a PR nester in 15, and a PO nester in six. Johnsgard (1979) shows breeding confined to the northeastern sector but the TBBAP disclosed nesting extending throughout the two eastern tiers of counties. Only four of the occupied quadrangles were located west of the 101st meridian: two in Hutchinson, one in Armstrong, and one in Randall County. A study of Wood Ducks conducted in the eastern Panhandle (Magill, 1996) found that of 80 nest boxes equipped with a smaller cavity for nongame species, six were occupied by nesting Great Crested Flycatchers.

Although the species was never confirmed nesting in Hutchinson County, Thompson (1952) collected an adult male Great Crested Flycatchers in breeding condition on both 17 and 20 June 1950 in that county, and observations later (Duncan Ranch, Frying Pan Ranch) point to almost certain nesting. On 13 July 1996 a nest with young was found east of Pampa, Gray County. The PDCSP is another locality in the central sector where in recent years the species has been found during summer, and where confirmation of nesting was made 21 June 1997. The Kritser Ranch on the Canadian River in north Potter County is a site where regular summer residence points to almost certain nesting, and in June of 1972 a single bird was found near Dumas, Moore County.

Ligon (1961) reported Great Crested Flycatchers in the Clayton area, Union County, New Mexico, during four summers in the 1940s, including two immatures, 22 July 1948. A juvenile was found in the same area, 23 July 1967 (Williams, 1967).

SPECIMENS: Two specimens of *M. c. boreus* were collected in Hutchinson County (17 and 20 June 1950, TNHC). They are Thompson's birds already mentioned and are probably the source of Oberholser's (1974) citation. Oberholser also shows specimens collected in Randall and Lipscomb counties, again without details. The Randall County bird is possibly McCauley's (1877).

Cassin's Kingbird *Tyrannus vociferans* Swainson

STATUS: Uncommon to fairly common migrant. Vagrant breeder.

OCCURRENCE: The Cassin's Kingbird has been recorded in nine counties: Castro, Dallam, Hartley, Hemphill, Oldham, Parmer, Potter, Randall, and Swisher. Oberholser (1974) shows it in Randall County only. It has been seen from April to October.

Reported sightings of the Cassin's Kingbird in the study area have been confined almost exclusively to the two westernmost tiers of counties. The source of a Hemphill County sighting in the extreme northeastern sector is unknown, and its presence should possibly be questioned. Baumgartner and Baumgartner (1992) refer to the species in northwest Oklahoma in fall as "rare," while Tyler (1979b) questions a single spring sighting reported in Jackson County in the southwest.

Reports of spring Cassin's Kingbirds are rare. The species possibly follows a more westerly route than on its return later in the year. The early and late spring dates are for one at BLNWR, 22 April 1967, and one in southeast Swisher County, 24 May 1988. The fall passage occurs after most Western Kingbirds have left. The earliest date on record, and the only August sighting, is for a single bird in Amarillo, Randall County, 20 August 1985—all others fall between 14 and 28 September. The latest date is for one near Amarillo, Randall County, 16 October 1964, one of only a very few October sightings. The movement of birds in fall is normally only a trickle; however, 40 were counted at nearby Clayton, Union County, New Mexico, 11 September 1972 (Williams, 1973). Perhaps an observer residing in a far western county would pick up a similar passage. The single observer prior to mid-century to name the Cassin's Kingbird is Russell (1935), who classified it as "very common on the plains and occasionally seen in the canyon." Such plenitude is hard to credit: his birds were possibly misidentified Western Kingbirds. Often the identifications of Cassin's are made solely on the basis of the absence of white outer tail feathers, the observers not taking into consideration the fact that these become quite worn later in the year, making them hard to see, and are absent during molt.

NESTING: The first reported summer presence of the Cassin's Kingbird was a bird heard calling in Texline, Dallam County, 11 June 1981 (BBS). The first nesting was discovered two years later on 14 June 1983, when a pair was observed feeding young in a nest on the Rita Blanca National Grasslands. Farther east on the same day another pair of Cassin's was encountered, this time along with a pair of Western Kingbirds, but nesting was not discovered. On 14 June 1998, a Cassin's was heard on the outskirts of Texline (BBS). On the previous day I had observed several in Clayton, Union County, some ten miles to the west, as I did again in June of 1999—and where nesting had been discovered for the first time in the summer of 1971 (Williams, 1971). One observed on the BLNWR on 30 July 1995 is the sole summer sighting reported outside Dallam County—most likely an early migrant.

In the Oklahoma Panhandle Sutton (1967) said: "Three pairs observed June 3 and 4, 1965, along the Cimarron River near Kenton, were building nests, each nest being well up in a large cottonwood. Western Kingbirds and Eastern Kingbirds occupied the same general area, and ecological requirements of the three species appeared to be much the same. . . . Cassin's nest (four eggs) observed June 23, 1935, at river level ten to eleven miles northwest of Boise City."

Thick-billed Kingbird *Tyrannus crassirostris* Swainson

STATUS: Vagrant.

OCCURRENCE: On the afternoon of 30 October 1998, a first-year Thick-billed Kingbird was observed for some 20–30 minutes in the PDCSP (R. Scott, E. Kutac, J. Elston, R. Cadra; TBRC; TP-RF). The bird was heard calling repeatedly (*purr-eet*), and occasionally made sallies to catch insects. The day was overcast with intermittent misty rain, followed that night by more turbulent weather and heavy rainfall. Over eight inches fell locally, flooding the canyon and closing it to public access for a week. Efforts to find the bird again after the park reopened were unsuccessful.

There have been ten accepted records of the Thick-billed Kingbird in Texas, all from Big Bend NP, Brewster County, and none later in the year than 24 September (Lasley and Sexton, 1995a).

Western Kingbird *Tyrannus verticalis* Say

STATUS: Common breeder and migrant.

OCCURRENCE: The Western Kingbird has been recorded in every Texas Panhandle county and has been seen from March to October.

This kingbird is the most common and widespread of the tyrant flycatchers in the study area. The only place where it is not found commonly, except as a bird of passage, is in the deeper canyonlands. This is based on observations in the PDCSP, where I have but one record of a kingbird found nesting below the escarpment. It differs from those of two earlier observers, for Carlander (1934) held that kingbirds "are very much in evidence in the Palo Duro," and Stevenson (1942) said the species "occasionally nests in cottonwoods and other trees on the canyon floor."

Returning Western Kingbirds can be looked for in the third week of April (average 21 April). There are only two March sightings: 20 March (Hawkins, 1945; year and site unspecified) and one in the PDCSP, 22 March 1953. The species rarely remains beyond September (average 18 September). Hawkins (1945) gives the departure date as "early October." There have been 11 October sightings reported since then, the latest for two birds at BLNWR, 26 October 1963. As evidence of how early fall migration may begin, "hundreds" were observed between Boise City and Kenton, Oklahoma, 1 August 1975 (Williams, 1976), just north of the study area. Large movements of Western Kingbirds are seldom reported. On 16 May 1993, I witnessed a movement of 100+ along an eight-mile stretch of road crossing a treeless plain north of Texline, Dallam County (a day of strong north wind), and on the morning of 1 September 1980, following a frontal passage, I counted 85 kingbirds passing overhead in a ten-minute period at BLNWR.

The averages on the BBSS give an indication of the Western Kingbird's abundance and distribution: *Booker*—19; *Childress*—8; *Miami*—17; *Waka*—9; *Pantex*—16; *Clarendon*—25; *Panhandle*—20; *Skellytown*—20; *Channing*—29; *Texline*—33; *Dalhart*—19.

NESTING: The Western Kingbird has been recorded nesting in all 26 study area counties. The TBBAP found it to be among the most widespread and common of the breeding birds. It was a CO nester in 85 survey blocks, a PR in 37, and a PO in six. The respective numbers of occupied quadrangles: 100th to 101st meridian, 23–2-1; 101st to 102nd, 28–15-4; west of 102nd, 34–2-1.

Although the Western Kingbird arrives in late April, nest building begins only much later, after a noisy courtship. Early and late dates: 23 May 1970 (BLNWR); two families of newly fledged young in Amarillo, Potter County, 12–13 August 1981. Nests are usually placed in crotches of tree limbs anywhere from head high to the canopy. On the treeless plains nests are often built on the cross arms and among transformers on power poles. I have found them placed in or very near the bulky nests of Swainson's, Red-tailed, and Ferruginous hawks, and once in the top of a dead tree stump projecting some ten feet above water some 50 yards from shore. Recently, one was found on the platform of an occupied Purple Martin house. Strecker (1910) speaks of finding kingbirds "nesting in bushes, on the tops of tall gate-posts, and rarely, on wind-mill platforms," and McCauley (1877) found a nest that in turn had a nest of a "tree-Mouse" safely ensconced beneath it. From this safe retreat it had "eaten all the eggs but two" and was working on them as well ("the little thief at White Fish").

On 6 September 1982, I observed an albinistic Western Kingbird at BLNWR. It was examined at length from a short distance and found to be entirely snow white—no shading was discernible. Its mandibles were yellow, its legs and feet flesh-colored, and its eyes appeared dark red. The ragged ends of the tail made it seem shorter than normal. As I watched, a Red-tailed Hawk circling overhead dived at the bird, causing it to fly off. The bird could possibly have been a Cassin's and not a Western Kingbird, however, for it was not heard calling. On such an early date the latter species is more likely as Cassin's normally are later migrants. Another albinistic kingbird, also thought a western, was observed near Dumas, Moore County, in September 1974.

SPECIMENS: Specimens have been collected in Armstrong (1905, SM), Hutchinson (15 and 17 June 1950, TNHC), Potter (4 May 1939, WTAMU), and Randall (29 May 1985, TCWC; 7 May and 3 August 1939, and 8 May 1970, WTAMU) counties. The Hutchinson County birds are the two taken by Thompson (1952). McCauley (1877) collected specimens at Palo Duro (25 May), Red River Canyon (31 May), White Fish Creek (19 June), McClellan Creek (20 June), and Mulberry Creek (17 June). The counties would have been present-day Randall, Armstrong, Gray, and Armstrong. Where they were deposited is unknown. In that he was a member of a government expedition, one would think they would have been placed in the U.S. National Museum in Washington, D.C.; if so, they have never been located (letter, Richard C. Banks, 8 July 1986). Oberholser (1974) shows specimens collected in Dallam, Oldham, Hutchinson, and Wheeler counties, and a specimen record of breeding in Armstrong County.

Eastern Kingbird *Tyrannus tyrannus* (Linnaeus)

STATUS: Uncommon to common breeder (eastern half) and migrant.

OCCURRENCE: The Eastern Kingbird has been recorded in every Texas Panhandle county except Swisher. It has been seen from April to October.

Most observers prior to mid-century had little or nothing to say about the Eastern Kingbird. Mention of the species was notably absent from the accounts of Strecker (1910) and Carlander (1934), and it was not named as a bird of the Palo Duro Canyon by either Russell (1935) or Stevenson (1942). Hawkins (1945) classified it as a "fairly common resident below the cap rock in the eastern Panhandle; rare in the western Panhandle." The species today is fairly common to common throughout most of the two eastern tiers of counties, but only locally westward. As a breeder west of the 101st meridian, the species is found primarily along the Canadian River as far west as Boys Ranch in Oldham County and north (Rico and Rita Blanca creeks). It can also be found south of the river in Hutchinson County (White Deer Creek) and in the headwaters of McClellan Creek. To emphasize how local it is in the southwestern sector, the Eastern Kingbird nests in both Canyon and the BLNWR in Randall County, but not in surrounding areas, including Amarillo. A sighting at any time in the PDCSP is considered rare. As indicators of the relationship of Eastern to Western kingbirds at isolated localities in the central and western sectors, on the BLNWR my records show a ratio of Westerns to Easterns of 3:1 (May 21–Aug 21). Just west of the 101st meridian along White Deer Creek in Hutchinson County the ratio is 1.5:1.

The Eastern Kingbird can be expected in spring in late April, the earliest date being 13 April 1999 at Lake Marvin, Hemphill County, and it is seldom seen past September. Four on the BLNWR on 26 October 1963 were exceptional. The only other October record is of a single bird on the refuge, 5 October 1969. The averages on the BBSS give an indication of its presence and distribution in summer: *Booker*—5; *Childress*—0.2; *Miami*—5; *Waka*—0.05; *Pantex*—0.05; *Clarendon*—6; *Skellytown*—0.3; *Panhandle*—0; *Channing*—0.5; *Texline*—0; *Dalhart*—(1994–96) 1. Testimony to how common it is in late summer in the eastern sector, an estimated 70 Eastern Kingbirds were observed between Canadian and Lake Marvin, Hemphill County, 23 August 1997. Although the species has never been recorded on the Texline BBS, a single Eastern Kingbird was observed near the Thompson Grove Picnic Area northeast of Texline, 12 June 1976 and 11 June 1997. Nearby at Clayton, Union County, New Mexico, a pair nested in the summer of 1952 (Baumgartner, 1953).

NESTING: The Eastern Kingbird has been confirmed nesting in 15 study area counties: Armstrong, Collingsworth, Donley, Gray, Hall, Hartley, Hemphill, Hutchinson, Lipscomb, Ochiltree, Oldham, Potter, Randall, Roberts, and Wheeler. The TBBAP found it a CO nester in 16 survey blocks, a PR in 23, and a PO in eight. Of the 47 occupied quadrangles, 29 were between the 100th and 101st meridians, 11 between the 101st and 102nd, and seven west of the 102nd.

The earliest nest-building dates are 17 May 1987 (BLNWR), and 17 May 1988 (Lark, Armstrong County). An adult on a nest was found west of Canadian in Roberts County, 14 July 1990, and an adult feeding fledglings east of Canadian, Hemphill County, 12 August 1990. An adult observed on 15 June 1981 at Wolf Creek Park, Ochiltree County, was just beginning a nest placed some ten feet up in a small hackberry tree.

SPECIMENS: Specimens are available for Hutchinson County (13, 15, and 16 June 1950, TNHC). These are Thompson's (1952) birds and are probably the source of Oberholser's (1974) reference to specimens from that county. McCauley (1877) collected specimens along White Fish Creek (Armstrong County) and McClellan Creek (Gray County).

Scissor-tailed Flycatcher *Tyrannus forficatus* (Gmelin)

STATUS: Fairly common to common breeder and migrant, common to abundant in fall.

OCCURRENCE: The Scissor-tailed Flycatcher has been found in every Texas Panhandle county and has been recorded from March to November.

As shown by the reports of early observers, the scissor-tail was formerly common to abundant in the Texas Panhandle. McCauley (1877) said it was "one of the species most frequently seen. . . . They were found frequenting the fringe of timber bordering the steams as far as their headwaters in the Staked Plain, as well as along the streams in the Indian Territory—Wolf Creek." Strecker (1910) found it "abundant on the plains, especially so in the neighborhood of farm and ranch houses"; Reeves and Reeves (1914) said "in Canyon, Common"; Russell (1935) reported it as "common in the mesquite areas"; Hawkins (1945) said "it covers practically the entire Panhandle"; and Thompson (1952) noted it as "common, concentrating in certain areas, but occurring in nearly all the associations." There is reason to believe that the scissor-tail is no longer as common in the western half of the study area as formerly.

The Scissor-tailed Flycatcher's present status across the study area is indicated by the averages on the BBSS: *Childress*—57.4; *Clarendon*—26.6; *Miami*—12.9; *Channing*—7.5; *Booker*—6.2; *Waka*—2.1; *Pantex*—1.4; *Texline*—0.05. As can be seen, the area of greatest abundance is in the southeast, while it is uncommon to almost absent in areas of the southwest and extreme northwest. There is evidence of a recent decline in the southwestern sector. Using my records of 30

Scissor-tailed Flycatcher

years (1964–93), broken down into ten-year periods, the average numbers per trip recorded at BLNWR, as well as those seen while driving to and from the refuge, are as follows: *1964–73*—3.7; *1974–83*—1.04; *1984–93*—1.09. The 72 percent decline began abruptly in 1974 and has continued, if not intensified. Based on birds seen per man-hour, 1.32 were recorded in 1965–69 and 0.23 in 1989–93, an 83 percent decline. Ten to twelve pairs of scissor-tails summered on the refuge in 1958, while only two were found in 1987 during the TBBAP. It is not known if there have been similar declines in other areas as there are no figures available for comparisons. Most of the BBSs were not started until 1975 and do not reflect any apparent change in status. Nationwide there has been a -0.4 percent annual decline (1966–91; Peterjohn and Sauer, 1993), but statewide records show a 1.9 percent annual increase (1980–94; letter, B. Ortego, BBS State Coordinator, 19 February 1996).

The Scissor-tailed Flycatcher is first seen in spring around the second week of April. One in Amarillo, 12 March 1966, and one in Potter County, 22 March 1997, represent the only March sightings; the early date otherwise is 1 April 1967 at Amarillo. Few are seen past October, the latest being one at BLNWR, 17 November 1959. Scissor-tails may be found migrating in large flocks in fall. Hawkins (1945) reported a movement of 350 in one flock near Goodnight, Armstrong County, 1 September 1945; 350 were observed at BLNWR, 22 September 1960; 100+ in migration south of Canadian, Hemphill County, 18 September 1977; 200+ in Lipscomb County, 21 September 1996; 100+ in Wheeler County, 3 October 1996. Comparable numbers have never been reported in spring.

NESTING: The TBBAP found CO nesting in 44 survey blocks, PR in 29, and PO in 15. Forty-two of the occupied quadrangles were between the 100th and 101st meridians, 32 between the 101st and 102nd, the remaining 14 west of the 102nd. Scissor-tails were not encountered in any of the eight quadrangles surveyed in Deaf Smith, Carson, and Parmer counties in the southwest sector, and of the ten surveyed in Dallam and Sherman counties in the northwest sector, it was found in only one quadrangle in each county.

A comparison can be made in the number of quadrangles between meridians that were occupied by the three *Tyrannus* flycatchers:

	100th–101st	101st–102nd	102nd–103rd
Western Kingbird	26	47	37
Eastern Kingbird	29	11	7
Scissor-tailed Flycatcher	42	32	14

Thirty-eight quadrangles were occupied by all three species.

The Scissor-tailed Flycatcher has been confirmed nesting in all the study area counties except Carson, Deaf Smith, Parmer, and Castro, the latter three in the southwestern sector. No doubt it would be confirmed in Carson with more searching. While most begin nest building in May, one nest in Ceta Glen, South Ceta Canyon, Randall County, was found occupied on the early date of 19 April 1985. The latest initiation of nesting was observed near Canyon, Randall County, 8 July 1987, and adults have been observed feeding fledglings as late as 25 July 1987 (near Palo Duro Canyon). Concerning the PDCSP, Carlander (1934) thought the location "a perfect setting in which to study these beautiful birds." Today the species is considered uncommon in the state park: when encountered it is usually found around the park entrance, rarely on the canyon floor.

SPECIMENS: Specimens have been taken in Briscoe (May 1972, WTAMU), Hutchinson (9 July 1950, TNHC), Potter (ACMNH; 8 July 1947, TCWC), and Randall (7 October 1939, P-PHM; 20 August and 1 September 1939, 24 June 1969, WTAMU) counties. The Hutchinson County birds shown by Oberholser (1974) without details are probably those collected by Thompson (1952). In addition, McCauley (1877) took specimens in Armstrong, Briscoe, Gray, and Randall counties.

Family Laniidae (Shrikes)

Loggerhead Shrike *Lanius ludovicianus* Linnaeus

STATUS: Fairly common to common migrant and breeder. Uncommon winter visitor.

OCCURRENCE: The Loggerhead Shrike has been recorded in all 26 counties of the Texas Panhandle and has been seen in every month.

The Loggerhead Shrike is on the Blue List of birds thought to be declining in some parts of the country (Arbib, 1971). A look at my records for the periods 1965–79 and 1980–93 does not lend support to this belief for the study area. The first period shows that I recorded 1.10 shrikes per trip afield (985 trips), while the latter shows 1.24 (1,010 trips). There are no data published on the status of the Loggerhead Shrike prior to mid-century. McCauley (1877) failed to name the species at all. Others, such as Carlander (1934), Russell (1935), and Stevenson (1942), thought it fairly common to common as a summer resident. Hawkins (1945) encountered only one shrike in June and two in July "in covering hundreds of miles of roads through the Plains in 1945"; he thought it common only in migration. My records reveal the following monthly incidence of occurrence per trip afield: January 1.11; February 0.61; March 0.74; April 2.06; May 0.81; June 0.75; July 0.88; August 1.73; September 1.55; October 0.80; November 1.12; December 1.90.

The CBC averages show the Loggerhead Shrike to be more common in early winter in the Canadian River Valley than in the canyonlands and plains: *Lake Meredith* (*east*)—11.0; *Lake Meredith* (*west*)—10.3; *Quitaque*—5.9; *Buffalo Lake* NWR—4.4; *Amarillo*—2.4; *Friona*—1.3.

NESTING: The TBBAP disclosed a fairly even distribution of the Loggerhead Shrike across most of the study area. It was a CO nester in 14 survey blocks, PR in 16, and PO in 33—27 between the 100th and 101st meridians, 17 between the 101st and 102nd, and 19 west of the 102nd. The only sector where it was absent was the extreme southwest.

Nest-building has been observed as early as 30 April 1995 (Palo Duro Lake, Hansford County), and adults feeding fledglings on 7 May 1991 (near Waka, Ochiltree County). An adult on the nest has been found as early as 18 May 1991 (near Perryton, Ochiltree County) and as late as 18 June 1972 (BLNWR). Young in the nest were being fed on 14 July 1990 (west of Canadian, Roberts County), and fledglings were seen as late as 26 July 1989 (Channing, Hartley County). In nearby southwestern Oklahoma, Tyler (1992) found the extreme date for first evidence of nest construction to be 23 February, and the earliest egg discovery was 13 March. Peak nesting occurred about the first week of April, with a second, though shorter, period of activity taking place between 21 May and 20 June.

SPECIMENS: Specimens have been taken in Dallam (26 August 1964, FMNH), Hutchinson (26 June 1950, TNHC), and Randall (18 January, 30 April, 12 June, 11 and 20 August, 23 September 1939, 12 June 1969, 10 October 1987, WTAMU) counties. In addition, Oberholser (1974) shows specimens taken in Hutchinson, Roberts, Oldham, Wheeler, Randall, and Armstrong counties, without naming the collections in which they were deposited. His Hutchinson County bird is very likely the one taken by Thompson (1952) and identified as the race *excubitorides*. The Dallam County bird was also of this race, as were the two taken in Roberts and Oldham counties referred to by Oberholser. The Randall County specimen named by Oberholser was indentified as *nevadensis* and the Armstrong County specimen as *gambeli*. The former was the bird Stevenson (1942) said was taken on 26 September 1938 near Canyon.

Northern Shrike *Lanius excubitor* Linnaeus

STATUS: Rare winter visitor.

OCCURRENCE: The Northern Shrike has been found in 18 Texas Panhandle counties: Armstrong, Briscoe, Castro, Dallam, Donley, Hansford, Hartley, Hemphill, Hutchinson, Moore, Ochiltree, Oldham, Parmer, Potter, Randall, Sherman, Swisher, and Wheeler. Oberholser (1974) names it in three. It has been seen from October to March.

When a Northern Shrike was discovered at BLNWR on 19 January 1966, observers thought it the first sighting for the study area. Not until later was it learned that one had previously been seen on 22 December 1961 near Friona, Parmer County—"the first sighting since the 1958–59 season" (C. D. Littlefield). Undoubtedly it had been overlooked by earlier observers: had every shrike tagged as a loggerhead been examined more closely, the northern would surely have been discovered much sooner. As of the end of March 1998, 108 Northern Shrikes had been reported, with hardly a winter season passing without at least one being seen. The following is a breakdown of sightings by county: *Armstrong* (2); *Briscoe* (3); *Castro* (1); *Dallam* (4); *Donley* (1); *Hartley* (1); *Hemphill* (7); *Hutchinson* (4); *Moore* (2); *Ochiltree* (1); *Oldham* (1); *Parmer* (2); *Potter* (7); *Randall* (68); *Sherman* (2); *Swisher* (1); *Wheeler* (1). The first documentation was an adult found southwest of Dumas, Moore County, 14 January 1973 (TP-RF).

The Northern Shrike is rarely seen before mid-November. The earliest of three October sightings is one in PDCSP, 23 October 1977. Normally none is found past February. Of six recorded in March the latest is a singing bird in the PDCSP, 27 March 1996. The species has been found in a variety of habitats, most often at BLNWR and in PDCSP, localities intensively birded. In the state park it has been found both topside and on the canyon floor. It has been encountered on the open plains as well as in city cemeteries. Two observers watched from an alley in Fritch, Hutchinson County, 30 December 1978, as a shrike captured and fed on a House Sparrow.

With few exceptions, Northern Shrike reports have been of single birds. The four reported on the Amarillo CBC of 21 December 1975 represented a publishing error: the birds were in fact Loggerhead Shrikes.

Family Vireonidae (Vireos)

White-eyed Vireo *Vireo griseus* (Boddaert)
STATUS: Casual migrant.
OCCURRENCE: There have been eight sightings of the White-eyed Vireo in the study area, all from Potter and Randall counties and a single bird in each instance: Canyon, 1 May 1956; Canyon City Club, 5 May 1956; BLNWR, 6 May 1956; Amarillo, 19 September 1964; Amarillo, 12 May 1967; Lake Tanglewood, 1 May 1977; Palo Duro Club near Canyon, 9 May 1977; Amarillo, 19 May 1991.

Two reports of White-eyed Vireos seen earlier in the century probably should be dismissed. Hibbets et al. (1914–36) cite a 20 November 1927 date. This matches the late date for north-central Texas, which Pulich (1988) says is "exceptionally late"—in an area where the species is a summer resident. A Reeves and Reeves (1914–36) citation reads: "1924: Usually seen each spring and fall in vines around house" (Canyon, Randall County). It is doubtful that the White-eyed Vireo has ever occurred in the Texas Panhandle with any regularity, despite Johnsgard (1979) showing the breeding range in North Texas extending as far west along the Red River Valley as the extreme southeastern tip of the study area. None has been recorded farther west in Oklahoma than Dewey and Comanche counties (Baumgartner and Baumgartner, 1992), and near Durham, Roger Mills County, but the species has occurred in Hamilton, Stanton, and Morton counties in extreme southwestern Kansas (Thompson and Ely, 1992).

There have been three reported sightings of the White-eyed Vireo in Lubbock, 21–24 April 1970, 22–26 April 1971, and 4 May 1984 (*fide* C. Stogner), and one in Dickens County, 17 and 24 April, year unspecified (*fide* C. Stogner).

Bell's Vireo *Vireo bellii* Audubon
STATUS: Rare to uncommon migrant. Rare breeder in eastern counties.
OCCURRENCE: The Bell's Vireo has been reported in 13 counties: Armstrong, Briscoe, Childress, Collingsworth, Dallam, Donley, Hemphill, Lipscomb, Oldham, Potter, Randall, Roberts, and Wheeler. It has been seen from April to October.

There has been a marked decline in Bell's Vireos in the study area since the 1960s, lending support to its placement on the Blue List (Arbib, 1971). My records reveal scarcity since the beginning of observations in the mid-1960s: during subsequent years I have recorded it but seven times in the central Panhandle during migration. It is doubtful that the species was ever common. None of the early observers named it, although they did cite other vireo species. With the exception of McCauley (1877), who spent only one season in the area, none carried out extensive or sustained observations in the eastern Panhandle where the species would be expected. Little work has been done by anyone in those counties, and such information as we have on the status of the Bell's Vireo there has been gathered haphazardly.

Almost all reports of migrant Bell's Vireos are of birds seen in May, with only a few reported in September. One in Amarillo, Potter County, 16 April 1955, was extremely early, and equally late for fall were one in Miami, Roberts County, 24 October 1980, and one in Canyon, Randall County, 29 October 1955. These latter sightings, if in order, are remarkable because most Bell's Vireos have left the United States by early October (Brown, 1993). These exceed by far the late record for Oklahoma (Durham, Roger Mills County, 6 October 1968; Baumgartner and Baumgartner, 1992), and there is but a single late October date (24th) for north-central Texas (Tarrant County; Pulich, 1988).

NESTING: The only record of nesting Bell's Vireos is a sight record of breeding in Hemphill County (Oberholser, 1974). Details of this event are not provided. Johnsgard (1979) shows the breeding range extending throughout the eastern two-thirds of the Texas Panhandle, "possibly extending rarely or locally to the New Mexico border." The basis for this belief is not given, and it certainly cannot be sustained by those working in the field today. It is probable that even Brown (1993) extends the breeding range too far westward. Sightings of the species in western counties have been rare even during migration.

The strongest evidence of nesting centers around the Lake Marvin–Gene Howe WMA areas in Hemphill County, going back to 1953. If more time were spent in brushy areas along the Canadian River nearby, the Bell's Vireo would probably be encountered more often and nesting might be confirmed. I explored such an area on 15 June 1981 and quickly encountered three singing Bell's Vireos in thickets of Russian olive, plum, and salt cedar and have found the species there in subsequent years.

Another location where the Bell's Vireo has been found fairly regularly in summer is the Lelia Creek–Salt Fork of Red River area in Donley County. One was found on 13 and 20 June 1971, four on 4 June and one 18 June 1972, and two on 3 June 1973. Birds on territory were observed on the O'Neill Ranch southwest of Shamrock, Collingsworth County, 8 June 1989, and multiple singing males and birds in breeding habitat east of Childress, Childress County, 7 June 1992. A singing bird exhibiting nesting behavior was observed along Willow Creek in southeastern Lipscomb County, 8 June 1983. Possibly nesting was a singing bird on the BLNWR, 4 July 1956. Oberholser (1974) shows summer sight records for Lipscomb, Roberts, Hemphill, Potter, Wheeler, Randall, and Armstrong counties, without providing details.

SPECIMENS: Oberholser (1974) cites a summer specimen collected in Lipscomb County, but its present location is not given.

Yellow-throated Vireo *Vireo flavifrons* Vieillot

STATUS: Rare migrant.

OCCURRENCE: The only counties where the Yellow-throated Vireo has been reported are Donley, Gray, Potter and Randall—in spring, April–May, and in autumn, August–October.

The Yellow-throated Vireo has been reported 20 times in the study area. It is a species not named by early observers. The following is a listing of those recorded, in each instance a single bird: *Amarillo* (Potter and Randall counties)— 11 May 1953; 20 September 1953; 4 May 1954; 19 April 1957; 28 April 1960; 10 May 1960; 23 September 1980; 14 May 1994. BLNWR—1 May 1955; 6 May 1956; 6 September 1965; 24 April 1966; 9 May 1967; 18 May 1975; 6 May 1985; 4 October 1992; 9 April 1999. *Canyon* (Randall County)—22 October 1956; 23 August 1958. *Pampa* (Gray County)—9 September 1995. *Kritser Ranch* (Potter County)—11 May 1998. *Taylor Lakes WMA* (Donley County)—19 April 1999.

On 13 June 1986 a pair of Yellow-throated Vireos was found attending two recently fledged young 17 miles northwest of Boise City, Cimarron County, Oklahoma (Shackford, 1992). This was a remarkable discovery as only one other Yellow-throated Vireo had ever been reported in the Oklahoma Panhandle, that one also in Cimarron County (Sutton, 1967). The farthest west in the state that any had been found previously was Comanche County in the southwestern sector (Tyler, 1979b). The habitat of the nesting pair was "a small but dense thicket of close-set hackberry, soapberry and cottonwood trees near a small stream. Although cattle had removed most of the undergrowth below four feet, the trees themselves were enmeshed with luxuriant tangles of grapevines." Such habitat exists in the study area, and observers should be on the alert for possible nesting.

Plumbeous Vireo *Vireo plumbeus* Coues

STATUS: Uncommon migrant.

OCCURRENCE: See Blue-headed Vireo entry for a discussion on the status of this species in the Texas Panhandle. The two were formerly considered races of the Solitary Vireo.

Blue-headed Vireo *Vireo solitarius* (Wilson)

STATUS: Uncommon migrant.

OCCURRENCE: What the relative distribution and status of the Blue-headed and Plumbeous Vireo are in the study area remains to be discovered. The data on file pertain almost entirely to birds referenced simply as "Solitary" Vireo, a species now split into three (AOU, 1997)— *V. solitarius* (Blue-headed), *V. cassinii* (Cassin's), and *V. plumbeus* (Plumbeous). From the sparse data on hand it appears that the Blue-headed may be the most common of the three in the study area. My notes show that for the period 1984–86, 25 of the Solitary Vireos recorded were of the "eastern" (= Blue-headed) race and eight were "Rockies" (= Plumbeous). In one year the ratio was only 7:5. All observations were limited to the south-central sector. The Solitary Vireo was recorded in 14 Texas Panhandle counties: Briscoe, Castro, Dallam, Donley, Gray, Hall, Hansford, Hartley, Hemphill, Hutchinson, Oldham, Parmer, Potter, and Randall. Oberholser (1974) shows it in two. It was seen April–May and August–November.

The first spring vireos of this complex can be expected during the first week of May and the last ones not later than the third week. There are three April sightings, the earliest a singing bird in Amarillo, Randall County, 21 April 1988. The latest date is for one bird (*plumbeus*) at the BLNWR, 30 May 1982. Returning birds in fall can be looked for from early September to the third week of October. The earliest date is for one at BLNWR, 24 August 1974, and the latest for one in Vega, Oldham County, 30 October 1995 and 1996, the latter a *solitarius*. There are two November records: a single *solitarius* at BLNWR, 9 November 1986, and one in Caprock Canyons SP, Briscoe County, 13 November 1977.

Sutton (1967) cites specimens of the two "western" races, *plumbeus* and *cassinii*, and one of the "eastern" race, *solitarius*, collected in the Oklahoma Panhandle. For this reason, area observers should become familiar with the defining characteristics of all three (Heindell, 1996).

Warbling Vireo *Vireo gilvus* (Vieillot)

STATUS: Uncommon to common migrant. Fairly common to common breeder in the eastern third.

OCCURRENCE: Oberholser (1974) shows the Warbling Vireo in eight counties: Donley, Gray, Hemphill, Lipscomb, Oldham, Potter, Roberts, and Wheeler. Nine others have been added: Armstrong, Castro, Collingsworth, Hansford, Hartley, Hutchinson, Ochiltree, Parmer, and Randall. It has been seen from April to October.

The Warbling Vireo normally returns in spring during the second week of May. There are two April records: one at Lake Marvin, Hemphill County,

21 April 1968, and a singing bird at BLNWR, 24 April 1967. Migration is over by the end of the third week of May, and returning birds begin trickling through in late August; few are seen later than the third week of September. There are three October records, the latest a single bird in Amarillo, Potter County, 10 October 1956.

Although the Warbling Vireo is on the Blue List (Arbib, 1971), there probably has not been a significant change in its status in the study area. McCauley (1877) reported: "This exquisite little songster was frequently met with in the groves and thickets, except along alkali water, where none were heard or observed. Very many specimens might have been obtained if desired." Prior to the middle twentieth century, little time was spent by observers in the relevant eastern counties; as a result, there are hardly any data available for comparison. Hawkins (1945) did say that this vireo was a "fairly common resident in the eastern Panhandle; rare in the western Panhandle" in the mid-1940s. More recent work has shown the species still to be fairly common to common.

NESTING: Although numerous birds acting "nesty" have been reported, there have been few confirmations: three fledglings being fed at Lake Marvin, Hemphill County, 5 July 1971; a fledgling being fed at Lake McClellan, Gray County, 17 July 1977 and again 14 July 1988; a copulating pair at Lake Marvin, Hemphill County, 16 June 1981; one singing on nest at Indian Creek, Roberts County, 6 June 1987; one nest building near Turner Memorial Park along Wolf Creek, Lipscomb County, 10 June 1990; one singing on nest at Wolf Creek Park, Ochiltree County, 8 June 1995; one singing on nest on Taylor Lakes WMA, Donley County, 12 July 1996, and an adult feeding a fledgling, 20 August 1996. Other counties where summering Warbling Vireos have shown evidence of probable nesting are Armstrong, Collingsworth, Hutchinson, Potter, and Wheeler.

SPECIMENS: Oberholser (1974) shows summer specimens collected in Lipscomb, Gray, and Oldham counties (one for each), without naming their locations. The Gray County bird may have reference to the adult male collected by McCauley (1877) along McClellan Creek, 20 June 1876.

Philadelphia Vireo *Vireo philadelphicus* (Cassin)

STATUS: Casual migrant.

OCCURRENCE: The Philadelphia Vireo has been reported in three counties of the Texas Panhandle: Parmer, Potter, and Randall. It has been seen April–May and August–October.

There have been 15 reported sightings of the Philadelphia Vireo in the study area, nine in spring and six in autumn. Many are probably questionable, particularly those birds reported in fall. As is pointed out by Pulich (1988), fall Philadelphia Vireos "take an eastern path toward the Mississippi River drainage after entering northeastern Oklahoma." The Philadelphia and Warbling Vireo may easily be confused, and any vireo thought to be the former should be examined with extra care, always bearing in mind the important points of identification set forth by Kaufman (1990a). Furthermore, few Philadelphias have been reported in the study area in recent years, indicative possibly not of a decline in the species but of more care being taken by observers as they became conversant with the finer points of identification. This is a species for which a specimen or photograph is needed to place it firmly on the area's list of birds.

Red-eyed Vireo *Vireo olivaceus* (Linnaeus)

STATUS: Rare migrant.

OCCURRENCE: The Red-eyed Vireo has been found in seven counties: Castro, Gray, Hemphill, Oldham, Parmer, Potter, and Randall. It has been seen from May to October.

This vireo is not reported every year. My records show that I recorded it during 19 of 33 years. It probably would be found more often if the eastern counties were surveyed regularly. Its passage in spring lasts from early to late May and in fall from early September to early October. The early and late spring dates are: one near Friona, Parmer County, 1 May 1963; one at BLNWR, 30 May 1982. The early and late fall dates are: one at BLNWR, 14 August 1966; one in Amarillo 21 October 1967. The reference to the species being "abundant at Amarillo 8 September to 21 October" in 1967 is a puzzler (Williams, 1968), as I have been able to find but two reported sightings for the fall of that year. Although the Red-eyed Vireo has never been found nesting in the Panhandle, there are four summer sightings: a singing bird at Lake Marvin, Hemphill County, 14 June 1977; one singing in PDCSP, 8 June 1978; one singing at BLNWR, 29 June 1997; one at Lake Marvin, 17 July 1990.

Sutton (1967) cites summer records of the Red-eyed Vireo in Oklahoma west to Ellis and Roger Mills counties: "Two birds were seen June 2, 1957, along Cimarron River thirteen miles north of Boise City, Cimarron County, appeared to be a pair, but neither was singing (G. M. Sutton). Singing male taken July 10, 1964, along Cimarron River in Union County, New Mexico, just west of Oklahoma state line, had 'somewhat enlarged' testes (D. M. Niles)." Another singing male was found in Black Mesa SP, Cimarron County, 17 June 1984 (Williams, 1984). A short distance to the south, a Red-eyed Vireo was observed at the Muleshoe NWR, Bailey County, 4 July 1984 (Williams, 1984), as was a singing bird near Lubbock, 22–23 June 1989 (Lasley and Sexton, 1989). Two found in the Corrumpa Creek area of Union County, New Mexico, 26 May 1996 "seemed territorial" (Williams, 1996). The Red-eyed Vireo is not known to nest in Texas outside the eastern half of the state (TOS, 1995).

Family Corvidae (Crows and Jays)

Steller's Jay *Cyanocitta stelleri* (Gmelin)
STATUS: Casual winter visitor.
OCCURRENCE: The Steller's Jay has been recorded in seven counties: Briscoe, Collingsworth, Deaf Smith, Hall, Oldham, Potter, and Randall. It has been seen from September to April.

There have been nine winters since mid-century in which the Steller's Jay has been reported. Prior to that of 1972–73, each sighting was of a single bird: *1952*—Amarillo, Potter County, 23 November; *1957*—Amarillo, Randall County, 29 October; *1967*—Amarillo, Potter/Randall counties, 21 November; *1968*—Amarillo, Randall County, 21–24 November; *1970*—Amarillo 12 and 25 October.

The first "invasion winter" occurred in the 1972–73 season, when numerous Steller's Jays were observed in Amarillo from September to April. The first one was seen on 21 September in the Woflin Addition. Thereafter through the first week of April, jays regularly visited three separate feeders in that section of town, occasionally six or more birds at one time. In addition, four jays were found in Memorial Park Cemetery, Potter County, 8 October, and one at the Palo Duro Club near Canyon, Randall County, 4 October. It was during this winter that a "massive invasion occurred into the lower elevations" of New Mexico, "including in the eastern plains (Clayton, Portales)" (Hubbard, 1978).

In 1978 a Steller's Jay was seen in a group of Blue Jays in Amarillo, Potter County, in mid-October, and in 1980 one in Amarillo, Potter County, 21 November. The winter of 1989–90 witnessed another invasion. The Amarillo sightings, each at a different location, were as follows: one regularly at a feeder, 22 December–16 March; one during the last week of October; one or more regularly during the latter part of October (TP-RF); one, 24 November. In addition, observers noted one Steller's Jay or more in Quitaque, Briscoe County, and Turkey, Hall County, late October–early December, and one or more on the Tom Green Ranch north of Vega, Oldham County, in mid-October. The same winter was unprecedented for Steller's Jays in the Oklahoma Panhandle (Oliphant, 1991), where 57 were recorded on the Kenton CBC of 31 December; unusual numbers were also found in nearby areas of Kansas and New Mexico.

Oberholser (1974) shows sight records of Steller's Jays in Deaf Smith and Oldham counties and a specimen collected in Collingsworth County, but details are lacking.

The Steller's Jay in Colorado is a "fairly common to common resident in foothills and lower mountains" (Andrews and Righter, 1992); in New Mexico it is a "resident in mountainous areas statewide" (Hubbard, 1978), including the upper Piñabetitos Creek area of Union County (NMOS, 1992); in Texas it is a "locally common resident in the Davis and Guadalupe Mountains of the Trans-Pecos" (TOS, 1995). The fall and winter movements of these populations are normally altitudinal, with only occasional winter irruptions into adjacent plains areas.

SPECIMENS: As indicated, Oberholser's (1974) citation of a specimen taken in Collingsworth County is not supported with details.

Blue Jay *Cyanocitta cristata* (Linnaeus)

STATUS: Fairly common to common resident.

OCCURRENCE: The Blue Jay has been recorded in every Texas Panhandle county and has been seen in every month.

The Blue Jay is common in the eastern sector of the study area; however, McCauley (1877) failed to include it in his species accounts during his traversal of the region in May and June of 1876. It is in the south-central sector, particularly in the Amarillo and Canyon areas, that the history of its more recent dispersal can be followed.

Strecker (1910) did not name it on his trip to Armstrong County. The sole comment of Reeves and Reeves (1914–36) for 1918 was: "There are more now than when first seen." Hibbets et al. (1926–36) called it a "permanent resident" without comment on numbers. The Blue Jay's absence from Carlander's (1934) accounts is puzzling considering the extensive scope of his study of bird life in the region. Russell (1935) did not name it as a bird of the PDCSP and vicinity, and Stevenson (1942) thought it noteworthy that "two migrants were noted at Canyon on September 30, and three . . . in Palo Duro Canyon on October 1, 1937 . . . and Palisades State Park on September 26, 1938." Hawkins (1945) thought the Blue Jay was "fairly common during certain months in the western Panhandle. Between March 1 and April 20, 1945, none was seen in the Amarillo area, but several were present throughout the summer and fall months." The notes of an Amarillo observer in 1952 (P. Acord) read: "fairly common in wooded areas—found around town and in Palo Duro Canyon from mid-April until October—seen occasionally in town in winter."

The Blue Jay today is fairly common to common year-round in Amarillo and nearby towns. However, it is only a summer resident in PDCSP, where a two-year breeding bird census (Seyffert, 1967–68) disclosed an average density of 10 per 100 acres. Common as it is during that season, it is rarely found past 1 October and does not return to the park until late March or early April. In all the Amarillo CBCs (1954–96), it has been recorded within the park boundaries only twice, both times a single bird. The Blue Jay does winter upcanyon at Lake Tanglewood. Farther to the west at BLNWR (Tierra Blanca Creek), the Blue Jay has only recently taken up summer residence.

In the western sector of the study area, the Blue Jay is a breeder in the Canadian River Valley and its wooded tributaries. It is found in almost all the larger towns that dot the plains and sometimes around ranch and farm sites containing extensive growth of trees. To what degree, if any, the birds withdraw in winter is unknown. That some remain in the larger towns in the northwestern Panhandle is probable, as wintering jays are known for Clayton, Union County, New Mexico (Williams and Hubbard, 1993).

The Blue Jay has been recorded on six of the eight BBSs, being absent on the Pantex and Waka routes, which run almost entirely through croplands. Only once has it appeared on the Texline count in the extreme northwest (a single bird at a farmsite), and only four times on the Childress count in the extreme southeast. The averages on the remaining counts are as follows: *Clarendon*—9; *Booker*—2; *Miami*—2; *Channing*—1. The averages on the CBCs are as follows: *Quitaque*—4; *Lake Meredith* (*west*)—3; *Amarillo*—3; *Lake Meredith* (*east*)—0.3; *Buffalo Lake* NWR—0.

Migrating flocks of Blue Jays can be seen in spring and fall, but little attention has been given them and their numbers have seldom been recorded. A 1954 report is the only one I know of that gives any depiction of a spring movement: "April 25—large flocks along the Canadian—had arrived just a few days before in rather large flocks" (A. S. Jackson). Thirty+ were in a flock in an Amarillo cemetery, Potter County, 2 October 1966, and a flock of 43 was seen at the BLNWR, 3 October 1982.

NESTING: The Blue Jay has been found nesting in 20 of the 26 study area counties and has been seen during summer in five of the remaining ones, Parmer County the exception. The TBBAP recorded CO nesting in 29 survey blocks, PR in 23, and PO in 15. Thirty were located between the 100th and 101st meridians, 20 between the 101st and 102nd, and 17 west of the 102nd. The only occupied quadrangles in the extreme northwest sector included the towns of Dalhart and Texline in Dallam County, and in the extreme southwest sector, Hart and Nazareth in Castro County showed occupation. Otherwise, the distribution was fairly evenly spread across the region.

Some Blue Jay pairs are probably two-brooded. Nest building has been observed as early as 17 April 1988 (Amarillo, Potter County), a nest with eggs was found on 10 June 1987 (Dumas, Moore County), and young were still being fed as late as 30 August 1987 (BLNWR).

SPECIMENS: Specimens have been taken in Hemphill (30 July 1971, TCWC), Hutchinson (12, 21 and 27 June 1950, TNHC), Potter (ACMNH; 8 October 1987, WTAMU), and Randall (28 June 1956, MNH; 1 October 1937, MVZ; 9 and 11 August 1939, spring 1983, WTAMU), counties. In addition, Oberholser (1974) shows specimens collected in Armstrong, Hutchinson, Lipscomb, and Randall counties, without giving details. Five of the birds collected (Hemphill, Hutchinson, Randall) were identified as the race *cyanotephra*. Three of these (Hutchinson) were collected by Thompson (1952) and are probably the source of the Oberholser reference to birds taken in that county.

Western Scrub-Jay *Aphelocoma californica* (Vigors)

STATUS: Fairly common to common resident in the canyonlands, rare winter visitor elsewhere.

OCCURRENCE: The Western Scrub-Jay has been found in 11 counties: Armstrong, Briscoe, Deaf Smith, Hansford, Hartley, Hutchinson, Moore, Oldham, Potter, Randall, and Roberts. It has been recorded year-round.

Is the Western Scrub-Jay a recent addition to the avifauna of the study area? The accounts of the earliest observers fail to mention the species; it was not until the work of Hibbets et al. (1926–36) that it was first named: "Winter and spring—October 25, 1927, Winter 1929, June 1930." Sightings were recorded later in South Ceta Canyon, Randall County (four on 8 November, two on 15 November, and two on 6 December 1936). The authors called the species the "Florida Jay." Stevenson (1942) found four Scrub-Jays near Dripping Springs, 15 miles south of Claude, Armstrong County, 24 September 1938, and several north of Amarillo and along the Canadian River, Potter County, 27 September 1938. These were the only reported sightings prior to mid-century.

It was not until the 1950s that the Scrub-Jay began being reported with any regularity, and even then a sighting was thought noteworthy. No observer thought the species was resident. Still later, Oberholser (1974) was unable to pronounce it as nesting: "fairly common (some winters) to scarce in canyons of northern Panhandle (breeding unconfirmed)." In the early 1950s scrub-jays began making news in nearby areas. When they appeared in Boise City, Cimarron County, Oklahoma, during the winter of 1950–51, it was "the first time in 32 years of observation" (Baumgartner, 1951), and a few found at Clayton, Union County, New Mexico, in the winter of 1953–54 were thought "erratic" (Baumgartner, 1954).

As often as the PDCSP had been censused during CBCs, beginning in 1954, it was not until the count of 22 December 1965 that the first Western Scrub-Jay, a single bird, was recorded. Even as recently as 1973, summering jays at that location were thought noteworthy (Williams, 1973). The species today is a fairly common to common resident in PDCSP, South Ceta Canyon, Lake Tanglewood area, and Caprock Canyons SP, Briscoe County. It has also been seen regularly throughout the year in the canyonlands of Armstrong County. None of the sightings in the other counties took place during summer. Scrub-jays have been recorded on six of 24 Lake Meredith (west) CBCS (1975–94), and a single bird was observed in the Bates Canyon area, 12 May 1987.

The Western Scrub-Jay is thought to be an altitudinal migrant only; however, there are irruptive winters when it moves into surrounding regions. There have been five such "invasion winters" in the study area—1957–58, 1972–73, 1978–79, 1989–90, 1994–95. During such times the scrub-jay may be found in numbers from mid-September to mid-May in areas where otherwise it is never seen. During the winter of 1972–73 the species was particularly common in and around Amarillo. During the same period, Clark's Nutcrackers, Steller's Jays, and Pinyon Jays also were present in the city. In the fall of 1989, I observed several flocks as they passed through the BLNWR, all headed south.

NESTING: The TBBAP found CO nesting in three survey blocks, PR in three, and PO in one. The COS were at Lake Tanglewood and PDCSP, Randall County, and on the Goforth Ranch (Luttrell Springs) in Armstrong County. The PRS were in Ceta Glen, South Ceta Canyon, Randall County, near Paloduro, Armstrong County, and Caprock Canyons SP, Briscoe County. The single PO was near Quitaque, Briscoe County. The only report of an actual nest found is one at Lake Tanglewood: young fledged on 2 July 1985. Testimony to how early nesting may begin, a Western Scrub-Jay carrying nesting material was observed in the PDCSP, 21 February 1997.

SPECIMENS: Stevenson (1942) collected a specimen near Dripping Springs, 15 miles south of Claude, Armstrong County, 24 September 1938. Its present location is not known. Oberholser (1974) assigned it to the race *woodhousii*. The TOS (1995), however, says the resident race is *texana*.

Pinyon Jay *Gymnorhinus cyanocephalus* Wied
STATUS: Casual fall and winter visitor.
OCCURRENCE: The Pinyon Jay has been recorded in five counties: Briscoe, Deaf Smith, Hutchinson, Potter, and Randall. It has been seen from September to April and once in June.

Pinyon Jays are normally encountered in flocks, some of these quite large. Hibbets et al. (1926–36) said of the species: "Fall, winter, spring. October 10, 1936, two very large flocks on plains about 30 miles north of Canyon." Two collected by Stevenson (1942) were "from a large flock found in junipers in Palo Duro Canyon on the Harold Ranch" (Randall County). Hawkins (1945) observed "flocks composed of up to twenty-seven . . . over Amarillo . . . during September and October 1944 and 1945." Near Burson Lake, Briscoe County, 100+ were seen, 12 February 1973, and 18 over west Amarillo, Potter County, 24 September 1975. The fall and winter of 1978 were unusual: 150 over southwest

Amarillo, 16 September; 30 over White Deer Creek (Duncan Ranch), southeastern Hutchinson County, 24 September; 40 over Bates Canyon, Lake Meredith, Potter County, 23 December. On 23 September 1988, 22 were seen at McBride Canyon, Lake Meredith, Potter County.

Smaller groups and single birds are occasionally seen. Reeves and Reeves (1914–36) reported: "1926. Three came for short periods during severe winter." One came to a feeder in Amarillo in March of 1953. Between 14 October 1961 and 8 March 1962, one to six jays were seen regularly at BLNWR. Two were at BLNWR, 19 September 1972, and one, 1 October 1978. A single bird at Lake Tanglewood, Randall County, 15 April 1979, is the latest on record. Oberholser (1974) does not name the source of his spring sight record for Deaf Smith County. Unaccountable, if correctly identified, were two Pinyon Jays at the Palo Duro Club near Canyon, Randall County, 10 June 1945 (Hawkins, 1945). The nearest to the study area that the Pinyon Jay is resident is the pinyon-juniper mesas of northwestern Cimarron County, Oklahoma (Sutton, 1967), and the species has been found during the breeding season in the pinyon-juniper-aspen-ponderosa pine area of Sierra Grande Mountain southwest of Des Moines, Union County, New Mexico (NMOS, 1992).

SPECIMENS: Oberholser (1974) refers to one or more specimens collected in Randall County and assigns them to the race *cassinii*. They may pertain to two mounted birds in the L. E. Simms collection mentioned by Stevenson (1942), which were taken in January or February 1929. Where they were deposited is not known, although it is known that some of Simms's birds were placed in the Panhandle-Plains Historical Museum in Canyon. If so, I have not found them.

Clark's Nutcracker *Nucifraga columbiana* (Wilson)
STATUS: Casual winter visitor.
OCCURRENCE: The Clark's Nutcracker has been recorded in six counties: Armstrong, Hemphill, Hutchinson, Moore, Potter, and Randall. It has been seen from October to April.

The first report of Clark's Nutcracker in the study area occurred in the fall of 1955. Two birds were found at two widely separated locations: one in Canyon, Randall County, 19–24 November, and one in Amarillo, Randall County, 19–20 November (photo). It was 15 years before another was reported—one on the Jokerst Ranch south of Amarillo, 13 October 1970.

When the species was next reported in the winter of 1972–73, it was truly an invasion: one near Canadian, Hemphill County, 29 October; one in Umbarger, Randall County, 6 November; one approximately seven miles northeast of Umbarger, Randall County, 19 November; one in Dumas, Moore County, latter part of November; one in Amarillo, Potter County, 1 January. One bird or more came regularly to feeders in Amarillo until as late as 5 April. Unreported at the time were a flock of 20 or more encountered in November along the rim of the Palo Duro Canyon five miles west of Wayside at the Armstrong–Randall County line, an unspecified number south of Canyon, Randall County, 16–17 November, and a single bird on the Jack Allen Ranch east of Borger, Hutchinson County, around 1 March. During this same winter Sutton (1974b) reported an irruption of Clark's Nutcrackers in Oklahoma involving at least 25 birds at various locations. Other places on the southern Great Plains where the species was found were Lubbock, Brownfield, Lamesa, Midland, and Burkburnett in Texas, and Clayton in New Mexico (Williams, 1973).

The most recent sighting of a Clark's Nutcracker was one observed in Amarillo, Potter/Randall counties, 19 January 1979. On 14 December 1996, one was at a rural residence a short distance south of Quitaque in Floyd County (TBRC; TP-RF).

Black-billed Magpie   *Pica pica* (Linnaeus)

STATUS: Casual winter visitor.

OCCURRENCE: Prior to the winter of 1997–98, there had been five reported sightings of the Black-billed Magpie in the Texas Panhandle: Dallam, Hemphill, Potter, Randall, and Swisher counties. During that winter at least seven were observed in Hansford County. Besides a pair that became resident, magpies have been seen in January, March, April, July, and December.

The first account of the Black-billed Magpie is found in Hibbets et al. (1926–36), where it is listed as rare: "1 July 1928 and 7 July 1929." No other details are provided. All the species cited in the report were seen within 40 miles of Canyon, Randall County. The next report involves a pair that took up residence in Canadian, Hemphill County, 1 April 1956 (Baumgartner, 1956), and nested. Shortly afterward the unlikely event in such an unlikely location received an explanation, for it was discovered that the pair had been brought to Canadian from Wyoming and had subsequently escaped and nested (TOS, 1956).

The files of the National Park Service at Lake Meredith contain a record of a Black-billed Magpie seen on the Recreation Area (Potter County): "30 April 1970. On Coldwater Ranch about 1 mile east of McBride—mesquite grassland. Flew across road flying north." The sighting was that of a park biologist (letter, Barbara Lund, 29 May 1972). The next magpie was reported near Happy, Swisher/Randall County, 5 January 1975 (Williams, 1975)—details are lacking.

The first confirmed Black-billed Magpie record is that of a single bird found in Texline, Dallam County, 27 December 1983 (TBRC). Earlier on that day, two magpies had been seen at nearby Clayton Lake, Union County, New Mexico. During the evening a strong cold front moved through, and when the observer returned to Texline he was surprised to see a magpie in town (letter, Mark Lockwood, 21 November 1995). The latest magpie sightings occurred during the winter of 1997–98 in Hansford County, involving possibly seven or more birds. On 5 December 1997, a single bird was observed at Coldwater Creek some 7–8 miles south of the Oklahoma state line in the northwestern sector of the county (D. and M. Tomlinson; TBRC), and on the following 16 January 1998, a magpie was watched at this same location as it retrieved food items cached in a fence post (D. Fisher, J. Windsor; TBRC). Still later, two pairs of magpies were observed a number of times during the first week or two of March on the Murrell Ranch, located on Coldwater Creek two miles or more southwest of this site. The birds reported earlier were possibly from this group. South of Gruver on Palo Duro Creek, a pair of magpies was observed on the Reynolds Ranch for a few weeks in late December and early January, and one bird again a short distance east of there during December. Some 4.5–5 miles southwest of these sightings, a magpie was seen north of Morse on two occasions in January, the latest date being 30 January. These observations were made by local landowners (letters, D. Hudson, 21 and 27 March 1998). It is possible that all of the birds seen in the Palo Duro Creek area were of the same group.

Wolfe (1956) classified the magpie in Texas as a "winter straggler in western area 1"; however, his "area 1" encompasses a larger region than the Panhandle, and on what basis the claim is made he fails to show.

The question arises of why the Black-billed Magpie has not been found more often in the Texas Panhandle, particularly in the northwestern sector, for it is resident in nearby northwestern Oklahoma (Cimarron County) and has occasionally been found eastward to Texas, Beaver, Woods, Grant, and Payne counties (Sutton, 1967). At nearby Clayton, Union County, New Mexico, one was present during all of summer 1968 (Williams, 1968). Another was found on 18 November 1990, and the species was thought to be possibly increasing in the county (Williams and Hubbard, 1991). Also in Union County, in an area only some 30 miles from the Texas line, I have recorded magpies northeast of Grenville on ten of 29 BBSS (1968–96), and the species is known to breed approximately 20–30 miles southwest of Clayton in the upper Piñabetitos Creek area (NMOS, 1992). With the initiation of the Texline BBS in Dallam County in 1975, I began exploring that area yearly for magpies but never found one.

The absence of proper breeding habitat of sufficient extent, coupled with the fact that outside of altitudinal movements, the Black-billed Magpie evinces little migratory behavior in the southern portions of its range, probably accounts for the dearth of sightings in the Texas Panhandle. The previously named ranchers in Hansford County, however, say the magpie has been seen in the area before, and the species may in fact occur there more often than we know.

American Crow *Corvus brachyrhynchos* Brehm

STATUS: Fairly common to abundant resident.

OCCURRENCE: The American Crow has been recorded in every county and has been seen year-round.

There are few references to the crow in the accounts of early observers. McCauley (1877) spent May and June in the eastern and central Panhandle where the species is presently a common resident, yet he found only "a few specimens . . . along McClellan Creek, etc." Furthermore, he encountered the Raven ("*Corvus corax*") frequently, and the White-necked Raven ("*Corvus cryptoleucus*") he thought "more abundant than any other of the *Corvidae*." Today the Common Raven is rarely, if ever, found in the regions he visited, and while the Chihuahuan Raven is still a resident, the crow is more common by far. This switch in status can possibly be attributed to the elimination of the buffalo as the dominant grazer and to widespread agricultural practices favorable to the crow.

Strecker (1910) did not name the crow as a bird seen on his trip to Armstrong County but noted the "White-necked Raven." Reeves and Reeves (1914–36) thought the crow "common near Canadian and near Memphis. 1919. 1926"; but they limited its presence in the area of Canyon, Randall County, to "once seen above Canyon Club." Hibbets et al. (1926–36) had this to say: "October 13, 1936. First seen in the Panhandle of Texas by these observers." Neither Russell (1935) nor Stevenson (1942) named it as a bird of the Palo Duro Canyon, but Hawkins (1945) said it was a "fairly common year-round resident of eastern Panhandle; uncommon winter resident of western Panhandle." Even Thompson (1952) did not encounter the crow in an area of Hutchinson County where it is found today.

The American Crow today is a common resident in the eastern third of the study area, diminishing westward. Changes in agricultural practices since mid-century in the southwestern sector, principally the extensive cultivation of sorghum grains, have caused the crow to become abundant there in winter; it is not uncommon to see 1,000+ in a day. The crow is rarely found in the extreme northwestern sector. An indication of its summer and winter status can be gleaned from the average numbers recorded on the BBSS and CBCS. BBS: *Clarendon*—35.5; *Childress*—12.5; *Miami*—1.8; *Channing*—1.6; *Booker*—0.4; *Pantex*—0.3; *Texline*—0.05; *Waka*—0. CBC: *Quitaque*—80.7; *Lake Meredith* (*west*)—26.9; *Amarillo*—4.3; *Lake Meredith* (*east*)—2.0; *Buffalo Lake* NWR—0.7; *Friona*—0. Examples of numbers during migration: 1,170 in Briscoe County, 23 November 1975, and 1,000+, 4 and 11 April 1976; 1,000+ in Wheeler County, 6 October 1985.

NESTING: The TBBAP (1987–92) found CO nesting in nine survey blocks, PR in 32, and PO in 16. Thirty were between the 100th and 101st meridians, 15 between the

101st and 102nd, and 12 west of the 102nd, many of the latter in the Canadian River Valley. There are few data concerning nesting and much remains to be learned. Nest building: 17 March 1995 (PDCSP) to 30 May 1989 (Moore County). Egg dates: 3 May 1970 (PDCSP) to 1 June 1987 (Hemphill County).

SPECIMENS: Specimens are available from Wheeler County (29 February, 4, 6, and 20 March 1972, WTAMU).

Chihuahuan Raven *Corvus cryptoleucus* Couch

STATUS: Uncommon to common resident.

OCCURRENCE: The Chihuahuan Raven has been recorded in all the Texas Panhandle counties except Hansford, Lipscomb, Ochiltree, and Swisher. It has been seen year-round.

McCauley's (1877) assessment of the status of the Chihuahuan Raven in the study area as "more abundant than any other of the *Corvidae*" is no longer true. As grasslands and scrublands have been converted to croplands, the crow has displaced the raven in predominance. A little over 30 years after McCauley, Strecker (1910) spoke of the Chihuahuan Raven as "apparently not a common species, as but two specimens were noted. They were flying over the plains." Later (1912) he classified the raven as "not common on the northern plains (Panhandle) as far as my observations go." Hawkins (1945) spoke of it as "a year-around resident in small numbers, but it is common in the eastern Panhandle."

Today the Chihuahuan Raven is found most commonly in the western third of the study area and is fairly common locally in the eastern third. It has been recorded on seven of 12 BBSS, but consistently and commonly on only two, the Texline and Dalhart routes in the northwest sector. This raven has been recorded on two of eight Clarendon counts, six of 20 Childress, two of 20 Pantex, one of 22 Miami, and 11 of 30 Channing counts. On the latter route, crows are usually encountered in the Canadian River Valley and ravens at higher elevations in the mesquite-scrub plains.

Most Chihuahuan Ravens withdraw from the northern areas in winter. Of 139 CBCs it was found on only eight. A gathering of 34 near Vega, Oldham County, 25 January 1995, was unusual. Of note: "Ravens shot by hunters in the Clayton, N. Mex. area proved to be the White-necked [Chihuahuan] species; previously birders had thought that only Com. Ravens wintered in the area" (Williams, 1969). No migrant groups have ever been reported in fall, but there is evidence of a spring movement: 100+ near Quitaque, Briscoe County, 4 and 11 April 1976, and 63 in one field in Hartley County, 16 May 1993.

NESTING: The TBBAP (1987–92) found CO nesting in four survey blocks, PR in 18, and PO in nine. Eight were between the 100th and 101st meridians, one between the 101st and 102nd, and the remaining 22 west of the 102nd. There is a paucity of information concerning nesting. The Chihuahuan Raven has been confirmed nesting in seven counties: Armstrong, Dallam, Deaf Smith, Donley, Hartley, Parmer, and Randall. Most nests have been found built on windmill platforms, less often in dead trees and on cliff walls.

SPECIMENS: Oberholser (1974) shows specimens taken in Hall and Childress counties but does not give their present whereabouts.

Common Raven *Corvus corax* Linnaeus

STATUS: Rare winter and casual summer visitor.

OCCURRENCE: The Common Raven has been recorded in ten counties: Armstrong, Childress, Collingsworth, Dallam, Deaf Smith, Hartley, Hemphill, Oldham, Potter, and Randall. It has been seen October–February and April–June.

The status of the Common Raven in the Texas Panhandle has changed dramatically since the time of McCauley (1877): "As may be imagined, this most striking of the *Corvidae* was frequently seen. No place could be found that would better suit its preference for a habitat than the great Llano Estacado. Fearfully monotonous, and with solitude as its main characteristic, rarely crossed by man . . . it is perfectly congenial to the Raven, offering adequate sustenance in the carcasses of animals that are often too numerous to the traveler."

The abundant food source no doubt accounted for the presence of ravens in such numbers, but whether the species was as common prior to the wholesale slaughter of buffalo witnessed by McCauley is unknown. What is known is that with the departure of the buffalo, the raven departed as well. When speaking of the Common Raven as a resident species in the Black Mesa country of the northwestern Oklahoma Panhandle, Sutton (1967) refers to Nice's belief that the species was "abundant in the days of the buffalo." He is skeptical of subsequent reports of its abundance, however, and thinks the birds were probably misidentified Chihuahuan Ravens, the more likely species. At the time I began my observations in the 1960s, the Common Raven was thought to be common in nearby Union County, New Mexico, until collecting proved that many were in fact Chihuahuans. None of the other early observers named this raven in the study area, and few have been reported since mid-century: BLNWR, 21 November 1964; Frying Pan Ranch, Potter/Oldham counties, 23 April 1972; near Masterson, Potter County, 24 October 1974; near Texline, Dallam County, 20 December 1982; near Channing, Hartley County, 2 December 1995; near Dalhart, Dallam County, 23 February 1997; near Boys Ranch, Oldham County, 7 February 1998. Probably more would be reported in the northwestern counties if they were surveyed more often in winter.

It is in the Lake Meredith Recreation Area west of McBride Canyon that a number of Common Raven sightings have occurred of late. This raven was recorded on the Lake Meredith (west) CBC on 2 January 1983, 22 December 1984, and 26 December 1993. Another was observed in that area on 10 May 1987. On 23 May 1987, I observed two Common Ravens at the Turkey Creek Plant near the Alibates–McBride Canyon road. As the ravens circled low overhead they were attacked by several kingbirds. One was again seen a short distance south of there on 5 June 1994. This recurrence points to possible residency.

Oberholser (1974) shows a winter sight record of a Common Raven for Potter County, a summer sight record for Armstrong County, and a spring sight record for either Childress or Collingsworth County. The Armstrong County sighting probably has reference to McCauley (1877), but the basis for the others is not known. This is also true of a Hemphill County report. I am skeptical of all these eastern county sightings and believe they were more likely Chihuahuan Ravens. Six reported on the Lake Meredith (west) CBC of 20 December 1997 must be questioned. The Common Raven is a much larger bird than the Chihuahuan, with a pronouncedly wedge-shaped tail that can be clearly seen during its hawk-like flight, alternately flapping and soaring. Perched birds display their shaggy throat feathers and heavier bills.

NESTING: The only report of nesting Common Ravens in the Texas Panhandle is that of Oberholser (1974), who shows a summer sight record of breeding in Deaf Smith County. Details are not given. A diligent search would possibly turn up breeding in western Dallam, Hartley, and Oldham counties. Ranches in these rugged and remote areas are largely inaccessible to the public and are rarely if ever birded. A nest with young was found on Perico Creek near Clayton, Union County, New Mexico, 25 June 1993 (Williams and Hubbard, 1993), and the species is known to breed in the upper Piñabetitos Creek area southwest of Clayton (NMOS, 1992).

Family Alaudidae (Larks)

Horned Lark *Eremophila alpestris* (Linnaeus)
STATUS: Common to abundant resident.
OCCURRENCE: The Horned Lark has been found in every Texas Panhandle county and has been seen year-round.

McCauley (1877) summed up the Horned Lark's presence on the High Plains: "This bright little songster was almost a constant companion in the daily surveys of the Staked Plain proper, being there especially noticeable and extremely abundant." Carlander (1934) attempted to estimate just how abundant: "I would say that there are at least fifty larks for each square mile of the Panhandle. This would make a total of 2,500,000 birds in this country." He based his estimate on "following the telephone wires and fences in the heat of a summer day and counting the birds standing in the shade." His figure is twice as high as it should be, however, as the 26 counties of the Texas Panhandle are of 25,610 square miles in extent (x 50 = 1,280,500 birds). How many there are in winter is anyone's guess, for Horned Larks are then flocking and appear even more plentiful than in summer.

Our methods of gathering numerical data today, such as BBSS and CBCS, differ greatly from that adopted by Carlander. The following are the averages per route on the BBSS: *Pantex*—328; *Texline*—130; *Booker*—111; *Miami*—90; *Waka*—60; *Panhandle*—56; *Dalhart*—49; *Channing*—48; *Skellytown*—5; *Childress*—4; *Clarendon*—0. The Pantex route encompasses primarily cropland mixed with mesquite-shrub/grassland, while the Clarendon route, located only a short distance to the east, is comprised of sandsage–Harvard shin oak brush mixed with small units of cropland. The number of larks tallied can vary widely from year to year. For example, the Pantex high and low are 667 and 164. All the older routes show evidence of long-term declines.

The following are the averages on the CBCS: *Buffalo Lake* NWR—460; *Friona*—265; *Amarillo*—189; *Quitaque*—105; *Lake Meredith (east)*—29; *Lake Meredith (west)*—5. The BLNWR average is not representative of the actual abundance of the Horned Lark in that area, for many of the earlier counts were restricted to the refuge itself, not taking in the surrounding plains where most larks are found. Also, as is true of most of the CBCS, in some winters unpaved roads are impassable and valid lark counts cannot be secured. As an example of wide variation in numbers, the BLNWR count has tallied zero birds up to 1,500.

NESTING: The Horned Lark has been confirmed nesting in 19 of the 26 study area counties and would be in the remainder with better searching. The TBBAP produced CO nestings in 30 survey blocks, PR in 63, and PO in 13. They were fairly evenly distributed: 29 between the 100th and 101st meridians, 41 between the 101st and 102nd, and 36 west of the 102nd. In arriving at breeding status, a majority of the confirmed nestings were based on the observation of fledglings or adults feeding young, mostly during the period 8 June–10 July. The earliest nesting date is for a nest with three recently hatched young (eyes still closed) near the BLNWR, 16 April 1975, and the latest date for a nest with eggs near Lake Tanglewood, Randall County, 10 July 1989. Courting birds have been noted as early as 16 February 1958.

SPECIMENS: Specimens have been collected in Armstrong (31 July 1968, MVZ; 13 July 1968, TCWC), Dallam (17 July 1984, TCWC), Deaf Smith (20 August 1978, CMNH), Hansford (28 October 1956, MNH; 25 November 1954, OMNH), Hemphill (13 June 1905, SM), Lipscomb (8 January 1986, WTAMU), Moore (MCHM), Potter (18 November 1972, OMNH; 16 June 1979, TCWC; 8 February 1970, WTAMU),

Randall (28 December 1936, 30 September 1937, MVZ; 10 April, 8 June, 21 July, 16 November 1985, 8 July 1986, 1 March 1987, TCWC; 30 December 1938, 9 and 15 January, 20 September 1939, 30 July 1970, 20 April 1990, WTAMU), Sherman (11 June 1958, MNH), and Swisher (21 July 1985, TCWC) counties. McCauley cites a specimen taken in Randall County, 20 May 1876, but it is not known where his birds were deposited.

Stevenson (1942) says of the Horned Lark (*Otocoris alpestris*): "Four taken on December 28, 1936, in Randall County, have been identified as *O. a. enthymia.* According to Dr. Oberholser, this is the breeding horned lark of the Panhandle. A specimen of *O. a. leucolaema* was taken by Smith in Randall County on December 28, 1936. An example of *O. a. lamphrochroma,* collected near Canyon, February 9, 1936, was reported by the writer in the Condor (39, 1937:44)." These specimens were deposited in the MVZ collection and are discussed by Oberholser (1974). In addition, a specimen of *leucolaema* taken on 31 July 1968 in Armstrong County is also in the MVZ. As far as I can determine, none of the other specimens has been identified as to subspecies. Oberholser (1974) shows specimens collected in Lipscomb, Moore, Hutchinson, Potter, Deaf Smith, Randall, Armstrong, and Castro counties, without naming the collections in which they reside. Some of the specimens mentioned in these collections represent those on his list. In addition, he refers to a specimen of *E. a. occidentalis* taken in Armstrong County ("Aug 22").

It is of interest to note the continental and seasonal distribution of these subspecies (AOU, 1957; Beason, 1995). *E. a. enthymia* breeds over much of the Great Plains from Saskatchewan and Manitoba to the Texas Panhandle, and southward in winter. Whether those that breed in the study area remain in winter or migrate is not known. *E. a. leucolaema* breeds from southern Alberta and extreme western Minnesota to central Colorado and eastern New Mexico, wintering southward. The TOS (1995) says *leucolaema* is resident in the southern half of the Panhandle and *enthymia* in the northern half. *E. a. lamphrochroma,* collected near Canyon in the winter of 1936, is a breeder in the northwestern United States and winters in southern Nevada, the Sacramento Valley and San Joaquin Valley south to Los Angeles County and the Imperial Valley in California, and southern Arizona. The subspecies *occidentalis,* taken in Armstrong County in August, breeds from northern and central Arizona to central New Mexico and winters in its breeding range, ranging also to Sonora, Chihuahua, and western Texas. It would add to our knowledge if all specimens that have been collected were identified as to subspecies. A full-scale year-round study of the status and distribution of the Horned Lark in the Texas Panhandle is a project worthy of an enterprising student.

Family Hirundinidae (Swallows)

Purple Martin *Progne subis* (Linnaeus)

STATUS: Uncommon to fairly common breeder in eastern two-thirds; rare to uncommon transient in the west.

OCCURRENCE: The Purple Martin has been reported in seventeen counties: Childress, Collingsworth, Deaf Smith, Donley, Gray, Hansford, Hartley, Hemphill, Hutchinson, Lipscomb, Ochiltree, Oldham, Parmer, Potter, Randall, Roberts, and Wheeler. It has been seen February to October.

The Purple Martin is a relatively recent addition to the avifauna of the Texas Panhandle. Few early observers mentioned the species, and then only tersely. Strecker (1912) asserted that it was a "summer resident, distributed over the entire state"; however, he was not specific as to any actual nestings taking place in the study area. Purple Martins were not recorded by McCauley (1877) in the eastern and south-central sectors during spring and summer of 1876. The first references to specific locations of occurrence are found in Carlander (1933, 1934), who reported martins in Amarillo between 13 August and 4 September 1932 and cited a single nesting record for Shamrock, Wheeler County. Hawkins (1945) later classified the species as only a "possible rare summer resident." It was not until the 1950s and 1960s that intermittent sightings of Purple Martins began to accumulate, and their number increased steadily thereafter.

The early and late dates for Purple Martins are 19 February 1992 at Canyon, Randall County, and 10 October 1997 in Potter County and at Lake McClellan, Gray County. The four-year average date of return (1992–95) in Canyon is 11 March. October is late indeed, for nesting birds are thought to be gone by the end of July. No large gatherings of migrants have been reported.

NESTING: It was in the summer of 1972 that the first survey was made to determine the nesting status of the Purple Martin in the Texas Panhandle (J. C. Williams). Colonies were found in the following counties: Collingsworth (Wellington); Gray (Pampa); Hemphill (Canadian); Ochiltree (Perryton); Roberts (Miami); Wheeler (Wheeler). Twenty-two martin houses located in Pampa contained 333 compartments; at these were 110 adult martins and 448 House Sparrows. There were about ten nesting pairs each in Canadian, Miami, and Perryton. Prior to the study, Purple Martins had been reported nesting in Childress, Childress County, in the summer of 1968, and in Pampa in the summer of 1970. On 3 May 1977, three pairs of were observed at a martin house in Borger, Hutchinson County. Although martins had been observed in Amarillo during summer prior to 1980, it was not until that decade that observers learned they were nesting.

Presently known martin colonies are located in the following towns: Amarillo, Borger, Canadian, Canyon, Childress, Clarendon, Howardwick, Lefors,

Miami, Pampa, Perryton, Shamrock, Spearman, Wellington, and Wheeler (Ray, 1995b). Some are quite large. As an example, 33–34 pairs with 89 young were reported at a site in the Avondale area of Amarillo, Potter County, in July 1995. In 1997, 79 martins were banded in Amarillo, 39 in Canyon, and 72 in Spearman, and up to 200 yearly thereafter (J. Ray).

Those interested in establishing a martin colony should consult Ray (1995a), and all colonies discovered should be reported, particularly any found west of a line running from Spearman to Amarillo. Of equal interest are nestings that may be discovered in housing not supplied by humans—in cavities in tree snags, cliff faces, and embankments.

Tree Swallow *Tachycineta bicolor* (Vieillot)

STATUS: Common to abundant migrant and vagrant breeder.

OCCURRENCE: The Tree Swallow has been reported in 19 Panhandle counties: Armstrong, Briscoe, Carson, Castro, Childress, Deaf Smith, Donley, Gray, Hartley, Hemphill, Hutchinson, Moore, Oldham, Parmer, Potter, Randall, Roberts, Swisher, and Wheeler. Oberholser (1974) shows it in four. It has been seen from February to November.

Often the Tree Swallow is the first of the swallows to return in spring. The earliest dates are for one at Ceta Glen, South Ceta Canyon, Randall County, 26 February 1956, and one at BLNWR, 27 February 1983. The normal date is around mid-March, and few remain beyond mid-May. The latest is a single bird east of Clarendon, Donley County, 2 June 1989.

It is not uncommon to encounter returning southbound birds in late July, the earliest date being for an unspecified number in Parmer County, 8 July 1962, and it is in fall that the largest gatherings occur. An estimated 700 Tree Swallows were at BLNWR, 5 September 1970, and 1,000+ on both 3 and 10 September 1978. Of an estimated 10,000 mixed swallow species at Cactus Lake, Moore County, 9 August 1997, 10 percent were thought to be of this species. There is one sighting past October, a single bird at BLNWR. 12 November 1968.

NESTING: The first nesting of the Tree Swallow was reported in Hemphill County in 1997. A pair was found occupying a Wood Duck box on the Gene Howe WMA (R. Magill); by 17 May six eggs had been laid. Five young hatched and successfully fledged. A pair was again observed feeding young in the same box, 21 June 1999 (J. Ray, M. Schoenhals). Prior to this discovery, other nestings of the Tree Swallow had been discovered in nearby areas of Oklahoma and New Mexico. Newell (1979) reported a pair feeding young in the nest at Lake Etling, Black Mesa SP, Cimarron County, Oklahoma, 28 June 1979, a first for the state. On 12 June of that summer, I found a nesting pair at Clayton Lake, Union County, New Mexico, a first record for northeastern New Mexico. I continued monitoring this site in subsequent years and again found swallows nesting on 12 June 1981, 16 June 1985, and 15 June 1986 (young being fed 28 June–5 July; Hubbard, 1986). Other potential nesting sites in the Panhandle that need watching are Lake Rita Blanca in Hartley County and Palo Duro Lake in Hansford County.

The Tree Swallow is a rare breeder in Texas. It formerly bred in Bexar, Jackson, and possibly Bandera counties, and more recently in Delta, Mason, and Wood counties (TOS, 1995).

Violet-green Swallow *Tachycineta thalassina* (Swainson)

STATUS: Casual migrant.

OCCURRENCE: The Violet-green Swallow has been recorded in five counties: Castro, Hemphill, Parmer, Potter, and Randall. It has been seen from February to September.

There have been 15 reported sightings of the Violet-green Swallow in the study area: *Castro*—6–7 August 1992; 10, 18, and 30 September 1993. *Hemphill*—25 April 1971 (Canadian). *Parmer*—7 September 1961 (Friona); 17 July 1990 (Lazbuddie). *Potter*—22 April 1972 (Bushland). *Randall*—26 February 1956 (South Ceta Canyon); 7 September 1961 (PDCSP); 27 August 1966 (near Amarillo); 28 March (BLNWR), 9 April (BLNWR) and 7 May (near Amarillo) 1967; 19 August 1974 (BLNWR); 29 August 1975 (BLNWR); 30 August 1977. The highest number for any sighting was 5–6. The Violet-green Swallow is often highly gregarious in migration; that flocks have never been reported in the study area is indicative of just how few of this montane species stray eastward.

From nearby in the Oklahoma Panhandle, three sightings of the Violet-green Swallow have been reported at Lake Etling, Black Mesa SP, Cimarron County: 24 August 1970; 5 July 1971; 17 April 1976 (Baumgartner and Baumgartner, 1992). On 4 July 1980, it was observed on the Muleshoe NWR, Bailey County ("remarkable at that date"; Williams, 1980b). In addition, the species is on the "rare visitors" list in the Clayton area, Union County, New Mexico (Weske, 1968). Hubbard (1978) says it migrates statewide in New Mexico, "including occasionally eastward to Clayton." Closer examination of swallow flocks would possibly turn up more violet-greens in the study area.

Northern Rough-winged Swallow *Stelgidopteryx serripennis* (Audubon)

STATUS: Uncommon to fairly common breeder locally; common to abundant migrant.

OCCURRENCE: The Northern Rough-winged Swallow has been reported in every county except Deaf Smith, Parmer, and Sherman. Oberholser (1974) shows it in three: Hemphill, Potter, and Roberts. It has been seen from March to October.

The Northern Rough-winged Swallow is one of the earliest of the swallow species to return in spring, the earliest being a single bird at Lake Tanglewood, Randall County, 14 March 1976—normal arrival date is the first week of April. Few are seen past mid-September. There are four October records, the latest a single bird in Potter County, 10 October 1997. Large flocks are seldom reported: 150–200 at BLNWR, 6 and 27 May 1961; 50+ near Amarillo, Randall County, 28 April 1995; 75+ (mostly juveniles) on Taylor Lakes WMA, Donley County, 20 August 1996, and 100 there, 26 August 1997. Of a mixed flock of an estimated 10,000 swallows observed at Cactus Lake, Moore County, 10 October 1997, 5 percent were thought to be rough-wingeds.

NESTING: In summer the Northern Rough-winged Swallow is widespread in the study area, as evidenced by its presence in the following counties: Armstrong, Briscoe, Collingsworth, Donley, Gray (adult with young, Lake McClellan, 23–24 June 1956), Hall, Hansford, Hartley, Hemphill (six fledglings, 15 July 1990), Hutchinson (two juveniles collected on Bugbee Ranch, 1 July 1950), Ochiltree (pair feeding young in nest at Lake Fryer, Wolf Creek Park, 3 June 1975), Oldham, Randall (nests yearly in Lake Tanglewood area and in PDCSP), Roberts, Swisher, and Wheeler. Many of the observations in these counties pointed to probable nesting.

SPECIMENS: The two specimens are available taken by Thompson (1952) in Hutchinson County (1 July 1950, TNHC).

Bank Swallow *Riparia riparia* (Linnaeus)
STATUS: Fairly common to abundant migrant.
OCCURRENCE: The Bank Swallow has been recorded in 18 counties: Armstrong, Briscoe, Carson, Castro, Deaf Smith, Donley, Gray, Hartley, Hemphill, Hutchinson, Moore, Ochiltree, Oldham, Parmer, Potter, Randall, Roberts, and Swisher. Oberholser (1974) shows it in five. It has been seen from April to November.

The migration dates of the Bank Swallow range from mid-April to mid-May, and from early August to mid-September. The early and late spring dates are: 8 April 1990, a single bird at Lake Tanglewood, Randall County, and 23 May 1987, two in Randall County. The early and late fall dates are: 16 July 1987, six or more at Hart, Castro County, and 8 November 1964, one at BLNWR. Occasionally large flocks have been observed: 800 at BLNWR, 13 May 1961; 100+ in Carson County, 9 August 1964; numerous large flocks, some of 200+, in Randall County, 3–17 August 1986; of an estimated 10,000 mixed swallow species at Cactus Lake, Moore County, 9 August 1997, 5 percent were thought to be Bank Swallows.

Evidence of possible nesting Bank Swallows in the study area has never been discovered. McCauley (1877) spoke of the species as "not uncommon along parts of Red River, where occasionally banks . . . rise up perpendicularly for a hundred

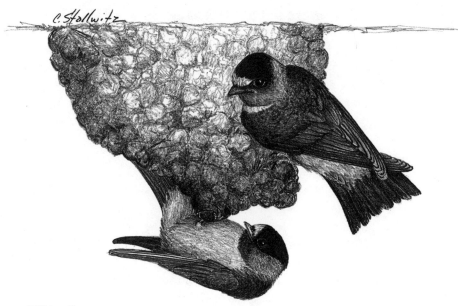

Cliff Swallows

feet from the dry alkali bed below"—implying that Bank Swallows could possibly be nesting in this seemingly favorable habitat. To my knowledge none have ever been reported in the canyonlands during summer since. Hawkins (1945) classified the Bank Swallow as a "rare summer resident. . . . mainly along the Canadian River and its tributaries," and two were recorded on the Clarendon BBS (Donley County), 2 June 1970. The Bank, Northern Rough-winged, and immature Tree Swallow are similar in appearance and can easily be confused unless scrutinized closely.

Bank Swallows reportedly have nested at Great Salt Plains NWR in northwest Oklahoma and attempted to nest in Cimarron County, Oklahoma, in 1920 (Baumgartner and Baumgartner, 1992). The TBBAP did not turn up any Bank Swallows in the Texas Panhandle.

Cliff Swallow *Petrochelidon pyrrhonota* (Vieillot)
STATUS: Common to abundant migrant and breeder.
OCCURRENCE: The Cliff Swallow has been recorded in every Texas Panhandle county and has been seen from April to October.

Most early observers in the study area spoke of the Cliff Swallow in terms of its commonness or abundance. As a rule, it does not return as early in spring or linger as late in fall as other swallow species. It can be looked for in mid- or late April, the earliest date being 2 April 1966 and 2 April 1995, both in Randall

County. It is usually gone by the first of October, the latest date being 31 October 1986 at BLNWR. Large flocks of migrants may be encountered. As an example, of an estimated 10,000+ swallows of mixed species at Cactus Lake, Moore County, 9 August 1997, 60 percent were thought to be Cliff Swallows.

NESTING: There are records of nesting Cliff Swallows from every county except Castro. Most early observers spoke of it nesting primarily, if not exclusively, in the canyonlands: Hawkins (1945) noted it "in only a few places," and Carlander (1934) said, "In the Panhandle these swallows have kept to their original nesting places, the cliffs. I do not believe they have taken to the walls of buildings here." I have observed large colonies of nesting swallows on brick buildings on the university campus in Canyon, Randall County, as did Reeves and Reeves (1914–36). Today almost every bridge crossing the Canadian River, and many on other waterways, hosts nesting swallows, some colonies quite large. The species may be found nesting on a wide assortment of man-made structures. One of the larger colonies I have seen occupies the gate tower at the Lake Rita Blanca dam, Hartley County. Other structures that it utilizes are road culverts, the sides of houses (usually of stucco), and the canopies of carports. Colonies may be abandoned periodically, particularly if there has been a buildup in ectoparasites such as fleas, ticks, and bedbugs, and then reinhabited after a lapse of a few years. Some bridge and culvert sites may also contain a few Barn Swallow nests, while the House Sparrow often occupies the gourd-shaped structures. I once found an Eastern Bluebird nest with young in one. Unfortunately, there is a paucity of data on the commencement and completion of this swallow's nesting cycle. The earliest date for nest building we have is 22 April 1988 near Dumas, Moore County.

The BBSS illustrate the variation and extent in the occupation of nest sites. Almost all swallows encountered are concentrated at or near bridges or road culverts. In some years the colonies may contain large numbers, in others few or none. The following are the averages, highs, and lows for each count: *Childress*—192 (1,179, 11); *Booker*—162 (436, 2); *Channing*—102 (424, 27); *Dalhart*—61 (80, 38); *Miami*—59 (171, 8); *Clarendon*—19 (97, 0); *Waka*—9 (51, 0); *Texline*—0.9 (5, 0); *Pantex*—0.4 (6, 0). The TBBAP found CO nesting in 63 survey blocks, PR in six, and PO in 19—36 between the 100th and 101st meridians, 31 between the 101st and 102nd, and 21 west of the 102nd. Only five quadrangles were occupied in the southwestern sector.

SPECIMENS: Specimens have been collected in Gray (16 June 1978, 10 June 1979, TCWC), Hartley (8 June 1979, TCWC), and Randall (30 May and 13 June 1985, TCWC) counties. Oberholser (1974) shows a specimen taken in Randall County but fails to give details. The TOS (1995) says nominate *pyrrhonota* is the resident race.

Barn Swallow *Hirundo rustica* Linnaeus

STATUS: Common breeder and common to abundant migrant.

OCCURRENCE: The Barn Swallow has been recorded in every Texas Panhandle county and has been seen from March to November.

In light of the species' present-day commonness as a breeder, it is of interest to note what earlier area observers had to say about the status of the Barn Swallow. McCauley (1877) was terse in his account: "Frequenting settlements in Indian Territory, not as common as *P. lunifrons*" (the Cliff Swallow)—he does not record Barn Swallows farther south in the study area. Strecker (1912) classified the species as an "abundant migrant" in Texas, but with limited breeding locally (San Antonio and Tyler areas), and did not name it on his earlier trip to Armstrong County (1910). Reeves and Reeves (1914) and Hibbets et al. (1926–36) named the Cliff Swallow in their lists of Panhandle birds, but not the Barn Swallow. Carlander (1934), among his many species accounts, failed to devote one to it. Neither Russell (1935) nor Stevenson (1942) list it as a bird of the central Panhandle, and Hawkins (1945) thought it a "probable summer resident. Two were seen during the spring migration of 1945, but none was seen during the summer months." Thompson (1952) spoke only of the Northern Rough-winged Swallow in Hutchinson County during his summer work in that area. Oberholser (1974) showed the Barn Swallow in only 15 of the 26 study area counties.

The Barn Swallow normally returns to the area in spring around mid-April. Very early was a single bird at Lake Tanglewood, Randall County, 14 March 1976. In 34 years of birding the area, I have yet to see one in March. Few are seen past the third week in October. The only sightings for November are a single bird at BLNWR, 6 November 1987, and two at Lake Tanglewood, 19 November 1994. It is in fall that the largest numbers can be seen. On the mud flats at the BLNWR, 750–1,000 congregated on 29 September 1968 and 1,000+ on 8 October 1972. In an hour's time during the morning of 15 October 1984, 2,000+ were estimated passing over the refuge, and the movement was continuing as the observer left. Of an estimated 10,000 mixed swallow species observed at Cactus Lake, Moore County, 9 August 1997, 20 percent were thought to be Barn Swallows. The averages on the BBSS are: *Panhandle—17; Booker—14; Childress—10; Texline—11; Miami—9; Skellytown—8; Waka—8; Pantex—5; Clarendon—4; Channing—3; Dalhart—2.*

NESTING: The Barn Swallow has been confirmed nesting in every study area county. The TBBAP found CO nesting in 80 survey blocks, PR in 27, and PO in 15. The occupied quadrangles were evenly distributed: 43 between the 100th and 101st meridians, 42 between the 101st and 102nd, and 37 west of the 102nd. Such distribution can be contrasted to that of an earlier day when a nest found at the BLNWR in the summer of 1967 was thought "unusual for western Texas" (Williams, 1967). Today many bridges and culverts may be found occupied by one Barn Swallow nest or more. Farm and ranch houses and outbuildings may have nests placed under eaves or on ledges above windows and doorways, and the species often nests within small towns and on the outskirts of large ones. Almost every abandoned house and barn scattered across the plains, and there are many, contains swallow nests plastered on the inner walls.

Nest building begins soon after the swallows return in spring. The earliest date of nesting activity is 27 April 1991 in Collingsworth County. A nest containing young was found near Quitaque, Briscoe County, 2 May 1987. The Barn Swallow is two-brooded, possibly three-brooded. A nest built in a highway culvert at the BLNWR (1970) was found occupied on 12 May (five eggs), 1 July (five young), and 2 August (four eggs). This 2 August date was duplicated by another nest containing five eggs found in an abandoned house on the plains in Castro County in 1987. A nest containing one young was found in the Thompson Grove Picnic Area northeast of Texline, Dallam County, 27 August 1984. Twenty or more swallows were flying about in this quite small oasis on the open plains. The latest date of nesting activity was a nest with three young in Moore County during the week of 7–13 September 1997. The Barn Swallow is not known to nest on the canyon floor in the Palo Duro; however, a nest, along with four flying birds, was discovered in a road culvert in the state park, 6 July 1995.

SPECIMENS: Specimens have been taken in Oldham (8 June 1979, TCWC) and Wheeler (August 1963, TCWC) counties.

Family Paridae (Chickadees and Titmice)

Carolina Chickadee *Poecile carolinensis* (Audubon)

STATUS: Fairly common to common resident in the eastern third and along the Canadian River and tributaries westward. Rare to uncommon resident in the canyonlands.

OCCURRENCE: Oberholser (1974) shows the Carolina Chickadee in seven Texas Panhandle counties: Collingsworth, Donley, Gray, Hemphill, Hutchinson, Lipscomb, and Ochiltree. Ten more can be added: Armstrong, Briscoe, Childress, Hall, Hartley, Oldham, Potter, Randall, Roberts, and Wheeler. It has been seen in every month.

Few references are made to the chickadee in the accounts of early observers, and then only to the Black-capped Chickadee (Hibbets et al., 1926–36; Hawkins, 1945; TPAS, 1955)—surely misidentifications. Hawkins's assessment of the Black-capped Chickadee as a "fairly common permanent resident of the cottonwood bottomlands in the eastern Panhandle" can be applied to the Carolina Chickadee today. The latter's range now extends westward along the Canadian River at least as far as the Boys Ranch area in Oldham County (confirmed nesting, 19 May 1988), including the Rico Creek drainage to the north, and two were found still farther north along Rita Blanca Creek (Reynolds Ranch) in central Hartley County, 4 July 1990.

The appearance of the Carolina Chickadee in the upper reaches of the Palo Duro Canyon, including the state park, is relatively recent. Neither Russell (1935) nor Stevenson (1942) named it for the park, and Hawkins (1945) thought the chickadee "rare or absent on the High Plains, even in the wooded canyons." Hibbets et al. (1926–36) mention two chickadee sightings in the Canyon area in Randall County (19 May 1929; 5 and 10 September 1933), and Reeves and Reeves (1914–36) note one for the Canyon Country Club (1925). It was not until 1978 that another was reported in that area (Palo Duro Club, 29 April). The first report of a "chickadee sp." in the PDCSP occurred on the CBC of 27 December 1958, and it was not until 28 November 1984 that another was reported, despite the park having been intensively birded during the intervening years. Since then the chickadee has been found regularly, though in small numbers, with confirmation of nesting on 8 May 1986. During the same period the first Carolina Chickadees (2) were found in Ceta Glen, South Ceta Canyon, 31 October 1982, where the species has become established. It is now resident in the Lake Tanglewood–Timbercreek communities and the Palo Duro Club. The first Carolina Chickadees were reported in the Caprock Canyons SP, Briscoe County, on 1 January 1989, followed by the discovery of several singing birds during the summer of 1990, a single bird on 1 January 1991, and others thereafter.

The presence of the Carolina Chickadee in Amarillo dates back to earlier years than those observed in the canyonlands, but it has been reported in the city only intermittently: 25 August 1969, 31 July 1972, October and November 1972, 26 June 1974, 27 August and 6–9 September 1976, 13 June 1977; 17 September and 22 October 1979; 4 December 1963, 7 January 1964, 20–21 November 1969; 26 January 1996. The southwesternmost sighting was a singing bird at BLNWR, 10 May 1987.

The CBCs and BBSs are poor indicators of the chickadee's presence and status. No CBC count circles are located in the eastern Panhandle, and BBS routes there have few stops that include chickadee habitat. The one CBC that provides a good idea of numbers in the Canadian River Valley is Lake Meredith (west), where the average number recorded is 23 (high 69).

NESTING: The TBBAP turned up CO nesting in 14 survey blocks, PR in 18, and PO in six. Twenty-five were between the 100th and 101st meridians, eight between the 101st and 102nd, and five west of the 102nd. Singing birds have been found as early as 8 March 1987 (PDCSP) and a pair setting up territory on 11 April 1988 (McBride Canyon, Lake Meredith Recreation Area, Potter County). Nest building has been observed from 19 April 1985 (Ceta Glen, South Ceta Canyon, Randall County), to 19 May 1990 (Gene Howe WMA, Hemphill County). A nest containing young was found on 27 April 1991 (near Wellington, Collingsworth County). Adults feeding young have been seen from 2 May 1988 (Duncan Ranch, Hutchinson County) to 19 July 1989 (near Shamrock, Collingsworth County). These dates point to possible two-broodedness.

SPECIMENS: Specimens have been collected in Hutchinson County (17 and 30 June 1950, TNHC). These are the two collected by Thompson (1952) and referred to by Oberholser (1974). Oberholser also shows a summer specimen taken in Lipscomb County, without supplying details.

Mountain Chickadee *Poecile gambeli* (Ridgway)

STATUS: Casual fall and winter visitor.

OCCURRENCE: The Mountain Chickadee has been recorded in five western counties of the Texas Panhandle: Castro, Dallam, Oldham, Potter, and Randall. It has been seen from October to March.

The first sighting of the Mountain Chickadee in the study area was reported incorrectly (Williams, 1967): "Mountain Chickadees were common at Amarillo, Oct. 23 to the end of the period." In reality, one bird was seen in Amarillo, Potter County, 22 October 1966, and two others in Amarillo, Randall County, the following 27 November. On 23 October, one day after the first sighting, a flock of eight Mountain Chickadees was encountered some 15–20 miles north of Adrian, Oldham County (Canadian River breaks), during an outing of the TPAS. There have been six subsequent sightings: one in Amarillo, Potter County, 11 and 14 January and 11 March 1979; six in the Thompson Grove Picnic Area northeast of Texline, Dallam County, 20 December 1982; one in Amarillo, Potter County, 5–24 October 1985; two in Ceta Glen, South Ceta Canyon, Randall County, 15 November 1985; one in Texline, Dallam County, 27 October 1989; and one in southwest Castro County, 18 February 1993.

Sutton (1967) cites the Mountain Chickadee as a winter visitor in northwestern Cimarron County, Oklahoma, where 13 specimens have been collected. In New Mexico, Hubbard (1978) says it is "resident in mountainous areas almost statewide," with an occasional occurrence as far east as Clayton, Union County.

Tufted Titmouse *Baeolophus bicolor* (Linnaeus)

STATUS: Uncommon to common resident in the southeastern sector and canyonlands. Casual visitor elsewhere.

OCCURRENCE: The Tufted Titmouse has been found in 12 counties: Armstrong, Briscoe, Childress, Collingsworth, Deaf Smith, Donley, Gray, Hall, Hemphill,

Potter, Randall, and Wheeler. Oberholser (1974) shows it in three: Armstrong, Hemphill, and Randall. It has been seen year-round.

The subspecies of crested titmouse resident in the study area is the Black-crested Titmouse of the *atricristatus* group. There have been three reports of titmice thought possibly of nominate *bicolor,* all of birds seen outside areas where the black-crested is normally found: one at Lake McClellan, Gray County, 7 November 1982, and a pair, 4 March 1996 (three observed on the following 1 May, however, were clearly black-cresteds). Another was observed in McBride Canyon, Lake Meredith Recreation Area, Potter County, 31 March–11 April 1988. All were possibly Black-crested x Tufted hybrids; although lacking black in their crests, they also lacked the black foreheads typical of *bicolor* as illustrated by Dixon (1955). Oberholser (1974) assigns summer and winter sightings in Hemphill County to *bicolor,* without naming dates or observers. I know of no other titmouse sightings from that county, and the black-crested has never been found north of 35 degrees 7.5 minutes north latitude. Sutton (1967) names *bicolor* as resident in Oklahoma as far west as Ellis and Roger Mills counties, adding that "the only titmouse specimens thus far taken in Jackson County are two females, one a Black-crested Titmouse, the other a Black-crested x Tufted hybrid." Dixon (1955) in his analysis of interbreeding among the crested titmice in Texas found the race in the Panhandle to be *paloduro* and restricted its range to Armstrong and Randall counties (Palo Duro Canyon). Later, Arnold (1972) examined two specimens collected in Cottle and Foard counties southeast of the canyon and found them to be *paloduro* also, thus extending the known range of this sub-species significantly. *Paloduro* was subsequently incorporated into the *atricristatus* group (AOU, 1983). Following Arnold's discovery, titmice have been found in Donley, Collingsworth, Briscoe, Hall, Childress, Gray, and Wheeler counties, all black-cresteds; no birds were collected.

Stray titmice are occasionally found farther west than the Palo Duro Canyon. A pair was seen in a church encampment along Palo Duro Creek in north-central Randall County, 19 March 1988, and one at BLNWR, 19 January 1964, 23 May and 1 September 1991, and 3 April 1994. Still farther west in the Tierra Blanca Creek drainage, two black-cresteds regularly visited a feeder in Hereford, Deaf Smith County, during the winter of 1986–87. There has been only one reported sighting in Amarillo, a single bird (Potter County) in early May 1968.

The Black-crested Titmouse is found most commonly in the Palo Duro Canyon. A two-year Breeding Bird Study conducted in the state park (Seyffert, 1967–68) disclosed a density of three titmice per 100 acres. The Amarillo CBC, which incorporates the PDCSP, has averaged 10.5 titmice, while the Quitaque CBC, which incorporates Caprock Canyons SP, has averaged 5.0.

NESTING: The TBBAP found CO nesting in five survey blocks, PR in six, and PO in five. Eight were between the 100th and 101st meridians, six between the 101st and 102nd, and two west of the 102nd. There are few data on nesting: nest building, 29 March 1992 (PDCSP) and 9 April 1996 (Taylor Lakes WMA, Donley County); young being fed in the nest, 7 May 1985 (Lake Tanglewood, Randall County); fledglings being fed, 10 July 1988 (Caprock Canyons SP, Briscoe County).

SPECIMENS: Twenty-two specimens are available from Armstrong (19 February 1952, MVZ; USNM) and Randall (CAS; 21 February 1936, USNM) counties, all assigned to the race *paloduro*. They are possibly those referenced by Oberholser (1974).

Family Remizidae (Verdins)

Verdin *Auriparus flaviceps* (Sundevall)
STATUS: Rare resident in the canyonlands.
OCCURRENCE: The Verdin has been recorded in Briscoe and Randall counties in the Texas Panhandle, where it has been seen in every month.

The first reference to a Verdin in the study area is that of Dowler et al. (1978), who name a specimen collected at an unspecified point in Randall County in September 1950. Prior to this publication it was thought that the first discovery had been made on 22 December 1965 during the Amarillo CBC in the PDCSP (C. D. Littlefield; Seyffert, 1971). These discoveries represented a significant extension in the Verdin's then known range, for the AOU (1957) placed it no nearer the Palo Duro Canyon than the areas of Monahans, Texas, and Carlsbad, New Mexico, both some 250 miles distant. Following the state park find, 9 January 1966, a Verdin was seen entering a winter roosting nest at the Sad Monkey Railroad Station not far distant from the initial discovery. Verdins continued to be found regularly at various locations in the state park until 1976. During that year I recorded the species on 1 February, 8, 15 and 31 May, and 18 and 25 July. A Verdin has not been reported there since.

With the establishment of Caprock Canyons SP in Briscoe County, I began exploring that area in the fall of 1975 and found the first Verdin on 19 September. I continued encountering the species in subsequent years, and last recorded it there on 8 September 1980. Although not reported, it probably can still be found in the park; few birders explore the rough, brushy flats of mesquite, sumac, and agarita that are its preferred habitat. A nest in good condition, possibly a winter roosting nest, was found at Cottonwood Lake a few miles southwest of Quitaque, Briscoe County, 1 January 1989, and Verdins have been seen in the Quitaque area more recently. Vast areas of the Palo Duro Canyon system in Randall, Armstrong, Briscoe, and Hall counties remain unexplored by birders, and it is likely that Verdins could be found with diligent searching.

It was during this same period that Verdins were first reported at localities near to the study area: Lubbock County, 30 December 1966; Wilbarger and Throckmorton counties, 5 December 1967; Archer County, 27 February 1968; Stonewall County, 10 May 1970 (unpublished records). Pulich (1988) says the first nesting of a Verdin in Wichita County was discovered in 1974, with others still being found in 1982. On 3 May 1971, I found a nesting pair near Eldorado, Jackson County, southwestern Oklahoma (Seyffert, 1972; Baumgartner and Baumgartner, 1992), the first occurrence in the state. Unlike in the PDCSP, the Verdins of Jackson County continue being found (OOS, 1993). The species is also now classified as "uncommon" year-round on the South Plains (LEAS, 1995).

NESTING: Other than the roosting nest already cited, the first Verdin nest in the PDCSP was discovered on 26 March 1967 (Seyffert, 1971). It was under construction and by 21 May contained three young. Another nest was found on 28 June 1970, and three juvenal-plumaged birds were seen in the vicinity later. A nest with three eggs was found in the same area on 6 May 1973 (TP-RF). On 7 July 1974, a juvenile was seen in Timbercreek Canyon west of the previous discoveries, and on 4 August a group consisting of two adults and two juveniles.

SPECIMENS: One specimen has been taken in Randall County (September 1950, MTTU).

Family Aegithalidae (Bushtits)

Bushtit *Psaltriparus minimus* (Townsend)
STATUS: Fairly common resident in the canyonlands and adjacent areas; rare to casual elsewhere.

OCCURRENCE: The Bushtit has been found in ten counties: Armstrong, Briscoe, Childress, Dallam, Donley, Hall, Hemphill, Oldham, Potter, and Randall. Oberholser (1974) shows it in two: Potter and Randall. It has been seen in every month.

None of the early observers in the study area named the Bushtit as a member of its avifauna. Even as recently as the mid-1930s Russell (1935) did not include it as a bird of the Palo Duro Canyon, a locality where it is most commonly found today. Stevenson's (1942) is the first published account of its presence and he restricted the number of sightings to just two flocks, both found in the Palo Duro Canyon (1936, 1938). Hawkins (1945) added another sighting in 1945. This paucity of reported sightings led Oberholser (1974) to conclude that the Panhandle was "outside its regular breeding range."

Observers who came upon the scene in the early 1950s had no difficulty in finding the Bushtit, and classified it on the first area checklist (TPAS, 1955) as "permanent" in the "Canyons." This is the area today where it is most common and where it is a breeding resident. A Winter-Bird Population Study conducted inthe PDCSP (Seyffert, 1968–78) disclosed an average density of ten per 100 acres. The Amarillo CBC, which includes the state park, has registered the Bushtit on 25 of 40 counts (high 100, average 15.5). Similarly, on the Quitaque CBC in Briscoe County, which includes Caprock Canyons SP, Bushtits have been found on ten of 21 counts (high 72, average 13.5). Winter is the most productive for seeing this tiny and unobtrusive bird for it is then that feeding flocks are formed, often of ten or more birds.

The Bushtit is a wanderer and may occasionally turn up unexpectedly in areas beyond its known breeding range: *Amarillo, Potter/Randall County*—two, 10 March 1959; six, 17 January and three, 2 April 1967; one, 17 April 1971. BLNWR—four, 14 November 1964; one, 9 December 1984. *Lake Marvin, Hemphill County*—1952 (unspecified date and number); five, 15 December 1968; two, 5 May 1969; one, 3 February 1995. There is one record of a Bushtit from Ellis County, Oklahoma, adjacent to Hemphill County to the east, and one from Woodward County to the northeast (Sutton, 1967). *Hall County*—two near Turkey, 21 May 1989. *Childress County*—an unspecified number east of Childress, summer of 1988. *Dallam County*—a single bird on the Rita Blanca National Grasslands east of Texline during the BBS of 14 June 1986. The Bushtit is a resident in northwestern Cimarron County, Oklahoma, just north of Dallam County (Sutton, 1967), and near Clayton, Union County, New Mexico, adjacent to the west (Ligon, 1961; Hubbard, 1978). *Lake Meredith, Potter County*—recorded twice on the Lake Meredith (west) CBC, 20 on 22 December 1984 and 12 on 17 December 1991, both times on the south side of the Canadian River; one in Plum Creek on the north side of the river, 17 October 1976. *Oldham County*—one on the Tom Green Ranch north of Vega, 24 October 1972.

NESTING: The earliest record of nesting is that of a pair I observed nest building in the PDCSP during a snow storm, 22 March 1987. With a 12-day incubation period, a pair observed feeding young in the nest at Lake Tanglewood, Randall County, 2 April 1965, provide evidence of a still earlier date of nest initiation. The Bushtit is known as being single-brooded; however, one was observed carrying nesting materials on the very late date of 31 May 1982 in the PDCSP. Unexpected was a nest found at Lake Marvin, Hemphill County, 5 May 1969. It was placed in a grapevine tangle growing on the trunk of a small cottonwood tree only a few yards from the north shore of the lake; young were being fed by the adults.

SPECIMENS: One specimen is available from Randall County (13 April 1977, WTAMU). Both Stevenson (1942) and Oberholser (1974) make reference to a

Bushtit collected on the Elkins Ranch in the Palo Duro Canyon, Randall County, 26 December 1936 (T. F. Smith), but neither names the collection in which the specimen was deposited.

Family Sittidae (Nuthatches)

Red-breasted Nuthatch *Sitta canadensis* Linnaeus

STATUS: Rare to uncommon migrant and winter visitor.

OCCURRENCE: The Red-breasted Nuthatch has been recorded in 18 counties: Armstrong, Briscoe, Castro, Dallam, Deaf Smith, Donley, Gray, Hansford, Hemphill, Hutchinson, Moore, Oldham, Parmer, Potter, Randall, Roberts, Sherman, and Wheeler. Oberholser (1974) shows it in four: Armstrong, Parmer, Potter, and Randall. It has been seen in every month.

Other than in a few "invasion" years, the number of Red-breasted Nuthatches reported at any one time or season is never large. More are seen in fall and early winter than at other times. The first returning birds in fall are normally found in early or mid-September, with a few notable exceptions: one in Vega, Oldham County, 8 July 1994; one in Amarillo, Potter County, 24 July 1982—seen regularly thereafter until 27 August; one in Pampa, Gray County, 5 August 1996; three together at BLNWR, 6 August 1989; one in Amarillo, Potter County, 10 August 1991. Rarely is one recorded past the third week of April, the latest being one at the BLNWR, 19 May 1979. Exceptional was a nuthatch observed at a feeder in Amarillo, Randall County, 24 May 1970, joined later by another and both remaining through summer. The Red-breasted Nuthatch breeds no nearer the Texas Panhandle than central Colorado (AOU, 1983). One "lingered in Cimarron County, OK, into June 1985" (Williams, 1985).

Indicative of its status in early winter are the CBCs. Of 145 counts, the Red-breasted Nuthatch has been recorded on only 14, half of them on the Lake Meredith (west) count in Canadian River Valley of Potter County.

White-breasted Nuthatch *Sitta carolinensis* Latham

STATUS: Rare to uncommon migrant and winter visitor. Casual breeder in eastern sector.

OCCURRENCE: The White-breasted Nuthatch has been recorded in 13 counties: Armstrong, Briscoe, Castro, Donley, Gray, Hemphill, Hutchinson, Moore, Oldham, Potter, Randall, Roberts, and Wheeler. Oberholser (1974) shows it in three: Armstrong, Potter, and Randall. It has been seen in every month except July.

The winter status of the White-breasted Nuthatch in the study area is indicated by the CBCs. Of 145 counts (1954–96), it has been recorded on ten—Lake

Meredith (west) seven times and Amarillo three times. The early date of arrival in fall is quite variable: in areas outside its breeding range it can be looked for in October.

NESTING: The White-breasted Nuthatch was not known to nest in the study area until a pair was discovered nest building in a roadside park a few miles east of Miami, Roberts County, 25 April 1989 (F. and J. Elston), with young being fed on 10 May (TP-RF). On 20 March 1993, a pair in the Wheeler Town Park in Wheeler, Wheeler County, gave every indication of nesting: "They were observed repeatedly throughout the day entering and leaving a woodpecker hole and calling repeatedly" (letter, G. Keiran, 8 May 1993). On 1 May 1996, an adult bird was observed carrying food to a nest in a dead cottonwood tree at Lake McClellan, Gray County (K. Seyffert). A number of summer sightings in recent years at Lake Marvin, Hemphill County, point to probable nestings. Other late spring birds of the past dismissed as transients are worthy of note: one in the Palo Duro Club near Canyon, Randall County, 7 May 1973; one at Lake Marvin, Hemphill County, 29 May 1983; one in Amarillo, Potter County, 27 April 1985; one in Llano Cemetery, Amarillo, Randall County, 9 May 1986; one at BLNWR, 1 June 1986.

Sutton (1967) places probable nesting of the White-breasted Nuthatch in Oklahoma no farther west than Dewey and Comanche counties, while Baumgartner and Baumgartner (1992) say the species has been recorded irregularly on the Beckham County BBS. Hubbard (1978) places the eastern limits of residency in New Mexico as the "upper Dry Cimarron" and "upper Canadian valley" in the northeastern sector. This may have led Pravosudov and Grubb (1993) to extend the year-round distribution of this nuthatch into much of the western Texas Panhandle; clearly in error, for the species has rarely been recorded west of Potter and Randall counties. More accurately, the species' range should have included the eastern and not the western Panhandle.

Pygmy Nuthatch *Sitta pygmaea* Vigors

STATUS: Casual winter visitor.

OCCURRENCE: The only location where the Pygmy Nuthatch has been reported in the Texas Panhandle is Amarillo, Potter/Randall counties, where it has been seen October–April during five winters.

Sightings are as follows: A single bird, 27 February and 14 March, and two daily thereafter until 12 April 1954; one observed several times during November–December 1954; one, 25 March 1956; 1–6 regularly, 18 October 1966–22 January 1967; 2–7 at one site, 27–29 October, and 1–9 at another, 12 and 26 November 1985. Concerning the 1995 birds, the flock of 27 October included a White-breasted Nuthatch, and the single bird of November 12 was accompanied by a Red-breasted Nuthatch.

The Pygmy Nuthatch may be a resident in the Black Mesa country of Cimarron County, Oklahoma (Sutton, 1974a): a female in breeding condition was taken on 22 May 1937 and a juvenile on 22 August 1972. The species is classified as an "accidental transient" in the Clayton area, Union County, New Mexico (Krehbiel, 1955) and as "accidental" on the South Plains in October (LEAS, 1994).

Family Certhiidae (Creepers)

Brown Creeper *Certhia americana* Bonaparte
STATUS: Rare to uncommon winter visitor.
OCCURRENCE: The Brown Creeper has been found in 16 counties: Armstrong, Briscoe, Castro, Donley, Gray, Hall, Hartley, Hemphill, Hutchinson, Ochiltree, Oldham, Parmer, Potter, Randall, Roberts, and Swisher. Oberholser (1974) shows it in five. It has been seen from September to June.

The Brown Creeper normally arrives during fall in mid-October and is last seen in spring in late March. There have been a few exceptions. A single bird was recorded on the BLNWR, 16 September 1984 and 25 September 1985, and there are four April sightings and two in May—a single bird on the BLNWR, 11 May 1996 and 21 May 1967. Unaccountable was one listed in the Canyon area, Randall County, for 27 June 1935 (Hibbets et al., 1926–36). The Brown Creeper is not known to breed any nearer the study area than the upper Piñabetitos Creek area southwest of Clayton, Union County, New Mexico (NMOS, 1992).

The CBCS give some idea of the incidence of the Brown Creeper in early winter: *Lake Meredith (west)*—16 of 24 (high 19); *Amarillo*—20 of 40 (high 5); *Quitaque*—9 of 20 (high 2); *Lake Meredith (east)*—4 of 18 (high 2); *Buffalo Lake NWR*—1 of 29 (high 1). The 19 on the Lake Meredith (west) count of 18 December 1976 in Potter County were all found in the heavily wooded Bonita Creek area on the LX Ranch.

Family Troglodytidae (Wrens)

Cactus Wren *Campylorhynchus brunneicapillus* (Lafresnaye)
STATUS: Casual breeder in far western sector, vagrant visitor elsewhere.
OCCURRENCE: The Cactus Wren has been observed in seven counties: Briscoe, Deaf Smith, Donley, Moore, Oldham, Potter, and Randall. It has been recorded in every month except January, May, and November.

The expansion of the Cactus Wren into the study area closely parallels that documented for north-central Texas by Pulich (1988), where the species began appearing in the western part of the region in the 1970s. Prior to then Oberholser (1974) had placed its range in the state no farther north than the Lubbock area.

Sightings for the study area by county are as follows: *Briscoe*—one in Caprock Canyons SP, 4 December 1977. *Deaf Smith*—one on the Bridwell Ranch south of Glenrio, 4 April 1998. *Donley*—one on the Sawyer Ranch eight miles northeast of Clarendon, September 1972. *Moore*—two in the Plum Creek area at Lake Meredith, 17 October 1976. *Oldham*—one midway between Vega and Boys Ranch, 7 August, and another on the Tom Green Ranch northwest of Vega, 18 September 1977; one south of the Canadian River at Boys Ranch, 2 June 1987; one on the Barfield Ranch northwest of Wildorado, 14 August, three on 22 August, one on 29 September, three on 1 December 1997, and one on 13 March 1998; "several" heard on the LS Ranch, 16 May 1998. *Potter*—the first Cactus Wren reported in the study area was one found in an alley in Amarillo, 21 July 1967. This was not the last wren to be found in the city, for one remained in another neighborhood 8 February–31 March 1976, a bird often heard singing. *Randall*—one on the BLNWR, 17 December 1973 and 7 September 1980.

In nearby Oklahoma, G. M. Sutton believed that he saw a Cactus Wren in Cimarron County on 21 May 1955, but "the identification was not unequivocal" (Baumgartner and Baumgartner, 1992), and a single bird was observed south of Durham, Roger Mills County, 30–31 August 1975. Weske (1968) cited the Cactus Wren as being on the "rare visitor" list for the Clayton area, Union County, New Mexico. In recent years the species has "continued to press north, with June reports at . . . Glenrio," Quay County (NMOS, 1992–93), and two north of Ute Lake, Harding County, 2 June 1995 (Williams and Hubbard, 1995). South of the study area, it is classified as "casual" (nesting) in the Lubbock area (LEAS, 1994).

NESTING: On the TPAS field trip to the Tom Green Ranch in Oldham County, 18 September 1977, the remains of two Cactus Wren nests were found in cholla cactus. The rancher said he had been encountering wrens regularly all summer and thought the birds were nesting. In the mid-1990s, wrens at nests were observed in northwest Oldham County by TPWD personnel, and on 29 September an old nest built in a cholla cactus and occupied by a mouse with her young was found on the Barfield Ranch in that county. Also in Oldham County, several nests (contents not checked) were seen during the 1998 encounter. The Deaf Smith County observation of 1998 included a bird on the nest. There is a Cactus Wren nest on display in the Moore County Historical Museum in Dumas that was collected during the 1970s. It had been placed in cholla cactus in pastureland five miles southwest of Dumas on the Stallwitz farm.

Rock Wren

Rock Wren *Salpinctes obsoletus* (Say)

STATUS: Uncommon to common resident.

OCCURRENCE: The Rock Wren has been recorded in every Texas Panhandle county except Carson and Collingsworth. It has been seen year-round.

Although they are common in the Palo Duro Canyon and Canadian River breaks in summer, there is a partial withdrawal of Rock Wrens in winter. This shift is supported by CBC data. The following are the percentages of counts in which Rock Wrens were recorded, along with averages: *Quitaque*—81 percent, 2.5; *Lake Meredith* (*east*)—78 percent, 3.4; *Amarillo*—80 percent, 2.1; *Lake Meredith* (*west*)—63 percent, 1.0; *Buffalo Lake* NWR—39 percent, 0.9. In comparison, my records for the Caprock Canyons SP (Quitaque) show the Rock Wren recorded on 90 percent of trips made from April to September (average five per trip), and almost every time on trips to the BLNWR. Furthermore, a movement is discernible in spring and fall. At such times it is not uncommon to encounter wrens along roadsides far out on the plains as well as in other atypical habitats.

NESTING: The Rock Wren has been confirmed nesting in nine counties: Armstrong, Briscoe, Deaf Smith, Hutchinson, Moore, Oldham, Potter, Randall, and Sherman. The TBBAP discovered PR or PO nesting in five others: Gray, Hall, Hartley, Hemphill, and Roberts. Four of the quadrangles were between the 100th and 101st meridians, 11 between the 101st and 102nd, and nine west of the 102nd.

Nest building has been observed as early as 3 April 1966 at BLNWR. A nest with recently hatched young was found on the refuge on 10 May 1981 and an adult still on a nest on 4 July 1974. During the TBBAP most observations of fledglings being fed came during the period 28 May–18 June. Further evidence of two-broodedness is provided by Thompson (1952), who observed a wren bringing dried grass to a crevice in a canyon wall (Hutchinson County) in mid-June 1950, and an adult carrying food items was observed on the Barfield Ranch near Wildorado, Oldham County, 22 July 1997. Stephenson (1942) reported a family group of adults with four young in the PDCSP on the late date of 9 August 1936.

In the PDCSP on 24 July 1986, I observed a pair of Rock Wrens feeding a juvenile Brown-headed Cowbird, and another young cowbird being fed by adult wrens was observed in the state park on 26 August 1995.

SPECIMENS: Specimens have been collected in Hartley (WTAMU), Hutchinson (11 and 23 June 1950, TNHC), and Swisher (November 1969, MTTU) counties. Ober-holser (1974) shows specimens taken in Deaf Smith, Hansford, and Lipscomb counties, but in what collections they reside he does not say. The Hutchinson County birds he names are probably those collected by Thompson (1952). Car-lander (1933) also cites a specimen taken but provides no details.

Canyon Wren *Catherpes mexicanus* (Swainson)

STATUS: Fairly common to common resident in the canyonlands.

OCCURRENCE: The Canyon Wren has been recorded in eight counties: Armstrong, Briscoe, Deaf Smith, Hutchinson, Oldham, Potter, Randall, and Swisher. It has been seen year-round.

Among the earlier observers there was a wide divergence of opinion concerning the status of the Canyon Wren. Both McCauley (1877) and Strecker (1910) found it to be common. Four observers who worked in the Palo Duro Canyon during the period 1933–45 differed in their assessments. Carlander (1934) thought it a "fairly common summer resident," Russell (1935) did not name it at all for the state park where Stevenson (1942) considered it a common resident, and Hawkins (1945) classified it as a rare summer resident: "It was observed in this survey only one time, although the song of this bird is unmistakable." Unless one hears it singing or is familiar with its *jeet* call, this wren can easily be overlooked, even when nearby. Also, it is not only along canyon walls that it can be found, for it is attracted to man-made structures, where it will nest. An example was a singing bird observed in a lumber yard in Amarillo, Potter County, 20 July 1984.

The Canyon Wren is rarely reported beyond the canyonlands. In 31 years of intensive birding on the BLNWR, a locality containing rocky draws seemingly favorable to it, I have encountered a Canyon Wren but once—a singing bird, 24 April 1993. Oberholser (1974) shows a fall sight record for Deaf Smith County, but details are lacking.

The TBBAP failed to turn up any Canyon Wrens outside the Palo Duro Canyon. On the Lake Meredith Recreation Area Checklist (NPS, 1976), the species is classified as an uncommon resident, with presumed nesting. The two CBCs conducted on the recreation area show this wren to be scarce in winter. Of 24 Lake Meredith (west) counts, it was recorded on two, and only once on 18 Lake Meredith (east) counts. I have encountered it twice in that area, both times in McBride Canyon, Potter County: 9 October 1977 and 21 March 1982. On the Amarillo CBC, the average number tallied is 2.5. Even in such prime habitat this wren was missed on five of the 40 counts. The Quitaque CBC average is 2.1.

NESTING: There are scarcely any data on the breeding of the Canyon Wren in the study area. Most accounts are not specific as to nest initiation, egg laying, young in nest, and fledging dates. An adult on a nest was found on 19 July 1990 in the PDCSP, and McCauley (1877) collected a nest with six eggs in "Red River Canyon" (= Palo Duro Canyon), 12 June 1876.

SPECIMENS: Specimens of Canyon Wrens have been taken in Armstrong (19 February 1952, MVZ), Randall (20 October 1939, P-PHM), and Swisher (November 1969, MTTU) counties. The two from Armstrong County were identified as the race *conspersus* and are probably the ones referred to by Oberholser (1974).

Carolina Wren *Thryothorus ludovicianus* (Latham)

STATUS: Rare to fairly common resident in eastern third, rare locally westward.

OCCURRENCE: Oberholser (1974) shows the Carolina Wren in four Texas Panhandle counties: Hemphill, Potter, Randall, and Wheeler. Eight others have been added: Briscoe, Castro, Childress, Donley, Gray, Hutchinson, Oldham, and Roberts. It has been seen year-round.

Outside the eastern counties, and to a certain extent even in them, there has been a history of ebb and flow in the presence of the Carolina Wren in the study area. As recently as the early 1960s the species was reported with great irregularity in most areas, and not until later did it become established in places such as Lake Marvin and Gene Howe WMA in Hemphill County. The PDCSP is perhaps most illustrative of this on-again, off-again presence, for this wren may be found year-round in the park for several years running and then disappear, not to return until after a lapse of several more years. Or it may return in winter and be absent in summer, and vice versa. This irregularity is in part a reflection of where birders reside; were several in place in the eastern counties, the picture would no doubt be clarified. Sutton (1967) says the Carolina Wren is well established in Oklahoma "westward to state line in Ellis, Roger Mills, Beckham (probably), and Harmon counties." There is no reason to believe that westward residence stops at the state line and that the same would not hold true of the eastern study area counties. The breeding range shown by Johnsgard (1979) is probably correct, with nesting occurring locally within the area. Mapping the breeding distribution of the Carolina Wren in the Texas Panhandle is an undertaking worthy an enterprising student.

NESTING: There has been little direct evidence of nesting by the Carolina Wren despite the number of sightings of birds during the breeding season. Carlander (1933) was the first to report this wren in the study area, and he found it "with young" at an unnamed point between 18 and 24 July 1933. On 8 March 1992, I first heard a singing wren in my neighborhood in Amarillo, Potter County. One bird or more continued to be seen or heard regularly thereafter until 12 August, when an adult wren was observed followed by a begging juvenile.

Bewick's Wren *Thryomanes bewickii* (Audubon)

STATUS: Fairly common to common resident.

OCCURRENCE: The Bewick's Wren has been recorded in every county except Carson and would be there with better coverage. It has been seen in every month.

The Bewick's Wren is the most common and widespread of the wrens in the study area. It is found in a variety of environments, most commonly in the canyonlands, where its cheerful song and scolding buzz is the "voice" of the canyons, more so even than either the Canyon or Rock Wren. The Bewick's Wren was found to be the seventh most common species in the PDCSP during a Winter-Bird Population Study (Seyffert, 1968–78), averaging 13 per 100 acres. In a two-year Breeding Bird Study conducted on the same plot, a density of 18 per 100 acres was found (Seyffert, 1967–68).

The averages on the CBCs are indicative of the status of the Bewick's Wren in early winter: *Amarillo*—10.4; *Lake Meredith* (*west*)—8.9; *Quitaque*—8.1; *Lake Meredith* (*east*)—5.5; *Buffalo Lake* NWR—1.0. The BBS averages reveal not only where the Bewick's Wrens are but, as important, where they are not: *Childress*— 8.6; *Clarendon*—5.0; *Miami*—1.5; *Channing*—1.0; *Booker*—0.3; *Pantex*—0; *Texline*—0; *Waka*—0.

The Bewick's Wren has been on the Blue List of birds since its inception (Arbib, 1971), signaling a significant decline in numbers over much of its range. A look at the average number recorded per party hour on the Amarillo CBCs shows a slight fluctuation: *1954–63*—0.38; *1964–73*—0.58; *1974–83*—0.43; *1984–*

93—0.29. My own records for the PDCSP show a stability based on average number recorded per man-hour: *1965–75,* 1.59; *1976–86,* 1.34; *1987–97,* 1.60. There is a slight movement of Bewick's Wrens in spring and fall. This is noticeable in cities, where the species is seldom found at other times of the year.

NESTING: The TBBAP (1987–92) found CO nesting in 11 survey blocks, PR in 29, and PO in four. Twenty-six of the occupied quadrangles were located between the 100th and 101st meridians, 13 between the 101st and 102nd, and five west of the 102nd. Except for one quadrangle (Umbarger), the Bewick's was absent from the southwest sector, and it was missing entirely from the extreme northwest and north-central sectors.

Nest building has been observed as early as 20 March 1987 in Miami, Roberts County ("in a gourd hanging on the porch swing on the patio"). A pair of wrens was observed disputing a tree nest hole with Eastern Bluebirds at Lake McClellan, Gray County, 23 February 1972. This wren may be two-brooded. A nest containing three eggs (in a bicycle seat cover that had been hung up to dry after a rain) was found in the PDCSP, 17 July 1997, and an adult feeding young was observed in the state park, 19 July 1993. Stevenson (1942) refers to "a nest with young in a soapberry tree" in the state park, 16 July 1935.

SPECIMENS: Specimens have been taken in Hansford (25 November 1954, OMNH), Hemphill (29 July 1971, TCWC), Hutchinson (10 and 26 June 1950, TNHC), and Randall (27 June 1956, MNH; 3 May and 26 December 1936, MVZ) counties. Five of the seven were assigned to the race *cryptus,* including the two adult males in breeding condition taken by Thompson (1952) in Hutchinson County (TNHC). Oberholser (1974) refers to specimens collected in Armstrong, Lipscomb, and Oldham counties but fails to name their locations. All Bewick's Wrens in the Texas Panhandle he assigns to *cryptus.*

House Wren *Troglodytes aedon* Vieillot

STATUS: Fairly common to common migrant. Fairly common to common breeder in eastern third, rare to uncommon westward along the Canadian River and tributaries. Casual winter visitor.

OCCURRENCE: The House Wren has been recorded in every Texas Panhandle county except Carson, Childress, Hall, Sherman, and Swisher. Oberholser (1974) shows it in four: Hemphill, Parmer, Potter, and Randall. It has been seen in every month.

Normally the House Wren is first recorded in spring during the second or third week of April. Three have been seen in March, the earliest a single bird in the PDCSP, 14 March 1997. Migration is over by early or mid-May, and returning birds in fall can be looked for in early September. Few are seen past mid-October. Sightings from November to February have been fewer than a dozen.

Of these all but two were in the canyonlands, the exceptions being single birds at BLNWR and Amarillo. A summer presence was almost unknown (or went unreported) until recently, despite Hibbets et al. (1926–36) classifying the species as a "permanent resident" prior to mid-century. Species lists of birds found on summer excursions to the Lake Marvin area by the TPAS in Hemphill County during the 1950s failed to include the House Wren, although that is the area where it is most commonly found today. The first time that I observed this wren in that area in summer was on 5 July 1971 (4). The next encounter was on 14 June 1977 (17). On my first trip to Lake Fryer, Wolf Creek Park, Ochiltree County, on the previous 8 June I had found one singing wren, and three singing birds were found at Lake McClellan, Gray County, on 17 July, a first for that locality in summer. The first Wheeler County birds reported were four on 9 July 1978. Eleven singing wrens were found along White Deer Creek on the Duncan Ranch, southeastern Hutchinson County, 19 June 1981.

A look at two eastern county BBSS discloses the emergence of the House Wren during the late 1970s or early 1980s. The Booker count in Lipscomb County was initiated in 1975, but it was not until June 1981 that the first House Wrens (4) were recorded. The Miami count in Roberts County was also started in 1975, and it was in June of 1979 that the first wrens (2) were recorded. Wrens continue to be found on both counts. The Clarendon, Donley County, BBS was made from 1968 to 1973 (when it was terminated) without a House Wren being recorded; however, subsequent surveys over the same route turned up one wren in 1984 and ten in 1994.

NESTING: The TBBAP found CO nesting in nine survey blocks, PR in 17, and PO in three. Twenty-two of the occupied quadrangles were between the 100th and 101st meridians, four between the 101st and 102nd, and three west of the 102nd. All were located north of 34 degrees, 45 minutes north latitude. The quadrangles were in Collingsworth, Donley, Gray, Hartley, Hemphill, Hutchinson, Lipscomb, Ochiltree, Potter, Randall, Roberts, and Wheeler counties. Finding nesting House Wrens in central Hartley County was unexpected as the species was not thought to be a breeder much farther west than the 101st meridian; finding a pair at Lake Tanglewood (The Palisades), Randall County, was also a surprise. Although only a single singing wren was recorded in the Miami quadrangle while atlassing, it was later discovered that numerous nest boxes erected along Red Deer Creek in town are occupied yearly. In fact, the House Wren is one of the more common nesting species in that area.

Neither Oberholser (1974) nor Johnsgard (1979) included the Texas Panhandle within the breeding range of the House Wren. Both made reference to a single nesting in Randall County based on Russell (1935), who observed a House Wren "carrying food into a hole in a cottonwood," 15 July 1935, in the PDCSP.

Russell said further that he found the species "common all through the canyon areas." This is remarkable in light of its almost complete absence in summer today. I have surveyed the state park hundreds of times and have encountered a House Wren but twice during summer (5 and 30 June 1967), and then without observing any evidence of nesting. It is to be noted that Stevenson (1942) makes reference to a Bewick's Wren nest found by Russell, without mentioning his House Wren. Carlander (1934) scoured the area thoroughly in the 1930s but did not include the House Wren in his list of Palo Duro Canyon birds, and Hawkins (1945) classified it only as an "uncommon migrant." Single House Wrens observed on the BLNWR on 19 June 1966 and 4 and 11 July 1976 gave no evidence of possible nesting. The first reported breeding since Russell's was a House Wren observed nest building at Lake Marvin, Hemphill County, 6 June 1984, and on 13 June 1984 a juvenile was observed along East Lelia Creek, Donley County.

It was considered noteworthy to find House Wrens nesting in Oklahoma City ("both south and west of their normal breeding range") as recently as 1967 (Williams, 1967). Brown (1985) documented the arrival of the House Wren as a nesting species in Beckham County, west-central Oklahoma, in 1970, and nesting birds were found in and around Elk City from 1980 to at least 1984. Singing males were found for the first time in Roger Mills County in June of 1980 and 1982, and a pair attempted to nest in Jackson County in 1979. These events closely parallel those taking place in the northeastern Texas Panhandle around the same time. A pair nested in Lubbock in the summer of 1977 (*fide* C. Stogner).

SPECIMENS: Two specimens are available, one taken in Oldham (29 April 1989, TCWC) and one in Randall (8 May 1993, TCWC) county. There is a House Wren nest on display (MCHM) recovered in a residential yard in Dumas, Moore County.

Winter Wren *Troglodytes troglodytes* (Linnaeus)

STATUS: Uncommon migrant and rare winter visitor.

OCCURRENCE: The Winter Wren has been found in nine counties—Briscoe, Castro, Donley, Gray, Hemphill, Hutchinson, Potter, Randall, and Roberts—and has been seen September–May.

It would be more appropriate to call the Winter Wren the "Fall" Wren. A Winter-Bird Population Study (Seyffert, 1968–78) conducted in the PDCSP disclosed its presence only twice, in both instances a single bird. My records of 33 years show wintering birds in 13 of them. The CBCs also disclose its rarity during that season. It has been recorded five times on the Amarillo counts, five times on Lake Meredith (west) and twice on the Quitaque counts, and never on the BLNWR and Lake Meredith (east) counts.

The Winter Wren is even rarer in spring. Those I have found overwintering have always been gone by mid-February; otherwise, I have encountered the species only three times: 28 April 1967, 4–10 May 1968, and 20 April 1991. This is in sharp contrast to its presence in fall, when I have recorded it in 19 of 33 years. My records show that I have recorded 29 percent of all Winter Wrens in October, 49 percent October–November, 67 percent October–December, and 83 percent October–January. The normal range of fall dates is mid-October to early or mid-November, with early and late dates of 20 September 1964 (BLNWR) and 21 November 1990 (PDCSP). The very earliest date is a "live bird in hand" in Canyon, Randall County, 17 September 1955.

Sedge Wren *Cistothorus platensis* (Latham)
STATUS: Casual migrant.
OCCURRENCE: The Sedge Wren has been recorded in Donley, Hutchinson, Potter, and Randall counties in March–April and October–December.

There have been six reports of the Sedge Wren: Hawkins (1945) spoke of it as an "uncommon migrant ... found on several occasions among the cattails at Palo Duro Club (Randall County) between March 11 and April 21, 1945. One spent several days in the shrubbery of this writer's garden" (Canyon); one "in tall weeds at Wolflin [Lawrence] Lake," Amarillo, Potter County, 10 October 1954; one along the creek at the Jokerst Ranch south of Amarillo, Randall County, 19 March 1967; one at Weatherly Lake near Borger, Hutchinson County, 3 November 1973; and a chattering bird at Cattail Lake on the Taylor Lakes WMA, Donley County, 18 December 1997.

From nearby areas in Oklahoma, Sutton (1967) cites a female Sedge Wren taken in Cimarron County, 24 September 1932 ("from the grasslands between two mesas"), and Tyler (1979b) reports a male seen near Hollis, Harmon County, 24 March 1963. A first for Guymon, Texas County, was one found on 23 October 1953 (Baumgartner, 1954), and one remained at Ross's Lake south of Durham, Roger Mills County, 19–21 November 1965 and 12–13 March 1966 (*fide* R. Ross). In the Lubbock area of the South Plains the species is listed as "casual" or "rare" in February and October–December (LEAS, 1994).

Marsh Wren *Cistothorus palustris* (Wilson)
STATUS: Fairly common to common winter visitor.
OCCURRENCE: The Marsh Wren has been found in 12 counties: Briscoe, Castro, Donley, Gray, Hansford, Hartley, Hemphill, Hutchinson, Parmer, Potter, Randall, and Swisher. Oberholser (1974) shows it in two. It has been seen from August to May.

When in the 1950s systematic and widespread field observations began in the study area, the reported presence of the Marsh Wren was questioned by outside "experts." An editor of the CBCs would not include the species without proof, preferably in the form of a specimen. As a result, it was not until the mid-1960s that reports of Marsh Wrens on CBCs were acknowledged. A clue to this reluctance may lie in an early 1950s Oklahoma report (Baumgartner, 1951): "[the wrens] seen at Lake Altus in March represent the first record for southwestern Oklahoma. Two were seen at Oklahoma City on Dec. 28, suggesting that this wren may occasionally winter in Oklahoma." The CBC averages and highs give an indication of the Marsh Wren's presence: *Lake Meredith (east)*—9.9 (21); *Lake Meredith (west)*—3.3 (15); *Quitaque*—2.7 (11); *Amarillo*—2.3 (12); *Buffalo Lake NWR*—1.2 (7). The Sanford Dam marsh at Lake Meredith, Hutchinson County, is an excellent locality for observing Marsh Wrens; far more than the 21 recorded on the CBC of 3 January 1982 would have been tallied had the entire marsh been covered.

The Marsh Wren can be looked for during the fall in mid-October. There are five September sightings, the earliest being for three birds at South East Park, Amarillo, Randall County, 5 September 1997. Exceptional were two heard at Lake Rita Blanca, Hartley County, 15 August 1997. The only other regional August records are of one seen south of Durham, Roger Mills County, Oklahoma, 18 August 1984, and two at Tucumcari Lake, Quay County, New Mexico, 4 August 1995 (NMOS, 1995). Few wrens remain past the second week of April. There are five May sightings, the latest being for one bird west of Canyon, Randall County, 8 May 1955. More and Strecker (1929) reported the Marsh Wren nesting in nearby Wilbarger County, Texas, leading Wolfe (1956) to speculate on possible nesting in "eastern area 1," an area inclusive of the Panhandle. Pulich (1988), however, says there is no positive evidence of nesting in north-central Texas.

Family Regulidae (Kinglets)

Golden-crowned Kinglet *Regulus satrapa* Lichtenstein
STATUS: Uncommon to fairly common winter visitor.
OCCURRENCE: The Golden-crowned Kinglet has been recorded in 15 counties: Armstrong, Briscoe, Castro, Dallam, Deaf Smith, Donley, Gray, Hall, Hemphill, Hutchinson, Oldham, Parmer, Potter, Randall, and Roberts. It has been seen from October to June.

The single reference by McCauley (1877) to the Golden-crowned Kinglet pertains to a bird seen in Cañoncito Blanco on 4 June 1876, the site of present-day Ceta Glen, South Ceta Canyon, Randall County, located just west of the Armstrong County line. The citation is possibly the source of the summer sight record for the latter county shown by Oberholser (1974). This kinglet breeds no nearer the study area than the mountains of New Mexico (Hubbard, 1978), and

I long viewed the observation with skepticism. However, on 3 June 1996, almost 120 years to the day after McCauley's discovery, a group from the Sutton Avian Research Center in Oklahoma observed a Golden-crowned Kinglet in the Thompson Grove Picnic Area northeast of Texline, Dallam County.

The Golden-crowned Kinglet arrives in fall in mid-October, the earliest date one at BLNWR, 4 October 1971, and rarely is one seen past late March. There are eight April sightings and one in May, the latest a single bird at BLNWR, 8 May 1993. It is seldom seen in groups of more than four or five birds and may often be found in feeding flocks with other small passerines. The most that I ever encountered at one time were ten at Bonita Creek, Lake Meredith Recreation Area, Potter County, 20 January 1979. Only occasionally does it outnumber the Ruby-crowned Kinglet. In the fall of 1955 it was "unusually common" and was observed "migrating in the grain fields with thrushes" (P. Acord).

The averages and highs on the CBCs give an idea of the golden-crowned's presence in winter: *Amarillo*—5.5 (18); *Quitaque*—2.2 (8); *Lake Meredith (west)*—2.2 (8). It has been recorded on only three of 18 *Lake Meredith (east)* counts and never on the BLNWR count. A Winter-Bird Population Study conducted in the PDCSP disclosed an average density of three per 100 acres (Seyffert, 1968–78). December is when most golden-crowneds are encountered. My records show the following incidence of observations: October, 9 percent; November, 24 percent; December, 34 percent; January, 18 percent; February, 8 percent; March, 6 percent; April, 1 percent.

SPECIMENS: There is one specimen taken in Randall County (30 December 1936, MVZ). Oberholser (1974) shows another taken in Armstrong County, but details are lacking.

Ruby-crowned Kinglet *Regulus calendula* (Linnaeus)

STATUS: Fairly common to common migrant and winter visitor.

OCCURRENCE: The Ruby-crowned Kinglet has been found in every Texas Panhandle county except Collingsworth, Lipscomb, Sherman, and Wheeler. Oberholser (1974) shows it in four. It has been recorded from August to May.

The Ruby-crowned Kinglet was seldom mentioned by early observers. One to note it was McCauley (1877), who spoke of "a few individuals observed along the Washita and Canadian, evidently migrating." Hibbets et al. (1926–36) recognized it as a winter resident. Hawkins (1945), based on some records of Stevenson's, thought "that a few may winter in the Panhandle."

The first ruby-crowneds of fall can be expected in mid-September; one in the first week of August 1982 was extremely early. Most are gone by the third week of May, the latest being a single bird in Amarillo, Randall County, 24 May 1970. October is the month of this kinglet's greatest presence. Of those that I have recorded, the following are percentages by month: September—9 percent; October—34 percent; November—13 percent; December—10 percent; January—6 percent; February—4 percent; March—4 percent; April—10 percent; May—10 percent. These can be compared with those shown for the Golden-crowned Kinglet, for which December is the month of greatest incidence (34%). On a yearly basis, the ruby-crowned outnumbered the golden-crowned at a ratio of 4:1; however, the ratio dropped to 3:2 in winter (December–February). A Winter-Bird Population Study in the PDCSP (Seyffert, 1968–78) yielded in an average density of three birds per 100 acres for both species.

The largest number of Ruby-crowned Kinglets that I recorded in a single day in spring was 18 at the BLNWR, 12 May 1968, and in fall 37 at Lake McClellan, Gray County, 7 October 1981. The averages and highs on the CBCs also give an idea of the ruby-crowned's early winter presence: *Amarillo*—5.7 (30); *Quitaque*—4.6 (10); *Lake Meredith (west)*—3.3 (9); *Lake Meredith (east)*—1.1 (3). In 29 counts conducted on the *Buffalo Lake NWR*, the ruby-crowned was recorded once.

SPECIMENS: Two specimens have been taken in Randall County (23 September 1939, P-PHM; 7 October 1939, WTAMU). Oberholser (1974) names one taken in Potter County (September 27), but its whereabouts is not given.

Family Sylviidae (Gnatcatchers)

Blue-gray Gnatcatcher *Polioptila caerulae* (Linnaeus)
STATUS: Fairly common migrant and breeder. Vagrant winter visitor.
OCCURRENCE: Oberholser (1974) shows the Blue-gray Gnatcatcher in four Texas Panhandle counties: Armstrong, Parmer, Potter, and Randall. Seventeen others have been added: Briscoe, Carson, Castro, Childress, Dallam, Donley, Gray, Hartley, Hemphill, Hutchinson, Lipscomb, Moore, Ochiltree, Oldham, Roberts, Swisher, and Wheeler. The species has been seen in every month except February.

Early April is when the Blue-gray Gnatcatcher may be expected in spring, rarely earlier (27 March), and one is seldom seen past October, the latest date being 24 November 1956 at BLNWR and 24 November 1985 in PDCSP. There are two winter records: one at Blue West, Lake Meredith, Moore County, 29 December 1972, and one in Amarillo, 1 January 1970. The ten shown on the Amarillo CBC of 2 January 1955 were a publishing error as the birds were in fact Ruby-crowned Kinglets. Others have been observed during winter in nearby areas: one at Clayton, Union County, New Mexico, 18 December 1982 (Hubbard, 1983); Lubbock, 23–30 December 1981 (Williams, 1982); Lubbock 18 December 1991 and

2 January 1992 (Lasley and Sexton, 1992); Muleshoe NWR, Bailey County, CBC of 19 December 1993.

On 7 September 1995 I observed on the BLNWR a gnatcatcher with tertials a prominent snow-white ("fluffy white epaulettes").

NESTING: The Blue-gray Gnatcatcher's breeding range follows closely that shown by Johnsgard (1979)—the Canadian River and Red River drainages. The TBBAP found CO nesting in four survey blocks (Hemphill), PR in two (Briscoe), and PO in four (Lipscomb, Potter, Gray, Armstrong). Nesting had previously been confirmed in Armstrong and Randall counties. Summering birds have also been found in Childress, Donley, Roberts, and Wheeler counties. Nest building commences soon after spring arrival (PDCSP, 22 April 1945), and a nest with young has been seen as late as 10 August 1936 (Armstrong County). On 21 June 1970, I watched a pair in the PDCSP as they picked apart an old gnatcatcher nest placed in a juniper, using the material to construct a new one less than 100 yards away—at the same time feeding a Brown-headed Cowbird fledgling.

Family Turdidae (Thrushes)

Eastern Bluebird *Sialia sialis* (Linnaeus)

STATUS: Fairly common to common resident in the eastern third and westward along the Canadian River and tributaries; locally elsewhere. A winter visitor in many areas.

OCCURRENCE: The Eastern Bluebird has been recorded in every Texas Panhandle county except Carson, Moore, Parmer, Sherman, and Swisher. It has been seen in every month.

The counties where the Eastern Bluebird is most commonly found in summer lie in the eastern sector. It also breeds locally in the Canadian River Valley and tributaries westward as far as eastern Oldham County (Boys Ranch), northward along Rita Blanca Creek and Punta de Aqua Creek to central and western Hartley County (Reynolds Ranch, Whiteaker Ranch), locally and irregularly in the upper reaches of Palo Duro Canyon (Lake Tanglewood–Palo Duro Club), and the Tierra Blanca Creek area westward to BLNWR (occasionally). Summering birds have been found in Hall, Donley, and Deaf Smith counties without confirmation of nesting. The winter range is widespread.

The CBCs provide an indication of winter distribution and abundance. The Eastern Bluebird has been recorded on 21 of 40 Amarillo counts (high 126). A few miles to the west on the BLNWR, only four birds have been recorded in 29 counts. A similar contrast exists on the adjacent Lake Meredith counts: 21 of 24 west counts (high 186); one of 18 east counts. On the Quitaque CBC it has been found on four of 21 counts (high 29), although absent in summer.

NESTING: Adults feeding young in the nest have been found as early as 15–18 April 1986 in the PDCSP, a rare event for that location, and a bird was still on the nest on the Reynolds Ranch (Rita Blanca Creek), Hartley County, 2 June 1990—a far western location. Nesting continues still later, for fledglings or juveniles were found on 16 August 1991 (western Hartley County), 17 August 1980 (Chicken Creek, Lake Meredith, Potter County), and 31 August 1969 (Lake Tanglewood, Randall County). A Cliff Swallow colony under a bridge in Roberts County contained a nest occupied by young bluebirds, 31 May 1987. The TBBAP found CO nesting in 12 survey blocks, PR in six, and PO in five.

SPECIMENS: There are specimens taken in Hall (8 February 1977, WTAMU) and Hutchinson (10, 13, and 22 June and 7 July 1950, TNHC) counties. The Hutchinson County birds are those collected by Thompson (1952) and probably are the ones referred to by Oberholser (1974).

Western Bluebird *Sialia mexicana* Swainson

STATUS: Casual winter visitor.

OCCURRENCE: The Western Bluebird has been recorded in six Panhandle counties—Armstrong, Briscoe, Hemphill, Potter, Randall, and Swisher—and has been seen from September to May.

The first Western Bluebird reported was a single bird in Hemphill County, 23 March 1945 (Hawkins, 1945), the only instance of one found in an eastern county. This species is not seen every year. My records reveal encounters in 15 of 34 winter seasons. Inexperienced observers may easily confuse the Western with the Eastern Bluebird, and even some of our few reports must be viewed with caution. The Western Bluebird is usually encountered in discrete flocks, although some observers have reported them in mixed flocks with other bluebird species. The most that I have ever encountered at one time was 17 in the PDCSP, 20 December 1970.

It is rare for a Western Bluebird to be seen before late October. There are two September sightings: one in the Palo Duro Club near Canyon, Randall County, 8 September 1968, and westerns in a mixed flock with easterns and mountains near Amarillo, 16 September 1965. There are but four sightings later than March, three of them in the first week of April and a single bird in the PDCSP, 14 May 1997. The CBCs are illustrative of the Western Bluebird's presence in early winter. It has been recorded on six Amarillo counts, three Lake Meredith (west) counts, and three Quitaque counts. The largest number on any was 50 on the Amarillo CBC of 21 December 1975. A Winter-Bird Population Study in the Palo Duro Canyon SP (Seyffert, 1968–78) found it present in two of the years.

SPECIMENS: There is one specimen collected in Randall County (1972, WTAMU).

Mountain Bluebird *Sialia currucoides* (Bechstein)

STATUS: Fairly common to abundant winter visitor.

OCCURRENCE: The Mountain Bluebird has been recorded in every county except Childress, Collingsworth, Hall, Lipscomb, and Sherman and has been seen from September to May.

The presence of the Mountain Bluebird in winter may vary from abundance to an almost total absence. This is shown by the CBCs. The number on the Amarillo count has varied from zero birds on six to 514 (average 81); on the Quitaque count from zero on four to 663 (average 130); on the Lake Meredith (west) count from zero on one to 269 (average 57). A Winter-Bird Population Study conducted in the PDCSP (Seyffert, 1968–78) found the Mountain Bluebird to be the fifth most common species present (average 23 per 100 acres).

It is rare for a Mountain Bluebird to be seen before mid-October. My earliest sighting is of a male in Ceta Glen, South Ceta Canyon, Randall County, 6 October 1985. The earliest on file is an unspecified number in a mixed flock of Mountain, Eastern and Western bluebirds observed near Amarillo, 18 September 1965. Most are gone by the end of March. Often a drive across the plains in mid-March will reveal large numbers strung out on power lines and fences. I have encountered one but three times in April, the latest a lone bird at BLNWR, 15 April 1990. The several May sightings, along with a possible one or two in June, are of particular interest in light of the several nestings of Mountain Bluebirds discovered in nearby areas of Oklahoma. The Oberholser (1974) reference to Carlander's observations must be clarified. He is cited as having seen a Mountain Bluebird in the Palo Duro Canyon between "June 15 and Sept. 15, 1933." While the Carlander paper from which this observation is derived is headed "June 15 to September 15, 1933," the header on the page on which the Mountain Bluebird is listed reads "August 15 to September 3, 1932, and June 19 to September 15, 1933." It is possible that the species was seen in summer but not certain. Oberholser (1974) also cites a bird for June 23, 1933. Is this based on a Carlander sighting? I have been unable to locate this reference in the papers in my possession, but I do find reference to a dead bird found sometime between either 19–22 June or 10–17 July 1933. The present location of this specimen, if preserved, is unknown. Another late observation is that reported by Hibbets et al. (1926–36), who cite an unspecified number in the Canyon area, Randall County, on 12 May 1931. More recent May sightings are as follows: one in Amarillo, 7 May 1954; one in the PDCSP, 10 May 1981; one in Pampa, Gray County, 6 May 1983; one on the LX Ranch, north-central Potter County, 12 May 1984 and 11 May 1985; one in the PDCSP, 13 May 1994; a female at the BLNWR, 3 May 1997.

Schwilling and Comer (1972) are of the opinion that any Mountain Bluebirds seen after the first week of April, possibly even earlier, should be kept under close observation for the possibility of nesting. They reported on a nest found on 9 May 1971 about nine miles east of Kenton, Cimarron County, Oklahoma. The nest was placed in a small woodpecker hole "about 9 feet up in a partly dead willow. . . . The seven eggs were slightly incubated. Nowhere in the vicinity did we see or hear an Eastern Bluebird . . . a species known to breed in that area." The authors also cite the R. Crompton Tate findings of "4 or 5 nests . . . near Kenton in 1922 and 1923" and "a pair observed by George M. Sutton on 28 February 1954, near Vinson, Harmon County, southwestern Oklahoma . . . a nest that appeared to be ready for eggs." W. Marvin Davis observed a pair near Kenton on 22 April 1961, that "might well have been breeding." An unfinished nest was found in central Oklahoma (Norman, Cleveland County) on 21 April 1951 (Harold and Hazel Cooksey). These findings should alert Panhandle birders to the possibility of the Mountain Bluebird nesting in the study area. I have observed singles and pairs in the PDCSP in late winter and early spring investigating old woodpecker holes.

A Mountain Bluebird recovered near Stratford, Moore County, in the fall of 1972 had been banded near Edmonton, Alberta, 26 June 1971, while still too young to fly (letter, James E. Dillard, TPWD, Dumas, Texas, 16 June 1973). A female observed near Vigo Park, Swisher County, 12 February 1973 "had a white spot on the top of the head—one on the nape—the entire primaries were white and the outer tail feathers were white . . . a second female was normal except for white outer tail feathers like a junco" (P. Acord).

SPECIMENS: Specimens have been collected in Gray (10 February 1939, WTAMU), Hansford (28 October 1956, MNH), Randall (7 March and 14 October 1939, P-PHM; 7 March and 26 October 1939, WTAMU), and Wheeler (6 and 16 March 1939, WTAMU) counties.

Townsend's Solitaire *Myadestes townsendi* (Audubon)

STATUS: Uncommon to fairly common winter visitor.

OCCURRENCE: Oberholser (1974) shows the Townsend's Solitaire in five Texas Panhandle counties: Armstrong, Deaf Smith, Parmer, Potter, and Randall. Fifteen others have been added: Briscoe, Castro, Dallam, Donley, Gray, Hansford, Hartley, Hemphill, Hutchinson, Moore, Ochiltree, Oldham, Roberts, Sherman, and Swisher. It has been seen from September to May.

Returning solitaires in autumn can be looked for in early October, seldom before. There are three September records, the earliest a single bird in Amarillo, Randall County, 9 September 1959. Few are seen beyond mid-April and there are but six records for May, the latest a single bird in Amarillo, Randall County, 19 May 1979.

Averages and highs on area CBCs reflect the solitaire's status in early winter: Amarillo—9.0 (38); *Lake Meredith (west)*—6.9 (35); *Quitaque*—5.2 (16); *Lake Meredith (east)*—1.3 (6). There is evidence pointing to fewer solitaires wintering in the PDCSP than formerly. The Amarillo CBCs for the ten-year period 1954–63 show an average of 1.08 per party hour, while for the ten-year period 1984–93 it is 0.06. The Townsend's Solitaire is aptly named for it is seldom that more than two or three birds are encountered at a time. The winter of 1974–75 was exceptional for numbers in that as many as 30 could be found in the PDCSP in a single day. Often its presence is revealed only by the bird's clear and mellow bell-like call echoing off the canyon walls, and occasionally on warm days in late winter it can be heard singing.

Veery *Catharus fuscescens* (Stephens)

STATUS: Rare migrant.

OCCURRENCE: The Veery has been recorded in six counties: Dallam, Hutchinson, Oldham, Parmer, Potter, and Randall. It has been seen March–May and September–October.

Testimony to the rarity of the Veery in the study area, my records reveal seeing one but ten times in 34 years. Almost all records on file are for May, the latest being for a single bird at BLNWR, 30 May 1995. A singing bird was observed at Lake Tanglewood, Randall County, 27 May 1979. There have been two sightings reported earlier than May: one in Amarillo, 16 March 1982, and another on 16 April 1968. There have been only seven fall birds reported, the earliest one in Amarillo, 8–9 September 1967, and the latest one in Amarillo, 14 October 1974.

Pulich (1988) questions the few March records and single September record for north-central Texas. There are no March records for Oklahoma and only four for September (birds either netted or found dead), plus another for October without details (Baumgartner and Baumgartner, 1992). It is probable that our March record is not in order, for the Veery typically arrives in the United States in April after crossing the Gulf of Mexico from the Yucatan Peninsula, according to Moskoff (1995). This author offers a possible explanation of why so few Veeries are reported during migration in the Southwest: "Veeries breeding in Arizona and Rocky Mtns. are virtually absent from Mexico or sw. U.S. in the spring, suggesting they may first migrate east and then circle back to breed in that area."

Gray-cheeked Thrush *Catharus minimus* (Lafresnaye)

STATUS: Casual migrant.

OCCURRENCE: The Gray-cheeked Thrush has been recorded in Ochiltree, Potter, and Randall counties in the Texas Panhandle. It has been seen in May, October, and November.

My records reflect the rarity of the Gray-cheeked Thrush in the study area, for I recorded it only eleven times in a 34-year period. All spring records are for May, ranging from one bird in the Palo Duro Club near Canyon, Randall County, 1 May 1969, 1977, and 1979, to one at BLNWR, 22 May 1983. There are three fall records: one bird at BLNWR, 22 September 1984 and 4 October 1981, and one in Amarillo, Randall County, 7 November 1968. The sighting for Randall County in February 1934 must be dismissed (Hibbets et al., 1926–36). Perhaps this is the source of the winter sighting for Randall County that Oberholser (1974) also questions.

Swainson's Thrush *Catharus ustulatus* (Nuttall)

STATUS: Fairly common to common spring migrant; rare to uncommon fall migrant.

OCCURRENCE: Oberholser (1974) shows the Swainson's Thrush in two counties, Oldham and Randall. Eleven others have been added: Briscoe, Castro, Dallam, Gray, Hartley, Hemphill, Moore, Ochiltree, Parmer, Potter, and Roberts. It has been seen March–June and August–November.

Returning Swainson's Thrushes in spring can be looked for in the first week of May. In 33 years of observations I have seen one only four times in April, the earliest a single bird at BLNWR, 18 April 1965. I know of only one other April sighting. There are two March reports: one bird in Amarillo, Potter County, 28 March 1954, and one at the Palo Duro Club near Canyon, Randall County, 29 March 1966. My records reveal that 94 percent of all Swainson's Thrushes were seen in spring, 72 percent during the seven-day period 13–19 May. The species is usually encountered singly. Notable exceptions were 65 at BLNWR, 19 May 1968, and 45, 14 May 1993. All on the latter date were found within a small area, 15 in one rather compact group. It is not uncommon to hear late migrants singing.

The Swainson's Thrush often is found as late as the last week in May. There are seven June records: two at BLNWR, 1 June 1969; one in Amarillo, Potter County, 1 and 3 June 1975, 5 June 1976, and 3 June 1983; one in Wolf Creek Park, Ochiltree County, 7 June 1983; one in the Thompson Grove Picnic Area northeast of Texline, Dallam County, 9 June 1984 and 14 June 1983.

What migratory pathway does the Swainson's Thrush follow in autumn? Most certainly not through the central Texas Panhandle. During the period 1963–96, I recorded only 20 Swainson's during fall, the dates ranging from 8 September to 27 October. In 13 of the years the species was recorded only once. The records of another observer (R. Scott) show that during the period 1987–93 only one Swainson's was seen in autumn. There are one August and two November records: 30 August 1963, Parmer County; 3 November 1988, Amarillo, Randall County; 8 November 1958, Amarillo, Potter County.

All winter sightings of the Swainson's Thrush must be dismissed, for the species winters principally through Middle and South America and only casually in southern Texas and on the Gulf Coast (AOU, 1983). A Swainson's reported on the BLNWR CBC of 20 December 1971, without supporting documentation, was questioned by the regional editor, as well it should have. Hibbets et al. (1926–36) cite dates of 21 and 27 January 1935 for the Canyon area, Randall County. This is the source of the Randall County winter sighting that Oberholser (1974) questioned. It is more than probable that all winter sightings, and possibly some of the late fall ones, were in fact of Hermit Thrushes, a species known to winter in small numbers.

Hermit Thrush *Catharus guttatus* (Pallas)

STATUS: Fairly common to common migrant. Uncommon winter visitor.

OCCURRENCE: Oberholser (1974) shows the Hermit Thrush in three Texas Panhandle counties: Parmer, Potter, and Randall. Twelve others have been added: Briscoe, Castro, Dallam, Donley, Gray, Hansford, Hartley, Hemphill, Hutchinson, Moore, Oldham, and Roberts. It has been seen from September to July.

The Hermit Thrush is the only thrush found wintering in the study area, and then only in small numbers. This is illustrated by the number of times it has been recorded on the CBCs: *Amarillo*—16 of 40; *Buffalo Lake NWR*—4 of 29; *Lake Meredith (west)*—6 of 24; *Lake Meredith (east)*—1 of 18; *Quitaque*—10 of 20. The highest number on any count was six. A Winter-Bird Population Study conducted in the PDCSP (Seyffert, 1968–78) found wintering hermits in two of the years.

The first Hermit Thrushes of spring arrive during the first or second week of April, and most have passed through by the end of the third week of May. There are three records as late as 30 May. Three summer reports are difficult to account for: a singing bird in Amarillo as late as 31 July 1971; a singing bird in Amarillo as late as 28 June 1972; one in the Canyon County Club near Canyon, Randall County, 14 June 1998.

It is of interest to compare the May status of the Hermit Thrush in the Panhandle with that in north-central Texas as reported by Pulich (1988). He recognized that "no doubt a few Hermit Thrushes linger or pass through north central Texas in early May, but birders should take extra care to distinguish them from Swainson's Thrushes, which are commonly found in the study area in May." Sightings reported in Tarrant County as late as 17 and 20 May he questions. In contrast, my records disclose that in the Panhandle 71 percent of all spring migrants (April–May) occurred in May. Spring birds were fairly evenly distributed over the period 24 April–20 May, the greatest numbers occurring in the seven-day period 6–12 May (29%) and the 14-day period 29 April–12 May (51%). The largest numbers for single days were 22 on 1 May and 20 on 7 May 1983, and 19 on 8 May 1993, all at BLNWR. This contrast in dates between the two regions is supported by data from Oklahoma. Grzybowski et al. (1992) place a limiting date of 18 May for spring migrants in the Oklahoma Panhandle, while for the rest of the state it is 22 April.

Of all migrant Hermit Thrushes, 73 percent occurred in spring (April–May) and 27 percent in fall (September–October). The first fall migrants can be expected in the first or second week of September, the earliest date being for a single bird at BLNWR, 1 September 1968. My records show that fall birds are evenly distributed throughout the season, with no significant valleys or peaks.

SPECIMENS: Specimens have been collected in Oldham (15 October 1993, TCWC), Potter (2 May 1984, TCWC), and Randall (26 December 1936 and 23 October 1978, TCWC; 25 October 1939 and 25 February 1990, WTAMU) counties. Oberholser (1974) names a specimen of nominate *guttatus* taken in Randall County but does not give its location. As far as I know, the other specimens have not been identified as to race.

Wood Thrush *Hylocichla mustelina* (Gmelin)

STATUS: Casual migrant.

OCCURRENCE: The Wood Thrush has been found in five Texas Panhandle counties: Castro, Hutchinson, Oldham, Potter, and Randall. It has been recorded March–May and September–November.

Hibbets et al. (1926–36) give two dates for the Wood Thrush: 3 March 1929 and 20 March 1930. Such extremely early dates must be questioned, for both are much earlier than those for north-central Texas (Pulich, 1988) and Oklahoma (Sutton, 1974a) where the species is to be expected.

The following is a listing of reported sightings in the study area, in all instances but one a single bird: *1957*—BLNWR, 26 May; *1964*—BLNWR, 13 September; *1968*—Amarillo, 31 October; *1969*—Amarillo, 8 September; *1971*—Amarillo, Potter County, 19 May; *1972*—Borger, Hutchinson County, 1 November; *1976*—near Canyon, Randall County, 22 April; *1977*—BLNWR, 3 and 8 May; *1978*—BLNWR, 1 May and 29 October; *1980*—Vega, Oldham County, 29 April, and BLNWR, 11 September; *1983*—BLNWR, 2 May; *1987*—Amarillo, Randall County, 10 November; *1988*—Lake Tanglewood, Randall County, 15 May; *1993*—Castro County, 14 May; *1996*—one reported on the Lake Meredith (west) CBC on 28 December is without documentation and must be dismissed. There are only isolated reports of wintering Wood Thrushes in Texas, and then only from the coast and Lower Rio Grande Valley (TOS, 1995).

American Robin *Turdus migratorius* Linnaeus

STATUS: Uncommon to common breeder; common to abundant winter visitor.

OCCURRENCE: The American Robin has been recorded in every county and in every month. Oberholser (1974) shows it in nine counties.

The robin's increasing presence in the study area during summer parallels expansion of human settlement. Reeves and Reeves (1914–36) said that "in 1914 robins were seldom seen in Canyon [Randall County]. As trees, shrubs, and lawns and available water increased, they became more common." Hibbets et al. (1926–36) did not know the robin as a year-round resident but classified it as a "winter resident." In the central Panhandle, Stevenson (1942) said it was a "migrant and common winter visitor to the juniper thickets of the park [Palo Duro Canyon] and vicinity." Hawkins (1945) was the first to affirm that "an occasional pair may remain to nest." Even as recently as 1955, one observer spoke of seeing the first robin of the season in Amarillo on 14 October. As evidence of its increasing presence in the city, a count was made in the Country Club area on 20 July 1967 and 150+ robins were tallied.

Winter remains the season of the robin's greatest abundance. The CBCs display this, showing as well extremes in numbers (high, low, average): *Amarillo*— 4,874, 0, 433; *Lake Meredith (west)*—1,472, 0, 301; *Quitaque*—598, 1, 172; *Lake Meredith (east)*—150, 0, 150; *Buffalo Lake* NWR—58, 0, 4. The robin was found to be the second most common species in the PDCSP during a Winter-Bird Population Study (Seyffert, 1968–78), averaging 106 per 100 acres.

NESTING: Hawkins's (1945) suspicion that the robin was nesting in Amarillo was based on a single bird seen in the city on 7 and 8 July 1945: "Four were present on September 8, two of this group having the spotted breasts of juveniles." The first confirmed nestings within the city were an adult carrying nesting material, 28 April 1958, and an adult with newly fledged young, 9 May 1959. To date the robin has been confirmed nesting in 19 counties: Briscoe, Childress, Collingsworth, Dallam, Donley, Gray, Hall, Hansford, Hartley, Hemphill, Hutchinson, Lipscomb, Moore, Ochiltree, Oldham, Potter, Randall, Roberts, and Wheeler; it would be in the others with better coverage. The TBBAP found CO nesting in 30 survey blocks, PR in 13, and PO in 17. Twenty-eight were located between the 100th and 101st meridians, 19 between the 101st and 102nd, and 13 west of the 102nd. The BBSS are poor indicators of the robin's summer presence as few of the stops sample proper habitat, principally towns and farm or ranch lots. Neither Johnsgard (1979) nor Oberholser (1974) shows the species nesting in the study area.

The robin is two-brooded. Nest building has been observed as early as the last week of March 1988 (Amarillo, Potter County) and as late as 21 June 1988 (Boys Ranch, Oldham County) and 22 June 1986 and 1996 (Amarillo, Potter

County). Fledglings have been seen as early as 5 May 1987 (Pampa, Gray County) and as late as 2 August 1987 (Glazier, Lipscomb County).

What appeared to be a "mosaic" robin was observed in Amarillo, Potter County, 9 March 1967 (P. Acord). The left half of the tail was white and the right half was normal. The face and wings on the left side had extensive white blotchings throughout, while the right side had noticeably few.

SPECIMENS: Specimens have been taken in Hall (7 March 1977, WTAMU), Potter (ACMNH; 30 August 1978, TCWC), and Randall (13 May 1939, 10 June 1969, April 1972, WTAMU) counties. The TCWC specimen is a juvenal-plumaged bird.

Varied Thrush *Ixoreus naevius* (Gmelin)

STATUS: Vagrant winter visitor.

OCCURRENCE: There has been a single report of the Varied Thrush in the Texas Panhandle. One first appeared in Amarillo, Potter County, 3 February 1964 (T. Fox), and was seen repeatedly thereafter by many observers until 31 March.

The Varied Thrush winters from southern British Columbia and northern Idaho south through Washington, Oregon, and California to northern Baja California, while it is casual through much of central and northeastern North America (AOU, 1983). As of 12 September 1995, there had been twenty-seven reported sightings in Texas (Lasley and Sexton, 1995a). The nearest confirmation to the study area was a bird seen at Idalou, Lubbock County, 18 February–21 March 1979 (TBRC). Another Varied Thrush was reported in Lubbock, 15 December 1990 (Lasley and Sexton, 1991).

Family Mimidae (Mockingbirds and Thrashers)

Gray Catbird *Dumetella carolinensis* (Linnaeus)

STATUS: Uncommon to fairly common migrant. Rare summer and casual winter visitor.

OCCURRENCE: The Gray Catbird has been recorded in 16 counties: Armstrong, Briscoe, Castro, Deaf Smith, Donley, Gray, Hartley, Hemphill, Hutchinson, Moore, Oldham, Parmer, Potter, Randall, Roberts, and Swisher. Oberholser (1974) shows it in six. It has been found in every month except March.

Returning catbirds in spring can be expected in the second week of May. There are five April records, all of single birds, the earliest being 2 April 1994 at Ceta Glen, South Ceta Canyon, Randall County. Most are gone by the end of the third week of May. Fall birds arrive in the second week of September, with few remaining past October. The normal winter range of the Gray Catbird in Texas is along the coast and in the Lower Rio Grande Valley (TOS, 1995). Occasionally one winters in the study area: 4 February 1956, Canyon, Randall County;

3 December 1964–2 February 1965, Amarillo; 19 December 1982, PDCSP; 28 December 1985, Lake Meredith National Recreation Area, Potter County; 19 December 1992–20 February 1993, PDCSP; 22 November–25 December 1997, Kress, Swisher County.

NESTING: The only reference to nesting of the Gray Catbird in the study area is the sight record of breeding in Hemphill County shown by Oberholser (1974). A search of the Oberholser files, however, did not turn up any background material pertaining to this record (*fide* W. Pulich). Oberholser is possibly the basis for Johnsgard's (1979) reference to nesting in Hemphill County and for his including the northeastern third of the study area in the species' breeding range. Summer sightings, including singing birds, have since been made in Hemphill, Oldham, Potter, and Randall counties, without evidence of nesting. A typical catbird nest with an adult bird nearby was found in a plum thicket along Rico Creek north of the Canadian River at Boys Ranch, Oldham County, 3 and 9 July 1977, but there was no indication of occupancy and young birds were not seen.

The Gray Catbird has been confirmed nesting in two localities in Oklahoma near the study area. Sutton (1967) makes reference to a nest in Cimarron County in the Panhandle, 1 June 1910. A pair nested successfully in Clinton, Custer County, in the summer of 1970 ("for the first time in 14 years"; Williams, 1970). On the basis of Hubbard (1978), Johnsgard (1979) says the catbird has been found nesting in Clayton, Union County, New Mexico. A perusal of the Hubbard account, however, fails to confirm this: his reference to the species in that area is limited to its being a migrant only. Oberholser (1974) shows a sight record of breeding in Wilbarger County.

Northern Mockingbird *Mimus polyglottos* (Linnaeus)

STATUS: Common resident.

OCCURRENCE: The Northern Mockingbird has been recorded in all 26 counties of the Texas Panhandle and in every month.

Although the species is common in summer, significantly fewer mockingbirds are encountered outside towns during winter. Many observers do not look upon the species as being a migrant. Only once have I encountered what I thought to be a possible movement of birds. On 6 August 1989, I observed at least 24 mockingbirds in one group in a field of sunflowers at BLNWR. The species is not normally gregarious, and I suspect that many more birds were present than limited access allowed me to discover. The extent of such population shifts, their timing, routes of movement, and how far south the birds go is little known (Derrickson and Breitwisch, 1992). A look at my records from BLNWR throws some light on this population shift. On 29 May 1978 there were 40+ birds present but by 4 September none—another was not seen until the following 15 April.

The spans between arrival and departure dates for the years 1978–86 are: *1978*—9 April–4 September; *1979*—15 April–3 September; *1980*—23 March–21 September; *1981*—19 April–6 September; *1982*—25 April–19 September; *1983*—10 April–25 September; *1984*—22 April–19 August; *1985*—6 April–1 September; *1986*—10 April–4 September. Occasionally one or two birds overwintered on the refuge. My records for PDCSP also illustrate the extent of seasonal variation in mockingbird populations, in this case birds in a more sheltered environment. A Breeding Bird Study (Seyffert, 1967–68) revealed an average density of 15 birds per 100 acres, while a Winter-Bird Population Study (Seyffert, 1968–78) conducted on the same plot produced an average density of 6 birds per 100 acres. A comparison of average numbers of mockingbirds recorded per trip afield in June and January at PDCSP and BLNWR (1965–96) further demonstrates the extent of population shift: PDCSP 8.2 and 2.9; BLNWR 10.0 and 0. 3. The summer BBS averages are: *Childress*—106.0; *Clarendon*—67.5; *Channing*—35.5; *Skellytown*—34.7; *Miami*—22.0; *Dalhart*—15.0; *Panhandle*—10.3; *Texline*—6.2; *Booker*—5.2; *Pantex*—3.6; *Waka*—0.8. The winter CBC averages are: *Amarillo*—16.5; *Quitaque*—9.0; *Lake Meredith (west)*—0.8; *Lake Meredith (east)*—0.6; *Buffalo Lake NWR*—0.3. Is the mockingbird more common in the study area today than formerly, as some believe? Using these same PDCSP and BLNWR records for June, the period 1965–79 produced an average of 8.2 per trip afield, and the period 1980–96 yielded 11.5.

NESTING: The TBBAP found the Northern Mockingbird to be one of the most widely and evenly distributed of nesting species in the study area. It was a CO nester in 29 survey blocks, a PR in 64, and a PO in 17. Forty quadrangles were located between the 100th and 101st meridians, 37 between the 101st and 102nd, and 33 west of the 102nd. Unfortunately for such a common and conspicuous species, there is little nesting data. The earliest date of nest building is 14 April 1958 in Amarillo, Randall County, and the latest date for a nest containing young is 1 August 1982 at BLNWR.

SPECIMENS: Specimens have been taken in Hutchinson (9 June and 1 July 1950, TNHC), Potter (15 August 1981, TCWC), and Randall (18 September 1939 and 2 April 1977, WTAMU) counties. The Hutchinson County birds were taken by Thompson (1952) and represent the ones shown by Oberholser (1974) for that county. Oberholser also names a specimen taken in Oldham County but fails to give its location. The Potter County specimen is an albino juvenile.

Sage Thrasher *Oreoscoptes montanus* (Townsend)
STATUS: Uncommon to fairly common migrant. Rare winter visitor and vagrant summer visitor.

OCCURRENCE: The Sage Thrasher has been found in 13 counties: Armstrong, Briscoe, Castro, Dallam, Deaf Smith, Hartley, Hutchinson, Moore, Oldham, Parmer, Potter, Randall, and Roberts. It has been recorded in every month except June.

Sage Thrashers tend to be overlooked and the species is underreported as a result. The brushy prairie and plains habitats where the species can usually be found are the very ones least birded; consequently, we do not have a good handle on migration dates. In spring the Sage Thrasher can normally be expected from early or mid-March to mid- or late April and in autumn from mid-September to late October. The latest spring date is for two birds at BLNWR, 22 May 1965, and the early fall date for one at BLNWR, 15 August 1976. Seldom are many seen at a time. Ten were at BLNWR on 1 October 1993 and ten in PDCSP on the late date of 10 December 1956.

A few Sage Thrashers overwinter. I found a single bird during one year of a Winter-Bird Population Study in the PDCSP (Seyffert, 1968–78). Altogether, I have encountered the species in eight winters (1963–96). During CBCs Sage Thrashers have been recorded on four Amarillo counts (1954–96), four times on the Quitaque counts (1975–96), and once on the BLNWR (1961–96). It has never been recorded on the two Lake Meredith counts (1970–96). As can be seen, wintering Sage Thrashers are to be found primarily in the canyonlands. The few records of those found elsewhere are almost invariably from earlier in the season and probably represent late migrants. As an example, one found in Memorial Park Cemetery, Amarillo, Potter County, 12 December 1982, did not overwinter.

Three midsummer sightings of Sage Thrashers have raised speculation on the possibility of an occasional nesting. One was seen near Amarillo, 29 July 1960; one in the PDCSP, 19 July 1962; and one near Friona, Parmer County, 23 July 1960. It is unlikely that they were nesting. Wolfe (1952) classified the species as a "summer resident in area 1," of which the study area is a part, but on what basis he does not say. Sutton (1967) cites one record of nesting in the Oklahoma Panhandle: "June 13, 1920, three adult birds and nest (four eggs) found in 'pasture' on ranch in southern Cimarron County," while for New Mexico Hubbard (1978) refers to the few July records of Sage Thrashers in the Clayton area of Union County as probable migrants and not nesters. Johnsgard (1979) refers to the single Oklahoma record and names one other for southwestern Kansas (Morton County), where the species is very rare in summer (Cable et al., 1996). There is a record of breeding in Baca County in extreme southeastern Colorado (Andrews and Righter, 1992).

Brown Thrasher *Toxostoma rufum* (Linnaeus)

STATUS: Fairly common to common resident in the eastern half, and uncommon westward along the Canadian River and tributaries; rare and local elsewhere. Uncommon to fairly common migrant and winter visitor in other areas.

OCCURRENCE: The Brown Thrasher has been recorded in all the Texas Panhandle counties except Sherman and Swisher and would be in them with better coverage. Oberholser (1974) shows it in seven. It has been found in every month.

Early observers in the study area regarded the Brown Thrasher as primarily a bird of the eastern counties, making few references to its presence westward. As recently as the 1970s, Johnsgard (1979) thought it was "probably" a breeder only in the eastern tier of counties. Today it is known as a summer resident throughout the eastern third of the region; in the central third locally from Moore and Hutchinson counties in the north to Randall and Armstrong counties in the south; and in the western third from Hartley and Moore counties in the north to Deaf Smith and Randall counties in the south.

The BBSS present a rather poor picture of the presence and distribution of the Brown Thrasher. No routes sample the eastern counties where the species is most commonly found, and few of those located farther west contain stops at proper habitats. If BBS data were relied upon as indicators, the species would be thought of as almost absent in summer. The CBC averages are better indicators of winter status, although none of these are made in the eastern counties either: *Amarillo*—1.6; *Lake Meredith* (*west*)—0.9; *Quitaque*—0.8; *Buffalo Lake* NWR— 0.4; *Lake Meredith* (*east*)—0.1; *Friona*—0.1.

NESTING: The TBBAP results are as follows: CO nesting in five survey blocks, PR in 14, PO in 22. Twenty-four were between the 100th and 101st meridians, ten between the 101st and 102nd, and seven west of the 102nd.

There is a dearth of nesting data: nest with four eggs, Lake McClellan, Gray County, 12 June 1955; adult feeding nestlings, Rico Creek near Boys Ranch, Oldham County, 2 July 1972; nest with four thrasher eggs and one cowbird egg, Salt Fork of Red River north of Wellington, Collingsworth County, 25 May 1987. There are more records of adults with fledglings or juveniles: Lake McClellan, Gray County, 19–20 July 1958; BLNWR, 24 August 1980; Lake Tanglewood, Randall County, 25 June 1987; near Dumas, Moore County, 30 June 1987; Pampa, Gray County, June 1987; Gene Howe WMA, Hemphill County, 24 June 1990; Taylor Lakes WMA, Donley County, 22 July 1998. A pair of Brown Thrashers was observed on the Reynolds Ranch, Rita Blanca Creek, Hartley County, 4 July 1984, and a single bird on the Whiteaker Ranch in far western Hartley County near the New Mexico line, 20 July 1991—the westernmost extension of the species' known range in the study area. It may nest still farther north as the Brown

Thrasher is classified as a breeder/summer bird (rare) in the Perico Creek area of nearby Union County, New Mexico (NMOS, 1992).

SPECIMENS: Specimens have been taken in Hemphill (30 July 1971, TCWC) and Hutchinson (14 and 21 June 1950, TNHC) counties. The two birds from Hutchinson County are those collected by Thompson (1952) on the Bugbee Ranch and identified as the race *longicauda*. They are the specimens shown for that county by Oberholser (1974), who also assigned all Brown Thrashers in the study area to *longicauda*. The Hemphill County bird, however, was identified as nominate *rufum*.

Curve-billed Thrasher *Toxostoma curvirostre* (Swainson)

STATUS: Fairly common to common resident in the western half, rare to fairly common in the eastern half.

OCCURRENCE: The Curve-billed Thrasher has been found in all but six counties: Carson, Collingsworth, Hartley, Lipscomb, Ochiltree, and Wheeler. Oberholser (1974) shows it in one (Potter) and Johnsgard (1979) not at all. It has been recorded in every month.

None of the early observers in the study area named the Curve-billed Thrasher, including Carlander (1933, 1934), Stevenson (1942), and Hawkins (1945), who all worked in areas where the species is most commonly found today. When and where the first bird was observed went unrecorded. The first mention of the species in the literature was for the spring of 1955, when it was said to be "quite common at Palo Duro" (Baumgartner, 1955). However, in the winter of 1956–57 it was thought noteworthy when one was found in the Amarillo area (Baumgartner, 1957).

Two CBCs initiated prior to 1970 announced the arrival of the Curve-billed Thrasher as a winter visitor. The Amarillo count, started in 1954, recorded the first two birds on 30 December 1967, and the species was present on 20 of 28 subsequent counts. Started in 1961, the BLNWR CBC recorded its first thrasher on 30 December 1974, and the species continued to be found on 11 of the following 20 counts. Illustrative also of an increasing presence in winter, a Winter-Bird Population Study (Seyffert, 1968–78) conducted in the PDCSP found this thrasher on the study plot in six of the years.

The Channing and Childress BBSs are the only two of eight routes on which the Curve-billed Thrasher has been recorded, the former located in the northwestern sector and the latter in the far southeastern sector. It has been found six times on the Channing route in Oldham County and 16 times on the Childress route in Childress and Cottle counties.

NESTING: The Curve-billed Thrasher has been confirmed nesting in Hansford,

Moore, Oldham, Potter, and Randall counties and has been found in summer in Armstrong, Briscoe, Castro, Deaf Smith, Donley, Gray, Hall, Hutchinson, and Sherman counties. Nest building has been observed as early as 21 April 1998 in Gruver, Hansford County, and a nest with three eggs near Lake Tanglewood, Randall County, as late as 12 August 1973 (TP-RF). All nests discovered were built in cholla cactus. The TBBAP found CO nesting in eight survey blocks, PR in three, and PO in six. Three of the quadrangles were located between the 100th and 101st meridians, six between the 101st and 102nd, and eight west of the 102nd.

SPECIMENS: There are specimens taken in Hall (27 June 1968, FMNH, MNH) and Oldham (August 1974, SRSU) counties. One from Hall County (FMNH) was identified as the race *celsum*.

Family Sturnidae (Starlings)

European Starling *Sturnus vulgaris* Linnaeus

STATUS: Common to abundant resident.

OCCURRENCE: The European Starling has been recorded in every Texas Panhandle county and has been seen year-round.

The starling is a recent addition to the avifauna of the Texas Panhandle. In tracing its introduction in Texas, Oberholser (1974) had this to say: "First Texas record . . . was established when one was found dead at Cove (Chambers Co.) in late December, 1925. It was next taken at Beaumont (Jefferson Co.) January 8, 1926. Both of these localities are on the upper coast." Dickerson (1938) tracked the further expansion of the starling in the state and said it "invaded the Panhandle about 1937. Stevenson and two co-workers who studied birds in the Amarillo area between 1935 and 1938 apparently failed to find the species." His placement of the western and northern boundaries of its range in the High Plains at Shamrock (Wheeler County), Memphis (Hall County), and Hale Center (Hale County) was based on observations of winter birds: no summer birds had been reported. Reeves and Reeves (1914–36) observed: "1940: The first we saw here, when during a light wet snow dozens appeared in our trees." This was in Canyon, Randall County. By 1942 Hawkins (1945) was able to say that "the Starling was numerous and already a nuisance in downtown Amarillo during November and December. It leaves the Panhandle during the spring, summer, or early fall months." These observations support studies showing that starlings invading new territories were migrant and wandering flocks composed primarily of first-year and nonbreeding second-year birds (Kessel, 1953).

Observer P. Acord's records for the 1950s show steady increases. In 1952 she found the starling a "fairly common winter resident—arriving about the first of November and being present until about the last of March. Some scattered pairs around town and in a few areas of the canyons." In 1956 she noted a "few breeding pairs around town and at Palo Duro Club—most common from Nov. to mid-Mar." By 1957 starlings were "reported in unusually large flocks at Amarillo"; in 1958 they "continued to increase in numbers in Amarillo." And in 1959 "a definite increase in nesting pairs was noted . . . at Amarillo." An example of what at the time was considered a large number was "a tremendous flock of 800–1000 just at daylight—others flying west . . . across the fields" at BLNWR in January 1958 (P. Acord). Today the starling is one of the more common birds of the study area and is present wherever one goes.

The CBCs give an indication of starling abundance in early winter. The Amarillo count, which includes the Palo Duro Canyon and surrounding plains, was started in 1954 and the first starlings (9) were recorded on 29 December 1959. Since then they have averaged 182 per count (high 786). The BLNWR count, begun in 1961, recorded its first starlings (4) on 22 December 1971. Farther west in Parmer County, starlings (80) were recorded on the first Friona count of 22 December 1961. Showing the rapid growth in numbers, 51,000 were tallied on the Friona CBC of 24 December 1972.

It is the Lake Meredith (east) CBC in Hutchinson County that illustrates the tremendous change in the winter status of the starling in the study area. The first count of 30 December 1970 tallied 2,303 birds. An attempt was later made to ascertain the number that roosted nightly in the Sanford Dam marsh, with resulting estimates of 285,000 on 29 December 1973 and 270,000 on 22 December 1974. These numbers were surpassed by 500,000 estimated on 29 December 1984.

NESTING: The European Starling is found throughout the study area in summer. The averages on the BBSs are indicative of its presence on the sparsely inhabited plains: *Channing*—9.0; *Waka* —8.6; *Booker*—7.9; *Texline*—4.7; *Childress*—4.5; *Pantex*—3.7; *Miami*—2.7; *Clarendon*—0.75. The TBBAP found CO nesting in 61 survey blocks, PR in 14, and PO in 16. Thirty-six of the quadrangles lay between the 100th and 101st meridians, 30 between the 101st and 102nd, and 25 west of the 102nd.

The starling is two-brooded and begins nesting quite early (18 March 1994, Amarillo, Potter County). Nest building continues through June (8 June 1988, Carson County) and July (14 July 1988, Lake McClellan, Gray County). A bird on the nest was observed as late as 1 August 1988 (Wheeler, Wheeler County), and one carrying nesting material on 12 August 1997 (Amarillo, Potter County). Of late the starling has become increasingly common in summer in the PDCSP, usurping old woodpecker holes for nesting. What effect this is having on other cavity-nesting species is unknown and warrants study.

SPECIMENS: Specimens have been collected in Moore (MCHM) and Randall (11 and 15 May 1969, 17 and 21 March 1970, May 1970, and one in 1975, WTAMU) counties.

Family Motacillidae (Pipits)

American Pipit *Anthus rubescens* (Tunstall)
STATUS: Fairly common to common migrant. Uncommon to fairly common winter visitor.

OCCURRENCE: The American Pipit has been seen in 17 counties: Armstrong, Briscoe, Carson, Castro, Childress, Dallam, Deaf Smith, Donley, Gray, Hansford, Hartley, Moore, Oldham, Parmer, Potter, Randall, and Wheeler. Their scattered locations across the study area indicate that the pipit would also be found in the missing counties with better coverage. It has been seen from September to May.

For those familiar with its sharp and clear flight notes (*pip-pit*), the American Pipit is more often heard than seen. Single birds or small flocks often alight around the margins of playa lakes to feed and drink, and it is from such locations that most pipits are reported. Observers should also be on the alert for it in open country, plowed fields, and short grass and overgrown fields. Large flocks have only occasionally been reported: "Flocks of about 50" (Randall County), 2 April 1952, and several hundred, 12–16 November 1974; 50 (Potter County), 24 October 1996; 35 (Briscoe County), 27 April 1997. Pipits may also be found in association with Horned Larks and longspurs, making it difficult to single them out.

Fall birds begin arriving in mid- or late September, the earliest dates being for six at BLNWR, 2 September 1979, and four in Gray County, 5 September 1983. Few are seen past early May, the latest a single bird at BLNWR, 19 May 1968. Most pipits are recorded between mid-September and early November, and between mid-March and early May.

The CBCs reflect winter scarcity. The American Pipit has never been recorded on the Friona, Lake Meredith (west), or Lake Meredith (east) counts and appears but once on the Quitaque, twice on the BLNWR, and six times on the Amarillo counts. The Amarillo CBC tallied 40 pipits on 18 December 1993, by far the highest number for any count. It is my opinion that the species is underreported in winter and that more are around than are noticed.

Sprague's Pipit *Anthus spragueii* (Audubon)
STATUS: Rare migrant.

OCCURRENCE: The Sprague's Pipit has been recorded in five counties—Carson,

Hutchinson, Oldham, Randall, and Wheeler—and has been seen March–April and September–November.

Although the area is within its migratory pathway, the Sprague's Pipit is considered rare in the Texas Panhandle. It is among the most overlooked and under-reported species primarily because most observers are unfamiliar with its call note and spend little time surveying proper habitat. The few records on file are quickly listed: one at BLNWR, 19 September 1954; an unspecified number near Amarillo, Randall County, 27 March 1964; 6–10 at BLNWR, 27 September 1964; two near Canyon, Randall County, 5 October 1965; one in Randall County, 10 April 1966; one on the Duncan Ranch in southeast Hutchinson County, 24 September 1978; one in Carson County, 22 March 1986; 3–5 near Wheeler, Wheeler County, 6–10 April 1988; one near Amarillo, Randall County, 23 November 1993; three near Amarillo, Randall County, 9 November 1995; one near Wildorado, Oldham County, 29 September 1997.

Family Bombycillidae (Waxwings)

Bohemian Waxwing *Bombycilla garrulus* (Linnaeus)

STATUS: Casual fall and winter visitor.

OCCURRENCE: The Bohemian Waxwing has been found in Dallam, Moore, Parmer, Potter, Randall, and Roberts counties and has been seen from November to May.

An irruptive species from northern boreal regions, the Bohemian Waxwing appears but irregularly in the study area. Although usually found in discrete flocks, it sometimes associates with the Cedar Waxwing and probably would be reported more often if flocks of the latter were scrutinized closely. Occasionally the area is invaded by fairly large numbers.

There are two reports of the Bohemian Waxwing prior to mid-century. Hibbets et al. (1926–36) cited it for the winters of 1926 and 1928 and for 30 January 1927. The observations of this group were confined principally to Canyon, Randall County, or to within 40 miles of the city. Stevenson (1942) reported "a flock of 12 flying over Palo Duro Creek, on the Elkins Ranch, Randall County, on December 26, 1936"—from which a male bird was collected. He evidently was unaware of the Hibbets sightings as he thought this was "the first record of the species for Texas": surely the first confirmation.

The following list gives sightings since 1950. *1958–59*—an invasion winter in the southern Great Plains region, the first Bohemian Waxwing observed in Amarillo was on 9 November—"the first record in a number of years" (P. Acord). Later, an injured bird was found in Amarillo, 27 December. It was rescued from dogs and placed in the care of two Amarillo birders. The bird was without a tail and one wing was badly damaged; not until the following fall did it molt into fresh plumage. On 21 November 1959, the bird was taken from the house and placed on a birdbath in the yard so that visiting photographers could take pictures of it. To everyone's surprise, the waxwing then took flight and was never seen again. The last sighting of the season occurred on 10 March, when 22 were found in Amarillo.

1961–62—large flocks were recorded during the winter season. The first birds were seen in Amarillo around 4 November, and by 30 December their number had increased to some 20–30. On 27 January an estimated 300 were observed feeding and bathing in the Ellwood Park area (P. Acord, J. G. Newell), and smaller flocks continued to be seen regularly through late February. The last sighting was on the very late date of 13 May. Smaller flocks were also found during the season in Canyon and nearby Palo Duro Club, Randall County. *1966*—1–2, Amarillo, Randall County, 17–19 March. *1967*—one or more on the Jokerst Ranch south of Amarillo, Randall County, 14 January, and four at Lake Tanglewood, Randall County, 1 April. *1968–69*—50 birds in the PDCSP, 27 January, 50 in Amarillo in January, and 6–8 on 3 and 24 February. One was observed at length in Miami, Roberts County, 15 February, as it visited a feeder. *1969*—12 near Friona, Parmer County, 23 December.

1972–73—54 birds in the PDCSP, 14 January, one at Lake Tanglewood and three in The Palisades, Randall County, 16 March, and 20 in Amarillo, 18 March. *1986*—one southwest of Dumas, Moore County, 9 December. *1993*—one in a flock of Cedar Waxwings in the PDCSP, 28 January (TBRC). *1997*—one in a group of 20 Cedar Waxwings in Texline, Dallam County, 12 January (TBRC; TP-RF).

SPECIMENS: The specimen reported by Stevenson (1942) as having been taken in Randall County on 26 December 1936 was deposited in the USNM (#597272). Oberholser (1974) places the collection site as the Palo Duro Canyon SP; the Elkins Ranch, however, is adjacent to the state park.

Cedar Waxwing *Bombycilla cedrorum* Vieillot

STATUS: Fairly common to abundant fall, winter, and spring visitor. Vagrant summer visitor.

OCCURRENCE: The Cedar Waxwing has been recorded in every county except Childress and Lipscomb. Oberholser (1974) shows it in three counties. Waxwings have been seen in every month except July.

The Cedar Waxwing normally is present in fairly large numbers during winter and early spring; however, in some years it may be almost totally absent. This variability is illustrated by a Winter-Bird Population Study conducted in the PDCSP in which the Cedar Waxwing was found to be the fifth most common species on the study plot, averaging 23 per 100 acres (Seyffert, 1968–78). The average ranged from a high of 123 to its absence in one winter. Such variability is also illustrated by the species' absences, highs, and averages on the CBCs: *Amarillo*—absent on 15 of 40 (286, 43); *Quitaque*—absent on 9 of 21 (434, 39); *Lake Meredith* (*west*)—absent on 11 of 24 (179, 16); *Lake Meredith* (*east*)—absent on 16 of 18 (11, 9); *Buffalo Lake* NWR—absent on 28 of 29 (8).

The CBCs do not present a true picture of the winter status of the Cedar Waxwing for they are conducted early in the season when the species is least common. My records show an elapsed period of three months from the time the first waxwings are recorded in fall, usually in small numbers, until the next ones are seen, most often in January (Seyffert, 1991). It is in late winter and early spring that the species is most abundant, during which times it may often be found in the "thousands." As an example, on 7 April 1995 at PDCSP, I counted 1,440 pass over me in a few minutes.

The first waxwings can be looked for in mid- or late September. The earliest recorded are five in Amarillo, Potter County, 17 August 1985 and 20 August 1968, and one at BLNWR, 18 August 1996. Most are gone by mid- or late May. The latest on record are six at Lake Tanglewood, Randall County, 1 June 1981, and two in Amarillo, Randall County, 7 June 1997. Not uncommonly the earliest waxwings are juvenal-plumaged birds, or young birds in the company of adults, raising the question of possible nesting (Seyffert, 1991). Juvenal-plumaged birds have been found in Amarillo, Potter County, 13 September 1959 (two together), 20 August 1968 (one), 29 September 1974 (one), 17 August 1985 (five together), 12 October 1998 (two together); at BLNWR, 23 September 1970 (two together) and 24 September 1972 (one with an adult); in PDCSP, 19 September 1991 (3–5 together). In addition, a flightless juvenal-plumaged Cedar Waxwing, accompanied by two adults, was recovered from a yard in Borger, Hutchinson County, 19 October 1989. Sutton (1967) reported a "bird in streaked juvenal feather taken Guymon, Texas County, September 10, 1959 (J. D. Ligon), another seen near Kenton, September 21, 1954 (G. M. Sutton)." The nearest locations to the study area where the Cedar Waxwing has been confirmed nesting are in the Oklahoma Panhandle (Sutton, 1967): near Kenton, Cimarron County, 15 June 1914 and 3 June 1920; and near Gate, Beaver County, 1921.

SPECIMENS: Specimens have been collected in Hansford (24 December 1955, MNH), Hutchinson (21 October 1989, TCWC), Moore (MCHM), Potter (ACMNH; 20 January 1980, TCWC), and Randall (30 January 1977, TCWC; May 1967, 15 April 1969, 1 May 1970, 2 May 1972, 16 May 1979, 4 March 1986, 2 February 1992, WTAMU) counties.

Family Ptilogonatidae (Silky-Flycatchers)

Phainopepla *Phainopepla nitens* (Swainson)

STATUS: Casual fall and winter visitor.

OCCURRENCE: The Phainopepla has been recorded in Briscoe, Deaf Smith, Moore, Oldham, and Randall counties of the Texas Panhandle. It has been seen in February, August, October, and November.

Though the species is known to withdraw in winter from the northern limits of its range, two Phainopepla sightings in the study area occurred in February. The first was a single bird observed southwest of Dumas, Moore County, in February 1972; it remained for three days. In mid-February 1985, another was found in Hereford, Deaf Smith County. On the morning of 21 August 1983, a female Phainopepla was observed at length at BLNWR; the same bird was seen later in the day, along with possibly one other. A male was watched closely and at length as it bathed in a yard in Vega, Oldham County, 26 August 1986. The October and November sightings were of a female found in the South Prong of Caprock Canyons SP, Briscoe County, 4 October 1983, and a male in PDCSP, 27 November 1993.

The Phainopepla in Texas is a locally common resident throughout most of the Trans-Pecos, rare to Howard County (Big Spring) and along the Rio Grande to Webb County (TOS, 1995). There are several reports of birds seen near the study area: Muleshoe NWR, Bailey County, 14 July 1958 (TOS, 1958) and 3 September 1978 (Williams, 1979); Hale County, 8 January 1980 (Williams, 1980b); Crosby County, 10 August and 14 October 1980 (Williams, 1981); Floyd County, 25 June 1985 (Williams, 1985).

The two sightings in Oklahoma are of interest (Baumgartner and Baumgartner, 1992): 4 February 1962 (Wakita, Grant County); 18 August 1987 (Lake Etling SP, Cimarron County).

Family Parulidae (Wood-Warblers)

Blue-winged Warbler *Vermivora pinus* (Linnaeus)

STATUS: Vagrant migrant.

OCCURRENCE: There have been but three sightings of the Blue-winged Warbler in the Texas Panhandle. The first was a male observed off and on over a 20-minute period in Vega, Oldham County, 2 May 1994 (R. Scott). A dirt driveway flooded to attract birds lured the bird several times to bathe. On 6 June 1996, a singing Blue-winged Warbler, identified by a person familiar with its distinctive song on its breeding grounds, was located on the Bar H Ranch west of Clarendon, Donley County (letter, Frank Schaff, Frederick, Maryland, 18 June 1996). The latest sighting was of two birds in the Red Deer Creek area ("Sleepy Hollow") between Miami and Canadian, Hemphill County, 7 September 1996 (E. Kutac, R. Scott, et al.).

An explanation for the several recent Blue-winged Warbler sightings may lie in the expansion of the species' breeding range into states as far west as southern Michigan and Minnesota. With this extension, more vagrants are being found in western North America—those in California since 1982 (Dunn and Garrett, 1997).

The Blue-winged Warbler has not been recorded in the Oklahoma Panhandle (Baumgartner and Baumgartner, 1992) but has occurred several times on the Southern Plains: in Crosby County, 4 September 1982 (Williams, 1983); and at Lubbock, 23 June 1984 (Williams, 1984—"third county record"), 6 May 1989 (Lasley and Sexton, 1989), and 26 April 1992 (Lasley and Sexton, 1992). The nearest that it has been seen to the east is Comanche County, Oklahoma, but only once (Tyler, 1979b); twice in Wichita County to the southeast in Texas (Pulich, 1988); and to the west a single bird at Clayton, Union County, New Mexico, 5 May, 1997 (Williams, 1997). It is a rare to locally common migrant in the eastern half of Texas (TOS, 1995).

Golden-winged Warbler *Vermivora chrysoptera* (Linnaeus)

STATUS: Casual migrant.

OCCURRENCE: The Golden-winged Warbler has been reported six times in the Texas Panhandle, as follows: a male at BLNWR, 12 May 1966; a male at BLNWR, 10 May 1968; a singing male at a rural residence near the southwestern outskirts of Canyon, Randall County, 1 June 1977 (TBRC); a male at Tierra Blanca Creek near the previous year's sighting, 23 September 1978; a male at Lake Tanglewood, Randall County, 8 May 1993; a male on the Taylor Lakes WMA, Donley County, 5 May 1997.

Even as near the study area as central Oklahoma and north-central Texas, the Golden-winged Warbler is classified as a rare to casual transient (Baumgartner and Baumgartner, 1992; Pulich, 1988), and it is a rare to uncommon migrant in the eastern half of Texas (TOS, 1995). It is classified as an "accidental" on the South Plains (LEAS, 1994).

Tennessee Warbler *Vermivora peregrina* (Wilson)

STATUS: Rare migrant.

OCCURRENCE: The Tennessee Warbler has been reported in Hemphill, Hutchinson, Moore, Oldham, Potter, and Randall counties of the Texas Panhandle. It has been seen April–May and August–October.

As of the end of 1998, there had been 35 reported sightings of the Tennessee

Warbler in the study area: April (8), May (21), August (1), September (1), October (4). Spring dates range from 14 April 1975 (Amarillo, Potter County) to 26 May 1992 (BLNWR), and fall dates from 27 August 1986 (BLNWR) to 24 October 1998 (Jim's Lake, Hutchinson County). With the exceptions of one each in Hutchinson, Hemphill, and Moore counties and two in Oldham, all occurred in Potter and Randall counties. Surprisingly, a Tennessee Warbler has never been reported in the PDCSP despite the frequency with which that site has been birded.

Inexperienced observers tend to misidentify the similar and much more common Orange-crowned Warbler as the Tennessee Warbler, particularly fall birds and juveniles, and it is my belief that the Tennessee is the most overreported of the less common warbler species in the study area. Besides plumage differences, observers should keep in mind that the Tennessee is more likely to be found feeding high in the tree canopy, while the Orange-crowned Warbler prefers the lower elevations and brushy areas.

The Tennessee Warbler is an uncommon to abundant migrant in the eastern half of Texas, rare in the western half (TOS, 1995).

Orange-crowned Warbler *Vermivora celata* (Say)

STATUS: Fairly common to common migrant. Casual winter visitor.

OCCURRENCE: The Orange-crowned Warbler has been observed in 20 counties: Briscoe, Carson, Castro, Collingsworth, Dallam, Donley, Gray, Hall, Hansford, Hartley, Hemphill, Hutchinson, Lipscomb, Moore, Oldham, Parmer, Potter, Randall, Roberts, and Wheeler. Oberholser (1974) shows it in two. It has been recorded in every month except July.

The Orange-crowned Warbler is one of the more common warbler migrants. My records show that 6 percent of all warblers seen were of this species, following the Yellow-rumped (51%), Wilson's (19%), and Yellow (12%). Its normal arrival and departure dates in spring range from the third week in April to the second week in May, the extreme dates being for a single bird in Amarillo, 30 March 1953, and one in PDCSP, 4 June 1976. In contrast to those in spring, fall migrants are more evenly distributed. The normal dates for arrival and departure range from the last week of August or first week of September to the third or fourth week of October, the extreme dates being one at BLNWR, 14 August 1966, and one in Amarillo, Randall County, 22–25 November 1989. There have been only four other November sightings. It is in fall that the highest number seen in a single day has been posted, a group of 45 birds moving through Lake McClellan, Gray County, 7 October 1981. The seven-day periods of greatest abundance are 30 April–6 May and 2–8 October. My records also show that 49.4 percent of all orange-crowneds were recorded in spring, 50.2 percent in fall, and

0.4 percent in winter. No other warbler species except the Yellow-rumped Warbler displays such an even seasonal distribution.

Although Orange-crowned Warblers winter fairly regularly on the South Plains (LEAS, 1994; Midland Naturalists, 1992), there have been only seven reports of the species in the Panhandle: Amarillo, Randall County, 4 December 1963; Lake Theo, Caprock Canyons SP, Briscoe County, 1 January 1980, 30 December 1982 (3), and 1 January 1997; Blue West, Lake Meredith Recreation Area, Moore County, 25 January 1995; Thompson Park, Amarillo, Potter County, 26 January 1996 (2); Amarillo, Randall County, 3 February–23 March 1998.

The Texas Panhandle is a meeting ground for both the eastern race (*celata*) and a western race (*orestera*) of the Orange-crowned Warbler, and much variation in plumages may be observed, ranging from drab olive-gray for *celata* to olive-yellow for *orestera*. A few individuals have been reported of so pronounced a yellow that observers were led to speculate that they may have been the far western race, *lutescens*.

SPECIMENS: Oberholser (1974) shows specimens of *celata* collected in Potter and Randall counties but fails to name the collections in which they reside.

Nashville Warbler *Vermivora ruficapilla* (Wilson)

STATUS: Uncommon to fairly common migrant.

OCCURRENCE: The Nashville Warbler has been recorded in 14 Texas Panhandle counties: Armstrong, Briscoe, Castro, Donley, Gray, Hemphill, Hutchinson, Moore, Oldham, Parmer, Potter, Randall, Roberts, and Wheeler. Oberholser (1974) shows it in three. It has been seen in the periods April–May and August–November.

The Nashville is one of the earliest of the warbler species to return in spring. It can be looked for in the third week of April, and by the last week of May it is usually gone. The extreme dates are for one at Lake Tanglewood, Randall County, 2 April 1967, and one in Amarillo, Potter County, 24 May 1963. Fall birds begin arriving in early September and continue through the third week of October. There are two August observations, the earliest one bird at BLNWR, 20 August 1989, and two November observations, the latest for two in Amarillo, Potter County, 7 November 1978.

Pulich (1988) speaks of the Nashville Warbler as being more common in north-central Texas in fall than in spring. The opposite is true for the study area, where 65 percent of all Nashvilles have been reported in spring, the seven-day period of greatest abundance being 1–7 May. Unlike most warbler migrants, the Nashville shows no peaks or valleys in its fall passage, as illustrated by the three seven-day periods of greatest abundance: 4–10 September (17%); 20–26 September (22%); 4–10 October (21%).

Virginia's Warbler *Vermivora virginiae* (Baird)

STATUS: Rare migrant.

OCCURRENCE: The Virginia's Warbler has been found in four counties: Carson, Castro, Potter and Randall.

This warbler has been recorded 31 times in spring (19 April–16 May) and six times in fall (26 August–7 October). Normally only one or two birds will be seen in a day. Exceptional were 8+ at the Palo Duro Club near Canyon, Randall County, 2–3 May 1964. Even more so were "at least a dozen" at Amarillo, 1 May 1967 (Williams, 1967). A review of the records shows that numbers in fact were four birds on 3 May, one on 4 May, and two on 5 May.

The Virginia's Warbler is a summer resident in the mountains of New Mexico almost statewide and occasionally a migrant on the eastern plains (Hubbard, 1978). One "was seen among the scrub oaks in the crater of Capulin Mountain Natl'l Monument [Union County], N. Mex., June 11," 1970 (Williams, 1970). The species is known to breed in the higher elevations of northeastern New Mexico, and one would think more would stray into the Texas Panhandle. However, the Virginia's Warbler winters mainly in western Mexico and its migratory pathway lies through mountains, not the adjacent lowlands (Dunn and Garrett, 1997). Perhaps more intensive birding in the far western counties during the appropriate seasons would turn up more in the study area. In Texas, it is an uncommon migrant in the Trans-Pecos and a rare summer resident in the Davis and Guadalupe mountains (TOS, 1995).

SPECIMENS: There is a specimen taken in Potter County (26 August 1978, TCWC).

Northern Parula *Parula americana* (Linnaeus)

STATUS: Rare migrant.

OCCURRENCE: The Northern Parula has been recorded in Hutchinson, Moore, Oldham, Parmer, Potter, and Randall counties of the Texas Panhandle. It has been seen 28 March–28 May, once in June, and 29 August–25 October. All but five of the sightings occurred in spring. This conforms to Dunn and Garrett's (1997) assertion that the Northern Parula in fall migration "is strongly biased toward the Atlantic Coast."

Unless otherwise noted in the listing that follows, a single bird was recorded in each instance: *1957*—Amarillo, Potter County, 20 May. *1958*—Amarillo, Randall County, 14 April. *1961*—Parmer County, 28 and 30 April and 6 June. *1963*—Amarillo, Potter County, 9 and 14 April. *1966*—Amarillo and BLNWR, 7 April; BLNWR, 24 April. *1967*—Randall County, 28 and 31 March; Lake Tanglewood, Randall County, 1 April; Amarillo, Potter County, 2 April. *1969*—two at BLNWR, 26 April, and one, 27 April and 9 May. *1970*—Amarillo, Randall County, 14 May; BLNWR, 29 August and 7 September. *1971*—Amarillo 4 and 28 May; BLNWR,

6 May. *1973*—BLNWR, 6 and 17 May. *1976*—Amarillo, Randall County, 7 April. *1979*—Amarillo, Randall County, 29 April. *1982*—BLNWR, 23 May. *1983*—BLNWR, 29 April. *1984*—BLNWR, 29 April. *1990*—Vega, Oldham County, 1, 4, and 7 May. *1991*—PDCSP, 17 April. *1992*—PDCSP, 30 March. *1993*—PDCSP, 5 and 8 April; Vega, Oldham County, 5 May; BLNWR 8, 14, and 23 May. *1994*—Canyon, Randall County, 25 October. *1996*—Amarillo, Randall County, 17 April. *1997*—PDCSP, 29 April; Vega, Oldham County, 12 May; near Dumas, Moore County, 22 September. In addition, the species has been seen in Hutchinson County, but details are lacking.

The Northern Parula is a common migrant and summer resident in eastern Texas (TOS, 1995).

Yellow Warbler *Dendroica petechia* (Linnaeus)

STATUS: Common migrant and rare summer visitor.

OCCURRENCE: The Yellow Warbler has been recorded in every county except Childress and Sherman and would be in them with better coverage. Oberholser (1974) shows it in six: Armstrong, Deaf Smith, Oldham, Parmer, Potter, and Randall. It has been seen from April to October.

The Yellow Warbler is the third most common warbler species in the study area (12%), following the Yellow-rumped (51%) and Wilson's (19%). It arrives in spring later than most others, rarely before the first week of May—(five April records, the earliest for a single bird at Lake Marvin, Hemphill County, 24 April 1954, and Amarillo, Randall County, 24 April 1964)—and may still be rather common during the last week of the month. My records show an average late date of 27 May. Returning birds in fall can be expected in early or mid-August, the earliest a single bird at Amarillo, Randall County, 1 August 1998; this warbler is rarely encountered past mid-September, a notable exception being one at BLNWR, 2 October 1983.

The most Yellow Warblers recorded in a single outing were 50+ in Amarillo cemeteries, 11 May 1967 and 8 September 1969; 35+ at BLNWR, 29 August 1975, and 30, 16 May 1982; and 40+ at Lake Rita Blanca, Hartley County, 16 May 1993. My records reveal that 72 percent of all Yellow Warblers were recorded in spring. The seven-day period of greatest abundance in spring is 12–18 May and in fall 23–29 August.

NESTING: The summer status of the Yellow Warbler in the Texas Panhandle has changed dramatically since mid-century. Prior to then it was classified by most observers as rather common. McCauley (1877) found the species "very common among the groves occurring near the upper part of Red River and heads of its tributaries. . . . The birds were nesting." He collected a nest with three eggs in Red River Canyon (Palo Duro Canyon), Armstrong County, 30 May 1876, and another with two eggs in Cañoncito Blanco (South Ceta Canyon), Randall County, 3 June. Hibbets et al. (1926–36) gave its status as "spring, summer and fall." Carlander (1933) reported a "nest with young and first brood still around" at an unnamed point sometime between 18 and 24 July 1933: "I found a nest with young 12 feet up in tree at Palisaides [sic]. The first brood of young birds was still in the vicinity." This was near Canyon, Randall County. Carlander later (1934) classified the Yellow Warbler as a "fairly common summer resident where there is underbrush and trees." Stevenson (1942) spoke of it as a "summer resident along wooded streams of the canyons and plains," and Hawkins (1945) considered it a "fairly common summer resident of the eastern Panhandle; rare in the western Panhandle. A pair appeared to be nesting at Palo Duro Club on June 10, 1945." This locality is also near Canyon. These reports are possibly the basis for Johnsgard (1979) showing the Yellow Warbler as nesting throughout the study area. This is no longer true, as the last reported breeding was a nest with three young and one egg found at Lake McClellan, Gray County, 23 June 1956 (P. Acord).

Since the late 1950s there have been only a few summer sightings: *1969*—one in Amarillo, Potter County, 29 July. *1977*—two singing males at Lake Marvin, Hemphill County, 14 June; a singing male at Lake Tanglewood, Randall County, 3 July. *1984*—a singing male in the Kiowa Creek area of northwest Lipscomb County, 6 June. *1986*—a singing male along with a female at BLNWR, 1 June. *1988*—a singing male, 4 June, at the Lipscomb County site of 1984. *1989*—a singing male at Lake Tanglewood, Randall County, 20 June. *1990*—a singing male in Amarillo, Potter County, 20 June. *1992*—a male in southwest Castro County, 1 and 2 June; a singing male approximately 10.5 miles east of Texline, Dallam County, 13 June. *1995*—a singing male at Boys Ranch, Oldham County, 1 June. *1996*—two singing males in territorial dispute on the Taylor Lakes WMA, Donley County, 17 June. Yellow Warblers are not uncommon throughout much of the study area in late May. It has always been assumed that they were migrants; however, the possibility that a few may remain to nest should not be discounted, particularly those found in areas where the species is known to have nested in the past.

Sutton (1967) discusses the "puzzlingly spotty" distribution of summering Yellow Warblers in Oklahoma. He points out that nesting begins in early May (11 May) while migration is under way, and that while orchards, shade trees, and shrubbery in towns are utilized in central and eastern Oklahoma for nesting, the species prefers cottonwoods in the wild areas of the west. The counties in western Oklahoma where nesting has been found are Cimarron, Woodward, Ellis, and Roger Mills, but not in recent years. Not far west of the study area, "highs were 50+ pairs of Yellow Warblers" in the Tucumcari Lake area of Quay County, New Mexico, in the summer of 1987 (Hubbard, 1987).

SPECIMENS: Oberholser (1974) refers to specimens (one each) collected in Oldham, Randall, and Armstrong counties and assigns them to the western race *morcomi*. He makes reference to the eggs collected by McCauley but not the specimens. McCauley collected an adult male on 17 May 1876 at "Mulberry Creek" (Armstrong County), an adult female on 26 May at "Palo Duro" (Randall County), and two adult males on 6 June at "Cañoncito Blanco" (Randall County). The present whereabouts of his specimens is unknown.

Chestnut-sided Warbler *Dendroica pensylvanica* (Linnaeus)

STATUS: Rare migrant.

OCCURRENCE: The Chestnut-sided Warbler has been recorded in six counties—Castro, Moore, Oldham, Parmer, Potter, and Randall—and has been seen February, April–May, and September–October. Spring dates range from 29 April to 29 May and fall dates from 1 September to 9 October.

The following is a listing of all reported sightings, a single bird in each instance unless otherwise noted: *1956*—two at Amarillo, Potter County, and one near Canyon, Randall County, 5 May. *1957*—Amarillo, 20 May. *1962*—near Friona, Parmer County, 28 May. *1963*—one in nonbreeding plumage in PDCSP, 15 February; Amarillo, Potter County, 5 May. *1965*—Amarillo, 9 May. *1967*—Amarillo, 7 May and 17 September. *1967*—Amarillo, Potter County, 7 and 11 May; Amarillo, Randall County, 15 May and 17–19 September. *1968*—BLNWR, 7 May. *1969*—BLNWR, 4 May. *1970*—two at BLNWR, 17 May; Amarillo, 1 September. *1973*—BLNWR and PDCSP, 11 May. *1974*—BLNWR, 26 May; Amarillo, Potter County, 14–15 and 23 September. *1975*—BLNWR, 18 May. *1976*—BLNWR, 9 May; McBride Canyon, Potter County, 17 May. *1978*—near Canyon, 29 April; near Lake Tanglewood, Randall County, 14 May; BLNWR, 21 May. *1982*—BLNWR, 19 September. *1985*—BLNWR, 16 May. *1988*—Amarillo, Potter County, 29 May. *1989*—PDCSP, 9 October. *1992*—Castro County, 14 May; Vega, Oldham County, 25 September. *1993*—Vega, Oldham County, 7 May. *1995*—BLNWR, 12 May; Lake Tanglewood, Randall County, 21 May. *1996*—BLNWR, 20 May; Amarillo, Randall County, 21 May.

There is one other out-of-season report from the region: one recorded on the Lubbock CBC, 17 December 1994. For an October sighting for Moore County, details are lacking.

The Chestnut-sided Warbler is an uncommon to locally common migrant in the eastern half of Texas (TOS, 1995). Specimens have been taken in nearby Cimarron and Harper counties, Oklahoma (Sutton, 1967).

Magnolia Warbler *Dendroica magnolia* (Wilson)

STATUS: Rare migrant.

OCCURRENCE: The Magnolia Warbler has been recorded in seven Texas Panhandle counties: Castro, Dallam, Hartley, Moore, Oldham, Potter, and Randall. It has been seen May–June and August–October. Spring dates range from 2 May to 2 June and fall dates from 7 August to 27 October.

The following listing includes all reported sightings, a single bird in each instance unless otherwise noted: *1953*—Amarillo, Potter County, 29 September. *1954*—Amarillo, Potter County, 27 September. *1963*—Amarillo, Potter County, 19 May. *1965*—Amarillo, 6 May. *1967*—Amarillo, Potter County, 12 and 31 May; BLNWR, 14 May. *1968*—Amarillo, Potter County, 2 May; BLNWR, 16 May; PDCSP, 23 May; Canadian River, Potter County, 29 September. *1969*—BLNWR, 25 May. *1970*—BLNWR, 9 and 30 May. *1974*—BLNWR, 22 September; Amarillo, 6 October. *1976*—Amarillo, Potter County, 19 May. *1977*—Reynolds Ranch, Rita Blanca Creek, Hartley County, 5 September; Randall County, 27 October. *1978*—BLNWR, 21 and 28 May. *1980*—Palo Duro Club near Canyon, Randall County, 3 May. *1981*—BLNWR, 10 May. *1983*—BLNWR, 24 September. *1984*—near Dumas, Moore County, 3 May. *1985*—BLNWR, 16 May. *1991*—BLNWR, 21 May. *1992*—BLNWR, 8 May; Castro County, 4 October. *1993*—BLNWR, 8 May. *1994*—Amarillo, Randall County, 2 June. *1996*—Thompson Grove Picnic Area northeast of Texline, Dallam County, 3 June; Amarillo, Randall County, 29 September. *1997*—Amarillo, Randall County, 2, 19, and 21 May. *1998*—Amarillo, Randall County, 21 May; PDCSP, 7 August.

The Magnolia Warbler is an uncommon to locally common migrant in the eastern half of Texas (TOS, 1995). Specimens have been taken in nearby Cimarron and Ellis counties, Oklahoma (Sutton, 1967).

Cape May Warbler *Dendroica tigrina* (Gmelin)

STATUS: Casual migrant.

OCCURRENCE: The Cape May Warbler has been found in four counties: Moore, Oldham, Potter, and Randall. With the exception of one sighting in October, all others occurred in April and May.

Hibbets et al. (1926–36) were the first to report a Cape May Warbler in the study area: one on 16 October 1936 in Canyon, Randall County. Twenty years later another was seen near Canyon, 5 May 1956. Another sixteen years elapsed before a male was found in Dumas, Moore County, 1–7 May 1972 (TP-RF). The next occurrence involved three birds: a male at the Palo Duro Club near Canyon, Randall County, 25–26 April, a male at BLNWR, 28 April, and a male in Amarillo, Potter County, 30 April, all in 1976. Sixteen years elapsed before one was again seen, a male in Vega, Oldham County, 14 May 1992.

The Cape May Warbler, a rarity anywhere in Texas, is found more often in the eastern half of the state (TOS, 1995). There are three records from nearby Cimarron County in the Oklahoma Panhandle (Baumgartner and Baumgartner, 1992).

Black-throated Blue Warbler *Dendroica caerulescens* (Gmelin)

STATUS: Rare migrant.

OCCURRENCE: The Black-throated Blue Warbler has been found in six counties—Briscoe, Castro, Gray, Hemphill, Potter, and Randall—in spring, 2–30 May, and in fall, 22 August–20 October. Three times as many have been seen in fall as in spring.

The following is a listing of all reported sightings, a single bird in each instance unless otherwise noted: *1954*—Amarillo, Potter County, 30 September. *1955*—near Canyon, Randall County, 19 October. *1956*—Amarillo, Potter County, 23–24 September. *1964*—at BLNWR, two on 2 May, one on 9 September, two on 11 October. *1965*—BLNWR, 4 October. *1966*—BLNWR, 10 and 13 October. *1968*—two at BLNWR, 6 October. *1971*—Amarillo, Potter County, 12 October. *1974*—BLNWR, 12 May and 21 September; Amarillo, Randall County, 19 October. *1982*—BLNWR, 16 May. *1983*—BLNWR, 30 May. *1984*—BLNWR, 9 September. *1986*—BLNWR, 19 October. *1991*—Amarillo, Randall County, 20 October. *1992*—Castro County, 30 September. *1993*—Lake Tanglewood, Randall County, 8 May. *1996*—Canyon, Randall County, 16 May; Pampa, Gray County, 18 October. *1998*—Lake Marvin, Hemphill County, 22 August; Caprock Canyons SP, Briscoe County, 17 October.

The Black-throated Blue Warbler is a rare migrant in the eastern half of Texas, "more numerous in fall than in spring" (TOS, 1995). A specimen (mummy) secured in Cimarron County in the Oklahoma Panhandle was assigned to the northern race *D. c. caerulescens* (Sutton, 1967).

Yellow-rumped Warbler *Dendroica coronata* (Linnaeus)

STATUS: Common to abundant migrant. Rare to uncommon winter visitor.

OCCURRENCE: The Yellow-rumped Warbler has been recorded in every county except Childress, Ochiltree, and Sherman, and would be in them with better coverage.

The most common of the area's warblers (51%), the Yellow-rumped Warbler was formerly considered two separate species—"Audubon's Warbler" and "Myrtle Warbler." Both races occur in the study area, the Audubon's outnumbering the Myrtle in the central sector at a ratio of 3:1; both may be observed in discrete as well as mixed flocks.

Returning Yellow-rumped Warblers in spring begin trickling through in late

Yellow-rumped Warbler

March and early April, but the main push begins in mid-month. The seven-day period of greatest abundance is 1–7 May (37%). Rarely is one seen past the third week of May: I have recorded only twelve later ones. A very few returning fall birds can be expected in early September, but significant numbers begin showing up in mid-month. I have recorded only seven birds during the first week of September. The earliest fall sighting is an Audubon's in Amarillo, Potter County, 25 August 1976. Fall migration occurs over a longer time span than does that of spring. The seven-day period of greatest abundance is 1–7 October (24%). Most are gone by mid-November.

The Audubon's lingers later in spring than does the Myrtle: the average departure date for the former 18 May and for the latter 10 May. The opposite takes place in fall. On average the Audubon's first appears on 16 September, the Myrtle on 2 October. These dates are somewhat clouded by the difficulty of correctly assigning immature birds and birds in fall and winter plumage to the proper race. Yellow-rumps are distributed fairly evenly between spring (52%) and fall (46%)—the remaining 2 percent occur in winter.

At times the Yellow-rumped Warbler can be found in large numbers. On 6 May 1956 they were "so common as to be found migrating in fields with Lark Buntings" (P. Acord); 100+ were seen in Memorial Park Cemetery, Amarillo, Potter County, 13 October 1963, 250+ in Llano Cemetery, Amarillo, Randall County, 2 October 1967, and 250+ on the Reynolds Ranch on Rita Blanca Creek, Hartley County, 5 May 1990. Of the 1990 assemblage, it was estimated that 60 percent were Myrtles and 40 percent Audubon's, this ratio a reverse of what was expected. I watched 50 or more at sunrise at BLNWR on 16 October 1994 as they left a night roost in a stand of tamarisk.

The Yellow-rumped Warbler is not reported every winter, as attested to by the CBCs. Of 132 counts, it was recorded on 37, and seldom more than a dozen on any one. A remarkable 50 were tallied on the Amarillo CBC of 20 December 1987 and 62 on 27 December 1997. Previously, 13 at Lake Tanglewood in the last week of December 1971, and "at least 12" in Thompson Park, Amarillo, Potter County, 2 February 1958, were thought unusually high numbers. The species was present in five years of a Winter-Bird Population Study conducted in the PDCSP (Seyffert, 1968–78). Rarely is one reported in a far northern county: one at Lake Marvin, Hemphill County, 3 February 1995; one in Texline, Dallam County, 7 January 1998. There have been several summer sightings of interest, the first that of Hawkins (1945), who cites a singing Audubon's that he and W. L. Thompson encountered "at Palo Duro," 17 June 1945. A "few" lingered in Amarillo, Potter County (Ellwood Park) until 2 June 1957. Unaccountable was what appeared to be a subadult in Amarillo, Potter County, 6 July 1986.

SPECIMENS: Oberholser (1974) names a specimen taken in Randall County and assigns it to the "Rocky Mountain" race of Audubon's, *D. a. memorabilis*. Its present whereabouts is not given. There are two specimens of *auduboni*, along with one of unspecified race, taken in Randall County (30 September and 7 October 1939, and May 1970, WTAMU).

Black-throated Gray Warbler *Dendroica nigrescens* (Townsend)

STATUS: Rare migrant.

OCCURRENCE: The Black-throated Gray Warbler has been found in four counties: Castro, Potter, Randall, and Roberts. It has been seen in the periods April–May and August–October, plus once in December.

Sightings of the Black-throated Gray Warbler are almost evenly divided between spring and fall. The spring dates range from 9 April to 21 May and fall dates from 24 August to 2 October. The date published for the bird on the BLNWR, 8 August 1974 (Williams, 1975), was in error; the correct date was 8 September.

The following is a listing of all reported sightings, in each instance a single bird unless otherwise noted: *1954*—two in Amarillo, Potter County, 13 April. *1955*—Canyon, Randall County, 22 and 28 April; near Canyon, 27 April. *1956*—Amarillo, Potter County, 23 and 30 September and 2 October. *1957*—Amarillo, Potter County, 25 April. *1964*—five at BLNWR, 29 August, and one, 26 September. *1965*—four at BLNWR, 6 September. *1966*—BLNWR, 17 April. *1967*—near Canyon, Randall County, 5 May; two at BLNWR, 26 April, and one, 21 May. *1968*—BLNWR, 6 May; Amarillo, Potter County, 23 and 29 September. *1969*—Amarillo, 9 April. *1970*—two at BLNWR 7 September. *1974*—Amarillo, Randall County, 24 August; two at BLNWR, 8 September, and one, 15 September. *1976*—BLNWR, 5 September. *1977*—Amarillo, Randall County, 9 May; BLNWR, 4 September. *1979*—PDCSP, 2 December. *1980*—Miami, Roberts County, 16–18 April. *1983*—two in Amarillo, Potter County, 16 April; BLNWR, 15 May. *1986*—BLNWR, 12 September. *1992*—Castro County, 26 and 30 August. *1993*—BLNWR, 8 May and 2 October. *1994*—BLNWR, 7 May. *1998*—BLNWR, 17 September.

The December sighting was unexpected as the Black-throated Gray Warbler winters from coastal southern California, southern Arizona, and (rarely) southern Texas south to Oaxaca and Veracruz, Mexico (AOU, 1983).

Black-throated Green Warbler *Dendroica virens* (Gmelin)

STATUS: Rare migrant.

OCCURRENCE: The Black-throated Green Warbler has been seen in nine counties: Briscoe, Castro, Gray, Hartley, Hutchinson, Oldham, Parmer, Potter, and Randall. It has been recorded in the periods April–May and August–November.

For this warbler 79 percent of all sightings in the study area have occurred in the fall of the year, 62 percent of those in October. The seven-day period of greatest abundance is 5–11 October. Fall dates range from one in Amarillo, 21 August 1970—the only August record—to one at BLNWR, 13 November 1983. There is but one other November sighting: a single bird in Amarillo, Potter County, 8 November 1959. The spring dates range from one at BLNWR, 21 April 1974, to one at the same location, 21 May 1978. My records (1964–96) show that I failed to record the species in only nine of the years.

The Black-throated Green Warbler is a common migrant in the eastern half of the state (TOS, 1995). Specimens have been taken in Cimarron, Beaver, and Harper counties of the Oklahoma Panhandle (Sutton, 1967).

Townsend's Warbler *Dendroica townsendi* (Townsend)

STATUS: Rare migrant.

OCCURRENCE: The Townsend's Warbler has been recorded in nine counties: Castro, Dallam, Hartley, Moore, Oldham, Parmer, Potter, Randall, and Roberts. It has been seen April–May, August–October, and once in December.

Records show that 70 percent of all Townsend's Warblers have been observed in the fall, 72 percent of those in September. The spring dates range from one on 22 April 1984 to one on 22 May 1966 and the fall dates from four on 27 August 1978 to one on 25 October 1970, all at BLNWR. Exceptional was a single bird observed near Dumas, Moore County, 4–5 December 1997.

The Townsend's Warbler is normally encountered singly or in groups of no more than two or three birds. It was reported as "seen in numbers" at Canyon, Randall County, 22 September, and at Amarillo, 24 September and 2–14 October 1956 (Baumgartner, 1957). The species was classified as "fairly common" in southwestern Castro County, 12, 14, and 16 September 1993. On 16 September 1984, six males and four females were observed on the BLNWR.

Hermit Warbler *Dendroica occidentalis* (Townsend)

STATUS: Vagrant migrant.

OCCURRENCE: There is but one record of the Hermit Warbler in the Texas Panhandle, a single bird observed in southwestern Castro County, 15 August 1993 (C. D. Littlefield). Although this may seem early, Hubbard (1978) says that autumn migration in New Mexico is "mainly in August."

All other regional sightings of the Hermit Warbler have been reported in spring: one on the Muleshoe NWR, Bailey County, 10 May 1980, the first documented record east of the Pecos River (TP-RF), and another at the same location, 7 May 1984 (*fide* C. Stogner); one in Lubbock, 12 May 1993 (*fide* C. Stogner), and another, 4 May 1995 (Lasley and Sexton, 1995b). The Muleshoe refuge is only a short distance south of Castro County. Ligon (1961) names the species on the "Clayton Area Check-list of Birds" (Union County, New Mexico), without details.

The Hermit Warbler is a summer resident of the far western United States and a migrant in the southwestern states (AOU, 1983). It is but a rare migrant in Texas, mostly in the Trans-Pecos (TOS, 1995).

Blackburnian Warbler *Dendroica fusca* (Müller)

STATUS: Rare migrant.

OCCURRENCE: The Blackburnian Warbler has been found in seven counties: Armstrong, Castro, Hutchinson, Moore, Oldham, Potter, and Randall. Oberholser (1974) shows it in two. It has been seen in May, September, and October.

Records show that 79 percent of all Blackburnian Warblers found in the study area have been seen in spring, the dates ranging from 3 to 30 May. There have been only six sightings in fall, the early date ambiguous (probably early September), the late date 4 October.

The following is a listing of all reported sightings, in each instance a single bird unless otherwise noted: *1932*—Carlander (1933) reported seeing one at

"Hall's Ranch" sometime between 13 August and 4 September. The location of this ranch is thought to be in Armstrong County. *1958*—Amarillo, Potter County, 12–13 May. *1965*—four at BLNWR, 22 May. *1966*—BLNWR, 7 May. *1967*—near Canyon, Randall County, 5 May, BLNWR, 14 May, PDCSP, 15 May. *1968*—BLNWR, 10, 12, and 19 May. *1970*—two at BLNWR, 30 May. *1973*—near Dumas, Moore County, 15 May; Amarillo 8 September. *1976*—near Canyon, Randall County, 6 May and 8 September; BLNWR, 9 and 30 May. *1978*—two at BLNWR, 21 May. *1980*—Borger, Hutchinson County, 20–21 May. *1981*—Canyon, Randall County, 15 September. *1983*—Amarillo, Randall County, 8 September and 4 October. *1987*—Amarillo, Potter County, 24 May. *1990*—Amarillo, Potter County, 6 May. *1991*—BLNWR, 21 May. *1992*—Castro County, 26 May. *1995*—Vega, Oldham County, 3 May. *1997*—Vega, Oldham County, 12 May.

The Blackburnian Warbler is a rare to uncommon migrant in the eastern half of Texas (TOS, 1995). A specimen was taken in nearby Cimarron County, Oklahoma (Wood and Schnell, 1984).

Yellow-throated Warbler *Dendroica dominica* (Linnaeus)

STATUS: Casual migrant.

OCCURRENCE: Potter and Randall are the only counties where the Yellow-throated Warbler has been recorded.

Considering its present-day rarity, the status of the Yellow-throated Warbler in the study area in the late nineteenth century as reported by McCauley (1877) is unexpected: "It is very probable that this species is not uncommon, though but few were noted in the localities of which *D. aestiva* [Yellow Warbler] seemed to have possession. More prevalent on Palo Duro than any other locality." His observations were made during May and June. Did McCauley perhaps misidentify his birds? Surprisingly, he did not name the "Audubon's" Warbler, a race of the Yellow-rumped Warbler common in the area today, especially during May—a species hard to overlook and one that also has a yellow throat. Other early observers did not name the species in their accounts. There have been four reported sightings since McCauley's: one in Amarillo, Randall County, 8–11 April 1956 and 24 April 1982; one at BLNWR, 3 May 1964 and 8 May 1991.

The Yellow-throated Warbler is a rare to common resident in the eastern half of Texas (TOS, 1995), and nowhere is it resident to the north of the study area. There is only one record from Cimarron County in the Oklahoma Panhandle (Baumgartner and Baumgartner, 1992). One was found to the south in Lamb County, 27–28 April 1994 (Lasley and Sexton, 1994b), only a few yards from the Castro County line. Considering the paucity of sightings in the Texas Panhandle and surrounding areas, surprisingly large numbers have been recorded westward in Colorado, Arizona, and California (Dunn and Garrett, 1997).

Grace's Warbler *Dendroica graciae* Baird

STATUS: Vagrant migrant.

OCCURRENCE: There have been but two reports of the Grace's Warbler in the Texas Panhandle, both without details: one in Canyon, Randall County, on an unspecified date in spring 1955 (Baumgartner, 1955) and one in Hemphill County, 12 April 1981. This is a species that can easily be confused with the similar Yellow-throated Warbler and Yellow-rumped Warbler, and for which a specimen, photograph, or detailed notes would be desirable in order to place it on a firmer bases as a valid species in the study area.

There are no records of Grace's Warbler in Oklahoma. It is on Krehbiel's "rare visitor" list for the Clayton area, Union County, New Mexico (Ligon, 1961; Weske, 1968). Although Hubbard (1978) says it summers statewide in the mountainous areas of that state, he does not acknowledge any sightings for the eastern plains. A first was one on the Muleshoe NWR, Bailey County, 15 May 1978 (*fide* C. Stogner). In Texas it is an uncommon resident in the higher elevations of the Davis and Guadalupe mountains and an uncommon migrant in the Trans-Pecos (TOS, 1995).

Pine Warbler *Dendroica pinus* (Wilson)

STATUS: Casual migrant.

OCCURRENCE: The Pine Warbler has been found in Gray, Potter, and Randall counties and has been recorded March, May, September, October, and December.

There have been ten reported sightings of the Pine Warbler in the study area, the first an out-of-season bird observed repeatedly at a feeder in Amarillo, Randall County, 5–10 December 1963. The following is a listing of subsequent sightings, a single bird in each instance: *1968*—BLNWR, 10 May; *1974*—Amarillo, Potter County, 18 October; *1976*—BLNWR, 9 May; *1980*—BLNWR, 11 September. *1982*—Ceta Glen, South Ceta Canyon, Randall County, 31 October; *1983*—a singing male (in a pine tree!) in Amarillo, Potter County, 12 March, and BLNWR, 25 September; *1990*—Pampa, Gray County, 6–12 May; *1992*—PDCSP, 21 October.

Four sightings have been reported on the South Plains, two in winter: Lubbock, 11 January 1975 (Williams, 1975); winter of 1987–88 (Williams, 1988); 16 November 1990 (Lasley and Sexton, 1991); 14–19 September 1992 (Lasley and Sexton, 1992). The Pine Warbler is an uncommon to common winter resident in the eastern third of the state (TOS, 1995), and while it is rare in north-central Texas, Pulich (1988) says there was a "rash of valid winter records" in the 1980s.

Prairie Warbler *Dendroica discolor* (Vieillot)

STATUS: Casual migrant.

OCCURRENCE: Despite its name, the Prairie Warbler is not a bird of the western plains. There have been but five reported sightings in the Texas Panhandle: one in Canyon, Randall County, 3 May 1955; one observed repeatedly southwest of Dumas, Moore County, 4–9 May 1975 (TP-RF); an immature in Pampa, Gray County, 21 September 1981; a male in Amarillo, Randall County, 2 September 1993; and a first fall male at BLNWR, 15 September 1994.

The Prairie Warbler is an uncommon migrant in the eastern half of Texas (TOS, 1995), and Pulich (1988) names but ten records for north-central Texas. Three sightings have been made on the South Plains: one on the Muleshoe NWR, Bailey County, 11 May 1980 (Williams, 1980b); one in Crosby County, 2 September 1980 (Williams, 1981); and one in Lubbock, 28 September 1993 (Lasley and Sexton, 1994b). There is one record for Cimarron County, Oklahoma (Baumgartner and Baumgartner, 1992).

Palm Warbler *Dendroica palmarum* (Gmelin)
STATUS: Casual migrant.

OCCURRENCE: The Palm Warbler has been recorded in four Texas Panhandle counties: Castro, Gray, Potter, and Randall. Sightings have been scattered over a period of seven months, as follows, a single bird in each instance: *1956*—Canyon Country Club, Randall County, 6–8 May. *1962*—BLNWR, 23 August. *1965*—Amarillo, 10 May. *1974*—BLNWR, 19 May. *1978*—BLNWR, 23 November. *1980*—Lake McClellan, Gray County, 27 April. *1981*—Amarillo, Potter County, 10 May. *1987*—BLNWR, 28 October. *1990*—Amarillo, Randall County, 6 September. *1992*—Castro County, 29 September. *1994*—Pampa, Gray County, 15–28 January, and Amarillo, Randall County, 11 May. *1995*—BLNWR, 26 April. *1996*—Amarillo, Randall County, 1 September. Both the "Yellow" (*hypochrysea*) and "Western" (*palmarum*) have been recorded.

There are three sightings from the South Plains: 23 October 1986 (Williams, 1987); 7 May (Lasley and Sexton, 1994b); and 16 August (*fide* C. Stogner) 1994, all in Lubbock. The Palm Warbler is an uncommon migrant in the eastern half of Texas, west to the Pecos River (TOS, 1995). A specimen was collected in Cimarron County of the Oklahoma Panhandle (Wood and Schnell, 1984); one was observed in Custer County, 12 November 1988 (Grzybowski, 1988), and one in Cimarron County, 28 April 1989 (Grzybowski, 1989).

Bay-breasted Warbler *Dendroica castanea* (Wilson)
STATUS: Rare migrant.

OCCURRENCE: The Bay-breasted Warbler has been recorded in three counties of the Texas Panhandle: Moore, Potter, and Randall. It has been seen April–May in spring, and August–October in fall. The following is a listing of all sightings, a single bird in each instance unless otherwise noted: *1956*—Amarillo, Potter

County, 5 May. *1963*—Amarillo, Potter County, 5 and 19 May, and Lake Tanglewood, Randall County, 24 May. *1964*—Amarillo, Randall County, 19 September. *1967*—Amarillo, Potter County, and near Canyon, Randall County, 5 May; BLNWR, 14 and 21 May. *1968*—BLNWR, 19 May. *1970*—PDCSP, Amarillo, and BLNWR, 9 May. *1972*—Amarillo, 5 May. *1974*—near Canyon, Randall County 26 May; Amarillo, Potter County, 24 August, 18 and 20 October. *1975*—BLNWR, 18 May. *1976*—BLNWR, 26 April; Amarillo, Potter County, 15 May. *1977*—BLNWR, 22 May. *1982*—5–6 at BLNWR, 25 September. *1990*—Amarillo, Randall County, 8 May. *1993*—BLNWR, 23 May. *1995*—BLNWR, 28 April. There are reports of April and May sightings in Moore County, but details are lacking.

The Bay-breasted Warbler is a common to locally abundant spring migrant and an uncommon fall migrant in the eastern half of Texas (TOS, 1995). Three specimens have been taken in Cimarron County of the Oklahoma Panhandle, including a female, 4 June 1936 (Sutton, 1967).

Blackpoll Warbler *Dendroica striata* (Forster)

STATUS: Rare migrant.

OCCURRENCE: The Blackpoll Warbler has been found in five counties: Castro, Oldham, Parmer, Potter, and Randall. With the exception of one October sighting, all have been seen in April and May, the dates ranging from 24 April to 31 May.

The following is a listing of all reported sightings, in each instance a single bird unless otherwise noted: *1955*—Amarillo, Potter County, 25 April. *1959*—Amarillo, Potter County, 29 April. *1961*—near Friona, Parmer County, 29 April. *1964*—Amarillo, Randall County, 24 April. *1966*—BLNWR, 7–8 May. *1967*—Amarillo, 7–10 May. *1968*—two at BLNWR, 7 May; Amarillo, Randall County, and BLNWR, 10 May. *1969*—BLNWR, 31 May. *1970*—BLNWR, 17 and 30 May. *1971*—BLNWR, 20 May. *1973*—BLNWR and Amarillo, Randall County, 11 May; BLNWR, 15 May and 14 October. *1975*—BLNWR, 4 May; Lake Tanglewood, Randall County, 25–26 May. *1976*—McBride Canyon, Lake Meredith National Recreation Area, Potter County, 17 May. *1977*—Amarillo, 3 May. *1979*—Amarillo, Potter County, 1 May. *1983*—near Canyon, Randall County, 4 May, and BLNWR, 7 May. *1984*—two at BLNWR, 6 May. *1986*—BLNWR, 10 May. *1987*—PDCSP, 9 May. *1990*—Amarillo, Potter County, 12 May. *1993*—Castro County, 14 May. *1995*—BLNWR, 27 May. *1997*—Vega, Oldham County, 12 May; Amarillo, Randall County, 13–14 May; BLNWR, 17 May. *1998*—Vega, Oldham County, 3 May; BLNWR, 8–9 May.

The Blackpoll Warbler is an uncommon spring migrant and rare fall migrant in the eastern half of Texas (TOS, 1995). It is of interest that there are only two fall reports of the species for north-central Texas (Pulich, 1988). One reported in Lubbock on 21 September 1980 "constituted a first fall record" (Williams,

1981), and one was banded in Cimarron County, Oklahoma, 3 October 1932 (Sutton, 1974a). Two out-of-season birds reported from nearby areas were one on the Muleshoe NWR, Bailey County, 4 July 1984 (Williams, 1984), and one in Lubbock, 1 March 1994 (*fide* C. Stogner).

Cerulean Warbler *Dendroica cerulea* (Wilson)
STATUS: Vagrant migrant.
OCCURRENCE: There has been but one reported sighting of the Cerulean Warbler in the Texas Panhandle, a single bird at the BLNWR on 11 May 1970 (M. Mayfield). The report does not state whether the bird was a male or a female.

This species is a rare summer resident in extreme northeastern Texas, and a rare to uncommon migrant in other eastern areas of the state (TOS, 1995). Pulich (1988) classified the Cerulean Warbler as "one of the rarest of the warblers that pass through north central Texas," with fewer than 25 records; it is one of the rarest of the "eastern" warblers to appear in all of western North America (Dunn and Garrett, 1997). The species is also one of the most difficult of the warblers to find and identify, for it spends most of its time foraging high in the tree tops; only its white underside is normally exposed to view. The only other regional record is one reported at Lubbock, 27 September 1981 (Williams, 1982).

Black-and-white Warbler *Mniotilta varia* (Linnaeus)
STATUS: Rare to uncommon migrant.
OCCURRENCE: The Black-and-white Warbler has been recorded in 14 counties: Briscoe, Castro, Dallam, Gray, Hansford, Hartley, Hemphill, Moore, Oldham, Parmer, Potter, Randall, Roberts, and Wheeler. It has been seen from March to October.

Sixty-three percent of all Black-and-white Warblers have been seen in spring. Spring birds can be looked for during the second week of April, and rarely is one found past mid-May, the latest date being 22 May 1971 in Amarillo. There are three sightings in March, the earliest being for a single bird in South Ceta Canyon, Randall County, 23–25 March 1963. The seven-day period of greatest abundance is 4–10 May (43%). Most fall birds move through between early and late September, the seven-day period of greatest abundance being 3–9 September (44%). There are eight records for August, the earliest 23 August 1974 in Amarillo, Potter County, and 23 August 1981 at BLNWR, and six for October, the latest 25 October 1992 at BLNWR.

Several summer birds have been encountered. One was in Amarillo, Randall County, in June 1967 (day not specified). A singing male spent the day in Amarillo, Randall County, 20 July 1972, and a female in Amarillo, Potter County, 20 July 1974. Hibbets et al. (1926–36) are the only observers of earlier days to name the species, referring to it as found in "late spring and summer." The Black-and-white Warbler nests no farther west in Oklahoma than Alfalfa, Major, Dewey, Caddo, Comanche, and Love counties (Sutton, 1967) and no farther west in Texas than the north-central area (Pulich, 1988). Sutton (1974a) speaks of two birds seen together in Cimarron County of the Oklahoma Panhandle, 30 May 1970, that "may have been a pair."

SPECIMENS: A specimen is available taken in Randall County (spring 1991, TCWC).

American Redstart *Setophaga ruticilla* (Linnaeus)

STATUS: Rare to uncommon migrant.

OCCURRENCE: The American Redstart has been reported in 14 counties: Briscoe, Castro, Dallam, Donley, Hall, Hartley, Hemphill, Moore, Ochiltree, Oldham, Parmer, Potter, Randall, and Roberts. It has been seen April–June and August–November.

The American Redstart does not arrive early in spring. It normally appears in the second week of May and is gone by the fourth week. Early and late dates and 25 April 1957 (Potter County) and 30 May 1976 and 1982 (BLNWR). The seven-day period of greatest occurrence is 8–14 May (44%). Returning birds in fall can be expected around 1 September, and few are seen past the end of the month. Early and late fall dates are 24 August 1969 (BLNWR) and 1974 (Amarillo) and 31 October 1986 (BLNWR). Extremely late was a male in Caprock Canyons SP, Briscoe County, 13 November 1977. The seven-day period of greatest occurrence is 5–11 September (44%). Migrants are fairly equally distributed between spring (48%) and fall (52%).

There have been three reports of American Redstarts seen in summer. On 14 June 1977, a female was observed at Lake Marvin, Hemphill County, and another redstart in Castro County, 7 June 1990. The Hemphill bird was in a moist, heavily wooded deciduous bottomland; the Castro bird in an isolated woodlot on the plains. On the same day of the redstart discovery at Lake Marvin, an out-of-season singing Red-eyed Vireo and two singing Yellow Warblers were also encountered. The other summer sighting is that of Oberholser (1974), who shows a summer sight record for Potter County without giving details. The American Redstart is not known to nest any nearer the study area than forested eastern Texas (TOS, 1995) and eastern Oklahoma (Sutton, 1967).

Prothonotary Warbler *Protonotaria citrea* (Boddaert)

STATUS: Casual migrant.

OCCURRENCE: The Prothonotary Warbler has been recorded in Briscoe, Hemphill, Potter, and Randall counties. McCauley's (1877) account of meeting with the species in May–June of 1876 provides little information: "Frequenting Wolf

Creek and the Canadian." The encounters presumably took place during the outward journey in early May. The Ruffner expedition left Camp Supply in Indian Territory on 3 May and arrived at Fort Elliott on Sweetwater Creek in present-day Wheeler County on 6 May, crossing Wolf Creek and the Canadian River en route (Hunnius, 1876). These crossings, however, probably lay in what is now northwestern Oklahoma, not the Texas Panhandle. A reference to the Prothonotary Warbler so far west is unexpected, for in Oklahoma today it is found only in the eastern and central portions of the state (Sutton, 1967).

There have been eight twentieth-century sightings of the Prothonotary Warbler in the study area: a male and a female in Llano Cemetery, Amarillo, Randall County, 5–8 May 1967; a singing male at Lake Tanglewood, Randall County, 3 May 1970; 2–4 at the Palo Duro Club near Canyon, Randall County, 29 April 1971; a female at BLNWR, 15 May 1983; a male in Caprock Canyons SP, Briscoe County, 24 April 1990; one in Thompson Park, Amarillo, Potter County, 30 April 1998; a female in Amarillo, Randall County, 5 May 1999; a female at BLNWR, 20 May 1999.

The Prothonotary Warbler is an uncommon to common summer resident and migrant in eastern Texas (TOS, 1995). One was observed in Lubbock, 8 September 1991 (Lasley and Sexton, 1992), and 29 April–4 May 1994 (Lasley and Sexton, 1994b). A specimen was taken in nearby Cimarron County, Oklahoma (Wood and Schnell, 1984), and the species is on the "Clayton Area Check-list of Birds," Union County, New Mexico (Ligon, 1961).

Worm-eating Warbler *Helmitheros vermivorus* (Gmelin)

STATUS: Casual migrant.

OCCURRENCE: The Worm-eating Warbler has been found in Castro, Donley, Hutchinson, and Randall counties (and possibly Hemphill) and has been recorded April, May, and August.

There have been ten reports of this secretive and unobstrusive warbler: *1966*—Amarillo, Randall County, 1 May, and BLNWR, 21 May. *1968*—three at BLNWR, 7 May. *1969*—Amarillo, Randall County, 25 August. *1976*—a stunned bird recovered after flying into a glass door in Borger, Hutchinson County, 22 April. *1977*—BLNWR, 9 May. *1978*—Currie Ranch near Lake Tanglewood, Randall County, 23 April. *1993*—Castro County, 16 May. *1997*—PDCSP and Taylor Lakes WMA, Donley County, 6 May.

McCauley (1877) reported seeing the Worm-eating Warbler at a site possibly located in present-day Hemphill County: "Occasionally noted near the crossing of the Canadian." He implies that several were encountered. The expedition of which he was a member crossed the Canadian River at a point between Camp Supply in Oklahoma and Fort Elliott in Texas.

The Worm-eating Warbler is an uncommon to locally common migrant in the eastern third of Texas, mostly on the coast, south to the Lower Rio Grande Valley (TOS, 1995). A female specimen was taken in Cimarron County, Oklahoma, 15 May 1966 (Sutton, 1967).

Swainson's Warbler *Limnothlypis swainsonii* (Audubon)

STATUS: Vagrant.

OCCURRENCE: The Swainson's Warbler has been found once in the Texas Panhandle. On 17 May 1999, a dead bird was recovered from a cat in Canyon, Randall County (D. Lee; TP-RF).

The Swainson's Warbler is an uncommon to locally common summer resident in the forested eastern third of Texas and an uncommon migrant in the eastern third of the state, mostly on the coast (TOS, 1995). On the South Plains it is classified as "accidental" in April and May (LEAS, 1994).

Ovenbird *Seiurus aurocapillus* (Linnaeus)

STATUS: Rare to uncommon migrant.

OCCURRENCE: The Ovenbird has been recorded in ten counties: Carson, Castro, Dallam, Gray, Hutchinson, Moore, Oldham, Parmer, Potter, and Randall. Only one lies in the eastern sector. It has been seen March–June and September–October.

In spring almost all Ovenbirds have been recorded in May, the seven-day period of greatest abundance being 4–10 May. There is one record for March—Canyon, Randall County, 21 March 1937—and three exist for April. The latest May date is for a single bird at BLNWR, 30 May in both 1970 and 1995. The sole June sighting is for Castro County, 4 June 1991. Fall sightings are evenly spread throughout September, the earliest for a single bird at BLNWR, 1 September 1986. There are three records for October, the latest for one in Amarillo, Randall County, 21 October 1985. Of all sightings, 60 percent are for spring, 40 percent for fall. "Astounding" was an Ovenbird in Lubbock on 16, 19, and 24 December 1981 (Williams, 1982).

The Ovenbird is an uncommon to common migrant in most of the eastern half of Texas and a rare winter resident along the coast, especially in the Lower Rio Grande Valley (TOS, 1995).

SPECIMENS: A specimen was recovered in Randall County (May 1996, WTAMU).

Northern Waterthrush *Seiurus noveboracensis* (Gmelin)

STATUS: Uncommon migrant.

OCCURRENCE: The Northern Waterthrush has been found in ten counties: Castro, Deaf Smith, Donley, Hartley, Hutchinson, Lipscomb, Oldham, Parmer, Potter, and Randall. It has been recorded March through June and in August, September, and November.

Although most spring sightings of the Northern Waterthrush have occurred within the seven-day period 4–10 May, there are three others much earlier. The report of one at Amarillo on 12 March 1969 (Williams, 1969) pertains in fact to two birds found on the Jokerst Ranch south of Amarillo, Randall County. Single birds were found at the Canyon City Club near Canyon, Randall County, 7 April 1956, and in Amarillo, Randall County, 15 April 1996. An unexpectedly late sighting was a singing bird in Amarillo, Randall County, 2 June 1994. Another summer sighting, this one for Parmer County, is shown by Oberholser (1974); however, a check of his files did not disclose any background data (*fide* W. Pulich). Only 31 percent of all sightings have occurred in fall, most of them between mid-August and late September. The early and late dates are for one in Castro County, 6 August 1992, and one at BLNWR, 26 September 1964. The latest occurrence is an isolated one—a single bird at BLNWR, 23 November 1978.

It must be borne in mind in reviewing sightings that the Northern and Louisiana waterthrushes can easily be confused in the field. Concerning March reports of the Northern Waterthrush in north-central Texas, Pulich (1988) questions them on the grounds that the Louisiana is the earlier migrant and the one more likely to occur.

SPECIMENS: Oberholser (1974) names a spring specimen collected in Oldham County without providing details.

Louisiana Waterthrush *Seiurus motacilla* (Vieillot)

STATUS: Casual migrant.

OCCURRENCE: The Louisiana Waterthrush has been found in five Texas Panhandle counties: Hutchinson, Oldham, Parmer, Potter, and Randall. It has occurred March–May and July, September, and October.

The following is a listing of all reported sightings, a single bird in each instance unless otherwise noted: *1939*—Ceta Glen, South Ceta Canyon, Randall County, 30 April. *1956*—near Canyon, Randall County, 28–29 April. *1959*—Amarillo, Potter County, 14 May and 21 September. *1960*—Amarillo, 15 May. *1964*—Amarillo, Potter County, 5–6 May. *1966*—Palo Duro Club near Canyon, Randall County, 25 March. *1967*—two at BLNWR, 3 May. *1968*—a singing bird at BLNWR, 16 and 19 May; Amarillo, 16 August. *1971*—near Friona, Parmer County, 5 September. *1973*—Palo Duro Club, 7 May. *1984*—one at Jim's Lake on Spring Creek, southeastern Hutchinson County, 21 July. *1992*—Amarillo, Randall County, 15 October. *1994*—Vega, Oldham County, 4 and 11 May. *1997*—BLNWR, 17 and 20 May.

Although seen in July, the 1984 bird was probably an early migrant and not a nester. As is pointed out by Dunn and Garrett (1997), the Louisiana Warbler is the earliest eastern wood-warbler migrant in fall, widely recorded by early and mid-July. The latest date in Oklahoma for young still in the nest is 25 June (Sutton, 1967), and for north-central Texas Pulich (1988) gives the early fall date for migrants as 30 June. A Louisiana Waterthrush was reported in Lubbock County in late July 1980 (Williams, 1980b).

Possibly all the mid- and late spring reports of Louisiana Waterthrushes should be questioned, for the species is among the earliest of all spring wood-warbler migrants, returning to the Gulf Coast during the second and third weeks of March, only a few stragglers remaining into early May (Dunn and Garrett, 1997): "Suspected Louisianas found late in spring should be distinguished carefully from Northern Waterthrushes, which are still commonly moving through then."

The Louisiana Waterthrush is an uncommon migrant in the eastern half of Texas and a rare to uncommon summer resident in the eastern third (TOS, 1995). A specimen was collected in nearby Ellis County, Oklahoma (Sutton, 1967).

Kentucky Warbler *Oporornis formosus* (Wilson)

STATUS: Casual migrant.

OCCURRENCE: The Kentucky Warbler has been reported in three Texas Panhandle counties—Gray, Potter, and Randall—all in April and May.

The following is a listing of all sightings, a single bird in each instance: *1930*—Hibbets et al. (1926–36) give a date of 8 May at "Hale's Park," presumably in Canyon, Randall County. *1955*—Canyon, Randall County, 25 April. *1957*—Amarillo, Potter County, 21 May. *1964*—Amarillo, Potter County, 23–25 April, and Randall County, 12 May. *1968*—Amarillo, Randall County, 10 May. *1970*—near Canyon, Randall County, 12 May. *1976*—near Canyon, 3 May; Lake Tanglewood, Randall County, 8 May. *1982*—BLNWR, 16 May. *1990*—Amarillo, Potter County, 15 May. *1991*—Amarillo, Potter County, 29 April–1 May; Amarillo, Randall County, 5–6 May. *1995*—Amarillo, Randall County, 24–25 April. *1996*—Pampa, Gray County, 28 April–1 May. *1997*—Amarillo, Randall County, 4 May. *1998*—Canyon, Randall County, 28 April. The majority were found in urban settings.

The Kentucky Warbler is an uncommon to common migrant and resident in the eastern half of Texas (TOS, 1995).

SPECIMENS: A specimen was collected in Potter County (15 May 1990, TCWC).

Mourning Warbler *Oporornis philadelphia* (Wilson)

STATUS: Vagrant migrant.

OCCURRENCE: There have been five reports of the Mourning Warbler in the Texas Panhandle: a male at BLNWR, 17 May 1975; a first-year male at BLNWR, 7 October

1996; one at BLNWR, 17 May 1997; either an immature or a female in Amarillo, Randall County, 23 September 1997; a singing bird at the Palo Duro Club near Canyon, Randall County, 23 May 1998. Concerning the September 1997 sighting, "separation of female and immature Mournings and MacGillivray's is more difficult, and some birds may not be identifiable in the field" (Dunn and Garrett, 1997). The MacGillivray's is the common *Oporornis* warbler in western and northwestern Texas, as the Mourning is in the eastern half of the state (TOS, 1995). The Mourning has been reported six times on the South Plains (*fide* C. Stogner): Crosby County, 2 September 1980, 1 June 1982, 13 October 1985; Lubbock County, 13 May 1979 and 3 May 1980; Muleshoe NWR, Bailey County, May 1977.

Perhaps some of these sightings should be questioned, for as time goes by more is being learned concerning variation in plumages in both the Mourning and MacGillivray's. Importantly, the presence and pattern of an eye-ring—too often used exclusively in telling the two species apart—are not always reliable indicators (Pyle and Henderson, 1990; Pitocchelli, 1993; Dunne, 1998), and hybridization is known to occur (Cox, 1973; Patti and Myers, 1976). That the Mourning Warbler occurs in the study area is supported by the fact that specimens have been obtained in nearby Ellis and Cimarron counties in Oklahoma (Sutton, 1967). The species is considered an uncommon transient in western Kansas, where it appears to be more common in fall than in spring (Thompson and Ely, 1992).

MacGillivray's Warbler   *Oporornis tolmiei* (Townsend)
STATUS: Fairly common migrant.
OCCURRENCE: The MacGillivray's Warbler has been found in 12 counties: Briscoe, Carson, Castro, Dallam, Deaf Smith, Gray, Hartley, Hutchinson, Oldham, Parmer, Potter, and Randall. Gray is the only eastern county.

Hawkins (1945) reported a summer encounter with the MacGillivray's: "A female was observed in a buttonbush thicket at Palo Duro Club on June 10, 1945, and two singing males were chased for an hour and finally identified at Palo Duro Canyon a week later—strong circumstantial evidence that this warbler may nest in West Texas." Both locations are in Randall County. There have been other June sightings: BLNWR, 9 June 1964; Lake Tanglewood, Randall County, 4 June 1973 and 4 June 1983; Thompson Grove Picnic Area northeast of Texline, Dallam County, 9 June 1984; Amarillo, Potter County, 1 June 1991; Amarillo, Randall County, 8 June 1996; Canyon County Club near Canyon, Randall County, 4, 13, and 14 June 1998. As Hubbard (1978) says of the MacGillivray's on the eastern plains of New Mexico: "Spring migrants persist into June." Nesting occurs only in the mountainous areas of that state.

The spring presence of the MacGillivray's Warbler is normally limited to the last three weeks of May. There are three April sightings on record, the earliest one in Pampa, Gray County, 18 April 1954. The seven-day period of greatest abundance (45%) is 14–20 May. Normally few are encountered in a day's outing. The greatest single-day counts were 12–30 seen repeatedly at BLNWR, 16–20 May 1996.

Returning birds in fall can be expected in the first week of September—the earliest record is one in Amarillo, Randall County, 15 August 1986—and rarely is one found beyond the second week in October—the latest being one in Amarillo, Randall County 19–20 October 1986. In contrast to spring, fall birds are evenly distributed throughout the season. Of all the wood-warblers, the MacGillivray's shows the greatest spread in the incidence of spring versus fall birds—85 percent to 15 percent.

SPECIMENS: There is a specimen taken in Potter County (20 May 1985, TCWC).

Common Yellowthroat *Geothlypis trichas* (Linnaeus)

STATUS: Fairly common to common migrant and breeder. Vagrant winter visitor.

OCCURRENCE: The Common Yellowthroat has been found in every Texas Panhandle county except Childress and Swisher and would be in them with better coverage. Oberholser (1974) shows it in six. It has been recorded in every month.

A fairly early spring migrant, the Common Yellowthroat is to be expected in the last week of April. Extremely early was a male at BLNWR, 26 March 1989. Most are gone by early October, an extremely late one being a bird in Caprock Canyons SP, Briscoe County, 17 November 1990. During the winter of 1998–99, a male and female remained from 31 December to 20 February at that site.

NESTING: The Common Yellowthroat has been found in summer in 19 of the 26 study area counties. Despite widespread summer observations, there have been few confirmed nestings: "Excited parents defending nests" were found "along the Canadian River bottomlands in Hemphill County on June 15, 1945" (Hawkins, 1945); a nest with four eggs was found at a playa east of Sunray, Moore County, 6 June 1978. During the TBBAP a bird in juvenal plumage was observed in the Sanford Dam marsh, Lake Meredith, Hutchinson County, 27 July 1987. A female carrying nesting material was at South East Park, Amarillo, Randall County, 19 May 1996. Fischer et al. (1982) name the species as a nesting summer resident in Castro County, but details are lacking.

The Common Yellowthroat can be found yearly during summer in the marshes of the larger impoundments as well as along the Canadian River and other waterways. Permanent playa lakes, small impoundments, and sewage ponds often contain pairs. Dallam County is sparing in nesting habitat, yet on 11 June 1988 a singing male was found at Buffalo Springs, a small oasis in the extreme northwest corner of the county. In June I have encountered singing males in fields of irrigated wheat growing alongside the road on the Waka BBS in Ochiltree County.

SPECIMENS: Oberholser (1974) names a specimen collected in Hemphill County, 14 July 1903 (A. H. Howell), and assigns it to the race *coloradonicola* Oberholser; without, however, specifying the collection in which it was deposited. This may be the specimen assigned to *occidentalis* by the AOU (1957), this being the race shown as resident in the Texas Panhandle by Dunn and Garrett (1997).

Hooded Warbler *Wilsonia citrina* (Boddaert)

STATUS: Casual migrant.

OCCURRENCE: The Hooded Warbler has been reported in Castro, Hutchinson, Moore, Oldham, Parmer, Potter, and Randall counties, and has been seen April– June and September.

With the exception of three times in September and once in June, all Hooded Warblers have been recorded April–May, the dates ranging from 3 April to 22 May. The following is a listing of all reported sightings, a single bird in each instance: *1957*—Canyon, Randall County, 3–6 April. *1966*—BLNWR, 7 May. *1967*—ten at BLNWR, 13 May—surely a misprint! *1968*—Amarillo, Randall County, 13 May. *1969*—Amarillo, 25 April–1 May. *1970*—Amarillo, 2–3 May. *1972*—near Dumas, Moore County, in April (TP-RF). *1973*—Palo Duro Club near Canyon, Randall County, 7 May. *1974*—Amarillo, Potter County, 30 April; Amarillo, Potter/Randall counties, 1 and 3 May; Amarillo, Potter County, 3 May. *1976*—Palo Duro Club near Canyon, Randall County, 6 May. *1978*—Amarillo, 26 April. *1982*—Borger, Hutchinson County, 22 April. *1986*—BLNWR, 1 September. *1987*—near Dumas, Moore County, 10 May (TP-RF). *1990*—Amarillo, Randall County, 2 September. *1991*—BLNWR, 8 May. *1992*—Castro County ("Dodd's Woodlot"), 10 April and 22 May; BLNWR, 1 May. *1993*—BLNWR, 30 April; Castro County ("Dodd's Woodlot"), 6 May. *1995*—Amarillo, Randall County, 11 September. *1996*—Amarillo, Randall County, 25 April; a singing male in PDCSP, 15 June. *1997*—Vega, Oldham County, 12–13 May. *1998*—Amarillo, Randall County, 13 April and 24 May.

This handsome warbler is an uncommon to common migrant in eastern Texas and an uncommon to common summer resident in the forested eastern third of the state (TOS, 1995).

Wilson's Warbler *Wilsonia pusilla* (Wilson)

STATUS: Common migrant.

OCCURRENCE: The Wilson's Warbler has been reported in all but six Texas Panhandle counties—Armstrong, Childress, Collingsworth, Lipscomb, Sherman, and Wheeler—and has been seen from April to November.

The Wilson's Warbler is the second most common (19%) warbler migrant in the study area, with 65 percent recorded in fall. No single day of notable numbers has ever been reported in spring, but several have in fall: 100+ in two Amarillo cemeteries, 8 September 1969; BLNWR—41 on 7 September and 50+ on 22 September 1970, 55 on 18 September 1978, 50 on 14 September 1980, 60 on 2 September 1992. Such numbers would lead one to think the species is common every year, but this is not so. As examples, I recorded only one bird in September 1971, six in September 1972, and none in the spring in 1989 or 1990. Such occasional absences have been noted previously: "At Amarillo the Wilson's Warbler was seen on only one date instead of being fairly common" (Baumgartner, 1958).

The first Wilson's Warblers usually arrive after mid-April, the earliest being 5 April 1981 at BLNWR. Numbers can still be seen into the third week of May, followed by a sharp decline after the 22nd, the latest dates being for one at BLNWR, 31 May 1969 and 1 June 1965. The seven-day period of greatest abundance is 6–12 May. There are two summer observations of interest. A singing Wilson's Warbler was found in Amarillo, 6 June 1966, and a singing bird at Lake Tanglewood in Randall County, first heard during the last week of June, was followed by two singing birds, 5 July 1993. Hibbets et al. (1926–36) in classifying the species as a "summer resident" surely were misled by late spring and early fall migrants, for the species nests no nearer the Texas Panhandle than north-central New Mexico (AOU, 1983).

Fall birds begin trickling through during the third week of August. An early date was for one at BLNWR, 6 August 1989—it was not until 27 August that another was seen. The seven-day period of greatest abundance is 22–28 September. Numbers drop off sharply after 3 October, with a few still around through the second week of the month, the latest a single bird in PDCSP, 23 October 1994. Most unusual was a male that remained in Miami, Roberts County, 11–30 November 1978.

SPECIMENS: Specimens have been taken in Potter County (1 October 1984 and 24 April 1990, TCWC). Another Potter County specimen is referenced by Oberholser (1974), but its location is not given. He assigned it to *W. p. pileolata*.

Canada Warbler *Wilsonia canadensis* (Linnaeus)

STATUS: Casual migrant.

OCCURRENCE: The Canada Warbler has been found in three counties—Parmer, Potter, and Randall—and has been seen in the periods May–June and August–October.

The following is a listing of all reported sightings, a single bird in each instance unless otherwise noted: *1962*—near Friona, Parmer County, 24 August. *1966*—Amarillo, Randall County, 8–9 September. *1967*—1–2 in Amarillo, Potter County, 5 and 12 May; Amarillo, Randall County, 6 and 8 May; BLNWR, 14 May and 3 September. *1969*—Amarillo, 9–10 September. *1983*—Amarillo, Randall County, 9 October. *1992*—Amarillo, Randall County, 3 June. *1996*—BLNWR, 16 May.

The Canada Warbler is an uncommon to locally common migrant in the eastern half of Texas (TOS, 1995). A specimen was taken in Cimarron County, Oklahoma, 8 September 1976 (Baumgartner and Baumgartner, 1992).

Painted Redstart *Myioborus pictus* (Swainson)
STATUS: Vagrant migrant.
OCCURRENCE: There is one record of the Painted Redstart in the Texas Panhandle. On 15 April 1977 one was recovered on the campus of West Texas A&M University in Canyon, Randall County (D. Brooks). The male, killed when it flew into a plate glass window, was deposited in the university's specimen collection (WTAMU #707).

The Painted Redstart is an uncommon and very local summer resident in the Big Bend National Park and Chisos Mountains of Texas and has bred in Jeff Davis County (TOS, 1995). There have been only two other documented records outside that area, both from Midland County (one photographed, 10 March 1961, and one collected, 22 May 1967). Other vagrants have been observed in Cameron, Culberson, El Paso, Galveston, Hidalgo, Kendall, Kinney, Lubbock, and Val Verde counties (TOS, 1995).

Yellow-breasted Chat *Icteria virens* (Linnaeus)
STATUS: Uncommon migrant. Rare summer resident and possible breeder.
OCCURRENCE: The Yellow-breasted Chat has been recorded in 12 counties: Armstrong, Briscoe, Castro, Deaf Smith, Donley, Hemphill, Moore, Oldham, Parmer, Potter, Randall, and Wheeler. It has been seen from April to November.

Changes in the summer status of the Yellow-breasted Chat during the twentieth century are illustrated by comparing McCauley's (1877) observations from the late nineteenth century with those of later observers. He speaks of the chat in the "Palo Duro at its head": "Though here very abundant and more noticeable than elsewhere, this species inhabited the woodlands skirting the stream throughout nearly all the route." Today one would be hard put to find the chat in those areas during summer. The first one reported in the PDCSP since McCauley, a location heavily birded, was on 6 July 1995.

There is no twentieth-century confirmation of nesting, although there have been a number of reports of probable or possible nesting. Hawkins (1945) reported "a singing male obviously defending a nesting territory in the bordering thickets of Lake Marvin" in Hemphill County. A chat was observed in this same area on 3–5 July 1954. On 5 June 1994, a singing male was found a short distance west of Lake Marvin on the Gene Howe WMA. More attention given to this area would probably result in the discovery of nesting. Other locations of possible nesting are areas of brush, salt cedars, and plum thickets along the Canadian River from Hemphill County westward to Oldham County, where singing and paired birds have been found: 6 July 1980; 22–29 June 1986; 12 July 1987; 19 May 1988; 28 May 1989; 30 May 1994; 7 July 1998.

Probable nestings also have been found in areas away from the Canadian River. The salt cedar thickets at the upper end of the BLNWR have contained singing chats in summer: 4 July 1956; 28–29 May 1978; 28 June 1987; 4 July 1988; 21 May 1992. On 25 June 1972, two chats were found along Skillet Creek in northeastern Donley County, and one was observed in the Lelia Creek area in the same county on 3 June 1973. Multiple singing males were found in the Kelton area on 18 June 1988, and one was seen near Mobeetie on 7 July 1988, both in Wheeler County.

The Yellow-breasted Chat is rarely reported before the first week of May, the earliest one near Canyon, Randall County, 24 April 1979, and few occur past late September, the latest being one at BLNWR, 9 October 1988. Extremely late was one in Ceta Glen, South Ceta Canyon, Randall County, 9 November 1954. As late as this sighting is, still later was a chat at Clayton, Union County, New Mexico, 11 January 1954 (Baumgartner, 1954).

SPECIMENS: McCauley (1877) collected six specimens during his trek across the study area in 1876: one male each at Palo Duro Creek on 20 May, Red River Canyon on 30 May, Mulberry Creek on 15 June, Cañoncito Blanco on 16 June, and Palo Duro on 17 June and a female at Palo Duro also on 17 June—sites located in present-day Armstrong and Randall counties. It is not known where these specimens were deposited. Oberholser (1974) shows summer specimens taken in Hemphill, Armstrong, and Randall counties and spring birds in Armstrong and Deaf Smith counties. Again, where they were deposited is not given: some may involve McCauley's birds. Oberholser assigns those he examined to the race *longicauda*.

Family Thraupidae (Tanagers)

Hepatic Tanager *Piranga flava* (Vieillot)
STATUS: Vagrant.
OCCURRENCE: The Hepatic Tanager has been reported once in the Texas Pan-

handle. On 26 April 1993, a female was observed in "Dodd's Woodlot" in south-western Castro County (C. D. Littlefield).

The Hepatic Tanager is an uncommon summer resident in the Chisos, Davis, and Guadalupe mountains of the Trans-Pecos (TOS, 1995). Only a few have been reported in areas adjacent to the study area: "one at Lubbock 18–19 April 1975 . . . provided a first record there and was only the second record of the species on the w. Texas plains" (Williams, 1975); a male was observed in Lubbock County, 2 May 1990 (Lasley and Sexton, 1990); Weske (1968) cites the species on Kreh-biel's "seen once or twice" list for the Clayton area, Union County, New Mexico; a male was observed, 15 May 1966, in Boise City, Cimarron County, in the Okla-homa Panhandle (Baumgartner and Baumgartner, 1992).

Summer Tanager *Piranga rubra* (Linnaeus)

STATUS: Rare to uncommon migrant. Casual summer visitor.

OCCURRENCE: The Summer Tanager has been recorded in ten Panhandle counties: Briscoe, Castro, Gray, Hartley, Hemphill, Hutchinson, Lipscomb, Oldham, Pot-ter, and Randall. It has been seen April–October.

The Summer Tanager is a species that can easily be overlooked. Like other bright red birds, the male appears dark when not seen in good light and is hard to detect in dense, shadow-filled foliage, while the golden-colored female tends to disappear amid flickering sunlit leaves. Also, as with other tanagers, it is often found in leafy tree tops, where it does not invite attention by abrupt and fre-quent movements. Perhaps for these reasons the species is not reported as often as its probable presence warrants.

Spring migrants can be expected from late April to late May. The early date is for one at BLNWR, 19 April 1964, and the late date a singing male at the same location, 24 May 1981. Surprisingly few fall sightings have been reported. My records show that I recorded a Summer Tanager but twice during autumn. The early date is for one in Amarillo, 26 August 1974, and the late date one at BLNWR, 5 October 1968. Several summer sightings have occurred. A single bird was seen near Lake Marvin, Hemphill County, 7 June 1953, and a male at the same loca-tion, 22 July 1973. A singing male was encountered in the upper reaches of Tim-bercreek Canyon in PDCSP, 28 June 1970. Subsequent visits failed to disclose the bird. What appeared to be an immature singing male visited a suburban yard in Amarillo, Potter County, 7 June 1977, and another singing bird was recorded on the Booker BBS in western Lipscomb County in June 1978. On 2 July 1989, a male was observed at Lake Tanglewood, Randall County, and one was found in the PDCSP, 12 June 1998.

McCauley (1877) spoke of the Summer Tanager as "observed along Wolf

Creek and the Canadian, always in pairs; too shy to permit me to secure speci-mens." This was in May–June 1876, in what was then Indian Territory; the actual location of some may possibly have been in today's Lipscomb and Hemphill counties. The species is a rare to common resident in much of Texas (TOS, 1995) and is known to nest (uncommonly) as far west in Oklahoma as Alfalfa, Wood-ward, Dewey, Comanche, and Love counties (Sutton, 1974a).

Scarlet Tanager *Piranga olivacea* (Gmelin)
STATUS: Casual migrant.
OCCURRENCE: The Scarlet Tanager has been reported in Hemphill, Hutchinson, Potter, and Randall counties and has been seen April–June and September–October.

There are but two records of Scarlet Tanagers observed in the study area prior to mid-century. Reeves and Reeves (1914–36) cite a single bird in Canyon, Randall County, in 1927: "on the college campus, right in front of the Ad. Bldg., on a rainy morning." Hibbets et al. (1926–36) name dates of 10 May 1930, 16 May 1931, and 7 May 1933—all in the Canyon area.

The following is a listing of sightings reported since mid-century, a single bird in each instance unless otherwise noted: *1955*—Canyon, Randall County, 22–24 April. *1964*—two at BLNWR, 16 May. *1966*—BLNWR, 8 May; Amarillo, 20 September; BLNWR, 4 October. *1967*—two at BLNWR, 13 May. *1968*—BLNWR, 6 May. *1970*—BLNWR, 4 October. *1973*—Amarillo, 6 May. *1974*—BLNWR, 12 May. *1975*—McBride Canyon, Lake Meredith National Recreation Area, Potter County, 11 May. *1976*—Amarillo, 5 May. *1977*—BLNWR, 22 May. *1978*—Duncan Ranch, Hutchinson County, 24 September. *1979*—BLNWR, 13 May. *1980*—McBride Canyon, Lake Meredith Recreational Area, Potter County, 14 September. *1982*—BLNWR, 25 September. *1984*—Palo Duro Club near Canyon, Randall County, 3 May. *1986*—first-year male, Canadian River, Lake Meredith National Recreation Area, Potter County, 22 June. *1993*—BLNWR, 19 September. *1996*—PDCSP, 8 and 23 May. *1998*—Gene Howe WMA, Hemphill County, 12 May.

On 6 July 1967, a nesting pair of Scarlet Tanagers was found in Boiling Springs SP, Woodward County, Oklahoma, a short distance east of the study area (Moorman, 1986). This location is far west of where the species is known to nest regularly in Oklahoma (Sutton, 1967). The Scarlet Tanager is an uncommon to locally common spring and rare to irregular fall migrant in the eastern half of Texas (TOS, 1995). Oberholser (1974) shows several summer sight records for north-central Texas, but these are dismissed by Pulich (1988) for lack of supporting details. On 9 July 1966, one was observed at Lubbock (Williams, 1966) and on 20 July 1991, one in Crosby County (Lasley and Sexton, 1991).

Western Tanager *Piranga ludoviciana* (Wilson)

STATUS: Uncommon to fairly common migrant.

OCCURRENCE: The Western Tanager has been recorded in 15 counties: Armstrong, Castro, Dallam, Donley, Gray, Hall, Hartley, Hemphill, Hutchinson, Moore, Oldham, Parmer, Potter, Randall, and Roberts. Oberholser (1974) shows it in four: Armstrong, Parmer, Potter, and Randall. It has been seen April–October and once in January.

The Western Tanager is not among the earlier spring migrants, the first birds usually arriving in the first or second week of May. There are only three April sightings on record: one in Amarillo, 21 April 1979; one at the Palo Duro Club near Canyon, Randall County, 26 April 1979; one in Amarillo, Potter County, 20 April 1994. The latest spring date is 30 May—one near Friona, Parmer County in 1962 and one at BLNWR in 1982. Carlander (1933) reported seeing the Western Tanager at an unnamed point between 19–22 June and 10–17 July 1933. There have been three other June sightings: one at BLNWR, 1 and 8 June 1968, and one at the Palo Duro Club near Canyon, Randall County, 10 June 1964.

Returning birds in fall can be looked for in the last week of August or the first week of September. A male was observed in Amarillo, Potter County, 2 August 1987, and another male in the PDCSP, 10 August 1936 (Stevenson, 1942). Seldom is one encountered as late as the second week of October, the latest a bird at BLNWR, 21 October 1973. Unexpected was one at Lake Tanglewood, Randall County, 1 January 1973.

Although the most common of the tanagers in the study area, the Western Tanager is never encountered in large numbers. The most I have tallied in one day is seven at BLNWR, 8 September 1985. While there are no peaks and valleys in seasonal occurrence, 25 percent have been recorded in spring, 75 percent in fall.

SPECIMENS: A specimen is available taken in Oldham County (5 October 1992, TCWC).

Family Emberizidae (Emberizids)

Green-tailed Towhee *Pipilo chlorurus* (Audubon)

STATUS: Uncommon to fairly common migrant and casual winter visitor.

OCCURRENCE: The Green-tailed Towhee has been found in ten counties: Briscoe, Carson, Castro, Dallam, Hutchinson, Moore, Oldham, Parmer, Potter, and Randall. It has been recorded in every month except July and August.

The Green-tailed Towhee, unlike the Spotted Towhee, is usually silent and is undoubtedly more common and widespread in the study area than records indicate. Normally no more than one or two are encountered in a day's outing. In 1983, along a 100-yard stretch of brush on the BLNWR, seven were observed on

1 May and eleven on 11 May, some of the birds singing. Occasionally the species visits feeders in suburban yards.

This towhee is found from the last week of April to the third week of May and from the second week of September to the first week of October. There are few records earlier or later. A singing bird was observed at the Palo Duro Club near Canyon, Randall County, 31 March 1972; one in west Amarillo, Potter County, 1 June 1992; and one in the Canyon Country Club near Canyon, Randall County, 14 June 1998. The early and late fall dates range from one at BLNWR, 4 September 1966, to one in the PDCSP, 29 November 1997. More have been recorded in spring (79%) than in fall (21%). The seven-day periods of greatest abundance are 25 April–1 May and 6–12 September.

The Green-tailed Towhee occasionally winters in the study area, most often in the Palo Duro Canyon. One was recorded in the state park on 29 December 1963, three were found on 22 December 1965, two on 30 December 1967, and two on 28 December 1968. One was found in North Ceta Canyon, 29 December 1974, and one at Lake Tanglewood, 18 December 1977. All of these sites are in Randall County. On 23 December 1970, one was seen near Friona, Parmer County, and two wintered in Vega, Oldham County, 3 November 1986–28 February 1987. The Green-tailed Towhee normally winters no nearer the Panhandle than western Texas (TOS, 1995).

The possibility that the Green-tailed Towhee may nest in the northwestern sector of the study area should not be discounted, for it has done so near Clayton, Union County (Hubbard, 1978), and on 8 May 1982, a nest with three eggs was discovered in Black Mesa SP, Cimarron County, Oklahoma (Downs, 1983).

Spotted Towhee *Pipilo maculatus* Swainson

STATUS: Fairly common to common migrant and winter visitor.

OCCURRENCE: Formerly called the Rufous-sided Towhee, that species was split into the Spotted Towhee and Eastern Towhee (AOU, 1995). In the Texas Panhandle, the Spotted Towhee has been recorded in 20 counties: Armstrong, Briscoe, Carson, Castro, Collingsworth, Dallam, Donley, Gray, Hall, Hartley, Hemphill, Hutchinson, Moore, Oldham, Parmer, Potter, Randall, Roberts, Swisher, and Wheeler. Oberholser (1974) shows it in five: Donley, Hemphill, Parmer, Potter, and Randall. It has been seen in every month except June and August.

In a Winter-Bird Population Study conducted in the PDCSP (Seyffert, 1968–78), the Spotted Towhee was found to be the seventh most common species on a 31-acre streamside plot, averaging 13 birds per 100 acres. Of all the ecosystems in the study area, wintering towhees have been found most commonly in the brushy canyonlands, as indicated by the average numbers recorded on the CBCS:

Amarillo (*canyonland*)—13.9; Quitaque (*canyonland*)—7.0; Lake Meredith (*west*) (*river valley*)—6.8; Lake Meredith (*east*) (*river valley, marshes, lake*)—2.3; Buffalo Lake NWR (*lake, plains, croplands*)—1.8; Friona (*plains, croplands*)—0.6. The numbers have ranged from one bird to 37 on the Amarillo count.

The Spotted Towhee returns in fall during late September. The early date is for one in Amarillo, Potter County, 15 September 1978. Few remain beyond mid-May, the latest a singing male at BLNWR, 30 May 1985. If the Spotted Towhee is ever found breeding in the study area, it will likely be in the extreme northwest sector, for the species has nested in Paradise Canyon three miles north of Clayton, Union County, New Mexico (Hubbard, 1978; NMOS, 1992). Unaccountable was one visiting a feeder at the Canyon Country Club, Randall County, 13 July 1997.

SPECIMENS: Two specimens have been collected in Randall County (31 December 1936, 30 September 1937, MVZ). The former was identified as the race *montanus* and the latter as *arcticus*. Both were referenced by Stevenson (1942) and are probably the ones cited by Oberholser (1974) without attribution.

Eastern Towhee *Pipilo erythrophthalmus* (Linnaeus)

STATUS: Casual winter visitor.

OCCURRENCE: Prior to the Rufous-sided Towhee being split into the Eastern Towhee and Spotted Towhee (AOU, 1995), the "eastern" race had been recorded four times in the Texas Panhandle, all in Randall County: a female in Amarillo, 24 February 1967 and January 1969; a male in the PDCSP, 14–19 January and 3 November 1968. Following the split, one, possibly two, towhees were seen in the state park—6 and 21 December 1996 and 23 February and 14 March 1997.

The Eastern Towhee is a migrant and winter resident in the eastern half of Texas, west to about Bexar, Brazos, and Cooke counties (TOS, 1995). Pulich (1988) cites specimens taken in Dallas and Denton counties. The species has been seen as far westward in Oklahoma as Beaver, Woodward, Blaine, Jackson, and Love counties (Sutton, 1967).

Canyon Towhee *Pipilo fuscus* Swainson

STATUS: Uncommon to fairly common resident in the canyonlands.

OCCURRENCE: The Canyon Towhee has been found in nine counties: Armstrong, Briscoe, Deaf Smith, Gray, Hall, Moore, Oldham, Potter, and Randall. It has been seen in every month.

The Canyon Towhee may be a fairly recent addition to the avifauna of the Texas Panhandle. Until recently it was thought resident only in the Palo Duro Canyon, but ongoing studies in the breaks north of Wildorado, Oldham County, show probable year-round residence (nesting) there also. It is likely that the species is more widely distributed than has been recognized. Early-day observers, who spent many hours studying the bird life of the "Big" canyon, failed to name it. Even Oberholser (1974) classified it as a "visitor" only, and most current field guides and other publications fail to show the Texas Panhandle within the species' nesting range.

The first published references to the Canyon Towhee (formerly called the Brown Towhee) in the study area are those of Baumgartner (1959, 1963): "A Brown Towhee observed at Palo Duro Canyon on Nov. 6 represents a rare migrant in that locality" and "One in the Palo Duro Canyon Jan. 1 was first winter record for the area." The species continued to be thought of only as a transient well into the 1960s. I began birding the area in the fall of 1963 and it was only on 23 April 1967 that I first encountered a Canyon Towhee in the state park. Today it is a resident, and there are an increasing number of reports from other localities. Its known range extends from the upper reaches of the Palo Duro Canyon in Randall County southeastward through Armstrong County to Caprock Canyons SP, Briscoe County. It is probable that the species now occupies the entire Palo Duro Canyon system, albeit in relatively small numbers.

Although the canyonlands are the places to look for the Canyon Towhee, the first one I ever saw was at BLNWR on Tierra Blanca Creek, upstream from its confluence with Palo Duro Creek near Canyon (1 March–26 April 1964). The towhees on the refuge, however, have always proven to be transients: 24 January and 21 March 1965; 4 May 1980; 25 September 1983; 16–27 October 1985; 19 April 1992; 23 May and 2 October 1993. On 4 July 1975, I observed one in the Sand Point Draw area in extreme northwest Deaf Smith County, a canyonland environment favorable to the species. I have found it twice during the Lake Meredith (west) CBC, both times in Plum Creek (National Recreation Area): a single bird, 31 December 1973, and another, 23 December 1978. I have never observed one there during other times of the year. Two Canyon Towhees were observed within the city limits of Canyon, Randall County, 21 November 1993, and one was seen there on 16 April 1997. It is evident that some individuals of this species are wanderers.

On 12 August 1986, in "Tumbleweed Canyon" on the Elkins Ranch, Randall County, I listened to a singing Canyon Towhee; phrases of its song closely resembled that of a Blue-gray Gnatcatcher. Had I not heard other parts of the towhee's song, I would have been led to believe a gnatcatcher was present.

NESTING: Johnsgard's (1979) work on the breeding birds of the Great Plains is a fairly recent publication that does not show the Canyon Towhee nesting in the Texas Panhandle. The only actual nest ever reported, one in the process of being built, was discovered in the PDCSP, 21 June 1996. Containing a single cowbird egg, it was found abandoned on 1 July. Although only one nest has been reported, many adults with young have been observed. An adult carrying food was observed in the state park as early as 8 May 1976, and adults with young were seen as late as 10 August 1980.

The Canyon Towhee is a common breeder in the Black Mesa country of Cimarron County, Oklahoma (Sutton, 1967) and the Dry Cimarron area of northeastern New Mexico (Hubbard, 1978). In the latter state, I have also found it nesting at Clayton Lake in Union County (nest with four eggs and a pair feeding fledglings, 12 June 1982). Such close proximities should further alert observers to possible nesting in Dallam and Hartley counties.

SPECIMENS: A specimen is available from Randall County (2 April 1976, WTAMU).

Cassin's Sparrow *Aimophila cassinii* (Woodhouse)

STATUS: Common breeder.

OCCURRENCE: The Cassin's Sparrow has been recorded in all 26 counties. It has been seen from March to September and once in December.

Over much of the grassland of the Panhandle the Cassin's Sparrow is the most common of the summering sparrows, yielding to the Lark Sparrow in more brushy environments. The plaintive flight song of the Cassin's is a familiar sound heard throughout the day, as well as on moonlit nights, from late April through July. The repetitive and conspicuous "skylarking," accompanied by song, makes the species ideal for recording on BBSS. The following are the averages, highs, and lows for each count: *Channing*—72.3 (134, 26); *Skellytown*—65.7 (93, 49); *Clarendon*—61.6 (83, 45); *Miami*—50.3 (86, 9); *Texline*—50.2 (82, 11); *Dalhart*—49.3 (59, 42); *Pantex*—21.3 (73, 0); *Childress*—19.9 (73, 2); *Booker*—12.9 (37, 0); *Panhandle*—1.3 (3, 0); *Waka*—0.3 (3, 0). The lower numbers on the Waka and Panhandle counts can be attributed to the fact that these routes run almost entirely through croplands.

As can be seen, the number of Cassin's Sparrows may vary widely from year to year. Some observers believe the species is less common in wet years: Cassin's Sparrows "tended to decrease at Amarillo with the wet season. In fact, not a single one was seen during this period" (Baumgartner, 1958). Severe drought conditions in 1996, however, reduced grasslands to stubble, resulting in dramatically reduced sparrow counts on BBSS. Changes in land use have a direct bearing. A factor seldom mentioned but affecting count results significantly is wind velocity. Surveyors are instructed not to run BBS routes when wind speed exceeds 12 mph. If this restriction were adhered to on the High Plains, few counts would be made. With an increase in wind speed it becomes more difficult to pick up birdsong. I have run routes containing lengthy stretches of uniform grasslands where, as the wind velocity picked up, the number of Cassin's recorded per stop dropped noticeably. Such a factor should be borne in mind before coming to a conclusion, based on BBSS alone, that the Cassin's Sparrow has undergone a significant population change on the High Plains. I feel sure that had all counts been conducted under the same wind conditions, the trend results would be different.

Returning Cassin's Sparrows in spring can be looked for during the third week of April. There are two March records: one at BLNWR, 26 March 1966, and one near Amarillo, Randall County, 31 March 1987. Most have left the area by the second week of September. The latest date is for two in Randall County, 27 September 1971. Unaccountable, and a sighting that must be questioned, was one recorded on the Amarillo CBC of 27 December 1958. The Cassin's Sparrow is an uncommon winter resident from El Paso County and south through the South Texas Plains (TOS, 1995), and is classified as "casual" in winter in the Lubbock area (LEAS, 1994). There are no winter records from nearby areas of New Mexico (Hubbard, 1978) or Oklahoma (Sutton, 1967).

Knowing the Cassin's Sparrow song well, I listened to a skylarking bird south of Lark, Armstrong County, 6 July 1988, that was producing a song totally different from the species' normal one. Neither the pattern nor the phrases resembled those of a Cassin's, nor could I link the song with that of any other species with which I was familiar.

NESTING: The TBBAP disclosed the Cassin's Sparrow uniformly present throughout the study area. CO nesting was found in 12 survey blocks, PR in 74, and PO in 14. Thirty-six of the quadrangles were located between the 100th and 101st meridians, 30 between the 101st and 102nd, and 34 west of the 102nd meridian. Only one nest was found—21 May 1989 near Turkey, Hall County. All other confirmations were based on adults feeding fledglings, the dates ranging from 10 June to 6 August.

For so common a species, nesting data is almost nonexistent: nest with three eggs, 28 May 1979 at BLNWR; Moore County, July 1971 (nest salvaged; MCHM). Oberholser (1974) shows sight records of nesting in Oldham, Potter, and Deaf Smith counties, without giving details.

SPECIMENS: Specimens have been taken in Randall County (10 August 1936, MVZ; 8 July 1985, TCWC). Oberholser (1974) names others taken in Lipscomb and Potter counties.

Rufous-crowned Sparrow *Aimophila ruficeps* (Cassin)
STATUS: Fairly common to common resident.
OCCURRENCE: The Rufous-crowned Sparrow has been found in 15 counties: Armstrong, Briscoe, Childress, Donley, Gray, Hall, Hansford, Hartley, Hutchinson,

Moore, Oldham, Potter, Randall, Roberts, and Swisher. Oberholser (1974) shows it in four: Armstrong, Hutchinson, Potter, and Randall. It has been recorded year-round.

There are few references to the Rufous-crowned Sparrow in the accounts of early observers, and those who did mention it were uncertain of its winter status. Carlander (1934) was the first to publish an account of what was then called the "Rock Sparrow," and he thought it rare in the canyons. Hawkins (1945) classified it as a "fairly common summer resident of canyon walls" and said it arrived in the area in late April. He referred to the one winter record of Stevenson's (1942). The winter status of the species long remained unclear: "A Rufous-crowned Sparrow at Palo Duro Canyon Jan. 2 was a first winter record" (Baumgartner, 1955). The sighting occurred during the CBC, and it was not until the winter of 1961 that another was recorded.

As the tempo of birding increased during the 1960s, more systematic and extensive coverage disclosed the true winter status of this sparrow. A Winter-Bird Population Study (Seyffert, 1968–78) conducted in the PDCSP found an average density of six per 100 acres. This winter presence was reinforced by CBCS. The following are the averages and highs on each count: *Amarillo*—7.7 (42); *Quitaque*—5.0 (22); *Lake Meredith* (*east*)—3.4 (10); *Lake Meredith* (*west*)—2.2 (7); *Buffalo Lake* NWR—0.3 (2). If there is a migratory movement, it has gone undetected.

NESTING: Johnsgard (1979) says of the Rufous-crowned Sparrow that it is only a probable nester in the Texas Panhandle; however, nesting had in fact been confirmed prior to the publication of that work: nest with four eggs at Lake Tanglewood, Randall County, 12 June 1964, and a fledgling captured at that location 23 June 1968; nest building in the PDCSP, 18 April 1970; nest containing three eggs in PDCSP, 18 July 1976; adult carrying food in Tumbleweed Canyon on the Elkins Ranch adjacent to PDCSP, 12 August 1986; adult carrying nesting materials in McBride Canyon, Lake Meredith National Recreation Area, Potter County, 29 June 1975, and a juvenal-plumaged bird there, 10 July 1985. On 4 July 1973, an adult Rufous-crowned Sparrow was watched as it fed a young cowbird in the PDCSP.

The TBBAP found CO nesting in two survey blocks, PR in eight, and PO in three. All but one of the quadrangles were located west of the 101st meridian and none north of 35 degrees, 45 minutes north latitude. Both confirmations involved adults with young: PDCSP, 29 July 1987; Luttrell Springs, Armstrong County, 7 July 1991.

These nesting dates indicate that the Rufous-crowned Sparrow is two-brooded. I have heard singing birds in the Caprock Canyons SP, Briscoe County, as early as 10 February 1996, and in the PDCSP as late as 14 September 1996.

Samples of early singing dates in the PDCSP are 12 March 1978; 16 March 1980; 8 March 1987; 26 February 1989; 25 February 1990; 21 February 1991; 23 February 1992; 20 February 1993; 4 March 1994; 20 February 1995. Late singing dates noted for PDCSP are 21 August 1985; 25 August 1987; 27 August 1992; 14 August 1994; 23 August 1995; 14 September 1996.

SPECIMENS: Specimens have been collected in Hutchinson (23 June 1950, TNHC) and Randall (25 December 1936, MVZ; 11 September 1993, TCWC) counties. The MVZ specimen is the one cited by Stevenson (1942), and the two TNHC birds are those cited by Thompson (1952). One of the latter could not be identified by subspecies "because of the covering of soot on the plumage." It had been collected near the carbon black plants at Borger/Phillips, where pollutants were released unchecked into the atmosphere at that time. A dense pall of black smoke often covered the area.

American Tree Sparrow *Spizella arborea* (Wilson)

STATUS: Uncommon to common winter visitor.

OCCURRENCE: The American Tree Sparrow has been recorded in 20 counties: Armstrong, Briscoe, Dallam, Deaf Smith, Donley, Gray, Hansford, Hartley, Hemphill, Hutchinson, Lipscomb, Moore, Ochiltree, Oldham, Parmer, Potter, Randall, Roberts, Sherman, and Wheeler. It has been seen from October to May.

The tree sparrow returns to the study area in late fall, usually around mid-November. There are four October records, the earliest being for two birds at BLNWR, 12 October 1971. Few remain beyond mid-March. My records disclose only three sightings in April, all at BLNWR: 4 April 1976; 5 April 1981; 8 April 1979. A single bird at Lake Tanglewood, Randall County, 3 May 1973, was exceptional.

The CBCS are indicative of the American Tree Sparrow's distribution and abundance. The following are the averages and highs for each: *Lake Meredith* (*west*)—65.3 (369); *Lake Meredith* (*east*)—61.4 (203); *Buffalo Lake* NWR—39.1 (300); *Amarillo*—18.6 (323); *Quitaque*—10.0 (148); *Friona*—2.6 (10). No counts are located in the eastern counties, where relatively little birding has been done in winter. This species may be more abundant there than is known, for on the Arnett CBC in Ellis County, Oklahoma, a short distance to the east, the average (1966–82) is 82 (high 780). A Winter-Bird Population Study (Seyffert, 1968–78) conducted in the PDCSP revealed the tree sparrow to be the seventh most common species, averaging 13 per 100 acres.

SPECIMENS: Of seven specimens collected in Hemphill County, 25 January 1929 (MVZ), one was assigned to the nominate eastern race *S. a. arborea* and six to the western race *ochracea*. Oberholser (1974) shows other *ochracea* collected in Deaf Smith and Oldham counties but does not specify where they were deposited.

Chipping Sparrow *Spizella passerina* (Bechstein)

STATUS: Common to abundant migrant. Irregular and rare winter visitor.

OCCURRENCE: The Chipping Sparrow has been seen in every county except Childress and Sherman and would be in them with better coverage. Oberholser (1974) shows it in five: Armstrong, Oldham, Parmer, Potter, and Randall. It has been recorded in every month.

The Chipping Sparrow is one of the most abundant of migrant sparrows. As an example, approximately 2,000 passed through west Amarillo, Potter County, between 8:00 and 8:30 a.m. on 15 September 1972 (P. Acord). These returning birds begin arriving in late summer, usually in early or mid-August. There are several late July records, the earliest being a single bird in Amarillo, Potter County, 24 July 1968. Fall migration is lengthy, the latest birds lingering into late October or mid-November.

Small numbers of Chipping Sparrows occasionally overwinter. The species has been recorded on most of the CBCs: *Amarillo*—12 of 40 (high 10); *Lake Meredith (west)*—6 of 24 (high 5); *Lake Meredith (east)*—2 of 18 (high 20); *Quitaque*—3 of 21 (high 3); *Buffalo Lake NWR*—1 of 29 (high 100). I cannot but be skeptical of some of these numbers, particularly the 100 at BLNWR. The area had been scouted prior to count day and American Tree Sparrows were found to be common—but no Chipping Sparrows were seen. I have had inexperienced observers submit sightings based solely on red crowns, unaware that "chippies" lose this distinctive feature in winter, and have been in the presence of others who have misidentified the much more likely American Tree Sparrow and Field Sparrow. My records reveal that I recorded the Chipping Sparrow during only eight winters, and then no more than 12 birds at a time. A Winter-Bird Population Study made in the PDCSP (Seyffert, 1968–78) found the species present only once (6 February 1972). The Chipping Sparrow is found in winter not far south of the study area (TOS, 1995), but only irregularly (LEAS, 1994; Midland Naturalists, 1992).

Returning birds in spring tend to arrive early. My records show early dates of 12 March (1978) and 13 March (1966, 1988). Ten at Lake McClellan, Gray County, 23 February 1972, were probably early migrants and not wintering birds. The main push normally begins in mid-April and is usually over by mid- or late May. There are two June records: one in Castro County, 3 June 1992, and one at BLNWR, 11 June 1987. The Chipping Sparrow is not known to nest any nearer the Texas Panhandle than Cimarron, Texas, Woodward, and Caddo counties in western Oklahoma, and there but rarely (Baumgartner and Baumgartner, 1992), and it is a summer bird of the Capulin Mountain National Monument, Union County, New Mexico (NMOS, 1992).

SPECIMENS: Oberholser (1974) names specimens collected in Oldham and Randall counties and assigns them to the western race *arizonae*. He does not give their locations.

Clay-colored Sparrow *Spizella pallida* (Swainson)

STATUS: Common to abundant migrant. Vagrant winter visitor.

OCCURRENCE: The Clay-colored Sparrow has been recorded in all but four of the 26 Texas Panhandle counties: Childress, Deaf Smith, Ochiltree, and Sherman. Oberholser (1974) shows it in only three: Oldham, Potter, Randall. It has been seen March–May and August–November. There are two winter records and one for summer.

The Clay-colored Sparrow normally returns in spring around mid-April, about two weeks later than the Chipping Sparrow. The earliest date is for an unspecified number found at the Canadian River, Potter County, 23 March 1964. Most have passed through by mid-May, the latest being two birds at BLNWR, 25 May 1975. As a rule, fewer Clay-colored than Chipping Sparrows are reported in spring.

Fall migration is another story as the Clay-colored may then equal or exceed the Chipping Sparrow in abundance. Its passage is compressed within a shorter time span, however, as the first Clay-coloreds normally arrive about three weeks later than "chippies" and few are to be found past mid-October. The earliest arrival date is for a single bird at BLNWR, 18 August 1985. There are but two November sightings: two at the BLNWR, 2 November 1979, and "several" at the same location, 15 November 1968. An example of how abundant the Clay-colored Sparrow can be during fall is the following account of a passage through Amarillo in 1955: "When the peak population occurred, about 20 September, several thousand birds drifted through the residential districts, with hundreds sitting on the wires and lawns at one time" (P. Acord). The observer's notes read further: "On 22 September, a partly cloudy and cool day, approximately 1000 sparrows in groups of 1 or 2 to 50–60, passed through the yard between 7:15 and 8:30 a.m. Although all were not identified, most were of this species. Small groups continued to move through the rest of the day and these were identified as Clay-coloreds."

There are but two winter sightings. A single bird was found feeding with a flock of juncos in Tub Springs Draw, PDCSP, 5 December 1984 (Seyffert, 1988c), and one was observed in the far northwestern sector at Texline, Dallam County, 7 January 1998. The Clay-colored Sparrow's winter range in Texas extends from the Trans-Pecos, the southern South Plains, and the southern Edwards Plateau regions south to the Rio Grande and the central coast (TOS, 1995).

Strecker (1912) reported the Clay-colored Sparrow (*"Spizella pallida"*) breeding "in the Panhandle region," naming McCauley (1877) as his authority: "Red

River Canyon, edge of the Staked Plains, Paloduro and Red River Valley." In reading McCauley's account, the only reference to a spizella sparrow that I find is "*Spizella pallida breweri*, (Cass.) Coues"—Brewer's Sparrow—for which he names nest and eggs collected. Johnsgard (1979) acknowledged nesting of the Brewer's Sparrow in these counties but says the Clay-colored has never been known to nest any nearer the Texas Panhandle than southwestern Kansas (Morton County). Even there the single event was thought "extraordinary," as the southern edge of the species' breeding range in Kansas lies several hundred miles to the north (Cable et al., 1996). It is probable that Strecker erred. I find only one reference to a summer sighting of the Clay-colored Sparrow in the study area, a single bird at BLNWR, 16 July 1960—a sighting open to question.

SPECIMENS: Specimens have been taken in Oldham (16 September 1920, CMNH) and Randall (2 October 1937, MVZ; 7 October 1939 and 7 October 1979, WTAMU) counties. The MVZ bird is the one named by Stevenson (1942), who also names one collected in Potter County. Specimens collected in these counties shown by Oberholser (1974) without attribution are possibly the same birds.

Brewer's Sparrow *Spizella breweri* Cassin

STATUS: Uncommon to fairly common migrant. Casual winter visitor.

OCCURRENCE: The Brewer's Sparrow has been found in 13 counties: Armstrong, Briscoe, Carson, Castro, Dallam, Hartley, Hutchinson, Oldham, Parmer, Potter, Randall, Roberts, and Swisher. It has been seen in every month except July.

Though less common than either the Chipping or the Clay-colored Sparrow, the Brewer's Sparrow is possibly more common in the study area than is generally thought, for observers tend to assign flocks of spizella sparrows to a single species based on the identification of only a few individuals. Mixed-species flocks often occur, and more attention should be given to determining their compositions. Also, if more time were spent in the far western counties during migration, more Brewer's would probably be found.

The first birds of spring are usually found in late April, and seldom are any seen past early May. The earliest date is for two at BLNWR, 9 March 1980, and the latest for two in Randall County, 30 May 1998. Fewer Brewer's Sparrows are reported in fall. They can be looked for from early September to late October. The early and late dates range from two at the BLNWR, 24 August 1980, to two in the PDCSP, 24 November 1987. The latter were feeding in a large mixed flock of juncos, Spotted Towhee, and Field, White-crowned, White-throated, and Song sparrows. The flock composition of the 9 March 1980 birds was also mixed: White-crowned, White-throated, and Lincoln's Sparrows. In both instances the Brewer's may have been overwintering with the others. There are four winter records: three in the PDCSP, 17 January and 13 February 1965, and one, 4 February

1995; three feeding with juncos in Caprock Canyons SP, Briscoe County, 1 January 1980, and two, 5 February 1995. The Brewer's Sparrow is classified as "rare" in winter in the Lubbock area (LEAS, 1994), becoming somewhat more common, but irregular, in Midland County (Midland Naturalists, 1992).

NESTING: Does the Brewer's Sparrow still nest in the Texas Panhandle? There is little or no evidence to support such a belief. The only report of nests found at any time is McCauley's (1877): 21 May 1876, a nest with three eggs; 23 May, two nests with six eggs—all in the "Red River Cañon"; 25–27 May, six nests with 20 eggs in the "Palo Duro"; 10–12 June, two nests with six eggs at "Camp's edge of Staked Plains." These sites are located in present-day Randall, Armstrong, and Briscoe counties. This report is possibly the basis for later assertions that the Brewer's Sparrow breeds in the Texas Panhandle (Oberholser, 1974; Johnsgard, 1979).

The nearest to the study area that the Brewer's Sparrow was confirmed nesting in the twentieth century is the Panhandle of Oklahoma: "In 1957 bred in considerable numbers in grazing land ten to twelve miles west of Boise City, Cimarron County, four nests, each about one and one-half feet up in sage and containing small young, found June 11–12" (Sutton, 1967). The species was reported in the Clayton area of Union County, New Mexico, in the summer of 1968 (Hubbard, 1978). Oberholser (1974) makes reference to nesting in "adjacent areas of New Mexico" in the 1950s. In southwestern Kansas (Morton County), two colonies were located in the summer of 1979 (Williams, 1979).

On 23 June 1991, Brewer's Sparrows were observed on the Rita Blanca National Grasslands east of Texline, Dallam County (B. Ortego). The observer's notes read: "A number of small groups. . . . Some were mixed with Lark Buntings and others were by themselves. Most were in groups of 2–3 with a max of about 6." "Streaked" birds were observed. This observation occurred along the BBS route that I have run yearly since 1975 in early or mid-June. I have never recorded a Brewer's Sparrow during any count, nor while scouring surrounding areas pre- and postcount. Most certainly the Brewer's Sparrow warrants closer study for possible nesting in the northern Texas Panhandle.

SPECIMENS: Oberholser (1974) shows specimens taken in Roberts, Armstrong, and Briscoe counties, based on McCauley (1877). That report, however, names only eggs collected.

Field Sparrow *Spizella pusilla* (Wilson)

STATUS: Uncommon to common resident in the eastern half, uncommon locally westward.

OCCURRENCE: The Field Sparrow has been recorded in all but five counties: Carson, Deaf Smith, Ochiltree, Sherman, and Swisher. It has been seen year-round.

The western boundary of the Field Sparrow's summer distribution lies along 101 degrees, 30 minutes west, extending from Hutchinson County in the north to Briscoe County in the south. Small numbers can be found locally in the Canadian River Valley from the Sanford Dam area at Lake Meredith, Hutchinson County, westward to Boys Ranch, Oldham County. The species is fairly common in summer on the brushy slopes overlooking the Palo Duro Canyon in central Armstrong County and on the JA Ranch to the south and east. In recent years (1994–98) singing birds have been remaining near the PDCSP entrance into summer, indicating probable nesting.

Little work has been done in winter in the eastern counties where the Field Sparrow is common in summer, and the extent and degree of any seasonal movement is unknown. The species is known as a migrant in the northernmost portions of its continental range and as a partial migrant elsewhere (Carey et al., 1994). Movement into an area not occupied in summer has been documented in some sections of the Panhandle. Taking Randall County as an example, my records show that the Field Sparrow normally arrives in the fall in mid-October and departs in spring in mid-April.

The number of wintering Field Sparrows at any given locality is always small, as reflected in the averages and highs on the CBCs: *Buffalo Lake NWR*—10.0 (159); *Lake Meredith (west)*—4.2 (47); *Amarillo*—4.2 (20); *Quitaque*—4.0 (10); *Lake Meredith (east)*—1.8 (17); *Friona*—0.1 (1). Several of the highs must be questioned, in particular the 159 reported on the BLNWR count of 20 December 1971. On this same count, 73 American Tree Sparrows were tallied. I made repeated trips to the refuge throughout that winter and found but one Field Sparrow— but as many as 97 Tree Sparrows in a single outing. I strongly suspect that almost all of the Field Sparrows reported were in fact the latter species. My records also reveal that I have seldom recorded more than three or four in a single day during winter.

NESTING: It is not generally known that the Field Sparrow is a breeding bird in the Texas Panhandle. This is reflected in even the most recent publications (Johnsgard, 1979; Carey et al., 1994). The TBBAP found CO nesting in two quadrangles, PR in 16, and PO in five. Fourteen of the survey blocks were located between the 100th and 101st meridians, eight between the 101st and 102nd, and one west of the 102nd. On 19 May and 12 August 1990, I observed adults feeding young on the Gene Howe WMA, and on 5 July 1971 a juvenal-plumaged bird at Lake Marvin, both locations in Hemphill County. At Lake McClellan, Gray County, a nest with three eggs was discovered, 24 May 1990, and adults feeding recently fledged young, 19 July 1990.

Black-chinned Sparrow *Spizella atrogularis* (Cabanis)

STATUS: Vagrant spring visitor.

OCCURRENCE: There is one reported sighting of the Black-chinned Sparrow in the Texas Panhandle. A male was observed in a residential yard in Amarillo, Randall County, 26 April 1974 (R. Ross, M. Moyer, K. Seyffert, E. Waddill). The bird was present for over two hours.

The Black-chinned Sparrow is an uncommon summer resident in the mountains of Trans-Pecos, with only scattered sightings east of the Pecos River (TOS, 1995). The nearest to the study area that the species has been documented is Howard County (Big Spring, 10 February 1980; TP-RF). Others have been found at the Muleshoe NWR, Bailey County, 1 October 1942 (*fide* C. Stogner); Lubbock County (2), 30 December 1966 (*fide* C. Stogner); Crosby County, 13 February 1982 (*fide* C. Stogner); and west of Logan, Harding County, New Mexico, in 1992 and on 2 June 1993 (NMOS, 1992–93). One reported in Comanche County, Oklahoma, 26 April 1996 (Grzybowski, 1996), is being reviewed by the Oklahoma Bird Records Committee.

Vesper Sparrow *Pooecetes gramineus* (Gmelin)

STATUS: Fairly common to common migrant. Rare winter (southern) and casual summer visitor.

OCCURRENCE: The Vesper Sparrow has been recorded in all the counties except Ochiltree in the north and Childress in the southeast and has been seen in every month.

In referring to Vesper Sparrow numbers during the 1950s and early 1960s, observers spoke in superlatives: "The migration of Vesper Sparrows at Amarillo was spectacular. Thousands were seen on 17 September 1954, and were still present at the end of the period" (Baumgartner, 1955); an observer (P. Acord) driving from Amarillo to Canyon, Randall County, 30 September 1954, saw "hundreds of them along the road"; "several hundred" were seen near Amarillo on 22 April 1959; and "several thousand—largest flock I've seen in years"—near Amarillo, 28 September 1964. In all the years that I have birded the area, I have never encountered Vesper Sparrows in quantities such as these. On 4 October 1983, during a drive through Randall, Armstrong, and Briscoe counties, I recorded several hundred in scattered flocks. On 11 April 1965, and again on 27 September 1986, I recorded 100+ on the BLNWR. In surveying my records for the refuge over a 30-year period (1 April–15 May and 15 September–28 October), I find that the average number of Vesper Sparrows recorded per trip dropped from 7.1 in the first 15 years (1965–79) to 4.5 in the last 15 (1980–94).

The Vesper Sparrow is an early migrant, normally appearing in late March or early April, and few are encountered beyond the second week in May. The early and late dates range from an unspecified number west of Amarillo, Randall County, 14 March 1964, and one at BLNWR, 14 March 1987, to a singing bird near Amarillo, 31 May 1952. The seven-day period of greatest abundance is 19–25 April (34%).

There have been six sightings of summer vagrants ranging from 5 June 1979 (Carson County) to 13 July 1968 (Randall County). Oberholser (1974) shows a summer record for Wheeler County without giving details. The nearest locality to the Texas Panhandle where the species is known to nest is the foothills of southeastern Colorado (Andrews and Righter, 1992). Ligon (1961) referred to vespers nesting at Clayton, Union County, New Mexico, but this was not recognized by Hubbard (1978). Fall migrants return around mid-September and are gone by the last of October. The early date is for an unspecified number in Parmer County, 28 August 1961, and the late date for one at Greenbelt Lake, Donley County, 27 November 1981. The seven-day period of greatest abundance is 29 September–5 October (41%).

The Vesper Sparrow winters in the extreme southwestern sector of the study area, appearing on the Friona CBC in Parmer County with fair regularity (high 51), but is reported only sporadically elsewhere. It has been recorded on six occasions in the Quitaque area, Briscoe County, five times on the CBC. The following are other winter records: *Armstrong*—one, 27 February 1998. *Moore*—several near Sunray, 3 February 1995. *Randall*—unspecified number, 18 January and 8 February 1953; one in the PDCSP, 2 January 1955; one, 4 December 1955; four, 23 January 1966; one, 9 February 1966; two, 15 February 1969: *Oldham*—one, 5 December 1981. Some were possibly early or late migrants.

SPECIMENS: Specimens have been collected in Randall (3 May 1936, 2 October 1937, MVZ; 30 September 1939, WTAMU) and Swisher (6 April 1986, TCWC) counties. Two of the Randall County specimens are those named by Stevenson (1942) and identified as *P. g. confinus*. The disposition of another he says was collected in that county, identified as *P. g. definitus*, is unknown. These three are also the ones to which Oberholser (1974) makes reference.

Lark Sparrow *Chondestes grammacus* (Say)

STATUS: Common breeder. Vagrant winter visitor.

OCCURRENCE: The Lark Sparrow has been recorded in every county of the Texas Panhandle and has been seen in every month except February.

Hawkins (1945) considered the Lark Sparrow "the most common nesting sparrow of the Plains," ranking the Cassin's Sparrow second. The BBSS have since reversed this ranking as one moves from east to west. Tracking this progression, the following are the averages per count (Lark/Cassin's): *Booker*—34/13; *Childress*—48/20; *Waka*—3/0.3; *Miami*—33/50; *Clarendon*—30/55; *Panhandle*—4/1;

Lark Sparrow

Skellytown—22/66; *Pantex*—3/21; *Channing*—29/73; *Dalhart*—16/49; *Texline*—4/50. It should be borne in mind that a bias exists in these results in that "skylarking" and singing Cassin's Sparrows are more easily registered than is the more silent and less conspicuous behavior of the Lark Sparrow.

Returning Lark Sparrows in spring can be looked for during the first week of April, the earliest being a single bird in Potter County, 23 March 1965. Flocking birds may be encountered as early as the first week of July, some in flocks of considerable size: 100+ in the Bugbee area of Lake Meredith, Hutchinson County, 3 July 1983; 126 in the McBride area of Lake Meredith, Potter County, 12 July 1981; 70 in Caprock Canyons SP, Briscoe County, 27 July 1980; 52 in the PDCSP, 22 August 1965. Such large flocks are rarely reported in spring. One of 75+ was observed at a playa near Amarillo, Randall County, 28 April 1979, and 40+ were seen in one flock at the BLNWR, 26 April 1995. The latter were feeding with Chipping and Brewer's sparrows. Few linger beyond the third week of September, the latest being two birds at Lake Tanglewood, Randall County, 24 October 1963. Sightings of wintering Lark Sparrows are scarce: one at Lake Meredith, Hutchinson County, 17 December 1970, and two, 27 December 1986; two in PDCSP, 20 December 1981, and one, 22 December 1995; one at Cottonwood Lake near Quitaque, Briscoe County, 19 December 1984; two near Lake Tanglewood, Randall County, 9 and 15 December 1990; one in Caprock Canyons SP, Briscoe County, 1 January 1994. The ten shown on the Amarillo CBC of 18 December 1993 were a reporting error.

NESTING: The Lark Sparrow is a common nester throughout the study area, perhaps less so in the southwestern sector. The TBBAP found CO nesting in 42 survey blocks, PR in 48, and PO in 17. Forty-one of the quadrangles were located between the 100th and 101st meridians, 38 between the 101st and 102nd, and 28 west of the 102nd. Nest building has been observed as early as 29 April 1989 (near Clarendon, Donley County) and as late as 2 June 1988 (PDCSP, and near Dumas, Moore County). Nests with eggs have been found from 16 May 1976 (BLNWR) to 11 July 1982 (BLNWR). An adult on the nest was found in Roberts County, 14 July 1990. Nests are most often placed on the ground. On 11 July 1982 at BLNWR, I found a nest containing three eggs built in a small clump of stunted ragweed and thistle growing in the middle of a well-traveled road.

On the Miami BBS in Roberts County, 4 June 1986, I observed a partial albino Lark Sparrow that flew up from the roadside and perched on a fence post nearby. It had several small insects in its mouth and appeared quite agitated, calling frequently during the three-minute stop.

SPECIMENS: Specimens have been collected in Hutchinson (9 and 23 June 1950, TNHC), Moore (22 June 1957, MNH), Oldham (6 July 1986, TCWC), and Randall (3 June and 20 August 1939, WTAMU) counties. The Hutchinson County birds

are the two collected by Thompson (1952) and assigned to the race *C. g. strigatus.*
Oberholser (1974) refers to birds collected in Hutchinson and Lipscomb counties; however, he assigns them to a new subspecies, *C. g. quillini,* a race that has not been accepted.

Black-throated Sparrow *Amphispiza bilineata* (Cassin)

STATUS: Rare breeder in canyonlands, possibly in western river breaks.
OCCURRENCE: The Black-throated Sparrow has been recorded in seven counties: Armstrong, Briscoe, Childress, Hutchinson, Oldham, Potter, and Randall. It has been seen in every month except February and October.

When McCauley (1877) made his trek through the Texas Panhandle in 1876, he called this handsome sparrow "*Euspiza americana,* (Gm.) Bp.—Black-throated Bunting." On 19 June, he collected a specimen along White Fish Creek, some three miles beyond the crossing of the Salt Fork of the Red River in Armstrong County (Hunnius, 1876). The next reference to the species is that of Strecker (1910): "This pale variety . . . is apparently rare. Only three or four individuals were noted." His encounters also took place in Armstrong County. In a later work (1912) he assigned the birds to the subspecies *A. b. deserticola* (Desert Sparrow) and gave its range in Texas as: "Trans-Pecos region, the southern plains and the Panhandle west of the edge of the Staked Plains, summer resident. Winters in the southern part of its breeding range."

Between Strecker's encounters in 1910 and Hawkins's (1945) published report near mid-century, there is but one mention of the Black-throated Sparrow in the accounts of area observers, that of Reeves and Reeves (1914–36). These authors name it as being seen in 1923 at an unspecified locality, probably in Randall County. Carlander (1934), Russell (1935), and Stevenson (1942), all of whom conducted extensive field work in the Palo Duro Canyon system, did not mention it in their accounts. Even Hawkins was quite terse: "Rare migrant. Thompson and the author saw one of these flashy sparrows in Palo Duro Canyon, April 22, 1945."

The next published report of a Black-throated Sparrow is that of two birds found on the Amarillo CBC of 21 December 1957, Randall County—"the first recorded since 1952." It has been recorded seven times on subsequent Amarillo CBCs. My records show finding it in the canyon yearly from 1964 through 1978, and irregularly thereafter. To show its rarity and monthly distribution, the following list gives the number of times that I have encountered it: January (5); February (0); March (3); April (7); May (8); June (3); July (4); August (6); September (2); October (0); November (1); December (5). Rarely were more than two birds observed in a day, and then usually adults with young.

It is not known whether the population in the PDCSP is resident or if the summering birds leave and those found in winter are migrants from farther north and west. Banks (1968), like Strecker, considered the Black-throated Sparrow as only a summer resident in the northern part of its range in Texas: "central northern [Texas] . . . (east of Pecos River, San Angelo, Wayland)."

It is doubtful that the Black-throated Sparrow of the Palo Duro Canyon is a disjunct population. In addition to those found by Strecker (1910) in Armstrong County, others have been found in the Caprock Canyons SP, Briscoe County. Still farther south and west, black-throateds have been recorded during almost every month in the Southern Plains area (LEAS, 1994). To the southeast, one was recorded on the Childress BBS, Childress County, 9 June 1974, and to the northwest, I have encountered Black-throated Sparrows 4–5 miles south of Boys Ranch in Oldham County (6 June 1976; 6 June 1982; 4 June 1991), all singing birds observed along the roadside: a systematic search of surrounding areas would probably disclose still others, for the habitat is favorable. Such an environment covers a vast area extending west and northwest of Amarillo on ranchlands largely inaccessible to the public and seldom explored by birders. A continuing connection might well exist with the breeding population in the Black Mesa area of the northwestern Oklahoma Panhandle (Johnsgard, 1979; Baumgartner and Baumgartner, 1992), where the species has also been recorded in winter on CBCs (22 December 1966; 27 December 1969; 28 December 1971; 31 December 1977; 3 January 1989). It was Sutton's (1974) belief that the birds of that area were "probably resident, though no valid record [exists] for period between January 2 and April 3." A single bird was observed at Clayton, Union County, New Mexico, 2 April 1971 (Williams, 1971), and Hubbard (1978) says the species summers locally in the Dry Cimarron and lower Canadian River valleys in the northeastern sector. Mapping the range of the Black-throated Sparrow in the Texas Panhandle and determining to what extent the birds are resident could well be a challenge for an enterprising student.

As evidence that the Black-throated Sparrow is also a migrant, it has been reported in suburban yards four times in spring: Amarillo, Potter/Randall counties, 6 April 1975, 15 May 1978, 26 March 1998; Borger, Hutchinson County, 28 April 1984.

NESTING: The only location in the study area where the Black-throated Sparrow has been confirmed nesting is the PDCSP: adult with one young, 2 September 1970; two adults with two young, 29 May 1975; a singing adult with one young, 16 August 1987. A courting pair was observed on 4 July 1971. Singing birds have been reported from 26 March to 21 August. An out-of-season songster was heard in the state park, 17 January 1965.

SPECIMENS: The only specimen named in the literature is a male taken by McCauley (1877) at White Fish Creek, Armstrong County, 19 June 1876. This is the bird referred to by Oberholser (1974). Where the specimen was deposited is unknown.

Sage Sparrow *Amphispiza belli* (Cassin)
STATUS: Vagrant fall and winter visitor.

OCCURRENCE: The Sage Sparrow has been reported four times in the Texas Panhandle, all in Randall County. Reeves and Reeves (1914–36) cited the species for 1923, without specifying number or location (probably Randall County). Ten were observed at BLNWR on 23 February 1964 and seven the following 1 March (K. Seyffert). The birds were encountered a short distance downstream from the dam during late afternoon. The group flew into a juniper near the mouth of a side canyon; by taking advantage of a small herd of cattle grazing slowly in their direction, I remained shielded until quite near them. The latest sighting was of a single bird at a feeder in Amarillo, 30 October 1967 (T. Fox, R. Ross, E. Waddill).

The Sage Sparrow is an uncommon migrant and local winter resident in the Trans-Pecos region (TOS, 1995). The following is a record of sightings in nearby counties of the South Plains: *Bailey*—one, 16 October 1977 (Williams, 1978); one, 23 December 1979 (*fide* C. Stogner); 28 March 1982 (Williams, 1982); one, 18 December 1994 (CBC); all were on the Muleshoe NWR. *Crosby*—one, 16 October 1973 (*fide* C. Stogner); one, 16 November 1975 (*fide* C. Stogner); 22 March 1980 (Williams, 1980b); one, 9 November and 30 November 1980 (Williams, 1981); one, 1 October 1984 (Williams, 1985). There are two records from Cimarron County in the western Oklahoma Panhandle: 2 January 1982 (Garrett, 1982), and 21 and 30 January 1988 (Shackford, 1989b).

Lark Bunting *Calamospiza melanocorys* Stejneger
STATUS: Abundant migrant. Uncommon to common and irregular breeder. Rare to common winter visitor, occasionally abundant.

OCCURRENCE: There are records of Lark Buntings from every Texas Panhandle county, and the species has been seen during every month.

Lark Buntings, some flocks numbering in the hundreds, are often encountered on the High Plains in spring, late summer, and early fall. In a typical year small flocks begin appearing during mid- or late March, the groups becoming larger by mid- or late April. The greatest numbers are normally encountered during the first two weeks of May, dwindling to only a few by the last of the month. Examples by county from my records: *Randall*—550, 7 May 1967; 500+, 12 May 1968; 1,000+, 30 April 1978. *Castro*—600, 6 March 1983. *Swisher*—3,000+, 3 May 1988. *Hartley*—500+, 5 May 1990. *Hartley* and *Dallam*—850 on 1 May and 1,750+ on 16 May 1993; 5,000+ on 7 May 1996. Rarely are any found other than in grasslands; only occasionally have a few appeared on the floor of Palo Duro Canyon.

The return movement in fall can often be detected as early as late July. Examples from my records of flocking birds: 40 in Briscoe County, 27 July 1980; 1,000+ in Sherman, 28 July 1985; 50+ in Carson, 30 July 1989, and 170, 25 July 1993; 50 in Castro, 20 July 1991. Normally the larger flocks begin arriving in early or mid-August, and most buntings have completed their passage by the end of October or early November. Most wintering birds are found in the southwestern sector. This is reflected in the CBC highs and lows: *Friona*—11 of 12 (271, 1); *Buffalo* NWR—12 of 29 (2,225, 12); *Amarillo*—9 of 40 (435, 1); *Quitaque*—12 of 21 (330, 5); *Lake Meredith (west)*—4 of 24 (107, 1); *Lake Meredith (east)*—1 of 18 (30). It has only been in relatively recent years (mid-1970s and thereafter) that the Lark Bunting has been found with any regularity in winter outside the extreme southwestern sector, events paralleled to the north in Colorado and Kansas (Shane and Seltman, 1995).

Exceptional was the winter of 1987–88. Not only were 2,225 Lark Buntings recorded on the BLNWR CBC, but 75 or more were encountered outside the count circle. Similarly, 90 were recorded on the Quitaque CBC and 1,000+ beyond the count circle. On 30 January 1988, 7,500 were tallied on a swing through Randall, Armstrong, Briscoe, and Swisher counties. The following are examples of numbers from another southwestern county, Castro: 155, 31 January 1982; 225, 12 December 1982; 60, 5 February 1983. Other counties in which Lark Buntings have been reported in winter (December–February) are Dallam, Lipscomb, Hartley, Moore, Oldham, Carson, Gray, Deaf Smith, Donley, and Hall. Little work has been done during winter in the southeastern counties, and it is probable that Lark Buntings would be found in them also, for they have been recorded in nearby areas of southwestern Oklahoma, sometimes in large numbers (Tyler, 1985).

NESTING: The Lark Bunting has been recorded during summer (June–July) in all but four counties: Collingsworth, Hall, Donley, and Hemphill. The species is found most often in the northern sector, as reflected by the BBSS: *Texline*—18 of 22; *Channing*—7 of 30; *Booker*—6 of 22; *Waka*—5 of 19; *Miami*—2 of 22; *Pantex*—12 of 21; *Childress*—1 of 21. The 443 on the Texline BBS of 9 June 1979 were remarkable. Recorded on 32 of the 50 stops, the birds were either singing males or pairs on territory, the majority on the Rita Blanca National Grasslands. In Sherman, another northern county, 60 nonflocking buntings were found, 6 June 1977. Unusual were 66 nonflocking birds in Deaf Smith County, 4 July 1975, and 140, 19 July 1981; 32+ in Swisher County, 13 July 1981; and 11 in Parmer County, 7 June 1977.

There have been but few confirmed nestings. Reeves and Reeves (1914–36) noted: "They have nested along Tierra Blanca Creek [Randall] where we have seen them with young." Stevenson (1942) reported: "Philip Allan [U.S. Soil Conservation Service] states that 'nests . . . were found two years ago (1939) north of Amarillo, near the Canadian River [Potter] and this year (1941) young birds have been seen at the same locality.'" A nest with four eggs was found southwest of Dumas, Moore County, 14 June 1973 (MCHM). On 13 June 1987 and 17 June 1995, adults feeding young were observed near Texline, Dallam County, and a bird was seen performing a distraction display near Hartley, Hartley County, the summer of 1987. On several occasions in summer I observed adult buntings carrying food items on the BLNWR but was never able to find nests or young. In the summer of 1997, many Lark Buntings were found throughout much of the area, and a pair feeding a fledgling was photographed in Castro County on 15 July (one of "many" pairs [K. Mote, J. Ray]).

SPECIMENS: Specimens have been taken in Armstrong (fall 1974, WFVZ), Deaf Smith (20 August 1978, CMNH), Hansford (28 October 1956, MNH), and Randall (29 May 1965, WFVZ; 12 April 1937, 7 March, 7 May, 3 and 20 August 1939, WTAMU) counties. Oberholser (1974) speaks of summer specimens taken in Lipscomb County ("June 30, and July 6, 1903, A. H. Howell"), but their locations are not given. He also refers to a May 3 bird collected in Randall County, not included in the above listing.

Savannah Sparrow *Passerculus sandwichensis* (Gmelin)

STATUS: Uncommon to common migrant. Uncommon to fairly common winter visitor, primarily in the southern half.

OCCURRENCE: The Savannah Sparrow has been recorded in every county except Childress, Hemphill, Lipscomb, and Ochiltree. It has been seen in every month except June.

The Savannah Sparrow returns early in spring. By mid-March or early April numbers have increased greatly over those of overwintering birds, and the passage is largely completed by early May. The latest date on record is for a single bird at BLNWR, 15 May 1965. Illustrative of how common this sparrow can be, 51 were recorded on the Taylor Lakes WMA, Donley County, 9 April 1996.

There are a few puzzling summer sightings. Six Savannahs were reported at BLNWR on 10 July 1958, and "young birds and adults that I can only call Savannahs" were observed on the plains in Randall County on 18 July of the same year (P. Acord). Oberholser (1974) shows a summer sight record for Dallam County. Nearby, the species has been reported in the breeding season at the municipal airport at Clayton, Union County, New Mexico (NMOS, 1992). The nearest to the study area that this sparrow has been known to nest is Baca County in south-eastern Colorado, and there only occasionally (Chase et al., 1982).

The return of the Savannah Sparrow in fall can be looked for in early September. The earliest date is for 12 at BLNWR, 18 August 1968. As with early spring migrants, the termination of fall migration is obscured by birds that overwinter; most, however, have passed through by early November.

Few early observers mentioned the Savannah Sparrow as wintering in the Panhandle. Strecker (1912) made a general assessment of its status, calling it a "common winter resident, occurring throughout the state," while Stevenson (1942) was hardly more explicit when he said that "some remain through the winter." We know now that the species winters regularly in the southern counties, primarily in the southwestern sector. During the period 1961–73 on the *Friona* CBC in Parmer County, it was recorded yearly, averaging 26 birds per count (high 58, low 5). It has been recorded only sporadically on the other area counts (highs are in parentheses): *Buffalo Lake* NWR—12 of 29 (18); *Amarillo*—10 of 40 (8); *Quitaque*—12 of 21 (9). The two northern counts reflect its scarcity in that area: *Lake Meredith* (*west*)—4 of 24 (3); *Lake Meredith* (*east*)—3 of 18 (2). As an example of numbers reported in winter outside the CBC period, 30 were seen near Amarillo, 26 January 1964. A one-time suburban occurrence was a Savannah Sparrow at a feeder in Amarillo, Randall County 7 January 1964.

SPECIMENS: There is a specimen available collected in Hansford County (28 October 1956, MNH). Oberholser (1974) names others collected in Oldham and Randall counties but fails to give their locations. The Randall County bird is probably the one named by Stevenson (1942) as "collected 6 miles southeast of Canyon on September 30, 1937, . . . referable to *P. s. nevadensis.*" *P. s. anthinus* is also found in the Panhandle (TOS, 1995).

Grasshopper Sparrow *Ammodramus savannarum* (Gmelin)

STATUS: Uncommon to common breeder.

OCCURRENCE: The Grasshopper Sparrow has been recorded in every Texas Panhandle county and has been seen from April to October. Oberholser (1974) shows it in nine counties.

Mid- or late April is the time for returning Grasshopper Sparrows to appear. The earliest date is 6 April 1991—six singing birds on the Britt Ranch, Wheeler County. Most are gone by mid- or late September. The latest date is for one on the Taylor Lakes WMA, Donley County, 17 October 1997. Almost all current accounts and range maps confine the summer range of the Grasshopper Sparrow to the northeastern sector. Perhaps the basis of such a limited range has been Oberholser (1974) and Johnsgard (1979). This has now been corrected by Vickery (1996), based on knowledge gained from BBSS and the TBBAP. The species' summer status in the southwestern counties may be more variable than elsewhere, although in most years I have found the Grasshopper Sparrow to be fairly common to common. Fischer et al. (1982) maintained that it was a "rare summer resident" in Parmer, Castro, and Swisher counties. A later observer (C. D. Littlefield), however, had this to say in 1993: "Nesting everywhere in Castro and Parmer counties where there is CRP [Conservation Reserve Program] lands—they are abundant." I have often found the species common in western Deaf Smith County, at times in fields adjacent to the New Mexico state line (11 birds, 4 July 1975), and it was found commonly during the TBBAP. As an example, I recorded 36 birds in the Nazareth quadrangle, Castro County, 7 July 1987.

Another factor bearing on arriving at a true picture of the Grasshopper Sparrow's summer status is the inability of some surveyors to detect its song—a highly pitched, insect-like buzz beyond the range of their hearing. On BBSS the ability to pick up song is critical. As examples, the Booker count registered only two Grasshopper Sparrows during its first three years; with a change in compiler, the number immediately jumped to 20. On the Miami count only two birds were recorded in the first four years, but numbers increased to 12, 32, 13, and 24 the next four with a change in compiler. The following is a listing, east to west, of averages and highs for each BBS route: *Childress*—0.1 (2); *Booker*—16.3 (41); *Miami*—12.1 (32); *Clarendon*—0.9 (3); *Waka*—1.7 (8); *Pantex*—15.8 (37); *Channing*—5.0 (15); *Dalhart*—13.7 (17); *Texline*—9.0 (18).

NESTING: The TBBAP found CO nesting in 31 survey blocks, PR in 49, and PO in 11. Twenty-eight were located between the 100th and 101st meridians, 31 between the 101st and 102nd, and 32 west of the 102nd. Twenty-six were between 34 and 35 degrees north latitude, 41 between 35 and 36 degrees, and 24 between 36 degrees and 36 degrees, 30 minutes. These figures show a rather even distribution across the study area. Nest building was observed in one quadrangle, near Amarillo, Randall County, 21 May 1987. Young being fed have been observed from 4 June 1992 (Roberts County) to 24 July 1983 (Armstrong County). On 8 July 1973, a nest containing one egg and three recently hatched young was found southwest of Dumas, Moore County (photos).

SPECIMENS: Specimens have been collected in Castro (19 July 1987, TCWC), Hutchinson (23 June 1950, TNHC), and Randall (7 July 1987, TCWC) counties. Oberholser (1974) shows others collected in Lipscomb and Hemphill counties, without naming where they were deposited, and assigns them to the race *A. s. perpallidus.*

Baird's Sparrow *Ammodramus bairdii* (Audubon)

STATUS: Rare migrant.

OCCURRENCE: The Baird's Sparrow has been found in six counties—Hemphill, Oldham, Parmer, Potter, Randall, and Sherman—and has been recorded in every month except June and July.

Probably no other species has raised more questions concerning its status in the study area, both today and in the past, than has the Baird's Sparrow. They center around possible former breeding and present wintering.

The question of possible past nesting originates with McCauley (1877). As a member of the Ruffner expedition that explored the area in May and June of 1876, he had this to say of the Baird's Sparrow: "Very few specimens noted." Even though few were seen, the species would certainly have been more common at that time than now, considering its decline throughout its range. However, in addition to birds sighted, he reported the following discovery: "Personally all my searches for a nest of this species were unsuccessful, the one secured having been found by one of the escort, Private Ruby . . . a German, who was a very enthusiastic oologist." McCauley described the nest containing three eggs in great detail and said it was found in Cañoncito Blanco, in what is now the Ceta Glen area of South Ceta Canyon, Randall County, on 7 June. The discovery was later discounted by Ridgway (1901–19): "Two alleged breeding localities are so far outside the really established breeding range of this species that I can only refer to them as doubtful. These are Camp Harney, eastern Oregon . . . and Cañoncito, northern Texas." The present-day southern boundary of the breeding range of the Baird's Sparrow lies in southern South Dakota (AOU, 1983), and it is doubtful that it ever extended much farther south. Did Lieutenant McCauley and Private Ruby possibly misidentify the owner of the nest? Nowhere in his accounts does McCauley name the Grasshopper Sparrow, a species found fairly commonly as a breeder today in the area of his travels.

The other point of controversy concerns the questionable status of the Baird's Sparrow as a winter visitor. There have been almost as many winter birds reported as migrants, which in itself make them suspect. The AOU (1983) places the Baird's northernmost extension in winter as north-central Texas. Pulich (1988), however, disallowed all winter sightings from that part of the state for lack of supporting evidence. Perhaps that should also be done for the study area sightings, none of them documented. The likelihood that most, if not all, were misidentified Savannah Sparrows—a species not uncommonly confused with the Baird's and one known to winter in the area—must be considered. However, the possibility of occasional wintering is supported by a recent study of winter grassland bird communities in nearby Bailey County, in which the work turned up two Baird's Sparrows on the grama-buffalograss plains of the Muleshoe NWR

(Grzybowski, 1982); and it is supported still further by specimens collected on the refuge on 27 November 1976, 18 January 1977, and 19 January 1977 (OMNH).

For the record, the following is a listing of all reported winter sightings: *1954*—"one feeding with sparrows in roadside weeds near Amarillo," Randall County, 30 December; *1955*—two on the BLNWR, 10 December, and two in Randall County, 29 December; *1958*—two in the PDCSP, 27 December; *1964*—one in the PDCSP, 19 January; *1965*—one in the PDCSP, 22 December; *1967*—one in the PDCSP, 2 February; *1970*—one in the PDCSP, 20 January, and one at BLNWR, 19 February; *1972*—one in the PDCSP, 1 and 9 January and 10 February, and two, 17 December; *1981*—one in the PDCSP, 25 January. Baird's Sparrows have also been reported in winter at Clayton, Union County, New Mexico, sightings that were unconfirmed (Hubbard, 1978), and one was observed in Crosby County on the South Plains, 14 December 1980, and on the Muleshoe NWR, Bailey County, 27 December 1997 (LEAS).

Spring dates range from 20 March to 17 May and fall dates from 12 August to 22 November. The following is a listing of all reported sightings: *1953*—one in Hemphill County, 22 April; *1955*—one in Randall County, 29 October; *1961*—three in Parmer County, 23 September; *1962*—one in Parmer County, 12 August, and two, 6–7 October; *1964*—one in Randall County, 16 October, and one in the PDCSP, 22 November; *1966*—one at BLNWR, 25 September; *1969*—one at BLNWR, 8 May; *1970*—one in Randall County, 20 March; *1976*—one at Lake Meredith, Potter County, 17 May; *1980*—one in Randall County, 22 September; *1982*—one in Oldham County, 24 October; *1983*—two at BLNWR, 9 October; *1984*—one at BLNWR, 6 May; *1994*—one at BLNWR, 30 April (TBRC); *1998*—one at Texhoma, Sherman County, 6 April. It is probable that additional work done in the far western counties would produce more sightings of Baird's Sparrow as the species' winter range lies to the southwest of the study area (AOU, 1983).

The nearest points to the Texas Panhandle where specimens of Baird's Sparrow have been taken lie in Union County, New Mexico (Rohwer, 1969); Cimarron County, Oklahoma (Baumgartner and Baumgartner, 1992); and Kent and Lubbock counties on the South Plains of Texas (OMNH).

Le Conte's Sparrow *Ammodramus leconteii* (Audubon)

STATUS: Rare migrant and casual winter visitor.

OCCURRENCE: The Le Conte's Sparrow has been reported in ten widely scattered Texas Panhandle counties: Armstrong, Briscoe, Donley, Hemphill, Hutchinson, Ochiltree, Parmer, Potter, Randall, and Wheeler. It has been seen from October to June.

The first mention of a Le Conte's Sparrow is that of Stevenson (1942): "One was collected on May 3, 1936, in a mesquite thicket along Palo Duro Creek on the Harold Ranch, Armstrong County." Twenty-two years elapsed before another was reported.

The following is a listing of all subsequent sightings, a single bird in each instance unless otherwise noted: *1950*—Gene Howe WMA, Hemphill County, 25–26 September. *1958*—near Bushland, Potter County, 23 February, and near Amarillo, Randall County, 1 March. *1960*—southwest of Friona, Parmer County, 21 December. *1968–69*—17 October–5 February "on a weedy playa" near Hub, Parmer County. *1973*—"right under the kitchen window," Borger, Hutchinson County, in May. *1978*—two at BLNWR, 23 November. *1984*—juvenile at BLNWR, 2 October; two in Plum Creek, Lake Meredith National Recreation Area, Potter County, 22 December; Sanford Dam marsh, Lake Meredith, Hutchinson County, 29 December. *1988*—northeast of Wheeler, Wheeler County, 10 April. *1990*—a singing bird in southeast Ochiltree County, 25 June. *1994*—BLNWR, 21 March. *1995*—Taylor Lakes WMA, Donley County, 14 November. *1996–97*—PDCSP, 19 November, 14 December, 3 January, and three on 7 March; three in Caprock Canyons SP, 1 January. *1998*—Taylor Lakes WMA, Donley County, 23 October.

With the exception of the single June sighting, the dates of 2 October to 9 May closely conform to those from areas to the east of the Panhandle where the Le Conte's is more commonly found. Grzybowski et al. (1992) give dates of 10 October–1 May for Oklahoma, and Pulich (1988) gives 8 October–3 May for north-central Texas. The unlikely suburban sighting in Borger in May 1973 may be questioned; however, another backyard bird was reported in Fort Worth on 21 April of that year (Williams, 1973). Concerning the juvenile at BLNWR in October 1984, Sutton (1967) has this to say of some Oklahoma specimens: "Earliest fall specimens at hand (October 2, 8) are in virtually complete *juvenal* feather despite probability that nearest breeding grounds are in southeastern South Dakota and northeastern Illinois." The June 1990 singing bird is a puzzler. I would dismiss it had it not been seen from a short distance by an experienced field observer familiar with its song. Upon learning of the find, I visited the site a few days later and found only Grasshopper Sparrows. The habitat was typical of that preferred by the latter species—rank and weedy upland grassland—and lacking the damp substrate preferred by the Le Conte's.

Those Le Conte's Sparrows found in Parmer County in the winters of 1960–61 and 1968–69 are of particular interest. A banding program conducted at playas in the San Angelo area, Tom Green County, in 1984 turned up an unexpected 25 Le Conte's during the period September–December (Williams, 1985). The Parmer County birds found in similar habitat point to the possibility of there being more of the species wintering in the study area than is thought. In nearby southwestern Oklahoma, the Le Conte's is classified as an "uncommon" and local winter resident (Tyler, 1979b).

SPECIMENS: The one specimen taken is that of Stevenson (1942) in Armstrong County (3 May 1936, MVZ). Oberholser (1974) mistakenly assigns it to Randall County.

Fox Sparrow *Passerella iliaca* (Merrem)

STATUS: Rare to uncommon winter visitor.

OCCURRENCE: The Fox Sparrow has been found in 12 counties: Briscoe, Castro, Dallam, Donley, Gray, Hartley, Hemphill, Hutchinson, Potter, Randall, Roberts, and Wheeler. It has been seen from October to May.

Most Fox Sparrows are seen during the period November–March. There are very few records for October, the earliest being for a single bird at BLNWR, 4 October 1964. Equally rare are those still present in April, and only four sightings have been reported in May, the latest a single bird in Amarillo, 30 May 1953. An indication of its winter status can be gleaned from the CBCs. The following are the number of times recorded on each: *Amarillo*—13 of 40; *Buffalo Lake NWR*—1 of 29; *Lake Meredith (west)*—2 of 24; *Lake Meredith (east)*—2 of 18; *Quitaque*—4 of 21; *Friona*—0 of 12. Eight on the Amarillo CBC of 20 December 1981 were exceptional.

The subspecies of Fox Sparrow found in the study area are *P. i. zaboria*, generally in the eastern sector, and *P. i. schistacea* westward.

Song Sparrow *Melospiza melodia* (Wilson)

STATUS: Fairly common to common winter visitor.

OCCURRENCE: The Song Sparrow has been found in every county except Carson, this exception arising only through oversight. It has been recorded in every month.

The nasal *tchuck* of the Song Sparrow is one of the more familiar bird calls one is apt to hear from October to April, particularly in the vicinity of streams, marshy areas, and playa lakes. This bird quickly sounds off when disturbed and can easily be called up for viewing. It is not unusual for one to burst into song on a bright, warm day in midwinter, while those in spring are often heard singing. In South Ceta Canyon, Randall County, 29 January 1978, three Song Sparrows were watched as they waded into a flowing stream and began picking up objects from the streambed. The half-submerged birds continued feeding for several minutes.

A Winter-Bird Population Study conducted in the PDCSP disclosed the Song Sparrow to be the third most common species on a 31-acre streamside plot

(Seyffert, 1968–78). The average number ranged from a low of 10 per 100 acres in one winter to a high of 60 per 100 acres in two others, the overall average 32 per 100 acres. The CBCs reflect its status in early winter. The following are the averages and highs for each count: *Amarillo*—33 (134); *Quitaque*—33 (80); *Lake Meredith* (*west*)—31 (180); *Lake Meredith* (*east*)—19 (36); *Buffalo Lake* NWR—20 (200); *Friona*—6 (27). Several earlier observers classified the Song Sparrow as less than common. Stevenson (1942) considered it an "uncommon winter visitor in the Palo Duro Canyon," while Hawkins (1945) thought it no more than a "fairly common winter resident along marshy creeks."

The Song Sparrow can be expected in fall during early or mid-October, and most are gone by mid-April. There is one record for August (BLNWR, 29 August 1964) and five exist for September. There are four May records, the latest for three birds in the Bates Canyon area, Lake Meredith National Recreation Area, Potter County, 14 May 1978, and for one at Lake Tanglewood, Randall County, 14 May 1994. Unaccountable for summer was an "individual seen in the brush near Palo Duro Creek, July 15" (Russell, 1935), and one in a residential yard in Amarillo, Randall County, 8 June 1998. Earlier, Hibbets et al. (1926–36) classified the Song Sparrow as a "permanent resident." The assessment was possibly based on the observation of late spring and early fall birds. There are breeding records for extreme southeastern Colorado (Chase et al., 1982), and Sutton (1967) notes a female specimen "in virtually complete juvenal feather" taken in Cimarron County, Oklahoma, 13 September 1959—"suggesting possibility that species occasionally nests in Oklahoma or Kansas." It is also listed as a "breeding/summer species" of Perico Creek, Union County, New Mexico (NMOS, 1992).

SPECIMENS: Two specimens have been collected, both in Randall County (31 December 1936, MVZ; 7 March 1939, WTAMU). The MVZ bird was assigned to *M. m. juddi*. Oberholser (1974) names a specimen of *montana* taken in Oldham County ("Oct. 27"), without specifying its present location. Other races probably occur, as wide variation in plumages has been observed.

Lincoln's Sparrow *Melospiza lincolnii* (Audubon)

STATUS: Fairly common migrant and uncommon winter visitor.

OCCURRENCE: The Lincoln's Sparrow has been recorded in all counties of the Texas Panhandle except Armstrong, Lipscomb, Ochiltree, and Sherman and has been seen from September to June. It is shown by Oberholser (1974) in six counties.

The Lincoln's Sparrow returns in fall around mid-September, the earliest date being for one at BLNWR, 4 September 1988. Seldom are more than half a dozen or so reported during a single outing. Exceptional were 35 encountered in the PDCSP, 29 November 1981. My records reveal that the seven-day period of greatest abundance in fall is 4–10 October. Because of overwintering birds, it is sometimes uncertain when the spring movement commences; normally is mid-April before an increase in numbers is detected, the seven-day period of greatest abundance 8–14 May. Of all the migrant emberizines, the Lincoln's Sparrow lingers the longest. Sightings for the last two days of May are numerous, while others have been found still later: one in Hartley County, 2 June 1990; one at BLNWR, 7 June 1969. A juvenile closely observed on the BLNWR on 29 September 1987 raised the question of possible nesting in or near the study area, for the juvenal feathering in this species is held only briefly. Such a possibility is unlikely as the Lincoln's Sparrow is known to nest no nearer than the mountains of southern Colorado and northern New Mexico (AOU, 1983).

As an indication of the status of the Lincoln's Sparrow in winter, it was found during six of the years of a Winter-Bird Population Study (Seyffert, 1968–78) conducted in the PDCSP, averaging three per 100 acres. The CBCs are indicative of early winter status. The following are the number of times it has been recorded on each: *Amarillo*—19 of 40; *Buffalo Lake* NWR—3 of 29; *Quitaque*—5 of 21; *Lake Meredith* (*west*)—5 of 24; *Lake Meredith* (*east*)—1 of 18; *Friona*—0 of 12. The highest number tallied on a single count was 22 on the Amarillo CBC of 20 December 1981.

SPECIMENS: There is a specimen on display taken in Potter County (AMNH) for which details are lacking. Oberholser (1974) names another taken in Potter County ("Sept. 27"), which he assigns to nominate *M. l. lincolnii*.

Swamp Sparrow *Melospiza georgiana* (Latham)
STATUS: Rare migrant and winter visitor.

OCCURRENCE: The Swamp Sparrow has been found in eight counties—Briscoe, Donley, Gray, Hartley, Hemphill, Hutchinson, Potter, and Randall—and has been seen September–May.

With three exceptions, all reported dates for the Swamp Sparrow fall between early October and late April. The exceptions are one in Hartley County, 22 September 1990; a dead bird recovered at Lake Tanglewood, Randall County, 19 September 1998; and one at BLNWR, 13 May 1979. Emphasizing its rarity in winter, the Swamp Sparrow has been found on only 28 of 143 CBCs, the highest number being six on the Amarillo count of 21 December 1991. The locations where it has been seen most often are the marshes at Lake Meredith (Hutchinson County), Lake Tanglewood–Currie Ranch (Randall County), and Lake Theo (Briscoe County).

The Swamp Sparrow is possibly more common than this short account indicates. The area's marshes are underbirded, and the species is seldom noticed until it pops up and sounds off with its loud metallic *chip*. Also, some young birds are possibly misidentified as juvenile White-throated Sparrows. The species is not mentioned in any accounts of early observers, and Oberholser (1974) does not name it.

White-throated Sparrow *Zonotrichia albicollis* (Gmelin)

STATUS: Uncommon to fairly common migrant and winter visitor.

OCCURRENCE: The White-throated Sparrow has been seen in 16 of the 26 Texas Panhandle counties: Briscoe, Castro, Dallam, Donley, Gray, Hall, Hansford, Hemphill, Hutchinson, Moore, Oldham, Parmer, Potter, Randall, Roberts, and Wheeler. It has been recorded September–May.

The White-throated Sparrow is usually encountered as a solitary bird or in groups of not more than two or three. It was found in five of the years of a Winter-Bird Population Study (Seyffert, 1968–78) conducted in the PDCSP, averaging three per 100 acres. The averages on the CBCs reflect a similar scarcity: *Amarillo*—4.5; *Quitaque*—1.7; *Lake Meredith (west)*—1.4. It has yet to be recorded on the Lake Meredith (east) and BLNWR counts. A notable exception to such low numbers was the winter of 1981–82. On 29 November 1981, 32 White-throated Sparrows were found in the PDCSP, 14 in one flock, and on the following 20 December, 70 were tallied there on the Amarillo CBC. An exceptional spring movement was observed in the state park on 16 April 1966, when 50+ white-throateds, many of them singing, were encountered in one loose gathering.

The White-throated Sparrow during fall is usually first observed in early or mid-October. There are only three September sightings, the earliest a single bird in Ceta Glen, South Ceta Canyon, Randall County, 9 September 1980, and few are found past mid-April, the latest being one at Lake Meredith, Potter County, 9 May 1982.

Harris's Sparrow *Zonotrichia querula* (Nuttall)

STATUS: Uncommon to fairly common winter visitor in the eastern half, less so westward.

OCCURRENCE: The Harris's Sparrow has been seen in all but six Texas Panhandle counties: Armstrong, Carson, Castro, Deaf Smith, Oldham, and Sherman. It has been seen October–May.

Oberholser (1974) classified the Harris's Sparrow in the study area as "rare, often absent." Its absence is local, not areawide. Early observers rarely mentioned it. Hawkins (1945) thought it strictly a migrant, while Wolfe (1956) did not place it in the region at all. It is doubtful that there has been any great change in the species' status, and its former absence can be attributed to lack of coverage.

The Harris's Sparrow seldom arrives before the second week of November, and few remain beyond mid-April. There have been only three sightings the third week of October or earlier, the earliest one in Miami, Roberts County, 13 October 1979. Only eight May records are on file, the latest a single bird at BLNWR, 13 May 1979. With a resident observer situated in a northeastern county, these dates would likely be extended. The averages and highs on the CBCs reflect the Harris's Sparrow's status in the central sector: *Lake Meredith* (*west*)—6.1 (33); *Lake Meredith* (*east*)—4.2 (26); *Amarillo*—1.4 (12); *Quitaque*—0.3 (3); *Buffalo Lake* NWR—0.3 (2); *Friona*—0.2 (1). No CBC is conducted in the eastern counties where the species is most commonly found. Numbers are higher on the Arnett CBC only a few miles east of the state line in Ellis County, Oklahoma, where the average is 67.2, high 209.

White-crowned Sparrow *Zonotrichia leucophrys* (Forster)

STATUS: Common to abundant migrant and winter visitor.

OCCURRENCE: The White-crowned Sparrow has been found in every county except Ochiltree, a northern county where little birding has been done other than in summer. It has been recorded in every month except July.

This bird of brushland and thicket is among the more common and familiar of the sparrows that winter in the study area. White-crowned Sparrows arrive early and remain late. Normally they are found in flocks, some quite large. Among the largest I have encountered are those that winter in extensive stands of *Kochia scoparia* at BLNWR. Singing birds may be heard all winter, particularly on warm days of sunshine, and their plaintive opening whistles followed by trills evoke a spirit of community. The first birds can be looked for in mid- or late September. Extremely early was an adult at BLNWR, 18 August 1985—the only August sighting. Prior to then the early date was an immature in Amarillo, Potter County, 9 September 1964. A Winter-Bird Population Study conducted in the PDCSP (Seyffert, 1968–78) found the White-crowned Sparrow to be the fourth most common species on the study plot, ranging from a low of three per 100 acres to a high of 81 per 100 acres. Averages and highs on the CBCs indicate its abundance in other habitats: *Friona*—259 (888); *Lake Meredith* (*west*)—197 (852); *Buffalo Lake* NWR—178 (985); *Quitaque*—97 (263); *Amarillo*—95 (336); *Lake Meredith* (*east*)—67 (374).

The composition of wintering flocks insofar as the ratio of adults to immatures is concerned has been given little or no attention. I examined one such a flock of some 160 birds at BLNWR, 1 November 1981, and found that 98 percent were immatures. Such a preponderance, however, is atypical. Most white-crowneds are gone by the end of the third week of May. One was found on the BLNWR, 29 May in both 1971 and 1978, and one in a suburban setting in Canyon,

Randall County, 30–31 May 1996. I observed an adult with a deformed bill in the Thompson Grove Picnic Area northeast of Texline, Dallam County, 9 June 1977.

NESTING: Unexpected was a nesting pair of White-crowned Sparrows found on the northern outskirts of Amarillo, Potter County, in late June 1994 (R. Thompson, R. Wilberforce). The nest was placed some 2–3 feet above ground in a juniper: one bird was sitting with the other in attendance. The professional wildlife photographers who discovered it were familiar with the species and sure of their identification. Several days were spent preparatory to taking pictures. When the foliage obscuring the nest was gradually parted and tied back for an unobstructed view, the tightly sitting bird appeared undisturbed. On 25 June, however, before pictures could be taken, a devastating wind struck the area, gusting to 70 mph and causing much damage. On the following morning, the nest with two eggs was found on the ground beneath the tree and the adult birds were nowhere to be seen.

The White-crowned Sparrow is not a breeding species of the Great Plains. The nearest locations to the study area where it nests are in the northern highlands of New Mexico in the Sangre de Cristo and San Juan mountains (Hubbard, 1978). Unfortunately, detailed notes were not kept of the nesting pair, and it is not known to what race the birds may have belonged.

SPECIMENS: Specimens have been taken in Potter (21 October 1988, TCWC) and Randall (16 November 1985, TCWC; 29 January, 6 March, 30 September, 7 October, 5 November 1939, 15 January 1969, 3 May 1971, WTAMU) counties. One of the two Randall County birds housed at TCWC was assigned to *leucophrys* and the other to *gambelii*. Oberholser (1974) assigns a specimen taken in Wheeler County to *leucophrys*, but he fails to name its location.

Golden-crowned Sparrow *Zonotrichia atricapilla* (Gmelin)
STATUS: Casual winter visitor.

OCCURRENCE: The Golden-crowned Sparrow has been recorded in three Texas Panhandle counties: Briscoe, Potter, and Randall. It has been seen from November to March and during two days in May.

There have been seven, possibly eight, sightings of the Golden-crowned Sparrow in the study area, in each instance a single bird: *1954*—Amarillo, Randall County, 17 January; Oberholser (1974) wrongly assigned this sighting to Potter County. *1955*—PDCSP, 2 January. *1964*—PDCSP, 8 December. *1976–77*—Amarillo, Randall County, 12 November–1 January (TBRC). *1981*—PDCSP, 20 December. *1985*—PDCSP, 16 and 24 March. *1990*—Caprock Canyons SP, Briscoe County, 1 January (TBRC). *1990–91*—an immature, 2 December–9 March in the Tierra Grande addition north of Amarillo, Potter County (TBRC; TP-RF); remarkably, a Golden-crowned Sparrow in adult plumage was observed at this site on the following 2–3 May.

Of 35 Golden-crowned Sparrows reported in Texas by the end of 1995, 22 percent had been seen in the study area (Lasley and Sexton, 1995a). A single bird was observed at Lubbock, 17–18 April 1979 (Williams, 1979). The Golden-crowned Sparrow's wintering range lies in the far western United States, with only casual appearances east to Utah, Colorado, and central New Mexico (AOU, 1983).

Dark-eyed Junco *Junco hyemalis* (Linnaeus)

STATUS: Common to abundant winter visitor.

OCCURRENCE: The Dark-eyed Junco has been reported in every Texas Panhandle county and has been seen from September to May.

Nominate *J. h. hyemalis* ("Slate-colored Junco"), *J. h. oreganus* ("Oregon Junco"), *J. h. caniceps* ("Gray-headed Junco"), and *J. h. aikeni* ("White-winged Junco") have all been found in the study area. Generally, the Oregon predominates in the western sector and the Slate-colored in the eastern. Of 55 juncos observed on the BLNWR, 31 January 1997, 90 percent were Oregons, 55 percent of them the "pink-sided" form. The Gray-headed is a rare to uncommon migrant and winter visitor, and the White-winged a casual winter visitor.

Juncos return in fall during the first or second week of October. In the central sector, the Oregon tends to arrive a week or two before the Slate-colored. The earliest date for each race: Oregon, 22 September 1987 at BLNWR; Slate-colored, 23 September 1956 at Amarillo, Potter County; Gray-headed, 21 September 1980 at BLNWR. Most have left the area by the first or second week of April, and rarely has one been reported as late as May: a Slate-colored at BLNWR, 14 May 1994; an Oregon in Hartley County, 5 May 1990; a Gray-headed in Canyon, Randall County, 3 May 1997, and at BLNWR, 11 May 1980.

The Gray-headed Junco has been reported in only ten counties: Armstrong, Castro, Dallam, Gray, Moore, Oldham, Parmer, Potter, Randall, and Roberts. With the exception of Gray and Roberts, all lie in the western sector. There is a tendency for this race both to arrive earlier and to linger later than the others. In fact, it is more a bird of passage than a winter resident. It is often found alone. The 26 reported on the Amarillo CBC of 2 January 1955 were remarkable, if in order.

There have been six reported sightings of the White-winged Junco: *1968*—an immature male collected on 19 December near Quitaque, Briscoe County (Weske, 1974), a first record for the state. The bird was alone in the canyon of Little Red River at the Haynes Boy Scout Camp, a site adjacent on the west to present-day Caprock Canyons SP; *1969*—a lone bird, 8 November, a mile or so upcanyon from the PDCSP; *1975*—a lone bird at BLNWR, 27 November; *1976*—one in a flock of other juncos at BLNWR, 30 October (postcard, Avis Newell, bander/naturalist, 1 November); *1983*—one in a mixed flock of juncos feeding at the roadside at Palo Duro Creek northeast of Umbarger, Randall County, 24 December; *1988*—one in a mixed flock of juncos near Cottonwood Lake southwest of Quitaque, Briscoe County, 1 January. The White-winged Junco is a sometime winter visitor in western Oklahoma, occurring from October to April (Sutton, 1967), and in the Clayton area of Union County, New Mexico (Williams and Hubbard, 1993). It would perhaps be found more often if the northwestern counties of the study area were birded extensively in winter.

The Dark-eyed Junco was found to be the most common species during a Winter-Bird Population Study conducted in the PDCSP (Seyffert, 1968–78). The average density was 117 per 100 acres (low 45, high 184 per 100 acres). The average flock size on the 31-acre study plot was 36 birds: the ratio of Oregons to Slate-coloreds varied from 16:1 to parity. The averages and highs on the CBCs are as follows: *Amarillo*—294 (716); *Lake Meredith* (*east*)—272 (833); *Quitaque*—250 (1057); *Lake Meredith* (*west*)—227 (719); *Buffalo Lake* NWR—131 (700); *Friona*—13 (27). A partial albino junco was observed at BLNWR, 27 February 1983: though it was otherwise entirely white, the top of the head and the back were a light tan.
SPECIMENS: The following specimens have been taken: *hyemalis*—Hemphill (25 and 31 January 1929, MVZ), Potter (23 November and 13 December 1982; TCWC), Randall (25 and 26 December 1936, 22 November 1993; TCWC) counties; *oreganus*—Hemphill (31 January 1929; MVZ) and Potter (8 November 1982; TCWC) counties; *aikeni*—Briscoe County (19 December 1968; USNM). In addition, Oberholser (1974) shows specimens of *oreganus* taken in Deaf Smith and Oldham counties, without naming where they were deposited.

McCown's Longspur *Calcarius mccownii* (Lawrence)
STATUS: Common to abundant winter visitor.
OCCURRENCE: The McCown's Longspur has been recorded in 18 counties: Armstrong, Briscoe, Carson, Castro, Dallam, Deaf Smith, Donley, Hansford, Hartley, Hemphill, Moore, Ochiltree, Oldham, Parmer, Potter, Randall, Sherman, and Swisher. It has been seen from October to April.

Except for brief periods, the McCown's is normally the most common of the wintering longspurs. Flock numbers may range from only a few up to hundreds. On 8 January 1968, a gathering of 8,000–10,000 was observed west of Amarillo, Randall County. The study area almost always produces the nationwide high on the annual CBCs. Illustrative are those conducted in Parmer (Friona) and Randall (BLNWR) counties. During the period 1961–73, a lone observer tallied an average of 1,008 McCown's on the Friona CBC (low 281, high 2,312), and during the period 1973–93, others recorded an average of 840 on the BLNWR CBC (low 37, high 2,720). Securing a good longspur count, however, may be prevented by impassable winter roads.

The last week of October and the first week of November are when the McCown's Longspur normally arrives in fall. The earliest date on record is a specimen collected in Oldham County, 15 October (Oberholser, 1974), while others recorded a small flock near Amarillo, Randall County, 16 October 1966. Most are gone by mid-March. The latest observation is of two birds in Randall County, 2 April 1966. Krause (1968) names Amarillo spring and fall dates of 4 April and 18 October. As recently as 1911 and 1914, the McCown's Longspur was known to breed in the western Oklahoma Panhandle (Sutton, 1967).

A familiarity with call notes and close attention given to the pattern and degree of white in tails are necessary in identifying flying McCown's Longspurs, particularly when in mixed flocks with other longspur species and Horned Larks ("larkspurs"). Longspur flocks are usually quite restless. Often when a flock lands, the birds almost immediately take flight again, circling about and re-peating the performance numberless times before settling down to feed, usually far from the observer. The optimal condition for viewing such restless flocks is when snow covers the ground, for then the birds tend to feed along partially cleared roadsides and allow a closer approach. Most often they are found in recently plowed fields, harvested grain fields, and fields of short winter wheat, occasionally visiting the margins of playa lakes to drink briefly.

On 18 November 1993 I found a flock of mixed McCown's and Lapland long-spurs feeding in a stubblefield near Umbarger, Randall County. One bird had a pure white head with a dark stripe running down the middle of its crown, while the rest of its plumage was that of a typical McCown's, including the pattern of the wing and tail feathers seen when in flight.

SPECIMENS: Specimens are available from Randall County (28 December 1936, MVZ). The location is not given for the one Oberholser (1974) cites as collected in Oldham County. The type specimen of McCown's Longspur was collected by Capt. John P. McCown, U.S.A., probably in the study area: "I fired at a flock of Shore Larks," he writes, "and found this bird among the killed" (Krause, 1968). Later, George N. Lawrence named the species for his friend, Capt. McCown, stating: "Two specimens were obtained . . . on the high prairies of Western Texas."

Lapland Longspur *Calcarius lapponicus* (Linnaeus)

STATUS: Common to abundant winter visitor.

OCCURRENCE: The Lapland Longspur has been recorded in all but six counties in the Texas Panhandle: Childress, Collingsworth, Hall, Hartley, Hutchinson, and Roberts. It has been seen from October to March.

The Lapland Longspur arrives later and leaves earlier than the McCown's and Chestnut-collared longspurs, and its presence is more variable. Mid- to late November is when it can be expected in the fall, and few are seen beyond February. There is an October record on file for Randall County that perhaps should be dismissed. My records show an early fall date of 18 November 1993 (10 in Randall County) and a late winter date of 10 February 1985 (200+ in Randall County). Those reported in a mixed flock with other longspurs on the very late date of 27 April 1970 must be questioned (Williams, 1970).

The BLNWR CBCs are indicative of the status of the Lapland Longspur in early winter. During the period 1973–93, it was recorded on 13 of 22 counts, averaging 215 per count (high 1,690). The most extraordinary winter for Laplands was that of 1978–79, when 7,000–20,000 were observed in Randall County on 13–14 January 1979. That was a conservative estimate. Enormous flocks that filled the sky ("a million," thought one observer) were encountered from PDCSP westward to BLNWR (specimen): that number is not unduly far-fetched, as an observer in Kansas is certain he saw over a million Laplands there in one day (Thompson and Ely, 1992), and hundreds of thousands have been seen in an hour. Interestingly, on the BLNWR CBC the preceding 16 December, not a single Lapland Longspur was recorded! How many may have been in the study area during the peak period is impossible to estimate. Such numbers are in sharp contrast to an observation that Hawkins (1945) made in mid-century: "The present author examined hundreds of longspurs through field glasses, but saw not a single Lapland Longspur." Wolfe (1956) classified the species as only a "casual winter visitor," and Oberholser (1974) said it was "locally fairly common to scarce."

Startling was a male Lapland Longspur in full breeding plumage that I observed feeding in a snow-covered stubblefield near the road northwest of Canyon, Randall County, 27 December 1997.

SPECIMENS: Specimens have been taken in Hansford (27 December 1955, MNH; 22 November 1954, OMNH), and Randall (14 January 1979 and 24 December 1983, TCWC) counties. One taken in Randall County was assigned to the race *C. l. alascensis* (Stevenson, 1942), and no doubt represents the one referred to by Oberholser (1974). The common race is nominate *lapponicus*.

Chestnut-collared Longspur *Calcarius ornatus* (Townsend)

STATUS: Common to abundant winter visitor.

OCCURRENCE: The Chestnut-collared Longspur has been recorded in 14 counties: Armstrong, Briscoe, Carson, Castro, Dallam, Deaf Smith, Donley, Gray, Moore, Oldham, Parmer, Potter, Randall, and Swisher. It has been seen from October to April.

The Chestnut-collared Longspur arrives earlier in the fall and remains later in the spring than do the other longspur species. The early and late dates are 20 at BLNWR, 1 October 1976, and two at the same location, 11 April 1970. The largest number in a single flock ever reported was approximately 2,000 northwest of Quitaque, Briscoe County, 1 January 1982. It is reported more often during winter in the southern counties.

The CBCs reflect an erratic presence in early winter that perhaps is misleading: *Buffalo Lake* NWR—10 of 29 counts, high 700; *Friona*—10 of 12 counts, high 49; *Quitaque*—5 of 21 counts, high 2,000; *Amarillo*—2 of 40 counts, high 12. The species has never been recorded on the Lake Meredith (east) and (west) counts. My records disclose seeing it during December in ten years, during January in five, and during February in four.

Pure flocks of Chestnut-collared Longspurs are more often reported in fall and spring than in winter, at which time the species may be found in mixed flocks with McCown's and Laplands. Large flocks of McCown's are seldom examined closely to determine species composition; as a consequence, the Chestnut-collared Longspur is probably overlooked in many instances and undoubtedly is more common than our records indicate. Much work remains to be done toward clarifying the relationship and status of the longspurs.

SPECIMENS: A specimen is available taken in Hansford County (28 October 1956, MNH). Oberholser (1974) shows specimens taken in Oldham and Randall Counties, but their locations are not given.

Snow Bunting *Plectrophenax nivalis* (Linnaeus)

STATUS: Vagrant.

OCCURRENCE: There has been one reported occurrence of the Snow Bunting in the Texas Panhandle. On 29 December 1983, two were observed in a flock of Lapland Longspurs approximately 17 miles northeast of Dalhart, Dallam County (M. Lockwood; TBRC). The birds were seen in flight and while feeding. The habitat was grasslands interspersed with occasional cultivated fields, and when first found the flock was feeding in a harvested maize field. At the time this represented only the second confirmed sighting of the species in Texas. The presence of Snow Buntings in a flock of longspurs emphasizes the need for examining such flocks carefully.

The Snow Bunting has been reported once in the Oklahoma Panhandle (Sutton, 1967): "December 22, 1960, three seen directly overhead near Kenton, Cimarron County." Krehbiel names it for the Clayton area, Union County, New Mexico (Ligon, 1961), as does Hubbard (1978).

Family Cardinalidae (Cardinals and Allies)

Northern Cardinal *Cardinalis cardinalis* (Linnaeus)

STATUS: Fairly common to common resident in eastern half, westward in Canadian River Valley and canyonlands; rare elsewhere.

OCCURRENCE: The Northern Cardinal has been recorded in every county except Sherman in the northwest and would be there with better coverage. It is present year-round.

The "redbird" is more common in the study area today than formerly, based on early accounts. In the latter part of the nineteenth century McCauley (1877) spoke of it in May and June as "occasionally observed on the Canadian and the McClellan and Wolf Creeks." Today it found considerably more often. Neither Carlander (1936) nor Hawkins (1945) names the species in his account, despite both Russell (1935) and Stevenson (1942) classifying the cardinal as common in the Palo Duro Canyon. The latter observer delineated its range in the study area as occurring from the central Panhandle eastward. Today it is common in the eastern half, the Canadian River Valley at least as far west as the Boys Ranch area in Oldham County, the canyon of the Prairie Dog Town Fork of the Red River as far upstream as its source in Randall County, and in Amarillo, Potter/Randall counties. A few can be found in western communities, such as Hereford (Deaf Smith County) and Vega (Oldham). Dalhart (Dallam/Hartley) is the farthest northwest where it has been reported. Cardinals have been reported twice in Cimarron County in the Oklahoma Panhandle (Newell, 1990), and in New Mexico a male was reported in Tucumcari, Quay County ("far n. of the usual range," 2 February 1993; Williams and Hubbard, 1993), and a female at Clayton Lake, Union County, 24 March 1994 (Williams, 1994).

Not only has the Northern Cardinal extended its range westward; it also has increased in number, as evidenced by its presence in the PDCSP. My records show that during the period 1964–78, I recorded an average of 5.0 cardinals per trip, while during the period 1979–93, the average was 10.8. These figures are based on 526 trips averaging three hours each. A two-year Breeding Bird Study conducted in the PDCSP (Seyffert, 1967–68) resulted in an average density of 19 per 100 acres, while a Winter-Bird Population Study (Seyffert, 1968–78) conducted on the same plot produced an average of 16 per 100 acres. The cardinal was the sixth most common species found on the site during winter.

The averages on the CBCs give an indication of winter numbers in varied habitats: *Amarillo* and *Quitaque,* held primarily in canyonlands, 37.1 and 19.4 respectively; *Lake Meredith* (*west*) and *Lake Meredith* (*east*), conducted in the Canadian River Valley, 26.7 and 6.0; *Buffalo Lake* NWR and *Friona,* predominantly grassland/cropland, 2.1 and 0.

The averages on the BBSs are somewhat misleading on the cardinal's summer status. With the exceptions of Childress and Clarendon, few stops on the other counts sample proper habitats: *Childress*—12.4: *Clarendon*—8.4; *Miami*—0.9; *Channing*—0.5; *Booker*—0.1; *Pantex*—0; *Texline*—0; *Waka*—0. The last three counts traverse prairie and croplands, with little sampling of wooded areas. A regionwide conclusion on the summer status of the Northern Cardinal based on the BBSs alone would be misleading, for no survey is conducted in the far eastern counties (with the exception of Childress) or in the Palo Duro Canyon system and Canadian River Valley, areas where the species can most commonly be found.

NESTING: The TBBAP (1987–92) discovered CO nesting in 17 survey blocks, PR in 31, and PO in four. Twenty-eight quadrangles were located between the 100th and 101st meridians, 17 between the 101st and 102nd, and seven west of the 102nd. The Northern Cardinal is probably two-brooded. Nests with eggs have been found as early as 9 May 1987 (Lelia Creek, Donley County) and as late as 10 July 1935 (PDCSP). Adults with fledglings were found at BLNWR, 30 August 1987.

SPECIMENS: Specimens have been taken in Hall (13 February 1977, WTAMU), Hutchinson (14 June 1950, TNHC), Potter (24 October 1974, WTAMU), and Randall (28 June 1956, MNH; 6 November 1991, TCWC; 15 January 1939, WTAMU) counties. The locations of those collected by McCauley (1877) and Stevenson (1942) in Armstrong County are unknown. The latter observer assigned a specimen taken on the Elkins Ranch in the Palo Duro Canyon, Randall County, to the subspecies *planicola,* the race Oberholser (1974) called the "Palo Duro Cardinal" (= *canicaudus*).

Pyrrhuloxia *Cardinalis sinuatus* Bonaparte

STATUS: Rare to uncommon winter visitor in the southern third.

OCCURRENCE: The Pyrrhuloxia has been recorded in Briscoe, Castro, Potter, Randall, and Swisher counties in the Texas Panhandle. It has been seen during every month except July.

Prior to the late 1970s, the Pyrrhuloxia was rarely reported. McCauley (1877), who had previously seen the species in Mexico, observed "about half a dozen individuals . . . in Cañoncito Blanco and elsewhere" and found them "too shy to be secured." Cañoncito Blanco is the location of present-day Ceta Glen in South Ceta Canyon, Randall County. Early in the twentieth century, Hibbets et al. (1926–36) recorded a "Texas Cardinal" in the Palo Duro, 20 March 1928. Reeves and Reeves (1914–26) said of it: "1936: A very dry spring, during a prolonged drouth. Three were seen at one time in a protected spot at Canyon Club [Randall County]. We never saw others and decided that probably they were out of usual range because of dry conditions." On 3 September 1954, three were observed in the PDCSP, and in 1961 (date not given), one was seen on the outskirts of Amarillo, Randall County.

The following is a listing of all sightings reported thereafter: *1977*—one in Amarillo, Randall County, 17 January–22 March (TBRC); two near Lake Tanglewood, Randall County, 18 December. *1978*—one in Caprock Canyons SP, Briscoe County, 1 January; two at BLNWR, 8 January, and one, 19 February; two in Ceta Glen, South Ceta Canyon, Randall County, 29 January. *1979*—one in PDCSP, 16 December.

1980—Fischer et al. (1982) reported an unspecified number in Castro County, 4 January; two in PDCSP, 24 February. *1981*—one near Amarillo, Randall County, 7 November to last of March 1982. *1982*—one near Amarillo, Randall County, 24 October. *1983*—four in the Sunday Canyon community, Palo Duro Canyon, Randall County, 11 January; two in Ceta Glen, South Ceta Canyon, Randall County, 15 January; two at BLNWR, 13 February, and one, 27 February and 10 April; one in PDCSP, 29 August; two in Caprock Canyons SP, 30 December. *1986*—one in Amarillo, Randall County, 8–11 February. *1988*—one on the Hugh Currie Ranch, Randall County, 17 December. *1989*—one near Bivins Lake, Randall County, 25 November.

1990—one in PDCSP, 28 March. *1993*—one north of Amarillo, Potter County, 17 January; one in PDCSP, 7 February–23 April; one in Caprock Canyons SP, Briscoe County, 20 March; one at Lake MacKenzie, Briscoe County, 27 November. *1995*—one in PDCSP, 19 August. *1997–98*—one in Kress, Swisher County, 28 November; 2–4 regularly at two locations in Canyon, Randall County, late September to the end of April, and 1–2 at the Canyon Country Club northwest of town during the same period.

The Pyrrhuloxia is notorious for wandering northward after the nesting season. It is an uncommon resident in western Texas from the Trans-Pecos region east through the southern South Plains, the southern Edwards Plateau, and south through the South Texas Plains and the Lower Rio Grande Valley (TOS, 1995). In Midland County it is common year-round (Midland Naturalists, 1992), while to the north in the Lubbock area it is classified as "uncommon" from October to April and "casual" in summer (LEAS, 1994). Breeding was confirmed in Crosby County when nestlings were found on 1 July 1979 (Williams, 1979). Oberholser (1974) attributes the Pyrrhuloxia's expansion northward to the spread of mesquite since the 1880s. Further expansion can be expected, and observers should be on the alert for possible nesting in the study area. Many of the males found March and later were singing birds.

Rose-breasted Grosbeak *Pheucticus ludovicianus* (Linnaeus)

STATUS: Uncommon to fairly common migrant. Casual summer and vagrant winter visitor.

OCCURRENCE: The Rose-breasted Grosbeak has been seen in 11 counties: Castro, Donley, Gray, Hartley, Hemphill, Hutchinson, Moore, Oldham, Potter, Randall, and Roberts. Oberholser (1974) shows it in two: Hutchinson and Randall. It has been recorded from April to December and once in February.

The Rose-breasted Grosbeak has been recorded more often in spring (84%) than in fall (16%). Its arrival can be looked for in the first week of May, and most are gone by the last week. There have been six sightings in April, the earliest a single bird in PDCSP, 27 April 1993, and another in Amarillo, Randall County, 27 April 1996. The latest spring date is 31 May: Lake Tanglewood, Randall County, in 1976, and Amarillo, Potter County, in 1992. Returning birds in fall can be looked for from mid-September to mid-October, the early and late dates being at BLNWR, 6 September 1965, and PDCSP, 13 November 1998.

There have been five sightings of this grosbeak in summer: a male on the Duncan Ranch in southeastern Hutchinson County (White Deer Creek), 26 June 1955; a female in Amarillo, Potter County, 30 July 1977; a male at BLNWR, 21 August 1983; what appeared to be a juvenile (possibly an adult and two young) in PDCSP, 7 July 1998.

To the south at Lubbock, one was found dead on 20 July 1966 (Williams, 1966), and a male was observed on 4 July 1984 (Williams, 1984). The species is not known to nest any nearer the study area than Kay and Oklahoma counties in central Oklahoma (Sutton, 1967). There have been two winter sightings. A male was observed in the PDCSP, 25 February 1996, very likely an early migrant, and an injured immature male was recovered in Amarillo, Randall County, 3 December 1998, when it struck a window. On 9 December 1979, one was observed in Lubbock (Williams, 1980b).

Caution is needed when identifying female and immature *Pheucticus* grosbeaks, particularly in the fall, as the Rose-breasted and Black-headed hybridize freely north of the Texas Panhandle (West, 1962; Anderson and Daugherty, 1974; Thompson and Ely, 1992).

Black-headed Grosbeak *Pheucticus melanocephalus* (Swainson)

STATUS: Uncommon to fairly common migrant.

OCCURRENCE: Oberholser (1974) shows the Black-headed Grosbeak in three Texas Panhandle counties: Oldham, Potter, and Randall. We now have records for 13 others: Armstrong, Briscoe, Castro, Collingsworth, Dallam, Donley, Gray, Hartley, Hemphill, Hutchinson, Lipscomb, Moore, and Parmer. It has been seen from April to November.

The Black-headed Grosbeak is not an early migrant, and its passage is relatively brief. The first birds of spring normally arrive during the first week of May. Single birds at BLNWR on 19 April 1964 and 19 April 1981 were exceptional. Most are gone by late May. Spring sightings predominate over those of fall (65%–35%).

There are two June and two July records, along with numerous sightings in August. A singing male was found in the Thompson Grove Picnic Area northeast of Texline, Dallam County, 7 June 1980, and a female at the BLNWR, 10 June 1967. A male and female (possibly an immature) frequented a yard in Amarillo, Randall County, 20–26 July 1994, and a female was seen in the PDCSP, 31 July 1966. The Black-headed Grosbeak nests as near the Texas Panhandle as southwestern Kansas (Johnsgard, 1979), and Capulin Mountain National Monument, Union County, New Mexico (NMOS, 1992), and summering birds have been encountered at Clayton, Union County (Hubbard, 1978). The AOU (1957, 1983) includes "western Oklahoma" in the species' breeding range, not indicating on what basis. The species is also a common summer resident in the Trans-Pecos mountains of Texas (TOS, 1995).

Fall birds begin arriving in mid-August, and few are seen beyond the third week of September. There are six records for October, the latest for a single bird at BLNWR, 19 October 1974. Three November sightings are exceptional: Lake Tanglewood, Randall County, 7 November 1987; PDCSP, 21 November 1990 and 2 November 1996 (photo).

SPECIMENS: A specimen was taken in Oldham County (29 August 1920, CMNH). It is the one referred to by Oberholser (1974).

Blue Grosbeak *Guiraca caerulea* (Linnaeus)

STATUS: Fairly common to common breeder.

OCCURRENCE: The Blue Grosbeak has been seen in every Texas Panhandle county and has been recorded from April to October.

This grosbeak is a species for which time of return in spring is more nearly predictable than for most. My records (1964–96) show that the first bird of the year is routinely seen around the first of May. My earliest date is of a male at the BLNWR, 26 April 1992, while the earliest on record is one in Caprock Canyons SP, Briscoe County, 21 April 1996. Few remain beyond the third week of September, the latest being two birds in Caprock Canyons SP, 10 October 1982.

NESTING: The Blue Grosbeak nests throughout the study area. The TBBAP found CO nesting in 10 survey blocks, PR in 38, and PO in 18. Twenty-seven were located between the 100th and 101st meridians, 16 between the 101st and 102nd, and 23 west of the 102nd. Nest building has been observed as early as 23 May 1987 (Lake Meredith, Hutchinson County) and as late as 6 August 1989 (female gathering nesting materials, BLNWR), indicating possible two-broodedness. On 27 June 1966, a nest found near Amarillo held one grosbeak egg and three cowbird eggs. Males may continue singing as late as the last week of August or first week of September.

The averages on the BBSS are as follows: *Clarendon*—4.5; *Dalhart*—3.3; *Skelly-town*—3.3; *Channing*—2.7; *Miami*—2.3; *Childress*—2.2; *Texline*—1.3; *Booker*—0.5; *Pantex*—0; *Waka*—0. A two-year Breeding Bird Study conducted in the PDCSP (Seyffert, 1967–68) disclosed an average density of seven Blue Grosbeaks per 100 acres.

SPECIMENS: Specimens have been taken in Hutchinson (25 and 30 June 1950, TNHC), Lipscomb (27 June 1903, USNM), and Randall (3 May 1936, TCWC) counties. Oberholser (1974) shows others taken in Hutchinson, Oldham, and Armstrong and assigns them to the race *mesophila* ("Texas Blue Grosbeak"). Other than the Lipscomb County bird, he does not give the names of the collections in which they were deposited; the Armstrong County bird is likely the one collected by McCauley (1877). Two specimens taken in Hutchinson County (Thompson, 1952) were assigned to the race *interfusa*, a race not recognized (AOU, 1957).

Lazuli Bunting *Passerina amoena* (Say)

STATUS: Fairly common migrant. Rare to uncommon summer visitor and possible breeder.

OCCURRENCE: The Lazuli Bunting has been recorded in 13 counties: Castro, Donley, Gray, Hansford, Hartley, Hemphill, Hutchinson, Moore, Oldham, Parmer, Potter, Randall, and Roberts. Oberholser (1974) shows it in three. It has been recorded March–October and once in December.

With three exceptions, Lazuli Buntings have not been reported earlier than the first week of May—the earliest a male in PDCSP, 11 March 1989—and migrants are rarely recorded past the third week of May. Returning birds in fall can be looked for in late August, with few occurring beyond late September, the latest a male at Lake Tanglewood, Randall County, 24 October 1963. Exceptional was a male observed at length on the Currie Ranch near Lake Tanglewood, 3 December 1984 (Seyffert, 1986). The Lazuli's wintering range lies from southern Baja California, southern Arizona, and Chihuahua south to Guerrero and central Veracruz (AOU, 1983). Oberholser (1974) cites three previous winter sightings in Texas, one each for McLennon, Bexar, and Hidalgo counties, all far south of the Panhandle.

NESTING: As stated by Johnsgard (1979), "Presumably the Texas Panhandle is part of the breeding range, but there have been no recent nesting records." I have been unable to determine the factual basis for any nesting. Wolfe (1956) says the Lazuli Bunting is a "summer resident" of area 1, an area that includes the Panhandle, but he too fails to provide nesting data. There had been little or no evidence of nesting in northeastern New Mexico until recently (Hubbard, 1978), although Ligon (1961) refers to the species being shown as a nester on the "Clayton Area Check-list of Birds" in Union County: "A local first was a pair of Lazuli Buntings nesting at Tucumcari L. [Quay County] in late July" (Hubbard, 1987). Nesting has been confirmed in Cimarron, Ellis, and Roger Mills counties in western Oklahoma (Sutton, 1967). In Colorado, confirmation has been made in Baca County in the extreme southeast sector (Andrews and Righter, 1992).

Although there are no recent records of nesting in the study area, there is evidence supporting possible, if not probable, nesting: *1953*—singing male near Lake Marvin, Hemphill County, 7 June. *1954*—singing male at the Palo Duro Club near Canyon, Randall County, 24 July. *1957*—female and singing male near Canyon, Randall County, 15 July–3 August. *1958*—what appeared to be a male in molt near Dimmitt, Castro County, 21 July. *1963*—a male and possibly four or five young at Lake Tanglewood, Randall County, 18 August. *1965*—a singing male in PDCSP (Chinaberry), 5 June. *1966*—singing male in PDCSP (Chinaberry), 5 June. *1968*—a singing male in PDCSP (Chinaberry), 2 and 12 June, and a singing male at Channing, Hartley County, 9 June. *1985*—female in PDCSP, 25 June; singing male between McBride and Mullanox canyons, Lake Meredith National Recreation Area, Potter County, 10 July. *1987*—two singing males on 12 May near the site of 10 July 1985 sighting; singing male in the Plum Creek area, Lake Meredith National Recreation Area, Potter County, 5 July—the Lazuli was attacked and driven off by a male Indigo Bunting; a singing male at BLNWR, 21 May. *1992*—two singing males near Dodd, southwest Castro County, 28 June.

The dates of these sightings are well within nesting dates recorded in nearby areas of Oklahoma (Baumgartner and Baumgartner, 1992): partially built nest in Roger Mills County, 4 May; nest with two eggs in Ellis County, 26 May; young in nest in Cimarron County, 1 and 3 July.

Indigo Bunting *Passerina cyanea* (Linnaeus)

STATUS: Fairly common migrant. Fairly common breeder in the eastern third, locally westward.

OCCURRENCE: The Indigo Bunting has been recorded in 16 counties: Armstrong, Briscoe, Castro, Collingsworth, Donley, Gray, Hall, Hartley, Hemphill, Hutchinson, Lipscomb, Moore, Oldham, Potter, Randall, and Roberts. It has been recorded from April to October.

The Indigo Bunting can be expected in spring during the first week of May. Three April dates are on record, the earliest a male at Caprock Canyons SP, Briscoe County, 16 April 1978. Migration is largely over by mid-May, and returning birds arrive in late August and early September. The passage is of short duration with few birds reported in comparison to those seen in spring. There are two October sightings: one in PDCSP, 12 October 1995, and one at Lake Tanglewood, Randall County, 19 October 1970.

NESTING: The Indigo Bunting's nesting range is expanding westward in the Panhandle. McCauley (1877) speaks of the species in May and June as "occasionally seen," and others who worked in the area prior to the mid-1950s name it only as an occasional migrant. Oberholser (1974) shows summer sight records for Hemphill and Randall counties without making reference to the possibility of nesting, while Johnsgard (1979) places the breeding range well to the east.

Singing males, paired birds, adults carrying food, and/or juveniles have been recorded in the following counties: *Briscoe*—Caprock Canyons SP; *Collingsworth*—Buck Creek west of Wellington; *Donley*—Lelia Creek; *Gray*—Lake McClellan; *Hall*—Indian Creek; *Hemphill*—Lake Marvin/Gene Howe WMA; *Hutchinson*—Sanford Dam area, Lake Meredith; *Oldham*—Boys Ranch, Rico Creek, Middle Alamosa Creek; *Potter*—Lake Meredith National Recreation Area, south side of river in Alibates, McBride, Mullanox area, and north side of river in Plum Creek area; *Randall*—BLNWR; PDCSP; Ceta Glen, South Ceta Canyon; *Roberts*—Chicken Creek. A nest at Lake Meredith, Potter County, contained a recently hatched chick and one cowbird egg, 10 July 1995.

Several of the locations where Indigo Buntings have been found were also occupied by the Lazuli Bunting, sometimes conjointly. The two species are known to hybridize (Emlen et al., 1975; Kroodsma, 1975). A male Indigo of 13 June 1970 (Boys Ranch, Oldham County) had all the markings of an Indigo except for the belly and undertail coverts, which were white, as in the Lazuli. Of three singing male Indigos encountered near Mullanox Canyon on 29 June 1975, one was of a lighter blue, more turquoise in color, with white feathers on its lower belly. Perhaps they were hybrids? As Kroodsma (1975) pointed out, "Identification of phenotypically pure Indigo Buntings was complicated by a delay in the completion of their prenuptial molt far into the summer, causing many of them to possess characteristics of the winter plumage that could be mistaken as indication of hybridization with Lazuli Bunting."

Painted Bunting *Passerina ciris* (Linnaeus)

STATUS: Uncommon to common breeder.

OCCURRENCE: Oberholser (1974) shows the Painted Bunting in seven Texas Panhandle counties: Armstrong, Briscoe, Childress, Hall, Potter, Randall, and

Wheeler. Fourteen others have been added: Castro, Collingsworth, Dallam, Donley, Gray, Hansford, Hartley, Hemphill, Hutchinson, Lipscomb, Moore, Oldham, Parmer, and Roberts.

Contrary to the range maps in most current field guides and other publications, as well as the accounts of several students of Texas birdlife (Wolfe, 1956; Oberholser, 1974; Johnsgard, 1979), the Painted Bunting is not absent from the study area. Anyone who has ever visited the Palo Duro Canyon in spring and summer is aware of this. A two-year Breeding Bird Study conducted in the state park disclosed an average density of 18 birds per 100 acres (Seyffert, 1967–68). The only places where it appears to be largely absent are the northernmost tier of counties and the southwestern sector. A reliance on BBSs in determining the summer range of the species would produce an inaccurate picture, for none except the Childress count is made in areas where the species is most common.

The Painted Bunting returns in spring during the first week of May. There are two April records, the earliest a male at BLNWR, 25 April 1972. The males normally leave in late summer earlier than do the females and young. I have encountered singing males (3) as late as 15 August 1996. Concerning this early departure, I have heard George M. Sutton say that there were no records of adult males in Oklahoma after 10 August: "Males apparently leave abruptly, arriving at wintering grounds in South America the first week of October" (speech). The females and young remain until mid-September. Unusual was a female that came to a feeder in Miami, Roberts County, 18–19 October 1980, the only October record. The latest September record is for two at Lake Tanglewood, Randall County, 26 September 1963. Truly exceptional was a Painted Bunting photographed in Lubbock, 26 December 1979 (Williams, 1980b). The citation does not specify the bird's gender.

NESTING: The TBBAP found CO nesting in one survey block, PR in 19, and PO in ten. Eleven of the quadrangles were between the 100th and 101st meridians, 12 between the 101st and 102nd, and seven west of the 102nd. Only one quadrangle lay north of 36 degrees north latitude (Dalhart West). The confirmed nestings were in the PDCSP and involved adults with fledglings. On 29 July 1987, an adult male bunting was observed feeding a cowbird fledgling.

My records show adults with young on dates ranging from 7 July to 27 August. An analysis of records for the PDCSP reveals the following average numbers of Painted Buntings found per trip during the nesting season: May, 5.2; June, 6.1; July, 8.7; August, 4. 3. On 10 July 1999, 30 singing males were encountered. No nests have ever been reported.

SPECIMENS: There is a specimen collected in Lipscomb County (3 August 1985, TCWC). McCauley (1877) speaks of a specimen collected on 26 May 1876 on a tributary of Mulberry Creek at about latitude 34 degrees, 50 minutes north. This would place the collecting point in present-day Armstrong County.

Dickcissel *Spiza americana* (Gmelin)
STATUS: Uncommon to common breeder.
OCCURRENCE: The Dickcissel has been observed in all 26 counties of the Texas Panhandle and has been seen during the period April–October.

References to the Dickcissel in the study area prior to mid-century are almost nonexistent. McCauley (1877) spent May and June in areas where the species is now common without mentioning it. The earliest reference is that of Reeves and Reeves (1914–36): "1925—in the open space south of the college campus" (Canyon, Randall County). Later, Hawkins (1945) classified it as a "rare summer resident," limiting its presence to Hemphill County in the northeast sector. As field work became more systematic in the 1950s, reports of Dickcissels became more frequent, although they remained noteworthy. Today it is found yearly in most areas of the eastern half, more irregularly westward.

Normally it is mid-May before the first Dickcissel is reported. One in Amarillo, Randall County, 30 April 1969, and another in Hall County, 30 April 1988, were unusually early. It is probable that were observers resident in the eastern counties earlier dates would be registered, for the normal arrival date in nearby areas of Oklahoma is 18 April (Grzybowski et al., 1992). By late summer singing has ceased and it is more difficult to find the species; seldom is one seen past mid-September. The only October birds reported were one on the Taylor Lakes WMA, Donley County, 1 October 1997; one in the PDCSP, 3 October 1997; and one in Castro County, 11 October 1993. A roadkilled Dickcissel was recovered in Lubbock, 16 January 1992 (Lasley and Sexton, 1992). Seldom is a movement of any size reported. Noteworthy was "a very heavy wave" that passed through Amarillo, 6–7 September 1962 (Baumgartner, 1963). To the south, a flock of 200 at Lubbock, 1 May 1982, "was the largest ever seen there" (Williams, 1982).
NESTING: The TBBAP (1987–92) found CO nesting in five survey blocks, PR in 53, and PO in 15. Thirty-two were located between the 100th and 101st meridians, 25 between the 101st and 102nd, and 16 west of the 102nd. A nest containing three young was found in eastern Moore County, 28 June 1993. Fledglings being fed have been observed from 8 June 1991 (Childress County) to 17 August 1987 (Randall). The BBSS give an idea of the distribution and variability of the Dickcissel. Averages per count are as follows: *Booker*—16.9; *Waka*—11.1; *Pantex*—3.9; *Childress*—3.8; *Clarendon*—1.9; *Miami*—1.2; *Texline*—0.4; *Channing*—0.1. The Booker and Waka routes lie in the northeastern sector where the Dickcissel is normally most common, and the Texline and Channing routes in the northwest-

ern sector where it is scarce. Only fairly recently has the species been recorded on these two western counts, Texline in 1983 and Channing in 1988. The Booker count is also illustrative of variability: numbers have ranged from 0 to 62.

SPECIMENS: There is a specimen from Hutchinson County (15 June 1950, TNHC), collected by Thompson (1952) and referred to by Oberholser (1974). Oberholser also names specimens collected in Oldham and Armstrong counties.

Family Icteridae (Blackbirds)

Bobolink *Dolichonyx oryzivorus* (Linnaeus)
STATUS: Casual migrant.
OCCURRENCE: The Bobolink has been reported in Carson, Hall, Moore, and Randall counties in the Texas Panhandle and has been seen in spring during April and May and in fall during August and September.

Only two sightings of the Bobolink were reported prior to mid-century. Reeves and Reeves (1914–36) recorded it in 1923: "Along the creek and on the fences near the Gordon-Cummins place, spring." This would have been in the Canyon, Randall County, area. Later, Hibbets et al. (1926–36) reported the species on 12 May 1935, also in the Canyon area. Neither of the reports specifies numbers.

By far the largest gathering of Bobolinks ever found in the study area was encountered near Canyon on 16 August 1954. The observers "followed the flock of brownish streaked birds for about a mile down a dirt road near Canyon—they heard the characteristic 'chink.'" Under the entry "Bobolink," the notes of another observer read: "1960: 5901 S. Western"—without naming date or numbers (R. Ross). The location was on the southwestern outskirts of Amarillo, Randall County, at that time an area undeveloped and still largely grassland. On 28 April 1962, one was observed near Memphis, Hall County. The files of the USFWS at BLNWR show two Bobolinks on the refuge, 18 September 1965.

A singing male Bobolink was observed at length near BLNWR on 9 May 1982 a short time before tornados skipped across the area. The first confirmed sighting was of a male observed southwest of Dumas, Moore County, 12 May 1984 (TP-RF). More recently, three singing males were found southeast of Amarillo, Randall County, 8 May 1993, and a male was seen in Carson County north of Washburn, 21 May 1999 (TP-RF).

Sutton (1967) speaks of the Bobolink in Oklahoma as "seen westward . . . infrequently to Beaver and Ellis counties; one record for Cimarron County: September 1, 1963, female in first feather taken near Boise City." In the southwestern sector of that state, Tyler (1979b) notes: "at least six males in mixed flock of blackbirds 1 1/2 M E of Mangum, Greer Co., 6 May 1967." Krehbiel (1955) classified the Bobolink in the Clayton area, Union County, New Mexico, as an "accidental transient," and its presence there was recognized by Hubbard (1978). One was seen in that area on 24 September 1996 (Williams, 1997). South of the study area on the South Plains, one was observed in Crosby County, 17 March 1978 and 4 April 1979 (*fide* C. Stogner), and another in Lubbock County, 3 April 1982 (Williams, 1982).

Farther east in Texas the Bobolink is considered rare to uncommon (TOS, 1995), and Pulich (1988) says of it for the north-central sector: "This gregarious species is not as numerous today as it was earlier. . . . Most fall reports are old and total only ten sightings."

Red-winged Blackbird *Agelaius phoeniceus* (Linnaeus)

STATUS: Common to abundant resident.

OCCURRENCE: The Red-winged Blackbird has been observed in every county and has been recorded in every month.

This blackbird is more common in the study area today than formerly. McCauley (1877) said of his encounters during May and June of 1876: "not as common as *M. ater*" (Brown-headed Cowbird). Even as late as mid-century, Hawkins (1945) classified the species as only "fairly common" in summer, although an "abundant migrant." Today the Red-winged Blackbird is common throughout most of the region in summer, particularly in areas of irrigated croplands, playa lakes, and impoundments, and outnumbers the cowbird at all times. Winter roosting flocks may range from several hundred to several million.

The Red-winged Blackbird's summer distribution is indicated by the averages on the BBSS: *Waka*—335; *Booker*—70; *Pantex*—63; *Texline*—39; *Childress*—27; *Channing*—14; *Miami*—9. The high average on the Waka count is accounted for by the irrigated croplands (wheat and maize) that the route traverses, while the low Miami and Channing averages reflect primarily grassland and rangeland habitats. There are few areas where the species is absent in summer.

Winter is the season of greatest abundance. "Clouds" of blackbirds are then encountered feeding on waste grain in stubblefields and around farm and ranch buildings, and "rivers" of them move from and to nighttime roosting sites. Royall et al. (1970, 1975) summarized results of blackbird censuses conducted during two winters (1969–70, 1974–75). Taking as an example the roost at Sanford Dam marsh, Lake Meredith, Hutchinson County, I estimated 1,800,000 birds present on 22 December 1974 (84% red-wingeds, 15% starlings, 1% Brewer's Blackbirds, 1% cowbirds). On the following 9–10 January 1975, the Royall party estimated 4,500,000 blackbirds present (94.9% red-wingeds, 5% starlings, 0.1% undetermined blackbird species). The following are the average numbers, highs, and

Red-winged Blackbird

lows of Red-winged Blackbirds recorded on the CBCS: *Lake Meredith (east)*—742,556 (3,000,000; 5,000); *Lake Meredith (west)*—35,346 (400,000; 9); *Quitaqua*—733 (8,720; 1); *Amarillo*—1,184 (10,028; 0); *Buffalo Lake NWR*—1,025 (20,250; 0); *Friona*—180 (856; 4).

NESTING: The Red-winged Blackbird has been found nesting in every county of the study area. During the TBBAP CO nesting was found in 59 survey blocks, PR in 57, and PO in 7. Forty-two of the quadrangles were located between the 100th and 101st meridians, 44 between the 101st and 102nd, and 37 west of the 102nd. Although nesting probably does not begin until mid- or late April, loose gatherings of displaying males have been observed as early as mid- or late February. During the TBBAP nest building was recorded from 5 May to 12 July, and nests with eggs were found from 30 May to 10 July, indicating two-broodedness. Most feeding activity of fledged young occurred from late May to late June.

SPECIMENS: Specimens have been taken in Deaf Smith (17 February 1977, WTAMU), Hutchinson (20 December 1977, TCWC; 9, 12, and 24 June 1950, TNHC), Moore (MCHM), Potter (ACMNH; 26 May 1939, WTAMU), and Randall (26 October 1939, 30 July 1970, 30 April 1978, WTAMU) counties. In addition, Oberholser (1974) shows specimens taken in Lipscomb, Hemphill, and Oldham counties, without naming their locations. Those he examined from Lipscomb, Hemphill, Deaf Smith, and Oldham counties were assigned to the race *fortis* ("Thick-billed Red-winged Blackbird"). The Hutchinson County birds were identified as nominate *phoeniceus,* and *stereus* is found as a migrant and winter resident in the western half of Texas (TOS, 1995).

Eastern Meadowlark *Sturnella magna* (Linnaeus)

STATUS: Fairly common to common resident in the eastern half, rare locally westward.

OCCURRENCE: The Eastern Meadowlark has been recorded in every county except Hansford, Moore, and Sherman in the north-central sector. It has been found year-round. Sightings in the western and southwestern counties—Dallam, Hartley, Oldham, Deaf Smith, Parmer, Castro, Swisher—all for summer, are based on Oberholser (1974). Neither Rohwer (1972) nor Fischer et al. (1982) found *S. magna* in those counties, nor have others who have birded these areas extensively. It is possible that a few may reside in extreme western Dallam and Hartley counties, for in recent years there have been reports of spring and summer *magnas* found south of Clayton in adjacent Union County, New Mexico (Williams and Hubbard, 1990, 1991). I have surveyed the Texas roads that run parallel to the state line south of Texline in Dallam County but heard only singing *neglecta,* the Western Meadowlark. With the initiation of the Dalhart BBS (1994), which runs south of town, I have on each of four counts heard what I thought were possibly singing *magna.* The pattern and rhythm of song closely resembled those of *magna,* and the pitch and timbre that of *neglecta.* Sightings in Carson, Armstrong, and Briscoe counties have been limited to their eastern portions. The only records of this species in Randall County are rare late fall singing birds, indicating a possible movement of *magna* into the county in winter. Although meadowlarks are thought to be sedentary throughout most of their range, there is a seemingly random movement among some wintering birds (Lanyon, 1995).

All anecdotal reports of Eastern Meadowlarks in the western portions of the study area should be viewed with caution. Lanyon (1957) explored the ecological aspects of the distribution of the meadowlarks and found "*magna* exhibiting a preference for the more moist areas and *neglecta* selecting the drier environments." His study indicated that "environmental moisture may be a major proximate factor in limiting meadowlark distribution." I have found this to hold true in the study area. There is widespread distribution of *magna* in the moister areas of the eastern tier of counties, with occupancy farther west limited primarily to the Canadian River Valley and lowlands adjacent to feeder streams. The species can be found in the river valley as far west as central Potter County; seldom is one found in the drier uplands overlooking the valley. Still farther west, I have explored the river valley in eastern Oldham County numerous times but have never heard a singing *magna*. As other examples, I have found the Eastern Meadowlark nesting in moist meadows along White Deer Creek in southeastern Hutchinson County but not in the higher and drier adjacent areas. The only place I have encountered any on the Miami, Roberts County, BBS is in the meadowlands adjacent to Chicken Creek, the route otherwise traversing prairie and grasslands at higher elevations.

In his study of the distribution of the meadowlarks in the central and southern Great Plains, Rohwer (1972) documented the relatively recent westward expansion of the Eastern Meadowlark in Kansas, Oklahoma, and the Texas Panhandle, pointing out for the last region the absence of sightings of *magna* in McCauley (1876), Stevenson (1942), Thompson (1952), and Wolfe (1956). Rohwer's findings closely parallel the presently known distributional boundaries, the only exceptions being a shift still farther westward in the Canadian River Valley and Briscoe County (Quitaque area). It is of interest that he also discovered an isolated population of *S. m. lilianae* (specimen), a morph of *S. magna*, at two sites near Springlake in Lamb County, only a short distance south of the study area. In light of another study by Rohwer (1976) indicating that *S. m. magna* and *S. m. lilianae* may be separate species, could the indeterminate songs of some western meadowlarks heard not far distant from this population belong indeed to *lilianae*? Lanyon (1995) says that not only genetic data but also analysis of their primary songs shows differences in the two forms.

Eastern and Western meadowlarks can be found closely intermingled in some areas in the eastern Panhandle. I have listened to spring males of both *magna* and *neglecta* singing vigorously from the same tree at Lake McClellan, Gray County, and have found the species closely associated at both Greenbelt Lake and Taylor Lakes WMA in Donley County. At these locations *magna* occupies the lower, moister grasslands near water, *neglecta* the higher and drier ground.

Lanyon (1957) found the call notes, whistles, and primary songs of the two meadowlark species to be the most distinguishable characteristics in making specific identifications in the field, and vocalizations are indeed relied on almost entirely by most field observers. This reliance could lead, however, to errors in the identification of birds heard in the western sector of the study area. As already noted, I have found some songs that contained elements characteristic of both *magna* and *neglecta*. Lanyon (1957) points out further that the primary song of both species is learned rather than inherited, and "males of either species are potentially capable of learning and rendering primary song of the other species." For these reasons, one should be cautious about viewing any meadowlarks occupying the higher prairies of the western Panhandle as *magna* when the assessment is based solely on songs and calls.

NESTING: The TBBAP found CO nesting of the Eastern Meadowlark in 10 survey blocks, PR in 29, and PO in five. Thirty-three were located between the 100th and 101st meridians, and 11 between the 101st and 102nd. The westernmost occupied quadrangle (Alibates Ranch) is located in the Canadian River Valley of northeast Potter County. Few nests have been reported: nest with five eggs near Lake Marvin, Hemphill County, 28 May 1975; nest with four eggs north of Glazier, Lipscomb County, 30 June 1987; nest with six eggs in southeastern Hutchinson County, 21 May 1988. Fledglings being fed have been observed as early as 9 May 1987 (Donley County), and as late as 25 June 1987 (Armstrong County). These dates point to possible two-broodedness. Oberholser (1974) shows a sight record of nesting in Deaf Smith County, but details are lacking and the record must be questioned.

SPECIMENS: Only two specimens are available, both from Hall County (27 June 1968, MNH). Oberholser (1974) shows a summer specimen taken in Hemphill County without naming its whereabouts.

Western Meadowlark *Sturnella neglecta* Audubon

STATUS: Common to abundant resident.

OCCURRENCE: The Western Meadowlark has been recorded in every Texas Panhandle county and has been seen year-round.

This meadowlark is one of the most common and widespread bird species in the study area—its joyful song greets the ear almost everywhere. In earlier days McCauley (1877) found it "very abundant, except upon the sterile plain itself. Descending thence, however, to the canyon bottoms, or to some wooded stream, the songster is again heard." Observers today would say quite the opposite, that the "sterile plain" has been claimed by the songster and fewer are found in the canyon bottoms.

The Western Meadowlark's winter status as shown by CBCs is similar to that in summer, as reflected in the following BBS averages: *Texline*—204; *Miami*—199; *Booker*—198; *Pantex*—195; *Channing*—154; *Waka*—95; *Childress*—47; *Clarendon*—13. CBC: *Quitaque*—228; *Buffalo Lake NWR*—202; *Friona*—187; *Amarillo*—159; *Lake Meredith (west)*—65; *Lake Meredith (east)*—54.

Little is known about meadowlark population shifts that may occur between summer and winter. Meadowlarks are thought to be stationary throughout most of their range (Lanyon, 1995), migrating only from the northernmost areas and higher elevations, some considerable distances (Lanyon, 1994); to what extent there may be an influx of birds into the study area is unknown. They migrate during the day and sometimes large gatherings may be encountered; these are not necessarily migrants, however, for such groups can also be encountered in midsummer and winter.

NESTING: The TBBAP found CO nesting of the Western Meadowlark in 56 survey blocks, PR in 67, and PO in three. Thirty-six were located between the 100th and 101st meridians, 48 between the 101st and 102nd, and 42 west of the 102nd. Nest building has been observed as early as 27 April and as late as 6 July 1988, indicating two-broodedness. There are records of nests with eggs: 7 May 1972 (2 eggs; Randall County), 31 May 1975 (5 eggs; Moore County), and 28 June 1988 (? eggs; Randall County). Most COs during the TBBAP were of recently fledged birds and young being fed (mid-June to mid-July). Nesting has been confirmed in every county except Hall and Hemphill and would be in them with more searching.

SPECIMENS: More specimens are available for the Western Meadowlark than any other species: Armstrong (20 April 1981, WTAMU), Deaf Smith (29 April 1971, WTAMU), Donley (23 February 1972, TCWC), Hall (27 June 1968, MNH; 23 January 1977, OMNH), Hemphill (8 October 1977, WTAMU), Hutchinson, (26 June 1968, MNH; 10 June and 7 July 1950, TNHC), Lipscomb (4 January 1986, WTAMU), Oldham (8 January 1921, 19 May 1991, CMNH), Potter (21 October 1977, TCWC; March 1981, WTAMU), Randall (28 December 1936, 24 November 1979, 27 September and 15 November 1986, TCWC; 30 December 1938, 13 March 1939, P-PHM; 22 February and 30 December 1939, 22 November 1967, 10 May 1970, 27 April 1971, 10 April 1972, 6 December 1977, 17 January 1978, March (no date), 20 April, 2 and 4 December 1981, 7 December 1987, 25 February 1990, WTAMU), and Swisher (17 September 1979, TCWC) counties. In addition, there are two *sturnella* sp. taken in Roberts County (MNH). Those shown by Oberholser (1974) without locations named may be included in these collections.

According to Thompson (1952) two specimens taken in Hutchinson County were examined by G. M. Sutton, who "found them to show primarily the characteristics of the western meadowlark, *Sturnella neglecta.* In addition, however, he found similarities to *S. magna,* the eastern meadowlark, which caused him to believe the specimens were hybrids." An albino meadowlark was observed in Parmer County, 22 December 1965, and a flying meadowlark at BLNWR, 14 August 1988, was an overall white with a sandy wash.

Yellow-headed Blackbird *Xanthocephalus xanthocephalus* (Bonaparte)

STATUS: Common to abundant migrant; fairly common breeder locally; rare winter visitor.

OCCURRENCE: The Yellow-headed Blackbird has been recorded in every county except Childress and has been seen in every month.

The Yellow-headed Blackbird normally returns during the last week of March or the first week of April. The earliest date is for two males near Amarillo, Randall County, 14 March 1992. The first arrivals usually are males, either singles or small groups, and such early birds may encounter severe weather—as did two forced to utilize a feeder near downtown Amarillo during a snowstorm, 27 March 1970. It is during late April or early May that the larger flocks occur, and most yellow-headeds are gone by late May. Those seen in late June and early July are often assumed to be summer residents, but in many instances they are not. As an example, the Sanford Dam marsh at Lake Meredith may contain a few scatterred males in the first week of July where none had been present earlier. These birds are most likely southbound migrants rather than residents, an opinion held by Sutton (1967) for midsummer sightings in western Oklahoma. This belief is supported by the findings of Royall et al. (1971) based on Yellow-headed Blackbird recoveries in the Texas Panhandle and southwestern Oklahoma during July through September of birds that had been banded earlier in North and South Dakota. The study showed a rapid and direct southward migration from the Dakotas after nesting, the birds traveling at least 70 miles per day: such migrants could certainly be in the study area by early July. These early returning birds are usually adult males; for example, 50 near Amarillo, Potter County, 5 July 1996, were all males.

Late August through September is the time when most Yellow-headed Blackbirds move through and when the larger gatherings may be seen. Flocks congregate around feedlots, farm and ranch buildings, and playas with emergent vegetation as well as in fields of waste grain. Sometimes large gatherings in spring or fall may be found within city limits. As an example, 400+ were estimated in a cemetery in Amarillo, Randall County, 1 May 1982. The passage often takes the form of groups of a dozen or so birds that follow one another at regular intervals. Some examples of large gatherings are: 5,000 near Amarillo, 2 May 1971; 10,000 in Randall County, 13 September 1971.

The Yellow-headed Blackbird is rarely encountered in winter. Exceptions notable for high numbers were an estimated 500 in a cattail marsh near Alanreed, Gray County, 23 January 1970 (Royall et al., 1970), and a flock of 80 near Pampa, Gray County, 17 February 1997. Beyond these reports, the dozen or so other winter records are of 1–6 birds each. Observers in the extreme southwestern sector should be on the alert for wintering birds as 220 were reported on the Muleshoe NWR, Bailey County, 27 December 1997 (LEAS).

NESTING: Prior to the finding of a nesting colony in south-central Castro County, 12 May 1978 (Seyffert, 1993), the Yellow-headed Blackbird had been reported nesting in the study area only twice: in 1876 in Armstrong County (McCauley, 1877) and in 1899 in Oldham County (Oberholser, 1974). The McCauley find occurred in late May and involved a single nest, "found in the canyon of the Red River, where the stream, sometimes but a few feet wide, occasionally widens into good-sized marshy pools—the resort of ducks and other waterfowl. A few yards out from the edge, on a clump of thick, rank grass that rose five feet out of water . . . the birds had built their home." The report of the Oldham County find is without details.

Three nests with eggs were found initially at the Castro County site (TP-RF; M. Traweek)—16 nests, 20 May, and 10 nests, 4 June. On 4 July 1982, 16 May 1987, and 28 June 1995, nesting birds were again found at this site. Unlike most playas, this one is not ephemeral but a feedlot playa that holds permanent water. On 6 June 1979, two other playas in northwestern Castro County were examined and fairly large numbers of yellow-headeds were found—along with strong indications of nesting. On 24 June, 72+ birds were found at three playas in that area. During this period Fischer et al. (1982) reported nesting not only in Castro County but also in Parmer and Swisher. On 19 June 1990, 50+ nest-building birds were observed at a playa approximately ten miles west of Kress, Swisher County, and on 28 June 1995, a small colony at a feedlot playa in Hart, Castro County. All of these confirmed nestings are located in the southwestern sector of the study area. Nesting has also been confirmed in the north-central sector, where a small colony of summering birds is found almost yearly at a playa half a mile east of Spearman, Hansford County. This site contained at least one nesting pair on 7 May 1989, and there were strong indications of nesting on 7 July 1997. On the latter date a number of adults and juveniles were found on a playa south of Spearman, the young being fed. Possible nesting sites have been discovered at other locations: cattail marsh 3.5 miles east of Sunray, Moore County, 6 June 1978; BLNWR, summer of 1972; cattail marsh on the south side of the Canadian River at Boys Ranch, Oldham County, June 1987 and 1988, and cattail marsh north of the river (Rico Creek), 26 June 1987. Rita Blanca Lake in Hartley County and playa lakes in Deaf Smith County are other locations where yellow-headeds have been seen in summer and where nesting may possibly be occurring.

Prior to the documentations cited above, the localities nearest the Texas Panhandle where nesting was known to occur with any regularity were eastern Colorado and southwestern Kansas (Johnsgard, 1979) and Tucumcari Lake, Quay County, northeastern New Mexico (Hubbard, 1978), where the Yellow-headed Blackbird has apparently become established (Hubbard, 1983). Sutton (1967) cited one breeding record for Oklahoma: nest with eggs collected near Kenton, Cimarron County, 19 June 1914. Nesting has since been confirmed at another site in western Oklahoma: Optima Lake, Texas County, 29 May 1986 (Shackford and Tyler, 1987).

On 13 July 1975, I observed a male bird with an extremely pale lemon head at Lake Meredith, Hutchinson County.

SPECIMENS: Specimens have been collected in Randall County (1 May 1985, TCWC; 10 September 1939, WTAMU).

Rusty Blackbird *Euphagus carolinus* (Müller)

STATUS: Casual winter visitor.

OCCURRENCE: The Rusty Blackbird has been recorded in six counties: Briscoe, Gray, Hemphill, Parmer, Potter, and Randall. It has been seen November–February, twice in April, and once in June.

The following is a listing by county of all reported sightings: *Briscoe*—five in Caprock Canyons SP, 30 December 1996; *Gray*—three at Lake McClellan, 27 April 1980; *Hemphill*—five at Lake Marvin, 14 December 1995; *Parmer*—eight near Friona, 4 February 1969; *Potter*—12 in the Bonita Creek area of Lake Meredith, Potter County, 31 December 1970; *Randall*—BLNWR: 2–5, 7 November 1965–16 January 1966; one, 20 December 1971; four, 23 December 1972; 7–30, 19–23 November 1978; one, 20 December 1980; 1–12, 27 November–5 December 1987; 10–14, 23 November–7 December 1993. Other Randall County sites: a "few" in the PDCSP, 6 November 1955; one near Amarillo, 5 November 1961; one at the Palo Duro Club near Canyon, 26 April 1969; one in Amarillo on unspecified day in February 1971; three near Amarillo, 15–18 November 1985; one at Lake Tanglewood, 19 November 1989. In addition, an out-of-season bird was reported at Lake McClellan, Gray County, 12 June 1955. These late spring and early summer sightings must be viewed with caution, for by then feather edgings on Rusty Blackbirds have become worn and the birds appear all black, making them more difficult to tell apart from the Brewer's Blackbird and Common Grackle. The

Rusty Blackbird does not breed south of Canada except for some areas of the extreme northeastern United States (AOU, 1983) and is a rare to uncommon migrant and winter resident in the eastern half of Texas (TOS, 1995).

Brewer's Blackbird *Euphagus cyanocephalus* (Wagler)
STATUS: Common to abundant winter visitor.
OCCURRENCE: The Brewer's Blackbird has been reported in every county except Childress, Dallam, and Sherman, and has been seen in every month.

The Brewer's Blackbird is the third most abundant "blackbird" species in the study area during winter, following the Red-winged Blackbird and European Starling. Returning birds in fall can be looked for in early or mid-October, and most have departed by late April. The early and late dates: an unspecified number near Amarillo, Randall County, 13 September 1973, and a tailless male at Lake Marvin, Hemphill County, 29 May 1983.

Occurrence, averages, and highs on the CBcs are indicative of the Brewer's status and distribution in early winter: *Lake Meredith (east)*—15 of 18 (8,304; 120,000); *Lake Meredith (west)*—12 of 24 (75; 1,000); *Amarillo*—12 of 40 (130; 5,000); *Buffalo Lake* NWR—21 of 29 (68; 350); *Quitaque*—7 of 21 (9; 56); *Friona*—2 of 12 (1; 10). A number of censuses of blackbird roosts have been made in the study area (Royall et al., 1970, 1975). A roost of 15,000 located in a two-acre cottonwood grove near Goodnight, Armstrong County, 25 January 1975, was composed of 90 percent Brewer's Blackbirds. Such a high percentage is an exception as other large roosts, some containing more than a million "blackbirds," were estimated at 0.1 percent to 8 percent Brewer's.

For lack of evidence, it cannot be said that the Brewer's Blackbird nests in the Texas Panhandle despite Bent (1958) citing "northern Texas (Canyon)" as within its breeding range. Until recently, the only report of nesting anywhere in Texas was a nest with eggs taken in Wilbarger County (Harrold) on 13 May 1928 (More and Strecker, 1929), a short distance southeast of the study area. Perhaps Bent based his citation on the reports of several early observers in the Canyon area (Hibbets et al., 1926–36; Carlander, 1934), who classified the Brewer's as a summer resident. As far as I have been able to discover, however, none of these observers named specific instances of nesting. Wolfe (1956) placed the species as a summer resident in "western Texas" without being specific.

On file are a number of June through August sightings of Brewer's Blackbirds: "a few pairs" near Lake Marvin, Hemphill County, 5 June 1955; "several small flocks" in Thompson Park, Amarillo, Potter County, 17 July 1955; "July 26—large flocks through Aug., only a few by first of Oct."—1956; an unspecified number in north Amarillo, Potter County, 3 August 1964; an unspecified number near Amarillo, 26 August 1964; "small flock" in west Amarillo, Potter

County, 24 July 1968; unspecified number near Amarillo, Randall County, 30 July 1969; unspecified number at BLNWR, 30 August 1974; "2–3 near a number of Com. Grackles" at Lake Rita Blanca, Hartley County, 23 June 1991. The late August birds were possibly early migrants. In addition, Oberholser (1974) shows a summer sight record for Deaf Smith County.

Beyond a single nest with eggs found near Kenton, Cimarron County, 1 June 1910 (Sutton, 1967), no other Brewer's Blackbirds have been reported nesting in western Oklahoma. Johnsgard (1979) says there are no definite breeding records for Kansas, but he does show the species' nesting range extending into the southeastern corner of Colorado. Later observers in Colorado (Andrews and Righter, 1992), however, say the Brewer's Blackbird has decreased dramatically in summer on the eastern plains in the last 25 years: "It may have been displaced from many areas (especially agricultural and urban areas) by the rapidly increasing Common Grackle. The blackbird is now quite local in summer." If it is true that the Brewer's formerly summered and perhaps nested in the study area, such a displacement may well have taken place here also, for there is no question that the Common Grackle has increased significantly with agricultural development and that it is now common throughout the study area. The Brewer's Blackbird is listed in the Lubbock area as "casual" during the period May–September (LEAS, 1994). A single nest was reported in the city, 5 June 1973 (Williams, 1973), and another in Crosby County, 14 June 1981 (*fide* C. Stogner).

SPECIMENS: There is an undated specimen available taken in Randall County (WTAMU).

Common Grackle *Quiscalus quiscula* (Linnaeus)

STATUS: Uncommon to common breeder. Rare to uncommon winter visitor locally.

OCCURRENCE: The Common Grackle has been recorded in every Texas Panhandle county and has been seen year-round.

Since mid-century the Common Grackle has become more plentiful and widespread in the study area, no doubt because of agricultural development and other changes in the environment. McCauley mentioned seeing "several" along McClellan Creek (Gray County)—"and in other places"—naming his bird *Quiscalus macrurus* = *Q. mexicanus*, the Great-tailed Grackle, surely a mistake in identification (see Great-tailed Grackle). Early in the twentieth century Strecker (1910) reported a few pairs nesting in Armstrong County, and he later (1912) classified the Common Grackle as a "rather rare resident of the Panhandle (Armstrong and Potter counties, etc.)." Carlander (1934) spoke of this grackle as a "summer resident in extreme eastern part," where still today it is more commonly found than elsewhere. Stevenson (1942) thought it worthy of note that "three were . . . at a ranch house 10 miles south of Claude (Armstrong Co.) on September 24, 1938." During this same period, however, Hawkins (1945), who covered the Panhandle rather extensively, failed to name the species.

Few Common Grackles winter in the study area, and those largely in the southeastern counties. For example, 200 were tallied at Lelia Lake, Donley County, 16 February 1992—possibly early returning birds rather than wintering ones. More work in those counties is needed to clarify winter status. The CBCs reflect an early winter scarcity. The Common Grackle has been recorded once on the *Amarillo* count, once on *Lake Meredith* (*west*), twice on *Quitaque*, once on *Buffalo Lake* NWR, and never on the *Friona* count. The *Lake Meredith* (*east*) CBC is an exception, where it has been recorded on 13 of 18. The birds are usually found among the millions of "blackbirds" that roost nightly in the Sanford Dam marsh or in nearby Sanford and Fritch.

Common Grackles begin returning to the area in numbers in late March and early April. Soon after nesting is completed in July, flocks begin forming and most birds have departed by mid- or late October. On 22 July 1998, 400 or more occupied a roost at Taylor Lakes WMA, Donley County; by mid-October still larger flocks have been recorded at that site—5,000+ on 15 October 1996, for example.

The BBSs reflect an absence of Common Grackles except where stops occur near human habitations, which is infrequently on most counts. The following are their averages: *Childress*—18.3; *Texline*—15.3; *Booker*—15.6; *Waka*—12.1; *Channing*—5.0; *Miami*—3.5; *Pantex*—1.4; *Clarendon*—0.3. All counts have registered significant increases since the mid-1980s. Four recent counts have been added to the survey: *Panhandle*—15.7; *Dalhart*—2.7; *Skellytown*—0.

Oberholser (1974) speaks of the decline of the Common Grackle in some marginal areas of its range in Texas, speculating that this may have been caused by the increased presence of the Great-tailed Grackle, the larger species driving out the smaller from prime habitats. The Great-tailed Grackle is a rather recent addition to the avifauna of the Panhandle (mid-1950s), and it will be enlightening to follow the fortunes of the two grackles in their bid for dominance. The Texline BBS may be the one to watch. It has always hosted fairly high numbers of Common Grackles, but recently (1991) great-taileds have moved in.

NESTING: The Common Grackle has been found nesting in every county. The TBBAP disclosed uniform breeding throughout much of the area. CO nestings were found in 67 survey blocks, PR in 17, and PO in 12. Thirty-seven were located between the 100th and 101st meridians, 33 between the 101st and 102nd, and 25 west of the 102nd. Fledglings being fed have been found as early as 2 May 1987 (Briscoe County) and as late as 28 June 1989 (Gray County).

SPECIMENS: Specimens have been taken in Randall County (2 June 1968, 21 April 1978, 5 December 1987, 15 February 1992, WTAMU). Oberholser (1974) shows one collected in Lipscomb County without naming its location.

Great-tailed Grackle *Quiscalus mexicanus* (Gmelin)

STATUS: Fairly common to common resident.

OCCURRENCE: The Great-tailed Grackle has been recorded in every Texas Panhandle county and has been seen in every month. Oberholser (1974) shows it in one county—Randall.

The Great-tailed Grackle is a recent addition to the avifauna of the Texas Panhandle. Observers in the 1950s announced its arrival. Today it is a bird of summer in most areas and a winter bird locally. Its arrival was the culmination of a northward expansion in the state that began in the early years of the twentieth century (1912), when it was apparently confined to the brush country from San Antonio to the mouth of the Rio Grande (Oberholser, 1974). During or soon after World War II its presence was first noted in the Fort Worth and Dallas areas (Pulich, 1988), where it quickly became established. By 1953 the Great-tailed Grackle had moved still farther north into southern Oklahoma, and its subsequent expansion in that state closely paralleled what was taking place in the study area (Davis, 1975). This expansion into northwest Texas was not generally known, for range maps published as late as 1975 did not show the species occupying either the South Plains or the High Plains (Pruitt, 1975).

The year of the Great-tailed Grackle's arrival in the study area went unrecorded. Probably the event took place in the early or mid-1950s as the first citation in the literature is that of Baumgartner (1958) for spring 1958: " Boat-tailed [Great-tailed] Grackle continue to spread northward apparently on a broad front . . . ; 3 were observed at Amarillo, the first record in many years." An observer (C. D. Littlefield) in the southwestern sector had this to say of the species in Castro County: "First bird arrived here 29 April 1962 (a male) and was joined by a female on 13 May. It appeared they tried to nest but water in the lake dried up and 28 July was the last that was seen of them."

The Great-tailed Grackle had been reported in the study area much earlier by McCauley (1877): "Several specimens observed along McClellan Creek and in other places." He named the birds "*Quiscalus macruras,* Sw.—Great-tailed Grackle." Although *Q. macruras* is synonymous with *Q. mexicanus,* it is questionable that the birds he observed were correctly identified. The annotator of the McCauley report, Dr. Elliott Coues, noted: "I deem it prudent to prefix a query to this species, which is one of a group in which identifications are difficult, and a bird not known, I think, to occur in the United States except in maritime portions." The Common Grackle, *Q. quiscula,* preceded the Great-tailed Grackle in the study area and surely is the species McCauley encountered.

The first Great-tailed Grackle was recorded in nearby northeastern New Mexico (Clayton area, Union County) on 23 March 1954, according to Cook and Krehbiel (1987). These authors say a pair was next found in 1958; however, it was in the spring of 1983 before another was seen (Hubbard, 1983). Nesting was first reported during the summer of 1990 (Williams and Hubbard, 1990), and by the fall of 1991 the total number of grackles had climbed to a record 60 (Williams and Hubbard, 1991).

Most summering birds are found in or around cities and towns and in outlying areas of human habitation near water or irrigated croplands. The BBSS, many of which are conducted away from such habitats, reflect a paucity of birds: *Channing* (1967–96)—first recorded 1979 (Boys Ranch area), periodically thereafter; *Childress* (1969–94)—first recorded 1975, periodically thereafter; *Pantex* (1974–96)—first recorded 1974, almost every year thereafter; *Booker* (1975–96)—first recorded 1978, twice thereafter; *Miami* (1975–96)—first recorded 1983, once thereafter; *Texline* (1975–96)—first recorded 1991, each year but one thereafter (but only in areas under cultivation, never on the Rita Blanca National Grasslands); *Waka* (1975–96)—first recorded 1980, every year thereafter (primarily in the area of a refinery).

The Great-tailed Grackle appears to be a year-round resident only within or in the neighborhood of the larger towns, principally those located in the southern counties. Much work remains to be done to clarify the picture. Amarillo hosts a winter population of several hundred. At what time birds began wintering in the city is uncertain; my first winter record is of 28 birds on 28 January 1967. As do the BBSS, the CBCS reflect a scarcity: *Amarillo* (1954–96)—1987 and 1994 (high 9; count circle does not include the city itself); *Buffalo Lake NWR* (1961–96)—1988, 1990, 1993, 1996 (high 15); *Friona* (1961–73)—0; *Lake Meredith* (*west*) (1970–96)—0; *Lake Meredith* (*east*) (1970–87)—1980, 1983, 1984, 1987 (high 40); *Quitaque* (1975–96)—0. Illustrative of how scarce the great-tailed is away from human settlement, I have encountered the species only five times on the BLNWR and but once in the PDCSP, despite hundreds of trips to each location during all seasons.

NESTING: The first reported nesting of the Great-tailed Grackle occurred in Memorial Park Cemetery, Amarillo, Potter County, 1 May 1964. In the following years the species was confirmed nesting in Sherman, Ochiltree, Hartley, Moore, Oldham, Carson, Gray, Wheeler, Deaf Smith, Randall, Parmer, Castro, Swisher, and Childress counties. Nest building has been observed as early as 25 April 1968, and adults have been seen feeding fledglings as late as 29 June 1966—both events in Amarillo, Potter County. The TBBAP found CO nesting in 24 survey blocks, PR in 31, and PO in 16. Twenty were located between the 100th and 101st meridians, 31 between the 101st and 102nd, and 20 west of the 102nd.

An imperfectly albinistic Great-tailed Grackle was observed in Amarillo, Potter County, 1 February 1993. The bird was all white except for some black feathers in its wings and tail.

Bronzed Cowbird *Molothrus aeneus* (Wagler)
STATUS: Vagrant summer visitor.
OCCURRENCE: The Bronzed Cowbird has been found but once in the Texas Panhandle. On 20 May 1995 a male was observed foraging on the ground near birdfeeders in the Hackberry Camping Area in the PDCSP (E. Kutac, R. Scott).

A common summer resident in South Texas and north to the Edwards Plateau (Coryell, Kerr, and Tom Green counties), the Bronzed Cowbird is rare but increasing in Midland County (TOS, 1995). Like the grackles, this is a southern species expanding its range northward, noticeably so in Texas after 1951 (Oberholser, 1974). Area observers should examine gatherings of blackbirds and cowbirds closely for possible Bronzed Cowbirds, as they are known to mix with roosting and feeding flocks of these migrants.

Brown-headed Cowbird *Molothrus ater* (Boddaert)
STATUS: Fairly common to common breeder and resident.
OCCURRENCE: The Brown-headed Cowbird has been recorded in every county and has been seen in every month.

Few early observers in the study area named the Brown-headed Cowbird in their accounts. A notable exception was McCauley (1877), who spoke of it as "a frequent visitor at our camps. . . . During a day's march over the plain, a good-sized flock, perceiving our wagon train, flew up to and followed it, keeping in rear of the last wagon, for a distance of eleven miles." Such a gathering in either May or June today would be unexpected, for cowbirds by then are well into their nesting cycle and are found singly or in small groups—postnesting flocks have yet to be formed. That the cowbird possibly wintered here was hardly recognized by these observers. Reeves and Reeves (1914–36) called it a bird of "spring, summer, and fall," and Carlander (1934) a "fairly common breeder throughout Panhandle, commoner during spring and fall migrations. Perhaps stays through lighter winters." Both Stevenson (1942) and Wolfe (1956) classified it as only a "summer resident," and Hawkins (1945) failed to name the species at all.

Even today movements of Brown-headed Cowbirds through the Panhandle are not well known. Most birders are not close observers of cowbirds, and the enormous flocks of "blackbirds" encountered in fall and winter are seldom examined for species composition. That the cowbird does winter yearly is now known, but numbers can be highly variable. Data from my records indicate that flocks begin forming in early or mid-September; whether these are composed of local postbreeding birds or migrants from farther north is undetermined. Numbers peak in early winter and decline rapidly thereafter. A study of cowbird populations in Custer County, western Oklahoma (Washita NWR), a short distance east of the Texas Panhandle, reflect a similar pattern (Goddard, 1971). A small incursion into that area was noted by 1 September, numbers that could not be accounted for by the local production of cowbirds. In both years of the study (1964, 1965), populations increased dramatically in early October and peaked in early November (1964) and early December (1965). Numbers then declined sharply in early January. Both winters of the study were thought mild.

The CBCs are indicators of the status of the Brown-headed Cowbird in early winter. The following show the number of times it has been recorded on each count and the averages: *Amarillo*—13 of 40 (4.6); *Buffalo Lake NWR*—9 of 29 (21.3); *Friona*—3 of 12 (8); *Lake Meredith* (*east*)—14 of 18 (3,035); *Lake Meredith* (*west*)—11 of 24 (2.8); *Quitaque*—9 of 21 (5.4). The higher average on the Lake Meredith (east) count can be attributed to the enormous number of "blackbirds" roosting nightly in the Sanford Dam marsh. An estimated 2 percent of a million or more birds there were thought to be cowbirds (Royall et al., 1970).

Is there a discernible spring migration of cowbirds through the study area that has gone undetected? If it has been missed, this is undoubtedly the result of not examining blackbird flocks closely enough. The Oklahoma study (Goddard, 1971) disclosed a spring movement during the first part of April, but the number of Brown-headed Cowbirds then tallied was considerably less than in fall. The spring dispersal of breeding cowbirds into the study area is shown most clearly by the species' arrival dates in the PDCSP, where none winter. My records show that the first birds appear during the first or second week of March—somewhat earlier in mild winters—and that the first groups normally are composed of 3–4 males.

NESTING: The TBBAP found CO nesting of the Brown-headed Cowbird in nine survey blocks, PR in 39, and PO in 39. They were distributed uniformly across the study area, with fewer occupied quadrangles in the extreme northwest and southwest sectors. Adults of other species feeding cowbird fledglings accounted for three of the confirmations: Blue-gray Gnatcatcher, Lake Marvin, Hemphill County, 6 June 1987; Painted Bunting, PDCSP, 29 July 1987; Orchard Oriole, Lipscomb County, 8 July 1990. A nest containing four Brown Thrasher eggs and one cowbird egg was found along the Salt Fork of the Red River in Collingsworth County, 25 May 1987. The remaining confirmations were based on unattended cowbird fledglings. An Indigo Bunting nest containing a recently hatched bird and a cowbird egg was found at Lake Meredith, Potter County, 10 July 1995.

Adult Rock Wrens were observed feeding cowbird fledglings in the PDCSP, 24 July 1986 and 26 August 1995. The Brown-headed Cowbird is known to parasitize more than 220 species of birds (Friedmann et al., 1977).

The BBS averages show a higher number of summering Brown-headed Cowbirds in the eastern counties than on the High Plains farther west: *Childress*— 17.1; *Clarendon*—9.3; *Miami*—6.8; *Booker*—6.0; *Channing*—3.6; *Pantex*—0.8; *Texline*—0.6; *Waka*—0.1.

SPECIMENS: Specimens have been collected in Hutchinson (13 and 15 June 1950, TNHC), Randall (9 August 1936, MVZ; 9 August 1936, TCWC), and Sherman (19 April 1990, WTAMU) counties. In addition, Oberholser (1974) shows specimens taken in Hutchinson and Randall counties. The former, which he assigns to nominate *ater*, probably represent the birds taken by Thompson (1952) and deposited in the TNHC. Those taken in Randall County he assigns to both *ater* and *buphilus*, the latter a race not recognized (AOU, 1957).

Orchard Oriole *Icterus spurius* (Linnaeus)

STATUS: Uncommon to fairly common breeder in the eastern third, locally westward.

OCCURRENCE: The Orchard Oriole has been reported in every county except Deaf Smith. Oberholser (1974) shows it in eleven, almost all in the eastern half. It has been seen May–October.

My records reveal that in 24 of the 33 years of record keeping, the return date of the Orchard Oriole fell in the seven-day period 1–7 May, missing it in the others by only a day or so. Few remain past early September, the latest a single bird at BLNWR, 26 September 1970. Unexpected was an immature male on the refuge feeding in a field of sunflowers with a flock of White-crowned Sparrows, 24 October 1992.

Although scant data are available for a close comparison, the Orchard Oriole appears to have been more common in the study area formerly than at present, based primarily on McCauley (1877), who notes that the species was "found frequenting most of the heavily wooded creeks, as Mulberry, McClellan, Etc., in Texas, and Wolf Creek above in the Indian Territory. Along the dry Washita and Canadian, many were also seen and heard." Furthermore, he says neither the Baltimore nor the Bullock's was as "numerous" as was the Orchard Oriole. This is no longer true, and I doubt if "many" would be proper in describing its presence in any area. Even as recently as Hawkins (1945) at mid-century, the species was considered an uncommon resident in the eastern Panhandle.

A closer look at the Orchard Oriole by county is in order, based on BBSS and the TBBAP. *Lipscomb*—Booker BBS: 14 of 22, average 1.5 per count. TBBAP: 21.5 hours at 0.6 per man-hour. *Hemphill*—TBBAP: 22 hours at 0.2 per man-hour.

In 13 visits to the Lake Marvin area, I recorded it ten times at an average of 1.7 per trip. *Wheeler*—TBBAP: 131.75 hours, no orioles. *Collingsworth*—TBBAP: 14.5 hours, one oriole. *Ochiltree*—TBBAP: 21.5 hours, a "few" singing males. My records for the same location (Wolf Creek Park) show an average of 2.2 per trip. *Roberts*—Miami BBS: 11 of 22, average 0.7 per count; TBBAP: 15 hours at 0.5 per man-hour. *Gray*—TBBAP: 14.5 hours at 0.3 per man-hour. *Donley*—Clarendon BBS: one of eight; TBBAP: 12 hours, one oriole. *Hall*—TBBAP: 18.5 hours, no orioles. *Hutchinson*—TBBAP: 12 hours at 1.2 per man-hour. *Armstrong*—TBBAP: 7 hours at 0.9 per man-hour. *Potter*—TBBAP: 26.5 hours at 0.1 per man-hour. *Randall*—my records disclose that on 251 visits to the BLNWR, the average number recorded was 4.7 per trip. *Oldham*—TBBAP: 21 hours at 0.7 per man-hour. *Hartley*—TBBAP: 12.45 hours at 0.3 per man-hour.

The Orchard Oriole breeds much farther west in the Texas Panhandle than was recognized by Oberholser (1974) and Johnsgard (1979). It penetrates the western half of the study area primarily via the Canadian River. I have found a higher concentration in eastern Oldham County in the Boys Ranch area than farther east in the Lake Meredith area. Outside the BLNWR, the chances of seeing an Orchard Oriole in the southwestern sector are slim, as evidenced by the remarks of one resident observer in Parmer County in the 1960s: "Usually lucky if I get one through per year" (C. D. Littlefield).

NESTING: The TBBAP found CO nesting in seven survey blocks, PR in 12, and PO in 12. Fifteen were located between the 100th and 101st meridians, eight between the 101st and 102nd, and eight west of the 102nd. Nesting has been confirmed in Hartley, Hutchinson, Lipscomb, Ochiltree, Oldham, and Randall counties.

SPECIMENS: Specimens have been taken in Hutchinson (14 and 27 June, and 8 July 1950, TNHC) and Potter (30 August 1978, TCWC) counties. Oberholser (1974) names a specimen collected in Lipscomb County without giving its location and assigns it to the race *I. s. capensis,* one not recognized (AOU, 1957).

Hooded Oriole *Icterus cucullatus* Swanson

STATUS: Vagrant summer visitor.

OCCURRENCE: There have been three reported sightings of the Hooded Oriole in the Texas Panhandle, all in Randall County. The first was that of Hibbets et al. (1926–36), who name a date of 6 May 1930: possibly the sighting for that county questioned by Oberholser (1974). The second occurrence took place in the PDCSP, where a male was reportedly found on 27 May 1991. Written documentation was submitted in verification; however, because of insufficient details and the fact that neither observer had ever seen a Hooded Oriole before, it was thought proper to dismiss the sighting. There are variations in plumages in the Bullock's Oriole, a species common in the park, and inexperienced observers could be led astray. The latest discovery, again in the state park, came on 18 May 1994 when a calling male was encountered (K. Seyffert).

The Hooded Oriole in Texas is a rare to locally common summer resident along the Rio Grande from El Paso County through the Lower Rio Grande Valley and north to Gillespie, Kerr, McMullen, and Nueces counties in the east, and the Davis and Guadalupe mountains of the Trans-Pecos (TOS, 1995). There have been sightings from the Muleshoe NWR, Bailey County, June–August 1956 (*fide* C. Stogner), and Crosby County, 4–5 September 1980 (Williams, 1981).

Baltimore Oriole *Icterus galbula* (Linnaeus)

STATUS: Uncommon to fairly common breeder in the eastern third, rare summer and fall visitor westward.

OCCURRENCE: The Baltimore Oriole has been recorded in 13 counties: Collingsworth, Donley, Gray, Hemphill, Hutchinson, Lipscomb, Moore, Ochiltree, Oldham, Potter, Randall, Roberts, and Wheeler. It has been seen from April to October.

Any attempt at a clear assessment of the distribution and status of the Baltimore Oriole in relation to the Bullock's Oriole is obscured by the two species having been "lumped" as a single species ("Northern Oriole") for many years, with the consequence that observers often did not break them down by race when recording observations. The problem is further compounded by the extent of hybridization occurring. Such knowledge as we have is based solely on sight records; results based on examination of specimens would undoubtedly modify the picture. In this regard, a study by Sutton (1968) of oriole specimens collected in nearby areas of Oklahoma is enlightening.

Sutton summarized the "pureness" or degree of hybridization of 96 specimens taken primarily in Cleveland (14), Ellis (22), and Cimarron (13) counties. As examples of specimens collected from counties near the study area, eight "pure" *bullockii* came from Cimarron County (of 13), two from Texas County (of 3), and one from Roger Mills County (of 3). Only one "pure" *galbula* specimen was collected in Beaver County (of 8), none in Ellis County (of 22), none in Roger Mills County (of 3), none in Beckham County (of 1), and none in Greer County (of 4). These results point to the degree of hybridization taking place, and one can assume that it is occurring in the study area also. Sutton speculates that "the zone of hybridization in Oklahoma may widen or shift as the decades pass. A hundred years from now pure *galbula* may have disappeared completely from Cleveland County and pure *bullockii* from Cimarron County; the Baltimore and Bullock's orioles of the entire state may by that time conceivably have become a 'hybrid swarm.' It is important that conditions as they now exist be documented with precision"—an admonition all observers in the study area should carry with them afield. My sight records reveal the following ratios of Bullock's Oriole to Baltimore Oriole in the eastern counties: Lipscomb, 3:2; Hemphill, 1:1; Wheeler, 7:1; Collingsworth, 21:1; Ochiltree, 2:1; Roberts, 17:1; Gray, 30:1; Donley, 19:1. Sight records of obvious hybrids have been reported in Gray, Hutchinson, Oldham, Potter, and Randall counties.

Most statements on the status of the Baltimore Oriole in former times are anecdotal. One account in the 1950s (P. Acord) speaks of the species as present in Amarillo in summer, where it is absent today. Revealing is the observation of Hawkins (1945) that the Baltimore Oriole was not only a fairly common summer resident of the eastern Panhandle but also probably the most common oriole species. The early and late dates for the Baltimore Oriole in the study area are 25 April 1971 and 1976 at BLNWR and 8 October 1978 in Miami, Roberts County.

NESTING: Almost all data pertaining to the nesting of the Baltimore Oriole were accumulated during the TBBAP. CO nesting was found in the following counties and survey blocks: Hemphill (Lake Marvin); Hutchinson (Adobe Creek SW); Lipscomb (Lipscomb, Glazier); Roberts (Dry Creek NE). PR and PO nestings were also observed in Collingsworth and Donley counties.

SPECIMENS: Oberholser (1974) names a specimen taken in Lipscomb County without specifying its whereabouts.

Bullock's Oriole *Icterus bullockii* (Swainson)

STATUS: Common breeder; vagrant winter visitor.

OCCURRENCE: The Bullock's Oriole has been found in every Texas Panhandle county and has been seen in every month.

The Bullock's Oriole returns in spring around mid-April, most often during the third week. The earliest dates are for a subadult in Amarillo, 28 February 1954, and one in Amarillo, Potter County, 14 March 1965. Most are gone by the third week of September. There are two sightings for 1 October and one for 20–22 November 1960 (Amarillo). The only confirmed overwintering bird was a female in Amarillo, Potter County, during the 1964–65 season. An immature in Miami, Roberts County, 5 December 1977, was not seen again.

The averages on the BBSS are as follows: *Booker*—3.4; *Childress*—14.4; *Waka*—0; *Miami*—8.3; *Clarendon*—14.4; *Pantex*—0.1; *Channing*—14.2; *Dal-hart*—5.3; *Texline*—3.3. A two-year Breeding Bird Study in the PDCSP yielded an average density of 23 orioles per 100 acres (Seyffert, 1967–68). This is in contrast to the view of Stevenson (1942), who thought the species an "uncommon summer resident."

NESTING: The TBBAP found CO nesting in 38 survey blocks, PR in 30, and PO in 15. Thirty-five were located between the 100th and 101st meridians, 23 between the 101st and 102nd, and 25 west of the 102nd. There are few data on the nesting status of this species. Nest building has been observed as early as 4 May 1989 in Potter County and as late as 13 June 1991 in Castro County. A nest with eggs was found as late as 20 June 1987 in Lipscomb County and an adult on the nest on 28 July 1988 at Lake Tanglewood, Randall County.

SPECIMENS: Specimens have been taken in Childress (19 July 1976, OMNH), Hutchinson (13, 14, 19, and 29 June, 10 July 1950, TNHC), Oldham (7 June 1981, TCWC), and Randall (11 August 1939, 29 June 1969, WTAMU) counties. Oberholser (1974) shows specimens collected in Collingsworth and Hutchinson counties without giving details. The Hutchinson County birds are probably those secured by Thompson (1952) and deposited in the TNHC.

Scott's Oriole *Icterus parisorum* Bonaparte
STATUS: Casual summer and fall visitor.

OCCURRENCE: There have been four reported sightings of the Scott's Oriole in the Texas Panhandle. The first occurrence was on 23 September 1978, when a first-year male was found at BLNWR (Seyffert, 1987; TBRC). The bird was under observation for some 30–40 minutes. The following spring another male was encountered, 27 May 1979, in Amarillo, Potter County (B. Zimmer). On 27 April 1984, a male was observed at BLNWR (P. Acord, F. Cain), followed by yet another male the next day at Ceta Glen, South Ceta Canyon, Randall County (F. Cain, J. Cepeda, K. Seyffert)—locations some 25 miles apart.

The Scott's Oriole is an uncommon to common summer resident in the Trans-Pecos and southern half of the Edwards Plateau (TOS, 1995). There have been several sightings reported from the South Plains, where it is classified as "accidental" (LEAS, 1994): one in Crosby County, 26 August 1980 (Williams, 1981), September 1983 (*fide* C. Stogner), and 24 August 1985 (*fide* C. Stogner); one on the Muleshoe NWR, Bailey County, 19 September 1982 (Williams, 1983). On 16 April 1967, a female Scott's was collected on the Cimarron National Grassland in Morton County, southwestern Kansas (Cable et al., 1996). The nearest location in New Mexico where one has been reported is west of Logan, Harding County, 2 June 1993 (NMOS, 1992–93).

Family Fringillidae (Fringilline and Cardueline Finches and Allies)

Pine Grosbeak *Pinicola enucleator* (Linnaeus)
STATUS: Casual fall and winter visitor.

OCCURRENCE: The Pine Grosbeak has been recorded in three counties: Gray, Potter, and Randall. It has been seen from October to March.

The first reference to the Pine Grosbeak in the study area is that provided by Wolfe (1956): "The files of the U.S. Fish and Wildlife Service contain the record of a bird picked up alive in Pampa, Gray County, in December 1933. It was kept as a pet for sometime and later preserved as a specimen." Oberholser (1974) published further details, adding that it was an "adult female found alive, but died two weeks later, preserved?, V. E. Moore." Pulich (1988) recently made an effort to locate the specimen but was unsuccessful and speculated that it may not have been saved. The AOU (1957) assigned the specimen to the subspecies *P. e. montana,* for which the normal wintering range extends from southern British Columbia and southern Alberta south to southeastern Oregon and western Nebraska.

There have been nine sightings of the Pine Grosbeak since mid-century: a pair in Amarillo, 10 October and 9 November 1953; one or more in company with "crossbills" at Amarillo, winter of 1960–61 ("arriving about Christmas"); one in Amarillo, 10 November 1962 ("the whole family watched for an hour"); two in Amarillo, third week of December 1968; two males and two females in Amarillo, 2 January–mid-March 1970; a singing male in PDCSP, 25 January 1970; five in Amarillo, 9 January 1978; a female in Amarillo, late February–early March 1981; a male in Amarillo, 21–24 November 1984 (feeding on the fruit of ornamental hawthorn trees on the grounds of the U.S. Postal Service Complex in Amarillo; TP-RF).

There have been three reported sightings of the Pine Grosbeak from nearby areas in New Mexico and Oklahoma: Clayton, Union County, New Mexico, spring of 1955 (Baumgartner, 1955); Goodwell, Texas County, Oklahoma, 2 and 3 December 1961; and Black Mesa State Park, Cimarron County, Oklahoma, 9 December 1979 (Baumgartner and Baumgartner, 1992). One male and two females were observed north of Elkhart, Morton County, Kansas, 26 May 1979 (Cable et al., 1996), a very late sighting. Another late sighting was one in Lubbock, 1 May 1988 (TBRC).

Purple Finch *Carpodacus purpureus* (Gmelin)

STATUS: Casual to rare fall and winter visitor.

OCCURRENCE: The Purple Finch has been seen in 12 counties—Briscoe, Deaf Smith, Donley, Gray, Hartley, Hemphill, Hutchinson, Oldham, Potter, Randall, Roberts, and Swisher—and from September to May.

The Purple Finch is of irregular occurrence in the study area. It is probable that with closer scrutiny, some birds accepted out-of-hand as House Finches would prove to be Purple Finches. Most are seen during the period October–March. There is one September record, a female in Amarillo, Potter County, 9 September 1964. There are four records for May, the latest a single bird in Amarillo, 18 May 1967. The September sighting may be questioned as it is far earlier than the earliest dates recorded at locations to the east of the study area, where the Purple Finch is much more common. As examples, the early date for Oklahoma is 2 October (Sutton, 1967), and for north-central Texas it is 27 October (Pulich, 1988). The earliest October date for the study area is 8 October 1994—two females at Greenbelt Lake, Donley County. I know of no instance of large flocks of Purple Finches having been seen, as often occurs with House Finches in winter; the most Purple Finches seen together were seven in South Ceta Canyon, Randall County, 8 March 1981.

Cassin's Finch *Carpodacus cassinii* Baird

STATUS: Vagrant winter visitor.

OCCURRENCE: There have been three reports of the Cassin's Finch in the Texas Panhandle, all for Potter and Randall counties. A single male was seen at a feeder in Amarillo, 24 January 1969. Several sightings occurred in the winter of 1972–73: a single bird in Amarillo, Potter County, 25 January–first week of April, and a male and female in The Palisades near Canyon, Randall County, 16 March. The 40 reported on the Lake Meredith (west) CBC of 20 December 1997 must be questioned.

The Cassin's Finch winters casually or irregularly as far east as western Nebraska, western Kansas, western Oklahoma, and central Texas (AOU, 1983). In the Oklahoma Panhandle, the Cassin's Finch is classified as a common but erratic winter visitant in Cimarron County (Baumgartner and Baumgartner, 1992), and in New Mexico it is an occasional visitant as far east as the Clayton area, Union County (Hubbard, 1978). Observers in Texline, Stratford, and Dalhart should be on the alert for the species' possible presence. In late summer and early fall Cassin's Finches form groups, often foraging with other montane species such as crossbills, and such mixed groupings, which visit feeders regularly, should be examined closely. Only a short distance south of the study area, eight Cassin's Finches were tallied on the Plainview CBC in Hale County, 21 December 1960, and one was seen in Lubbock, 15 December 1984 (Williams, 1985).

What McCauley (1877) named the Cassin's Finch, *Peucaea cassini,* (Woodh.) Bd., was surely the House Finch, *Carpodacus mexicanus,* a species common to the area and one he fails to name. The Cassin's Finch is a bird of the montane forests of western North America and would not be present in the Texas Panhandle during May and June, as McCauley was.

House Finch *Carpodacus mexicanus* (Müller)

STATUS: Fairly common to common resident.

OCCURRENCE: The House Finch has been recorded in every Texas Panhandle county and has been seen year-round.

The first account of what surely was the House Finch, not the Cassin's Finch as named, is that of McCauley (1877): "*Peucaea cassini,* (Woodh.) Bd.—Cassin's Finch: First met with in the thickets along the Palo Duro ... traveling up the stream, the pleasant notes of these birds could be heard as we rode by the thickets everywhere skirting it. It was heard often afterward, and occasionally seen, chiefly in the dense underbrush along Red River, near where it enters the canyon." He collected an adult female along the Palo Duro on 25 May 1876 and a nest with eggs the following day. A montane species of western North America, the Cassin's Finch occurs in the Panhandle only as a winter vagrant. It nests no nearer than south-central Colorado (Andrews and Righter, 1992) and the northern highlands of New Mexico (Hubbard, 1978). It was in the same areas where McCauley found his birds that the House Finch was first reported.

When Strecker (1910) visited the southeastern Panhandle near the beginning of the twentieth century, he failed to name the House Finch among the species encountered. However, he journeyed no farther west than Armstrong County and would perhaps have found it had he penetrated farther into the region. When he later published *The Birds of Texas* (1912), the range of the House Finch was given as: "Western Texas—trans-Pecos region and southern plains." Observations published later centered on the Potter–Randall County area, including the Palo Duro Canyon, and we have no knowledge of a possible presence of the House Finch elsewhere in the region. Reeves and Reeves (1914–36) gave the House Finch a single entry: "1928: Spring and fall, not nesting here so far as I know," and Hibbets et al. (1926–36) classified it as "rare in winter."

As mid-century neared, observers had more to say concerning the status of the House Finch in the Palo Duro Canyon. Russell (1935) said "flocks were common in the canyon after July 26"; Stevenson (1942) considered the species "resident in the Palo Duro Canyon and vicinity. Finches are present throughout the year but are more common in winter"; Hawkins (1945) reported the bird as a "fairly common permanent resident of the larger canyons." Observers in the 1950s considered the House Finch an uncommon permanent resident (TPAS, 1955), found primarily in the canyons, and it appears that the species did not become common until the 1960s.

The history of the arrival and eastward spread of the House Finch in the Oklahoma Panhandle (Oliphant and Brown, 1984) is of help in tracing what likely occurred in nearby northern and eastern areas of the Texas Panhandle during the same period. The first House Finch recorded in Oklahoma was during the summer of 1919, when fewer than a dozen were found near Kenton, Cimarron County. Nesting was confirmed in the county in 1922, and sightings continued intermittently thereafter; by 1952 the species had become established.

It was not until 1957 that the House Finch was found beyond Cimarron County, when two were found much farther to the east in Caddo County in west-central Oklahoma. By 1964 the species had arrived in Beckham County to the south (bordering the study area on the east), and it has since continued spreading eastward in the state. In the Clayton area of Union County in northeastern New Mexico, the House Finch was considered only an occasional resident during the 1950s (Krehbiel, 1955).

The House Finch is found today throughout the Panhandle region, most commonly in towns and around farm and ranch buildings. Its distribution and status are not accurately reflected by the BBSS, most of which are on routes that traverse open plains and croplands containing few areas of ornamental trees, lawns, and buildings—ideal finch habitat found principally in towns. By late summer finches have begun gathering in flocks. As examples, 50 or more were seen in a maize field near Amarillo, Randall County, 23 August 1986, and 75 in a weedy field on the Wildcat Bluff Nature Center in Amarillo, Potter County, 24 November 1995. An estimated 190 finches in one group were observed at a stock watering tank in the Plum Creek area of Lake Meredith, Potter County, 31 December 1977. Illustrating how common the House Finch has become in the eastern Panhandle, 50+ visited feeders daily at a residence in Miami, Roberts County, during the winter of 1994–95. The degree and extent of a migratory movement, if any, are unknown. The averages and highs on the CBCs reflect the species' winter status and distribution: *Lake Meredith (west)*—31.5 (190); *Amarillo*—28.3 (259); *Lake Meredith (east)*—7.6 (53); *Buffalo Lake NWR*—9.6 (82); *Quitaque*—6.4 (56); *Friona*—0.

NESTING: The TBBAP disclosed a wide summer distribution of the House Finch. CO nesting was found in 24 survey blocks, PR in 24, and PO in nine. Eighteen quadrangles were located between the 100th and 101st meridians, 21 between the 101st and 102nd, and 18 west of the 102nd meridian. The House Finch is two-brooded, possibly three-brooded. Adults building nests have been observed as early as 30 March 1968 at Lake Tanglewood, Randall County, and as late as 13 June 1991 in Parmer County. Newly fledged young being fed were seen in Amarillo, Potter County, 31 August 1995. During the TBBAP most nest building was found in the period 1–22 May. Closer observation would possibly disclose nesting earlier in March than our few records suggest. In far western Oklahoma (Cimarron County), the earliest date for a House Finch nest with eggs is 25 April 1968 (Parmelee, 1969).

SPECIMENS: Despite this being so common a town-dwelling species, there is but one specimen available, a bird taken in Potter County (4 April 1990, WTAMU). The whereabouts of the specimen collected by McCauley (1877) is unknown.

Red Crossbill *Loxia curvirostra* Linnaeus

STATUS: Rare summer, fall, and winter visitor.

OCCURRENCE: The Red Crossbill has been recorded in 11 counties: Briscoe, Dallam, Donley, Gray, Hansford, Hutchinson, Moore, Parmer, Potter, Randall, and Sherman. It has been seen in every month.

The following is a listing of all reported sightings: *1958*—Amarillo, 4 May (2). *1959*—Amarillo, 3, 14, and 19 May (1). *1960*—Amarillo, 11 November (100). *1961*—Amarillo in early June. *1963*—Amarillo in March. *1964*—Amarillo in February (2). *1966*—Amarillo, 17 September (5), 4 and 16 October (6), and 16 December; Lake Tanglewood, Randall County, 24 November (1). *1967*—Amarillo, 30–31 January, Amarillo, 5–7 May (1–18+); PDCSP, 20 May (5). *1969*—Amarillo, 16 October. *1970*—Amarillo, February–25 May and 6 June (2) *1972*—BLNWR, 22 October (3). *1973*—Amarillo, 24 January (7) and 12 February (4); BLNWR, 8 September (1). *1974*—Amarillo, 23–24 August. *1984*—Borger, Hutchinson County, 5 November (25). *1986*—Caprock Canyons SP, Briscoe County, 1 January (30). *1990*—Caprock Canyons SP, 17–18 November (20–30; TP-RF); Amarillo, 24 November (1). *1996*—Dumas, Moore County, 14 July (1); Clarendon, Donley County, 16–17 August (1); PDCSP, 1–17 November (1–21); Amarillo, 27 October–27 November (1–24); Pampa, Gray County, 29–30 November (6). *1997*—Amarillo, 10 January–4 March (2–16); Clarendon, Donley County, January–February; Borger, Hutchinson County, 27 January; Stratford, Moore County, 21 February (TP-RF); Hansford County, 22 February (TP-RF); Texline, Dallam County, 23 February (TP-RF); Dumas, Moore County, 11 April (5–6); Pampa, Gray County, 19 February–16 May (1–10). *1998*—Lake Tanglewood, Randall County, 26 April 1998 (1). The Parmer County bird was a November sighting, the year not specified.

The June and July sightings were unexpected. The Red Crossbill is a breeding bird of montane forests and is known to nest no nearer the study area than Colorado (Andrews and Righter, 1992), New Mexico (Hubbard, 1978), and the Guadalupe and Davis mountains of Trans-Pecos in Texas (TOS, 1995). There are several summer sightings for Oklahoma (Baumgartner and Baumgartner, 1992; Heck, 1996). Crossbills are known to wander widely and may appear at any place during any season: they will nest wherever food supplies are abundant.

SPECIMENS: There is one specimen available, a male salvaged in Potter County (24 November 1990, TCWC). It is not known to which of the four subspecies of Red Crossbill found in Texas this one belongs.

White-winged Crossbill *Loxia leucoptera* Gmelin

STATUS: Vagrant winter visitor.

OCCURRENCE: The White-winged Crossbill has been reported once in the Texas Panhandle. An adult male visited a feeder in Amarillo, Randall County, 12–16 March 1981 (R. Ross et al.; TP-RF). This was the second confirmed sighting of the species in Texas. The first was a male that visited a feeder regularly in Lubbock, 25 December 1975–8 March 1976 (Jury, 1976; TP-RF). The most recent confirmed Texas sighting was a single bird that visited a yard in Aledo, Parker County, 12 December 1992–27 February 1993 (TP-RF).

Sutton (1967) reported a male White-winged Crossbill hit by a car near Gate, Beaver County, Oklahoma, 23 August 1951 (specimen). Another nearby Oklahoma sighting was a single bird seen southeast of Elk City, Washita County, 22 January 1978 (Baumgartner and Baumgartner, 1992). Baumgartner (1955) reported a male found dead at Clayton, Union County, New Mexico, 3 November 1954—a bird recovered in Paradise Canyon three miles north of town.

The White-winged Crossbill winters throughout its breeding range in the far north and only irregularly and sporadically farther south (AOU, 1983).

Common Redpoll *Carduelis flammea* (Linnaeus)

STATUS: Vagrant fall and winter visitor.

OCCURRENCE: There have been three reported sightings of the Common Redpoll in the Texas Panhandle, one each for Ochiltree, Randall, and Wheeler counties. The months when they were seen range from November to February.

The first sighting of the Common Redpoll occurred on 25 November 1965, when six were observed on the BLNWR (K. Seyffert; TBRC). It was a day of northerly winds of gale force and the flock had sought shelter in a grove of trees near the lakeside, as had the observer. From one to six birds were seen repeatedly thereafter until 16 January 1966, when three were last seen. A report of 15 having been present was in error (Williams, 1966). The second encounter took place on 27 November 1977, when a single redpoll was observed feeding with a flock of American Goldfinches at Wolf Creek Park, Ochiltree County (K. Seyffert; TBRC). The latest sighting was a single bird that came to a feeder in Wheeler, Wheeler County, during February 1983 (*fide* R. DeArment).

South of the study area, three Common Redpolls were recorded on the Plainview CBC in Hale County, 21 December 1960. The birds were found in the town's cemetery and were studied repeatedly during the ensuing four weeks. Redpolls were reported wintering at Clayton, Union County, New Mexico, during the 1972–73 season (Williams, 1973). The Common Redpoll does not normally winter farther south than central Colorado and Kansas (AOU, 1983).

Pine Siskin *Carduelis pinus* (Wilson)

STATUS: Fairly common to abundant winter visitor; vagrant breeder.

OCCURRENCE: The Pine Siskin has been found in every county except Collingsworth and Hall and has been recorded in every month.

Normally the Pine Siskin returns to the area in September, occasionally earlier. My records show sightings during August in five years, the earliest being two birds at BLNWR, 7 August 1985. Typically, the first sightings involve no more than one or two birds. A few siskins may linger into mid- or late May.

The number of siskins wintering can fluctuate widely, but seldom does a trip afield fail to produce at least a few. A Winter-Bird Population Study in the PDCSP (Seyffert, 1968–78) found the species to be the seventh most common, averaging 13 birds per 100 acres. The average ranged from 1 per 100 acres to 61 per 100 acres. Averages on the CBCs are indicative of its early winter status: *Quitaque—*374.1; *Lake Meredith* (*west*)—22.0; *Amarillo—*22.5; *Buffalo Lake* NWR—8.5; *Lake Meredith* (*east*)—6.1. The exceptionally high average on the Quitaque count can be accounted for by the 6,952 siskins tallied on 1 January 1976. On that day, fields of cultivated sunflowers near the Caprock Canyons SP were swarming with clouds of siskins and goldfinches. As an example of other area numbers, at Clayton, Union County, New Mexico, flocks of migrating Pine Siskins on 15 April 1959 were estimated at 5,000 birds (Baumgartner, 1959).

NESTING: There are two records of the Pine Siskin nesting in the study area. On 3 May 1966, a nest with an adult feeding newly hatched young was found in southwest Amarillo, Randall County, and on 17 June 1969 a surviving young siskin a few days old was found, along with two dead nest mates, on the grounds of the Amarillo City Hall, Potter County, following a severe hail storm (Pulich, 1971).

There have been numerous sightings of Pine Siskins in late spring and summer: at BLNWR ten on 13 June 1970, three on 31 May and one on 26 July 1981, one on 30 May 1982; one in Amarillo, Potter County, 7 June 1978; one in the Thompson Grove Picnic Area northeast of Texline, Dallam County, 7 June 1980; one in PDCSP, 25 May 1981; one in Follett, Lipscomb County, 8 June 1983; one at Lake Tanglewood, Randall County, early June 1988; one coming to a feeder in Amarillo, Randall County, through the last week of June 1988; up to ten all summer in Gruver, Hansford County, in 1999. Oberholser (1974) shows a summer sight record for Deaf Smith County, without giving details.

In light of the confirmed nesting dates in early May and mid-June, all Pine Siskins encountered in the study area within that time frame should be watched closely for possible nestings. On 5 June 1911, a nest with three eggs was found in a pinyon tree near Kenton, Cimarron County, Oklahoma, and in the summer of 1950, a nest in Guymon, Texas County, Oklahoma (Baumgartner and Baumgartner, 1992). There are also summer records for the Clayton area, Union County, New Mexico (Hubbard, 1978).

The known nesting range of the Pine Siskin lies no nearer the Texas Panhandle than the mountainous areas of Colorado, New Mexico, and western Texas (Guadalupe Mountains of Trans-Pecos) (AOU, 1983).

SPECIMENS: Specimens are available from Randall (October 1990 and 9 December 1991, TCWC; 29 January 1939, WTAMU), and Potter (17 June 1969, WFVZ) counties.

Lesser Goldfinch *Carduelis psaltria* (Say)

STATUS: Uncommon breeder locally. Casual winter visitor.

OCCURRENCE: The Lesser Goldfinch has been seen in 12 counties: Armstrong, Briscoe, Donley, Gray, Hartley, Hutchinson, Lipscomb, Moore, Oldham, Potter, Randall, and Roberts. Oberholser (1974) shows it in two, Potter and Randall. It has been recorded in every month except January.

More attention should be directed to the Lesser Goldfinch to determine its true status in the study area. Other than in the Lake Tanglewood and Palo Duro Canyon areas in Randall County, few sightings have been reported—but those are widespread enough to suggest that with better coverage, the species would be found in many of the missing counties. Observers in the southeastern and northwestern counties should be particularly alert, for the species is classified as an uncommon migrant and summer resident, occasionally wintering, in nearby areas of southwestern Oklahoma (Tyler, 1979b) and as a summer resident in northwestern Cimarron County, Oklahoma (Sutton, 1967).

First sightings of the Lesser Goldfinch in spring are normally made during mid-May or later, only a few earlier, the earliest being one at Lake Tanglewood, Randall County, 12 March 1967. There have been an unexpected number of winter sightings: Stevenson (1942) cites birds seen in the Palo Duro Canyon in February and December (years not given). Others are of a male in PDCSP, 8 December, and four birds, 15 December 1974; a male at Lake Tanglewood, Randall County, 9 December 1990; one at Lake Meredith, Potter County, 31 December 1970; a male in Amarillo, Randall County, 2 February 1984; and several near Canyon, Randall County, 14 February 1998.

Occasionally pronouncedly green-backed Lesser Goldfinches are seen, but it is unlikely that they represent the western race *C. p. hesperophilus,* which supposedly occurs no nearer than south-central New Mexico (AOU, 1957). The Panhandle birds are probably first-winter males of *C. p. psaltria.* Kaufman (1993) discusses both green-backed and black-backed birds that may be found in Colorado and New Mexico and pinpoints the caution needed in assigning them to race.

NESTING: There have been few confirmed nestings of the Lesser Goldfinch in the study area. Hawkins (1945) observed a pair building a nest in the top of a juniper in the PDCSP, 17 June 1945. An adult feeding four newly fledged young was observed at Lake Tanglewood, 10 September 1966. On 10 September 1988, an adult male was seen accompanied by a begging juvenile in the PDCSP, and other adults were found with young at Lake Tanglewood on the same day. A pair was observed at a residence in Clarendon, Donley County, 31 May–1 June, followed by adults with young, 7 September 1997. Gross (1968) says that in the Kerrville area of Texas, most nests are not built until June and that active nests reported in September and October are probably second nestings.

Johnsgard (1979) does not show the Lesser Goldfinch breeding in the Texas Panhandle but does show it in the Oklahoma Panhandle. Sutton (1967) cites nests found in Cimarron County, and Tyler (1979b) names the species as a summer resident of southwestern Oklahoma. Birders in the study area seeking the nest of this goldfinch should note that those found in Oklahoma were located in a "tall rose bush," a "young willow," and a "small willow," while others have been found in red cedars (Newell, 1985). Gross (1968) names the cottonwood as a favored nest tree.

SPECIMENS: Stevenson (1942) cites "two immatures collected September 29, 1937, on the Elkins Ranch," Randall County, without citing where they were deposited. These are probably the ones referenced by Oberholser (1974).

American Goldfinch *Carduelis tristis* (Linnaeus)

STATUS: Common to abundant winter visitor. Rare breeder locally in northeastern sector.

OCCURRENCE: The American Goldfinch has been recorded in every county except Collingsworth and Deaf Smith. It has been seen in every month.

The American Goldfinch is among the more common of the wintering birds and one most familiar to those who maintain feeders. It normally returns in fall around the third week of September, the first sightings seldom numbering more than two or three birds, and most are gone by the third week of May. The species' abundance in winter is indicated by a Winter-Bird Population Study conducted in the PDCSP (Seyffert, 1968–78) and by the CBCs. The winter study found the American Goldfinch to be the fifth most common species, averaging 23 per 100 acres. CBC averages are: *Quitaque*—168.0; *Lake Meredith (west)*—52.5; *Lake Meredith (east)*—40.8; *Amarillo*—35.6; *Buffalo Lake* NWR—26.7. American Goldfinches apparently do not roost at night in a compact group. Before sunrise on 3 January 1988, at the Sanford Dam marsh, Lake Meredith, Hutchinson County, I observed goldfinches as they flew singly out of widely scattered salt cedars before assembling into a flock and flying off.

NESTING: The first confirmed nesting of the American Goldfinch took place during the late summer of 1990 in Hemphill County on the Gene Howe WMA. On both 12 August and 3 September, I observed an adult male and a juvenal-plumaged bird feeding in a field of sunflowers. Beginning on 24 June, this site and one other had been occupied by goldfinches. Yet another bird was discovered a few miles farther east at Lake Marvin, 3 September. The American Goldfinch is known to nest in late June or early July, continuing into September (Middleton, 1993).

Nesting in the Lake Marvin area had long been thought probable but had never been confirmed. Nine goldfinches were observed there, 14 June 1977, including a singing male on territory, which gave chase to an intruding male. On 24 July four birds were present, and three again on 25 September. Earlier, several had been found, 5 July 1971, and a single male, 22 July 1973. On 15 June 1981, a singing male followed by a female flew out of a large cottonwood tree at this site, and on 7 June 1986 a calling pair flew over the observer quite low. Return visits to the WMA sites of 1990 disclosed goldfinches present, 4 June 1994 and 8 June 1995. It is probable that the American Goldfinch nests yearly in this area. An adult male at Skillet Creek in northeastern Donley County, 25 June 1972, pointed to possible nesting. Oberholser (1974) shows summer sightings for Hemphill, Potter, Gray, Randall, Armstrong, Donley, Briscoe, and Hall counties, not indicating whose records are involved. Some possibly are derived from McCauley (1877), who says of the American Goldfinch: "Observed along the Washita, and Wolf, McClellan, and Mulberry Creeks."

The American Goldfinch breeds in Oklahoma no farther west than Woodward County: "September 17, 1954, well-developed young in nest twelve feet up in salt cedar" (Sutton, 1967). Oklahoma nesting dates range from 25 May to 25 September.

SPECIMENS: Specimens have been collected in Randall County (October 1990 and 9 December 1991, TCWC; 29 January 1939, WTAMU).

Evening Grosbeak *Coccothraustes vespertinus* (Cooper)

STATUS: Rare winter visitor.

OCCURRENCE: The Evening Grosbeak has been recorded in 15 counties: Briscoe, Donley, Gray, Hansford, Hartley, Hemphill, Hutchinson, Moore, Oldham, Parmer, Potter, Randall, Roberts, Sherman, and Swisher. Oberholser (1974) shows it in three: Parmer, Potter, and Randall. It has been seen from August to May.

This handsome bird, understandably a favorite of feeder watchers, is an irregular and unpredictable (usually winter) visitor in the study area. The Evening Grosbeak may appear in late summer and linger into late spring. Two visited a feeder in Amarillo on 30 August 1974, and an unspecified number were seen in the city on 9 September 1977. Five to six were observed regularly at Lake Tanglewood, Randall County, 19–26 May 1988, and six were seen in Amarillo, Randall County, 25 May 1956. It is not uncommon for this grosbeak to remain into May.

Flocks of Evening Grosbeaks may on occasion be quite large: an estimated 200 were observed at Lake Tanglewood on 28 February 1991 and 100+ on 16 March 1973. What appeared to be a movement of migrants was encountered in the PDCSP, 16 March 1986. As the observer moved downcanyon during the morning hours, flocks of 10, 7, 4, 8, 30, and 7 birds were observed passing low overhead in rapid flight, flying north without pausing. Evening Grosbeaks are often found in company with Cedar Waxwings, and flocks of the latter should be examined closely.

SPECIMENS: Specimens have been taken in Potter County (15 October 1992, TCWC; 10 April 1973, WTAMU).

Family Passeridae (Old World Sparrows)

House Sparrow *Passer domesticus* (Linnaeus)
STATUS: Common to abundant resident.
OCCURRENCE: The House Sparrow has been found in every Texas Panhandle county and has been seen year-round.

The House Sparrow is one of the most familiar and widespread bird species in the study area. Those who maintain bird feeders help support a large population, along with a lucky few other species. A student interested in all aspects of bird life would find the House Sparrow an ideal species for study.

Robins (1973) traced the introduction and range expansion of the House Sparrow in North America from the first eight pairs shipped from England to the Brooklyn Institute in New York City in 1850 and their subsequent release in early spring of 1851: "They did not thrive, so about 100 more were brought from England in 1852." Some of the earliest introductions also involved birds thought to have originated in Germany. House Sparrows were introduced "partly because European immigrants longed for the familiar birds of their homeland and partly because they believed this bird would serve a useful purpose in controlling insect pests." The first introduction in Texas was a group released in Galveston in 1867. By 1900 the species had spread to central New Mexico and central Colorado: "The birds flourished and spread, relying to a large extent upon the year-round supply of partially digested seeds in horse manure. Freight trains also probably played a big part in the spread of the House Sparrows, as many reports from western states at the turn of the century mentioned the bird as being well-established in cities along the railroads" (Robins, 1973).

Early in the twentieth century in the Texas Panhandle, Strecker (1910) found the House Sparrow to be "common at Goodnight (Armstrong County) and a few have scattered among farms and ranches." Reeves and Reeves (1914–36) reported it in Canyon, Randall County, in 1914, but gave no indication of numbers. By the 1930s observers were reporting the species as common around towns and farm houses, and it had invaded the Palo Duro Canyon.

NESTING: The House Sparrow nests throughout the area. Nesting activities begin in early or mid-March and continue through late summer. A study of captive sparrows conducted in Plainview, Hale County (Mitchell and Hayes, 1973), just south of the study area, found nests with eggs as early as 28 March and as late as 9 August, with last nestlings hatching on 20 August. A parallel study of wild birds (Mitchell et al., 1973) found early and late egg dates of 18 March and 16 August. The highest peak of egg laying occurred during the week ending 6 April, followed by progressively diminishing peaks during the weeks ending 11 and 28 May, 15 June, and 20 July. The earliest date of nest building that I have observed is 21 March 1996 in Amarillo, Potter County.

SPECIMENS: Numerous specimens are available from Hutchinson (WTAMU), Randall (WTAMU), and Swisher (WTAMU) counties.

Species of Uncertain Occurrence

This section includes reported species for which there is insufficient evidence to support their inclusion as confirmed members of the avifauna of the Texas Panhandle. I have placed these species in seven categories:

1. Those Review Species of the Texas Ornithological Society for which supporting documentation was submitted to the Texas Bird Records Committee and found lacking: Curlew Sandpiper; Ruff; California Gull.

2. Those species of possible occurrence seen by competent observers but for which there is insufficient or no supporting documentation—almost all are one-time observations and some of the species are difficult to identity with certainty in the field: Mottled Duck; Barrow's Goldeneye; White-tailed Kite; Gray Hawk; Crested Caracara; Gyrfalcon; Western Gull; Snowy Owl; Lesser Nighthawk; Black Swift; Blue-throated Hummingbird; Yellow-bellied Flycatcher; Acadian Flycatcher; Gray Vireo; Black-tailed Gnatcatcher; Connecticut Warbler; Red-faced Warbler; Smith's Longspur.

3. Those species correctly identified but of uncertain origin: Barnacle Goose; Mute Swan; Monk Parakeet.

4. Those species observed prior to the twentieth century but that no longer occur: Wood Stork; Sharp-tailed Grouse.

5. Introduced gamebirds that have not become established as breeding populations in the wild: Chukar.

6. Species of such doubtful occurrence or uncertain provenance, or surrounded with such uncertainty, that they probably should be dismissed: Least Grebe; Glossy Ibis; Great Black-backed Gull; Royal Tern; Mexican Jay; Black-capped Chickadee; Juniper Titmouse; Bendire's Thrasher. Several of these may well be confirmed in the future.

7. Species that I believe must be supported by a specimen or photograph, or be seen at one time by more than one reliable observer, although they have been documented in writing and approved by the Texas Bird Records Committee: Olive Warbler; Varied Bunting.

One may well ask why other species on the TOS's Review List that lack confirmation by the TBRC are not also included in this section of uncertain occurrence—species such as the Red-necked Grebe, Garganey, Thayer's Gull, Sabine's Gull, Varied Thrush, and Baird's Sparrow, all of which appear among the preceding species accounts. Realizing the arbitrariness of my decision in placing them on the confirmed list, my answer must be that these species have been seen a sufficient number of times by reliable observers, or under such circumstances (e.g., seen numerous times over a lengthy period of days) that placing them in a higher classification is warranted. It must be borne in mind that state bird records committees have been in existence for only a short time; furthermore, when such a committee declines to accept a sighting, this does not necessarily mean it was not valid but only that insufficient evidence was submitted for review. In the absence of a specimen, all sightings of rare and out-of-range species should be thoroughly documented, preferably with a photograph, regardless of whether there is a state bird records committee in place or not.

Least Grebe *Tachybaptus dominicus* (Linnaeus)

The Least Grebe has been reported once in the Texas Panhandle. Oberholser (1974) named (but questioned) a sighting for Roberts County in August 1934. A search of the Oberholser/Kincaid files failed to disclose documentation supporting the identification (*fide* W. Pulich). It is extremely unlikely that the sighting is valid. This is true also of a grebe identified as a Least that was shot near Clayton, Union County, New Mexico, 12 September 1954 (Baumgartner, 1955). A Least Grebe can be confused with a young Eared Grebe in fall, during which time the latter may be dingy gray on the neck and face and have yellow eyes. As an example of misidentification, Pulich (1988) was brought what was thought to be a Least Grebe recovered in Dallas County, "which proved to be an extremely small, immature Pied-billed Grebe."

The Least Grebe is an uncommon to locally common resident in South Texas from Val Verde, Bexar, and Calhoun counties south to the Rio Grande and is found only occasionally as a visitor in nearby areas (TOS, 1995). The TBRC has not accepted reports of birds seen farther north than the upper Coastal Prairies, with the exception of breeding attempts in Walker and Colorado counties.

Glossy Ibis *Plegadis falcinellus* (Linnaeus)

A Glossy Ibis was reportedly seen near Canadian, Hemphill County, 26 September 1954, "suggesting that this eastern species may have wandered west of its normal range" (Baumgartner, 1955). That this is a valid sighting is extremely unlikely, particularly for a bird that at this time of the year, in both juvenal and adult plumages, is very difficult to distinguish in the field from its look-alike congener, the White-faced Ibis, a migrant common to the area (Kaufman, 1990a). It is not unusual for inexperienced observers and those unfamiliar with its range to report

Glossy Ibis in the study area during fall, sometimes in large numbers. Only fairly recently (3–6 November 1983) has the Glossy Ibis been confirmed anywhere in Texas (Lasley and Sexton, 1995a). Although it is now being found with increasing frequency inland, most sightings have been limited to the upper coast (TOS, 1995).

In discounting this Panhandle sighting, I should note that two Glossy Ibis seen at Guymon, Texas County, Oklahoma, 15 April 1956 were acknowledged by Sutton (1967) and Baumgartner and Baumgartner (1992). Other Glossy Ibis have been reported in Oklahoma as close to the study area as Caddo and Comanche counties.

Wood Stork *Mycteria americana* (Linnaeus)

The Wood Stork has been reported twice in the Texas Panhandle, both times during the nineteenth century. McCauley's (1877) account of the encounters is worthy of close attention: "This large and notable bird has ventured to take up his dwelling in the Staked Plains, one having been observed on the Palo Duro, a few miles below its head; some days later, two others were met with near the upper part of the Tierra Blanca."

These sightings can be placed in present-day Randall County. The author continues: "As he has informed me, this species was previously observed by my friend, Dr. H. S. Turrill, assistant surgeon United States Army, when crossing the Staked Plain with a column of the Eighth Cavalry, under General Gregg, United States Army, in 1872. As usual, those seen were very shy. The one upon the Palo Duro, a magnificent bird, rose from the thick undergrowth bordering the stream, less than a hundred yards away." In describing the Tierra Blanca, Hunnius (1876) relates: "The upper course . . . lay through marshes and low flat meadows, and the whole evidently formed a choice grazing ground for a limited number of suitable animals."

Oberholser (1974) placed the McCauley sightings ca. 1 June 1876 in Deaf Smith County. However, the diary kept by Hunnius shows both encounters taking place in Randall County sometime between 21 and 28 May. On 20 May, the Ruffner party established permanent camp near the present-day Lake Tanglewood community, in northeastern Randall County, having traveled from Mulberry Creek to the east. Hunnius states that McCauley was in camp on the twenty-second, and on the twenty-third was detailed with a survey group "to run a Stadia line North to the Canadian." On the twenty-sixth he was with a detached party that digressed up an unnamed creek a short distance, returning to camp the same day. On the twenty-ninth the group arrived back at its base camp. The expedition then broke permanent camp and headed south. Although McCauley states that he found Wood Storks a few miles below the head of the Palo Duro as well as near the upper part of the Tierra Blanca, was he in fact at or near the actual heads of either stream? The head of Palo Duro Creek lies some 55 miles west of the permanent camp and that of Tierra Blanca Creek is in eastern New Mexico. By "head of the Palo Duro," McCauley was surely referring to that stream's confluence with Tierra Blanca Creek near present-day Canyon in Randall County, forming the head of the Prairie Dog Town Fork of the Red River, the actual headwaters of the Red. Members of the expedition journeyed a few miles up Palo Duro Creek beyond the confluence before turning south, striking Tierra Blanca Creek, and following it in turn a few miles farther upstream. The detailed map giving the route of march does not show the survey party ever entering present-day Death Smith County, however, and for McCauley to have struck out on his own to reach the heads of these streams would have required more than a day's journey. McCauley was not an assigned ornithologist acting independently from the survey group but was one of its working members. His ornithological work was done in conjunction with other duties. It is possible that the sighting by Dr. Turrill mentioned by McCauley was made in Deaf Smith County, for the 1872 Gregg expedition crossed the plains from Fort Bascom, New Mexico, on the Canadian River, to the head of Tierra Blanca Creek and then followed that stream to its confluence with Palo Duro Creek (Hunnius, 1876).

The Wood Stork in Texas is an uncommon to locally common postbreeding visitor in the coastal regions and inland to the eastern and central parts of the state. In the twentieth century, it has been recorded west as far as Concho County (TOS, 1995) and along the Red River in Grayson County (Pulich, 1988).

Barnacle Goose *Branta leucopsis* (Bechstein)

What Pulich (1988) says about the status of the Barnacle Goose in north-central Texas applies as well to the Panhandle: "*The Check-list of North American Birds* (AOU, 1983) states that the Barnacle Goose is casual in North America and on rare occasions can be expected inland through some of the prairie states—Colorado, Nebraska, and Oklahoma—south to the Gulf Coast of Texas. It also implies that some records may be of escapees since this goose is commonly kept in captivity and sometimes escapes. Oberholser (1974) included this species as hypothetical, based on coastal sight records. *The Checklist of the Birds of Texas* (TOS, 1984) has not accepted the species for Texas." The coastal records referred to are from Cameron (2) and Chambers (1) counties, the only inland record being a sighting in Grayson County. None of these being documented, the TBRC has declined placing the species on the official list of the birds of Texas (Lasley and Sexton, 1995a).

The single record of a Barnacle Goose found in the Texas Panhandle is that of a second-year female shot by a hunter northwest of Hereford, Deaf Smith County, 12 January 1986 (Bolen, 1987). A mounted specimen was made of the kill (TP-RF). The only question concerning the validity of the record pertained to the bird's wild status, and upon review by the TBRC the sighting was found unacceptable. The Barnacle Goose is common in wildlife collections, with some birds both full-winged and nonbanded; the chances of this bird being a wild vagrant were so small that the committee was reluctant to accept it as the first valid record for Texas. Ryff (1984) argues against any Barnacle Goose appearing in North America being a stray wild bird; however, the AOU (1998) now recognizes that "the seasonal pattern of distribution suggests that many are natural vagrants."

The nearest to the study area that the Barnacle Goose had previously been reported was in Oklahoma (Baumgartner and Baumgartner, 1992): Alfalfa County, 21 November 1958 (Salt Plains NWR) and 14 December 1963 (Amorita; specimen); Caddo County, 20 November 1985 (Anadarko); Custer County, 14 February 1980 (near Washita NWR). A Barnacle Goose found on the Tishomingo NWR, Johnston County, 16 December 1971, remained until 1 March 1972 (Jemison, 1972).

Mute Swan *Cygnus olor* (Gmelin)

The Mute Swan was introduced in North America as a domesticated species. Most feral birds are now found in the eastern United States from Massachusetts to New Jersey, and near Traverse City, Michigan (Palmer, 1962). Because of its popularity with bird fanciers and the desirability of having such a majestic bird swimming on a city park lake, it may appear almost anywhere. Although it may at times be found at a great distance from urban centers, the Mute Swan is not accepted as a valid species in Texas (Lasley and Sexton, 1995a). As examples of just how far from towns it may appear, on 2 June 1993 three swans were observed at a sand-and-gravel operation near Boys Ranch, Oldham County, and on the following 5–7 July, four on Cactus Lake, Moore County. Upon inquiry the observers were told by the owner of the latter site that the birds had not been introduced but had arrived on their own. From 8 to 12 November 1994, a Mute Swan was present on the South East Park lake, Amarillo, Randall County. According to the manager of city parks, it too was not a released bird. In checking into the matter, I discovered that un-pinioned captive swans were known to have escaped in the area more than once during the recent past. On 1–2 March 1996, another Mute Swan appeared on an Amarillo city pond, this time MediPark Lake in Potter County.

Mottled Duck *Anas fulvigula* Ridgway

There have been two reports of the Mottled Duck in the Texas Panhandle. Carlander (1935) saw one at "Wolfing's Lake" sometime between 13 August and 4 September 1932, and the recovery of one in Castro County on 3 November 1984 was reported by Moorman and Gray (1994).

Carlander did not elaborate on his sighting and I have been unable to determine the location of "Wolfing's Lake"—unless he meant "Wolflin" Lake (Lawrence Lake) in Amarillo, Potter County. An inquiry into the Castro County recovery disclosed that the specimen resembled a female Mallard and was thought to be either a Mottled Duck or a Mexican Duck (Fedynich and Rhodes, 1995), but whether it is a "pure strain" Mottled Duck remains undetermined (letter, Alan M. Fedynich, 25 September 1995). Several Mallard-like ducks collected at the time appeared to be one of several possible hybrid combinations involving Mallard–Black Duck and Mallard–Mottled Duck. Genetic fingerprinting of Mottled Ducks from coastal Texas and Florida is presently under way. When completed, it will allow a positive identification of the Castro County bird based on genetics rather than morphology and physical measurements alone.

The range of the Mottled Duck in Texas lies along the entire coast, extending inland approximately 100 miles in the middle portion (Stutzenbaker, 1988). The species was formerly thought to be largely sedentary. During this decade, however, Mottled Ducks have been reported with increasing frequency at locations far inland from their historical range, particularly in the northeast and north-central sectors of the state.

Barrow's Goldeneye *Bucephala islandica* (Gmelin)

There have been two reported sightings of Barrow's Goldeneye in the Texas Panhandle. One was recorded in Hartley County (probably Lake Rita Blanca) in December 1951 (H. Saunders) and the files of the USFWS at BLNWR show one for 22 December 1962—observer(s) not named. Neither of the birds was documented.

The Barrow's Goldeneye is on the Master List of Review Species of the TOS (Lasley and Sexton, 1995a). Only four sightings to date have been validated in Texas, one in Hunt County, two in Harris County, and one at Lake O'the Pines, Marion County. All of these sites are far downstate from where the species would be expected. Area observers should scrutinize every Common Goldeneye closely for a possible Barrow's.

The nearest locations to the Texas Panhandle where the Barrow's Goldeneye has been reported lie in New Mexico and Oklahoma. Ligon (1961) cited one in the Clayton area, Union County, New Mexico, 23 February 1957; Hubbard (1978), however, changed its status to "hypothetical." A more recent sighting at Clayton Lake was a "single probable female," 12 January 1984 (Hubbard, 1984). In Oklahoma Patti (1983) reported a male on Lake Carl Etling, Black Mesa SP, Cimarron County, during the Kenton CBC of 31 December 1979, and two more males at the same location during the CBC of 1 January 1983. On 14 January 1984, a male was shot by hunters on Lake Ellsworth, Comanche County (Rushing and Tyler, 1984).

The Barrow's Goldeneye occurs in winter mainly along the Pacific Coast, the upper Atlantic Coast, and inland in the northwest to southwestern Arizona and to Utah and Colorado (AOU, 1983).

White-tailed Kite   *Elanus leucurus* (Vieillot)

There is one report of a White-tailed Kite in the Texas Panhandle. The journal entry of the observer (R. Ross) reads: "Fall 1961—November—near Shamrock on trip to El Reno, coming and going." This would have been in Wheeler County in the eastern Panhandle. At that time the observer was a novice birder and the sighting was not advertised. However, because of a later reputation for reliability, and because there have been a number of reported recent sightings from nearby areas, the possibility of this one being valid must be recognized.

Records of White-tailed Kites found at locations not far distant from the study area are as follows: one in Howard County (Big Spring area), 24 April 1982 (Williams, 1982); in Wilbarger County, 2–3 south of Vernon, 8–9 February 1992 (Lasley and Sexton, 1992); one near Lake Electra, 27 February 1993 (Lasley and Sexton, 1993); and one in the Vernon area, 27 November–28 December 1993 (Lasley and Sexton, 1994b); one in Tillman County, Oklahoma, 21 October 1982 (Williams, 1983); one in Comanche County, Oklahoma, 26 March–9 April 1983 (Williams, 1983); one in Greer County, Oklahoma, 2 September 1988 (Grzybowski, 1989).

The White-tailed Kite in Texas is an uncommon to locally common resident along the coastal plains, inland to Bastrop, Harris, Starr, and Waller counties (TOS, 1995) and in counties along the Red River (Pulich, 1988).

Gray Hawk   *Asturina nitida* (Latham)

There has been one report of the Gray Hawk in the Texas Panhandle, an adult observed in the PDCSP, 11 May 1990 (T. Shane). The bird was seen from a near distance (60 yards) in riparian habitat of small cottonwoods by a skilled observer familiar with the species in Mexico. The written description rules out the possibility that the bird was either a Broad-winged Hawk or a Red-shouldered Hawk.

I have spent hundreds of hours in the area where this bird was found and the only buteo I ever recorded was an occasional Red-tailed Hawk, rarely a Broad-winged Hawk. Buteos are seldom encountered in riparian habitat anywhere in the state park.

In Texas the Gray Hawk is an uncommon local resident in the Lower Rio Grande Valley (TOS, 1995). I know of no extralimital sighting reported anywhere near the Panhandle.

Crested Caracara   *Caracara plancus* (Miller)

There have been three reports of the Crested Caracara in the Texas Panhandle. McCauley (1877) correlated the presence of the species in the study area during the late nineteenth century with that of the buffalo: "But a single one of the species observed near Lower Mulberry Creek, though a large number of buffalo carcasses were passed. This is almost the extreme northern limit of its range." This is possibly the source of Oberholser's (1974) summer sight record for Briscoe County. An examination of the route followed, however, places the Ruffner party on Mulberry Creek, Armstrong County, 16–19 June, where a diary kept by one of its members states that many buffalo were found (Hunnius, 1876). Baumgartner (1953) reported a caracara near Amarillo, 19 April 1953. This is possibly the source of the spring sight record shown for Randall County by Oberholser (1974). The bird was observed near the entrance to the PDCSP; however, its authenticity was thought highly questionable at the time. A caracara was reported "perched on a mesquite at the edge of some cultivated ground" approximately five miles east of Stinnett, Hutchinson County, 11 May 1983: "The bird was observed at a few hundred yards for 10–15 minutes by an observer very familiar with the species" (letter, Chuck Sexton, 31 August 1983).

The Crested Caracara is an uncommon to locally common resident from South Texas north along the eastern edge of the Edwards Plateau to Bosque, Hood, Kaufman, Johnson, and Van Zandt counties (TOS, 1995).

Gyrfalcon *Falco rusticolus* Linnaeus
The possibility that the Gyrfalcon has occurred in Texas was not known until recently. Clum and Cade (1994) affirm that the southern limits of the Gyrfalcon's winter range extend into northern Texas. In order to add the species to the official list of Texas birds, the TBRC has sought unsuccessfully to secure verification and locations of the alleged sightings. If the winter range of the Gyrfalcon does indeed extend to Texas, the Panhandle is a region where the sightings could well have taken place. There are three records of the species from Oklahoma (Baumgartner and Baumgartner, 1992): 12 January 1974, a white bird captured and photographed near Grainola, Osage County; 4 November 1982, a gray bird seen in Oklahoma County; 1–19 December 1982, a dark bird in Oklahoma City.

Chukar *Alectoris chukar* (Gray)
Several attempts have been made to introduce this Old World partridge into the Texas Panhandle, but all have failed. The history of two such introductions was related by Hawkins (1945): "Twelve pairs were released near Hereford in February, 1943. At least two pairs nested, but by the following year all had disappeared. Shortly before the war, about two hundred were released on the Coon Ranch in Moore County. . . . A few nested and some were found twenty-five miles north of the release point, but finally all disappeared."

Fifty-six Chukars from Spain were liberated in Lipscomb County in early 1956 by the Texas Game, Fish and Oyster Commission (Jackson, 1964). Fourteen remained by the end of the year and no broods were found. An additional 27 "redlegs" were released in February 1957 to join the 14; however, a March blizzard wiped out all but four, and the attempt at introduction failed.

During the period 1974–76, introduced Chukars, including young birds, could be observed near the entrance to the PDCSP, but they also soon disappeared. Single birds are reported periodically from scattered localities, most likely escapees from local game farms or those raised by bird fanciers. There is a Chukar specimen available (WTAMU).

Sharp-tailed Grouse *Tympanuchus phasianellus* (Linnaeus)

Oberholser (1974) classified the Sharp-tailed Grouse as hypothetical in Texas: "Reputedly common during 19th century in extreme corner of Panhandle (*fide* Mrs. R. L. Duke). Last sighting (only specific record available): Dallam Co., Buffalo Springs (1 in July, 1905, Mrs. Duke). Said to have largely disappeared from Texas range in 1906 (*fide* Mrs. Duke)." Wolfe (1956) recognized the sharptail's former presence in northwestern Texas based on accounts of the U.S. Fish & Wildlife Service. Carlander (1935) reported seeing a "covy [*sic*] of half grown young" on 23 August 1935, "within 30 miles of Amarillo." It is probable that these were locally raised and released birds, not wild ones.

Sutton (1967) says all records of the Sharp-tailed Grouse in Oklahoma are from Cimarron County in the Panhandle: "Formerly resident in northwestern Oklahoma, probably never very common." He cites records of 30 May 1910 ("six or seven"), 11 June 1912 (nest with four eggs), 6 June 1920 (three), and 7 June 1932 (one). In New Mexico Ligon (1961) found a "considerable number" of Sharp-tailed Grouse in 1926 on Johnson Mesa east of Raton, Colfax County. At the time of his writing, however, only a small remnant remained, and Hubbard (1978) thought they had probably since been extirpated.

Curlew Sandpiper *Calidris ferruginea* (Pontoppidan)

On 8 September 1995 what was thought to be a Curlew Sandpiper was observed at a playa located two miles north of Dawn, Deaf Smith County (E. Kutac, R. Scott; TBRC). The bird was observed from a distance of 40 yards or so through both binocular and scope. When seen initially it was in a mixed group of other shorebirds, including Greater and Lesser Yellowlegs, Least Sandpipers, Longbilled Dowitchers, Stilt Sandpipers, and Common Snipe; however, few characteristics were noted other than it being a rather slender and long-legged, grayish, medium-sized bird with a noticeably downcurved bill. The observers left the site but remained disturbed and puzzled by the length and the degree of decurvature in the bird's bill. Both had seen Curlew Sandpipers before. They returned to the playa after a lapse of some fifteen or twenty minutes but only a few Least Sandpipers and two dowitchers were still present. Concerning the bill shape, one TBRC member commented in declining the observation that he had recently photographed a Stilt Sandpiper with an odd bill very similar to a Curlew Sandpiper's.

At the time of this sighting only three Curlew Sandpipers had been documented in Texas, one each for Galveston, Bexar, and Travis counties (TOS, 1995).

Ruff *Philomachus pugnax* (Linnaeus)
The single report of a Ruff in the Texas Panhandle is that of an adult female in breeding plumage discovered at Greenbelt Lake, Donley County, 9 April 1996 (K. Seyffert). However, documentation did not pass muster with the TBRC. This is a Texas Review species, and at the time of writing 15 of 43 sightings of Ruffs reported in the state had been accepted (Lasley and Sexton, 1995a), 42 percent occurring in April.

The Ruff breeds in Eurasia from northern Scandinavia, northern Russia, and northern Siberia south to western and southern Europe, southern Russia, and southern Siberia; it is found only casually in western North America during migration (AOU, 1983).

California Gull *Larus californicus* Lawrence
There have been three reports of the California Gull in the Texas Panhandle. The first was a single bird seen in Hemphill County in June of 1935 (H. Saunders). Details are lacking and presumably it was seen at Lake Marvin. On 2 May 1987, two adults were reported on the sewage treatment playa southeast of Amarillo, Randall County (D. Myers). The California Gull is a Review Species requiring verification; written documentation was submitted to the TBRC but declined for lack of sufficient evidence. There is a reference to one sighting or more of the California Gull on the BLNWR (TOS, 1966), but details are lacking and I have been unable to discover on whose data this reference is based.

A California Gull was "shot or found dead on October 29, 1928, at Altus, Jackson County" Oklahoma (Sutton, 1967), and the author is of the opinion that "there is no reason why this species, which breeds . . . in Weld County, northeastern Colorado, should not pass through Oklahoma regularly." This could well apply to the Texas Panhandle. Another California Gull was collected at Lake Hefner, Oklahoma County, 9 September 1978 (Baumgartner and Baumgartner, 1992). More recently this gull has been found nesting in Bent/Kiowa counties in southeastern Colorado (Andrews and Righter, 1992). The nearest point to the study area in New Mexico where it has been found is Eagle Nest Lake, Taos County (Hubbard, 1978).

The California Gull in Texas is a rare migrant and winter visitor at scattered inland localities (TOS, 1995). One was reportedly seen at Lubbock, 7 November 1982 (Williams, 1983).

Western Gull *Larus occidentalis* Audubon

On 28 December 1967, what was thought to be a Western Gull was found at BLNWR (P. Acord, T. Fox). The bird was seen among Ring-billed and Herring gulls: "a herring-gull size gull—black or very dark wings—yellow bill and flesh legs—a Western Gull surely").

The single Western Gull sighting in Texas accepted by the TBRC was found at Ft. Bliss, El Paso County, 14 May 1986 (TP-RF). The observation was supported by an extensive series of photographs. Without them it would not have been accepted, and even with them the sighting was questioned by some members of the committee. This far western gull is listed on the *Check-list of Birds for Clayton, Union County, New Mexico* (Ligon, 1961), but the sighting is classified as "hypothetical" by Hubbard (1978).

The Western Gull winters from southern British Columbia south to southern Baja California and is casual in southwestern Arizona (AOU, 1983).

Great Black-backed Gull *Larus marinus* Linnaeus

There is a record of a Great Black-backed Gull in the files of the U.S. Fish and Wildlife Service at BLNWR. The bird was reportedly seen on 18 November 1961. Details are lacking, including the name of the observer(s), and the sighting should probably be dismissed.

There are 18 sightings of the Great Black-backed Gull in Texas accepted by the TBRC, all from coastal areas (Lasley and Sexton, 1995a). Presently under review is a first-summer bird observed at Lubbock, 28 June–2 July 1998 (TP-RF).

Royal Tern *Sterna maxima* Boddaert

There is an undocumented report of a Royal Tern seen in Deaf Smith County in October 1947, one that must be dismissed. The bird was possibly a misidentified Caspian Tern. The Royal Tern is a common resident along the Texas coast and has been found inland usually only after tropical storms (TOS, 1995). The species has never been reported anywhere near the study area.

Monk Parakeet *Myiopsitta monachus* (Boddaert)

The few Monk Parakeets that have been reported in the Texas Panhandle most likely were escaped cage birds. All were isolated sightings without recurrences: one in Amarillo, Potter County, 1 October 1985; 1–2 in southwest Amarillo, Randall County, in the early 1990s. Parrots of one species or another have been reported periodically in the parks, cemeteries, and suburban neighborhoods of Amarillo. All such birds should be identified by species if possible.

Snowy Owl *Nyctea scandica* (Linnaeus)

There have been periodic reports of a Snowy Owl in the Texas Panhandle, but upon investigation they proved to be either a Barn Owl or light-colored Great Horned Owl. The single report of one that was probably identified correctly is that of a "white owl" observed by Lewis Walker, a Swisher County farmer, approximately three miles east and two miles north of Kress, 31 January or 1 February 1989. Walker first saw the bird as it perched on a section of irrigation pipe lying on the ground. It then flew low across a field of short winter wheat and lit on a large clod of dirt in full view of the observer. He described the bird as a large owl, white (not cream colored), with a large rounded head ("domed head") that appeared "neckless." News of the encounter became known on the morning of 4 February, and Joel Reese and I made a search for the owl that afternoon, without success. Although looked for on subsequent days, the white owl was not seen again. One other sighting was possibly, if not probably, authentic: a bird seen during winter near Dalhart, Hartley County, in the mid- or late 1970s by a reliable observer (J. Ray).

There are records of Snowy Owls from nearby areas in Oklahoma (Shackford, 1975): one near Kenton, Cimarron County, in late December 1918 and 25 December 1929; one near Guymon, Texas County, 30 November 1974; one seen repeatedly from 18 to 28 January 1975 in Custer and Roger Mills counties; a dead bird found near Rosston, Harper County, 1 February 1975; one in Elk City, Beckham County, 22 February 1975. In addition, one was shot near Gate, Beaver County, in January 1912 (Baumgartner and Baumgartner, 1992). With this many sightings, surely the Snowy Owl will eventually be confirmed in the Texas Panhandle.

Lesser Nighthawk *Chordeiles acutipennis* (Hermann)

There have been two reported sightings of the Lesser Nighthawk in the Texas Panhandle. For only one are there details, and those but scant. Hibbets et al. (1926–36) say: "'Texas Nighthawk'—19 May 1929," near Canyon, Randall County. Oberholser (1974) shows a summer sight record for Potter/Randall counties but questions it. A search of the Oberholser/Kincaid files did not disclose the basis for the sighting (*fide* W. Pulich): perhaps it is the Hibbets account.

The Lesser Nighthawk has been recorded in counties adjacent to the study area. Sutton (1967) cites a bird taken in Boise City, Cimarron County, 23 April 1961: "very fat male with somewhat enlarged testes . . . shot in residential part" of the city—the only Oklahoma record. Williams (1975) reported three Lesser Nighthawks on the Muleshoe NWR, Bailey County, 31 May 1975. Others observed on the South Plains have been recorded in April, June, August, and September (LEAS, 1994).

All nighthawks should be examined closely for the possibility of one being a Lesser Nighthawk. Not only are there differences in plumages between the Lesser and the Common Nighthawk, but more readily noticeable are the differences in flight habits and calls.

The Lesser Nighthawk is a common summer resident from the Trans-Pecos east and south through the southern Edwards Plateau to the lower and central coast (TOS, 1995).

Black Swift *Cypseloides niger* (Gmelin)

The presence of the Black Swift in Texas has yet to be accepted (Lasley and Sexton, 1995a). The literature provides thirteen reported sightings, none verified by the TBRC.

Ten of those reports are from the study area, as follows: (1) "Two . . . were observed carefully at Amarillo 17 September 1959. This is apparently the first record of the species in Texas" (Baumgartner, 1960). The observer's notes read: "stiff bowed wings—slender notched tail—black—slower wing beat than other swifts—not very high under heavy storm clouds—going due south—watched for 1 minute, perhaps 2." (2) One over Memorial Park Cemetery, Amarillo, Potter County, 9 October 1959. (3) One in Parmer County, 26 May 1962: "seen in good light at 50–100 yards distance, following strong WSW winds that lasted most of the day." (4) One at Amarillo, 18 October 1966: "overhead wheeling." (5, 6, 7) "Observed daily, May 5–10, in a flock of Chimney Swifts at Amarillo" (Williams, 1967). In fact, two were seen on 7 and 8 May and one on 11 May 1967. One observer's notes read: "had seen them in Jamaica Christmas '66." (8) An unspecified number were observed flying over Llano Cemetery, Amarillo, Randall County, 13 May 1968. (9) "The most extraordinary record of the season was the appearance of Black Swifts in Palo Duro Canyon on 20 January 1970. They were seen by five experienced observers, all of whom were aware of the improbability of their identification, but who were nevertheless positive" (Williams, 1970). The notes of one observer read: "two flying just above the mesquite in front of the car in full light—went down the canyon—all saw well—no doubts." (10) unspecified number in Memorial Park Cemetery, Amarillo, Potter County, 7 May 1976, "along with Chimneys."

The Black Swift is a summering bird of the western United States, with breeding occurring as near the Texas Panhandle as central and western Colorado (Andrews and Righter, 1992) and the Jemez Mountains of north-central New Mexico (Johnson, 1990). With the birds present in such close proximity, it is probable that wayward swifts could appear in the skies of northwestern Texas from time to time. That appears to be the case in northeastern New Mexico: "Although Clayton, N.M. would seem to be east of the migration route . . . this species appears at that locality regularly each spring; this year 8 were recorded," 26 May 1970 (Williams, 1970). It is of interest that concurrent with the May 1967 sightings in Amarillo, a single Black Swift was seen at Clayton on 13 May (Williams, 1967).

The report that raises the most questions is that of 20 January 1970. If in order, it represents the first winter sighting not only for the state but possibly for the United States. All other Black Swift sightings in Texas have occurred in the period April–October (Lasley and Sexton, 1995a). Much remains to be learned about the winter distribution of the Black Swift as well as the other swifts. Currently the AOU (1983) places it "in Mexico (presumably), through the breeding range from Chiapas to Costa Rica, and in the Greater Antilles (except Puerto Rico)." Inclusion of both Mexico and Costa Rica in the wintering range of the Black Swift has been questioned, for all specimens collected in southern Mexico were taken during the breeding or migration periods, and those observed in Costa Rica were found during the same periods, according to Stiles and Negret (1994). From specimens collected in Colombia, the authors are of the opinion that the Black Swift probably winters exclusively in South America.

That Black Swifts would be found in the Palo Duro Canyon of Texas in winter is most unlikely. Could the two birds possibly have been misidentified White-throated Swifts? At the time of observation, the latter species was not known to winter in the canyon occasionally—this was established in later years (Seyffert, 1984). Given the observer's statement that the birds were "flying just above the mesquite in front of the car," would not white throats and breasts have been obscured from view from such a perspective? Such features of the White-throated Swift are certainly not easily noticeable with the unaided eye unless the birds are quite near, and these features are absent altogether in juveniles of duller coloring. A White-throated Swift may easily be mistaken for a Black Swift in poor light, and white-throateds found in the state park in winter were sometimes observed flying low above the canyon floor when foraging.

Although many of the sightings of this species are probably in order, I have elected to place the Black Swift in the "uncertain" category pending a specimen or good photographs confirming its presence in the state.

Blue-throated Hummingbird *Lampornis clemenciae* (Lesson)

There have been three unverified reports of the Blue-throated Hummingbird in the Texas Panhandle, all in Potter and Randall counties. A possible female Blue-throated Hummingbird was observed off and on during the first week of October 1996 in Amarillo, Potter County. This suburban yard where the bird was seen contains, along with feeders, an abundance of plantings set out specifically to attract hummingbirds; it plays host yearly not only to several pairs of summering Black-chinned Hummingbirds but to migrant species as well. It is of interest that on 4–5 October of the same year, another Blue-throated Hummingbird was observed at a feeder in Levelland, Hockley County, only a short distance south of the study area. Unreported at the time, a possible male Blue-throated Hummingbird was observed in The Palisades near Lake Tanglewood, Randall County, during late summer or early fall of 1995. On 15 August 1997, another possible female Blue-throated Hummingbird was observed at a feeder in Canyon, Randall County. Female hummingbirds of most species are difficult to identify in the field, and care is necessary in their identification.

The Blue-throated Hummingbird is an uncommon summer resident in the Chisos Mountains, rare in the Guadalupe and Davis mountains, and a vagrant to Howard and Midland counties (TOS, 1995).

Yellow-bellied Flycatcher *Empidonax flaviventris* (Baird and Baird)
The Yellow-bellied Flycatcher has been recorded once in the Texas Panhandle, a singing bird on the BLNWR, 14 May 1985 (K. Seyffert).

In Texas the Yellow-bellied Flycatcher is an uncommon to common migrant in the eastern half west to Cooke, Palo Pinto, Travis, Bexar, and Webb counties (TOS, 1995). Pulich (1988) found the species in north-central Texas no nearer the study area than Young County. Locations nearer the Panhandle where specimens have been taken lie in southwestern Oklahoma (Tyler, 1979b): "a female taken at Olustee, Jackson County 20 August 1961; a female in first winter feather collected at Vinson, Harmon County, 2 October 1954." In New Mexico Hubbard (1978) classifies the species as "casual in the extreme east-central plains."

In the absence of a specimen, it is questionable that the Yellow-bellied Flycatcher should be listed in the Texas Panhandle. As Pulich (1988) aptly notes, "sightings tend to be concentrated in areas where there are qualified observers." The extreme southeastern sector of the study area near where specimens have been collected in Oklahoma has received little attention by birders.

Acadian Flycatcher *Empidonax virescens* (Vieillot)
The Acadian Flycatcher has been reported four times in the Texas Panhandle. In an addendum to his final report, Carlander (1933) cites a specimen of Acadian Flycatcher taken at an unnamed location sometime between 15 August and 3 September 1932. His specimens were given to the "biology Department of the West Texas State Teachers College" in Canyon (West Texas A&M University), and to L. E. Simms of Canyon to be mounted and "put in the Historical Society's museum" in Canyon (Panhandle-Plains Historical Museum). There is not an Acadian Flycatcher specimen listed in the university's catalog of birds, nor is there a

mounted empid on display in the museum. Carlander further reports seeing an Acadian Flycatcher in the Palo Duro Canyon sometime between 13 August and 4 September 1932 as well as another at an unspecified location sometime between 18 and 24 July 1933. The only other Panhandle record pertains to a singing bird encountered in Llano Cemetery, Amarillo, Randall County, 6 May 1973.

The Acadian Flycatcher is a common migrant and summer resident in the eastern third of Texas, west to Cooke, Hays, Kerr, and Real counties (TOS, 1995). The nearest to the Panhandle that Pulich (1988) shows it in north-central Texas is Wichita County. Sutton (1967) cites one record for western Oklahoma: "Cimarron County: May 19, 1955, female with unenlarged ovary taken along Cimarron River thirteen miles north of Boise City."

The present whereabouts of the specimen taken by Carlander (1933) is unknown. Until found, the Acadian Flycatcher cannot be named as a confirmed species in the study area.

Gray Vireo *Vireo vicinior* Coues

There have been three reports of the Gray Vireo in the Texas Panhandle. Probably the most likely to be valid is the bird observed in PDCSP, 17 August 1952 (P. Acord): "plain olive-gray bird with narrow white eye ring—no wing bars—faint yellowish underparts—bigger than Bell's Vireo—about the size of Red-eyed Vireo—in bush at foot of embankment in canyon." The other sightings involve a bird seen in Ellwood Park in Amarillo, Potter County, 6 May 1964, and one on the outskirts of Amarillo, Randall County, 7–9 May 1967. Details on the last two birds are lacking.

The correctness of the latter two identifications must be questioned as—unlike in the Palo Duro Canyon sighting—neither bird was encountered in typical Gray Vireo habitat. For the bird seen at Palo Duro, although descriptive details were provided, indications of important behavioral characteristics (restlessness, tail-flicking) were not. Despite such lack of details, the sightings were recognized by Oberholser (1974) and the AOU (1983). Perhaps they were given credence because of substantiated records of breeding from nearby areas in New Mexico and Oklahoma. Ligon (1961) cites a Quay County, New Mexico record: "A breeding colony of the Gray Vireo was found, and one bird taken, on June 14, 1903 on Pajarito Creek near Montoya at 4,300 feet. There is no other nesting place known within 300 miles in any direction, and its presence there is unexplained." The Oklahoma occurrence is from Sutton (1967): "May 22, 1937, male shot . . . of breeding pair observed for some time among pinyons, junipers, and scrubby oaks 'in a little canyon among the mesas' several miles southwest of Kenton, Cimarron County: 'when first encountered, the male was singing while the female was gathering nesting material (Sutton)." These were both isolated occurrences. A Gray Vireo was recorded on one other occasion in Oklahoma, again in Cimarron County (Sutton, 1967): "December 2, 1952, one seen same general area: bird came close to observer and scolded briefly (R. R. Graber)." This December date is surprising as the Gray Vireo is not known to winter in the United States except in southern Arizona and the Big Bend region of Texas (AOU, 1983).

Maxwell (1979) cited recent nesting northeast of the Pecos River in Texas (Reagan, Irion, and Tom Green counties). In his opinion, "Gray vireos may have been present in this region all along, remaining undetected until now . . . apparently suitable habitat exists locally between the Trans-Pecos region and the Oklahoma Panhandle. The other possibility is that gray vireos are expanding their breeding distribution north." He describes the habitats in which the nestings were discovered as "contact zone between mesquite and juniper savannahs at an elevation of about 701m on a gentle slope," and "scrub oak and juniper." Such habitats exist in the study area and should be explored for possible Gray Vireos.

Mexican Jay *Aphelocoma ultramarina* (Bonaparte)

Periodically there are reports of a Mexican Jay in the Texas Panhandle. The sightings usually originate with novice birders who have had limited or no experience with either it or the resident Western Scrub-Jay. An observer who was most certain of his identification was Hawkins (1945), who called his bird the "Arizona Jay," presumably referring to *A. u. arizonae,* and who classified it as an accidental visitor: "In August, 1944, a jay spent a week or more in the author's yard, pecking holes in peaches." This was in Canyon, Randall County. He provided some details: "This jay lacked the streaked throat and brownish back of the Woodhouse's Jay. Uncrested, blue-backed jays with unmarked throats answer to the description of the Arizona Jay, which normally ranges only as far north as south Texas." At the same time, he classified the Woodhouse's Jay (Western Scrub-Jay) as only an "erratic visitor."

Although he was a reliable observer, Hawkins's identification must be questioned. Anyone who has carefully examined Western Scrub-Jays is aware that all do not exhibit clearly defined streaked throats or contrasting brownish backs. An illustration of this lack of contrast in some birds is provided by Kaufman (1990b), who also discusses other similarities in plumages. As he points out, "the Scrub Jays found in the interior of the West . . . are much less colorful and contrasty than the races in Florida and on the Pacific Coast—in other words, somewhat closer to the appearance of Gray-breasted [Mexican] Jays." The surest ways of telling the two apart lie in their very different shapes, actions, and voices, features that none of the observers who have reported Mexican Jays have discussed.

Other sightings of what were thought to be Mexican Jays were reported in Amarillo in April 1953 and 18 November 1953 (*fide* P. Acord). At the time the

Western Scrub-Jay was being reported only sporadically in the study area and it was not yet known to be resident. The Western Scrub-Jay is known as an irruptive species, while the Mexican Jay is sedentary and "strictly nonmigratory" (Brown, 1994). It must be noted that a Mexican Jay was collected in Clark County, southwestern Kansas, not far north of the Oklahoma state line, in March 1906 (Thompson and Ely, 1992).

The Mexican Jay is a common resident in Texas in the Chisos Mountains of the Trans-Pecos (TOS, 1995).

Black-capped Chickadee *Poecile atricapillus* (Linnaeus)

Despite Oberholser (1974) showing spring and fall sight records for Randall County, there is no confirmation of the Black-capped Chickadee in the Texas Panhandle. His inclusion of it is possibly based on Hibbets et al. (1926–36), who cited two records for the Canyon area in Randall County: 19 May 1929 and 5–10 September 1933. Also, the first checklist of Panhandle birds (TPAS, 1955) named the Black-capped Chickadee as a permanent resident in the "Canadian Breaks"; the Carolina Chickadee is not named. Similarly with Hawkins (1945): he discusses the status of the Black-capped Chickadee but fails to name the Carolina Chickadee.

The only confirmed record of a Black-capped Chickadee in the region is one found on the Laurance Regnier Ranch 4.5 miles south of Kenton, Cimarron County, Oklahoma, 29 December 1985 (Shackford, 1986b); it was netted on 30 January 1986, measured, and photographed. Sutton (1967) classified the species in Oklahoma as "uncertain" and believed all sight records of *P. a. atricapillus* were questionable. He cited a specimen of *septentrionalis* collected in Harper County but later added a qualifier (1974a): "specimen does not represent species unequivocally."

Baumgartner (1959) cited both Black-capped and Mountain chickadees at Clayton, Union County, New Mexico, in the fall of 1958: "This is only the second year when these species have appeared." Hubbard (1978) concluded that in migration and winter the Black-capped Chickadee "casually and occasionally moves into . . . Clayton area." One was reported in Union County, 20 January 1996 (Williams, 1996), and later that year the species was found east to Union County— one at Folsom, 23 November, and 14 near Clayton, 13 November (Williams, 1997). It is considered a rare winter visitor on the Kiowa National Grasslands of that area (USDA, 1973). It has been found in winter at Capulin Mountain National Monument in Union County (NMOS, 1992), and 21 were reported in Sugarite Canyon east of Raton, Colfax County, 17 October 1991 (Williams and Hubbard, 1992). It is not known whether any of the Union County birds were collected, surely necessary for confirmation.

There is but one confirmed record of the Black-capped Chickadee in Texas, a specimen collected in El Paso, El Paso County, 10 April 1881, deposited in the Yale Peabody Museum, Yale University (#9723). Prior to a recent publication about this "discovery" (Haynie, 1998), Pulich (1988) had rightly averred: "There are no valid records of this northern species for Texas, and occurrence . . . anywhere in the state is extremely doubtful. . . . Sight records are not acceptable since this species and the Carolina Chickadee cannot be identified in the field on the basis of song or even on the amount of white on the secondaries. Even ornithologists have difficulty distinguishing the two species in the hand."

The AOU (1983) includes central New Mexico in the Black-capped Chickadee's range, and Andrews and Righter (1992) place it in riparian areas of southeastern Colorado. The species has also been found in the southwestern tier of counties in Kansas (Thompson and Ely, 1992). It is possible that an occasional bird may drift into the northwestern sector of the Texas Panhandle, and all chickadees found in that area should be examined closely, particularly those encountered in the Canadian River drainage. The river acts as a corridor for the westward extension of the Carolina Chickadee's range into Oldham and Hartley counties, and it is possible that it could do the same for the eastward extension of the Black-capped Chickadee from New Mexico.

Juniper Titmouse *Baeolophus griseus* (Ridgway)

There have been periodic reports of the Juniper, formerly called Plain, Titmouse in the Texas Panhandle. All lacked documentation, and it is unlikely that any were correctly identified. These sightings have almost invariably occurred during summer or early fall—when young Black-crested Titmice are out of the nest—and have usually been made by inexperienced observers. Young black-cresteds with short gray crests are virtually indistinguishable from the Juniper Titmouse. None of the reports speak of the calls, which differ markedly. The only published account of the Juniper is Carlander's (1933), who listed "Plain" Titmouse at an unnamed point in the study area (probably Randall County) sometime between 19–22 June and 10–17 September 1933.

The Juniper Titmouse is a resident in the Black Mesa country of northwest Cimarron County, Oklahoma (Sutton, 1967), and in New Mexico Hubbard (1978) notes that it occurs occasionally in migration and winter in the Clayton area. The extreme northwest sector of the Texas Panhandle is the area where the species may eventually be found. A Juniper Titmouse reported south of the study area in Crosby County, 3 July 1985 (Williams, 1985), must be questioned.

Black-tailed Gnatcatcher *Polioptila melanura* Lawrence

There have been two reports of the Black-tailed Gnatcatcher in the Texas Panhandle. The first was a bird observed on a nest in the PDCSP in early June 1976. I visited the site on 5 June and found the nest placed approximately six feet up in a mesquite tree. Both adult gnatcatchers were in attendance. Superficially the male appeared to be a Black-tailed Gnatcatcher; however, closer examination in strong sunlight disclosed a head that was not black but rather a deep purple. Moreover, when the bird sat on the nest with its tail thrust upward, the undertail pattern was clearly typical for a Blue-gray Gnatcatcher. Its call also was that of a Blue-gray.

Another possible Black-tailed Gnatcatcher was observed in McBride Canyon, Lake Meredith Recreation Area, Potter County, 30 April 1993. The competent and reliable observer was familiar with the species, and the bird's dark head and tail were reportedly seen clearly, but flittingly. Such an out-of-range species requires detailed documentation for acceptance. The Black-tailed Gnatcatcher is not known to occur any nearer the study area than the Trans-Pecos (TOS, 1995), although a February sighting is listed for the South Plains (LEAS, 1994).

Bendire's Thrasher *Toxostoma bendirei* (Coues)

There have been two reported sightings of the Bendire's Thrasher in the Texas Panhandle, both from Randall County. Neither sighting was supported with documentation, and without this they cannot be accepted. The Bendire's Thrasher and the area's fairly common Curve-billed Thrasher are quite similar in appearance; the former species may even be confused with the Sage Thrasher in some stages of plumage (Kaufman, 1990a). The first sightings was of one bird in the PDCSP, 14 April 1955—"According to the Creagers, who are very familiar with southwestern thrashers from birding in Arizona, this bird had too short a tail for a curve-bill and too straight a bill" (P. Acord). The second was of one at Canyon, 9 November 1956: "watched for entire day at close range." These sightings were acknowledged by Oberholser (1974) and he placed the species on his "hypothetical" list.

At the time of these reports the status and distribution of the Curve-billed Thrasher in the study area were only beginning to be discovered. Also, other than the Creagers, none of the observers had any experience with Bendire's Thrasher. Weske (1968) cites the Bendire's Thrasher as being on A. J. Krehbiel's "seen once or twice list" for nearby Clayton, Union County, New Mexico, sightings unacknowledged by Hubbard (1978).

The Bendire's Thrasher breeds no nearer the study area than central New Mexico (Sandoval and Socorro counties), remaining in winter only in the far southern portion of the state, and there is one record of nesting in Otero County in southeastern Colorado (AOU, 1983). The species has yet to be acknowledged as valid in Texas (TOS, 1995; Lasley and Sexton, 1995a). Other than the single southeastern

Colorado sighting, all authenticated records of wandering birds have occurred to the north and west of the species' known range (England and Laudenslayer, 1993).

Olive Warbler *Peucedramus taeniatus* (Du Bus de Gisignies)

There has been one reported occurrence of the Olive Warbler in the Texas Panhandle. On 30 April 1995 an adult male was observed in Tule Canyon, Lake MacKenzie, Briscoe County (G. Whitten; TBRC). Although a majority (8–1) of the TBRC gave their assent to the identification, most voiced reservations concerning the "text-book" description. As one member commented: "I have no reason to reject it, but my instincts are to do so regardless of how it reads." The bird was under observation for some 30–45 seconds; other than noting that it was "alert," nothing was said about its behavior. It was found in a semiarid habitat composed of mesquite, catclaw, and juniper, and was seen "perched low in bush." The observer had seen Olive Warblers before this encounter (*fide* C. Stogner), although this was not stated in the report. It is my judgment that this species should not be placed on the confirmed list of Texas Panhandle birds without a specimen or photograph in support—or written documentation based on lengthy study.

The Olive Warbler breeds from central and southeastern Arizona and southwestern New Mexico south through the highlands of Mexico to north-central Nicaragua (AOU, 1983). There are three other accepted records for Texas: Brewster County (Big Bend NP), 3 May 1991; Jeff Davis County (Mt. Livermore, Davis Mountains), 19 May 1992; Presidio County (Big Bend Ranch), 7 September 1994 (Lasley and Sexton, 1995a).

Connecticut Warbler *Oporornis agilis* (Wilson)

The Connecticut Warbler has been reported in the study area three times. Hibbets et al. (1926–36) give dates of 15 May 1931 and 7 May 1933; presumably the sightings took place in the Canyon area, Randall County. The third sighting was of a male at BLNWR, 22 May 1983 (K. Seyffert). The bird remained in view for only a short time, however, and all the distinguishing plumage and behavioral characteristics were not observed clearly.

The Connecticut Warbler is a Review Species on the Rare Birds of Texas list, and there have been but six accepted sightings in the state out of 67 reported (Lasley and Sexton, 1995a). The species has been verified in the Oklahoma Panhandle; Sutton (1967) reported a "singing male taken May 18, 1937, near Gate, Beaver County."

Red-faced Warbler *Cardellina rubrifons* (Giraud)

This strikingly patterned warbler with a distinctive red, black, and white head was observed for approximately one hour in Vega, Oldham County, 28 April 1980

(R. Scott). At one time the bird bathed in a drainage ditch. Unfortunately, others were unable to visit the site until the following day and the bird was not found. Also unfortunate was the absence of detailed notes. The Red-faced Warbler is a Review Species in Texas and verification by the TBRC is desirable. As of 1995, ten Red-faced Warbler sightings had been confirmed in Texas, one was under review, and one had been rejected (Lasley and Sexton, 1995a). Seventeen unsubmitted sightings were on record, including the Oldham County bird.

This Panhandle location is no more out of range for the Red-faced Warbler than are some in other parts of the state where the species has been confirmed, such as Bastrop, San Saba, and Bexar counties in central and south-central Texas and Nueces County on the lower coast. In light of the recent discovery of breeding in the Sandia Mountains in north-central New Mexico (Hubbard, 1982), Red-faced Warblers wintering in southern Mexico that pass through the Big Bend and Trans-Pecos of Texas, where most of the confirmed sightings have occurred (Lasley et al., 1982), could well stray eastward on their passage north in spring.

Smith's Longspur *Calcarius pictus* (Swainson)

The Smith's Longspur has been reported in Carson, Hansford, and Randall counties of the Texas Panhandle. Detailed notes of the sightings, if made, are not available for review. For this reason, I think it inappropriate to include this species among birds on the confirmed list for the Texas Panhandle.

The first published report of the Smith's Longspur is that of Williams (1966), who spoke of large flocks of mixed longspurs seen from late January to mid-March, including "the first record for Smith's (TPAS)." The only observer notes I have found pertaining to this sighting give a date of 14 March 1966—"west of town [Amarillo, Randall County] in large flock mixed species." A single Smith's was reported near Panhandle, Carson County, during the latter part of October 1968. One was observed, or possibly three, east of Canyon, Randall County, during the fall meeting of the TOS, 20 November 1976; an attempt at the time to secure detailed notes from several of the observers was unsuccessful. One was seen, possibly two, south of Bushland, Randall County, 28 January 1981—both McCown's and Laplands were also in the area. In addition, Oberholser (1974) shows a winter sight record for Hansford County, but details are lacking. A search of his files failed to disclose any reference to this sighting (*fide* W. Pulich).

The Smith's Longspur has been reported twice in nearby Crosby County on the South Plains: 5–12 April 1979 (Williams, 1979), and 13 March 1981 (Williams, 1981; "carefully identified"). From nearby areas in Oklahoma Sutton (1967) has this to say of the species: "was considered 'common in migration' at Gate, Beaver County, by W. E. Lewis . . . ; one record for Cimarron County January 1, 1962 by W. M. Davis." There are also records from Beckham and Jackson counties

(Baumgartner and Baumgartner, 1992). From nearby Union County, New Mexico, Kemsies (1968) includes the Clayton area among casual records.

During migration the Smith's Longspur does not usually associate with Lapland Longspurs, and on its wintering grounds it is found in monospecific flocks (Briskie, 1993). These facts should be borne in mind when reporting Smith's Longspurs, and all sightings should be supported with detailed notes.

Varied Bunting *Passerina versicolor* (Bonaparte)
There has been one reported sighting of the Varied Bunting in the Texas Panhandle, a male observed in northeast Amarillo, Potter County, 5 May 1993 (R. Peterson; TBRC). The bird was observed in a backyard garden during the evening hours. This colorful bunting is a rare to locally uncommon summer resident along the Rio Grande from Cameron to Presidio counties and north to Crockett, Culberson, Kimble, Real, and Uvalde counties (TOS, 1995). The nearest to the study area that one had previously been reported was a male at a Lubbock feeder, Lubbock County, 21 April 1974 (Williams, 1974).

The vote of the TBRC was 8–1 in favor of acceptance. The comments of the dissenting member are worth noting: "Details don't rule out first spring male Indigo, or for that matter first spring Blue Grosbeak or Lazuli Bunting. The head color on Varied is bright red, not rust. I bet this was an Indigo not in full plumage." It must be recognized also that the observer had never before seen a Varied Bunting. For these reasons I have elected not to place this species on the confirmed list of birds in the Texas Panhandle. One hopes that any future sighting will be supported by a specimen or photograph.

CHECKLIST OF SPECIES IN THE COUNTIES

(1) Armstrong, (2) Briscoe, (3) Carson, (4) Castro, (5) Childress, (6) Collingsworth, (7) Dallam, (8) Deaf Smith, (9) Donley, (10) Gray, (11) Hall, (12) Hansford, (13) Hartley, (14) Hemphill, (15) Hutchinson, (16) Lipscomb, (17) Moore, (18) Ochiltree, (19) Oldham, (20) Parmer, (21) Potter, (22) Randall, (23) Roberts, (24) Sherman, (25) Swisher, (26) Wheeler

Species	1	2	3	4	5	6	7	8	9	10	11	12	13	14	15	16	17	18	19	20	21	22	23	24	25	26
Red-throated Loon	—	*	—	—	—	—	—	—	—	—	—	—	—	—	—	—	—	—	—	—	—	—	—	—	—	—
Pacific Loon	—	—	—	—	—	—	—	—	*	—	—	—	—	—	—	—	—	—	—	—	—	*	—	—	—	—
Common Loon	*	*	—	—	*	—	—	—	*	—	—	—	—	—	—	—	*	—	—	*	*	*	—	*	—	—
Pied-billed Grebe	*	*	*	*	*	*	—	*	*	*	*	*	*	*	*	*	*	*	*	*	*	*	—	*	*	—
Horned Grebe	*	*	—	*	—	—	—	—	*	—	*	*	*	*	*	—	*	—	*	—	*	*	—	—	*	—
Red-necked Grebe	*	*	—	—	—	—	—	—	—	*	—	—	—	—	—	—	—	—	—	—	*	*	—	—	—	—
Eared Grebe	*	*	*	*	—	—	*	*	*	*	*	*	*	*	*	—	*	*	*	*	*	*	—	*	*	—
Western Grebe	*	*	*	*	*	—	—	—	*	*	—	—	—	—	*	—	*	*	—	—	*	*	*	—	—	*
American White Pelican	*	*	*	*	*	*	*	*	*	*	*	*	*	*	*	*	*	—	*	*	*	—	*	—	—	*
Brown Pelican	—	—	—	—	—	—	—	—	—	—	*	—	—	*	—	*	*	—	—	—	—	*	—	—	—	—
Double-crested Cormorant	*	—	*	*	*	*	—	—	*	*	—	*	—	*	*	*	*	*	*	—	*	*	*	—	—	—
Anhinga	—	—	—	—	—	—	—	*	—	—	—	—	—	—	—	—	—	—	—	*	—	—	—	—	—	—
American Bittern	—	*	*	*	—	—	*	—	—	*	—	—	—	*	—	—	*	—	*	*	*	*	—	—	—	—
Least Bittern	—	*	*	—	—	—	—	—	—	—	—	—	—	—	—	*	—	—	—	—	*	*	—	—	*	—
Great Blue Heron	*	*	*	*	*	—	—	*	*	*	*	*	*	*	*	*	*	*	*	*	*	*	*	*	*	*
Great Egret	*	*	*	*	—	—	—	—	*	*	*	*	—	*	*	—	—	*	—	—	*	*	—	—	*	—
Snowy Egret	*	*	*	*	—	—	—	*	*	*	*	*	*	*	*	—	*	—	—	—	*	*	—	—	—	—
Little Blue Heron	*	—	*	*	—	—	—	—	*	*	—	—	*	—	—	—	*	—	*	—	*	*	—	—	—	*
Tricolored Heron	—	—	—	—	—	—	—	—	*	*	—	*	—	—	*	—	—	—	—	—	—	—	—	*	—	—
Cattle Egret	*	*	*	*	*	—	—	—	—	*	—	*	*	*	*	—	*	*	*	*	*	*	*	*	*	—

Species	1	2	3	4	5	6	7	8	9	10	11	12	13	14	15	16	17	18	19	20	21	22	23	24	25	26
Green Heron	—	*	—	*	*	*	*	—	*	*	*	*	—	*	*	*	—	*	*	*	*	*	*	*	—	*
Black-crowned Night-Heron	*	*	*	*	—	*	*	*	*	*	*	*	*	*	*	*	*	*	*	*	*	*	*	*	*	*
Yellow-crowned Night-Heron	—	*	*	*	*	—	—	—	*	*	*	*	*	*	*	*	*	*	*	*	*	*	*	*	*	*
White-faced Ibis	*	*	*	*	—	—	—	*	*	*	—	*	*	*	*	—	—	—	—	—	—	—	—	—	—	*
Roseate Spoonbill	—	—	—	—	—	—	—	*	*	—	—	—	—	—	—	—	—	—	—	—	—	—	—	—	—	—
Black Vulture	*	—	*	—	—	—	*	—	—	*	*	*	—	*	*	*	—	*	*	*	*	*	*	—	—	—
Turkey Vulture	*	*	*	*	*	*	*	*	*	*	*	*	*	*	*	*	*	*	*	*	*	*	*	*	*	*
Black-bellied Whistling-Duck	—	—	—	—	—	—	—	*	—	—	—	—	—	—	—	—	—	—	—	—	—	—	—	—	—	—
Fulvous Whistling-Duck	—	—	—	—	—	—	—	*	—	—	—	—	*	—	—	—	—	—	—	—	—	—	—	—	—	—
Greater White-fronted Goose	—	*	—	*	—	—	—	—	*	*	*	*	*	*	*	*	*	—	*	*	*	*	—	—	*	—
Snow Goose	*	*	*	*	—	—	—	—	*	*	*	*	*	*	*	*	*	*	*	*	*	*	*	*	*	*
Ross's Goose	—	—	*	—	—	—	—	*	—	*	*	*	*	*	—	—	—	*	*	*	—	*	—	—	—	—
Canada Goose	*	*	*	*	*	*	*	*	*	*	*	*	*	*	*	*	*	*	*	*	*	*	*	*	*	*
Brant	—	—	—	*	—	*	—	*	—	—	—	*	*	—	—	—	—	—	—	—	—	—	*	*	—	—
Trumpeter Swan	—	—	—	—	—	—	—	—	—	—	—	*	*	*	—	—	*	*	*	*	*	*	—	—	—	—
Tundra Swan	*	*	*	*	—	—	—	—	*	*	—	*	*	*	*	—	*	*	*	*	*	*	—	*	—	*
Wood Duck	*	*	*	*	*	*	*	*	*	*	*	*	*	*	*	*	*	*	*	*	*	—	*	—	*	*
Gadwall	*	*	*	*	*	—	—	*	*	*	*	*	*	*	*	*	*	*	*	*	*	*	—	*	*	*
Eurasian Wigeon	—	*	—	*	—	—	—	*	—	*	—	—	*	—	—	—	—	—	—	*	*	—	—	—	—	—
American Wigeon	*	*	*	*	*	—	*	*	*	*	*	*	*	*	*	*	*	*	*	*	*	*	*	*	*	*
American Black Duck	—	—	—	—	—	—	—	—	—	—	—	—	—	—	—	—	—	—	—	—	—	*	—	—	—	—
Mallard	*	*	*	*	*	*	*	*	*	*	*	*	*	*	*	*	*	*	*	*	*	*	*	*	*	*
Blue-winged Teal	*	*	*	*	*	*	*	*	*	*	*	*	*	*	*	*	*	*	*	*	*	*	*	*	*	*
Cinnamon Teal	*	*	*	*	—	—	—	*	*	*	*	*	*	*	*	*	*	*	*	*	*	—	*	—	*	*
Northern Shoveler	*	*	*	*	*	—	—	*	*	*	*	*	*	*	*	*	*	*	*	*	*	*	—	—	*	*

Species																									
Northern Pintail	*	|	*	|	*	|	|	*	|	|	|	|	*	|	|	*	|	|	*	|	*	|	*	*	*
Garganey	*	|	*	*	*	*	|	*	*	|	|	|	*	*	|	*	|	*	|	|	*	*	*	*	*
Green-winged Teal	*	|	*	|	*	|	|	|	|	|	|	|	|	|	|	|	|	*	|	|	|	|	*	|	|
Canvasback	|	|	*	|	|	|	*	|	|	|	|	|	|	|	*	|	*	|	|	|	*	*	*	*	*
Redhead	*	|	*	*	*	*	|	*	*	|	|	*	*	*	*	*	*	*	*	|	*	*	*	*	*
Ring-necked Duck	*	|	*	*	*	*	|	*	|	|	|	|	*	*	*	*	|	*	*	*	*	|	*	*	*
Greater Scaup	*	|	*	*	*	*	|	*	|	|	|	|	*	*	|	*	|	*	*	*	*	*	*	*	*
Lesser Scaup	*	|	*	*	*	|	|	*	|	|	|	|	|	|	|	|	|	*	|	|	*	*	*	*	|
Surf Scoter	*	|	*	*	*	*	|	*	|	|	|	|	*	*	*	*	|	*	*	|	*	*	*	*	*
White-winged Scoter	*	|	|	|	|	|	|	|	|	|	|	|	|	|	|	|	|	|	|	|	*	|	*	|	|
Black Scoter	*	*	*	*	*	*	|	*	|	|	|	*	*	*	*	*	*	*	*	|	*	*	*	*	*
Oldsquaw	*	|	*	*	*	*	*	*	*	|	|	|	*	*	*	*	*	*	*	|	*	*	*	*	*
Bufflehead	*	|	*	*	*	*	|	*	|	|	|	|	*	*	*	*	|	*	*	|	*	*	*	*	*
Common Goldeneye	*	|	*	*	*	*	|	*	|	*	|	|	*	*	|	*	|	*	*	|	*	*	*	*	*
Hooded Merganser	|	|	*	|	*	|	|	*	|	|	|	|	|	|	|	|	|	*	|	|	*	*	*	*	|
Common Merganser	*	|	*	*	*	*	*	*	|	|	|	|	*	*	|	*	|	*	*	|	*	*	*	*	*
Red-breasted Merganser	*	|	*	*	*	*	|	*	|	|	|	|	*	*	*	*	*	*	*	|	*	*	*	*	*
Ruddy Duck	*	|	*	|	*	|	*	*	*	|	*	*	|	*	|	|	*	*	*	|	*	*	*	*	|
Osprey	|	*	|	*	*	|	|	*	|	|	|	|	*	|	*	*	|	*	*	*	*	*	*	*	*
Swallow-tailed Kite	|	|	*	|	|	|	|	|	|	|	|	|	|	|	|	*	|	|	*	|	*	|	*	|	*
Mississippi Kite	*	|	*	*	*	*	|	*	|	|	|	|	*	*	*	|	*	*	*	|	*	*	*	*	*
Bald Eagle	*	|	*	*	*	*	|	*	|	|	|	|	*	*	*	*	|	*	*	|	*	*	*	*	*
Northern Harrier	*	|	*	|	*	|	*	*	*	|	|	|	*	|	*	*	|	*	*	*	*	*	*	*	*
Sharp-shinned Hawk	*	|	*	*	*	*	|	*	*	|	|	|	*	*	*	*	|	|	*	*	*	*	*	*	*
Cooper's Hawk	*	|	*	*	*	*	|	*	*	|	|	|	*	*	*	*	|	*	*	*	*	*	*	*	*

	1	2	3	4	5	6	7	8	9	10	11	12	13	14	15	16	17	18	19	20	21	22	23	24	25	26
Northern Goshawk	—	—	—	*	—	—	—	—	—	—	—	—	—	*	—	—	*	—	—	—	*	*	—	—	—	*
Common Black-Hawk	—	—	—	—	—	—	—	—	—	—	—	—	—	—	—	—	—	—	—	—	*	—	—	—	—	—
Harris's Hawk	—	*	—	—	—	—	—	—	—	—	—	—	—	—	—	—	*	—	—	—	—	*	*	*	—	—
Red-shouldered Hawk	—	—	—	*	—	—	*	—	*	*	—	—	—	—	*	—	*	*	—	—	*	*	*	*	*	—
Broad-winged Hawk	—	—	—	*	—	*	*	—	*	*	—	—	—	—	*	—	*	*	*	*	*	*	*	*	—	—
Swainson's Hawk	*	*	*	*	*	*	*	*	*	*	*	*	*	*	*	*	*	*	*	*	*	*	*	*	*	—
Red-tailed Hawk	*	*	*	*	*	*	*	*	*	*	*	*	*	*	*	*	*	*	*	*	*	*	*	*	*	*
Ferruginous Hawk	*	*	*	*	—	*	*	*	*	*	*	*	*	*	*	*	*	*	*	*	*	*	*	*	*	*
Rough-legged Hawk	*	*	*	*	*	—	—	—	—	—	—	*	*	*	*	*	*	*	*	*	*	—	*	*	*	*
Golden Eagle	*	*	*	*	*	*	*	*	*	*	*	*	*	*	*	*	*	*	*	*	*	*	*	*	*	*
American Kestrel	*	*	*	*	*	*	*	*	*	*	*	*	*	*	*	*	*	*	*	*	*	*	*	*	*	*
Merlin	*	*	—	*	*	*	—	—	—	—	*	—	—	—	*	*	*	*	*	*	*	*	*	*	*	*
Peregrine Falcon	—	—	—	—	—	—	—	—	—	—	—	—	*	—	—	*	*	*	*	*	*	*	*	*	*	*
Prairie Falcon	*	*	*	*	*	*	*	*	*	*	*	*	*	*	*	*	*	*	*	*	*	*	*	*	*	*
Ring-necked Pheasant	*	*	*	*	*	*	*	*	*	*	*	*	*	*	*	*	*	*	*	*	*	*	*	*	*	—
Lesser Prairie-Chicken	*	*	*	—	—	*	*	*	*	*	*	*	*	*	*	*	*	*	*	*	*	*	*	*	*	*
Wild Turkey	*	*	*	—	*	*	*	*	*	*	*	*	*	*	*	*	*	*	*	*	*	*	*	*	*	*
Scaled Quail	*	*	*	*	*	*	*	*	*	*	*	*	*	*	*	*	*	*	*	*	*	*	*	*	*	*
Northern Bobwhite	*	*	—	—	—	*	*	*	*	*	*	*	*	*	*	*	*	*	*	*	*	*	*	*	*	*
Yellow Rail	—	—	—	—	—	—	—	—	—	—	—	—	—	—	—	—	—	—	—	—	*	—	—	—	—	—
Black Rail	—	—	—	—	—	—	—	—	—	—	—	—	—	—	—	—	—	—	—	—	*	—	—	—	—	—
King Rail	—	—	*	—	—	—	—	—	—	—	—	—	—	—	—	—	—	—	—	—	*	*	—	—	—	—
Virginia Rail	—	—	*	*	—	—	—	*	*	*	*	—	—	—	—	—	*	*	*	*	*	*	—	—	*	—
Sora	*	*	*	*	*	—	—	—	—	—	—	—	—	—	—	—	*	*	*	*	*	*	*	*	*	—
Purple Gallinule	—	—	—	—	—	—	—	—	—	—	—	—	—	—	—	—	—	—	—	—	*	—	—	—	—	—

Common Moorhen
American Coot
Sandhill Crane
Whooping Crane
Black-bellied Plover

American Golden-Plover
Snowy Plover
Semipalmated Plover
Piping Plover
Killdeer

Mountain Plover
Black-necked Stilt
American Avocet
Greater Yellowlegs
Lesser Yellowlegs

Solitary Sandpiper
Willet
Spotted Sandpiper
Upland Sandpiper
Whimbrel

Long-billed Curlew
Hudsonian Godwit
Marbled Godwit
Ruddy Turnstone
Red Knot

	1	2	3	4	5	6	7	8	9	10	11	12	13	14	15	16	17	18	19	20	21	22	23	24	25	26
Sanderling	—	*	*	*	—	—	—	—	—	*	—	—	—	—	*	—	*	—	—	—	*	*	—	—	—	—
Semipalmated Sandpiper	*	*	*	—	—	—	—	*	*	*	—	*	*	*	*	—	*	*	*	*	*	*	—	—	*	*
Western Sandpiper	*	*	*	*	—	—	—	*	*	*	*	*	*	*	—	—	*	*	*	*	*	*	—	—	*	*
Least Sandpiper	*	*	*	*	*	—	—	*	*	*	*	—	*	*	—	—	*	—	*	*	*	*	*	—	*	—
White-rumped Sandpiper	*	—	—	*	—	—	—	—	*	*	—	—	—	—	—	—	—	—	—	*	—	*	—	—	—	—
Baird's Sandpiper	*	*	*	*	—	—	—	*	*	*	—	*	*	*	—	—	*	*	*	*	*	*	—	*	—	—
Pectoral Sandpiper	*	*	*	*	—	—	*	*	*	*	*	*	*	*	—	—	*	—	*	*	*	*	*	—	—	—
Dunlin	—	—	—	—	—	—	—	—	—	—	—	—	—	—	—	—	—	—	—	—	*	*	*	—	—	—
Stilt Sandpiper	*	*	*	*	—	—	*	*	—	*	—	*	*	—	*	—	*	*	*	*	*	*	—	—	*	*
Buff-breasted Sandpiper	—	—	—	*	—	—	—	—	—	—	—	—	—	—	—	—	—	—	—	—	*	*	—	—	—	—
Short-billed Dowitcher	—	*	*	*	—	—	—	*	*	*	—	*	*	—	*	—	*	*	*	*	*	*	*	*	*	*
Long-billed Dowitcher	*	*	*	*	—	*	*	*	*	*	—	*	*	—	*	—	*	—	—	*	*	*	*	—	*	*
Common Snipe	*	*	*	—	—	*	*	—	*	—	*	*	*	*	*	—	*	—	—	*	*	*	*	—	—	*
American Woodcock	—	—	—	—	—	—	*	—	—	*	—	*	*	*	*	—	*	*	*	*	*	*	*	—	—	—
Wilson's Phalarope	*	*	*	*	*	—	—	*	*	—	*	*	*	—	*	—	*	*	*	*	*	*	—	—	*	—
Red-necked Phalarope	*	—	—	*	—	—	—	—	—	*	—	—	—	—	—	—	*	*	*	*	*	*	—	—	—	—
Red Phalarope	—	—	—	—	—	—	—	—	—	—	—	—	—	—	—	—	—	—	—	—	*	*	*	—	—	—
Parasitic Jaeger	—	—	—	—	—	—	—	—	—	—	—	—	—	—	—	—	—	—	—	—	*	*	*	—	—	*
Laughing Gull	—	—	—	—	—	—	—	—	—	—	—	—	—	—	—	—	—	—	—	—	*	*	—	—	—	—
Franklin's Gull	*	—	—	—	—	—	—	*	—	*	*	*	*	*	*	—	*	*	*	*	*	*	*	*	*	*
Bonaparte's Gull	—	*	*	*	—	—	—	*	*	—	—	—	—	*	*	—	*	—	—	—	*	*	*	*	*	*
Ring-billed Gull	*	*	*	*	*	*	*	*	*	*	—	*	*	*	*	*	*	*	*	*	*	*	*	*	*	*
Herring Gull	—	—	—	*	*	—	—	—	—	—	—	*	*	*	*	*	*	—	—	—	*	*	—	—	—	*
Thayer's Gull	—	—	—	—	—	—	—	—	—	—	—	—	—	—	—	—	—	—	—	—	*	*	—	—	—	—
Glaucous Gull	—	*	—	—	—	—	—	*	—	—	—	*	—	—	—	—	—	—	—	—	*	*	—	—	—	*

Sabine's Gull
Black-legged Kittiwake
Caspian Tern
Common Tern
Forster's Tern

Least Tern
Black Tern
Rock Dove
Band-tailed Pigeon
Eurasian Collared-Dove

White-winged Dove
Mourning Dove
Inca Dove
Common Ground-Dove
Black-billed Cuckoo

Yellow-billed Cuckoo
Greater Roadrunner
Barn Owl
Western Screech-Owl
Eastern Screech-Owl

Great Horned Owl
Burrowing Owl
Barred Owl
Long-eared Owl
Short-eared Owl

	1	2	3	4	5	6	7	8	9	10	11	12	13	14	15	16	17	18	19	20	21	22	23	24	25	26
Northern Saw-whet Owl	-	-	-	-	-	-	-	-	-	-	-	-	-	-	-	-	-	-	-	-	-	*	-	-	-	-
Common Nighthawk	*	*	*	-	*	*	*	*	*	*	*	*	*	*	*	*	*	*	*	*	*	*	*	*	*	*
Common Poorwill	*	*	-	*	-	*	*	-	*	-	-	-	-	*	*	-	-	-	-	*	*	*	*	-	-	*
Chuck-will's Widow	-	-	-	-	-	-	-	-	*	-	-	-	-	-	*	-	-	-	-	-	-	*	-	-	-	-
Whip-poor-will	-	-	-	*	-	-	-	-	-	-	-	-	-	-	-	-	-	-	-	-	-	*	-	-	-	-
Chimney Swift	*	*	*	-	*	*	*	*	*	*	*	*	*	*	*	*	*	*	*	*	*	*	*	-	*	*
White-throated Swift	-	*	-	*	*	*	*	*	*	*	*	*	*	*	-	*	*	*	*	*	*	*	*	*	-	*
Ruby-throated Hummingbird	-	-	-	-	-	-	-	-	-	-	-	-	-	-	-	-	-	-	-	-	*	*	*	*	-	-
Black-chinned Hummingbird	-	-	-	*	-	-	-	*	*	*	-	-	*	*	-	*	-	*	*	*	*	*	*	*	-	*
Anna's Hummingbird	-	-	-	-	-	-	-	-	-	-	-	-	-	-	-	*	-	-	-	-	*	-	-	-	-	-
Calliope Hummingbird	-	-	-	-	-	-	-	-	*	*	-	-	*	-	-	*	-	-	-	-	*	*	-	-	*	-
Broad-tailed Hummingbird	-	-	-	*	*	-	-	-	*	*	-	-	-	-	-	-	-	*	*	*	*	*	*	-	-	-
Rufous Hummingbird	*	*	*	-	*	*	*	-	*	*	*	*	*	-	*	*	-	*	*	*	*	*	*	-	*	*
Belted Kingfisher	*	-	-	-	-	-	-	-	*	*	*	*	*	*	*	*	*	*	*	*	*	*	*	*	*	*
Green Kingfisher	-	-	-	-	-	-	-	-	-	-	-	-	-	-	-	-	-	-	-	-	*	*	-	-	-	-
Lewis's Woodpecker	-	-	-	-	-	*	-	-	-	*	-	-	*	-	-	-	-	-	-	-	-	*	*	-	*	-
Red-headed Woodpecker	*	*	*	*	*	*	*	*	*	*	*	*	*	*	*	*	*	*	*	*	*	*	*	*	*	*
Acorn Woodpecker	-	-	-	-	*	-	-	-	-	-	*	-	*	-	-	-	-	-	-	-	*	*	-	-	-	*
Golden-fronted Woodpecker	*	*	-	-	*	*	-	-	*	*	*	*	-	*	-	*	-	*	*	-	*	*	*	-	*	*
Red-bellied Woodpecker	*	*	-	*	*	*	*	-	*	*	*	*	*	*	*	*	*	*	*	*	*	*	*	*	*	*
Williamson's Sapsucker	-	-	-	-	-	-	*	*	-	-	-	-	-	-	-	-	-	-	-	-	*	*	-	-	-	-
Yellow-bellied Sapsucker	*	*	-	-	*	*	-	*	-	-	-	-	*	*	-	-	-	-	-	*	*	*	*	-	-	*
Red-naped Sapsucker	-	-	*	*	-	*	-	-	-	*	*	*	*	*	*	*	*	*	*	-	*	*	*	-	*	*
Ladder-backed Woodpecker	*	*	*	-	*	*	*	-	*	*	*	*	*	*	*	*	*	*	*	*	*	*	*	-	*	*
Downy Woodpecker	*	*	-	-	*	*	-	-	*	*	*	*	*	*	*	*	*	*	*	*	*	*	*	-	*	*

Hairy Woodpecker
Northern Flicker
Olive-sided Flycatcher
Western Wood-Pewee
Eastern Wood-Pewee

Empidonax sp.
Willow Flycatcher
Least Flycatcher
Hammond's Flycatcher
Gray Flycatcher

Dusky Flycatcher
Cordilleran Flycatcher
Black Phoebe
Eastern Phoebe
Say's Phoebe

Vermilion Flycatcher
Ash-throated Flycatcher
Great Crested Flycatcher
Cassin's Kingbird
Thick-billed Kingbird

Western Kingbird
Eastern Kingbird
Scissor-tailed Flycatcher
Loggerhead Shrike
Northern Shrike

	1	2	3	4	5	6	7	8	9	10	11	12	13	14	15	16	17	18	19	20	21	22	23	24	25	26
White-eyed Vireo	—	*	—	—	*	—	—	—	—	—	—	—	—	—	—	—	—	—	—	—	*	*	*	—	—	—
Bell's Vireo	*	*	—	—	—	*	*	—	*	*	—	—	—	—	—	*	—	*	*	—	*	*	*	—	—	*
Yellow-throated Vireo	—	—	—	—	—	—	—	—	—	—	—	—	—	—	—	—	—	—	—	—	*	*	*	—	—	—
Plumbeous Vireo	—	?	—	?	—	?	?	—	?	?	?	?	?	?	?	—	—	—	?	?	*	*	—	—	—	—
Blue-headed Vireo	—	?	—	?	—	?	?	—	?	?	*	?	?	?	?	—	—	—	*	?	*	*	—	—	—	—
[Solitary Vireo]	—	*	—	—	—	—	*	—	*	*	*	*	*	*	*	—	*	*	*	*	*	*	*	—	—	*
Warbling Vireo	*	—	—	*	—	*	*	—	*	*	—	—	—	—	—	*	—	*	*	*	*	*	*	—	—	—
Philadelphia Vireo	—	—	—	*	—	—	—	—	—	—	—	—	—	—	—	—	—	—	—	—	*	*	—	—	—	—
Red-eyed Vireo	—	—	—	*	—	—	—	—	—	—	—	—	—	—	—	—	—	—	—	—	*	*	—	—	—	—
Steller's Jay	—	*	—	—	—	*	*	*	—	*	*	—	—	*	—	*	*	*	*	—	*	*	—	—	—	*
Blue Jay	*	*	*	*	*	*	*	*	*	*	*	*	*	*	*	*	*	*	*	—	*	*	*	—	*	*
Western Scrub-Jay	*	*	—	*	—	*	*	*	*	*	*	*	*	*	*	—	—	—	*	—	*	*	*	*	—	*
Pinyon Jay	—	*	—	*	—	—	—	*	—	—	*	*	*	*	*	—	*	—	—	—	*	*	—	—	—	—
Clark's Nutcracker	*	—	—	*	—	—	—	—	—	—	—	—	—	—	—	*	—	—	—	—	*	*	—	—	*	—
Black-billed Magpie	—	—	—	—	—	*	*	—	—	—	*	—	—	—	—	—	—	—	—	—	*	*	—	—	—	—
American Crow	*	*	*	*	*	*	*	*	*	*	*	*	*	*	*	*	*	*	*	*	*	*	*	—	*	*
Chihuahuan Raven	*	*	*	*	*	*	*	*	*	*	*	—	*	*	*	*	—	—	*	*	*	*	*	—	*	*
Common Raven	*	—	—	*	*	*	*	—	—	—	—	—	*	—	—	—	*	—	—	—	*	*	*	*	*	—
Horned Lark	*	*	*	*	*	*	*	*	*	*	*	*	*	*	*	*	*	*	*	*	*	*	*	—	*	*
Purple Martin	—	—	—	—	—	*	—	—	*	*	—	—	—	—	—	*	*	*	*	*	*	*	*	*	—	*
Tree Swallow	*	*	*	*	—	*	*	—	*	*	—	—	*	*	*	*	*	—	*	—	*	*	—	—	*	*
Violet-green Swallow	—	—	—	*	—	—	—	—	—	—	—	—	—	—	—	—	—	*	*	*	*	—	*	*	—	—
Northern Rough-winged Swallow	*	*	*	*	*	*	*	*	*	*	—	—	*	*	*	—	*	*	*	*	*	*	*	*	*	*
Bank Swallow	*	*	*	*	—	—	—	—	*	*	—	*	*	*	*	—	*	*	*	*	*	*	*	—	*	—
Cliff Swallow	*	*	*	*	*	*	*	—	*	*	*	*	*	*	*	*	*	*	*	*	*	*	*	*	*	*

Barn Swallow
Carolina Chickadee
Mountain Chickadee
Tufted Titmouse
Verdin

Bushtit
Red-breasted Nuthatch
White-breasted Nuthatch
Pygmy Nuthatch
Brown Creeper

Cactus Wren
Rock Wren
Canyon Wren
Carolina Wren
Bewick's Wren

House Wren
Winter Wren
Sedge Wren
Marsh Wren
Golden-crowned Kinglet

Ruby-crowned Kinglet
Blue-gray Gnatcatcher
Eastern Bluebird
Western Bluebird
Mountain Bluebird

	1	2	3	4	5	6	7	8	9	10	11	12	13	14	15	16	17	18	19	20	21	22	23	24	25	26
Townsend's Solitaire	*	*	—	*	*	—	*	*	*	*	—	*	*	*	*	—	*	*	*	*	*	*	*	*	*	—
Veery	—	—	—	—	*	—	*	—	—	—	—	—	—	—	—	—	—	*	*	*	*	*	—	—	—	*
Gray-cheeked Thrush	—	—	—	—	—	—	—	—	—	—	—	—	—	—	—	—	—	—	—	—	*	*	—	—	—	—
Swainson's Thrush	—	*	—	*	*	—	*	—	—	—	—	*	*	*	*	—	*	*	*	*	*	*	*	—	—	—
Hermit Thrush	—	*	—	*	*	—	—	—	*	*	—	*	*	*	*	—	*	*	*	*	*	*	*	—	—	*
Wood Thrush	—	—	—	*	—	—	—	—	—	—	*	—	—	—	—	*	—	—	—	*	*	*	*	—	—	*
American Robin	*	*	*	*	*	*	*	*	*	*	*	*	*	*	*	*	*	*	*	*	*	*	*	*	*	*
Varied Thrush	—	—	—	—	—	—	—	—	—	—	—	—	—	—	—	—	*	—	—	—	*	*	—	—	—	—
Gray Catbird	*	*	—	*	*	—	—	*	*	*	*	*	*	*	*	—	*	*	*	*	*	*	*	—	*	—
Northern Mockingbird	*	*	*	*	*	*	*	*	*	*	*	*	*	*	*	*	*	*	*	*	*	*	*	*	*	*
Sage Thrasher	*	*	*	—	—	—	*	*	*	—	*	*	—	*	*	*	*	*	*	*	*	*	*	—	—	*
Brown Thrasher	*	*	*	*	*	*	*	*	*	*	*	*	*	*	*	*	*	*	*	*	*	*	*	—	*	—
Curve-billed Thrasher	*	*	*	*	*	*	*	*	*	*	*	*	—	*	*	*	*	*	*	*	*	*	*	*	*	—
European Starling	*	*	*	*	*	*	*	*	*	*	*	*	*	*	—	*	*	*	*	*	*	*	*	*	*	*
American Pipit	*	*	*	*	*	*	—	—	*	*	*	*	*	*	—	—	—	*	*	*	—	*	*	*	*	—
Sprague's Pipit	—	—	*	—	—	—	*	—	*	—	—	—	—	*	*	*	*	*	—	*	*	*	*	—	—	*
Bohemian Waxwing	—	—	—	—	—	—	*	—	—	—	—	—	—	—	—	*	—	*	*	*	*	*	*	*	*	—
Cedar Waxwing	*	*	*	*	—	*	*	*	*	*	*	*	*	*	*	*	*	*	*	*	*	*	*	*	*	*
Phainopepla	—	*	*	—	—	—	—	*	*	—	—	—	—	—	—	—	*	*	—	—	—	—	*	*	*	*
Blue-winged Warbler	—	—	—	—	—	—	—	—	*	—	—	—	—	*	—	—	—	*	*	—	—	—	—	—	—	*
Golden-winged Warbler	—	—	—	—	—	—	—	—	*	—	—	—	—	—	—	—	*	—	—	—	—	*	*	—	—	*
Tennessee Warbler	—	—	*	—	—	—	—	—	—	—	—	—	—	*	*	—	*	*	*	*	*	*	*	—	—	*
Orange-crowned Warbler	—	—	—	*	*	*	*	—	*	*	*	*	*	*	*	—	*	*	*	*	*	*	*	—	—	—
Nashville Warbler	*	*	—	*	—	—	*	—	*	—	—	*	—	*	*	—	*	*	*	*	*	*	*	—	—	*
Virginia's Warbler	—	—	—	*	—	—	—	—	—	—	—	—	—	—	—	—	*	—	—	*	*	*	—	—	—	—

Northern Parula
Yellow Warbler
Chestnut-sided Warbler
Magnolia Warbler
Cape May Warbler

Black-throated Blue Warbler
Yellow-rumped Warbler
Black-throated Gray Warbler
Black-throated Green Warbler
Townsend's Warbler

Hermit Warbler
Blackburnian Warbler
Yellow-throated Warbler
Grace's Warbler
Pine Warbler

Prairie Warbler
Palm Warbler
Bay-breasted Warbler
Blackpoll Warbler
Cerulean Warbler

Black-and-white Warbler
American Redstart
Prothonotary Warbler
Worm-eating Warbler
Swainson's Warbler

	1	2	3	4	5	6	7	8	9	10	11	12	13	14	15	16	17	18	19	20	21	22	23	24	25	26
Ovenbird	—	—	*	*	—	—	*	—	—	*	—	—	*	—	*	—	*	—	*	*	*	*	—	—	—	—
Northern Waterthrush	—	—	—	*	—	—	—	—	*	—	—	—	—	—	*	—	—	—	*	*	*	*	*	—	—	—
Louisiana Waterthrush	—	—	—	—	—	—	—	*	—	—	—	—	—	—	—	—	—	—	—	*	*	*	*	—	—	—
Kentucky Warbler	—	—	—	—	—	—	—	—	—	—	—	—	*	—	—	—	—	—	*	—	*	*	*	—	—	—
Mourning Warbler	—	—	—	—	—	—	—	—	—	*	—	—	—	*	*	—	—	*	*	*	—	*	*	*	*	—
MacGillivray's Warbler	—	*	*	*	—	—	—	*	—	—	—	—	—	—	—	—	—	—	*	*	*	*	*	*	—	*
Common Yellowthroat	*	*	*	*	—	*	*	*	*	—	—	—	—	—	*	*	*	—	*	*	*	*	*	*	—	*
Hooded Warbler	—	—	—	*	—	—	—	—	*	—	—	—	*	*	*	—	*	*	*	*	*	*	*	—	*	—
Wilson's Warbler	—	*	*	*	—	—	*	*	*	—	*	*	*	*	*	—	*	*	*	*	*	*	*	*	*	—
Canada Warbler	—	—	—	—	—	—	—	—	—	—	—	—	—	—	—	—	—	—	—	—	*	*	*	—	—	—
Painted Redstart	—	—	—	—	—	—	—	—	—	—	—	—	—	—	*	—	—	*	—	—	*	*	—	—	—	—
Yellow-breasted Chat	*	*	—	*	—	—	*	*	*	—	—	—	—	*	*	*	*	*	*	*	*	*	*	*	—	*
Hepatic Tanager	—	—	—	—	—	—	—	—	—	—	—	—	—	—	—	—	—	—	—	—	—	—	—	—	—	—
Summer Tanager	—	*	*	*	—	—	*	—	—	—	—	*	*	*	*	*	*	*	*	*	*	*	*	*	*	—
Scarlet Tanager	—	—	—	—	—	—	—	—	—	—	—	—	—	—	—	—	—	—	—	—	*	*	—	—	—	—
Western Tanager	*	—	—	*	*	—	*	—	*	—	*	*	*	*	*	*	*	*	*	*	*	*	*	*	*	—
Green-tailed Towhee	—	*	*	*	—	—	*	—	*	*	*	*	*	—	*	*	*	*	*	*	*	*	*	*	*	*
Spotted Towhee	*	*	*	*	—	*	*	*	*	*	*	*	*	*	*	*	*	*	*	*	*	*	*	*	*	*
Eastern Towhee	—	—	—	—	—	—	—	—	—	—	—	—	—	—	—	—	—	—	—	—	*	*	*	—	—	—
Canyon Towhee	*	*	*	*	—	*	*	*	*	*	*	*	*	*	*	*	*	*	*	*	*	*	*	*	*	*
Cassin's Sparrow	*	*	*	*	*	*	*	*	*	—	*	*	*	—	*	*	*	—	*	*	*	*	*	*	*	*
Rufous-crowned Sparrow	*	*	*	*	—	—	—	—	—	—	*	*	*	*	*	*	*	*	*	*	*	*	*	*	*	*
American Tree Sparrow	*	*	*	*	—	—	—	—	—	—	—	*	*	*	*	*	*	*	*	*	*	*	*	*	*	*
Chipping Sparrow	*	*	*	—	—	*	*	*	*	—	*	*	*	*	*	*	*	—	*	*	*	*	*	—	—	*
Clay-colored Sparrow	*	*	*	*	—	*	*	*	*	—	*	*	*	*	*	*	*	*	*	*	*	*	*	—	—	*
Brewer's Sparrow	*	*	*	*	—	—	*	*	—	—	*	—	—	—	*	—	*	*	*	*	*	*	*	*	*	—

```
 *  |  * *  |    |  * * *  |    * * * *  |    * * *  |  *    |    *    |  |  |  *
 |  |  * *  |    |  * * *  |    |  |  * *  |    |  |  * *  |  *    * * *  |  *
 *  *  |  * *  |  |  * * *  |    |  * * *  |    *  * * *  |    * * *  |  |  |
 *  *  |  * *  |  * * *  |      |  * * *  |    * * * *  |    * * *  |    |  *
 *  |  |  * *  |  |  * * *  |    * * * *  |    * * *  |    * * *  |    |  *

 *  |  * *  *    |  * * *  *    * * * *  *    * * *  |  *    |  |  |  *
 *  |  * *  |    |  *  |  * *    * * * *  *    * * *  |  *    * * *  |  *
 *  |  * *  |    |  * * *  |    |  |  * *  |    * * *  |  *    * * *  |  *
 *  |  * *  |    |  * * *  |    |  * * *  |    * * *  |  *    |  |  |  *

 *  |  * *  |    |  * * *  *    |  * * *  *    * * *  |  *    |  * * *    |  *
 *  |  * *  |    |  * * *  |    *  * * *  *    * * *  |  *    * * *  |  *
 *  |  * *  |    |  * * *  |    |  |  * *  |    * * *  |  *    |  |  |  *
 *  |  * *  |    |  * * *  |    |  |  * *  |    *  |  *    |  |  |  *

 *  *  |  |  *    |  *  |  |  *    *  *  |  |  *    |  |  |  *
 *  *  |  |  *    |  * * *  |    |  *  |  *    |  |  |  *
 *  |  * * *    |  * * *  |    |  |  * *    *  |  *    |  |  |  *
 *  *  |  |  |    |  * * *  |    |  |  *    |  |  |  *

 *  *  * * *    |  * *  |  *    |  * * *  *    |  *  *  *    *  |  *
 *  *  * * *    |  * * * *    |  * * *  |  *    * * *  |  *    |  *
 *  *  |  * *    |  * * *  |    *  |  *    |  |  |  *
```

Field Sparrow
Black-chinned Sparrow
Vesper Sparrow
Lark Sparrow
Black-throated Sparrow

Sage Sparrow
Lark Bunting
Savannah Sparrow
Grasshopper Sparrow
Baird's Sparrow

Le Conte's Sparrow
Fox Sparrow
Song Sparrow
Lincoln's Sparrow
Swamp Sparrow

White-throated Sparrow
Harris's Sparrow
White-crowned Sparrow
Golden-crowned Sparrow
Dark-eyed Junco

McCown's Longspur
Lapland Longspur
Chestnut-collared Longspur
Snow Bunting
Northern Cardinal

Species	1	2	3	4	5	6	7	8	9	10	11	12	13	14	15	16	17	18	19	20	21	22	23	24	25	26
Pyrrhuloxia	—	*	—	*	—	—	—	—	—	—	—	—	—	—	—	—	—	—	—	—	*	*	—	—	*	—
Rose-breasted Grosbeak	—	—	—	*	—	—	—	—	*	*	—	—	—	*	*	*	*	—	*	—	*	*	*	—	—	—
Black-headed Grosbeak	*	*	*	*	—	*	*	—	*	*	—	—	*	*	*	*	*	—	*	*	*	*	*	*	—	—
Blue Grosbeak	*	*	*	*	*	*	*	*	*	*	*	*	*	*	*	*	*	*	*	*	*	*	*	*	*	*
Lazuli Bunting	—	—	—	*	*	—	—	—	*	*	—	*	*	*	*	—	*	—	*	*	*	*	*	—	—	—
Indigo Bunting	*	*	—	*	—	*	—	—	*	*	—	—	*	*	*	*	*	—	*	—	*	*	*	—	—	—
Painted Bunting	*	*	—	*	*	*	*	—	*	*	*	*	*	*	*	*	*	—	*	*	*	*	*	—	—	*
Dickcissel	*	*	*	*	*	*	*	*	*	*	*	*	*	*	*	*	*	*	*	*	*	*	*	*	*	*
Bobolink	—	—	*	—	—	—	—	—	—	—	*	—	—	—	—	—	*	—	—	—	—	*	—	—	—	—
Red-winged Blackbird	*	*	*	*	*	*	*	*	*	*	*	*	*	*	*	*	*	*	*	*	*	*	*	*	*	*
Eastern Meadowlark	*	*	*	*	*	*	*	*	*	*	*	*	*	*	*	*	*	*	*	*	*	*	*	*	*	*
Western Meadowlark	*	*	*	*	*	*	*	*	*	*	*	*	*	*	*	*	*	*	*	*	*	*	*	*	*	*
Yellow-headed Blackbird	*	*	*	*	—	*	*	*	*	*	*	*	*	*	*	*	—	*	*	*	*	*	*	*	*	*
Rusty Blackbird	—	*	—	—	—	—	—	—	—	—	—	—	—	—	—	—	*	—	—	*	*	*	—	—	—	—
Brewer's Blackbird	*	*	*	*	—	*	—	*	*	*	*	*	*	*	*	*	*	*	*	*	*	*	—	—	*	*
Common Grackle	*	*	*	*	*	*	*	*	*	*	*	*	*	*	*	*	*	*	*	*	*	*	*	*	*	*
Great-tailed Grackle	*	*	*	*	*	*	*	*	*	*	*	*	*	*	*	*	*	*	*	*	*	*	*	*	*	*
Bronzed Cowbird	—	—	—	—	—	—	—	—	—	—	—	—	—	—	—	—	—	—	—	—	—	*	—	—	—	—
Brown-headed Cowbird	*	*	*	*	*	*	*	*	*	*	*	*	*	*	*	*	*	*	*	*	*	*	*	*	*	*
Orchard Oriole	*	*	*	*	*	*	*	—	*	*	*	*	*	*	*	*	*	*	*	*	*	*	*	*	*	*

Hooded Oriole	Baltimore Oriole	Bullock's Oriole	Scott's Oriole	Pine Grosbeak	Purple Finch	Cassin's Finch	House Finch	Red Crossbill	White-winged Crossbill	Common Redpoll	Pine Siskin	Lesser Goldfinch	American Goldfinch	Evening Grosbeak	House Sparrow
|	*	*	|	|	|	|	*	|	|	*	*	|	*	|	*
|	|	*	|	|	*	|	*	|	|	|	*	|	*	*	*
|	|	*	|	|	|	|	*	*	|	|	*	|	*	*	*
|	*	*	|	|	*	|	*	|	|	*	*	*	*	*	*
*	*	*	*	*	*	*	*	*	*	*	*	*	*	*	*
|	*	*	*	*	*	*	*	*	|	|	*	*	*	*	*
|	|	*	|	|	|	|	*	*	|	|	*	|	*	*	*
|	*	*	|	|	*	|	*	|	|	|	*	*	*	*	*
|	*	*	|	|	|	|	*	|	|	*	*	|	*	|	*
|	*	*	|	|	|	|	*	*	|	|	*	*	*	*	*
|	*	*	|	|	|	|	*	|	|	|	*	*	*	|	*
|	*	*	|	|	*	|	*	*	|	|	*	*	*	*	*
|	*	*	|	|	*	|	*	|	|	|	*	|	*	*	*
|	|	*	|	|	*	|	*	|	|	|	*	*	*	*	*
|	|	*	|	|	|	|	*	*	|	|	*	|	*	*	*
|	|	*	|	|	|	|	*	|	|	|	|	|	*	|	*
|	*	*	|	*	*	|	*	*	|	|	*	*	*	*	*
|	*	*	|	|	*	|	*	*	|	|	*	*	*	*	*
|	|	*	|	|	*	|	*	|	|	|	*	|	|	|	*
|	|	*	|	|	|	|	*	*	|	|	*	|	*	|	*
|	*	*	|	|	|	|	*	|	|	|	|	|	|	|	*
|	|	|	|	|	|	|	*	|	|	|	*	|	*	|	*
|	|	|	*	|	|	|	*	|	|	|	*	|	*	|	*
|	|	|	*	|	|	|	*	|	|	|	*	|	*	|	*
|	|	|	*	|	*	|	*	*	|	|	*	*	*	|	*
|	|	|	*	|	|	|	*	|	|	|	*	*	*	|	*

LITERATURE CITED

Abert, J. W. 1846. Journal of Lieutenant J. W. Abert from Bent's Fort to St. Louis in 1845. 29th Cong., 1st Sess., Sen. Doc. 438, Serial 477. H. B. Carroll (ed.). 1941. *Panhandle-Plains Hist. Rev.* 14:9–113.

Aldrich, J. W. 1946. The United States races of bob-white. *Auk* 63:493–508.

———. 1963. Geographic orientation of American Tetraonidae. *Jour. Wildl. Mngmt.* 27:529–45.

Allan, P. F., and P. R. Sime. 1943a. A hawk census on Texas Panhandle highways. *Wilson Bull.* 55:29–39.

———. 1943b. Distribution and abundance of the Mississippi Kite in the Texas Panhandle. *Condor* 45:110–12.

Allison, P. S., A. W. Leary, and M. J. Bechard. 1995. Observations of wintering Ferruginous Hawks (*Buteo regalis*) feeding on prairie dogs (*Cynomys ludovicianus*) in the Texas Panhandle. *Texas Jour. of Sci.* 47(3):235–37.

American Ornithologists' Union [AOU]. 1957. *Check-list of North American birds.* 5th ed. Baltimore.

———. 1973. Thirty-second suppl. to the A.O.U. *Check-list of North American birds. Auk* 90:411–19.

———. 1983. *Check-list of North American birds.* 6th ed. Washington, D.C.

———. 1985. Thirty-fifth suppl. to the A.O.U. *Check-list of North American birds. Auk* 102:680–86.

———. 1995. Fortieth suppl. to the A.O.U. *Check-list of North American birds. Auk* 112:819–30.

———. 1997. Forty-first suppl. to the A.O.U. *Check-list of North American birds. Auk* 114:542–52.

———. 1998. *Check-list of North American birds.* 7th ed. Washington, D.C.

Anderson, B. W., and R. J. Daugherty. 1974. Characteristics and reproductive biology of grosbeaks (*Pheucticus*) in the hybrid zone in South Dakota. *Wilson Bull.* 86:1–11.

Andrews, R., and R. Righter. 1992. *Colorado birds.* Denver Museum of Natural History, Denver.

Arbib, R. S., Jr. 1971. Announcing—the Blue List: an "early warning system" for birds. *Amer. Birds* 25(6):948–49.

———. 1972. The Blue List for 1973. *Amer. Birds* 26(6):932–33.

Archambeau, E. R. 1966. Old Tascosa: Selected news items from the *Tascosa Pioneer* 1886–1888 (C. F. Rudolph, ed.). *Panhandle-Plains Hist. Rev.* 39:111.

Arnold, K. A. 1972. Crested titmice from Cottle and Foard counties, Texas. *Bull. Texas Ornith. Soc.* 5(2):23.

Ault, J. W., III. 1975. Harris' Hawk in southwestern Oklahoma. *Bull. Oklahoma Ornith. Soc.* 8:34–36.

———. 1984. The Curve-billed Thrasher in southwestern Oklahoma. *Bull. Oklahoma Ornith. Soc.* 17:12–14.

Austin, J. E., and M. R. Miller. 1995. Northern Pintail (*Anas acuta*). In *The birds of North America,* no. 163 (A. Poole and F. Gill, eds.). Acad. Nat. Sci., Philadelphia, and Amer. Ornith. Union, Washington, D.C.

Bailey, A. M., and R. J. Niedrach. 1965. *Birds of Colorado.* Denver Museum of Natural History, Denver.

Banks, R. C. 1968. Texas Black-throated Sparrow. Pp. 990–92 in *Life histories of North American cardinals, grosbeaks, buntings and allies* (O. L. Austin, Jr., ed.). U.S. Nat'l. Mus. Bull. 237.

Banta, J. K., and J. McMahon. 1987. Harris' Hawk in Oklahoma during fall and winter, 1986–87. *Bull. Oklahoma Ornith. Soc.* 20:29–31.

Baumgartner, F. M. 1951. Southern Great Plains region. *Aud. Field Notes* 5(3):212–14; 5(4):263–65.

———. 1953. Southern Great Plains region. *Aud. Field Notes* 7(4):281–82; 7(5):315–16.

———. 1954. Southern Great Plains region. *Aud. Field Notes* 8(3):259–61; 8(4):320–22; 8(5):352–54.

———. 1955. Southern Great Plains region. *Aud. Field Notes* 9(1):36–38; 9(3):267–69; 9(4):340–41; 9(5):386–87.

———. 1956. Southern Great Plains region. *Aud. Field Notes* 10(1):35–37; 10(4):343–45.

———. 1957. Southern Great Plains region. *Aud. Field Notes* 11(1):35–37; 11(3):275–77.

———. 1958. Southern Great Plains region. *Aud. Field Notes* 12(4):364–65; 12(5):423–24.

———. 1959. Southern Great Plains region. *Aud. Field Notes* 13(1):43–45; 13(4):381–84.

———. 1960. Southern Great Plains region. *Aud. Field Notes* 14(1).

———. 1962. Southern Great Plains region. *Aud. Field Notes* 16(5):488–89.

———. 1963. Southern Great Plains region. *Aud. Field Notes* 17(1):45–46; 17(3):339–44; 17(4):414–15; 17(5):468–69.

Baumgartner, F. M., and A. M. Baumgartner. 1992. *Oklahoma bird life.* Univ. Oklahoma Press, Norman.

Beason, R. C. 1995. Horned Lark (*Eremophila alpestris*). In *The birds of North America,* no. 195 (A. Poole and F. Gill, eds.). Acad. Nat. Sci., Philadelphia, and Amer. Ornith. Union, Washington, D.C.

Bellrose, F. C. 1976. *Ducks, geese and swans of North America.* Stackpole Books. Harrisburg, Penn.

Bellrose, F. C., and D. J. Holm. 1994. *Ecology and management of the Wood Duck.* Stackpole Books. Mechanicsburg, Penn.

Bent, A. C. 1926. *Life histories of North American marsh birds.* U.S. Nat'l. Mus. Bull. 135 (Dover ed.). Washington, D.C.

———. 1929. *Life histories of North American shore birds* (part 2). U.S. Nat'l. Mus. Bull. 146 (Dover ed.). Washington, D.C.

———. 1932. *Life histories of North American gallinaceous birds.* U.S. Nat'l. Mus. Bull. 162 (Dover ed.). Washington, D.C.

————. 1938. *Life histories of North American birds of prey.* U.S. Nat'l. Mus. Bull. 170 (Dover ed.). Washington, D.C.

————. 1940. *Life histories of North American cuckoos, goatsuckers, hummingbirds and their allies.* U.S. Nat'l. Mus. Bull. 176 (Dover ed.). Washington, D.C.

————. 1958. *Life histories of North American blackbirds, orioles, tanagers and their allies.* U.S. Nat'l. Mus. Bull. 211 (Dover ed.). Washington, D.C.

Berthelsen, P. S., and L. M. Smith. 1995. Nongame bird nesting on CRP lands in the Texas Southern Plains. *Jour. of Soil and Water Conser.* 50(6):672–75.

Bolen, E. G. 1987. A specimen record of the Barnacle Goose in Texas. *Southwestern Nat.* 32(4):506–07.

Bolen, E. G., and D. Flores. 1993. *The Mississippi Kite: portrait of a southern hawk.* Univ. Texas Press, Austin.

Bolen, E. G., L. M. Smith, and H. L. Schramm, Jr. 1989. Playa lakes: prairie wetlands of the Southern High Plains. *BioScience* 39(9):615–23.

Boyd, R. 1991. First nesting record for the Piping Plover in Oklahoma. *Wilson Bull.* 103:305–308.

Brauner, J. 1952. Reactions of Poor-wills to light and temperature. *Condor* 54:152–59.

Briskie, J. V. 1993. Smith's Longspur (*Calcarius pictus*). In *The birds of North America,* no. 34 (A. Poole, P. Stettenheim, and F. Gill, eds.). Acad. Nat. Sci., Philadelphia, and Amer. Ornith. Union, Washington, D.C.

————. 1994. Least Flycatcher (*Empidonax minimus*). In *The birds of North America,* no. 99 (A. Poole and F. Gill, eds.). Acad. Nat. Sci., Philadelphia, and Amer. Ornith. Union, Washington, D.C.

Britten, T. A. 1993. Changing land uses in Carson County: A microcosm of the Panhandle experience. *Panhandle-Plains Hist. Rev.* 66:53–72.

Brown, B. T. 1993. Bell's Vireo (*Vireo bellii*). In *The birds of North America,* no. 35 (A. Poole, P. Stettenheim, and F. Gill, eds.). Acad. Nat. Sci., Philadelphia, and Amer. Ornith. Union, Washington, D.C.

Brown, I. S. 1973. The Black-chinned Hummingbird in west-central Oklahoma. *Bull. Oklahoma Ornith. Soc.* 6:9–11.

————. 1981. American Woodcock in Beckham County, Oklahoma. *Bull. Oklahoma Ornith. Soc.* 14:32.

————. 1985. Successful nesting of the House Wren in western Oklahoma. *Bull. Oklahoma Ornith. Soc.* 18:17–20.

Brown, J. M. 1994. Mexican Jay (*Aphelocoma ultramarina*). In *The birds of North America,* no. 118 (A. Poole and F. Gill, eds.). Acad. Nat. Sci., Philadelphia, and Amer. Ornith. Union, Washington, D.C.

Brown, L., and D. Amadon. 1968. *Eagles, hawks and falcons of the world.* McGraw-Hill Book Co., New York.

Browning, M. R. 1974. Comments on the winter distribution of the Swainson's Hawk (*Buteo swainsoni*) in North America. *Amer. Birds* 28(5):865–67.

Burgess, H., and A. Burgess. 1997. Trumpeter Swans once wintered in Texas—why not now? In *North American Swans. Bull. Trumpeter Swan Soc.* 26(2):50–53.

Butts, K. O. 1976. Burrowing Owls wintering in the Oklahoma Panhandle. *Auk* 93:510–16.

————. 1988. Juvenile Whooping Crane winters in western Oklahoma. *Bull. Oklahoma Ornith. Soc.* 21:13–15.

Byard, M. E. 1979. Caspian Tern in Cimarron County, Oklahoma. *Bull. Oklahoma Ornith. Soc.* 12:21.

Cable, T. T., S. Seltman, and K. J. Cook. 1996. Birds of Cimarron National Grassland. Tech. Rep. RM-GTR-281. U.S. Dept. Agric., Forest Svce., Rocky Mtn. Forest and Range. Exp. Sta., Fort Collins.

Cain, F. 1988. First Texas Panhandle record for Garganey. *Bull. Oklahoma Ornith. Soc.* 21:18.

Carden, J., and R. C. Rushing. 1987. Black Scoter: A new bird for Oklahoma. *Bull. Oklahoma Ornith. Soc.* 20:1–2.

Carey, M., D. E. Burhans, and D. A. Nelson. 1994. Field Sparrow (*Spizella pusilla*). In *The birds of North America,* no. 103 (A. Poole and F. Gill, eds.). Acad. Nat. Sci., Philadelphia, and Amer. Ornith. Union, Washington, D.C.

Carlander, K. 1933. The final report of the summer survey of the birds of the Panhandle of Texas, June 15 to September 15, 1933. Typewritten report, located at Panhandle-Plains Hist. Mus., Canyon. 21 pp.

————. 1934. Birds of the Palo Duro. *Amarillo Daily News,* 5 August–25 December 1934.

————. 1935. Birds seen in the vicinity of Amarillo, Texas, June 26 to September 23, 1936. Located at West Texas A&M Univ. Library, Canyon. 2 pp.

Carlson, P. H. 1980. Panhandle pastores: Early sheepherding in the Texas Panhandle. *Panhandle-Plains Hist. Rev.* 53:1–15.

Chase, C. A., III, S. J. Bissell, H. E. Kingery, and W. D. Graul. 1982. Colorado bird distribution latilong study. Colorado Field Ornith., Denver. 78 pp.

Clover, P. C. 1981. Breeding of Hooded Merganser in Alfalfa County, Oklahoma. *Bull. Oklahoma Ornith. Soc.* 14:28–29.

Clum, N.J., and T. J. Cade. 1994. Gyrfalcon (*Falco rusticolus*). In *The birds of North America,* no. 114 (A. Poole and F. Gill, eds.). Acad. of Nat. Sci., Philadelphia, and Amer. Ornith. Union, Washington, D.C.

Colwell, M. A., and J. R. Jehl, Jr. 1994. Wilson's Phalarope (*Phalaropus tricolor*). In *The birds of North America,* no. 83 (A. Poole and F. Gill, eds.). Acad. Nat. Sci., Philadelphia, and Amer. Ornith. Union, Washington, D.C.

Cook, W., and A. Krehbiel. 1987. When did the Great-tailed Grackle first invade northeastern New Mexico? *Bull. Oklahoma Ornith. Soc.* 20:32–33.

Cox, G. W. 1973. Hybridization between Mourning and MacGillivray's Warblers. *Auk* 90:190–91.

Crocoll, S. T. 1994. Red-shouldered Hawk (*Buteo lineatus*). In *The birds of North America,* no. 107 (A. Poole and F. Gill, eds.) Acad. of Nat. Sci., Philadelphia, and Amer. Ornith. Union, Washington, D.C.

Csada, R. D., and R. M. Brigham. 1992. Common Poorwill (*Phalaenoptilus nuttallii*). In *The birds of North America,* no. 32 (A. Poole, P. Stettenheim, and F. Gill, eds.). Acad. Nat. Sci., Philadelphia, and Amer. Ornith. Union, Washington, D.C.

Curson, J., D. Quinn, and D. Beadle. 1994. Warblers of the Americas: An identification guide. Houghton Mifflin, Boston.

Dallas Morning News. 1998–99. *Texas Almanac.* Dallas.

Davis, W. M. 1975. The Great-tailed Grackle in Oklahoma. *Bull. Oklahoma Ornith. Soc.* 8:9–18.

Dawson, J. W., and R. W. Mannan. 1989. A comparison of two methods of estimating breeding group size in Harris' Hawks. *Auk* 106:480–83.

Derrickson, K. C., and R. Breitwisch. 1992. Northern Mockingbird (*Mimus polyglottos*). In *The birds of North America*, no. 7 (A. Poole, P. Stettenheim, and F. Gill, eds.). Acad. Nat. Sci., Philadelphia, and Amer. Ornith. Union, Washington, D.C.

Dickerson, L. M. 1938. The western frontier of the European Starling in the United States as of February, 1937. *Condor* 40:118–23.

Dixon, K. L. 1955. An ecological analysis of the interbreeding of crested titmice in Texas. *Univ. California Publ. Zool.* 54(3):125–206.

Dowler, R. C., D. K. Dean, T. E. Herman, and A. C. Simon. 1978. County records in Texas housed in the Museum, Texas Tech University. *Bull. Texas Ornith. Soc.* 11:12–16.

Downs, J. 1983. Green-tailed Towhee nest in Cimarron County, Oklahoma. *Bull. Oklahoma Ornith. Soc.* 16:7.

Dunn, J. L., and K. L. Garrett. 1997. *A field guide to warblers of North America*. Houghton Mifflin, Boston.

Dunne, P. 1998. Looking close—overlooking the obvious. *Birding* 30 (1):67–68.

Dzubin, A. 1965. A study of migrating Ross' Geese in western Saskatchewan. *Condor* 67:511–34.

Ehrlich, P. R., D. S. Dobkin, and D. Wheye. 1988. *The birder's handbook*. Simon and Schuster, New York.

Ely, C. R., and A. X. Dzubin. 1994. Greater White-fronted Goose (*Anser albifrons*). In *The birds of North America*, no. 131 (A. Poole and F. Gill, eds.). Acad. of Nat. Sci., Philadelphia, and Amer. Ornith. Union, Washington, D.C.

Emlen, S. T., J. D. Rising, and W. L. Thompson. 1975. A behavioral and morphological study of sympatry in the Indigo and Lazuli buntings of the Great Plains. *Wilson Bull.* 87:145–77.

England, A. S., and W. F. Laudenslayer, Jr. 1993. Bendire's Thrasher (*Toxostoma bendirei*). In *The birds of North America*, no. 71 (A. Poole and F. Gill, eds.). Acad. of Nat. Sci., Philadelphia, and Amer. Ornith. Union, Washington, D.C.

Exedine, B. 1991. Sandhill Crane in Oklahoma in summer. *Bull. Oklahoma Ornith. Soc.* 24:6.

Farquhar, C. C. 1992. White-tailed Hawk (*Buteo albicaudatus*). In *The birds of North America*, no. 30 (A. Poole, P. Stettenheim, and F. Gill, eds.). Acad. of Nat. Sci., Philadelphia, and Amer. Ornith. Union, Washington, D.C.

Fedynich, A. M., and O. E. Rhodes, Jr. 1995. Mallard-like ducks in the Playa Lakes region. *Wilson Bull.* 107:548–51.

Fischer, D. H., M. D. Schibler, R. J. Whyte, and E. G. Bolen. 1982. Checklist of birds from the playa lakes of the southern Texas Panhandle. *Bull. Texas Ornith. Soc.* 15:2–7.

Flowers, T. L. 1985. Recent breeding of the Mountain Plover in Cimarron County, Oklahoma. *Bull. Oklahoma Ornith. Soc.* 18:9–12.

Frederick, R. B., and R. R. Johnson. 1983. Ross' Geese increasing in central North America. *Condor* 85:257–58.

Friedmann, H. 1950. *The birds of North and Middle America*. U.S. Nat'l. Mus. Bull. 50(11). Washington, D.C.

Friedmann, H., L. F. Kiff, and S. I. Rothstein. 1977. *A further contribution to knowledge of the host relations of the parasitic cowbirds.* Smithsonian Contr. to Zool. no. 235. Washington, D.C.

Garrett, J. S. 1982. Sage Sparrow in Cimarron County, Oklahoma. *Bull. Oklahoma Ornith. Soc.* 15:33.

Gehlbach, F. R. 1995. Eastern Screech-Owl (*Otus asio*). In *The birds of North America,* no. 165 (A. Poole and F. Gill, eds.). Acad. of Nat. Sci., Philadelphia, and Amer. Ornith. Union, Washington, D.C.

Gibbs, J. P., F. A. Reid, and S. M. Melvin. 1992. Least Bittern (*Ixobrychus exilis*). In *The birds of North America,* no. 17 (A. Poole, P. Stettenheim, and F. Gill, eds.). Acad. of Nat. Sci., Philadelphia, and Amer. Ornith. Union, Washington, D.C.

Goddard, S. V. 1971. Size, migration pattern, and structure of fall and early winter blackbird and starling populations in western Oklahoma. *Wilson Bull.* 83(4):371–82.

Godfrey, R. D., Jr., and A. M. Fedynich. 1987. Blue-winged X Cinnamon Teal hybrid in the southern High Plains, Texas. *Southwestern Nat.* 32:397–98.

Gould, F. W., G. O. Hoffman, and C. A. Rechenthin. 1960. Vegetational areas of Texas. Texas A&M Univ., Texas Agric. Exp. Sta. Leaflet no. 492.

Graham, D. S., and A. Wormington. 1993. Inca Dove: New to Ontario and Canada. *Birders Jour.* 2(3):153–59.

Gratto-Trevor, C. L. 1992. Semipalmated Sandpiper (*Calidris pusilla*). In *The birds of North America,* no. 6 (A. Poole, P. Stettenheim, and F. Gill, eds.). Acad. of Nat. Sci., Philadelphia, and Amer. Ornith. Union, Washington, D.C.

Graul, W. D., and L. E. Webster. 1976. Breeding status of the Mountain Plover. *Condor* 78:265–67.

Grieb, J. R. 1970. *The shortgrass prairie Canada Goose population.* Wildlife Soc. Mngrph. no. 22.

Gross, A. O. 1968. Lesser Goldfinch. Pp. 471–74 in *Life histories of North American cardinals, grosbeaks, buntings, towhees, finches, sparrows, and allies* (O. L. Austin, Jr., ed.). U.S. Nat'l Mus. Bull. 237.

Grzybowski, J. A. 1982. Population structure in grassland bird communities during winter. *Condor* 84:137–51.

———. 1983. Western Screech-Owl: A "new" bird for Oklahoma. *Bull. Oklahoma Ornith. Soc.* 16:17–20.

———. 1987. First nesting record of Gadwall in Oklahoma. *Bull. Oklahoma Ornith. Soc.* 20:5–6.

———. 1989. Southern Great Plains region. *Amer. Birds* 43(2):124–26; 43(3):499–501.

———. 1993. Southern Great Plains region. *Amer. Birds* 47(3):426–29; 47(5):1122–24.

———. 1995. Southern Great Plains region. *Field Notes* 49(2):162–64; 49(3):269–73.

———. 1996. Southern Great Plains region. *Field Notes* 50(1):74–77; 50(3):296–300.

———. 1998. Southern Great Plains region. *Field Notes* 51(5):1015–17.

Grzybowski, J. A., J. W. Arterburn, W. A. Carter, J. S. Tomer, and D. W. Verser. 1992. *Date guide to the occurrences of birds in Oklahoma.* 2nd ed. Oklahoma Ornith. Soc., Norman. 40 pp.

Grzybowski, J. A., and J. D. Webster. 1990. First documented occurrence of Clark's Grebe in Oklahoma. *Bull. Oklahoma Ornith. Soc.* 23:22–23.

Guthery, F. S., and F. C. Bryant. 1982. Status of playas in the southern Great Plains. *Wildl. Soc. Bull.* 10:309–17.

Haig, S. M. 1992. Piping Plover (*Charadrius melodus*). In *The birds of North America*, no. 2 (A. Poole, P. Stettenheim, and F. Gill, eds.). Acad. of Nat. Sci., Philadelphia, and Amer. Ornith. Union., Washington, D.C.

Hamilton, T. H. 1962. The habitats of the avifauna of the mesquite plains of Texas. *Amer. Midland Nat.* 76:85–105.

Haukos, D. A., and L. M. Smith. 1994. The importance of playa wetlands to biodiversity of the southern High Plains. *Landscape and Urban Planning* 28:83–98.

Hawkins, A. S. 1945. Bird life of the Texas Panhandle. *Panhandle-Plains Hist. Rev.* 18:110–50.

Hayman, P., J. Marchant, and T. Prater. 1986. *Shorebirds: An identification guide to the waders of the world.* Houghton Mifflin, Boston.

Haynie, C. B. 1992. Texas Bird Records Committee report for 1992. *Bull. Texas Ornith. Soc.* 25(2):30–41.

———. 1998. Texas Bird Records Committee report for 1996. *Bull. Texas Ornith. Soc.* 31(1):7–21.

Heck, B. A. 1996. The Red Crossbill invasion of Oklahoma during the summer of 1996. *Bull. Oklahoma Ornith. Soc.* 29(4):25–27.

Heindel, M. T. 1996. Field identification of the Solitary Vireo complex. *Birding* 28:458–71.

Herbert, L. 1997. First nesting record for the Cedar Waxwing in eastern Oklahoma. *Bull. Oklahoma Ornith. Soc.* 30(4):33–34.

Hibbets, A. I., L. A. Saunders, and D. Walker. 1926–36. Birds seen along the creeks, in canyons, or on plains within forty miles of Canyon, Texas. Typewritten report, located at West Texas A&M Univ. Library, Canyon. 20 pp.

Hill, L. A. 1993. Status and distribution of the Least Tern in Oklahoma. *Bull. Oklahoma Ornith. Soc.* 26(2):9–24.

Holm, S. F., H. D. Irby, and J. M. Inglis. 1978. First nesting record of Double-crested Cormorant in Texas since 1939. *Bull Texas Ornith. Soc.* 11(2):50–51.

Howe, B. 1993–94. New collar protocol for North American swans. *Trumpeter Swan Soc. Newsletter* 23(1):1–3. Maple Plain, Minn.

Hubbard, J. P. 1978. *Revised check-list of the birds of New Mexico.* New Mexico Ornith. Soc. Pub. no. 6.

———. 1982. Southwest Region: New Mexico. *Amer. Birds* 36(6):1006–1007.

———. 1983. Southwest Region: New Mexico. *Amer. Birds* 37(3):327–28; 37(5):900–901; 37(6):1015–17.

———. 1984. Southwest Region: New Mexico. *Amer. Birds* 38(3):346–47.

———. 1985. Southwest Region: New Mexico. *Amer. Birds* 39(5):949–51.

———. 1986. Southwest Region: New Mexico. *Amer. Birds* 40(2):313–14; 40(5):1240–42.

———. 1987. Southwest Region: New Mexico. *Amer. Birds* 41(1):128–30; 41(5):1473–75.

———. 1989. Southwest Region: New Mexico. *Amer. Birds* 43(5):1351–54.

Hundertmark, C. P. 1974. Breeding range extensions of certain birds in New Mexico. *Wilson Bull.* 86:298–300.

Hunnius, C. J. A. 1876. Survey of the sources of the Red River April 25th to June 30th [,]

1876. In T. L. Baker (ed.) 1985. The survey of the headwaters of the Red River, 1876. *Panhandle-Plains Hist. Rev.* 58:52–121.

Jackson, A. S. 1964. A study of the introduction, release, and survival of certain European and Asiatic game birds. *Trans. 29th N. Amer. Wildl. and Nat. Resources Conf.* Wildl. Mngmnt. Inst., Washington, D.C.

Jackson, A. S., and R. DeArment. 1963. The Lesser Prairie Chicken in the Texas Panhandle. *Jour. Wildl. Mngmnt.* 27:733–37.

Jaeger, E. C. 1949. Further observations on the hibernation of the Poor-will. *Condor* 51:105–109.

Jemison, E. J. 1972. Barnacle Goose winters in southeastern Oklahoma. *Bull. Oklahoma Ornith. Soc.* 5(4):27–28.

Johnsgard, P. A. 1973. *Grouse and quails of North America.* Univ. Nebraska Press, Lincoln.
———. 1979. *Birds of the Great Plains: Breeding species and their distribution.* Univ. Nebraska Press, Lincoln.

Johnson, P. W. 1990. Black Swift (*Cypseloides niger*) nesting in the Jemez Mountains of New Mexico. *Bull. New Mexico Ornith. Soc.* 18(3–4):13–15.

Jury, G. M. 1976. First record of White-winged Crossbill (*Loxia leucoptera*) for Texas. *Bull. Texas Ornith. Soc.* 9:7.

Kaufman, K. 1990a. *A field guide to advanced birding.* Houghton Mifflin, Boston.
———. 1990b. The practiced eye: Scrub Jay and Gray-headed Jay. *Amer. Birds* 44(1):5–6.
———. 1992. The practiced eye: Identifying monochrome grebes in winter. *Amer. Birds* 46(5):1187–90.
———. 1993. The practiced eye: Notes on goldfinch identification. *Amer. Birds* 47(1):159–62.

Kemsies, E. 1968. Smith's Longspur. Pp. 1628–35 in *Life histories of North American cardinals, grosbeaks, buntings and allies* (O. L. Austin, Jr., ed.). U.S. Nat'l. Mus. Bull. 237.

Kessel, B. 1953. Distribution and migration of the European Starling in North America. *Condor* 55(2):49–67.

King, R. 1978. Habitat use and related behaviors of breeding Long-billed Curlews. MS thesis, Colorado State Univ., Fort Collins. 69 pp.

Kirk, J. A. 1981. Swallow-tailed Kite in Alfalfa County, Oklahoma. *Bull. Oklahoma Ornith. Soc.* 14:22.

Klett, E. V. 1982. A new bird for Oklahoma: Garganey. *Bull. Oklahoma Ornith. Soc.* 15:9–10.

Krause, K. 1968. McCown's Longspur. Pp. 1564–97 in *Life histories of North American cardinals, grosbeaks, buntings and allies* (O. L. Austin, Jr., ed.). U.S. Nat'l. Mus. Bull. 237.

Krehbiel, A. 1955. Preliminary check list of the birds of the Clayton, New Mexico, vicinity. Located in author's personal files. 3 pp.

Kroodsma, R. L. 1975. Hybridization in buntings (*Passerina*) in North Dakota and eastern Montana. *Auk* 92:66–80.

Lane, J. 1968. Baird's Sparrow. Pp. 745–65 in *Life histories of North American cardinals, grosbeaks, buntings, and allies* (O. L. Austin, Jr., ed.). U.S. Natl. Mus. Bull. 237.

Lanyon, W. E. 1957. The comparative biology of the meadowlarks (*Sturnella*) in Wisconsin. *Pub. Nuttall Ornith. Club,* no. 1. Cambridge, Mass.

————. 1994. Western Meadowlark (*Sturnella neglecta*). In *The birds of North America,* no. 104 (A. Poole and F. Gill, eds.). Acad. of Nat. Sci., Philadelphia, and Amer. Ornith. Union, Washington, D.C.

————. 1995. Eastern Meadowlark (*Sturnella magna*). In *The birds of North America,* no. 160 (A. Poole and F. Gill, eds.). Acad. of Nat. Sci., Philadelphia, and Amer. Ornith. Union, Washington, D.C.

Lasley, G. W. 1990. Texas bird records committee report for 1989. *Bull. Texas Ornith. Soc.* 23(1&2):6–19.

Lasley, G. W., D. A. Easterla, C. W. Sexton, and D. A. Bartol. 1982. Documentation of the Red-faced Warbler (*Cardellina rubrifrons*) in Texas and review of its status in Texas and adjacent areas. *Bull. Texas Ornith. Soc.* 15(1&2):8–14.

Lasley, G. W., and C. Sexton. 1989. Texas region. *Amer. Birds* 43(1):127–33; 43(3):502–10; 43(5):1337–42.

————. 1990. Texas region. *Amer. Birds* 44(1):118–27; 44(3):458–65.

————. 1991. Texas region. *Amer. Birds* 45(1):124–29; 45(2):290–94; 45(3):469–73; 45(5):1135–39.

————. 1992. Texas region. *Amer. Birds* 46(1):117–23; 46(2):286–90; 46(3):446–51; 46(5):1153–56.

————. 1993. Texas region. *Amer. Birds* 47(2):274–78; 47(5):1124–28.

————. 1994a. Texas region. *Amer. Birds* 48(1):127–30.

————. 1994b. Texas region. *Field Notes* 48(2):224–28; 48(3):316–20; 48(5):960–64.

————. 1995a. Master List of Review Species [Updated, 12 September 1995]. Prep. for Texas Bird Records Committee, Austin. 130 pp.

————. 1995b. Texas region. *Field Notes* 49(1):68–71; 49(3):273–78.

Leachman, B., and B. Osmundson. 1990. Status of the Mountain Plover: A literature review. U.S. Fish and Wildl. Svce., Golden, Colo. 83 pp.

Lehman, P. 1980. The identification of Thayer's Gull in the field. *Birding* 12(6):198–210.

————. 1994. Franklin's vs. Laughing Gulls. A "new" problem arises. *Birding* 26(2):126–27.

Lewis, J. C. 1995. Whooping Crane (*Grus americana*). In *The birds of North America,* no. 153 (A. Poole and F. Gill, eds.). Acad. of Nat. Sci., Philadelphia, and Amer. Ornith. Union, Washington, D.C.

Ligon, J. S. 1961. New Mexico birds and where to find them. Univ. New Mexico Press, Albuquerque.

Littlefield, C. D. 1970. A Marsh Hawk roost in Texas. *Condor* 72:245.

————. 1973. Swainson's Hawks preying on fall armyworms. *Southwestern Nat.* 17:433.

Litton, G., R. L. West, D. F. Dvorak, and G. T. Miller. 1994. The Lesser Prairie Chicken and its management in Texas. Fed. Aid Rep. Series no. 33. Fed. Aid Proj. W-129-M. Texas Parks and Wildl. Dept., Austin. 22 pp.

Llano Estacado Audubon Society [LEAS]. 1994. *Birds of the Texas South Plains.* 6th ed. LEAS, Lubbock.

Lockwood, M. W. 1992. First breeding record of *Aechmophorus* grebes in Texas. *Bull. Texas Ornith. Soc.* 25(2):64–66.

Magill, R. T. 1996. Habitat selection of Wood Duck and cavity nesting nongame birds in northern Rolling Plains riparian zones: Annual report. Dept. Range, Wildl., and Fish Mngmnt., Texas Tech Univ., Lubbock. 24 pp.

Maisel, G. 1985. Laughing Gulls in Ellis County, Oklahoma. *Bull. Oklahoma Ornith. Soc.* 18:21.

Marcy, R. B. 1854. Exploration of the Red River in Louisiana in 1852. Senate Doc. no. 64, Thirty-first Congress, First Session. Washington, D.C.

Marshall, J. T., Jr. 1967. *Parallel variation in North and Middle American Screech-Owls.* Mngrph. Western Found. Vert. Zool. 1. 72 pp.

Martin, C. 1989. Texas colonial waterbird census summary. Special Admin. Rep. Texas Parks and Wildl. Dept. and Texas Colonial Waterbird Soc., Austin.

Maxwell, T. C. 1979. Vireos (Aves: *Vireonidae*) in west-central Texas. *Southwestern Nat.* 24:223–29.

McCabe, R. A. 1954. Hybridization between bobwhite and scaled quail. *Auk* 71:293–97.

McCament, D. 1985. Interior Least Tern distribution and taxonomy. Fed. Aid Proj. no. W-103-R-15. Perf. Rep., Texas Parks and Wildl. Dept., Austin. 11 pp.

McCauley, C. A. H. 1877. Notes on the ornithology of the region about the source of the Red River of Texas, from observations made during the exploration conducted by Lieut. E. H. Ruffner, Corps. of Engineers, U.S.A. Bull. U.S. Geol. and Geog. Surv. Terr. 3, no. 3. (K. D. Seyffert and T. L. Baker, eds.). *Panhandle-Plains Hist. Rev.* 61:25–88.

McMahon, C. A., R. G. Frye, and K. L. Brown. 1984. The vegetation types of Texas. Pittman-Robertson Proj. W-107-R. Texas Parks and Wildl. Dept. Austin.

Meyer, K. D. 1995. Swallow-tailed Kite (*Elanoides forficatus*). In *The birds of North America,* no. 138 (A. Poole and F. Gill, eds.). Acad. of Nat. Sci., Philadelphia, and Amer. Ornith. Union, Washington, D.C.

Middleton, A. L. A. 1993. American Goldfinch (*Carduelis tristas*). In *The birds of North America,* no. 80 (A. Poole and F. Gill, eds.). Acad. of Nat. Sci., Philadelphia, and Amer. Ornith. Union, Washington, D.C.

Midland Naturalists, Inc. [MN]. 1992. Field check list: Birds of Midland County, Texas. 10th ed.

Mitchell, C. J., and R. O. Hayes. 1973. Breeding House Sparrows, *Passer domesticus* in captivity. Pp. 39–48 in *A symposium on the House Sparrow* (Passer domesticus) *and European Tree Sparrow* (P. montanus) *in North America* (S. C. Kendeigh, chrmn.). Amer. Ornith. Union Mngrph. no. 14.

Mitchell, C. J., R. O. Hayes, P. Holden, and T. B. Hughes, Jr. 1973. Nesting activity of the House Sparrow in Hale County, Texas, during 1968. Pp. 49–59 in *A symposium on the House Sparrow* (Passer domesticus) *and European Tree Sparrow* (P. montanus) *in North America* (S. C. Kendeigh, chrmn.). Amer. Ornith. Union Mngrph. no. 14.

Mollhausen, B. 1858. *Diary of a journey from the Mississippi to the coasts of the Pacific with a United States government expedition.* 2 vols. Longmans, Brown, Green, Longmans and Roberts, London. Vol. 1, p. 167.

Moore, W. S. 1995. Northern Flicker (*Colaptes auratus*). In *The birds of North America,* no. 166 (A. Poole and F. Gill, eds.). Acad. of Nat. Sci., Philadelphia, and Amer. Ornith. Union, Washington, D.C.

Moorman, T. E., and P. N. Gray. 1994. Mottled Duck (*Anas fulvigula*). In *The birds of North America,* no. 81 (A. Poole and F. Gill, eds.). Acad. of Nat. Sci., Philadelphia, and Amer. Ornith. Union, Washington, D.C.

Moorman, Z. 1986. Nesting of Scarlet Tanager in Woodward County, Oklahoma. *Bull. Oklahoma Ornith. Soc.* 19:15–16.

More, R. L., and J. K. Strecker. 1929. *The summer birds of Wilbarger County, Texas.* Contr. Baylor Univ. Mus. no. 20. Waco.

Moskoff, W. 1995. Veery (*Catharus fuscescens*). In *The birds of North America,* no. 142 (A. Poole and F. Gill, eds.). Acad. of Nat. Sci., Philadelphia, and Amer. Ornith. Union, Washington, D.C.

Mueller, A. J. 1992. Inca Dove (*Columbina inca*). In *The birds of North America,* no. 28 (A. Poole, P. Stettenheim, and F. Gill, eds.). Acad. of Nat. Sci., Philadelphia, and Amer. Ornith. Union, Washington, D.C.

National Park Service [NPS]. 1976. A birder's checklist, Lake Meredith Recreation Area. Fritch, Tex.

Neill, R. L., and J. F. Kuban. 1986. Shorebird migration at Arlington, Texas: 1977–1986. *Bull. Texas Ornith. Soc.* 19(1&2):13–20.

Newell, D. B. 1990. Second record of Northern Cardinal in Cimarron County, Oklahoma. *Bull. Oklahoma Ornith. Soc.* 23:15–16.

Newell, J. G. 1979. Breeding of Tree Swallow in Cimarron County, Oklahoma. *Bull. Oklahoma Ornith. Soc.* 12:24.

———. 1985. A temporary colony of Lesser Goldfinches in central Oklahoma. *Bull. Oklahoma Ornith. Soc.* 18:1–4.

New Mexico Ornithological Society [NMOS]. 1983–84. *Field Notes* (R. Goodman, ed.) 22.

———. 1985–86. *Field Notes* (R. Goodman, ed.) 25(1).

———. 1991–92. *Field Notes* (P. R. Snider, ed.) 31(3); 31(4).

———. 1992. *New Mexico Bird Finding Guide* (D. A. Zimmerman, M. A. Zimmerman, and J. D. Durrie, eds.).NMOS, Albuquerque.

———. 1992–93. *Field Notes* (P. R. Snider, ed.) 32(3&4).

———. 1995. *Field Notes* (P. R. Snider, ed.) 34(4).

Nice, M. M. 1931. *The birds of Oklahoma.* Rev. ed. Publ. Univ. Oklahoma Biol. Surv. 3(1). 224 pp.

Oberholser, H. C. 1974. *The bird life of Texas* (E. B. Kincaid, Jr., ed.). 2 vols. Univ. Texas Press, Austin.

Oklahoma Ornithological Society [OOS]. 1993. *Scissortail* 43(4):36.

Oliphant, M. 1990. A new bird for Oklahoma: Pacific Loon. *Bull. Oklahoma Ornith. Soc.* 23:17–20.

———. 1991. An invasion of the Steller's Jay into the Oklahoma panhandle. *Bull. Oklahoma Ornith. Soc.* 24:14–15.

Oliphant, M., and I. S. Brown. 1984. Eastward expansion of the House Finch's range in Oklahoma. *Bull. Oklahoma Ornith. Soc.* 17:9–12.

Palmer, R. S. 1962. *Handbook of North American birds.* Vol. 1: *Loons through flamingos.* Yale Univ. Press, New Haven.

———. 1976. *Handbook of North American birds* Vol. 2: *Waterfowl.* Yale Univ. Press, New Haven.

———. 1988a. *Handbook of North American birds.* Vol. 4. *Diurnal raptors.* Yale Univ. Press, New Haven.

―――. 1988b. *Handbook of North American birds.* Vol. 5. *Diurnal raptors.* Yale Univ. Press, New Haven.

Parker, J. W., and J. C. Ogden. 1979. The recent history and status of the Mississippi Kite. *Amer. Birds* 33(2):119–29.

Parmelee, D. F. 1969. Early nesting of the House Finch in Oklahoma. *Bull. Oklahoma Ornith. Soc.* 2:16.

―――. 1992. White-rumped Sandpiper. In *The birds of North America,* no. 29 (A. Poole, P. Stettenheim, and F. Gill, Eds.). Acad. of Nat. Sci., Philadelphia, and Amer. Ornith. Union, Washington, D.C.

Patten, M. A., and M. T. Heindel. 1994. Identifying Trumpeter and Tundra Swans. *Birding* 26(5):306–18.

Patti, S. T. 1983. Barrow's Goldeneyes in Cimarron County, Oklahoma. *Bull. Oklahoma Ornith. Soc.* 16:29–30.

Patti, S. T., and M. L. Myers. 1976. A probable Mourning X MacGillivray's Warbler hybrid. *Wilson Bull.* 88:490–91.

Peterjohn, B. G., and J. R. Sauer. 1993. North American breeding bird survey annual summary 1990–1991. Bird Populations, Vol. 1 (Reprint).

Peterson, J. J., G. W. Lasley, K. B. Bryan, and M. Lockwood. 1991. Additions to the breeding avifauna of the Davis Mountains. *Bull. Texas Ornith. Soc.* 24(2):39–48.

Peterson, R. T. 1990. *A field guide to western birds.* Houghton Mifflin, Boston.

Phillips, A. R. 1975. Semipalmated Sandpipers: Identification, migrations, summer and winter ranges. *Amer. Birds* 29(4):799–806.

Pitocchelli, J. 1993. Mourning Warbler (*Oporornis philadelphia*). In *The birds of North America,* no. 72 (A. Poole and F. Gill, eds.). Acad. of Nat. Sci., Philadelphia, and Amer. Ornith. Union, Washington, D.C.

Ports, M. 1979. Spotted Sandpiper breeding in Texas County, Oklahoma. *Bull. Oklahoma Ornith. Soc.* 12:20–21.

Pravosudov, V. V., and T. C. Grubb, Jr. 1993. White-breasted Nuthatch (*Sitta carolinensis*). In *The birds of North America,* no. 54 (A. Poole and F. Gill, eds.). Acad. of Nat. Sci., Philadelphia, and Amer. Ornith. Union, Washington, D.C.

Prevett, J. P., and C. D. MacInnes. 1972. The number of Ross' Geese in central North America. *Condor* 74:431–38.

Pruitt, J. 1975. The return of the Great-tailed Grackle. *Amer. Birds* 29(5):985–92.

Pulich. W. M. 1971. Some fringillid records for Texas. *Condor* 73:111.

―――. 1980. A Thayer's Gull specimen from Texas: A problem in identification. *Southwestern Nat.* 25:257–58.

―――. 1988. *The birds of north central Texas.* Texas A&M Univ. Press, College Station.

Purdue, J. R. 1969. The Western Sandpiper in Oklahoma. *Bull. Oklahoma Ornith. Soc.* 2:17–21.

Pyle, P., and P. Henderson. 1990. On separating female and immature *Oporornis* warblers in fall. *Birding* 22(5):222–28.

Ray, J. D. 1995a. The Purple Martin and its management in Texas. Texas Parks and Wildl. Bull. PWD BK W7100–254. Austin. 27 pp.

―――. 1995b. Purple Martins in northwest Texas. *Purple Martin Update* 6(3):10–12.

Ray, J. D., and H. W. Miller. 1997. A concentration of small Canada Geese in an urban setting at Lubbock, Texas. *Southwestern Nat.* 42(1):68–73.

Ray, J. D., H. W. Miller, and B. D. Sullivan. *Breeding Ducks in the High Plains of Texas.* In prep.

Reeves, T. V., and L. Reeves. 1914–36. Birds seen in the Panhandle of Texas, 1914 and thereafter. Located at West Texas A&M Univ. Library, Canyon. 5 pp.

Regosin, J. V., S. Orr, and J. Sarnat. 1991. Recent breeding records of the Northern Harrier in southwestern Oklahoma. *Bull. Oklahoma Ornith. Soc.* 24:29–30.

Rhodes, M. J. 1978. Late nesting of Ruddy Duck in northwest Texas. *Bull. Texas Ornith. Soc.* 11(1):19–20.

———. 1979. Redheads breeding in the Texas Panhandle. *Southwestern Nat.* 24:691–92.

Rideout, D. W. 1979. Plains gliders. *Texas Parks & Wildlife* 37(4):3–5.

Rideout, D. W., D. A. Swepston, and B. C. Thompson. 1984. Golden Eagle nesting and food habits surveyed in the Trans-Pecos and Panhandle of Texas, 1979–1983. Fed. Aid Proj. W-103-R. Special Rep., Texas Parks and Wildl. Dept., Austin. 46 pp.

Ridgway, R. 1870. A new classification of the North American Falconidae, with descriptions of three new species. *Proc. Acad. Nat. Sci. Philadelphia* (22):138–50.

———. 1901–19. *The birds of North and Middle America.* Pts. 1–8. U.S. Nat'l. Mus. Bull. 50:203.

Rising, J. D., and F. W. Schueler. 1980. Identification and status of Wood Pewees (*Contopus*) from the Great Plains: What are sibling species? *Condor* 82:301–308.

Roberson, D. 1980. *Rare birds of the west coast of North America.* Woodcock Publications, Pacific Grove, Calif.

Robins, C. S. 1973. Introduction, spread, and present abundance of the House Sparrow in North America. Pp. 3–9. in *A symposium on the House Sparrow* (Passer domesticus) *and European Tree Sparrow* (P. montanus) *in North America* (S. C. Kendeigh, chrmn.). Amer. Ornith. Union Monogr. no. 14.

Rohwer, S. A. 1969. Spring specimen of Baird's Sparrow from northeastern New Mexico. *Bull. Oklahoma Ornith. Soc.* 6:21–22.

———. 1972. Distribution of meadowlarks in the central and southern Great Plains and the desert grasslands of eastern New Mexico and west Texas. *Trans. Kansas Acad. Sci.* 75:1–19.

———. 1976. Specific distinctness and adaptive differences in southwestern meadowlarks. *Univ. Kansas Occ. Pprs. Mus. Nat. Hist.* 44:1–14.

Rosche, R. C., and D. J. Rosche. 1991. A new bird for Oklahoma: Calliope Hummingbird. *Bull. Oklahoma Ornith. Soc.* 24: 6–7.

Rosenberg, K. V., J. P. Hubbard, and G. H. Rosenberg. 1981. Southwest region. *Amer. Birds* 35(6):966–69.

Rosenfield, R. N., and J. Bielefeldt. 1993. Cooper's Hawk (*Accipiter cooperii*). In *The birds of North America,* no. 75 (A. Poole and F. Gill, eds.). Acad. of Nat. Sci., Philadelphia, and Amer. Ornith. Union, Washington, D.C.

Ross, P. V. 1974. Ecology and behavior of a dense colony of Burrowing Owls in the Texas Panhandle. MS thesis, West Texas State Univ., Canyon.

Ross, R. 1982. Possible Garganey Teal in Roger Mills County, Oklahoma. *Bull. Oklahoma Ornith. Soc.* 15:7–8.

Royall, W. C., Jr., R. W. DeHaven, and O. E. Bray. 1975. Distribution and ecology of blackbird and starling roosts in regions 1, 2, and part of 6. Technical Report No. 24. Denver Wildl. Res. Ctr. 24 pp.

Royall, W. C., Jr., J. L. Guarino, J. E. DeGrazio, and A. Gammell. 1971. Migration of banded Yellow-headed Blackbirds. *Condor* 73:100–106.

Royall, W. C., Jr., P. P. Woronecki, and O. E. Bray. 1970. Distribution and ecology of blackbirds and starling roosts in regions 1, 2, and part of 3. Denver Wildl. Res. Ctr. 28 pp.

Rushing, R. C., and J. D. Tyler. 1984. A new bird for Oklahoma: Barrow's Goldeneye. *Bull. Oklahoma Ornith. Soc.* 17:25–26.

Russell, P. 1935. Wildlife survey of Palo Duro Canyon State Park, Texas, and vicinity. U.S. Dept. Inter. Rep. 34 pp.

Ryan, R. 1980. Letters to the editor. *Birding* 12(3):90.

Ryff, A. J. 1984. The long sea-flights: A precise tradition. *Birding* 16(4):146–54.

Sands, J. L. 1968. Status of the Lesser Prairie Chicken. *Aud. Field Notes* 22(3):454–56.

Schaefer, K. 1988. American Swallow-tailed Kite in Texas County, Oklahoma. *Bull. Oklahoma Ornith. Soc.* 21:29–30.

Schemnitz, S. D. 1964. Comparative ecology of Bobwhite and Scaled Quail in the Oklahoma panhandle. *Amer. Midland Nat.* 71:429–33.

Schmutz, J. K. 1987. Population size, distribution and survival of Ferruginous Hawks in n. w. Texas. Univ. Saskatchawan. Saskatoon. 36 pp.

Schmutz, J. K., and R. W. Fyfe. 1987. Migration and mortality of Alberta Ferruginous Hawks. *Condor* 89:169–74.

Schwartz, H. R. 1991. National grassland breeding bird report for 1991. Cibola Nat'l Forest, Albuquerque. 20 pp.

Schwilling, M. D., and C. W. Comer. 1972. Recent nesting of Mountain Bluebird in Cimarron County, Oklahoma. *Bull. Oklahoma Ornith. Soc.* 5:15–16.

Schwindt, K. E. 1982. Saw-whet Owl again in Texas County, Oklahoma. *Bull. Oklahoma Ornith. Soc.* 15:30–31.

Sedgwick, J. A. 1994. Hammond's Flycatcher (*Empidonax hammondi*). In *The birds of North America*, no. 109. (A. Poole and F. Gill, eds.). Acad. of Nat. Sci., Philadelphia, and Amer. Ornith. Union, Washington, D.C.

Senner, S. E., and E. F. Martinez. 1982. A review of Western Sandpiper migration in interior North America. *Southwestern Nat.* 27(2):149–159.

Seyffert, K. D. 1967–68. Breeding-bird census. *Aud. Field Notes* 21(6):659–61; 22(6):697–98.

———. 1968–78. Winter bird-population study. *Aud. Field Notes* 22(3):492–93; 23(3):542–43; 24(3):561–62; 25(3):650–51; 26(3):677–78; 27(3):685; 28(3):713; 29(3):775; 30(6):1057–58; 32(1):35.

———. 1971. The Verdin in northwestern Texas. *Bull. Oklahoma Ornith. Soc.* 4:1–3.

———. 1972. Discovery of the Verdin in southwestern Oklahoma. *Bull. Oklahoma Ornith. Soc.* 5:9–12.

———. 1984. Wintering White-throated Swifts in the Texas Panhandle. *Bull. Oklahoma Ornith. Soc.* 17:31.

———. 1985a. The breeding birds of the Texas Panhandle. *Bull. Texas Ornith. Soc.* 18(1–2):7–20.

———. 1985b. A first nesting of the Wilson's Phalarope in Texas. *Bull. Texas Ornith. Soc.* 18(1&2):27–29.

———. 1986. First winter sighting of the Lazuli Bunting in the Texas Panhandle. *Bull. Oklahoma Ornith. Soc.* 19:31–32.

———. 1987. The Scott's Oriole in the Texas Panhandle. *Bull. Oklahoma Ornith. Soc.* 20:33–34.

———. 1988a. Breeding status of the Eared Grebe in the Texas Panhandle. *Bull. Oklahoma Ornith. Soc.* 21:5–6.

———. 1988b. A Yellow Rail in the Texas Panhandle. *Bull. Oklahoma Ornith. Soc.* 21:31–32.

———. 1988c. First winter sighting of the Clay-colored Sparrow in the Texas Panhandle. *Bull. Oklahoma Ornith. Soc.* 21:34.

———. 1989a. Breeding status of the Black-necked Stilt in the Texas Panhandle. *Bull. Oklahoma Ornith. Soc.* 22:10–13.

———. 1989b. Common Moorhens nesting in the Texas Panhandle. *Bull. Oklahoma Ornith. Soc.* 22:23–24.

———. 1991. Does the Cedar Waxwing nest in the Texas Panhandle? *Bull. Texas Ornith. Soc.* 24(2):55–57.

———. 1993. Nesting of the Yellow-headed Blackbird in the Panhandle of Texas. *Bull. Oklahoma Ornith. Soc.* 26:1–4.

———. 1995. Birds of the Palo Duro Canyon State Park: A field checklist. Texas Parks and Wildl. Dept., Austin.

Shackford, J. S. 1975. The Snowy Owl in Oklahoma. *Bull. Oklahoma Ornith. Soc.* 8:29–34.

———. 1983. Spotted Sandpiper chick caught in Cimarron County, Oklahoma. *Bull. Oklahoma Ornith. Soc.* 16:4–5.

———. 1984. Cooper's Hawk nests in Cimarron County, Oklahoma. *Bull. Oklahoma Ornith. Soc.* 17:15.

———. 1986a. Laughing Gull in Cimarron County, Oklahoma. *Bull. Oklahoma Ornith. Soc.* 19:4–5.

———. 1986b. Black-capped Chickadee in Oklahoma. *Bull. Oklahoma Ornith. Soc.* 19:25–27.

———. 1989a. A Curved-billed Thrasher nest in Texas County, Oklahoma. *Bull. Oklahoma Ornith. Soc.* 22:28–29.

———. 1989b. Sage Sparrow: A new species for Oklahoma. *Bull. Oklahoma Ornith. Soc.* 22:1–2.

———. 1991. Breeding ecology of the Mountain Plover in Oklahoma. *Bull. Oklahoma Ornith. Soc.* 24:9–13.

———. 1992. Yellow-throated Vireo nest in Cimarron County, Oklahoma. *Bull. Oklahoma Ornith. Soc.* 25:15–16.

Shackford, J. S., and J. D. Tyler. 1987. A nesting Yellow-headed Blackbird colony in Texas County, Oklahoma. *Bull. Oklahoma Ornith. Soc.* 20:9–12.

Shane, T. G., and S. S. Seltman. 1995. The historical development of wintering Lark Bunting populations north of the thirty-seventh parallel in Colorado and Kansas. *Bull. Kansas Ornith. Soc.* 46(4):36–39.

Shane, T. G., S. J. Shane, K. A. Meinsenzahl, and S. K. Meinsenzahl. 1995. Oklahoma Owls: Northern Saw-whet Owl in Cimarron County, Oklahoma. *Bull. Oklahoma Ornith. Soc.* 28:17–19.

Sheffy, L. F. 1930. The experimental stage of settlement in the Panhandle of Texas. *Panhandle-Plains Hist. Rev.* 3:78–79.

Shorger, A. W. 1966. *The Wild Turkey.* Univ. Oklahoma Press, Norman.

Short, L. L., Jr. 1965. Hybridization in the flickers (*Colaptes*) of North America. *Bull. Amer. Mus. Nat. Hist.* 129(4).

Simpson, C. D., and E. G. Bolen. 1981. *Wildlife assessment of playa lakes.* U.S. Bur. of Recl., Southwest Region, Amarillo, Tex. 159 pp.

Smith, P. W. 1987. The Eurasian Collared-Dove arrives in the Americas. *Amer. Birds* 41(5):1371–79.

Sodhi, N. S., L. W. Oliphant, P. C. James, and I. G. Warkentin. 1993. Merlin (*Falco columbarius*). In *The birds of North America,* no. 44 (A. Poole and F. Gill, eds.). Acad. of Nat. Sci., Philadelphia, and Amer. Ornith. Union, Washington, D.C.

Spear, L. B., M. J. Lewis, M. T. Myres, and R. L. Pyle. 1988. The recent occurrence of Garganey in North America and the Hawaiïan Islands. *Amer. Birds* 42(3):385–92.

Stevens, D. 1979–80. Bird Notes. *Scissor-tail* (Llano Estacado Aud. Soc.) 7(12)–8(1). 14 pp.

Stevenson, J. O. 1937. The Red Phalarope in Texas. *Condor* 39:92.

———. 1942. Birds of the central Panhandle of Texas. *Condor* 44:108–15.

Stewart, A. 1973. Estimating numbers in a roosting congregation of blackbirds and starlings. *Auk* 90:353–58.

Stiles, F. G., and A. J. Negret. 1994. The nonbreeding distribution of the Black Swift: A clue from Colombia and unsolved problems. *Condor* 96:1091–94.

Stogner, C. 1983. Bird News. *Scissor-tail* (Llano Estacado Aud. Soc.) 11(8). 14 pp.

Strandtmann, R. W. 1962. Notes on nest building and mating in the Golden Eagle. *Southwestern Nat.* 7:267–68.

Strecker, J. K., Jr. 1910. Notes on the fauna of northwestern Texas. Baylor Univ. Bull. 13(4–5).

———. 1912. *The birds of Texas: An annotated check-list.* Baylor Univ. Bull. 15(1).

Stutzenbaker, C. D. 1988. *The Mottled Duck, its life history, ecology and management.* Texas Parks and Wildl. Dept., Austin.

Sullivan, R. S. 1976. Oklahoma records for the Black Rail. *Bull. Oklahoma Ornith. Soc.* 9:9–10.

Sutton, G. M. 1960. Flammulated Owl in Lubbock County, Texas. *Southwestern Nat.* 5:173–74.

———. 1967. *Oklahoma birds: Their ecology and distribution, with comments on the avifauna of the Southern Great Plains.* Univ. Oklahoma Press. Norman.

———. 1968. Oriole hybridization in Oklahoma. *Bull. Oklahoma Ornith. Soc.* 1:1–7.

———. 1969. The Red Phalarope in Oklahoma. *Bull. Oklahoma Ornith. Soc.* 2:26–28.

———. 1974a. *A check-list of Oklahoma birds.* Contr. Stovall Mus. of Sc. and Hist. Norman. 48 pp.

———. 1974b. An irruption of Clark's Nutcracker in Oklahoma. *Bull. Oklahoma Ornith. Soc.* 7:1–4.

Telfair, R. C., II. 1994. Cattle Egret (*Bubulcus ibis*). In *The birds of North America,* no. 113

(A. Poole and F. Gill, eds.). Acad. of Nat. Sci., Philadelphia, and Amer. Ornith. Union, Washington, D.C.

Terres, J. K. 1980. *The Audubon Society encyclopedia of North American birds*. A. Knopf, New York.

Texas Game, Fish and Oyster Commission. 1945. *Principal game birds and mammals of Texas*. Von Boeckmann-Jones Co., Austin. 149 pp.

Texas Ornithological Society [TOS]. 1956. *Newsletter* 4(10):1–4.

———. 1958. *Newsletter* 6(9). 8 pp.

———. 1959. *Newsletter* 7(9). 8 pp.

———. 1960. *Newsletter* 8(1). 8 pp.

———. 1962. *Newsletter* 10(3). 14 pp.

———. 1966. *Newsletter* 14(10). 14 pp.

———. 1984. *Checklist of the birds of Texas*. 2nd ed. Hart Graphics, Austin.

———. 1995. *Checklist of the birds of Texas*. 3rd ed. Capital Printing, Austin.

Texas Panhandle Audubon Society [TPAS]. 1955. *Field checklist of the birds of the Panhandle of Texas*. West Texas College Press, Canyon.

———. 1966. *Field check-list Potter-Randall counties, Texas*. 2nd ed. TPAS, Amarillo.

———. 1977. *Field check list: birds of Potter & Randall counties, Texas*. 3rd ed. TPAS, Amarillo.

———. 1989. *Field check list: birds of the Texas Panhandle*. 1st ed. TPAS, Amarillo.

———. 1996. *Field check list: birds of the Texas Panhandle*. 2nd ed. TPAS, Amarillo.

Thompson, B. C. 1984. Interior Least Tern distribution and taxonomy. Fed. Aid Proj. no. W-103-R-14. Perf. Rep., Texas Parks and Wildl. Dept., Austin. 11 pp.

Thompson, M. C., and C. Ely. 1989. *Birds in Kansas*. Vol. 1. Univ. of Kansas Museum of Natural History, Lawrence.

———. 1992. *Birds in Kansas*. Vol. 2. Univ. of Kansas Museum of Natural History, Lawrence.

Thompson, W. L. 1952. Summer birds of the Canadian "breaks" in Hutchinson County, Texas. *Texas Jour. of Sci.* 4:220–29.

Tomer, J. S. 1983. Nesting of Vermilion Flycatcher in Cimarron County, Oklahoma. *Bull. Oklahoma Ornith. Soc.* 16:1–3.

———. 1997. The first list of Oklahoma birds. *Bull. Oklahoma Ornith. Soc.* 30:13–21.

Trauger, D. L., A. Dzubin, and J. P. Ryder. 1971. White geese intermediate between Ross' Geese and Lesser Snow Geese. *Auk.* 88:856–65.

Traweek, M. S., Jr. 1975. Waterfowl die-off in the Texas Panhandle. Texas Parks and Wildl. Dept. rep., Austin.

———. 1978. Texas waterfowl production survey. Job 5, Fed. Aid Proj. W-106-R-5. Texas Parks and Wildl. Dept., Austin. 17 pp.

True, D. 1993. *Hummingbirds of North America*. Univ. New Mexico Press, Albuquerque.

Tyler, J. D. 1979a. Nest of Lewis' Woodpecker in Cimarron County, Oklahoma. *Bull. Oklahoma Ornith. Soc.* 12:14–15.

———. 1979b. *Birds of southwestern Oklahoma*. Contr. Stovall Mus. of Sc. and Hist. Univ. Oklahoma, Norman. 65 pp.

———. 1983. Fulvous Whistling-Duck in Comanche County, Oklahoma. *Bull. Oklahoma Ornith. Soc.* 16:25–26

————. 1985. The Lark Bunting in Oklahoma. *Bull. Oklahoma Ornith. Soc.* 18:25–28.

————. 1992. Nesting ecology of the Loggerhead Shrike in southwestern Oklahoma. *Wilson Bull.* 104(1):95–104.

Tyler, J. D., S. J. Orr, and J. K. Banta. 1989. The Red-shouldered Hawk in southwestern Oklahoma. *Bull. Oklahoma Ornith. Soc.* 22:17–21.

U.S. Department of Agriculture [USDA]. 1973. Birds of the Kiowa National Grassland: field checklist.

U.S. Fish and Wildlife Service [USFWS]. 1988. Playa lakes region waterfowl habitat concept plan, category 24 of the North American waterfowl management plan. Albuquerque. 37 pp.

Vickery, P. D. 1996. Grasshopper Sparrow (*Ammodramus savannarum*). In *The birds of North America*, no. 239 (A. Poole and F. Gill, eds.). Acad. of Nat. Sci., Philadelphia, and Amer. Ornith. Union, Washington, D.C.

Webster, J. D. 1990. Breeding pair of Vermilion Flycatchers in Cimarron County, Oklahoma. *Bull. Oklahoma Ornith. Soc.* 23:25–27.

Weese, A. C. (ed.). 1947. The journal of Titian Ramsey Peale, pioneer naturalist. *Missouri Hist. Rev.* 41:147–63, 266–84.

Weske, J. S. 1968. Birds to be looked for in the Black Mesa country. *Bull. Oklahoma Ornith. Soc.* 1:8–9.

————. 1973. Nest of Poor-will in Cimarron County, Oklahoma. *Bull. Oklahoma Ornith. Soc.* 6:22.

————. 1974. White-winged Junco in Texas. *Condor* 76:119.

————. 1976. Western Flycatcher in Oklahoma. *Auk* 93:655–56.

West, D. A. 1962. Hybridization in grosbeaks (*Pheucticus*) of the Great Plains. *Auk* 79:399–424.

Wiens, J. A., J. T. Rotenberry, and J. F. Ward. 1972. Avian populations at IBP grassland biome sites: 1971. Tech. Rep. no. 205. Colorado State Univ., Fort Collins.

Wilds, C., and M. Newton. 1983. The identification of dowitchers. *Birding* 15(4&5):151–66.

Williams, F. ed. 1966. Southern Great Plains region. *Aud. Field Notes* 20(1):64–66; 20(5):580–82.

————. 1967. Southern Great Plains region. *Aud. Field Notes* 21(1):51–54; 21(3):430–33; 21(4):517–20; 21(5):582–85.

————. 1968. Southern Great Plains region. *Aud. Field Notes* 22(1):57–60; 22(5):620–23.

————. 1969. Southern Great Plains region. *Aud. Field Notes* 23(3):492–95; 23(5):671–73.

————. 1970. Southern Great Plains region. *Aud. Field Notes* 24(1):63–66; 24(3):515–18; 24(4):619–22; 24(5):693–96.

————. 1971. Southern Great Plains region. *Amer. Birds* 25(3):596–99; 25(4):764–68; 25(5):872–74.

————. 1973. Southern Great Plains region. *Amer. Birds* 27(1):78–82; 27(3):633–37; 27(4):788–92; 27(5):886–90.

————. 1974. Southern Great Plains region. *Amer. Birds* 28(1):70–75; 28(3):656–60; 28(4):817–22; 28(5):918–22.

————. 1975. Southern Great Plains region. *Amer. Birds* 29(1):77–82; 29(3):707–11; 29(4):870–74; 29(5):999–1003.

————. 1976. Southern Great Plains region. *Amer. Birds* 30(1):90–95.

————. 1977. Southern Great Plains region. *Amer. Birds* 31(2):194–97; 31(6):1154–58.

————. 1978. Southern Great Plains region. *Amer. Birds* 32(2):223–27; 32(6):1178–82.

————. 1979. Southern Great Plains region. *Amer. Birds* 33(2):191–93; 33(5):784–87; 33(6):876–77.

————. 1980a. August migration: The Phalarope. *Midland Nat.* 25(9). 5 pp.

————. 1980b. Southern Great Plains region. *Amer. Birds* 34(3):286–88; 34(5):791–93; 34(6):908–10.

————. 1981. Southern Great Plains region. *Amer. Birds* 35(2):198–201; 35(3):313–15; 35(5):838–40; 35(6):955–57.

————. 1982. Southern Great Plains region. *Amer. Birds* 36(2):192–94; 36(3):307–309; 36(5):868–71; 36(6):992–95.

————. 1983. Southern Great Plains region. *Amer. Birds* 37(2):196–99; 37(5):886–88; 37(6):1002–1004.

————. 1984. Southern Great Plains region. *Amer. Birds* 38(2):218–21; 38(6):1035–37.

————. 1985. Southern Great Plains region. *Amer. Birds* 39(1):72–75; 39(2):182–85; 39(5):931–33.

————. 1986. Southern Great Plains region. *Amer. Birds* 40(1):134–38; 40(5):1222–24.

————. 1987. Southern Great Plains region. *Amer. Birds* 41(1):109–13.

————. 1988. Southern Great Plains region. *Amer. Birds* 42(2):282–86.

Williams, S. O., III. 1993. New Mexico. *Amer. Birds* 47(2):286–88; 47(5):1136–38.

————. 1994. New Mexico. *Amer. Birds* 48(1):137–39; 48(3):327–29.

————. 1996. New Mexico. *Field Notes* 50(2):203–206.

————. 1997. New Mexico. *Field Notes* 51(1):98–101; 51(4):907–910.

————. 1998. New Mexico. *Field Notes* 51(5):1032–36.

Williams, S. O., III, and J. P. Hubbard. 1990. New Mexico. *Amer. Birds* 44(5):1167–69.

————. 1991. New Mexico. *Amer. Birds* 45(1):137–39; 45(2):301–303; 45(3):481–83; 45(5):1146–49.

————. 1992. New Mexico. *Amer. Birds* 46(1):134–36.

————. 1993. New Mexico. *Field Notes* 47(2):286–88.

————. 1995. New Mexico. *Field Notes* 49(5):961–63.

Wilson, D. E. 1981. Upland game investigations. Fed. Aid Proj. no. W-108-R-4. Perf. Rep., Texas Parks and Wild. Dept., Austin. 70 pp.

Wilson, J. B. 1984. American Swallow-tailed Kite in Caddo County, Oklahoma. *Bull. Oklahoma Ornith. Soc.* 17:30.

Wolfe, Col. L. R. 1956. *Check-list of the birds of Texas.* Intelligencer Prtng. Co., Lancaster, Penn.

Wood, D. S., and G. D. Schnell. 1984. *Distribution of Oklahoma birds.* Univ. Oklahoma Press, Norman.

Wright, R. A. 1978. The vegetation of the Palo Duro Canyon. *Panhandle-Plains Hist. Rev.* 51:87–116.

INDEX